HISTORY IN DISPUTE

ADVISORY BOARD

Edited by Robert J. Allison

A MANLY, INC. BOOK

ST. JAMES PRESS

AN IMPRINT OF THE GALE GROUP

DETROIT • SAN FRANCISCO • LONDON
BOSTON • WOODBRIDGE, CT

HISTORY IN DISPUTE

Volume 2 ▪ American Social and Political Movements, 1945–2000: Pursuit of Liberty

Matthew J. Bruccoli and Richard Layman, *Editorial Directors.*

Karen L. Rood, *Senior Editor.*

Anthony J. Scotti Jr., James F. Tidd Jr., *In-house editors.*

Philip B. Dematteis, *Production manager.*

Kathy Lawler Merlette, *Office manager.* Ann M. Cheschi, Tenesha S. Lee, Joann Whittaker, *Administrative support.* Angi Pleasant, Kathy Weston, *Accounting.*

Phyllis A. Avant, *Copyediting supervisor.* Thom Harman, *Senior copyeditor.* Brenda Carol Blanton, Worthy B. Evans, Melissa D. Hinton, William Tobias Mathes, Jennifer Reid, Michelle L. Whitney, *Copyediting staff.* Ronald D. Aiken II, Nicole M. Nichols, Jennie Williamson, *Freelance copyeditors.*

Margo Dowling, *Editorial assistant.* Carol A. Fairman, *Editorial trainee.* Alex Snead, *Indexing specialist.*

Janet E. Hill, *Layout and graphics supervisor.* Zoe R. Cook, *Layout and graphics.*

Charles Mims, Scott Nemzek, Alison Smith, Paul Talbot, *Photography editors.* Joseph M. Bruccoli, *Digital photographic copy work.*

Cory McNair, *SGML supervisor.* Tim Bedford, Linda Drake, Frank Graham, Alex Snead, *SGML staff.*

Marie L. Parker, *Systems manager.* Kimberly Kelly, *Data entry.*

Kathleen M. Flanagan, *Typesetting supervisor.* Karla Corley Brown, Mark J. McEwan, Patricia Flanagan Salisbury, *Typesetting staff.* Delores Plastow, *Freelance typesetter.*

Linda Holderfield, *Librarian, Thomas Cooper Library of the University of South Carolina.* Virginia Weathers, *Reference-department head.* Marilee Birchfield, Stefanie Buck, Stefanie DuBose, Rebecca Feind, Karen Joseph, Donna Lehman, Charlene Loope, Anthony McKissick, Jean Rhyne, Kwamine Simpson, *Reference librarians.* Caroline Taylor, *Circulation-department head.* David Haggard, *Acquisitions-searching supervisor.*

St. James Press
27500 Drake Road
Farmington Hills, MI 48331

ISBN 1-55862-396-5

St. James Press is an imprint of The Gale Group

Printed in the United States of America

10 9 8 7 6 5 4 3 2

CONTENTS

PREFACE

History is more than a record of the past; it is more than a collection of names and dates. History is the story of how people lived, what they did, and what they thought about. Two people who participate in the same event may experience, interpret, and remember it in different ways. The story historians tell of the past is influenced by the sources—the records and people we study—as well as by their own biases or methods of interpretation. Students of history must weigh all the available evidence, taking into account all the limitations, flaws, or biases of the sources, and from all of this information try to imagine the past as it actually occurred.

In this book many different historians try to interpret American history since 1945. On some basic facts all agree. The major events are all here: the Cold War, the Civil Rights movement, the War on Poverty, the space program, the Vietnam War, the feminist movement, Watergate, the rise of suburbs, and the influence of television. Most historians will agree that these are important and significant factors in understanding the last half of the twentieth century. However, no two historians would ever agree on which of these was the most important. Nor would any two agree on why these events happened the way they did. Historians do not simply record what happened; they try to explain why things happened so that all of us can learn from the experiences of the past. In this book different historians look at these events, using the methods of historical inquiry, and try to explain events, people, and ideas.

Historians are trained to study the past, to think critically about their sources, and to scrutinize documents or analyze statistics. Some of the men and women who have written essays for this book have spent their entire careers thinking about a particular topic. Yet, though two scholars may be studying the same event, or the same person, they may not agree on the most fundamental issues. Sometimes their differences are profound; sometimes they are more subtle. For example, two scholars in this volume assess the American space program. Both agree on the program's significance, in fact each one studies it, but why did Americans begin their venture into space? One scholar argues that Americans entered the space race against the Soviets as part of a broader Cold War strategy. This argument is plausible. The other scholar argues that the race into space was part of the American cultural tradition, owing more to the days of covered wagons and pioneers and science-fiction fantasies such as Buck Rogers than to Cold War fears. This stance, also, is a valid one. Is one more right than the other? That judgment is for history to decide.

Scholars studying the American Civil Rights movement agree on the profound impact it has had on American life. Yet, why did it develop the way it did? Some look to the success of the National Association for the Advancement of Colored People (NAACP) and its Legal Defense Fund, under the leadership of Thurgood Marshall, which defended the rights of African Americans in court and fought for the constitutional principle that all Americans are equal before the law. None would deny the importance of *Brown* v. *Board of Education of Topeka, Kansas* (1954) and Marshall's other legal victories. On the other hand, telling the story of the Civil Rights movement without mentioning the brave men and women who defied the law by sitting down at lunch counters and on buses would be wrong. At the time, leaders of the Civil Rights movement disagreed on which factor was more important. Subsequent historians have followed these two lines of argument. Which is more important? Mass action or legal action?

Serious scholars will take into account all these different explanations for an event, and they usually do not see these as "either/or" propositions. The space program owed much to Cold War fears, but it is also inconceivable without taking into account the peculiarities of American culture; the Civil Rights movement depended on both the law and men and women who acted bravely to defy unjust laws. How much weight an historian gives to one set of influences over another is a matter of judgment. Historians are usually not partisans, committed to one ideological position. Some may have profound biases, prejudices, or opinions. Most vote in elections and sometimes voice their opinions on political issues. Nevertheless, as scholars they are trying to explain the past, not advance an agenda. The topics discussed in this volume, important social and political issues, in some cases bitterly divided the American people. The anticommunist crusade of Sen. Joseph R. McCarthy, the Civil Rights movement, the Vietnam War, Watergate, the arms race, and the abortion debate: all were contentious issues in which Americans and others divided over them, argued over them, and sometimes killed one another over them. Historians observe the past from a distance and must be able to detach themselves from the passions of the day as well as to take those passions into account and explain them.

As you read these interpretations, think about the arguments each scholar makes, the sources he or she relies upon, and the conclusions they draw from the evidence. Think about which arguments you find most plausible, which ideas you find most compelling. As you read the supporting materials presented as sidebars, think about how you interpret the evidence. The same critical inquiry these scholars use to interpret the past you can use to understand the present. History is an explanation of why things happened the way they did. It is not an assessment of blame or an offering of praise, though it can move us to make these judgments.

–ROBERT J. ALLISON

CHRONOLOGY

Boldface type refers to a pertaining chapter title.

1945

12 APRIL: President Franklin D. Roosevelt dies at Warm Springs, Georgia; Harry S Truman becomes president.

8 MAY: Germany surrenders to Allied forces, ending war in Europe.

5 JULY: U.S. troops reoccupy the Philippines in fierce fighting, suffering 12,000 casualties.

16 JULY: The United States successfully tests an atomic bomb at Alamagordo, New Mexico.

17–26 JULY: At Potsdam, Germany, Winston Churchill, Joseph Stalin, and Truman meet to discuss new war aims, and agree to demand Japan's unconditional surrender. Churchill's party loses elections at home during conference; Churchill replaced as prime minister by Labour Party leader Clement Atlee. (*See* **Cold War Causes**)

6 AUGUST: An American bomber drops an atomic bomb on Hiroshima, Japan, killing 50,000 people and destroying four square miles of the city.

8 AUGUST: The Soviet Union declares war on Japan and attacks Japanese forces in Manchuria.

9 AUGUST: The United States drops an atomic bomb on Nagasaki, Japan, killing 40,000 people.

10 AUGUST: The Japanese Supreme Council agrees to accept Allied terms for surrender.

2 SEPTEMBER: Japan formally surrenders, ending World War II.

21 NOVEMBER – 12 MARCH 1946: United Auto Workers strike against General Motors, ultimately winning 18.5 cent/hour raise.

1946

27 JANUARY – 15 FEBRUARY: Steel workers strike and win 18.5 cent/hour raise. (*See* **Organized Labor**)

5 MARCH: In Fulton, Missouri, Churchill warns that an "iron curtain" has descended across Europe with Soviet forces in control of the eastern part of the Continent.

2 JULY: For the first time since Reconstruction, blacks are able to vote in the Mississippi Democratic primary. (*See* **Civil Rights Movement: Methods, Goals of Civil Rights**)

4 JULY: The United States grants independence to Philippines.

5 NOVEMBER: Republicans win control of the House and Senate for first time since 1928. (*See* **Political Consensus**)

22 NOVEMBER: The French bomb the Vietnamese cities of Hanoi and Haiphong, trying to suppress an independence movement.

1947

10 APRIL: Jackie Robinson signs a contract with the Brooklyn Dodgers, becoming the first black player in major league baseball.

15 APRIL: Robinson plays his first game for the Dodgers.

5 JUNE: At Harvard University's commencement, Secretary of State George C. Marshall offers $12 billion to help European nations rebuild their economies. (*See* **Cold War Causes, Fear of Attack**)

23 JUNE: Congress overrides Truman's veto of the Taft-Hartley Act, which allows businesses to sue unions for damages caused by strikes, and forbids union contracts that require businesses to hire only union members. (*See* **Organized Labor**)

5 OCTOBER: Truman becomes the first president to address the nation on television. (*See* **Mass Media**)

18 OCTOBER: The House Un-American Activities Committee begins an investigation of communist influence in the motion-picture industry. (*See* **McCarthyism**)

29 OCTOBER: Truman endorses a report of his Committee on Civil Rights calling for an end to racial segregation. (*See* **Civil Rights Movement: Methods, Goals Of Civil Rights**)

3 DECEMBER: The Screen Actors Guild, under its president, Ronald W. Reagan, bars communists from holding office in union; the Motion Picture Association vows not to glorify crime on film. (*See* **McCarthyism**)

1948

14 MAY: The British mandate ends in Palestine and the state of Israel is created. Syria, Egypt, Iraq, Lebanon, and Transjordan invade Israel, but the United Nations secures a truce by 15 July. (*See* **Middle East Policy**)

24 JUNE: The Soviet Union, occupying the eastern part of Germany, closes off Berlin. Two days later, the United States mounts an airlift of supplies into the city. (*See* **Cold War Causes**)

26 JULY: Truman orders the military and federal civil service to end racial segregation. (*See* **Civil Rights Movement: Methods, Goals of Civil Rights, Meaning of Brown**)

3 AUGUST: Former communist Whittaker Chambers accuses high-ranking State Department official Alger Hiss of membership in the Communist Party. (*See* **McCarthyism**)

2 NOVEMBER: In a stunning upset, Truman defeats Republican Thomas E. Dewey, Progressive Henry A. Wallace, and "Dixiecrat" J. Strom Thurmond for the presidency.

6 DECEMBER: California congressman Richard M. Nixon accuses the Truman administration of concealing evidence that Hiss and other communists have infiltrated the government. (*See* **McCarthyism**)

1949

25 JANUARY: The Soviet Union and the Communist states of Eastern Europe form the Council for Mutual Economic Assistance. (*See* **Cold War Causes**)

2 MARCH: An American B-50 bomber flies around the globe. (*See* **Space Race, Fear of Attack**)

4 APRIL: The United States and eleven allies form the North Atlantic Treaty Organization (NATO). (*See* **Cold War Causes**)

12 MAY: The Soviets lift their blockade around Berlin.

29 JUNE: American forces withdraw from Korea.

23 SEPTEMBER: Evangelist Billy Graham begins an eight-week revival in Los Angeles.

1 OCTOBER: Mao Tse-tung proclaims the creation of the People's Republic of China. (*See* **Cold War Causes, Fear of Attack**)

1950

The U.S. Census Bureau reports a population of 150,697,361.

17 JANUARY: Tony Pino and accomplices rob $2.8 million from a Brink's armored-car company in Boston.

25 JANUARY: Hiss is sentenced to five years in prison for perjury.

9 FEBRUARY: Senator Joseph McCarthy charges that the State Department is riddled with 205 communist agents. (*See* **McCarthyism**)

25 JUNE: North Korea invades South Korea.

23 SEPTEMBER: Congress overrides Truman's veto of the Internal Security Act.

1 NOVEMBER: Two Puerto Rican nationalists attempt to assassinate Truman; a guard and one would-be assassin are killed.

1951

7 MARCH: General Douglas MacArthur urges Truman to allow U.N. forces to move against China.

29 MARCH: Julius and Ethel Rosenberg are convicted of passing atomic secrets to the Soviet Union. (*See* **McCarthyism**)

11 APRIL: Truman fires MacArthur for overstepping his authority.

9 AUGUST: McCarthy accuses twenty-six State Department employees of disloyalty. (*See* **McCarthyism**)

1952

23 SEPTEMBER: Republican vice presidential candidate Richard M. Nixon makes a television speech to answer charges he received gifts from political supporters; Nixon admits to receiving a cocker-spaniel puppy named Checkers.

24 OCTOBER: Republican presidential candidate Dwight D. Eisenhower pledges to go to Korea for an "early and honorable end" to the war.
(*See* **Eisenhower**)

4 NOVEMBER: Eisenhower is elected president, carrying thirty-nine states, defeating Adlai E. Stevenson 32.9 million to 26.5 million votes; the Republicans win control of both houses of Congress. (*See* **Eisenhower**)

1953

1 JANUARY: Country singer Hank Williams dies.

20 JANUARY: Eisenhower is inaugurated as the thirty-fourth president of the United States. (*See* **Eisenhower**)

5 MARCH: Joseph Stalin dies. (*See* **Cold War Causes**)

19 JUNE: Julius and Ethel Rosenberg are executed. (*See* **Rosenbergs**)

27 JULY: An armistice leaves Korea divided.

22 AUGUST: A coup in Iran deposes Prime Minister Mohammad Mossadeg, who had tried to nationalize Iranian oil reserves; Mohammad Reza Pahlevi comes to power as shah. (*See* **Middle East Policy**)

1954

18 FEBRUARY: McCarthy accuses the U.S. Army of harboring communists. (*See* **McCarthyism**)

1 MARCH: Puerto Rican nationalists shoot five members of Congress in the Capitol.

13 MARCH: Vietnamese forces attack French fortifications at Dien Bien Phu. (*See* **Vietnam Causes**)

17 MAY: The United States Supreme Court in *Brown* v. *the Board of Education of Topeka, Kansas* rules that separate schools for black and white students violate the Fourteenth Amendment. (*See* **Meaning of Brown, Goals of Civil Rights**)

19 JULY: Elvis Presley's first professional recording, "That's All Right, Mama" is released. (*See* **Rock and Roll**)

21 JULY: Representatives from the United States, China, the Soviet Union, France, and different factions in Vietnam agree to a temporary partition of Vietnam pending a national election to choose a new government. (*See* **Vietnam Causes**)

2 DECEMBER: After a long investigation of charges that McCarthy leveled at the U.S. Army, the Senate votes to condemn McCarthy. (*See* **McCarthyism**)

1955

19 JANUARY: Eisenhower holds the first televised press conference. (*See* **Eisenhower**)

2 FEBRUARY: The American Federation of Labor merges with the Congress of Industrial Organizations to form the AFL-CIO. (*See* **Organized Labor**)

12 APRIL: Jonas Salk's polio vaccine is successfully tested; millions of Americans now will be vaccinated against the disease.

17 MAY: In a second phase of *Brown* v. *the Board of Education of Topeka, Kansas,* the Supreme Court orders segregated school districts to dismantle separate systems "with all deliberate speed." (*See* **Meaning of Brown, Goals of Civil Rights**)

20 AUGUST: Chuck Berry's first recording, "Maybellene," is released. (*See* **Rock and Roll**)

24 SEPTEMBER: Eisenhower suffers a heart attack. (*See* **Eisenhower**)

30 SEPTEMBER: Actor James Dean dies in a car crash.

5 DECEMBER: Rosa Parks is arrested for refusing to give up her seat to a white passenger on a Montgomery, Alabama, bus. Blacks in Montgomery organize a successful yearlong campaign to end racial segregation on buses. (*See* **Civil Rights Movement: Methods, Goals of Civil Rights**)

1956

25 FEBRUARY: Senator Harry Byrd of Virginia urges "massive resistance" to school desegregation. (*See* **Civil Rights Movement: Methods, Goals of Civil Rights**)

10 AUGUST: Painter Jackson Pollock dies in a car crash.

23 OCTOBER – 4 NOVEMBER: The Hungarian uprising against the Soviet Union occurs. (*See* **Cold War Causes, Fear of Attack**)

6 NOVEMBER: Eisenhower is reelected over Adlai E. Stevenson. (*See* **Eisenhower**)

25 NOVEMBER: The American Cancer Society declares a significant link between smoking and lung cancer.

1957

8–19 MAY: South Vietnamese president Ngo Dinh Diem visits the United States and receives a promise of American aid. (*See* **Vietnam Causes**)

21 MAY: Lawrence Ferlinghetti, publisher and owner of San Francisco's City Lights bookstore, is arrested for selling lewd and indecent material, but is later acquitted.

24 SEPTEMBER: Eisenhower orders U.S. Army paratroopers to oversee integration of Central High School in Little Rock, Arkansas. (*See* **Meaning of Brown, Eisenhower, Civil Rights Movement: Methods, Goals of Civil Rights**)

5 OCTOBER: The Soviet Union launches the first artificial satellite, *Sputnik.* (*See* **Space Race, Fear of Attack**)

1958

16 APRIL: Eisenhower signs the Federal Highway Act, authorizing $1.8 billion to create

an interstate highway system. (*See* **Interstate Highway Act, Eisenhower**)

16 JULY: Congress creates the National Aeronautics and Space Administration (NASA). (*See* **Space Race, U.S. Space Program**)

2 SEPTEMBER: The National Defense Education Act, mandating teaching of science and math, passes Congress. (*See* **Space Race, Fear of Attack**)

1959

2 JANUARY: Fidel Castro assumes power in Cuba. (*See* **Cold War Causes**)

3 FEBRUARY: Singers Richie Valens, Buddy Holly, and J.P. "Big Bopper" Richardson die in a plane crash in Clear Lake, Iowa. (*See* **Rock and Roll**)

16 OCTOBER: A special congressional committee begins an investigation into television quiz shows, which it determines were fixed. (*See* **Mass Media**)

1960

The U.S. Census Bureau reports a population of 178,464,236.

1 FEBRUARY: Black college students sit down at a whites-only lunch counter in Greensboro, North Carolina, beginning a wave of nonviolent "sit-in" protests. (*See* **1960s Progressive Movement, Goals of Civil Rights, Civil Rights Movement: Methods**)

1 APRIL: The United States launches *Tiros 1,* the first weather satellite. (*See* **Space Race**)

5 MAY: The Soviet Union shoots down a U-2 spy plane, capturing American pilot Francis Gary Powers. Premier Nikita Khrushchev cancels a scheduled summit conference with Eisenhower. (*See* **Cold War Causes, Fear of Attack, Eisenhower**)

1 JUNE: The National Council of Churches criticizes sex and violence on television.

AUGUST: The United States tests the *Discoverer* satellite, which takes pictures of the Soviet Union from space. (*See* **Fear of Attack, Space Race, U.S. Space Program**)

26 SEPTEMBER: The first televised presidential debates occur between Republican candidate Richard M. Nixon and Democratic candidate John F. Kennedy. (*See* **Kennedy**)

8 NOVEMBER: In a narrow victory, Kennedy becomes the youngest man ever elected as president. (*See* **Kennedy**)

1961

3 JANUARY: The United States breaks off diplomatic relations with Cuba.

12 APRIL: In the first manned space flight, Soviet cosmonaut Yuri Gagarin orbits the earth in *Vostok.* (*See* **Space Race**)

17 APRIL: Cuban exiles, supported by the CIA, attempt to invade Cuba at the Bay of Pigs. (*See* **Kennedy**)

5 MAY: Alan Shepard makes the first spaceflight by an American. (*See* **Space Race, U.S. Space Program**)

3 NOVEMBER: General Maxwell Taylor and Walt W. Rostow report to Kennedy that quick U.S. military action can defeat communist aggression in South Vietnam. (*See* **Kennedy, Vietnam Causes**)

1962

20 FEBRUARY: John Glenn in the *Friendship 7* spacecraft is the first American to orbit Earth. (*See* **U.S. Space Program**)

16 JUNE: In the sixth Soviet spaceflight, Lieutenant Valentina Tershokova is the first woman in space, orbiting Earth forty-eight times in a two-day, twenty-two-hour and fifty-minute mission. (*See* **Space Race**)

10 JULY: *Telstar* satellite, which can receive and send radio signals from Earth, is launched by the United States; this innovation allows direct broadcasts between the United States and Europe. (*See* **Space Race**)

27 AUGUST: The United States launches *Mariner 2,* a spacecraft sent to investigate planet Venus. (*See* **U.S. Space Program**)

14 OCTOBER: The United States learns that the Soviet Union has placed strategic missiles in Cuba. Kennedy demands that the missiles be removed. (*See* **Cold War Causes, Kennedy**)

1963

2 JANUARY: NASA loses contact with *Mariner 2,* which at that time was 86.8 million kilometers from Earth, after it transmitted information on the planet Venus. (*See* **U.S. Space Program**)

2 APRIL: Dr. Martin Luther King Jr. begins a campaign to end segregation in Birmingham, Alabama. (*See* **Civil Rights Movement: Methods, 1960s Progressive Movement**)

12 JUNE: National Association for the Advancement of Colored People (NAACP) leader Medgar Evers is assassinated in Jackson, Mississippi. (*See* **Civil Rights Movement: Methods, Goals of Civil Rights, 1960s Progressive Movement**)

26 JUNE: In a speech at the Berlin Wall, Kennedy declares, "Ich bin ein Berliner" (I

am a Berliner). (*See* **Kennedy, Cold War Causes**)

28 AUGUST: In the largest civil rights demonstration in U.S. history, a quarter of a million people assemble in Washington, D.C. to pressure the administration and Congress to pass the Civil Rights Act. King delivers his "I have a dream" speech. (*See* **Civil Rights Movement: Methods, Goals of Civil Rights, 1960s Progressive Movement**)

15 SEPTEMBER: A bomb kills four young girls at a black Baptist church in Birmingham, Alabama. (*See* **Civil Rights Movement: Methods, Goals of Civil Rights**)

1 NOVEMBER: Coup leaders in South Vietnam, supported by the United States, kill Diem and install a military government. (*See* **Vietnam Causes**)

22 NOVEMBER: Kennedy is assassinated in Dallas, Texas; Lyndon B. Johnson is inaugurated as president. (*See* **Kennedy**)

24 NOVEMBER: Lee Harvey Oswald, accused of killing Kennedy, is shot to death by nightclub owner Jack Ruby while in police custody .

1964

8 JANUARY: In the State of the Union Address, Johnson declares a war on poverty. (*See* **War on Poverty**)

11 JANUARY: Surgeon General Dr. Luther Terry issues a report showing a link between cigarette smoking and lung cancer and other diseases.

9 FEBRUARY: The Beatles appear on *The Ed Sullivan Show.* (*See* **Rock and Roll**)

25 FEBRUARY: Cassius Clay becomes the heavyweight boxing champion when Sonny Liston fails to answer the bell for a seventh round in Miami. Later, Clay announces he is a member of Elijah Muhammad's Nation of Islam and changes his name to Muhammad Ali.

21 JUNE: Civil-rights activists Michael Schwerner, James Chaney, and Andrew Goodman disappear in Mississippi and are later found murdered. (*See* **Civil Rights Movement: Methods, 1960s Progressive Movement**)

2 JULY: The Civil Rights Act of 1964 becomes law. (*See* **Civil Rights Movement: Methods, Goals of Civil Rights, 1960s Progressive Movement**)

18 JULY: Racial riots occur in Brownsville, Texas, and Harlem, New York.

2 AUGUST: North Vietnamese patrol boats reportedly attack American ships in the Gulf of Tonkin. (*See* **Vietnam Causes**)

7 AUGUST: Congress gives the president the power to take action against communist aggression in Vietnam. (*See* **Vietnam Causes**)

27 SEPTEMBER: The Warren Commission reports that Oswald had acted alone in the assassination of Kennedy. (*See* **Kennedy**)

30 SEPTEMBER – 4 OCTOBER: Students at the University of California at Berkeley protest and stage a sit-in at the administration building, beginning the "Free Speech Movement." (*See* **1960s Progressive Movement**)

14 OCTOBER: King receives the Nobel Peace Prize. (*See* **Civil Rights Movement: Methods**)

3 NOVEMBER: Johnson defeats Barry Goldwater in a landslide presidential election.

1965

21 FEBRUARY: Malcolm X is assassinated in Harlem. (*See* **Goals of Civil Rights**)

2 MARCH: American aircraft begin bombing North Vietnam. (*See* **Vietnam Causes**)

23 MARCH: The first two-manned spaceflight, *Gemini 3,* with astronauts Virgil Grissom and John Young, occurs. (*See* **U.S. Space Program**)

25 MAY: In a rematch in Las Vegas, Ali knocks out former champion Liston in the first round.

3–7 JUNE: In *Gemini 4* mission, Edward White makes the first U.S. space walk. (*See* **U.S. Space Program**)

28 JULY: Johnson announces that 50,000 more American soldiers will be sent to Vietnam, bringing the number to 125,000. (*See* **Vietnam Causes**)

30 JULY: Congress passes the Medicare Act. (*See* **War on Poverty**)

6 AUGUST: The Voting Rights Act passes Congress. (*See* **Civil Rights Movement: Methods**)

11 AUGUST: Rioting breaks out in Watts, a predominantly black Los Angeles neighborhood; thirty-four people are killed and more than one thousand are injured.

22 NOVEMBER: Ali knocks out Floyd Patterson in the twelfth round.

1966

28 APRIL: Bill Russell is named the first black coach of a major-league team; he leads the Boston Celtics to the world championship.

5 JUNE: James Meredith begins a protest walk across Mississippi and is wounded the next

day by a shotgun blast. (*See* **Goals of Civil Rights**)

13 JUNE: In *Miranda* v. *Arizona*, the Supreme Court rules that individuals in police custody must be informed of their rights to an attorney and to remain silent. (*See* **Warren Court**)

16 JUNE: Stokely Carmichael calls for "black power" in a Mississippi rally. (*See* **1960s Progressive Movement, Goals of Civil Rights**)

12 JULY: Race riots break out in Chicago and violence spreads to other cities.

8 NOVEMBER: Republicans gain seats in Congress; Reagan is elected governor of California.

1967

27 JANUARY: Astronauts Grissom, Edward White, and Roger Chaffee die in a fire inside the *Apollo 1* spacecraft during prelaunch tests. (*See* **U.S. Space Program**)

24 APRIL: Soviet cosmonaut Vladimir Komarov dies when his spacecraft equipment fails. (*See* **U.S. Space Race**)

20 JUNE: Muhammad Ali is stripped of his boxing titles after failing to register for the draft. (*See* **Antiwar Movement**)

12–17 JULY: Rioting in Newark, New Jersey, kills twenty-six people.

22 JULY: The United States announces that by the end of 1968, 525,000 American soldiers will be in Vietnam. (*See* **Vietnam Causes**)

23–30 JULY: Rioting in Detroit, Michigan, kills forty-three people before federal troops restore order.

2 OCTOBER: Thurgood Marshall becomes the first black man to serve on the United States Supreme Court.

1968

30 JANUARY: Viet Cong and North Vietnamese forces attack Americans and South Vietnamese targets throughout South Vietnam in the Tet offensive. (*See* **Vietnam Causes**)

31 JANUARY: The Viet Cong infiltrate the American embassy in Saigon. (*See* **Antiwar Movement, Vietnam Causes**)

12 MARCH: In the New Hampshire Democratic primary, Senator Eugene McCarthy, an antiwar candidate, finishes a close second behind Johnson. Nixon wins the Republican primary easily. (*See* **Antiwar Movement**)

16 MARCH: Lieutenant William Calley Jr. orders the massacre of hundreds of men, women, and children at My Lai, South Vietnam; the U.S. Army suppresses news of the slaughter for more than a year. (*See* **Vietnam Causes**)

31 MARCH: Johnson announces that the United States, North Vietnam, and South Vietnam have agreed to hold peace talks, that he has ordered a halt to American bombing of North Vietnam, and that he will not be a candidate for reelection. (*See* **Vietnam Causes**)

4 APRIL: King is assassinated in Memphis, Tennessee. (*See* **Civil Rights Movement: Methods**)

12 MAY: Vietnam peace talks begin in Paris. (*See* **Vietnam Causes**)

4 JUNE: After winning the California primary, Senator Robert F. Kennedy is shot in Los Angeles. He dies the next day.

28 AUGUST: As Chicago police fight with antiwar protestors, Vice President Hubert H. Humphrey is nominated for president at the Democratic convention. (*See* **Antiwar Movement**)

5 NOVEMBER: Nixon is elected president, defeating Humphrey and independent candidate George C. Wallace.

26 NOVEMBER: O. J. Simpson wins the Heisman Trophy.

DECEMBER: In South Africa, Dr. Christian Barnard performs the first heart transplant.

1969

9 APRIL: Four hundred student strikers at Harvard University seize campus buildings; police break up the demonstration. (*See* **1960s Progressive Movement**)

20 JULY: American astronauts Neil Armstrong and Buzz Aldrin become the first men to walk on the Moon. (*See* **U.S. Space Program**)

9 AUGUST: Charles Manson and his cult followers murder actress Sharon Tate and four others.

15–17 AUGUST: The Woodstock Festival is held in Bethel, New York. (*See* **Rock and Roll**)

3 SEPTEMBER: Ho Chi Minh dies at the age of seventy-nine.

3 NOVEMBER: In a televised speech Nixon asserts that the "great silent majority of my fellow Americans" support his Vietnam policies. (*See* **Antiwar Movement, Vietnam Causes, Nixon's Foreign Policy**)

13 NOVEMBER: Vice President Spiro Agnew criticizes television newscasters as "nattering nabobs of negativism."

15 NOVEMBER: In Washington 250,000 gather to protest against U.S. involvement in the Vietnam War. (*See* **Antiwar Movement**)

1970

The U.S. Census Bureau reports a population of 203,302,031. For the first time suburbanites outnumber city dwellers.

18 FEBRUARY: A jury acquits the "Chicago Seven" of inciting riots during the 1968 Democratic convention. (*See* **1960s Progressive Movement**)

22 APRIL: The first celebration of Earth Day is held.

29 APRIL: American and South Vietnamese troops invade Cambodia. (*See* **Vietnam Causes**)

4 MAY: Four students at Kent State University are killed by National Guard troops during a protest over the Cambodian invasion. (*See* **Antiwar Movement**)

9 MAY: Walter Reuther, head of the United Auto Workers, dies suddenly. (*See* **Organized Labor**)

31 JULY: To combat inflation and unemployment, Congress grants Nixon the power to freeze wages, prices, and rents. (*See* **Nixon's Reputation**)

7 AUGUST: Armed black revolutionaries storm a courtroom in San Rafael, California, taking five hostages, including Judge Harold Haley, who is killed by his captors before they are killed in turn by the police. (*See* **Civil Rights Movement: Methods**)

2 OCTOBER: Congress creates the Environmental Protection Agency.

1971

10 JUNE: Nixon ends a twenty-year embargo against the People's Republic of China. (*See* **Nixon's Foreign Policy**)

13 JUNE: *The New York Times* begins publishing the *Pentagon Papers.*

30 JUNE: The Twenty-sixth Amendment, which lowers the voting age to eighteen, goes into effect.

21 AUGUST: George Jackson and five other prisoners die attempting to escape from San Quentin Prison.

9–13 SEPTEMBER: A riot at Attica Prison in New York leaves thirty-nine dead, twenty-nine of them inmates, after Governor Nelson Rockefeller orders police to retake the prison by force.

1972

5 JANUARY: Nixon announces the space-shuttle program. (*See* **U.S. Space Program, Nixon's Reputation**)

21–28 FEBRUARY: Nixon visits China. (*See* **Nixon's Foreign Policy**)

15 MAY: George C. Wallace, campaigning for Democratic presidential nomination, is seriously wounded in an assassination attempt.

22–30 MAY: Nixon becomes the first American president to visit Moscow. (*See* **End of Cold War, Nixon's Foreign Policy**)

17 JUNE: Five men are arrested concerning a break-in at Democratic Party headquarters at the Watergate Complex, Washington, D.C.

12 AUGUST: The last American combat troops leave Vietnam. (*See* **Vietnam Causes**)

29 AUGUST: Nixon says that no White House officials were involved in the Watergate affair. (*See* **Nixon's Reputation**)

15 SEPTEMBER: Two former White House aides and five burglars are indicted in the Watergate break-in.

8 OCTOBER: The United States and North Vietnam agree to end the war; the South Vietnamese government refuses to support the agreement.

2–8 NOVEMBER: Native American activists seize the Bureau of Indian Affairs building in Washington, D.C.

7 NOVEMBER: Nixon is overwhelmingly reelected, defeating George S. McGovern.

18 DECEMBER: As peace negotiations break down, Nixon orders massive bombing of Haiphong and Hanoi. (*See* **Nixon's Foreign Policy, Vietnam Causes**)

1973

22 JANUARY: The United States and North Vietnam sign a cease-fire agreement. (*See* **Vietnam Causes, Nixon's Foreign Policy**)

28 FEBRUARY – 8 MAY: The American Indian Movement (AIM) begins an occupation of Wounded Knee Reservation in Pine Ridge, South Dakota.

25–29 JUNE: Former White House counsel John Dean testifies before a Senate committee and reveals that Nixon kept an "enemies list" of political opponents and that Nixon and some of his advisers were involved in covering up the White House's role in the Watergate break-in. (*See* **Nixon's Reputation**)

13 JULY: Alexander Butterfield testifies at Senate hearings that Nixon taped all conversa-

tions held in the Oval Office. (*See* **Nixon's Reputation**)

26 JULY: Nixon refuses to release tape recordings subpoenaed by the Senate committee and special prosecutor Archibald Cox. (*See* **Nixon's Reputation**)

10 OCTOBER: Vice President Spiro T. Agnew resigns and pleads no contest to charges of tax evasion; Agnew receives a three-year suspended sentence and is fined $10,000.

12 OCTOBER: Under provisions of the Twenty-fifth Amendment to the U.S. Constitution, Nixon nominates Congressman Gerald R. Ford to be vice president; Ford will be confirmed by both houses of Congress.

16 OCTOBER: The Organization of Petroleum Exporting Countries (OPEC) embargoes all oil shipped to the United States and other industrial nations. (*See* **Middle East Policy**)

20 OCTOBER: Nixon orders the firing of special prosecutor Cox; both Attorney General Elliot Richardson and Deputy Attorney General William Ruckelshaus refuse to dismiss him and are fired; Solicitor General Robert Bork then dismisses Cox. (*See* **Nixon's Reputation**)

21 NOVEMBER: The White House announces that 18.5 minutes are missing from a crucial tape recording of an Oval Office conversation. (*See* **Nixon's Reputation**)

6 DECEMBER: Ford becomes vice president.

8 DECEMBER: An audit by the Internal Revenue Service (IRS) reveals that Nixon owes $432,787.13 in back taxes.

1974

5 FEBRUARY: Patricia Hearst is kidnapped by the Symbionese Liberation Army (SLA). In April she announces she will "stay and fight," joining her captors.

8 APRIL: Hank Aaron hits his 715th career home run, breaking the record set by Babe Ruth.

12 JUNE: Girls are allowed to play in Little League Baseball. (*See* **Feminism**)

24 JULY: The U.S. Supreme Court rules 8–0 that Nixon's claim of executive privilege does not allow him to withhold evidence in a criminal investigation. (*See* **Nixon's Reputation**)

30 JULY – 5 AUGUST: Nixon delivers the tapes subpoenaed by the Court and Congress; the tape of 23 June 1972 reveals that Nixon had ordered aides to block the investigation of the Watergate break-in.

9 AUGUST: Nixon resigns as president of the United States; Ford becomes president.

20 AUGUST: Ford nominates Nelson A. Rockefeller for vice president; Congress confirms Rockefeller in December, making Ford and Rockefeller the only men to hold the offices of president and vice president without being elected.

8 SEPTEMBER: Ford pardons Nixon for crimes he may have committed while in office.

14 SEPTEMBER: White mobs in Boston attack school buses bringing black students into white neighborhoods during massive protests against court-ordered integration of city schools. (*See* **White Flight**)

30 OCTOBER: Muhammad Ali regains the heavyweight championship by knocking out George Foreman.

13 NOVEMBER: Karen Silkwood dies in a car accident on her way to meet with a *New York Times* reporter to deliver evidence about safety violations at Kerr-McGee nuclear power plant.

1975

1 JANUARY: H. R. Haldeman, John Ehrlichman, and John Mitchell are convicted of conspiracy and obstruction of justice in relation to the Watergate scandal.

17 APRIL: Khmer Rouge rebels capture the Cambodian capital, Phnom Penh.

30 APRIL: Saigon falls to North Vietnamese forces, who rename it Ho Chi Minh City and announce the unification of Vietnam.

14 MAY: Ford refuses federal assistance to help New York City avoid bankruptcy.

26 JUNE: One AIM member and two FBI agents die in a shoot-out at Pine Ridge Reservation in South Dakota.

30 JULY: Former Teamsters Union president Jimmy Hoffa disappears. (*See* **Organized Labor**)

30 SEPTEMBER: In the "Thrilla in Manila" Ali defeats Joe Frazier, who had defeated Ali in 1971.

1976

20 MARCH: Hearst is convicted of bank robbery and will serve two years in prison.

16 JUNE: American ambassador Francis E. Meloy Jr. and an aide are assassinated in Beirut. (*See* **Middle East Policy**)

2 JULY: The Supreme Court rules that capital punishment does not violate the Eighth or Fourteenth amendments.

19 AUGUST: Ford defeats Reagan for the Republican presidential nomination.

2 NOVEMBER: Jimmy Carter defeats Ford in the presidential election. (*See* **Carter**)

1977

17 JANUARY: Gary Gilmore is executed in Utah, the first execution in the United States in ten years.

21 JANUARY: Carter pardons most Vietnam-era draft evaders. (*See* **Carter**)

17 MARCH: Carter tells the United Nations that the international goal of the United States and the United Nations should be support of human rights. (*See* **Carter, Human Rights**)

5 APRIL: In the longest sit-in protest in a federal building, disabled people occupy San Francisco offices of the Department of Health, Education, and Welfare to demand more federal funds be spent to make government facilities accessible to the disabled.

15 APRIL: The Apple II computer is introduced at the West Coast Computer Fair.

1978

15 FEBRUARY: Leon Spinks defeats Muhammad Ali to become heavyweight champion.

6 JUNE: California voters approve a state constitutional amendment reducing property taxes by 57 percent.

28 JUNE: In *Regents of the University of California* v. *Bakke* the Supreme Court declares universities may take race into account in admitting students in order to promote racial diversity, but universities cannot have racial quotas.

15 SEPTEMBER: Ali defeats Spinks, regaining the heavyweight championship for the third time.

27 NOVEMBER: San Francisco city supervisor Dan White murders Mayor George Moscone and supervisor Harvey Milk for their support of gay rights.

1979

1 JANUARY: The United States recognizes the People's Republic of China.

26 MARCH: Anwar Sadat of Egypt and Menachem Begin of Israel sign a peace treaty at the White House. (*See* **Middle East Policy**)

28 MARCH: A serious accident occurs at the Three Mile Island nuclear plant in Pennsylvania.

6 MAY:In Washington, D.C., 65,000 people demonstrate against nuclear power.

22 OCTOBER: The deposed shah of Iran arrives in the United States for medical treatment. (*See* **Middle East Policy**)

4 NOVEMBER:Iranian militants seize the U.S. embassy in Tehran, holding it and fifty-two Americans hostage in an attempt to force the United States to deliver the shah to Iran for trial. (*See* **Carter, Middle East Policy**)

29 DECEMBER: The Soviet Union invades Afghanistan. (*See* **Human Rights**)

1980

4 JANUARY: Carter responds to the Soviet invasion of Afghanistan with an embargo of U.S. grain sold to the Soviet Union and withdraws the SALT II arms treaty from the Senate for ratification. (*See* **Carter, Human Rights**)

12 APRIL: The United States Olympic Committee votes to boycott the summer Olympics in Moscow.

24 APRIL: American special forces fail in an attempt to rescue the hostages in Iran.

18 MAY: The volcano Mt. St. Helens in Washington erupts.

4 NOVEMBER: Ronald Reagan is elected president, defeating Carter and independent candidate John Anderson. (*See* **End of Cold War**)

1981

20 JANUARY: Reagan is inaugurated as president. Iran frees the American hostages after 444 days of captivity; the United States releases $8 billion in Iranian assets. (*See* **Middle East Policy, End of Cold War**)

30 MARCH: Reagan is wounded by would-be assassin John Hinckley Jr.

12 APRIL: NASA successfully launches the space shuttle *Columbia*. (*See* **U.S. Space Program**)

24 APRIL: Reagan lifts the U.S. grain embargo of the Soviet Union. (*See* **End of Cold War**)

4 JULY: The Centers for Disease Control reports on the spread of a fatal new illness, marked by weakening of the immune system. The new disease is called Acquired Immune Deficiency Syndrome (AIDS).

7 JULY: Reagan nominates Sandra Day O'Connor to the U.S. Supreme Court, where she will become the first female justice. (*See* **Feminism**)

19 AUGUST: American fighter jets shoot down two Libyan planes over the Gulf of Sidra. (*See* **Middle East Policy**)

1982

6 APRIL: Secretary of State Alexander Haig says the United States will not rule out first use of nuclear weapons, reversing a long-term U.S. policy.

30 JUNE: The Equal Rights Amendment fails to achieve ratification. (*See* **Feminism**)

1 DECEMBER: National unemployment reaches 10.7 percent, the highest rate since 1940.

2 DECEMBER: Barney Clark receives the first artificial heart; he lives for four months.

1983

23 MARCH: Reagan proposes the Strategic Defense Initiative, including missile defenses based in outer space, which becomes known as the "Star Wars" defense plan. (*See* **End of Cold War**)

18 APRIL: Sixty-three people die in a terrorist bombing of the U.S. embassy in Beirut. (*See* **Middle East Policy**)

24 MAY: The United States Public Health Service declares AIDS to be the nation's number-one priority.

23 OCTOBER: Nearly 250 marines and sailors are killed by a suicide bomber at barracks in Beirut. (*See* **Middle East Policy**)

25 OCTOBER: U.S. troops invade the Caribbean nation of Grenada. (*See* **End of Cold War**)

1984

JANUARY: The CIA mines Nicaragua's harbors to weaken the country's leftist government.

20 SEPTEMBER: The U.S. embassy in Beirut is destroyed in a terrorist bombing, killing twenty-three people, including two Americans. (*See* **Middle East Policy**)

Former heavyweight boxing champion Muhammad Ali reveals that he is suffering from Parkinson's disease.

6 NOVEMBER: Reagan is reelected, defeating former vice president Walter Mondale.

15 NOVEMBER: "Baby Fae" dies twenty days after surgeons replaced her defective heart with a baboon's heart.

26 NOVEMBER: The United States and Iraq resume diplomatic relations after seventeen years.

1985

15 MAY: The U.S. Census Bureau reports that one-quarter of all American families with children have only one parent in the home.

1 SEPTEMBER: Dr. Robert Ballard discovers the wreck of the *Titanic*.

2 OCTOBER: Actor Rock Hudson dies of AIDS.

11 NOVEMBER: The Centers for Disease Control reports that 7,418 of the reported 14,739 people with AIDS have died.

14 DECEMBER: Wilma Mankiller becomes the principal chief of the Cherokee Nation of Oklahoma, the first woman to head a major Native American nation in the contemporary United States. (*See* **Feminism**)

1986

28 JANUARY: The space shuttle *Challenger* explodes after liftoff, killing all seven crew members. (*See* **U.S. Space Program**)

26 APRIL: An accident at the Chernobyl nuclear power plant in Ukraine releases nuclear fallout across much of Europe.

10 JULY: The National Institute on Drug Abuse reports that deaths from cocaine use have risen from 185 in 1981 to 563 in 1985.

NOVEMBER: The Iran-Contra Affair, in which illegal arms sales to Iran are used to fund the Contras in Nicaragua, is uncovered. (*See* **End of Cold War**)

1987

9 MARCH: Scientists announce that the ozone layer in the atmosphere is dangerously depleted.

27 APRIL: The United States bars former U.N. secretary general and current president of Austria Kurt Waldheim from visiting the United States after he is linked to Nazi war crimes.

19 OCTOBER: The stock market plummets, beginning a recession.

1988

7 JANUARY: New York City mayor Ed Koch approves a ban on smoking in retail stores and other public places.

29 SEPTEMBER: NASA successfully launches *Discovery,* the first shuttle launched since the *Challenger* disaster. (*See* **U.S. Space Program**)

8 NOVEMBER: George H. W. Bush is elected president, defeating Michael S. Dukakis. (*See* **New World Order**)

1989

4 JANUARY: U.S. planes shoot down two Libyan fighters in the Mediterranean.

20 JANUARY: Bush is sworn in as president.

24 MARCH: The oil tanker *Exxon Valdez* runs aground, spilling thousands of gallons of crude oil into Prince William Sound in Alaska.

19 APRIL – 4 JUNE: Prodemocracy demonstrators rally in Tiananmen Square in Beijing before being massacred by Chinese armed forces.

17 OCTOBER: San Francisco is rocked by an earthquake that kills ninety people.

20 OCTOBER: Federal judge Alcee Hastings is impeached and convicted for bribery; later he will be elected to Congress.

11 NOVEMBER: The Berlin Wall is taken down, allowing unlimited access between East and West. (*See* **End of Cold War**)

1990

3 JANUARY: Panamanian president Manuel Noriega surrenders to U.S. forces and is extradited to the United States.

11 FEBRUARY: Nelson Mandela is released from prison in South Africa. (*See* **Human Rights**)

26 JULY: The Americans with Disabilities Act, requiring all public buildings to be accessible to people with disabilities, becomes law.

2 AUGUST: Iraq invades Kuwait.

31 AUGUST: East and West Germany reunite.

1991

15 JANUARY: The Persian Gulf War begins as the United States and its allies invade Kuwait to force out the Iraqis. (*See* **Middle East Policy, New World Order**)

25 FEBRUARY: The Warsaw Pact is dissolved. (*See* **End of Cold War**)

3 APRIL: The Gulf War ends with the liberation of Kuwait. (*See* **New World Order, Middle East Policy**)

15 OCTOBER: Despite allegations of sexual misconduct, the Senate confirms Clarence Thomas to be associate justice of the U.S. Supreme Court.

1992

JANUARY: The text-based web browser is introduced, enabling access to information on what will become the world wide web.

29 APRIL: Rioting in Los Angeles occurs after a jury acquits white Los Angeles police officers accused in the beating of black motorist Rodney King.

3 NOVEMBER: William J. Clinton is elected president of the United States, defeating Bush and independent candidate H. Ross Perot. (*See* **Perot**)

1993

28 FEBRUARY: The United States begins airlifting supplies into Bosnia, which is besieged by hostile Serb forces from Yugoslavia. (*See* **New World Order**)

29 MARCH: Terrorists bomb the World Trade Center in New York City.

19 APRIL: Federal agents besiege the Branch Davidian complex in Waco, Texas, to arrest cult leader David Koresh on weapons charges; a fire set in the complex kills seventy-two, including many children.

18 NOVEMBER: South Africa adopts a new constitution allowing majority rule.

1994

17 JANUARY: An earthquake in Los Angeles kills fifty-one people.

29 APRIL: Mandela is elected president of South Africa.

6 MAY: Clinton is accused of sexually harassing state employee Paula Jones while he was governor of Arkansas.

18 JUNE: O. J. Simpson is arrested for the murder of his former wife and her friend Ronald Goldman.

6 NOVEMBER: Former president Reagan announces that he is suffering from Alzheimer's disease.

8 NOVEMBER: Republicans win control of both houses of the U.S. Congress for the first time since 1952.

1995

24 JANUARY – 3 OCTOBER: Simpson's trial for murder dominates the news; he will be acquitted.

19 APRIL: Right-wing terrorists bomb a federal building in Oklahoma City, killing 168 people.

27 JUNE: An American space shuttle docks with the Soviet space station, *Mir.* (*See* **U.S. Space Program**)

16 OCTOBER: African American men assemble in Washington for the Million Man March to affirm values and take responsibility for their lives.

14 DECEMBER: Warring factions in Bosnia sign a peace treaty.

20 DECEMBER: Republicans in Congress shut down the federal government.

1996

6 JANUARY: After a compromise between the administration and Congress, the U.S. government resumes operations.

25 JULY: A bomb at the Olympics in Atlanta kills one, while another tourist dies of a heart attack.

21 SEPTEMBER: The Virginia Military Academy admits women for the first time. (*See* **Feminism**)

5 NOVEMBER: Clinton is reelected president, defeating Republican Bob Dole.

1997

4 JULY: An American space probe begins exploration of Mars. (*See* **U.S. Space Program**)

14 AUGUST: Timothy McVeigh is sentenced to death for the Oklahoma City bombing.

29 OCTOBER: Iraq expels American members of an international team sent to inspect its weapons.

24 DECEMBER: The first commercial spy satellite is launched by the United States.

1998

9 JANUARY: Ramzi Ahmed Youssef is sentenced to life in prison for the 1993 World Trade Center bombing.

21 JANUARY: Clinton is accused of having sexual relations with a White House intern.

3 FEBRUARY: Clinton proposes the first balanced federal budget in thirty years.

1 APRIL: The Paula Jones sexual-harassment suit against Clinton is dismissed.

3 MAY: The European Union introduces a new currency for all European nations, the euro.

4 MAY: Theodore Kaczynski is sentenced to four life terms for being the "Unabomber," who sent bombs through the mail.

7 AUGUST: Terrorists bomb the U.S. embassies in Tanzania and Kenya.

17 AUGUST: Clinton admits to having had an inappropriate relationship with a White House intern.

20 AUGUST: In retaliation for the bombing of American embassies, the United States launches missile attacks on terrorist bases in Sudan and Afghanistan.

11 SEPTEMBER: Special Prosecutor Kenneth Starr releases a report outlining Clinton's relationship with the White House intern, and suggests impeachment since Clinton had lied about it.

29 OCTOBER: John Glenn, the first American to orbit the Earth, returns to space in a seven-day shuttle mission. (*See* **U.S. Space Program**)

15–19 DECEMBER: American and British forces bomb Iraq to destroy its capacity to make chemical weapons.

19 DECEMBER: The House of Representatives impeaches Clinton.

1999

12 FEBRUARY: The Senate acquits Clinton, by votes of 45–55 and 50–50 (a two-thirds vote being needed to convict).

6 MARCH: *The New York Times* reports that China has been stealing nuclear secrets from American installations.

24 MARCH: U.S. forces participate in seventy-eight days of bombing missions in Kosovo to end the genocide of ethnic Albanians. (*See* **New World Order**)

HISTORY IN DISPUTE

ANTIWAR MOVEMENT

Was the Vietnam Era antiwar movement successful?

Viewpoint: Yes, the antiwar movement succeeded in inhibiting further American escalation of the Vietnam War.

Viewpoint: No, the antiwar movement received too much credit for bringing the war to an end, because other factors influenced American foreign policy.

The Vietnam War generated greater strife in American public life than any episode since the Populist uprising of the 1890s and was the most divisive force since the Civil War. The crux of the division lay between the antiwar movement and American political leaders, who had shaped policy in Vietnam in the late 1950s and early 1960s mostly without consulting public opinion or conducting open debate. The antiwar movement made the war the most prominent public issue after 1965, the year of the first significant deployment of American troops and the first large protest against U.S. policy. In addition, the movement was a constant presence in national life through the duration of the conflict.

Because of its endurance, the fact that national leaders appeared to react toward public opposition to the war, and the many assessments of the antiwar movement that have been written by sympathetic scholars or activists, it has often been taken for granted that the antiwar movement succeeded in limiting American belligerence and eventually forcing the Nixon administration to make peace. These writers argue that the movement succeeded by maintaining constant pressure on public officials to justify the war, and because the war was unjustifiable, the movement exposed America's deeply flawed policy. Moreover, the movement changed the hearts and minds of many thousands, even millions of Americans, who had too long accepted whatever their leaders told them as irrefutable truth.

By maintaining constant and even boisterous public pressure and gradually convincing the American public that the war was irrational and immoral, the movement changed the equation in national politics. In so doing, the movement made it impossible for a leading politician to be aggressively prowar and greatly limited the range of American military options. Unable to prosecute a widened war, U.S. officials were left with two choices: to continue fighting in a losing cause or to negotiate a way out.

However, there are many good reasons to doubt this interpretation of the war's history. More-skeptical scholars have pointed out that the movement itself was always quite diffuse, disorganized, and usually rent by some internal division among its various factions. A prominent part of the movement was its most vocal wing, young student activists who engaged in active resistance through draft-card burning, sit-ins, marches, and other high-profile demonstrations. Especially after a series of violent demonstrations in 1967, this wing of the movement took on an increasingly anti-American tone, which greatly put off the majority of Americans. Many people objected to the antipatriotic attitudes of the protestors; many could not help but notice that the protestors were middle- and upper-class college students who had avoided the draft through college deferments. To a significant part of the public, the antiwar protestors appeared to be spoiled children rejecting the nation that had given them so much.

Moreover, it is not clear that the antiwar movement itself was responsible either for creating significant opposition to American policy or for limiting the options that war planners could deploy. Long before the movement arose, there were many influential men, including military leaders, who had grave reservations over U.S. policy in the region and who took stands against the growing military involvement after 1961. It was they, more than the noisy protestors, who were responsible for raising public skepticism concerning U.S. policy. So, too, events in Vietnam were more important than what happened at home: the longer the war dragged on and the more U.S. personnel died, the stronger public opposition to the war became. Finally, those skeptical about the success of the movement argue that U.S. policymakers were self-consciously limited in their military options not by public opinion but by the realities of the Cold War, which prevented an all-out assault on North Vietnam in the form of either the bombardment of civilian targets or an outright invasion, both of which, it was feared, would trigger a formal Chinese entry into the war, as had happened in Korea in the early 1950s. Ultimately, U.S. policymakers limited themselves, for the prospect of a catastrophic World War III was never out of the question.

Viewpoint: Yes, the antiwar movement succeeded in inhibiting further American escalation of the Vietnam War.

Debate over the impact of domestic opposition to the Vietnam War has been raging since before the war ended. Activists-turned-academics and the first historians to take up the subject generally credited the antiwar movement with ending the war and, they implied, saving lives in the process. Other scholars, particularly those who believe the United States could have won the war, have judged the antiwar movement as ineffective. Their most damning critique, clearly articulated by Adam Garfinkle in *Telltale Hearts: The Origins and Impact of the Vietnam Antiwar Movement* (1995), argues that the antiwar movement was counterproductive. "It did not help stop the war," Garfinkle asserts, "but rather helped prolong it," and therefore bears some responsibility for the death and destruction that continued in the war's later years.

Both interpretations are too simplistic. In fact, the impact of the antiwar movement on the prosecution of the war was much more complicated. Many factors influenced Presidents Lyndon B. Johnson and Richard M. Nixon when they chose to seek peace without victory in Vietnam (most notably the tenacity of the enemy and their apparent willingness to fight indefinitely), and the organized protest of American citizens was one of them. Still, to either give credit to the antiwar movement for ending the war or to blame it for prolonging the conflict overstates its long-term significance. The most that can be said is that, at a few crucial stages, policymakers in the Johnson and Nixon administrations viewed the antiwar movement as a key factor when they decided not to escalate the war further. For movement activists, this could be viewed only as a success.

The first of these instances occurred in the fall of 1967. Since the escalation of the war by President Johnson in 1965, organized protest of the war had little impact on either the president or public opinion. Most expressions of opposition were limited to letters written to elected officials, teach-ins on college campuses, and occasional protest marches, all of which the White House easily ignored. Polls showed that most Americans supported the administration's handling of the conflict, making it easy to dismiss protesters as a vocal minority.

By the end of the summer of 1967, however, certain segments of the antiwar movement began to take steps that guaranteed a confrontation with the government that the administration could not ignore. In a massive show of civil disobedience, an organized draft-resistance movement known as The Resistance collected more than one thousand draft cards on 16 October and four days later delivered them to the Department of Justice in Washington, D.C. Draft resisters, most of whom held deferments that protected them from conscription, distinguished themselves from draft dodgers by openly defying Selective Service laws and inviting prosecution. Their protest was one of moral witness, but it also had a strategic aim: to undermine the draft and overwhelm the federal court system with draft cases in a way that would cause the administration to take steps to end the war. They also hoped that their status as sons of the middle class (most were college students) would influence public opinion and erode support for the president's policies in Vietnam. The day after the draft cards were delivered to the Justice Department, the largest march to date con-

SDS-sponsored antiwar rally in Washington, D.C., on 17 April 1965

(State Historical Society of Wisconsin, Social Action Collection)

verged on the Pentagon, resulting in clashes with police and members of the armed forces.

Almost immediately, President Johnson reacted to the draft-card turn-in and the Pentagon march by ordering investigations into both by the Federal Bureau of Investigation (FBI) and into the antiwar movement in general by the Central Intelligence Agency (CIA). The Selective Service responded by reclassifying some draft resisters and calling them for induction. By January 1968 the Justice Department indicted noted pediatrician Dr. Benjamin Spock, Yale chaplain William Sloane Coffin, and three others for conspiracy to counsel, aid, and abet draft resisters. Most important, according to historian Melvin Small, the administration, "spurred by the increasing levels of dissent," recalled General William Westmoreland, commander of military forces in Vietnam, from the field for a public-relations campaign at home. In six different press briefings and public statements, Westmoreland assured the nation that he was "very, very encouraged" and that American forces were "making real progress." Suddenly it became clear that the antiwar movement had at last captured the administration's attention. The war, however, grinded on, and the full impact of the fall protests did not become apparent until March 1968, when the president decided to change course in Vietnam.

The Tet Offensive launched by the North Vietnamese on 31 January shocked the American public. Although the offensive did not constitute a military victory for communist forces, it effectively erased the rosy picture of progress painted by General Westmoreland and the president in previous months. The ambitious coordinated attack on dozens of targets in South Vietnam (including the American embassy in Saigon) made it clear that an end to the fighting was nowhere in sight. If Small is correct in crediting the antiwar movement for prompting the administration's campaign of reassurances in the fall, then the public shock in the wake of Tet can also be linked to such efforts. This point is important because as public opinion turned against the war, it soon began to affect policy.

The Tet Offensive occurred just as the administration considered General Westmoreland's request for 206,000 additional troops–

an increase of approximately 40 percent and a significant escalation of the administration's commitment to winning the war. The surprise of the offensive, and the public outcry that followed, caused a reevaluation of American policies among many officials in the departments of state and defense. In particular Phil G. Goulding, undersecretary of defense for public affairs, and Townsend Hoopes, undersecretary of the air force, warned of increased draft resistance and widespread domestic dissent following the higher draft calls and reserve activations that would be needed to fill the manpower request. "Until a few weeks ago, the people were being told that we were moving toward victory," Goulding wrote in a memo. "No one was suggesting extra troops, hardships, more spending, Reserve call-ups, high draft calls and increased casualties. Now, suddenly, the picture has changed. . . ." Hoopes argued that a further manpower commitment in the face of the public's "growing disaffection" with the war risked provoking increased draft resistance, unrest in the cities, and ultimately "a domestic crisis of unprecedented proportions."

Such reports moved Secretary of Defense Clark Clifford to favor a rejection of Westmoreland's request and urged that, instead, the first steps toward a negotiated peace should be taken. He received unexpected support from a group of senior advisers to the president known as the Wise Men who were particularly concerned with the changing tide in public opinion. According to one of them, McGeorge Bundy, the majority of the Wise Men agreed that "we could no longer do the job we set out to do in the time that American opinion would permit us." Consequently, on 31 March 1968 Johnson, citing "division in the American house tonight," announced a bombing halt that he hoped might lead to negotiations with the North Vietnamese, and also that he would no longer seek reelection to the office of president. Here, then, was a clear victory for the antiwar movement. The draft resistance of the fall, coupled with the march on the Pentagon, affected policymakers both directly and indirectly. Now they hoped for a quick end to the war.

Of course, the war continued long after 1968. Richard M. Nixon, the new president, promised "peace with honor" during the election campaign, and by the summer of 1969 began to outline his program of Vietnamization, in which South Vietnamese ground forces would gradually assume more responsibility for the fighting as American soldiers came home. According to one confidant, public opinion was a "crucial variable" in Nixon's decision to institute Vietnamization. At the same time, however, Nixon expanded the war by secretly bombing Cambodia for more than a year and by sending ground troops into neighboring Laos. In addition, away from the public eye, Nixon's negotiation strategy in 1969 consisted primarily of a threat to North Vietnam that if they did not become more conciliatory at the peace table, he would unleash the full fury of American power as they had never seen it. Their deadline was 1 November 1969. Consistent with this, Nixon considered escalating the war in various ways in a proposed assault known as Operation Duck Hook. According to historian Marilyn Young, Duck Hook "explored a new range of options [intended to end the war], including a land invasion of the North, the systematic bombing of dikes so as to destroy the food supply, and the saturation bombing of Hanoi and Haiphong."

Here again, however, the antiwar movement intervened and, as historians Small and Tom Wells have described it, made it impossible for Nixon to seriously consider implementing Operation Duck Hook. On 15 October 1969 more than two million Americans participated in the largest expression of dissent in the country's history when they skipped work and school to participate in rallies, demonstrations, church services, candlelight vigils, and organized forums as part of the first Vietnam moratorium. In the biggest demonstration of the day, more than one hundred thousand people gathered on Boston Common to hear a long list of speakers.

Inside the White House on the day of the moratorium, National Security staffer William Watts worked on a speech announcing Operation Duck Hook. According to Nixon's secretary of defense, Melvin Laird, however, the moratorium had "a tremendous influence" on the president, and ultimately Duck Hook was shelved. Nixon himself wrote in his memoirs that after the moratorium, he felt that "American public opinion would be seriously divided by any military escalation of the war."

Nixon actually blamed the moratorium for subverting the path to peace because he believed he could end the war with Operation Duck Hook if not with a threat to put such plans into action. This theme has become a common one for critics of the antiwar movement: by undermining public support for the two administrations, the antiwar movement gave the enemy reason to keep fighting and, more important, kept American policymakers from using overwhelming force that might have ended the war quickly.

It is a point worth considering. The United States did not, after all, withdraw from Vietnam until 1973, and the war between North and South Vietnam dragged on into 1975. Did the antiwar movement actually achieve the opposite of what it hoped to achieve? That is, instead of ending the war, did the antiwar movement prolong it and, therefore, cause more deaths on both sides? It is entirely possible and indeed probable that the successes that protesters achieved in inhibiting the escalation of the war in March 1968 and October 1969 actually prolonged the war, but only because they could not force those with the authority to simply end the war to do so. The charge that the protesters prolonged the war assumes that they were satisfied merely to have prevented escalation, that it was acceptable for Presidents Johnson and Nixon simply to forgo further escalation. It was not. If Nixon sought "peace with honor," the antiwar movement sought only an end to the war and did not care if the United States had to lose it to end it. The supporters of the movement sought peace alone, with or without honor.

Perhaps more important is that such a question would have been regarded as academic to most opponents of the war. Protesters saw a war they regarded as obscene taking the lives of millions of people; they simply had to act in any way they could to end it. For them, protesting was a question of morality. Ultimately they succeeded in keeping the war from expanding at key points in the conflict's history and pushing their government toward the peace table. The responsibility for a war that continued until 1975 must rest with those who were in a position to end it.

—MICHAEL S. FOLEY, UNIVERSITY OF NEW HAMPSHIRE

Viewpoint: No, the antiwar movement received too much credit for bringing the war to an end, because other factors influenced American foreign policy.

In judging the effectiveness of the Vietnam Era antiwar movement, it is important to distinguish between the active movement and the many other opponents of the war, between movement influence and changes in public opinion, and between policies shaped for public consumption and policies compelled by the brute facts of foreign relations. A close look at each of these distinctions strongly suggests that the antiwar movement has taken far too much credit for bringing the war to an end.

There has been an unexamined tendency among writers to give the antiwar movement credit for all of the opposition to the war, organized and otherwise. The organized antiwar groups were an extremely varied lot, and from the earliest days of protests there were tensions and profound disagreements over strategy and ideology. When Students for a Democratic Society (SDS) and assorted radical pacifists such as David Dellinger and Staughton Lynd assumed the leadership of the most notable active protests after 1965, many mainstream opponents of the war felt obliged to distance themselves, both because they disagreed with the radical analysis of the war and because they saw the movement tending toward confrontation with authorities. The most notable effort to join the various organizations into a unified front, under the Mobilization to End the War in Vietnam (MOBE), mostly revealed the dominance of radicals in the activist part of the movement. Only the aging pacifist A. J. Muste was able to keep any sense of mutuality alive. Hence the movement itself, that wing of antiwar sentiment that engaged in active protest, was not necessarily representative of antiwar opinion as a whole.

Because of its notoriety, the activist movement is given credit for swaying national leaders to the antiwar cause. Yet, such an interpretation of events ignores just how divided the government was and how many influential men and women opposed the war from the outset, well before the movement gained any steam. We now know, for example, that while the Joint Chiefs of Staff, America's military high command, were consistently hawkish, many highly placed military leaders were deeply skeptical over and quietly opposed to the war.

More important, the slow but steady escalation of American military involvement in Vietnam raised the active opposition of many in Congress. It is true that the Gulf of Tonkin Resolution, the 1964 decree that gave President Johnson a free hand to take whatever actions necessary to protect U.S. personnel and ensure national interests in Southeast Asia, sailed through Congress with only two, lonely dissenting voices—from Ernest Gruening (D-Alaska) and Wayne Morse (D-Oregon). Many in Congress, most notably J. William Fulbright, chair of the influential Senate Foreign Relations Committee, took the president at his word when he promised to act with prudence and restraint; what they did not

ONE BIG LIE

Don Duncan served in the Special Forces in Vietnam. When first drafted into the army, he was a militant anti-Communist. After eighteen months "in country," he denounced the war and U.S. involvement in Southeast Asia.

The whole thing was a lie. We weren't preserving freedom in South Vietnam. There was no freedom to preserve. To voice opposition to the government meant jail or death. Neutralism was forbidden and punished. Newspapers that didn't say the right thing were closed down. People are not even free to leave and Vietnam is one of those rare countries that doesn't fill its American visa quota. It's all there to see once the Red film is removed from the eyes. We aren't the freedom fighters. We are the Russian tanks blasting the hopes of an Asian Hungary.

It's not democracy we brought to Vietnam—it's anticommunism. This is the only choice the people in the village have. This is why most of them have embraced the Viet Cong and shunned the alternative. . . .

When I returned from Vietnam I was asked, "Do you resent young people who have never been in Vietnam, or in any war, protesting it?" On the contrary, I am relieved. I think they should be commended. I had to wait until I was 35 years old, after spending 10 years in the Army and 18 months personally witnessing the stupidity of the war, before I could figure it out. That these young people were able to figure it out so quickly and so accurately is not only a credit to their intelligence but a great personal triumph over a lifetime of conditioning and indoctrination. I only hope that the picture I have tried to create will help other people come to the truth without wasting 10 years. Those people protesting the war in Vietnam are not against our boys in Vietnam. On the contrary. What they are against is our boys being in Vietnam. They are not unpatriotic. Again the opposite is true. They are opposed to people, our own and others, dying for a lie, thereby corrupting the very word democracy.

Source: *Judith Clair Albert and Stewart Edward Albert, eds.,* The Sixties Papers *(New York: Praeger, 1984), p. 300.*

know was that the administration had been planning a bombing campaign against North Vietnam for at least three months. They had been lied to, and when the administration inaugurated sustained bombing in early 1965, many congressmen were incredulous not only that the president would violate his promise but also that he was raising the stakes in a hopeless gamble in a tiny and inconsequential corner of the globe.

As early as 1966 many moderate congressional leaders with long experience in foreign affairs began to voice their dismay. Mike Mansfield, who had been one of the earliest supporters of American aid to South Vietnam in the mid 1950s, for example, came out in opposition to the war. Eventually even some of the most conservative congressmen harbored serious doubts. However, no one was more influential than Fulbright himself. Foreign policy was Fulbright's forte, and he expected to exercise some influence in the White House. He took the decision to escalate as a personal betrayal, and when he voiced his opposition to Johnson in private he found himself increasingly pushed out of the circle of influence. In response he began in 1966 to hold public hearings on the war under the auspices of his Senate committee, and the tone of the hearings was decidedly hostile to administration policy.

Fulbright was arguably the single most important opponent of the Vietnam War, but he was not alone as an establishment critic. Several of the most powerful establishment figures regarding foreign policy also opposed the war, and they did so even earlier than Fulbright. George Kennan, the father of America's Cold War containment policy, opposed the first dispatch of American military personnel under John F. Kennedy in 1961 and consistently opposed escalation thereafter. Hans Morgenthau, the nation's leading international-relations scholar, spoke and wrote widely against the war and was the object of administration ridicule during the Teach-In Movement of 1965. Walter Lippmann, a journalist whose expertise in international relations reached back to his participation in Woodrow Wilson's peace plans during World War I, used his widely syndicated newspaper column to issue steady arguments against a policy he eventually came to see as sheer madness.

Because of their influential positions, wide experience in foreign policy, generally conservative domestic politics, and, above all, their wisely stated reasons for opposing the war, the establishment critics introduced formidable opposition to the war from the earliest days of American involvement. Fulbright's Senate hearings and Lippmann's regular columns carried more weight both in shaping public opinion and in putting the administration on the defensive than the public protests of the movement. Indeed, these men were conservative of temperament and naturally disdainful of the movement's exhibitionist activism, and by no means can they be associated as part of the antiwar movement. If anything, it confuses the matter to say that the movement influenced them: the arguments that the establishment critics developed resounded again and again in protest speeches and writings, and activists regularly dropped their names in an effort to exploit the ring of authority.

It is impossible to sort out who was influencing public opinion and how, but the evidence strongly suggests that the reasoned opposition of liberals and the establishment critics was far more important than the radical creeds of movement activists. Always hard to measure, public opinion regarding the Vietnam War is particularly hard to gauge because it shifted regularly in response to specific events and was, in the end, deeply ambivalent. Opinion polls regularly showed a tendency to rally around the flag; any increase in military activity in response to a specific event usually enjoyed majority support. However, that support was fleeting at best. Along with this well-known tendency there was a constant apprehension that the nation might be dragged into a war it had no business being in. As casualty tolls mounted after 1966, the two competing tendencies hardened into an almost schizophrenic opinion that the United States should either win the war at any cost or withdraw. After the Tet offensive of January 1968 the bulk of opinion shifted toward the latter view.

The antiwar movement can take credit for precious little of the war-weariness of the American public. On the whole the mainstream regarded the antiwar activists as ungrateful, unpatriotic, foul-mouthed radicals, an image that was reinforced by the media's tendency to exaggerate the influence of hippies and Communists in the movement. Antiwar protesters usually ended up lower in the public's estimation than President Johnson himself. The widespread contempt, even hatred, expressed for the movement only added to the ambiguity of public opinion. A good deal of anecdotal evidence, which appears in interviews and testimonies of the day, suggests that the typical attitude was that of a man who told one author that "I hate those damn protesters. I think we should win the war or get the hell out."

It is even more doubtful that the antiwar movement affected the actual policies of either the Johnson or Nixon administrations. Johnson would not even listen to Fulbright, and he considered Defense Secretary Robert McNamara's resignation akin to treason; how much less was he inclined to heed the antiwar movement? Only Senator Robert Kennedy's meddling in foreign policy worried him, and Kennedy can hardly be considered part of the movement. Nixon, meanwhile, exploited the ambivalence of public opinion and turned public contempt for antiwar activists to his own political ends. His famous "Silent Majority" speech was a cynical—and effective—attempt to justify his policies in contrast to the radicals who only wanted to tear America apart. If anything, the movement was counterproductive to the cause of ending the war during the Nixon years.

Given the significant opposition from establishment figures, in the absence of any determined public support, it is hardly a surprise that both the Johnson and Nixon administrations found themselves limited in the means they could employ in Vietnam. Yet, the limitations that they faced were imposed not by public opinion but by the hard realities of Cold War geopolitics—and it ought to be stated that within those limits the United States prosecuted a vigorous and terribly destructive campaign. U.S. policy was limited, first of all, by the threat that China might enter the conflict as it had in the Korean War in 1950. Such a development would greatly raise the stakes for the entire world. Beyond that possibility the United States had to keep its eye on the Soviet Union, perhaps not so much in Indochina as in Western Europe. The 1968 Soviet quelling of the Czechoslovakian democracy movement reminded American policymakers that Vietnam was, after all, only on the periphery of American interests and that the prosecution of the war there objectively weakened their ability to respond to communist power in Europe.

The limits on American options were reached in the objective character of international power relations. Any way it was figured, Vietnam simply was not essential to American national interests, and any full-throttled prosecution of war was not worth the serious risks to American security elsewhere. For all his belligerence, Nixon recognized as much, and for all the violence he unleashed—the United States dropped one ton of bombs for every minute Nixon was in office—his intention was to shore up American power in relation to the Soviets and Chinese by ending the war in Vietnam. The antiwar movement can hardly take credit for the brutal reality that American policymakers had to face up to: that the war in Vietnam was a lost cause, the wrong war with the wrong foe at the wrong time.

—DAVID STEIGERWALD,
OHIO STATE UNIVERSITY, MARION

References

William Berman, *William Fulbright and the Vietnam War: The Dissent of a Political Realist* (Kent, Ohio: Kent State University Press, 1988);

Charles DeBenedetti and Charles Chatfield, *An American Ordeal: The Antiwar Movement of the Vietnam Era* (Syracuse, N.Y.: Syracuse University Press, 1990);

Michael Ferber and Staughton Lynd, *The Resistance* (Boston: Beacon, 1971);

Michael S. Foley, "Confronting the War Machine: Draft Resistance During the Vietnam War," dissertation, University of New Hampshire, 1999;

Michael B. Friedland, *Lift Up Your Voice Like a Trumpet* (Chapel Hill: University of North Carolina Press, 1998);

Adam Garfinkle, *Telltale Hearts: The Origins and Impact of the Vietnam Antiwar Movement* (New York: St. Martin's Press, 1995);

Todd Gitlin, *The Sixties: Years of Hope, Days of Rage* (New York: Bantam, 1987);

Phil G. Goulding, *Confirm or Deny: Informing the People on National Security* (New York: Harper & Row, 1970);

Fred Halstead, *Out Now! A Participant's Account of the American Movement Against the Vietnam War* (New York: Pathfinder, 1978);

Tom Hayden, *Reunion: A Memoir* (New York: Random House, 1988);

Townsend Hoopes, *The Limits of Intervention* (New York: McKay, 1969);

Irving Horowitz, *The Struggle is the Message: The Organization and Ideology of the Anti-War Movement* (Berkeley, Cal.: Glendessary, 1972);

Walter Isaacson and Evan Thomas, *The Wise Men: Six Friends and the World They Made* (New York: Simon & Schuster, 1986);

Thomas Powers, *Vietnam: The War at Home* (New York: Grossman, 1973);

Melvin Small, *Johnson, Nixon and the Doves* (New Brunswick, N.J.: Rutgers University Press, 1988);

Small and William D. Hoover, eds., *Give Peace a Chance: Exploring the Vietnam Antiwar Movement* (Syracuse, N.Y.: Syracuse University Press, 1992);

Irwin Unger, *The Movement: A History of the American New Left, 1959–1972* (New York: Dodd, Mead, 1974);

Sandy Vogelgesang, *The Long Dark Night of the Soul: The American Intellectual Left and the Vietnam War* (New York: Harper & Row, 1974);

Tom Wells, *The War Within: America's Battle Over Vietnam* (Berkeley: University of California Press, 1994);

Lawrence S. Wittner, *Rebels Against War: The American Peace Movement, 1933–1983* (Philadelphia: Temple University Press, 1984);

Nancy Zaroulis and Gerald Sullivan, *Who Spoke Up? American Protest Against the War in Vietnam, 1963–1975* (Garden City, N.Y.: Doubleday, 1984).

CARTER

Was Jimmy Carter a successful president in the realm of foreign policy?

Viewpoint: No, Jimmy Carter's overwhelming defeat in 1980 was a repudiation of his failed foreign policies, which were ill-conceived and poorly executed.

Viewpoint: Yes, Jimmy Carter's administration produced some remarkable triumphs in American diplomacy in pursuit of his morality-based goals.

James Earl "Jimmy" Carter, former governor of Georgia, won the presidency in 1976 with the slogan: "For America's third century, why not her best?" Carter offered a change, not only from the policies of Gerald R. Ford, his opponent, but also from the failures of previous Democratic and Republican administrations. He was narrowly elected in November, and promised a weary and divided nation a new beginning both at home and abroad. As governor, Carter had broken with the South's racist past; as president he promised to free the United States from the burdens of imperialist wars.

After delivering his inaugural address, Carter and his family walked from the Capitol to the White House, the first of many attempts by Carter to open up the presidency, a contrast to the fortress that had surrounded presidents Lyndon B. Johnson and Richard M. Nixon. He offered a simplicity and openness that would prevent catastrophes such as Watergate or the Vietnam War from further weakening the nation, invoking the Book of Micah's call for a quiet strength and simple dignity.

Carter used simplicity and openness as a way of achieving the highest possible national goals. However, Carter, like Ford, was a victim of a domestic economy neither could master. The huge debts incurred in fighting the Vietnam War and increases in the cost of petroleum had driven up the rate of inflation; at the same time, these and other economic factors triggered relatively high unemployment. These domestic factors might have undone any administration, but Carter also was victim to some international events he could not control. The Soviet Union, perceiving Carter's weakness, invaded Afghanistan and increased Soviet support to leftists in countries including Nicaragua, Ethiopia, and Angola. In Iran the revolution against Shah Mohammed Reza Pahlevi turned into a revolution against the United States, and in 1979 Iranian students seized the American embassy in Tehran, holding fifty-two embassy employees hostage. Carter's administration was not able to release them.

In November 1980 the American people rather decisively voiced their judgment of Carter's failure by replacing him with Ronald W. Reagan. What had gone wrong? In one essay, Jürgen Scheunemann of Yale University delivers a verdict on Carter's foreign policy as one of failure, from its misguided inception to its ignominious end. In the second essay, though, Itai Sneh of Columbia University argues that Jimmy Carter had some notable international successes: in negotiating arms reductions and in the Middle East. Carter brought together President Anwar Sadat of Egypt and Prime Minister Menachim Begin of Israel, a remarkable achievement that earned both Sadat and Begin the Nobel Peace Prize. Perhaps Carter should have shared in this honor, but it was characteristic of him to allow others to take credit. Since his forced retirement Carter has emerged as an international spokesman for human rights, overseeing elections in Haiti and other nations that have begun the process of moving from dictatorship to democracy. The American electorate judged Carter harshly; history may take a different view.

Viewpoint: No, Jimmy Carter's overwhelming defeat in 1980 was a repudiation of his failed foreign policies, which were ill-conceived and poorly executed.

The presidency of James Earl "Jimmy" Carter was successful in many foreign-policy arenas: Carter brought a new style to U.S. foreign policy; introduced human rights as a foreign-policy goal in itself for the first time; brokered some of the twentieth century's most important agreements and treaties, such as the Middle East Peace Accord and the Panama Canal Treaty; and began a new era in North-South relations. In addition, Carter almost succeeded in implementing a new disarmament treaty with the Soviet Union, Strategic Arms Limitation Treaty II (SALT II). These are milestones in international diplomatic history that no critique of the Carter presidency can diminish. Even Carter's worst defeat, which was partly responsible for Ronald W. Reagan's election in November 1980, namely the hostage crisis in Tehran, was, in reality, a success for Carter, since the hostages were freed unharmed, thanks to shrewd and skillful diplomacy.

By the same token, however, these diplomatic achievements only reflect some of the highlights of the Carter administration. They by no means fully represent the greater part of his foreign policy in the years from 1977 to 1981. In fact, most of Carter's goals for a new foreign policy proved to be failures, because they were ill conceived and often poorly executed. Measured by the Carter administration's own goals and standards, a great deal of his foreign policy was confusing and confused. Even though many of the crises Carter faced around the globe were beyond his control, ultimately the responsibility for having not successfully resolved many of them remained in the hands of his administration.

Carter, in a sense, was the first post–Cold War U.S. president. Supporting himself with the theoretical concept of trilateralism, Carter tried to break free from the frozen, but stable, confrontational Cold War pattern of bipolar military and ideological warfare between the United States and the Soviet Union. Trilateralism, perceived by an international group of thinkers, including Carter and some of his top foreign-policy advisers such as Secretary of State Cyrus Vance and National Security Advisor Zbigniew Brzezinski, interprets the international system of nation-states as an increasingly multilateral system. With new powers emerging (for example, China), so the theory suggests, the traditional U.S.-Soviet conflict would eventually lose much of its significance. Economic and cultural factors would rival the military and ideological confrontation. Even more important, trilateralism subtly implied a weakened United States, as it saw the world dominated and led by three blocs of power: the United States, the Western European nations, and Japan. One of the most important aspects of this model, multilateralism, was introduced by the Carter administration as an improvement of North-South relations. The aim was not only to integrate Latin American states into the international community but also to break away from the Johnson and Nixon administrations' focus on the Soviet Union and the many local theaters of conflict that were so typical of the Cold War era. In the end, however, Carter stayed within the familiar framework of the Cold War.

A good example is Carter's successful rapprochement with China. Given his administration's goals, its China policy was marked by double standards and hypocrisy that ultimately showed the failure of Carter's multilateralism. Plans to intensify ties and, ultimately, to establish an official diplomatic relationship with the People's Republic of China dated back to the foreign-policy reviews of the Carter presidential race. The incoming administration felt that China, with close to one billion people, was too important to be neglected. In addition, a new China policy would signal to the world's threshold nations that the United States was now committed to a multilateral world, by demonstrating a more open and constructive attitude to international politics beyond the classic Cold War thinking. Once implemented, however, this policy—with the SALT II disarmament talks placed in a gridlock by the Soviets and the Soviet invasion of Afghanistan in December 1979—slowly metamorphosed into a classic power policy that primarily served immediate U.S. national interests. Carter, like his predecessor Nixon and Nixon's national security adviser Henry Kissinger, ended up adopting a triangular

Anwar Sadat, Jimmy Carter, and Menachim Begin celebrate the signing of the Camp David peace agreements in 1978

(Jimmy Carter Library)

power policy primarily designed to gain leverage over the Soviet Union. In 1980 Carter played the "China Card" he had so vehemently despised earlier. Deepening the ties with China was a subtle threat to the Soviet Union. The administration hoped that it would be useful in "softening up" the Soviets. By adopting this approach Carter's proclaimed new beginning in international relations not only came to an end but also fell back into the old pattern of bipolar global confrontation.

This all became abundantly clear when the Soviets invaded Afghanistan on 25 December 1979. The U.S. reaction was quick, decisive, and morally correct. Among other measures, the United States stopped its grain supplies to the U.S.S.R. and boycotted the Olympic Games in 1980. In addition, Carter asked the Senate not to vote on the SALT II treaty. But the success of these measures was more than doubtful. In fact, they seemed to be primarily designed to send a strong signal to the Soviet Union, but not to really interfere with superpower relations. In the long run it made U.S. foreign policy look weak and indecisive, a fact both Democratic and Republican hopefuls in the presidential race dwelled upon at length. It also added new daubs of color to the picture of a hypocritical president who favored symbolism over substance.

One of Carter's most historically significant policies regarded international human rights. Though the president undoubtedly raised human rights as a policy issue, not only in the international community but also in the bilateral relations conducted with other nations, the outcome remained questionable. Measured by Carter's own goals and standards, his human-rights policy fell short of his promises and even jeopardized U.S. national interests in some cases. The cause was noble, and the launch looked promising, but its execution was poor. The human-rights policy turned out to be, at times, an erratic and confusing experience, with standards that were indecisive and contradictory. Some countries with horrible human-rights records, such as Anastacio Somoza's Nicaragua, did, in fact, receive less (and finally no) U.S. foreign assistance in order to pressure them to comply with international human-rights accords. Other nations of much higher strategic value to the Carter administration, however, such as Iran or the Philippines, had equally poor human-rights records. Yet, the Carter administration (in Iran, for example) tried to push the sale of AWACs military-reconnaissance airplanes to the shah, and it prolonged the Ferdinand Marcos dictatorship in the Philippines, fearing it would otherwise endanger the U.S. military

bases in the archipelago. No doubt the starkest contradiction was Carter's ignoring of some of the world's most vicious violators of human rights: the Soviet Union and the Eastern bloc nations. Despite the administration's early and stern public criticism of the Soviet suppression of dissidents and its restrictive handling of Jewish emigration, human rights did not play an important part in U.S.-Soviet relations. Again, strategic considerations (the United States did not want to jeopardize the SALT II talks) superseded human rights. In the case of some Eastern bloc countries, most notably Romania, the Carter administration–even though it had much more leverage with these nations than with the Soviet Union–ignored gross and open human-rights abuses by, for example, dictator Nicolae Ceausecu, who was perceived as the head of state of an independent nation that seemed to be chipping away at the Eastern bloc. Finally, the breakdown of Carter's multilateralism was highlighted by the human-rights policies themselves and the reasons, in so many instances, they were neglected for strategic or global political reasons. In his human-rights policies Carter was forced to acknowledge that the international system had to continue to be steered by the bipolar confrontation between the Soviet Union and the United States. Dealing with nations outside this frame of reference proved to be more difficult in reality because the Soviets were incapable of perceiving the international system differently from what it still was in the late 1970s, namely a world dominated by the Cold War. Carter's foreign-policy concept came years too soon. A multilateral foreign policy was to make sense about six years later with the rise of Mikhail Gorbachev.

Carter's foreign policy with regard to the leading allies of the United States also failed. Given the administration's adherence to the theories of trilateralism, it appears even more amazing that U.S.-European relations in the years from 1977 to 1981 turned out to be quite as bad as they did. Right from the start, veteran European leaders such as German chancellor Helmut Schmidt and French president Giscard d'Estaing were suspicious of Carter's lack of experience in foreign affairs and his firm commitment to morality in foreign policy. They disagreed strongly with Carter's explicit style of public diplomacy during the first year of his administration, especially in that one area that was most important to the American president: human rights. For them, publicly condemning the Soviet Union or key Western allies for their poor human-rights records meant jeopardizing more-important foreign-policy goals such as international trade agreements and disarmament talks. Schmidt, in particular, favored a more covert, quiet diplomacy in dealing with human rights abroad. So despite the fact that trilateralism as a theoretical concept underlines the close cooperation between the United States, the West European nations, and Japan, Carter actually subscribed to an extremely unilateral style of foreign policy. In international human-rights and disarmament policy, the United States followed its own path rather strictly and did not really integrate European leaders.

Another example of this poor style and Carter's misunderstanding of European foreign-policy tradition was his unilateral decision to stop development of the Enhanced Radiation Weapon, popularly known as the neutron bomb. This new weapon, first perceived as a counterbalance to presumed Soviet superiority in conventional arms in the European theater, quickly grew into a foreign-policy disaster for the Carter administration. Initially Carter had made it clear that his administration would begin manufacturing the bomb only if the Europeans, primarily the Germans, explicitly committed themselves to deploying it in their countries. Carter, however, underestimated the growing domestic opposition to the neutron bomb in European countries. He remained too passive and let the European leaders discuss the weapons system as they were increasingly pressed, at times by their own parties, to weaken their commitment. Carter, faced with the choice between developing the weapon system without knowing if the Europeans would eventually deploy it or canceling it, opted for the latter. Although this was an understandable step, it revealed a lack of leadership and decisiveness–and it certainly supported the Soviet perception of a weak and hedging United States. In addition, the long process of (often publicly) discussing the neutron bomb with the European leaders further alienated them from the United States, especially when Carter suddenly and unilaterally came to his own decision. For transatlantic relations, the Carter years were a major crisis that was only resolved in the first Reagan years.

Carter's effort remains one of the most fascinating and noble attempts to change ideas, patterns, and implementation of U.S. foreign policy. One has to credit Carter for his personal courage, but also criticize him for his many shortcomings. In a way, as a devoted Christian, Carter later acknowledged his failures when he began his work at the nonprofit, private Carter Center, where his presidential foreign policy continues in private. Thanks to this new setting, Citizen Carter has implemented more of his original foreign policy than President Carter ever did.

—JÜRGEN SCHEUNEMANN, FOX FELLOW, YALE UNIVERSITY

Viewpoint: Yes, Jimmy Carter's administration produced some remarkable triumphs in American diplomacy in pursuit of his morality-based goals.

James Earl "Jimmy" Carter, a Democrat from Georgia, having won the 1976 election against incumbent Gerald R. Ford, served as the thirty-ninth president of the United States of America from 1977 to 1981. Carter succeeded in restoring a degree of faith in earnest governance in general and, especially, in the rectitude of American foreign policy. He demonstrated a conscience for social justice. In particular, Carter displayed a respectful treatment of the weaker elements within the United States and elsewhere in the world. His morality-based goals enshrined a more ethical approach in the formation and execution of American foreign policy. His agenda was based on the universal promotion of human rights, broadly defined, and on their protection in specific cases, such as in several problematic Latin American countries.

His conduct helped mend the breach of public trust caused by the corruption evident in the Watergate scandal, the Vietnam War, and revelations of a pattern of illicit operations by the Central Intelligence Agency abroad, as well as social turmoil caused by the Civil Rights movement, which fought segregation in the South and which included widespread racial riots. The 1963 assassination of President John F. Kennedy marked the beginning of an era largely characterized by a lack of credible, visionary leadership from the White House and by widespread cynicism and an almost collective disillusionment with the sense of American grandeur that had been evident since the 1945 victory in World War II. Despite his reelection defeat by Ronald W. Reagan in 1980, Carter's principled, normative approach to the conduct of the U.S. government at home and abroad restored much legitimacy to the presidency and confidence in politicians as servants of the people. His legacy for his successors, for Americans, and particularly for how people view American foreign policy, have been formidable.

Carter's gradual emergence from obscurity as a peanut farmer and occasional preacher in his church to becoming a national leader and international pacesetter began in his 1970 election as the governor of Georgia. He witnessed and supported the activities of the Civil Rights movement during the 1960s, when it was led by African Americans such as the Reverend Martin Luther King Jr. His campaign brought many white and black groups together. Indeed, in his 1971 inaugural address, Carter took a bold step, establishing a pattern for his actions. He tried to right moral wrongs by taking public stands, even ones that were not popular among the general population. Carter apologized to African Americans for the abuses and degradation they endured during their prolonged ordeal of slavery and segregation. He did so despite the antagonism that his statements created among segregationists in his own constituency, the Democratic Party. His administration, moreover, fought to eradicate any remnants of discrimination.

After his term as governor ended in 1975, Carter launched a presidential campaign in which he promised an honest, transparent, and accountable government, making a commitment to the American people: "I'll never lie to you." Carter conveyed his beliefs as a born-again Christian. He also espoused nationally the values of the Civil Rights movement, such as equality, integration, and nonviolence. As a candidate he committed himself to a trustworthy leadership founded on moral judgments. Carter frequently reiterated his conviction that human rights constituted "the soul" of American foreign policy. Carter advanced this discourse during his successful 1976 presidential campaign. In particular, he highlighted the positive role a president could play in endorsing and promoting human rights and in fighting racism and eradicating apartheid South Africa.

To be sure, Carter had failures. He encountered, moreover, major ideological and practical problems during his administration. Many of them were delineated by Jeanne Kirkpatrick in an article that was widely read at the time, "Dictatorships and Double Standards," published in the conservative monthly, *Commentary,* in November 1979. The article was highly critical of Carter's foreign-policy philosophy and of his actual deeds (subsequently securing for Kirkpatrick the position of U.S. Ambassador to the United Nations in the Reagan administration).

The issues involved included the wide perception at home and abroad that the United States was weak and hesitant about projecting its economic force and military might beyond

THE CAMP DAVID ACCORDS

Between 5 September and 17 September 1978, Anwar Sadat, president of the Arab Republic of Egypt, and Menachem Begin, prime minister of Israel, met with Jimmy Carter, president of the United States of America, at Camp David, Maryland, and agreed on the following framework for peace in the Middle East. They invited other parties in the Arab-Israel conflict to adhere to it.

Preamble

The search for peace in the Middle East must be guided by the following:

The agreed basis for a peaceful settlement of the conflict between Israel and its neighbors is United Nations Security Council Resolution 242, in all its parts.

After four wars during 30 years, despite intensive human efforts, the Middle East, which is the cradle of civilization and the birthplace of three great religions, does not enjoy the blessings of peace. The people of the Middle East yearn for peace so that the vast human and natural resources of the region can be turned to the pursuits of peace and so that this area can become a model for coexistence and cooperation among nations.

The historic initiative of President Sadat in visiting Jerusalem and the reception accorded to him by the parliament, government, and people of Israel, and the reciprocal visit of Prime Minister Begin to Ismailia, the peace proposals made by both leaders, as well as the warm reception of these missions by the peoples of both countries, have created an unprecedented opportunity for peace which must not be lost if this generation and future generations are to be spared the tragedies of war.

The provisions of the Charter of the United Nations and the other accepted norms of international law and legitimacy now provide accepted standards for the conduct of relations among all states.

To achieve a relationship of peace, in the spirit of Article 2 of the United Nations Charter, future negotiations between Israel and any neighbor prepared to negotiate peace and security with it are necessary for the purpose of carrying out all the provisions and principles of Resolutions 242 and 338.

Peace requires respect for the sovereignty, territorial integrity and political independence of every state in the area and their right to live in peace within secure and recognized boundaries free from threats or acts of force. Progress toward that goal can accelerate movement toward a new era of reconciliation in the Middle East marked by cooperation in promoting economic development, in maintaining stability and in assuring security.

Security is enhanced by a relationship of peace and by cooperation between nations which enjoy normal relations. In addition, under the terms of peace treaties, the parties can, on the basis of reciprocity, agree to special security arrangements such as demilitarized zones, limited armaments areas, early warning stations, the presence of international forces, liaison, agreed measures for monitoring and other arrangements that they agree are useful.

Source: *Jimmy Carter Library, Atlanta, Georgia.*

its borders, although most events were the result of endemic local problems or were clearly beyond American control. They included, in 1979, the collapse of Anastasio Somoza's pro-American regime in Nicaragua and the Soviet invasion of Afghanistan. Particularly important was the fall of the shah of Iran, causing a rise in oil prices, an energy crisis in the United States, a global economic recession, and the subsequent taking of American hostages in Tehran. The latter is by far the most memorable and painful crisis of Carter's presidency, dooming his prospects for reelection.

Carter took the unusual step of having two speeches upon accession to the presidency in January, 1977: one to Americans, another to the rest of humanity. In his inaugural address to the people of the world, Carter promised to address the needs of non-Americans. He repeated and acted upon his beliefs during his presidency, a time when regular vigilance with respect to abuses of human rights all over the world was evident. His strategy, especially in

Latin America, took the form of outreach to people rather than collaboration with their oppressive leaders or outright interventions in their internal affairs.

The agenda was largely kept, even to the detriment of traditional clients, such as the "Banana Republics" in Latin America, and of short-term U.S. interests. The reservoir of distrust toward perceived American aggression in Vietnam, domination in corrupt regimes in the Americas, and clandestine operations by the CIA was considerably diluted by a fresh outpour of goodwill caused by his dignified conduct. When Carter could control events—unlike in Iran—he implemented a noninterventionist policy, especially in Latin America, where, for example, he chose not to help Somoza's corrupt and failing regime, urgent requests by the long-term U.S. ally notwithstanding.

Of particular importance was Carter's strong support of the 1976 recommendations of the Trilateral Commission concerning the Panama Canal. Thus, he tried to open a new era in U.S. actions in the Western Hemisphere by signing in September 1977, in the presence of many leaders from the Americas, the Panama Canal Treaties. These agreements will yield the Canal Zone to Panama on 31 December 1999, while protecting American security and commercial interests. Carter did so even in the face of strong opposition from right-wing elements who opposed any surrender of American territory or influence. Only his personal involvement secured the 1978 passage of these treaties in Congress. Conceding control and sovereignty to the local people amounted to actively endorsing the principles of self-government and territorial integrity, thus helping to reverse—even if only in part—the long legacy of American control in that isthmus.

The Carter administration also censured, reduced aid, and imposed sanctions against American allies who abused human rights. These actions were coupled with political activism that vigorously challenged authoritarian regimes in Latin America—including Argentina, Brazil, Chile, and Paraguay—and in the Philippines, although there were exceptions for "strategically placed states" such as South Korea and Indonesia. Carter also denounced the apartheid regime in South Africa, a staunch American ally in the fight against Soviet interventions in its continent. The strength of this approach was its promotion of civil institutions that facilitated the development of democracy; its weakness was to make local activists appear to be supported by outsiders, helping their tyrannical opponents portray them as agents of a foreign cause and a hegemonic superpower.

Carter frequently denounced the Soviet bloc for its oppression of human rights, as well as condemned the 1978 deployment of a brigade in Cuba and the 1979 Soviet invasion of Afghanistan. He spoke in favor of democratic activism in Poland in 1980, helping to undermine the Cold War status quo as the popular Solidarity movement challenged the legitimacy of the communist government. Carter's administration also accorded a full recognition to the People's Republic of China in 1979, even in the face of a stern resistance by the considerable pro-Taiwan lobby. This act resolved a long-term obstacle in American relations with the communist regime representing the vast majority of the Chinese people.

Carter's most impressive achievement was probably his personal negotiation of the September 1978 Camp David Agreements that facilitated the March 1979 Peace Treaty between Egypt and Israel. Only thanks to Carter's tenacity and personal involvement did these two archenemies reach a deal, such highly problematic issues as the Israeli settlements in the Sinai Peninsula and whether the Palestinians had a right to self-determination notwithstanding. Even the subsequent Reagan and Bush administrations, while repudiating Carter's policies, did not move far away from his positions.

Subsequently, Carter's own personal stature has been tremendous in the developing world. He has been asked to negotiate transitions to democracy and monitor elections. Carter demonstrated, in performing personal diplomacy after leaving the White House, his commitment to and advocacy of the cause of human rights through his own prestige and the Carter Center he established in Atlanta, Georgia. His personal stature has grown steadily thanks to his efforts, regardless of intimidation, financial constraints, and political pressures at home and in the targeted areas, in helping to organize communities of advocates in such diverse places as India and Mexico and monitoring elections in countries such as South Africa and Nicaragua.

—ITAI SNEH, COLUMBIA UNIVERSITY

References

Douglas Brinkley, *The Unfinished Presidency: Jimmy Carter's Journey Beyond the White House* (New York: Viking, 1998);

Lloyd de Mause and Henry Ebel, eds., *Jimmy Carter and American Fantasy: Psychohistori-*

cal Explorations (New York: Two Continents, 1977);

John Dumbrell, *The Carter Presidency: A Re-Evaluation* (Manchester, U.K. & New York: Manchester University Press, 1993);

Stanley Hoffman, *Duties Beyond Borders: On the Limits and Possibilities of Ethical International Politics* (Syracuse, N.Y.: Syracuse University Press, 1981);

Burton I. Kaufman, *The Presidency of James Earl Carter, Jr.* (Lawrence: University Press of Kansas, 1993);

Jeanne Kirkpatrick, "Dictatorships and Double Standards," *Commentary* (November 1979): 34–45;

Linda B. Miller, "Morality in Foreign Policy: A Failed Consensus?" *Daedalus,* 109 (1980): 143–158;

Kenneth E. Morris, *Jimmy Carter, American Moralist* (Athens: University of Georgia Press, 1996);

Joshua Muravchik, *The Uncertain Crusade: Jimmy Carter and the Dilemmas of Human Rights Policy* (Lanham, Md.: Hamilton, 1986);

David D. Newsom, ed., *The Diplomacy of Human Rights* (Lanham, Md.: University Press of America, 1986);

Wesley G. Rippert, ed., *The Spiritual Journey of Jimmy Carter: In His Own Words* (New York: Macmillan, 1978);

Herbert D. Rosenbaum and Alexej Ugrinsky, eds., *Jimmy Carter: Foreign Policy and Post-Presidential Years* (Westport, Conn.: Greenwood Press, 1994);

Lars Schoultz, *Human Rights and United States Policy Toward Latin America* (Princeton: Princeton University Press, 1981);

Gaddis Smith, *Morality, Reason, and Power: American Diplomacy of the Carter Years* (New York: Hill & Wang, 1986).

CIVIL RIGHTS MOVEMENT: METHODS

Which was more important to the Civil Rights movement: Legal procedures or mass mobilization?

Viewpoint: The Civil Rights movement owed much of its success to national publicity.

Viewpoint: Despite the high drama of the public campaign against segregation, the mass movement would not have succeeded without the less dramatic work of legal pioneers such as Thurgood Marshall and Charles Houston.

Viewpoint: The Civil Rights movement was more than just an accretion of legal precedents: it was a change in the hearts and minds of a people, and it is best understood as a mass action.

Thurgood Marshall was not an overly sensitive man, but still he could be rankled. For sixteen years he had traveled the back roads of the American legal system, as chief counsel for the Legal Defense Fund (LDF) of the National Association for the Advancement of Colored People (NAACP), not only defending African American men and women accused of crime, but also arguing cases involving their civil rights. He argued cases in courthouses where he could not use the bathroom because he was black. Marshall, however, worked within the law, arguing one case at a time that the law forbids the government to treat black men and women differently from white men and women. Black school teachers had to be paid the same as white teachers; private contracts that forbid the sale of property to blacks could not be enforced in a court of law; and graduate schools could not refuse to admit qualified black applicants and, once admitted, could not separate them from other students. On 17 May 1954, Marshall enjoyed a moment of triumph, when the U.S. Supreme Court ruled that separate but equal, the justification for race segregation the Court had established in 1896, was unconstitutional.

At that moment no other American had done more to advance the cause of civil rights than Marshall. However, his singular role was not to last. In 1955 in Montgomery, Alabama, a boycott of segregated buses not only propelled into leadership the Reverend Martin Luther King Jr., it also ushered in a new era of civil-rights struggle. Instead of patiently building a body of law that protected the civil rights of all, African Americans took direct action against the forces of segregation. It was a bold strategy, but also a dangerous one. Courts could find boycotts illegal and jail boycotters, and the social disruption the boycott caused probably would not be worth the potential benefit. Marshall counseled against direct action, in Montgomery and later, when college students began sitting in at lunch counters. For his caution and his insistence on working within the law, he was regarded as too conservative and not in touch with the movement, though when the movement's leaders and foot soldiers wound up in jail, they called on Marshall and the LDF to bail them out.

History has slighted Marshall. Though he was rewarded for his service to the law and to the Civil Rights movement with a seat on the U.S. Supreme Court, King was honored with a Nobel Prize and a national holiday. In the essays that follow, Bryn Upton, Matthew Mason, and Adam Mack assess the role of the law, and the role of mass mobilization, in the Civil Rights movement. It is too easy to slight one or boost the other. A real understanding of history requires us to understand both.

Andrew Young, once an aide to King and later American ambassador to the United Nations, once asked a black South African in the days of apartheid why South Africa's blacks did not use the tactics of nonviolent direct action against the repressive regime. The South African replied that King and his followers, though they were breaking unjust laws, had the law on their side.

The *Brown* v. *Board of Education of Topeka, Kansas* decision, which Marshall had helped to achieve, made the Constitution of the United States color-blind and allowed the brave men and women of Montgomery and other towns and cities to protest against laws that violated it. Could the mass movement have succeeded without Marshall's patient effort to establish equality before the law? On the other hand, could equality before the law have been achieved without the mass movement of women and men who demanded it?

Viewpoint: The Civil Rights movement owed much of its success to national publicity.

Throughout the Civil Rights movement in the 1950s and 1960s, the press was a constant companion to the protestors, activists, and students. Many individuals in the movement became well known through newspapers, magazines, and television. This recognition was sometimes a tool used to gain sympathy, raise funds, and generally increase the national (and international) awareness for civil-rights issues. As one prominent member of the movement said, looking back, "If it had not been for instantaneous news reporting, our movement would not have been as successful as it was."

In 1954, with the historic decision in *Brown* v. *Board of Education of Topeka, Kansas,* black activists around the country, who had been frustrated for years by the lack of federal support in their efforts to gain the rights guaranteed to all citizens by the Fourteenth Amendment, were now even more frustrated. They had a major victory in the Supreme Court but felt that progress was once again being thwarted. Plans began to take shape within days of the Court's decision to force the hand of integration throughout the South. Images in newspapers and on the new medium of television were crucial to this phase of the Civil Rights movement. Looking back on the 1950s and early 1960s, Wyatt Tee Walker said: "We consciously manipulated television in the movement. . . . Television was an unwitting ally, but it had a greater power of persuasion than the print media." With the media watching, black students began to integrate Southern high schools. The resistance of local law enforcement and white citizens was often violent, and the pictures of this resistance shocked the world.

Nine black students were scheduled to enter Central High School in Little Rock, Arkansas, on 5 September 1957. The students had been selected for their academic excellence to be the first wave of integration. On Labor Day, 2 September, Governor Orval Eugene Faubus dispatched the National Guard to Little Rock's Central High School. No one was certain what the meaning of this action was, but that night the governor made everything clear. From the chair of the highest office of the state and to a live television audience, Faubus delivered the infamous words, "blood will run in the streets" if black students should attempt to enter Central High School.

When the first day of school finally came, again the showdown was covered by the media. One of the students, Elizabeth Eckford, did not arrive with the others and consequently faced a huge angry mob alone. As local National Association for the Advancement of Colored People (NAACP) leader Daisy Bates would later write in *The Long Shadow of Little Rock: A Memoir* (1962), "Elizabeth, whose dignity and control in the face of jeering mobsters had been filmed by television cameras and recorded in pictures flashed to newspapers over the world, had overnight become a national heroine."

Prior to the fall of 1960 few people knew the name Ruby Bridges. That fact would change on 14 November of that year when she became the first black student to enter the William Frantz Elementary School. On the same day three other six-year-old black girls were integrating another school in New Orleans, but Ruby was a special case in that she was the only black student going to her school. Some 150 whites, mostly housewives (who were later nicknamed the Cheerleaders) and teenage youths, clustered along the sidewalks across from the William Frantz School when the pupils marched in at 8:40 A.M. As reported by *The New York Times,* one youth chanted, "Two,

Martin Luther King Jr. giving a speech in Washington, D.C., in May 1957

(Moneta Sleet Jr., Ebony)

four, six, eight, we don't want to integrate; six, four, two, we don't want a chigaroo."

> Forty minutes later four deputy marshals arrived with a little Negro girl and her mother. They walked hurriedly up the steps and into the yellow brick building while onlookers jeered and shouted taunts.
>
> The girl, dressed in a stiffly starched white dress with a white ribbon in her hair, gripped her mother's hand tightly and glanced apprehensively toward the crowd.
>
> Almost immediately, a teacher who refused to give her name strode from the building and drove away. A short time later, white parents began arriving to remove their children.

Although there were television cameras and a documentary-film crew present, the pictures were not shown on New Orleans television. Local coverage was in the print media only. ABC News, however, went national with the documentary crew's coverage of Bridges. Those images were shown in New York; Washington, D.C.; Boston; and the rest of America–images that had an important impact on those who viewed it. No newspaper could print the words that the white demonstrators shouted, and television producers purposely blurred the obscenities. The visual images of screaming angry faces of middle-aged housewives and white teens, spewing their venom on a six-year-old girl, nonetheless were powerful enough.

Not all integration challenges were major media events; those cases, however, that did capture national media attention featured substantially more women than men. Young women were conspicuously placed on the front row of marchers to give integration the least confrontational face.

Other demonstrations were filmed by television cameras. Marches and boycotts derived support from all over the country after the nation was shown firsthand the conditions that were being faced. The Montgomery Bus Boycott of 1955–1956 became a media event and thereby made a minor celebrity of the young reverend who was its leader. Martin Luther King Jr. clearly had a gift for oration and was beginning to gain notoriety in the press, first in publications such as *Jet, Hue, Crisis,* and *American Negro.* Soon the white press took up the story: King and the Montgomery Improvement Association (MIA) were featured in *Newsweek, The New York Times,* and *Time.* Even network television began covering the events there, with one ABC commentator comparing the protestors to Mohandas Gandhi and the bankruptcy of white Montgomery's position to that of the British in India.

It was because of the successes of the Montgomery campaign that King first found himself on the cover of *Time* on 18 February 1957. The profile of King was laudatory, although some black leaders felt it gave King too much credit at the expense of others, and it helped make King a nationally known figure. After the feature in *Time, The New York Times Magazine* ran a history of the Montgomery Boycott that was mostly about King, and NBC's Lawrence Spivak invited him to become only the second African American to appear on "Meet the Press." Over the years King would appear on many television programs and magazine covers, and he was named "Man of the Year" by *Time* in 1963.

King was often the focus for the media, but the movement desired press coverage for all of its direct assaults on segregation. Leaders within the movement believed that if the world could see the injustices being wrought upon them, there would be popular outcry and support. One major news incident came on 7 March 1965 when a group of civil-rights demonstrators attempted to march from Selma to Montgomery. The marchers, largely from the Student Nonviolent Coordinating Committee (SNCC) and Southern Christian Leadership Conference (SCLC), met heavy police resistance crossing the Edmund Pettus Bridge. Troopers used tear gas to disorient the marchers, then attacked with nightsticks. It was early evening by the time the news reports of the bloody attack on Highway 80 began to spread across the country. Many television viewers were astounded by the graphic film of the troopers' assault on the peaceful marchers as ABC interrupted a movie broadcast, *Judgment at Nuremberg,* to present footage that depicted how racial hatred could generate awful violence in contemporary America, not just Nazi Germany.

Time after time during the Civil Rights movement the violence that came down upon nonviolent protestors was reported in the mass media. John Lewis describes in *Walking With the Wind* (1998) an incident in Selma: "I watched Sheriff Clark's temper play right into our hands. Again it was a woman he confronted, and again the press delivered a blow-by-blow account of the fight."

Support for the movement continued to grow in the North, outside of the United States, and even in parts of the South because of explicit coverage by the media. Through television millions of people saw the brutality of racial repression for the first time. U.S. attorney general Robert Kennedy, who had long been an advocate for civil rights from a basic legal standpoint, was deeply affected by pictures of teenage students being attacked by dogs and pummeled by water cannons. It forever changed Kennedy and his approach to dealing with civil-rights issues.

The media was not always on the side of protestors during the Civil Rights movement, and the press did not always agree with its leaders, but through the act of reporting on the demonstrations the press became an ally to the movement. Without the media, especially television, the Civil Rights movement might not have happened as it did. Some of the most powerful and lasting images came from the newspaper photos and television footage taken across the South during the 1950s and 1960s. Money, sympathy, support, and understanding were by-products of this press coverage. There is also a lasting legacy of video images that have been used to teach later generations about the struggle in a way that most history lessons can never be taught.

–BRYN UPTON, BRANDEIS UNIVERSITY

Viewpoint:
Despite the high drama of the public campaign against segregation, the mass movement would not have succeeded without the less dramatic work of legal pioneers such as Thurgood Marshall and Charles Houston.

In the past two decades scholars writing about the Civil Rights movement have focused largely on the grassroots level, attending to the mobilization of African American communities above all else. Accompanying this focus has also been a tendency to downplay the national arena, to shift attention and explanatory power away from the civil-rights leaders who sought to effect change through the courts and the national political process. In many ways this new focus has been salutary, giving us a fuller picture of how the changes wrought in the 1950s and 1960s came to pass.

It is, however, unfair and inaccurate to dismiss the importance of the work done in the courts and with the federal government more generally—either to neglect or dismiss it as too conservative to notice. The victories won by the legal arm of the National Association for the Advancement of Colored People (NAACP) from the 1930s through the 1960s and the efforts to enlist the power of the entire federal government on the side of civil rights were of tremendous significance on both moral and practical levels. Legal victories played an important role in convincing all Americans that fundamental American ideals were in accord with the Civil Rights movement, and the weight of white American opinion moved a hesitant federal government to play a key role as a third player in the South. It is most constructive to view the legal and legislative wing and the grassroots wing of the Civil Rights movement not only on equal footing, but indeed as working together, if not always in perfect harmony, to effect change.

This description is not to say that there was no difference between the legalistic approach that predominated from the 1930s to the early 1950s and mass mobilization that began in earnest in Montgomery, Alabama, in 1955. The people involved in the movement experienced this shift toward grassroots activism as a real change. Joseph Lowery, a black minister in Alabama who became an ardent supporter of the Montgomery bus boycott of 1955–1956, said that the movement begun by Rosa Parks and led in time by Martin Luther King Jr. marked "the beginning of self-determination." "Prior to the bus boycotts," he explained, "the determination of our freedom rested with the courts. With the bus boycott, *we* determined it. It didn't make any difference what the court said. The court could say what it liked, we weren't gon' ride—in the back of the bus. We'd walk." Lowery unduly minimized the courts' importance in Montgomery. Yet, his observation concerning the difference between mass mobilization and the legalistic approach was powerful and accurate. While the two approaches complemented each other, the bus boycott brought a vigor to the movement, a new sense of self-determination to African Americans in the South, in a way that even spectacular legal successes wrought by a few lawyers in distant courts could not.

Nevertheless, it would also be a mistake to interpret statements such as Lowery's as evidence of the conservative nature of the legal assault on Jim Crow. The legal and legislative challenges, while unavoidably involving a federal government hesitant to embrace and participate in change, did have a major transformative impact.

One consequence of the legal victories of the NAACP has to do with the power of law to establish norms and teach values of a society. The extent of this power is in dispute and cannot be resolved here. Yet, Supreme Court decisions striking down the legality of various features of Jim Crow—such as the Democratic white primary and discrimination in the Southern judicial system, interstate travel and commerce, and graduate and law schools—had enormous significance in signaling, and even teaching, a new interpretation of basic American documents and ideals.

This significance is true particularly for *Brown* v. *Board of Education of Topeka, Kansas,* the landmark 1954 Supreme Court ruling that declared segregation in all levels of education unconstitutional. In overturning the doctrine of "separate but equal," which had reigned since the Supreme Court declared segregation constitutional in its 1896 *Plessy* v. *Ferguson* decision, the court also sought to overturn racial separation and de facto subjugation. Back in 1896, Justice John Marshall Harlan, in his dissent from the *Plessy* decision, argued forcefully that the cultural and moral power of law is great. He thus protested that upholding segregation was tantamount to permitting "the seeds of race hate to be planted under the sanction of law." Lifting that sanction in 1954 should not be underestimated. Contrary to those who tell us that we cannot legislate morality, law by its nature prescribes morality; it is a measure of what lawmakers and/or their constituents deem to be immoral or moral. Thus, a shift in the constitutional doctrine of the highest court is a shift of no small significance.

Granted, the effect of Supreme Court decisions on African Americans' conception of the morality of their cause was probably slight and thus should not be overestimated. African Americans struggling for freedom and equality, whether as slaves or nominally free people, have long insisted that those American ideals were on their side, and thus the Supreme Court's reversal of interpretation seems to have had small effect on black Americans' attitudes toward what freedom and equality mean. Furthermore, as Richard H. King has so powerfully argued in *Civil Rights and the Idea of Freedom* (1992), the Civil Rights movement was not so much about trying to get respect from whites as it was about African Americans asserting their own self-respect.

Yet, having the prevailing constitutional winds in the movement's favor did give its participants a greater measure of moral authority and confidence in addressing America as a whole. It allowed civil-rights spokesmen to appeal to white Americans as advocates of the Constitution and of the law, which was important given the general veneration of American institutions and the Cold War context of touchiness concerning criticism of those institutions. Thus Martin Luther King Jr. could speak to a key ally, the American Jewish Committee:

> Civil disobedience in its true sense has not been employed by Negroes in their struggle. To utilize civil disobedience in its authentic, historical form involves defiance of fundamental national law. . . . We must see that the Negro today, when he marches in the streets, is not practicing civil disobedience because he is not challenging the Constitution, the Supreme Court, or the enactments of Congress. Instead, he seeks to uphold them. He may be violating local municipal ordinances or state laws, but it is these laws which [contradict] basic national law. Negroes by their direct action are exposing the contradiction. The civil disobedience, or I should say, uncivil disobedience in this situation, resting on unjust foundations, is that of the segregationists.

Only after decisions such as *Brown* could King take this powerful position. The position could only help the movement gain support among Northern whites, which was key to bringing the federal government in as a third player in the struggle against the Southern power structure. Local African American demonstrations also helped greatly in this process, attracting national and international attention and thus putting pressure on the federal government to at least partially abandon its usual modus operandi of delay tactics and half-measures. Yet, the outside attention was much more likely to be favorable if the movement seemed to be about squaring American practice with American ideals, or, as King maintained, if it seemed to be in harmony with the fundamental law of the land.

The realities of the situation required a strong outside presence for change to occur. Advocates of change faced a South wherein whites were in the majority and segregationists controlled the levers of power and influence. Courageous stands by local African Americans and some white Southern moderates were key to challenging this power structure, but insufficient in themselves. Civil-rights leaders understood that forcing the federal government to act in their behalf was necessary, and that meant continued activity in the courts, as well as using direct-action techniques (and the media coverage they attracted) to prod elected officials.

Indeed, civil-rights leaders' willingness to use a combination of direct action and legal means belies the subsequent tendency of scholars to establish a dichotomy between the two approaches. For instance, in Montgomery, rightly held up as the beginning of the mass mobilization that would thereafter characterize the movement in most people's minds, successful court actions combined with the better-publicized bus boycott to achieve change. In December 1955 King argued the need for both tactics. As he understood it, the nonviolent direct action of the bus boycott was a tool of "persuasion," whereas court decrees and legislation were tools of "coercion," and success would require both. King's formulation and the fact that the boycott ended successfully only when the circuit courts and Supreme Court ruled that segregated busing was unconstitutional contradict those who envisage the legalistic approach as inherently conservative and nonthreatening.

Recent works that heavily emphasize the grassroots aspects of the movement have made great contributions to the literature, but (sometimes despite themselves) they also demonstrate the need for outside intervention. For instance, JohnDittmer's excellent study of the movement, despite the emphasis suggested by his title, *Local People: The Struggle for Civil Rights in Mississippi* (1994), deftly illustrates the interplay between national and local people in working for change. His account details the need for outside activists to reinvigorate sometimes dispirited local organizations. Yet, Dittmer hesitates to recognize the key role of outside attention and power, for his tendency is to emphasize the local. In discussing the failure of school integration in Mississippi (in 1968 only 3.9 percent of black children went to previously all-white schools), his evidence suggests–but he is hesitant to acknowledge–that the lack of outside attention to the problem severely hampered integration efforts. Despite the unprecedented level of violence against school integrators in the town of Grenada in the mid 1960s, national civil-rights leaders and media paid only passing notice, distracted by talk of Black Power and urban riots. Hence, local people were left to themselves in the struggle against white domination and despite their courage wrought less change than when they had that vital third player from outside.

Yet, on the other hand, without local activists, the decisions and enactments won in circuit courts and in Washington, D.C., would likely have gone unenforced. As Donald G. Nieman has pointed out in *Promises to Keep: African-Americans and the Constitutional Order, 1776 to the Present* (1991), the Supreme Court in fashioning decisions such as *Brown* tried to retain its unanimity and ensure the enforcement of its decisions by hedging its language and urging all deliberate speed. Yet, massive resistance by white Southerners to these decisions betrayed these hopes, and it was left to local African Americans to enforce these laws, largely by means of pressing court action against local authorities. Furthermore, the much-celebrated Civil Rights Act of 1964 would likely have been a dead letter in places such as Mississippi were it not for determined local people who forced integration of public places despite intimidation and harassment.

Recent scholars writing in the grassroots vein have taken this evidence to mean that federal intervention was of only secondary importance, but a view of the whole scene shows that one cannot separate local and national aspects of the Civil Rights movement. It is an incomplete picture and a faulty understanding of the movement that emphasizes one aspect at the expense of the other. The same is true for the tactics of mass mobilization on the one hand and the legal and legislative approach on the other. As Nieman has written, "neither law nor mass protest was, by itself, sufficient to end the caste system; only a combination of the two would accomplish that monumental task."

Finally, perhaps the best evidence that the legal/legislative approach to change was a threat to the Jim Crow establishment was the response to the NAACP's legal successes. This threat is particularly evident in the segregationist response to *Brown,* aptly referred to as "massive resistance." Desegregating schools struck home with segregationists in a dramatic way and produced a dramatic resurgence of the Ku Klux Klan, as well as the introduction of a new organization, the White Citizens' Council.

The White Citizens' Council presented itself as more "genteel" or moderate than the Klan. While it tended to rely on economic intimidation (its members were largely the employers of the South) rather than physical violence, it did not constitute a mild response to the proposed desegregation of schools. During the Birmingham bus boycott, a leaflet circulated at a White Citizens' Council rally read, in part: "When in the course of human events it becomes necessary to abolish the Negro race, proper methods should be used. Among these are guns, bow and arrows, slingshots and knives. We hold these truths to be self-evident: that all whites are created equal with certain rights; among these are life, liberty and the pursuit of dead niggers." While this rally was not a specific response to *Brown,* this rhetoric does illustrate that there was precious little moderation in the main organizational embodiment of that response.

NAACP legal successes clearly threatened the white establishment in the South. The legal and legislative approach to working for change formed a key part of the Civil Rights movement. While many in the movement grew impatient with its slow pace, and some historians have joined these dissenters in labeling it overly conservative, the freedom struggle's successes came when grassroots direct action was combined with appeals to the courts and the national government. The two aspects formed two sides of the same coin and should be remembered as such.

—MATTHEW MASON, UNIVERSITY OF MARYLAND, COLLEGE PARK

Viewpoint: The Civil Rights movement was more than just an accretion of legal precedents: it was a change in the hearts and minds of a people, and it is best understood as a mass action.

In 1989 veteran activist Bob Moses wrote that the Civil Rights movement was characterized by two distinct organizing traditions. The first was concerned with large-scale community mobilization, generally for national goals, and was represented by familiar events such as the March on Washington and the protests in Birmingham and Selma. The second tradition involved work at the local level, focusing on grassroots organizing and development of indigenous leadership. Representing departures from the legalistic strategy practiced by the National Association for the Advancement of Colored People (NAACP), these two organizing traditions were primarily responsible for the major changes brought by the Civil Rights movement. Community mobilization prompted the federal government to pass transformative civil-rights legislation that dismantled the system of legalized segregation in the South, and grassroots organizing empowered black communities by helping develop leaders and institutions to carry forth the struggle for the long term. The Civil Rights movement was a collaborative effort, and legalistic activism made significant contributions to its success, but mass mobilization and local organization did the most to transform the racial landscape of the South.

There can be no doubt that legalistic activism furthered the civil-rights cause. A key point is that for the first half of the twentieth century racial segregation was entrenched in state law and, since the 1896 *Plessy* v. *Ferguson* decision, endorsed by the Supreme Court. Victories won by the legal arm of the NAACP from the 1930s through the 1950s—which included judgments against the white primary (1944), segregation in interstate travel (1946), racially restrictive covenants (1948), separate graduate and professional schools for blacks, and eventually segregation in all levels of public education (1954)—thus made critical contributions to the freedom struggle by undermining the legal structure of Jim Crow in the South. At the same time, these victories put the weight of the Constitution behind the emerging Civil Rights movement, giving moral as well as legal credibility to its goals.

Nevertheless, the NAACP's legalistic strategy was a limited instrument for racial change. As much as legal victories seemed to promise the downfall of Jim Crow, court decisions were not self-enforcing; without strong federal support, they could be evaded relatively easily by Southern obstructionists. This situation became painfully obvious in the aftermath of the court victories of the 1940s and 1950s. Although the Supreme Court removed a major obstacle to African American disfranchisement by outlawing the white primary, whites continued to keep blacks from the polls through a combination of intimidation and technical devices such as literacy tests. Moreover, the Court's ruling against segregated interstate travel was ignored in most of the South, and discrimination in housing and employment remained a fact of life. Perhaps the best example of Southern racial intransigence was white resistance to *Brown* v. *Board of Education of Topeka, Kansas,* the 1954 Supreme Court decision that declared segregation in public schools unconstitutional. Although *Brown* had an immediate effect on school desegregation in parts of the Upper South, it had essentially no impact in the Deep South, as whites mounted a campaign of massive resistance to the ruling. While the NAACP undertook the time-consuming business of filing desegregation suits, obstructionists used violence, token integration plans, and a host of creative legal devices to prevent implementation of the *Brown* decision. Meanwhile, the federal government refused to aggressively enforce the decision, enduring if not promoting Southern defiance.

Only when African Americans mobilized for direct confrontations with the Jim Crow system was the entire federal government compelled to intervene to help make real changes in the South. By the early 1960s, civil-rights proponents had learned that the best way to force the federal government to take decisive action was to create a crisis that drew national attention to the overt denial of basic citizenship rights to African Americans. More than any other civil-rights organization, Martin Luther King Jr.'s Southern Christian Leadership Conference (SCLC) succeeded in mobilizing black communities for dramatic nonviolent protest campaigns that captured media attention, aroused public support, and prompted federal intervention, including the passage of civil-rights legislation.

This strategy was used most effectively in nonviolent direct-action campaigns in Birmingham and Selma, Alabama. Both these campaigns brought the brutality of white supremacy to light by generating shocking scenes of local law enforcement using violence to suppress peaceful demonstrations. Appearing on the front pages of national newspapers and on television, events in Birmingham and Selma led to significant increases in public sympathy for the movement and moved the ever hesitant officials in Washington to take a stronger stand for civil rights. According to Adam Fairclough in *To Redeem the Soul of America: The Southern Christian Leadership Conference and Martin Luther King, Jr.* (1987), the turbulent events of the Birmingham campaign and the spinoff demonstrations that followed convinced the Kennedy administration—which had been following a piecemeal civil-rights policy—that racial crises would continue to occur in the South unless the federal government took action by passing strong civil-rights legislation. This decision, Fairclough argues, led John F. Kennedy to introduce legislation that was eventually passed as the Civil Rights Act of 1964, a measure that expanded the federal government's power to challenge segregation in public accommodations. Two years after the Birmingham protests, SCLC launched a campaign in Selma to address the problem of black disfranchisement, an issue not adequately addressed in the Civil Rights Act. As Fairclough has pointed out, the public reaction to the suppression of demonstrations in Selma energized the Johnson administration's efforts to produce a strong voting-rights law, increased Congressional support for such legislation, and thus paved the way for the Voting Rights Act of 1965.

The 1964–1965 federal civil-rights legislation was not a panacea for problems facing African Americans in the South, but its significance should not be underestimated. Unlike previous Supreme Court decisions and earlier civil-rights laws, the 1964 Civil Rights Act and the 1965 Voting Rights Act included strong enforcement measures and brought dramatic change to the South. Although there was some resistance to the Civil Rights Act, within a relatively short time after its passage, Jim Crow signs came down in much of Dixie, and public accommodations were opened, in a legal sense, to blacks. Described by Fairclough as the "crowning achievement of the civil rights movement," the Voting Rights Act transformed the South's political landscape. By providing new methods of enforcement such as federal registrars and election observers, as well as the suspension of literacy and other voting tests, the act streamlined the government's ability to protect African American voting rights. In the decade after its passage black voter registration increased significantly (in Mississippi it leapt from 6.7 percent to 67.4 percent), more and more African Americans were elected to public office, and unfavorable white candidates were defeated. Although whites continued to hold the lion's share of regional political power, the growth in the black electorate ushered in a new racial tone in southern politics as white politicians openly courted black votes; visible political racism generally became a thing of the past.

However, direct action alone did not engender the transformative civil-rights legislation of the mid 1960s. Indeed, part of the credit must go to NAACP lobbyists who helped push the measures through Congress. Similarly, while the NAACP did not fully embrace direct-action tactics, the protest campaigns of the mid 1960s benefited from timely legal and financial aid from the association. As King and other civil-rights proponents realized, the success of the movement depended on the interplay of NAACP-style legalism and direct action practiced by other groups; scholars should think twice before separating the two approaches completely. As King put it, "Direct action is not a substitute for work in the courts and the halls of government. Bringing about passage of a new and broad law by a city council, state legislature or the Congress, or pleading cases before the courts of the land, does not eliminate the necessity for bringing about the mass dramatization of injustice in front of a city hall. Indeed, direct action and legal action complement one another; when skillfully employed, each becomes more effective."

Of course, the movement would not have accomplished anything without local people who took to the streets to challenge Jim Crow. Yet for ordinary African Americans, the gains achieved through direct-action protest went beyond the passage of strong civil-rights legislation. The act of striking a blow for their own freedom–something difficult to do when activism was focused in faraway courtrooms–promoted a new sense of self-determination and self-respect. Reflecting on the movement in the mid 1970s, Franklin McCain, one of the four black students who started the Greensboro, North Carolina, sit-in movement, described his feelings after participating in his first demonstration: "If it's possible to know what it means to have your soul cleansed–I felt pretty clean at that time. I probably felt better on that day than I've ever felt in my life. Seems like a lot of feelings of guilt or what-have-you suddenly left me, and I

"I HAVE A DREAM"

In the summer of 1963 more than 200,000 men and women, black and white, gathered in Washington, D.C., for one of the most significant moments of the Civil Rights movement. The March for Jobs and Freedom was also the occasion of a landmark speech in American history delivered by Martin Luther King Jr.: "I Have a Dream."

I say to you today, my friends, that in spite of the difficulties and frustrations of the moment I still have a dream. It is a dream deeply rooted in the American dream.

I have a dream that one day this nation will rise up and live out the true meaning of its creed: "We hold these truths to be self-evident; that all men are created equal."

I have a dream that one day on the red hills of Georgia the sons of former slaves and the sons of former slaveowners will be able to sit down together at the table of brotherhood.

I have a dream that one day even the state of Mississippi, a desert state sweltering with the heat of injustice and oppression, will be transformed into an oasis of freedom and justice.

I have a dream that my four children will one day live in a nation where they will not be judged by the color of their skin but by the content of their character.

I have a dream today.

I have a dream that one day the state of Alabama, whose governor's lips are presently dripping with the words of interposition and nullification, will be transformed into a situation where little black boys and black girls will be able to join hands with little white boys and white girls and walk together as sisters and brothers.

I have a dream today.

I have a dream that one day every valley shall be exalted, every hill and mountain shall be made low, the rough places will be made plains, and the crooked places will be made straight, and the glory of the Lord shall be revealed, and all flesh shall see it together.

This is our hope. This is the faith with which I return to the South. With this faith we will be able to hew out of the mountain of despair a stone of hope. With this faith we will be able to transform the jangling discords of our nation into a beautiful symphony of brotherhood. With this faith we will be able to work together, to pray together, to struggle together, to go to jail together, to stand up for freedom together, knowing that we will be free one day.

Source: Peter B. Levy, ed., 100 Key Documents in American Democracy *(Westport, Conn. & London: Praeger, 1999), pp. 392–395.*

felt as though I had gained my manhood, so to speak, and not only gained it, but had developed quite a lot of respect for it. Not Franklin McCain only as an individual, but I felt as though the manhood of a number of other black persons had been restored and had gotten some respect from just that one day."

In recent years scholars have looked closely at how the movement changed the lives of local people, turning their attention from the familiar protest campaigns led by King and the SCLC to the less-glamorous work of organizing at the grassroots level. Sustained local organizing, these historians argue, wrought remarkable change by empowering black communities through the cultivation of indigenous leadership and the creation of institutions to support movement activity for the long term.

One of the best examples of the grassroots organizing tradition, and a movement that has received considerable attention from scholars, is the work done by the Student Nonviolent Coordinating Committee (SNCC) in Mississippi. Starting in the early 1960s, SNCC organizers dug in across the Magnolia state and began the slow and steady work of organizing black communities to challenge the racial status quo. Refusing to back down in the face of white violence and intimidation, these activists' persistence had a transformative impact on local blacks. As Charles M. Payne suggested in his study of the Mississippi movement, *I've Got the Light of Freedom: The Organizing Tradition and the Mississippi Freedom Struggle* (1995), when SNCC activists proved that challenges to white supremacy could be survived, much of the fear that had governed race relations in Mississippi broke down, giving local people the confidence to join the movement. For SNCC, unlike some other groups, the purpose of drawing local people into the movement was not so much an attempt to develop a steady stream of volunteers for demonstrations aimed at securing outside intervention; instead, SNCC sought to help local blacks fight for themselves. Through participation in voter-registration campaigns, mass meetings, and citizenship-education classes, thousands of local people were politicized and, significantly, began to believe that they could affect the decisions that impacted their lives. Out of these movements emerged indigenous leaders such as Fannie Lou Hamer, a former timekeeper on a Mississippi plantation who provided a dramatic example of the empowerment of local people by helping lead the Mississippi Freedom Democratic Party in its challenge to the state's all-white delegation at the 1964 Democratic National Convention.

Payne's study also reveals how the efforts of grassroots organizers promoted the creation of movement-related institutions at the local level. Focusing on Greenwood, Mississippi, Payne shows how local blacks activated by the movement went on to establish a variety of political organizations, activist groups, and educational programs. Well after the full-time SNCC organizers left town, these organizations continued working to transform race relations in Mississippi. For instance, the Greenwood Movement, an organization led by local blacks, sponsored a highly successful boycott of downtown merchants in the mid 1960s. While this boycott was initiated to protest discriminatory hiring practices and disrespectful treatment of black customers, it was also meant to win larger goals by putting indirect pressure on city hall. By the end of the 1960s, the city, under pressure from the boycott as well as civil-rights lawsuits, began hiring African Americans and making improvements in black neighborhoods such as paving roads and putting up street lights. Although these gains were significant in the context of Mississippi, the important point is that local blacks had begun organizing on their own to challenge the white power structure. Considering the lack of large-scale, organized resistance in Mississippi before the Civil Rights movement and the state's historically stifling racial climate, this local-level organizing was a transformation of no small significance; it was one of the main accomplishments of the grassroots movements.

The Civil Rights movement did not end the problem of race in America. It did, however, destroy the system of legalized segregation that imposed second-class citizenship on African Americans in the South. Equally important, the movement empowered blacks at the local level by helping indigenous leadership and movement-related institutions take root. Only when the focus of reform efforts shifted from a legalistic approach to a strategy based on community mobilization and grassroots organizing did these changes become possible. Court victories and legislative lobbying helped effect change, but the real credit belongs to the activists and ordinary people who confronted Jim Crow in the streets.

–ADAM MACK, UNIVERSITY OF SOUTH CAROLINA

References

Daisy Bates, *The Long Shadow of Little Rock: A Memoir* (New York: McKay, 1962);

David L. Chappell, *Inside Agitators: White Southerners in the Civil Rights Movement* (Baltimore: Johns Hopkins University Press, 1994);

Robert Cook, *Sweet Land of Liberty? The African-American Struggle for Civil Rights in the Twentieth Century* (London: Longman, 1998);

John Dittmer, *Local People: The Struggle for Civil Rights in Mississippi* (Urbana: University of Illinois Press, 1994);

Adam Fairclough, *Race & Democracy: The Civil Rights Struggle in Louisiana, 1915–1972* (Athens: University of Georgia Press, 1995);

Fairclough, *To Redeem the Soul of America: The Southern Christian Leadership Conference and Martin Luther King, Jr.* (Athens: University of Georgia Press, 1987);

David J. Garrow, *Bearing the Cross: Martin Luther King Jr. and the Southern Christian Leadership Conference* (New York: Morrow, 1986);

Martin Luther King Jr., *In Search of Freedom: Excerpts from his Most Memorable Speeches* (New York: Polygram Records, 1995), compact disc;

King, *Why We Can't Wait* (New York: Harper & Row, 1964);

Richard H. King, *Civil Rights and the Idea of Freedom* (New York: Oxford University Press, 1992);

Steven F. Lawson, "Freedom Then, Freedom Now: The Historiography of the Civil Rights Movement," *American Historical Review*, 96 (April 1991): 456–471;

John Lewis and Michael D'Orso, *Walking With the Wind: A Memoir of the Movement* (New York: Simon & Schuster, 1998);

August Meier and John H. Bracey, Jr., "The NAACP as a Reform Movement, 1909–1965: 'To Reach the Conscience of America,'" *Journal of Southern History*, 59 (February 1993): 3–30;

Robert P. Moses, Mieko Kamii, Susan McAllister Swap, and Jeffrey Howard, "The Algebra Project: Organizing in the Spirit of Ella," *Harvard Educational Review*, 59 (November 1989): 423–443;

Donald G. Nieman, *Promises to Keep: African-Americans and the Constitutional Order, 1776 to the Present* (New York: Oxford University Press, 1991);

Charles M. Payne, *I've Got the Light of Freedom: The Organizing Tradition and the Mississippi Freedom Struggle* (Berkeley: University of California Press, 1995);

Howell Raines, *My Soul is Rested: The Story of the Civil Rights Movement in the Deep South* (New York: Putnam, 1977);

Belinda Robnett, *How Long? How Long? African-American Women in the Struggle for Civil Rights* (New York: Oxford University Press, 1997);

Robert Weisbrot, *Freedom Bound: A History of America's Civil Rights Movement* (New York: Norton, 1990).

COLD WAR CAUSES

What caused the Cold War?

Viewpoint: Joseph Stalin's insecurity and desire to expand the Soviet sphere of influence provoked the United States into responding with policies of containment and massive retaliation.

Viewpoint: Recently released information from Russian archives suggest that American policymakers misinterpreted Soviet designs and capabilities.

Viewpoint: U.S. nationalism and aggressive capitalism provoked fears in the Soviet Union that the United States was trying to reduce their level of security.

Who started the Cold War? American and Soviet policymakers disagreed about the Cold War's origins, each side believing their side was in the right. American and Russian historians also disagree about how the Cold War began, but their disagreement has more to do with their sources than with their loyalties. With the collapse of the Soviet regime the Kremlin archives are being opened, revealing for the first time what Moscow's planners knew, what they thought they knew, and what they expected from the United States.

Erik Benson traces the origins of the Cold War to the various alliances of World War II, showing how the United States, though allied with the Soviet Union and Great Britain, still had to keep its own interests first and foremost. However, the American people and their leader, Franklin D. Roosevelt, did believe that they and the Soviets could remain friends. Roosevelt tried by various means to convince Stalin, but he could not overcome Soviet fears about the West.

Kenneth A. Osgood gives a tantalizing glimpse into what Soviet policymakers thought as the war ended and how they reacted to American policies. By focusing on the Soviet side of the story, Osgood is able to evaluate both Soviet intentions and whether American planners were correct about them. On the one hand, we now know that American fears of Soviet capabilities were exaggerated. More importantly, Americans had no way of knowing that their fears were exaggerated, so they could not have acted any differently. In this case not knowing the truth about one another forced both the Soviets and Americans into a long, costly, and terrifying Cold War, which neither wanted but neither knew how to avoid.

James Carter argues that the United States was responsible for the Cold War because it rebuilt the natural enemies of the Soviets, Germany and Japan, as well as built bases around the periphery of the Soviet Union. The Soviets were distrustful of American intentions, and the U.S. leadership did little to allay their fears.

Viewpoint: Joseph Stalin's insecurity and desire to expand the Soviet sphere of influence provoked the United States into responding with policies of containment and massive retaliation.

The Cold War was a contest between two different systems: one, championed by the United States, was open, democratic, and capitalistic; the other, headed by the Soviet Union, was closed, totalitarian, and communistic. Yet, the Cold War was not simply the result of systemic differences. Other nations have had strong differences of opinion that did not lead to a cold war. For example, during World War II the British and Americans found themselves ideologically opposed on various issues, most notably concerning colonialism. Yet, their association was so intimate and friendly that historians have referred to it as the "special relationship." Admittedly the differences between the United States and the Soviet Union were greater and more plentiful. However, they were not insurmountable. After all, the two nations had engaged in normal diplomatic relations during the 1930s and had allied against the Nazis in the 1940s. Why then did they become embroiled in the Cold War? The answer lies in the Soviet system and Joseph Stalin.

The argument is not a new one. In the early years of the Cold War the consensus among American historians was that Soviet aggression had produced the conflict. Soviet leaders, as automatons of a monolithic communist system, had sought global domination after World War II. They had subjugated Eastern Europe, and only the once-naive-but-now-wiser United States had prevented further conquest. In this tale the good and bad guys were easy to identify. However, in the midst of the turbulent 1960s a new group of historians reversed the roles. Known as revisionists, they claimed that the United States was responsible for the Cold War. The most prominent early revisionist, William Appleman Williams, argued that the conflict resulted from U.S. efforts to impose a capitalist economic system upon the world. The Soviets, understandably, opposed this and tried to protect themselves by expanding their sphere of influence. In essence, Williams contended that American imperialism had forced the Soviet Union to defend itself.

To their credit Williams and later revisionists offered a much-needed corrective to the early Cold War consensus. In particular, they made two good points. First, the United States did emerge from World War II in the best condition of any nation in the world. It had lost only 400,000 people in the conflict, as compared to the 20 million or more lost by the Soviet Union. While every other major combatant had suffered severe infrastructural damage, the United States was untouched. As war ravaged the economies of Europe and Asia, the U.S. gross national product more than doubled. By 1945 the United States controlled one-half of the world's industry, two-thirds of its gold, and three-quarters of its investment. It also emerged with the largest navy, the leading air force, and the atomic bomb.

Second, the Soviets did have legitimate interests, a fact often ignored by American historians in the 1950s. The Soviets had suffered greatly at the hands of the Germans in two world wars. Understandably, they wanted to prevent a German resurgence and secure their borders by having friendly governments in the nations of Eastern Europe. Moreover, Germany was not the only entity that worried the Soviets. In 1918 various powers, among them Britain and the United States, sent troops to Russia to battle the fledgling Soviet government. The British kept the Soviets out of the 1938 negotiations at Munich, arousing fears in Moscow that the Western powers were encouraging Adolf Hitler to expand eastward. During the war the Soviets had to bear the brunt of German arms while their allies laboriously prepared to invade France. In 1943 the British and the Americans left the Soviets out of the negotiations for Italy's surrender. Without doubt there was ample justification for Soviet suspicion of the West.

However, the revisionist argument has serious flaws. It overemphasizes American power in 1945 while ignoring the great potential of the Soviet Union. When the war ended, the United States immediately began a crash program of demobilization. Its armed forces shrank from 12 million in 1945 to 1.5 million in 1947. Many of the U.S. Navy's ships were mothballed, and most aircraft production ceased immediately. As for its atomic monopoly, the United States constructed parts for less than fifty bombs and had only a handful of planes equipped to carry them. Yet, as John Lewis Gaddis notes, it had to rely on atomic weapons as a deterrent because its conventional forces were so depleted. In contrast, the Soviet military, while scaled back in numbers, remained a much larger force. More importantly, the proximity of the Soviet Union to the European heartland gave it a key advantage over the United States. It had large numbers of troops located throughout eastern Europe and Germany and could deploy sizable forces throughout the continent with relative ease by means of secure overland routes. The United States, on the other hand, had a comparative handful of troops in Europe. To reinforce them it would have to send men and matériel over thousands of miles of potentially hostile ocean, a costly and time-consuming operation. In essence, the Soviets could more easily project power in Europe than could the United States.

The revisionist argument also ignores the fact that the United States had legitimate interests in Europe. It too had been involved in the two wars in Europe. While it had not suffered as much as the Soviets, the effort had not been without its political and human costs. The United States did not want a sequel. Moreover, the U.S. stake in Europe had increased dramatically during the twentieth century. Its growing economic investment in and trade with Europe gave it a vested interest in European affairs. In the strategic realm, advances in military technology had rendered the Atlantic Ocean obsolete as a defensive barrier against attack. In light of this fact, the United States could not afford to allow a hostile power to dominate the European continent. If one did, it would be able to draw upon military, economic, and human resources far in excess of what was available in the Western Hemisphere, thereby placing the United States at a grave disadvantage in commerce, diplomacy, and war. In summation, U.S. prosperity and security was intimately connected to Europe, and it was because of this link that the United States had battled Germany twice in a century.

However, Germany was not the only U.S. concern. While the West had a "history" with regard to the Soviet Union, the Soviets had one of their own with regard to the West. While the West had sent troops to Russia in 1918, the Soviet government had backed various revolutionary communist organizations in the West for decades. While the Soviets suspected the West of directing Hitler eastward in 1938, Stalin had actually signed a nonaggression pact with the Nazis in 1939. During the war, while Stalin balked at not being consulted in Italy, he himself had pursued secret talks with Germany for a separate peace. Quite simply, the United States had little reason to like or trust the Soviets and their leader.

Does all of this fear mean that the Cold War was inevitable? Were mutual suspicions too great? As tempting as such a conclusion may be, it ignores certain dynamics in the relationship. Specifically, the United States did try to overcome the differences. The Soviets, particularly Stalin, were unreceptive to such overtures. Their mistrust led them to take aggressive actions that caused the Cold War.

As World War II drew to a successful close, few Americans anticipated a falling-out with the Soviets. Public-opinion polls consistently revealed that most Americans had a positive image of the Soviets and expected that the two allies would continue to enjoy a good relationship. President Franklin D. Roosevelt certainly hoped so. In a late 1943 radio address he stated, "I believe that we are going to get along very well . . . with the Russian people–very well indeed." He made a concerted effort to fulfill this expectation. He provided the Soviets with billions of dollars' worth of Lend Lease aid with no strings attached. He pressed both his military leaders and the British to meet Soviet demands for a second front in France. In the diplomatic arena he went out of his way to avoid giving the Soviets the impression that the United States and Britain were "ganging up" against them. He refused to meet privately with British prime minister Winston Churchill before going to the Teheran Conference in 1943. At the conference he joked publicly with Stalin at Churchill's expense and privately confided in the dictator that the Americans and British were not getting along all that well. He was clearly trying to distance himself from the British and get closer to the Soviets. In his effort to ensure placid postwar relations with the Soviets, he ignored some of their more unsavory activities. For example, in the fall of 1944, as the Red Army closed in on Warsaw, Soviet radio encouraged the city's residents to rise up against their German occupiers. When they did, the Red Army suddenly and mysteriously ground to a halt. As the citizens of Warsaw struggled mightily, Stalin denied his allies permission to airdrop supplies to the Poles and held his armies back. After the Germans crushed the revolt (and eliminated most of the potential Polish opposition to the Soviet domination of Poland), the Red Army swept in and secured the city. Churchill was appalled, but FDR refused to comment on the affair. He was determined not to split the alliance by criticizing the Soviets.

FDR was not so kind to Great Britain. British colonial policy, especially as it pertained to India, was subject to official public criticism. Nor was this the only area in which the United States accorded its "special" ally worse treatment than its Soviet partner. One need only examine the Lend Lease program. Admittedly it was a good deal for the British. The United States agreed to "loan" them war material for which they could not immediately pay, thereby allowing them to continue the struggle against Hitler. However, there was a price. In exchange for its generosity Washington demanded that London hold British dollar and gold reserves to a maximum of $1 billion. In effect, this stipulation limited Britain's ability to compete with the United States in international commerce and finance. Moreover, at various wartime conferences the United States held Lend Lease over the heads of the British, compelling them to agree to U.S. plans for the postwar world. In contrast, the

DEPARTMENT OF STATE

INCOMING TELEGRAM

INFORMATION COPY

ACTION MUST BE END[ORSED] ON ACTION COPY

PEM-K-M
No paraphrase necessary.

8963

Moscow via War

~~SECRET~~

Dated February 22, 1946

Rec'd 3:52 p.m.

Secretary of State,

Washington.

511, February 22, 9 p.m.

Answer to Dept's 284, Feb 3 involves questions so intricate, so delicate, so strange to our form of thought, and so important to analysis of our international environment that I cannot compress answers into single brief message without yielding to what I feel would be dangerous degree of over-simplification. I hope, therefore, Dept will bear with me if I submit in answer to this question five parts, subjects of which will be roughly as follows:

(One) Basic features of post-war Soviet outlook.

(Two) Background of this outlook.

(Three) Its projection in practical policy on official level.

(Four) Its projection on unofficial level.

(Five) Practical deductions from standpoint of US policy.

I apologize in advance for this burdening of telegraphic channel; but questions involved are of such urgent importance, particularly in view of recent events, that our answers to them, if they deserve attention at all, seem to me to deserve it at once. THERE FOLLOWS PART ONE: BASIC FEATURES OF POST WAR SOVIET OUTLOOK, AS PUT FORWARD BY OFFICIAL PROPAGANDA MACHINE, ARE AS FOLLOWS:

(A) USSR still lives in antagonistic "capitalist encirclement" with which in the long run there can be no permanent peaceful coexistence. As stated by Stalin in 1927 to a delegation of American Workers:

'In course

~~SECRET~~

DECLASSIFIED
E.O. 11652, Sec. 3(E) and 5(D) or (E)
Dept. of State letter, Aug. 10, 1972

The first page of George F. Kennan's "Long Telegram," which provided the basis for U.S. foreign policy toward the Soviet Union

United States offered Lend Lease to the Soviets with no strings attached. They were able to accumulate large dollar and gold reserves without limit, and the United States refrained from using Lend Lease to pressure them into diplomatic agreements. If Lend Lease was a bargain for the British, it was a steal for the Soviets.

Neither the U.S. efforts to please the Soviets nor the comparatively poor treatment of the British served to assuage Stalin's suspicions. He ignored the windfalls of Lend Lease to emphasize its shortcomings. When American and British shipping failed to deliver materials because of German U-boats and the demands of various military campaigns, Stalin charged his allies with deliberately hurting the Soviet war effort. He was certain that the delay in opening a second front in France was a Western plot to let the Germans bleed Russia white. He ignored the difficulties of such an operation and the demands of the war effort in the Pacific, to which he was contributing nothing (a fact his allies chose not to bring to his attention). For Stalin such considerations meant nothing.

Stalin's mistrust of his erstwhile allies stemmed from suspicions rooted in national history and ideology. As Vojtech Mastny has written, Stalin's psychological perspective of the world was shaped by the history of Russia and the Soviet Union, as well as by the teachings of communism. Both history and ideology imbued him with a sense of being surrounded by hostile powers. In his mind these powers were always seeking to attack Russia and crush the Soviet revolution. Whatever they might proffer, they could not be trusted. For Stalin only one thing provided security: territory. Thus, much like the czars of old, Stalin was determined to expand the Soviet sphere of control. Yet, as Mastny cautions, he was not a crazed ideologue nor a nationalist zealot bent on world domination. He was cool and calculating, a political opportunist who could make deals and wait for the opportune moment to strike.

Stalin's opportunistic expansionism was quite evident in the prewar period. In 1939 he signed a pact with the Soviet Union's most hated enemy, Nazi Germany. Under the terms of the deal, Stalin was given a free hand to act in the eastern Baltic. He quickly took advantage of the opportunity. He forced the Baltic states of Estonia, Latvia, and Lithuania to sign treaties that effectively ended their independence. Finland was the only state in the region that resisted his encroachments. The Finns refused to agree to Soviet demands for large tracts of territory near Leningrad. They offered to sign a nonaggression treaty with the Soviets, but Stalin refused. Agreements would not provide for Leningrad's security, he declared; only land would suffice. To get it he launched a war against the Finns, who, despite heroic resistance, had to acquiesce. Stalin had seen a chance to expand and took it.

The postwar period presented him with another potential opportunity. With Germany shattered, Britain battered, and the United States seeking to withdraw as quickly as possible, there was no one to oppose the Soviet Union in Europe. During the early stages of the war Stalin had insisted that he only wanted to restore the Soviet sphere to its 1941 boundaries. His allies, while not entirely comfortable with his claims (which included parts of Poland he had acquired in his deal with Hitler in 1939), acquiesced. However, as the Red Army rolled into Eastern Europe, Stalin made new demands and took provocative actions. In 1944 he declared that the Soviets wanted to build bases in the Dardenelles, near Britain's sphere of influence in the eastern Mediterranean. He also installed a puppet government in Poland, using the Red Army to crush all democratic opposition. While his two allies had agreed that the Soviets were to oversee matters inPoland, they were stunned by the blatant disregard for Polish self-determination. In Iran the Soviets attempted to carve out an oil-rich preserve in the north by fomenting a rebellion against the Iranian government. Red Army troops remained in the region for several months after the war in violation of an allied agreement.

These and other Soviet actions strained the wartime alliance. The break came in early 1946. In a February speech Stalin, using classic communist rhetoric, blamed Western capitalism for the world war, emphasized the ongoing conflict between capitalism and socialism, and predicted the ultimate victory of the latter. The speech shattered any hopes in the United States for the continuation of the wartime alliance. In late February, U.S. diplomat George F. Kennan composed his famous "long telegram" in which he warned that the Soviets were not interested in a modus vivendi with the West. Unlike the West, he argued, the Soviets did not believe that a lasting peace was possible and thus did not regard international agreements as permanent or binding. The Soviets only believed in the use of force. Because of this, Kennan declared, the United States must take a firm stand against Soviet aggression in key areas of the world. Kennan's analysis made sense to his superiors in Washington. As the United States toughened its stance vis-à-vis the Soviets, the Cold War ensued. Ultimately, Soviet actions had aroused concerns in the West and led to the hardening of U.S.-Soviet relations.

Could the United States have been more flexible? Could it have "given" on some of the divisive issues? For revisionists who would answer "yes" to both questions, there are points to consider. First, the United States had just fought a war to prevent one power from dominating the Eurasian landmass. Could it trust the Soviets not to take advantage of the power vacuum in Europe? Soviet actions before, during, and immediately after the war would suggest not. Second, the United States had given much to the Soviet Union—one need only consider the Lend Lease program. The generosity of the terms under which the Soviets had received this aid is unparalleled in the history of international relations. Yet, such actions had not changed Stalin's perspective. To him, security did not come from agreements and friendship. It came from territorial acquisition and force of arms. Considering Stalin's paranoia about threats to his power, even from within Soviet ranks, it is difficult to say what would have made him feel secure in the postwar world. One thing is certain: the price tag for Stalin's security was too high for the United States.

—ERIK BENSON, UNIVERSITY OF GEORGIA

Viewpoint: Recently released information from Russian archives suggests that American policymakers misinterpreted Soviet designs and capabilities.

In the summer of 1989, Yale historian Gaddis Smith complained that Cold War history was "the history of one hand clapping." For decades scholars relied heavily on Western records and were not allowed to examine official materials from the "other side." Whereas scholars of American foreign policy had massive quantities of "behind-the-scenes" declassified documentary materials, scholars of Soviet foreign policy were forced to rely on "open sources," such as newspapers. The best estimates of Soviet motivations and goals remained, essentially, educated guesses. This changed in the early 1990s, when scholars from foreign countries were finally allowed to use archives from "behind the iron curtain." Many were hopeful that these new materials would finally answer questions about Soviet intentions and capabilities. The new evidence, however, is murky, incomplete, and contradictory. Historians continue to debate the meaning and significance of the sources now available from the former Soviet Union.

Although there is not widespread agreement, the emerging picture suggests that the U.S.S.R. was not as monolithic, ideological, and expansionist as Americans in the 1940s and 1950s believed. As Melvyn P. Leffler observes, new work based on Soviet sources leads to the conclusion that "the Cold War was not a simple case of Soviet expansionism and American reaction." Rather, the leaders in the Kremlin sought cooperation with the United States. Whereas many Americans feared a possible Soviet invasion of Western Europe, the Soviet archives have produced no evidence indicating plans for a European offensive. Soviet dictator Joseph Stalin dreaded the prospect of war—particularly because until 1949 the United States was the sole possessor of the atomic bomb. As Stalin's successor, Nikita Khrushchev, recalled years later: "In the days leading up to Stalin's death [in 1953] we believed that we would go to war. Stalin trembled at this prospect. How he quivered! He was afraid of war. . . . Stalin never did anything that might provoke a war with the United States. He knew his weakness." Stalin knew that American military power far outstripped that of the Soviet Union and wanted to avoid conflict with the United States.

Documents from the Russian archives thus inspire a greater appreciation of the genuine security fears felt in Moscow. One such document is the so-called Novikov Telegram of September 1946. The document was authored by the Soviet ambassador to the United States, Nikolai Novikov. He sent the telegram to Soviet Foreign Minister Vyasheslav Molotov in Moscow as the United States was beginning to adopt an increasingly hard-line policy toward the Soviet Union. Novikov cautioned the Soviet leadership that the United States was adopting a confrontational foreign policy and was "striving for world supremacy." He expressed considerable concern for the military might of the United States. He reported that American defense expenditures had "risen colossally," amounting to about 40 percent of the total budget. The United States had developed plans for establishing an extensive system of military bases around the world, including some 228 bases and points of support in the Atlantic and 258 in the Pacific. Because many of these bases were located miles from American soil, Novikov concluded they could not be for strictly defensive purposes. Moreover, the United States was considering an alliance with Great Britain and possibly Japan, and was working to undermine Soviet control over Eastern Europe. "All of these facts," Novikov concluded, "show clearly . . . plans for world dominance by the United States." The immediate aim of American policy, in his eyes, was to force the Soviet Union to accept U.S. plans for the postwar world.

If nothing else, the Novikov Telegram is an important reminder that actions Americans believed to be defensive in nature were interpreted as offensive by Soviet government officials. Nothing illustrates this better than the Soviet response to the Marshall Plan in the summer of 1947. The Marshall Plan, named after American secretary of state George C. Marshall, proposed massive economic aid to European countries. It intended to rebuild European economies not only because they were devastated by World War II but also because American leaders feared that their weakness made them appealing targets for communist subversion. Americans saw the plan as a defensive measure to prevent Soviet expansion into Western Europe. According to historian Scott D. Parrish, the Marshall Plan marked a turning point in Stalin's attitude toward the West. Up to that point Stalin had hoped that he might be able to reach an agreement with the United States on the most contentious issues, such as the fate of Germany. With the announcement of the Marshall Plan, however, Stalin came to believe that even limited cooperation with the United States was impossible. He saw the plan as an offensive attempt to subvert Soviet security interests in Eastern Europe. In response, he rapidly moved to solidify his as yet incomplete control over the communist countries of Eastern Europe. It was in reaction to an apparently defensive action on the part of the United States that Stalin abandoned his hope for a more cooperative relationship with the West.

Such a view differs greatly from the way that most Americans saw Soviet behavior at the time. American officials believed that Soviet policies were determined by their "fanatical" ideology. Because communism was implacably hostile to capitalism, most Americans believed that the Soviets would continue to expand unless "contained" by the West. Contrary to American perceptions, Soviet leaders were not determined to promote worldwide communist revolution at any cost. Instead, they appear more concerned with ensuring the security of the U.S.S.R. and protecting their sphere of influence in Eastern Europe.

In contrast to the traditional view of Stalin as possessing a "master plan" to expand Soviet influence, he appears more pragmatic and indecisive than American decision makers believed. As far as the German question was concerned, most American policymakers (with a few notable exceptions) concluded between 1946 and 1948 that Stalin was determined to establish a communist Germany under Soviet influence. The Truman administration thus came to support a divided Germany, with an independent West German state aligned with the West, because they believed Stalin would never accept an agreement for a unified, neutral Germany. Yet, Stalin appears to have been more flexible than expected. Stalin could not decide what he wanted: a divided Germany with a separate communist East German state; a unified procommunist Germany; or a unified, but neutral and disarmed, independent Germany. In contrast to the prevailing Western view, Stalin kept his options open. He was motivated less by an ideologically driven master plan for a communist Germany than by pragmatic political and security concerns.

Similarly, historians have unearthed no concrete plans for turning Poland, Hungary, Romania, and other East European states into the communist dictatorships they eventually became. To be sure, Stalin insisted that the regimes bordering the U.S.S.R. remain "friendly" to Soviet interests. The experience of two world wars and two devastating invasions by German armies meant that Stalin needed a buffer zone in Eastern Europe to meet his basic security requirements. However, Stalin did not have a definite design for transforming the economies and societies of Eastern Europe along the Soviet model. In many cases local communists within these countries played a far more decisive role in establishing communist regimes in Eastern Europe than did Stalin. In Eastern Europe, as in Germany, Stalin acted cautiously and indecisively.

The same is true in China. American policymakers saw Stalin as ideologically wedded to the Chinese communists. The revolution in China was seen as yet another example of communist expansion directed from Moscow, and Mao Tse-tung, the leader of the Chinese Communist revolution, was believed to be a tool of Stalin. In Asia, however, Stalin initially sought to maintain a cooperative relationship with the West. He nurtured ties with both parties to the Chinese Civil War–nationalists and communists–and again kept his options open.

Stalin's decisions were shaped by security concerns and threat perceptions rather than class struggle and the ideology of world revolution. Ideology clearly influences Stalin's foreign policy, but much more subtly than American analysts assumed. Stalin's adherence to the principles of Marxism-Leninism guided his understanding of the world and influenced his interpretation of Western actions, but it did not determine it. Communist ideology, like all firmly held beliefs, was flexible and frequently manipulated by Stalin. Ideological statements were constantly used to legitimize and justify policies, but rarely did ideology determine Soviet foreign policy.

If Stalin appears cautious and indecisive in the newly available Soviet documents, he also appears a little naive and, at times, just plain reckless. In addition to the provocative foolishness of Stalin's blockade of Berlin in 1948, consider his role in the Korean War in 1950. Americans at the time believed that Stalin ordered North Korean leader Kim Il Sung to attack South Korea to test American resolve. New evidence reveals that this is not exactly correct: the primary force behind the Korean invasion was Kim, not Stalin. Kim relentlessly pushed Stalin for permission to invade the South. He was dependent on Stalin's support, and Stalin hesitated. Eventually Stalin acquiesced and authorized the North Korean attack when he deduced that the Americans would not intervene. If Stalin hoped for a passive response from the West, he grossly miscalculated. As historian John Lewis Gaddis observes, "nothing could have been better calculated to provoke a sharp American response . . . than the first overt military assault across an internationally recognized boundary since the end of World War II." In response to the invasion, the United States and the United Nations mounted a swift and concerted attempt to repel the North Koreans. The Korean War crystallized American fears of Soviet expansionism and led to a tripling of the American defense budget. By confirming the American belief in Moscow's hostility and inherent aggressiveness, the Korean War ended, almost for good, any chance of East-West cooperation.

What does the new evidence suggest about the wisdom of American foreign policy? On the one hand, it appears that Americans exaggerated the threat posed by the Soviet Union. They misinterpreted the influence of communist ideology on Soviet decision-making and overestimated the extent to which communist revolutions were inspired, controlled, and directed from Moscow. They failed to appreciate the genuine security concerns shaping Soviet thinking and did not account for how Stalin could perceive Western "defensive" policies as threatening.

On the other hand, Stalin himself did much to fuel these perceptions. If he sought cooperation with the West, he did little to make these intentions clear. He remained deeply suspicious of American designs for Western Europe and feared the American monopoly of atomic weapons. Moreover, the closed nature of Soviet society made it extremely difficult for American analysts to arrive at accurate assessments of Soviet intentions. Soviet decision making remained shrouded in secrecy, and the United States had little hard data on which to base their conclusions about Soviet behavior. American evaluations came to be based on how Americans believed totalitarian dictatorships in general, and communist countries in particular, acted. In the absence of contradictory information they assumed that totalitarian nations seek unlimited expansion and that communists seek worldwide revolution. They also had little concrete information on Soviet military capabilities, which only exacerbated fears of "worst-case" scenarios. For Americans who had witnessed the Nazi conquest of Europe and the Japanese surprise attack at Pearl Harbor, the possibility of a massive Soviet invasion of Western Europe was not easily disregarded.

It is difficult to see, therefore, exactly how U.S. officials could have acted differently in the early years of the Cold War. Nevertheless, in evaluating the origins of the Cold War, historians must account for Soviet perceptions, fears, and security concerns as much as they do those of the United States.

–KENNETH A. OSGOOD, UNIVERSITY OF CALIFORNIA, SANTA BARBARA

Viewpoint: U.S. nationalism and aggressive capitalism provoked fears in the Soviet Union that the United States was trying to reduce their level of security.

Historians remain as divided today as they were two or three decades ago about the nature and origin of the intense global anxiety termed the Cold War between the United States and the Soviet Union. Naturally there were other participants. These two nations, however, more than any others, found themselves in a position to assert power in the aftermath of World War II. The debate among historians centers largely on which side sought to assert that power to the detriment of the other and which sought to do so first. Generally the histories have been divided into categories: the orthodox, revisionist, and postrevisionist perspectives, though allowing for considerable overlap and often similar specific arguments. This essay advances a revisionist interpretation that argues the United States initiated what became a cold war between the two nations, first in Europe and then globally.

The United States emerged from World War II virtually unscathed, while the rest of western and eastern Europe and much of Asia had been devastated by the conflict. Further, America's industrial output soared some 90 percent as a direct result of the war. To continue this growth and avoid another 1930s-type economic depression (a not-too-distant memory for Americans), U.S. policymakers determined to break the old balance-of-power or spheres-of-influence system that had dominated the global economy throughout the nineteenth century. The United States moved with clear direction (despite some regional ambivalence) to expand into global markets and gain access to cheap raw materials

CLOSED SKIES: THE U-2 INCIDENT

In early May 1960 Soviet anti-aircraft defenses shot down a U.S. U-2 spy plane over the Ural Mountains near Sverdlovsk. Not only did the Soviet military recover substantial pieces of wreckage, but they also captured the pilot, Francis Gary Powers. The incident could not have come at a worse time, as the major powers were meeting at a summit conference in Paris. An angry Nikita Khrushchev demanded an apology from the United States. When the United States admitted responsibility for the flight but did not make a formal apology, Khrushchev stormed out of the conference. President Dwight D. Eisenhower then made the following statement explaining his position:

. . . In my statement of May 11 and in the statement of Secretary Herter of May 9 the position of the United States was made clear with respect to the distasteful necessity of espionage activities in a world where nations distrust each other's intentions. We pointed out that these activities had no aggressive intent but rather were to assure the safety of the United States and the free world against surprise attack by a power which boasts of its ability to devastate the United States and other countries by missiles armed with atomic warheads. As is well known, not only the United States but most other countries are constantly the targets of elaborate and persistent espionage of the Soviet Union.

There is in the Soviet statement an evident misapprehension on one key point. It alleges that the United States has, through official statements, threatened continued overflights. The importance of this alleged threat was emphasized and repeated by Mr. Krushchev. The United States has made no such threat. Neither I nor my Government has intended any. The actual statements go no further than to say that the United States will not shirk its responsibility to safeguard against surprise attack. . . .

***Source:** Department of State press release no. 271, 17 May 1960.*

through the full implementation of the Open Door policy, first issued decades earlier. Briefly, the Open Door sought reduced trade barriers, liberalization of economic policies, and, most importantly, free and unrestricted access to raw materials as well as world markets. Having suffered the least after World War II, the United States was in a superior position to take advantage of such a "liberal" trade system. Obviously, the capacity of its European allies to absorb U.S. industrial output would be vital to sustain the American economy following the war. Also important, given the economic and political weakness of those allies, were a rebuilt Japan and China. American objectives were clearly ambitious.

The Soviet Union, on the other hand, had its own set of postwar objectives. Joseph Stalin's actions stemmed from immediate security concerns. Russia had been attacked twice in the first half of the twentieth century by Germany. Furthermore, eastern European nations such as Romania had aided the Nazis in attacking the U.S.S.R. As historian Melvyn P. Leffler has written, "Stalin was determined after World War II to gain control over the East European periphery so that countries like Poland could not serve as a springboard for an offensive against the Union." World War II had devastated Russia, destroying 1,700 towns and 70,000 villages, killing 600,000 at the siege of Leningrad alone, and ultimately costing Russia 25 million lives. As the Soviet leader declared after the war, "Give [the Germans] twelve to fifteen years and they'll be on their feet again. And that is why the unity of the Slavs is important." Stalin's actions were primarily in defense of Russian territorial integrity and security. From his point of view, the West, that is Great Britain and the United States, was quite menacing. Historian Walter LaFeber has written, "the West had poured thousands of troops into Russia between 1917 and 1920, refused to cooperate with the Soviets during the 1930s, tried to turn Hitler against Stalin in 1938, reneged on promises about the second front, and in 1945 tried to penetrate areas Stalin deemed crucial to Soviet security." Indeed, Stalin had reason to be concerned about the motivations and actions of the West, particularly in Eastern Europe but also in Asia.

During the war Russia and the United States remained reluctant allies against a common enemy, Adolf Hitler's Germany. Even during those years, however, serious tensions between the two were clearly evident. From at least 1943 the United States and Great Britain began to consider the postwar world as both now believed allied victory would eventually be obtained. They enjoyed time to calculate the postwar world primarily because the Russians kept the German military occupied in the east after the German invasion of 20 June 1941. The imbalance between the allies became a point of serious contention and division during the course of the war, as the West repeatedly reneged on promises to relieve the pressure on the Soviets by opening a second front.

In the spring of 1942 and during the following year, both the U.S. president and the English prime minister promised the opening of a second front somewhere along the Atlantic coast. Repeatedly the promise was broken owing to certain ambiguous military pressures. Actually, the Americans were much more desirous of a second front than were the British. In any event, neither could agree on when and where such aid to the Russians should occur. In the meantime, the Russians were beaten back deep into their own territory. Eventually the Germans overran a vast area encompassing 45 percent of the prewar Soviet population. The Germans destroyed thousands of Russian villages and towns, killed hundreds of thousands of livestock, destroyed countless farms, and killed millions of people in the process. Stalin repeatedly pleaded with his allies to launch an attack in the west to divide the German forces or the Soviet Union might be entirely overrun. Operation OVERLORD, which was the code name of the eventual western attack, was delayed until the summer of 1944. In the interim American-Russian relations had suffered a great deal. Stalin now believed, with reason, that the Americans did not mind seeing the Germans significantly weaken his country as they feared Russian control of eastern Europe in the postwar period anyway. As Senator Harry S Truman put it in 1941, "If we see that Germany is winning we should help Russia and if Russia is winning we ought to help Germany and that way let them kill as many as possible, although I don't want to see Hitler victorious under any circumstances." The refusal to open the second front and the broken promises certainly indicated to Stalin the nature of the alliance and would shape relations between East and West in the postwar period.

On questions concerning the postwar surrender and settlement of not only Western but Eastern Europe as well, Russia was often shut out of discussions or had its involvement severely limited, as in the case of Italy during 1943 and 1944. In the end Soviet leaders acquiesced on Italy and other Western nations, thinking that the "Italian formula" had set an important diplomatic precedent. Surely when it came time to discuss the future of Eastern European nations, the West would similarly indulge Stalin. Such was not the case. At the Yalta Conference, held in February 1945, the United States challenged Russian control of Eastern European nations such as Poland and Romania. The previous October, British prime minister Winston Churchill had somewhat clandestinely offered Stalin control of Bulgaria and Romania in exchange for English control of Greece to secure Mediterranean shipping, to which Stalin agreed. U.S. president Franklin D. Roosevelt was furious that the Soviets expected control of Eastern Europe. Stalin had, prior to Yalta, recognized a procommunist government in Poland. Now the United States demanded that the government be broadened to include pro-Western elements. Procommunist governments represented, to U.S. policymakers, closed markets and a return to the old spheres-of-influence arrangement. The United States refused to permit Stalin total control in the East. The Soviet leader accepted Western demands regarding Poland, though admittedly the agreement was so shot through with ambiguities as to be basically meaningless. Consequently, Stalin left the Yalta meeting believing the other allies would allow him a greater degree of control and autonomy in Eastern Europe than had been the case in Western Europe, though not a total reversal of the Italian formula.

As Stalin tightened down on Romania, however, it became clear the United States would not permit the Soviets to play the dominant role in the East. In mid April, Roosevelt died and Truman inherited the thorny problem of East-West relations. Traditional historians viewed Truman as an insecure man who sought to take the hard line with the Soviets, lest his policies be criticized as appeasement. While his position certainly can accurately be characterized as hard-line, the United States had already begun to take this position by 1945 through efforts such as insisting on sole responsibility for rebuilding Japan and including China among the so-called great powers, which Stalin perceived, not without reason, as "capitalist encirclement." Truman's advisers only reinforced this hard-line, though some, such as Secretary of War Henry Stimson, explicitly recognized the effect such a policy might have on U.S.-U.S.S.R. relations. As Stimson predicted, the Soviet leader began to tighten his hold on places such as Romania and Poland as the United States increased its demands on Soviet policy in the region.

To make an important distinction, however, Soviet policy in Eastern Europe still varied widely. The reason for this is quite simple: the Soviets had no clear plan to expand into and take control of the countries of Eastern Europe and certainly no plan for world domination through revolution. In fact, Soviet leaders believed the wartime coalition with the British and Americans would continue and should continue if the U.S.S.R. was to achieve its own security aims following the war. This position is reinforced by the opening in recent years of the archives of the U.S.S.R. and former Soviet-bloc nations. These archival sources reveal, according to Leffler, a far more nuanced reality than that suggested by orthodox historians or the post-revisionists. Rather than the "messianic" nature of communist ideology shaping events, the Soviets responded to a multitude of immediate threats and responded in different ways. "Governing a land devastated by two world wars, they feared a resurgence of German and Japanese strength. They felt threatened by a United States that alone among the combatants emerged from the war wealthier and armed with the atomic bomb," and when American leaders began to signal their intention to rebuild Germany and Japan, the threat of "capitalist encirclement" became quite real.

By contrast with the U.S. position, the "Soviets had nothing comparable to Joint Chiefs of Staff memo 1067, the American blueprint for the occupation of Germany." The overriding theme in Soviet policy in Eastern Europe during these years was pragmatism, emphasizing Russian territorial security, not world revolution. The Soviet Union had sought only to protect its own security interests throughout the war and into the late 1940s.

Immediately following the war Stalin perceived his main threat as being a rejuvenated Germany. By mid 1947, however, the Russian leader began to "reassess the threat, shifting [the] focus from a resurgent Germany in fifteen to twenty years' time, to a capitalist coalition led by the English-speaking powers that would be ready for war in five to six years." To make matters worse for the Russians, a revived Germany and a rebuilt Japan would now be part of that coalition. Challenging Stalin in Eastern Europe reinforced this perception, as did the emphasis on rebuilding Germany and Japan along capitalist lines. To the Soviets, the United States had now completely changed its earlier goals for the postwar world, particularly in Germany, moving from "the extreme of [Henry] Morganthau's pastoralization plan to the opposite policy of rehabilitation" and the merging of western occupied zones that encompassed Germany's industrial heartland, knowing this was anathema to the Soviets for obvious reasons. By 1947 the United States had embarked on a highly ambitious foreign policy in Europe and Asia that excluded and, at the same time, sought to control the Soviet Union.

The introduction of Marshall Plan aid beginning in 1948 only confirmed the true intent of the West to the Soviets. The United States officially extended an offer to the Soviets to participate in rebuilding Europe. The real intention of the plan, however, soon became clear. When the Russian foreign minister suggested changes in the organization of aid to Europe, the West refused to consider them. For Russia to participate, it would have to open its economic records to world scrutiny, send raw materials to Europe (in the midst of a famine), and allow for a rebuilt Germany. It is sometimes asserted that the Soviet Union refused to participate in the Marshall Plan just to be belligerent and anticapitalist. Given the recent history between the United States and the U.S.S.R., however, this position quickly breaks down. The Soviets had every reason to fear the nature of American aid in Europe. It seemed that the United States, according to historian Michael MccGwire, was attempting "to lure as many countries as possible into a binding relationship with the West, by integrating their economies into the capitalist bloc." After the Soviets declined to participate and sacrifice national security, they embarked on a similar plan for Eastern Europe in defense against the American plan: the Molotov Plan. The East now became an isolated trading bloc to a large extent with trade in the region quadrupling by 1950.

By the late 1940s the East and West had become fairly rigidly divided and remained so until around 1990. After 1948 the emphasis shifted away from Europe to various places around the Third World such as Korea, Indonesia, Malaya, Vietnam, and Guatemala. The basic outlines of the Cold War had solidified, and conflict in each of the aforementioned locations became the scene of proxy wars in which the East (Soviet Union) and the West (United States) fought for control and a dominant position around the world.

The Soviets, during and after World War II, had real and immediate concerns about aggression from the West, especially Germany. So long as the Balkans remained unstable, the threat persisted and worsened. If Stalin could achieve even a modicum of stability there, then the opportunities for an aggressive Germany in the future diminished exponentially. Indeed, Soviet policy in the East was often aggressive and at times brutal in seeking stability, or the creation of what was termed a buffer zone. Nevertheless, it is important to point out that the U.S.S.R. sought security, not world dominance. Stalin was not in a position to achieve or take advantage of a position of world dominance. As former premier Khrushchev later revealed, Stalin "trembled at this prospect" of going to war with the United States. "How he quivered! He was afraid of war... Stalin never did anything that might provoke a war with the United States. He knew his weakness."

American policymakers were aware of the Russian leader's weakness as well. The Joint Logistic Plans Committee and the Military Intelligence Division had conducted their own investigation into Soviet capabilities after World War II. Estimating that the Russians would need from fifteen to twenty years to rebuild, the report concluded, "the offensive capabilities of the United States are manifestly superior to those of the U.S.S.R. and any war between the U.S. and the U.S.S.R. would be far more costly to the Soviet Union than to the United States." Armed with this information, however, the United States moved ahead with plans to rebuild Germany and Japan and to move China into a position of world power through membership in the new United Nations, all the while securing military bases around Europe and Asia and opening access to important sources of raw materials. For obvious reasons the Soviet Union perceived U.S. actions as aggressive nationalism, all the more dangerous because the United States appeared to be abandoning its wartime ally in favor of that ally's historic enemies.

–JAMES CARTER, UNIVERSITY OF HOUSTON

References

Bruce Cumings, "'Revising Postrevisionism,' Or, The Poverty of Theory in Diplomatic History," *Diplomatic History,* 17 (Fall 1993): 20–62;

David Dimbleby and David Reynolds, *An Ocean Apart: The Relationship Between Britain and America in the Twentieth Century* (New York: Random House, 1988);

John Lewis Gaddis, *The United States and the Origins of the Cold War, 1941–1947* (New York: Columbia University Press, 1972);

Gaddis, *We Now Know: Rethinking Cold War History* (New York: Oxford University Press, 1997);

Sergei N. Goncharov, John W. Lewis, and Xue Litai, *Uncertain Partners: Stalin, Mao and the Korean War* (Stanford, Cal.: Stanford University Press, 1993);

David Holloway, *Stalin and the Bomb: The Soviet Union and Atomic Energy, 1939–1956* (New Haven: Yale University Press, 1994);

Gabriel Kolko, *The Politics of War: The World and United States Foreign Policy, 1943–1945* (New York: Random House, 1968);

Walter LaFeber, *America, Russia and the Cold War, 1945–1990* (New York: McGraw-Hill, 1991);

Melvyn P. Leffler, *A Preponderance of Power: National Security, the Truman Administration, and the Cold War* (Stanford, Cal.: Stanford University Press, 1992);

Leffler, "Inside Enemy Archives: The Cold War Reopened," *Foreign Affairs,* 75 (July–August 1996): 120–135;

Ralph B. Levering, *The Cold War: A Post-Cold War History* (Arlington Heights, Ill.: Harlan Davidson, 1994);

Vojtech Mastny, *The Cold War and Soviet Insecurity: The Stalin Years* (New York: Oxford University Press, 1996);

Mastny, *Russia's Road to the Cold War: Diplomacy, Warfare and the Politics of Communism, 1941–45* (New York: Columbia University Press, 1979);

Michael MccGwire, "National Security and Soviet Foreign Policy," in *The Origins of the Cold War: An International History,* edited by Leffler and David S. Painter (New York: Routledge, 1994): pp. 81–118;

Thomas J. McCormick, *America's Half-Century: United States Foreign Policy in the Cold War* (Baltimore: Johns Hopkins University Press, 1989);

Norman M. Naimark, *The Russians in Germany: A History of the Soviet Zone of Occupation, 1945–1949* (Cambridge, Mass.: Belknap Press of Harvard University Press, 1995);

Scott D. Parrish, "The Turn Toward Confrontation: The Soviet Reaction to the Marshall Plan, 1947," Cold War International History Project, Working Paper No. 9;

Gaddis Smith, "Glasnost, Diplomatic History, and the Post-Cold War Agenda," *Yale History Journal of World Affairs,* 1 (Summer 1989): 50;

"The Soviet Side of the Cold War: A Symposium," *Diplomatic History,* 15 (Fall 1991): 523–564;

"Symposium: Soviet Archives: Recent Revelations and Cold War Historiography," *Diplomatic History,* 21 (Spring 1997): 215–305;

William Appleman Williams, *The Tragedy of American Diplomacy* (Cleveland: World, 1959);

Vladislav Zubok and Constantine Pleshakov, *Inside the Kremlin's Cold War: From Stalin to Khrushchev* (Cambridge, Mass.: Harvard University Press, 1996).

COMMUNISM AND CIVIL RIGHTS

Did the American Civil Rights movement encourage sympathy with communism?

Viewpoint: By focusing attention on Soviet totalitarianism and mistreatment of minorities, the Cold War compelled Americans to change their own position on race relations and advance a civil-rights agenda.

Viewpoint: The Cold War made apparent to many Americans the hypocrisy of their own nation.

Is it a coincidence that the American Civil Rights movement emerged just as the United States was getting involved in the Cold War? Probably not, as Jonathan Rosenberg argues in his essay. The Cold War, pitting American freedom against Soviet totalitarianism, made Americans look at themselves and see that all was not well in their own "house." President Harry S Truman, who oversaw the Berlin Airlift, the Korean War, and the Marshall Plan, which were all aimed at combating Soviet aggression, also ended segregation in the American armed forces and appointed the President's Committee on Civil Rights in 1946.

On the other hand, as Anthony Connors maintains, if the conflict pointed to the discrepancy between American ideals and American practices, not all Americans believed the United States was bound to reform. W. E. B. Du Bois, one of the most influential thinkers of the twentieth century, came to believe that American racism was endemic to the American system. Rather than joining Martin Luther King Jr. and Thurgood Marshall in overturning segregation, Du Bois at this time publicly embraced Marxism, ran for the U.S. Senate on the Socialist Labor ticket, and then renounced his native land for exile in Ghana.

Du Bois's exile has been something of a puzzle and at the time caused many, black and white, to reevaluate Du Bois's intellectual position. Nevertheless, Du Bois, a powerful critic of society, must also cause us to reevaluate our own notions of how history happens and how men and women analyze and interpret the events they experience. Why did the Cold War and the Civil Rights movement begin almost simultaneously? Was there a relationship between the two? Truman and Du Bois certainly thought so, but they differed on what was the definition of that relationship. The difference forms one of the intellectual puzzles of history. We must remember that though the relationship is a puzzle today, at the time of Du Bois's exile it seemed to have grave consequences.

Viewpoint: By focusing attention on Soviet totalitarianism and mistreatment of minorities, the Cold War compelled Americans to change their own position on race relations and advance a civil-rights agenda.

Few would question the proposition that the post-1945 struggle between the United States and the Soviet Union had a transformative effect on international relations. Before it ended with the dissolution of the Soviet Union in 1991, the Cold War had touched the lives of people on every continent, consumed vast wealth, and contributed to the development and proliferation of weapons of mass destruction that still plague the security of nations. Lest one forget, the East-West conflict was no mere "cold war," for in that it never became a shooting war between the superpowers, it did contribute to the course of hot wars throughout the developing world—struggles responsible for the deaths of countless soldiers and civilians. It seems difficult, then, to overestimate the profound implications the Cold War has had on the lives of peoples and nations in the post–World War II era.

However, the East-West confrontation did more than shape world politics; it also influenced domestic life in the United States, leaving few aspects of society unaffected. Perhaps the most obvious effect was the emergence of the "national security state." Defense expenditures increased dramatically as a proportion of government spending, the buildup of complex systems of nuclear and conventional weapons, and governmental support for the technologies and industries that attended the development of these novel instruments of war, became a top priority. The fundamental aim of this massive increase in military spending was to deter war with the Soviet Union, which was itself developing a highly destructive arsenal, and to enable the West to prevail in the event of a clash between superpowers.

One consequence of the East-West conflict, then, was to increase the size of the U.S. government, as it became essential to plan and implement the military buildup that flowed inexorably from the global competition. Moreover, during the Cold War, American policymakers came to believe that developments in every corner of the world—from Korea to Guatemala, from Germany to the Horn of Africa—were vital to national security. Those charged with formulating U.S. foreign and defense policy saw international politics as a zero sum game, a notion that led the United States to commit vast resources to preserve its expanding security interests and to assume much of the burden for defending other nations from Soviet communism, which was seen as a threat to world freedom.

In addition to transforming American foreign and defense policies and causing an enlargement in government, the East-West conflict reconfigured domestic life in myriad ways that were far from clear at the time and that often remain obscure. The Cold War profoundly affected social, cultural, and political life in postwar America; it influenced what Americans read, what they saw at the movies and on television, how they worshiped and were educated, and where they lived and worked. It shaped the contours of family life, gender relations, and childhood and profoundly affected the trajectory of domestic politics. The Cold War also powerfully influenced the most significant social question of the postwar era—the struggle for racial justice—supplying the Civil Rights movement with heightened energy and, many believed, greater legitimacy.

Perhaps it is not surprising that a global conflict that many thought pitted democracy and freedom against tyranny and oppression would have significance in the context of a domestic struggle, at the heart of which lay questions about democracy, freedom, tyranny, and oppression. One consequence of the Cold War—at a time when the United States had become the international guarantor of democracy—was that it compelled many Americans to question the legitimacy of Jim Crow, the system of legal racial oppression that scarred life in the South. In retrospect it seems obvious that America's self-proclaimed role as world protector of freedom and democracy (whether either was actually threatened is arguable) would have collided with the reality of a system of state-sanctioned racial persecution that denied the blessings of freedom and democracy to one in ten of its citizens. Thus, the Cold War called into question the validity of the American creed.

For those leading the crusade for racial justice, the Cold War served as a perfect vehicle with which to advance their domestic aims. From the late 1940s on, as the American government began to assume responsibility for defending the world from the perceived threat of Soviet communism, civil-rights leaders pointed time and again to the inconsistency between the country's mission abroad and the persistence of segregation at home. Reference to this discrepancy, which civil-rights leaders often described as rank hypocrisy, became a central element in the rhetoric of the Civil Rights movement.

Further strengthening the view that Jim Crow and the Cold War were uneasy partners was a transformative international development, the anti-imperial struggles waged around the world. Race-reform leaders asserted repeatedly that if the United States wished to command the loyalty of peoples of color in the developing world—and they

Protesters in San Francisco, ca. 1967

(Flax Hermes/Pathfinder Press)

claimed this to be vital during the Cold War—it was necessary to end domestic racial persecution. In the words of one black leader, the Reverend James H. Robinson, the creation of a real democracy in the United States would make it possible to gain the support of colonial peoples and "to win this great mass to our way and use their whole weight on the scales against communism."

In a variety of places—at conferences and meetings, in newspapers and magazines, on the radio, and in churches—those who fought for racial justice asserted relentlessly that Jim Crow was incompatible with America's international role. Leading figures in the Civil Rights movement made this point repeatedly, and the words, for example, of Walter White of the National Association for the Advancement of Colored People (NAACP); W. E. B. Du Bois, one of the century's foremost race activists; A. Philip Randolph, head of the Brotherhood of Sleeping Car Porters; and Martin Luther King Jr., were unambiguous: effective world leadership demanded that the United States practice at home what it preached abroad. White declared in 1947 that this country had no business spending "dollars and lives" to demand democratic governments throughout the world when it had failed "completely to provide democracy in Mississippi." Throughout the Cold War this view was articulated time and again by virtually every important civil-rights leader.

Those listening to civil-rights rhetoric in the Cold War years would have recognized that race leaders were determined to use America's posture in the East-West struggle to help advance the movement's aims. Beginning in the late 1940s, the reformers' unrelenting message—that Jim Crow would prove costly to the United States on the international scene—began to take hold. At the NAACP's annual conference in 1947, President Harry S Truman observed that the "support of desperate populations of battle-ravaged countries must be won. . . . We must have them as allies." Linking the Cold War to civil rights, he declared, "Our case for democracy should be as strong as we can make it. It should rest on practical evidence that we have been able to put our own house in order." The president argued that the nation could "no longer afford the luxury of a leisurely attack upon prejudice and discrimination" and claimed it was up to the federal government to "show the way."

The chief executive established an organic connection between Cold War foreign-policy concerns and progress on civil rights. If Truman was the first president to make explicit this interrelationship, he would not be the last. Presidents Dwight D. Eisenhower, John F. Kennedy, and Lyndon B. Johnson, along with leading government officials, offered similar observations throughout the Cold War, averring in public comments, as well as in private conversations and correspondence, that the persistence of Jim Crow weakened America's position in a dangerous world. Acting Secretary of State Dean Acheson observed in 1946, "discrimination against minority groups in this country has an adverse effect upon our relations with other countries," often making "it next to impossible to formulate a satisfactory answer to our critics" in other lands.

Not only presidents and policymakers advanced the idea that U.S. race relations was a liability in the East-West conflict; it was acknowledged in the legal arena that domestic racial oppression weakened the position of the United States on the world stage. The amicus curiae brief filed by the U.S. Department of Justice in the celebrated case of *Brown* v. *Board of Education of Topeka, Kansas,* in which the Supreme Court ruled in 1954 that the "separate but equal" doctrine in education was unconstitutional, argued that desegregation was in the national interest, in part because of foreign-policy concerns. The Justice Department noted that *Brown* was significant because the "existence of discrimination against minority groups . . . furnishes grist for the Communist propaganda mills, and raises doubts . . . as to the intensity of our devotion to the democratic faith." Clearly, it was impossible to disentangle the challenge of domestic race relations from the Cold War.

In the wake of this landmark decision, newspapers in the United States and throughout the world declared that *Brown* had weakened the communist cause, and Channing Tobias, a civil-rights activist, declared that the "propaganda value of this ruling for America and the free world in the . . . struggle against communism is beyond measure." Even Eisenhower, hardly a supporter of the Civil Rights movement, declared that the case was enormously important to the "cause of freedom in the world." The idea that progress on civil rights was inextricably connected to the struggle abroad was put forward explicitly in several other key civil-rights cases, and civil-rights leaders were largely responsible for pushing the idea that American world preeminence depended on the construction of a genuine democracy in the United States.

Progress in civil rights after 1945 flowed from a complex set of factors: economic and demographic changes, an extraordinarily effective group of black leaders, and a gradual but undeniable evolution in public attitudes that delegitimized institutionalized racial oppression. These are some of the elements that aided the process whereby Jim Crow would be dismantled in the South, a slow but steady transformation that by the mid 1960s enabled African Americans to participate more fully in the American democracy. In addition to these critical developments, America's determination to fight communism around the world—a commitment that had broad appeal and a deep impact on postwar America—played a key role in helping the country realize that legal racial persecution and democratic government were incompatible.

The Cold War altered domestic politics and culture in the United States after 1945, and Americans saw the competition between capitalism and communism as a struggle between freedom and tyranny. As the global contest unfolded, it compelled Americans to consider more fully the domestic inequities and international implications of race relations in the United States, and it convinced presidents, policymakers, and average people that the fight against communism overseas made it imperative to create a genuine democracy at home. In so doing, the Cold War provided the Civil Rights movement with considerable energy and supplied it with a degree of momentum and legitimacy that it would not otherwise have had.

—JONATHAN ROSENBERG, UNIVERSITY OF VIRGINIA

Viewpoint: The Cold War made apparent to many Americans the hypocrisy of their own nation.

In 1961 African American leader and NAACP founder W. E. B. Du Bois applied for membership in the Communist Party of the United States of America (CP-USA) and soon thereafter became a citizen of the newly independent, Marxist-oriented African nation of Ghana. Some critics attributed his decision to senility—he was, after all, ninety-three years old. Others considered it a meaningless gesture of defiance, more an expression of anger than of considered opinion. It was, however, an altogether logical decision, one that reflected a lifetime of frustration over intractable racism in America as well as a growing conviction that economic factors were at the root of racial inequality. Communism, with its theoretical emphasis on the economic welfare of all, held a powerful attraction for him. Beyond the abstract appeal, Du Bois's own personal history—of harassment and discrimination in the United States and of respect and privilege behind the Iron Curtain—was a strong determinant in his decision.

Du Bois was the preeminent black intellectual in America in the first half of the twentieth century. The first African American to earn a Ph.D. from Harvard University (1895), he published more than two thousand essays, editorials, and articles, as well as nineteen books. In 1903, in *The Souls of Black Folk*–still one of the most lyrical and powerful expressions on race relations in America–he announced that "the problem of the twentieth century is the problem of the color line," and he spent the remaining sixty years of his life in an uncompromising effort to resolve that problem. While he occasionally enjoyed public esteem (*The Souls of Black Folk* was well received), his life was one of growing separation from the mainstream American way that he saw as continuing on a path that would never willingly allow social, political, and economic equality to African Americans. His increasingly global outlook, evidenced by his participation in several Pan-African and United Nations–sponsored congresses, convinced him that the problem of color was worldwide and directly related to Western imperialism and the exploitation of African and Asian peoples and resources. This internationalism is critical to understanding his attitude toward communism. He was attempting to resolve not just an American problem, but one that required a global solution.

For the most part, Du Bois was not an uncritical advocate of communism. In his application letter to CP-USA Chairman Gus Hall, he noted that he had once been a member of the Socialist Party but resigned after endorsing Democratic candidate Woodrow Wilson for President in 1912, and that he had castigated the CP-USA in the 1930s for its handling of the Scottsboro case, in which nine black youths were convicted of gang-raping two white women. In particular, he disagreed with the Communists' dogmatic unwillingness to support desegregation because if desegregation were to succeed without the revolution of the working class, it would contradict communist theory. As late as 1940 he claimed, "I was not and am not a communist. I do not believe in the dogma of inevitable revolution to right economic wrong." Communism, though, appeared to be the only viable alternative to capitalism. Furthermore, the Soviets proclaimed economic equality as their highest goal and in some sense fostered a real cross-racial society (although hidden under the cloak of communist brotherhood–a bond that later dissolved in the breakup of the Soviet Union). In comparison, Du Bois saw little evidence of economic and social progress for blacks in the United States. His personal treatment in communist countries, as well as the suspicion and harassment of his own government, makes the logic of his communism intelligible.

One of the paradoxes of Du Bois's support for Soviet communism was his elitism, a haughty attitude that earned him little affection among black leaders. Early in his career Du Bois had developed the theory of the Talented Tenth, an elite corps of black intellectuals who would lift the masses–their "duller brethren," as he put it–to higher ground. No nation, Du Bois claimed, had ever become civilized from the bottom up. This fundamentally anti-egalitarian principle would seem at odds with the communist doctrine of revolutionary dictatorship of the working class. Du Bois, however, was convinced that intellectuals were at the top of the Soviet hierarchy, thus working-class rhetoric combined with high status for intellectuals suited him well. In a letter to his daughter Yolande, written from Russia in 1958, he expressed his delight that "we have servants for every wish" and for the "hotel suite, car, chauffeur and the most georgeous [*sic*] honors ever bestowed on me." He had of course received special treatment as an American dissident; Soviet intellectuals, on the other hand, were often closely watched and often imprisoned in the Gulag. It is important to bear in mind that Du Bois sincerely believed people like him were revered by the communist leadership. This special treatment was seductive to a man whose courage, intellect, and accomplishments had never been respected in his own country.

If Du Bois's head could be turned by foreign acclaim, it does not sufficiently explain his attraction to communism, nor his tendency to ignore the harsh realities of the Soviet Union. He was by no means alone in his hope for a permanent cure to the economic and social turmoil of the Great Depression–a time when radical social and economic alternatives were considered by many, including intellectuals, workers, and African Americans. The Communist Party of America, at its peak membership (about one hundred thousand) in the mid 1930s, actively helped the hungry and unemployed during the depression and courageously promoted racial justice at a time when most political organizations and the public were indifferent or openly hostile. Du Bois's attraction to communism is therefore not surprising.

More problematic, however, was his propensity to ignore negative factors, such as Joseph Stalin's 1939 pact with Adolf Hitler, Russia's aggression against her formerly independent neighbors after World War II, and the brutal suppression of the 1956 Hungarian revolt–not to mention the disclosure of Stalin's purges. Many American communists deserted the CP-USA from the late 1930s to the early 1950s for these reasons. Yet, in an embarrassingly flattering tribute to Stalin in 1953, Du Bois almost identifies with the Soviet leader: "As one of the despised minorities of man, [Stalin] first set Russia on the road to conquer race prejudice and make one nation out of its 140 groups without destroying their individuality." A half decade later Russia's brutal suppression of individuality in the Baltic countries and Eastern Europe is better known. Du Bois was certainly aware of Stalin's crimes, but he ignored them: his final autobiography (written mostly from 1958 to 1960) barely mentions Stalin at all.

Yet, how could he disregard such harsh reality? Du Bois simply needed to believe in a viable alternative to capitalism. It was primarily the theory of communism–the abstraction–that he believed in, and in doing so he found himself forced to ignore negative aspects in the only country seemingly making economic and social strides without capitalism. The Russians were, in fact, making progress, although much of it proved to be a sham. *Sputnik I*–the Russian satellite launched in 1957–delighted Du Bois because "it taught the United States the superiority of Communist thought and calculation." In retrospect, communist superiority was hardly the case, although fear of it did frighten the United States into renewed effort in the space program. Du Bois truly believed that Russia was not the villain portrayed in the Western press. His own experiences demonstrated to him that communist societies were open, and he naively believed his warm reception in Russia and China was representative of how communist states really operated. "Few police are in evidence," he wrote of Moscow in the late 1950s. If it ever occurred to him that his treatment was related to his anti-Americanism, he never acknowledged it.

Fundamentally, Du Bois considered America's obsessive focus on Russia beside the point. The real issue of inequality was being obscured by the rhetoric of the Cold War. "It is not Russia that threatens the United States so much as Mississippi," he wrote in 1947. A few years later he articulated this theme more broadly:

> If tomorrow Russia disappeared from the face of the earth, the basic problem facing the modern world would remain: and that is, why is it, with the earth's abundance and our mastery of natural forces, and miraculous technique; with our commerce belting the earth, and goods and services pouring from our stores, factories, ships and warehouses–why is it that nevertheless, most human beings are starving to death, dying of preventable diseases and too ignorant to know what is the matter, while a small minority are so rich that they cannot spend their income?

The real issue was not Russia but the inherent problem of wealth, distribution, and indifference in a capitalist-dominated world. By actively promoting programs of economic reform on a massive scale, Soviet communism appeared to have loftier aims than democratic capitalism.

Du Bois was also convinced that democracy was simply not working in America. Most blacks were denied the ballot and most whites did not bother to vote; McCarthyism had done irreparable damage to free speech; the economic and social innovations of the New Deal had been largely reversed; and Cold War militarism threatened the world. He was embittered and discouraged by his harassment by the State Department and the Federal Bureau of Investigation (FBI). He had been denied permission to travel abroad for much of the 1950s and was arrested in 1951 for distributing the "Stockholm Appeal," an international petition to abolish the atomic bomb. Although this appeal collected 2.5 million signatures in the United States, and similar antiwar appeals were circulated by the Red Cross and the Quakers, the State Department considered it a Soviet propaganda ploy. Du Bois retorted that, "Today in this country it is becoming

THE APPLICATION

W. E. B. Du Bois's application for membership in the Communist Party USA (CP-USA) was followed by this letter, which appeared in the 26 November 1961 issue of The Worker.

On the first day of October, 1961, I am applying for admission to membership in the Communist Party of the United States. I have been long and slow in coming to this conclusion, but at last my mind is settled. . . .

Capitalism cannot reform itself; it is doomed to self-destruction. No universal selfishness can bring social good to all.

Communism—the effort to give all men what they need and to ask of each the best they can contribute—it has and will make mistakes, but today it marches triumphantly on in education and science, in home and food, with increased freedom of thought and deliverance from dogma. In the end Communism will triumph. I want to help bring that day.

The path of the American Communist Party is clear: It will provide the United States with a real Third Party and thus restore democracy to this land. It will call for:

1. Public ownership of natural resources and all capital.
2. Public control over transportation and communications.
3. Abolition of poverty and limitation of personal income.
4. No exploitation of labor.
5. Social medicine, with hospitalization and care of the old.
6. Free education for all.
7. Training for jobs and jobs for all.
8. Discipline for growth and reform.
9. Freedom under the law.
10. No dogmatic religion.

These aims are not crimes. They are practiced increasingly over the world. No nation can call itself free which does not allow its citizens to work for these ends.

standard reaction to call anything 'communist' and therefore subversive and unpatriotic, which anybody for any reason dislikes." The case against Du Bois for failing to register as an "agent of a foreign principal" was thrown out of court. Yet, even with his innocence established, Du Bois was ignored or consciously avoided: "all that dammed-up wisdom and experience had no outlet into the mainstream or American life." The effect was to alienate him further from America and to reinforce his commitment to a more hopeful alternative.

Finally, did Du Bois's adoption of communism either help or hinder the Civil Rights movement in America? According to Taylor Branch, in *Parting the Waters: America in the King Years, 1954–1963* (1988), the FBI reacted indifferently to Du Bois' joining the CP-USA because they no longer viewed him as important. Martin Luther King Jr. was wary because he realized his program could be destroyed by association with the fractured Communist Party, but King never forgot that they had preached and practiced racial equality, and he clearly had Du Bois in mind in late 1961 when he warned: "There can be no doubt that if the problem of racial discrimination is not solved in the not too distant future, some Negroes, out of frustration, discontent, and despair, will turn to some other ideology." A few years later King could be more open about Du Bois's legacy. In a speech delivered at Carnegie Hall on 23 February 1968, the one hundredth anniversary of Du Bois's birth, King said:

> We cannot talk of Dr. Du Bois without recognizing that he was a radical all of his life. Some people would like to ignore the fact that he was a Communist in his later years . . . it is time to cease muting the fact that Dr. Du Bois was a genius and chose to be a Communist. Our irrational, obsessive anti-communism has led us into too many quagmires to be retained as if it were a mode of scientific thinking.

Neither senility nor thoughtless anger, Du Bois's choice of communism was a courageous stand for social and economic justice made in the face of McCarthyism—a contrary view that is remarkable for its incisive assessment of racism in America, its understanding of the fundamental role of economics in race relations, and its boldness in suggesting an alternative vision during a period of controlled opinion. What led Du Bois to communism was the logic of his entire life. "I believe that all men, black and brown and white, are brothers," he wrote in 1920, "varying through Time and Opportunity, in form and gift and feature, but differing in no essential particular, and alike in soul and the possibility of infinite development." This belief was the credo from which he never retreated. But when it became obvious to him that democratic capitalism was not going to fulfill his dream of racial equality, he turned his attention to the only major alternative. He may have been a poor prophet—communism obviously did not triumph—yet, his assessment of what needed to be fixed provided much of the foundation of the Civil Rights movement. King is revered partly because he took another path—working nonviolently within the democratic system. Our appreciation for the accomplishments of Du Bois should be no less because he chose the other political system.

—ANTHONY CONNORS, CLARK UNIVERSITY

References

Taylor Branch, *Parting the Waters: America in the King Years, 1954–1963* (New York: Simon & Schuster, 1988);

Alan Brinkley, *The Unfinished Nation: A Concise History of the American People* (New York: Knopf, 1993);

W. E. B. Du Bois, *The Autobiography of W. E. B. Du Bois: A Soliloquy On Viewing My Life From the Last Decade of Its First Century* (New York: International Publishers, 1968);

Du Bois, *Dusk of Dawn: An Essay Toward An Autobiography of a Race Concept* (New York: Harcourt, Brace, 1940);

Du Bois, *The Oxford W. E. B. Du Bois Reader*, edited by Eric J. Sundquist (New York: Oxford University Press, 1996);

Du Bois, *The Souls of Black Folk: Essays and Sketches* (Chicago: McClurg, 1903);

Mary Dudziak, "Desegregation as a Cold War Imperative," *Stanford Law Review*, 41 (November 1988): 61–120;

Gerald Horne, *Black and Red: W. E. B. Du Bois and the Afro-American Response to the Cold War, 1944–1963* (Albany: State University of New York Press, 1986);

Brenda Gayle Plummer, *Rising Wind: Black Americans and U.S. Foreign Affairs, 1935–1960* (Chapel Hill: University of North Carolina Press, 1996);

Benjamin Quarles, *The Negro in the Making of America* (New York: Collier, 1964);

William M. Tuttle, ed., *W. E. B. Du Bois* (Englewood Cliffs, N.J.: Prentice-Hall, 1973);

Penny M. Von Eschen, *Race Against Empire: Black Americans and Anticolonialism, 1937–1957* (Ithaca, N.Y.: Cornell University Press, 1997).

EISENHOWER

Was President Dwight D. Eisenhower a Cold Warrior or Peacemaker?

Viewpoint: President Eisenhower was committed to preventing a nuclear holocaust, and his administration successfully kept the nation out of war.

Viewpoint: Though President Eisenhower spoke often of the need for peace, his administration relied mainly on American military strength and preparedness to counter Soviet aggression.

How does history evaluate a president? When Dwight D. Eisenhower left the White House in 1961, he was one of the most admired men of his time. Within a few years, though, his historical reputation suffered, while that of his predecessor, Harry S Truman, rose. At one point in the 1960s historians rated Eisenhower in the lower tier of presidents. After the experiences of the late 1960s and early 1970s, however, Eisenhower's reputation rose once again.

This kind of historical exercise—rating and ranking presidents or other historical figures—is meaningless as history, but it is important to understanding the present. Comparisons are made to men and women who came before, and just as historians evaluate past actions, citizens ponder how the future might evaluate their own.

Eisenhower came into the White House offering change. He was the first Republican elected president since Herbert Hoover, and for twenty years the Democratic Party had held both the White House and Congress. Though Eisenhower was a Republican, he had professed his political allegiance only months before his nomination—in fact, in 1951 Truman had asked Eisenhower to run for the presidency as a Democrat. Eisenhower was a man above party, but he quickly moved to take control of the Republicans, replacing the conservative Senator Robert A. Taft as the party's leader.

How did Eisenhower, a career military officer, respond to the challenges of the Cold War? In the first essay Eisenhower is presented as a skillful organizer sincerely committed to keeping the United States out of war and preventing the country from responding to Cold War threats by becoming itself a military dictatorship. Horrified by the prospect of nuclear holocaust, Eisenhower proposed bold plans to end the arms race.

The second essay evaluates Eisenhower more critically, suggesting that his and other Americans' misreading of the Soviet Union, particularly after the death of Joseph Stalin in March 1953, led to continued escalation of the arms race. Eisenhower, Kenneth Osgood argues, made his Atoms for Peace and Open Skies proposals knowing that the Soviets could not accept them and that even if the Soviets did, both these plans were to the strategic advantage of the United States.

Viewpoint: President Eisenhower was committed to preventing a nuclear holocaust, and his administration successfully kept the nation out of war.

Dwight D. Eisenhower was an enigmatic man, often underestimated both in his lifetime and afterward. During his military career he was overshadowed by more visibly brilliant officers, notably Field Marshall Bernard Law Montgomery, General Douglas MacArthur, and General George S. Patton. However, Eisenhower, who had an average record at West Point, proved to be a more skillful officer than any of his contemporaries. It was he, not Montgomery, who was chosen to be supreme allied commander of the European theater, and he, not MacArthur, who was elected president of the United States. Eisenhower cultivated an image as an amiable and even-tempered man, uninterested in the tedious details of administration. But it was his mastery of administration and his ability to delegate responsibility that made him a formidable officer and a successful president.

Eisenhower was a master at seeming to do one thing while actually doing another. A joke circulated during his presidency of an aide asking a foursome on the golf course, "Do you mind if the President plays through? New York has just been attacked." Another said that while Franklin D. Roosevelt showed that a man with a physical disability could be president and Truman proved that a man without a formal education could be president, Eisenhower showed that the United States really did not need a president. Eisenhower, according to political scientist Fred Greenstein, in *Hidden Hand Presidency: Eisenhower as Leader* (1982), "cultivated the impression that he was not involved even in the most successful of the maneuvers in which he directly participated." His talent as both a general and a president was to accomplish what needed to be done without drawing attention to himself, which also meant that if his policy failed, he would not be seen as responsible. He had developed this managerial style over his long military career: it was essential to the success of an organization that it have a clearly articulated chain of command, and the commander must have absolute confidence in each member of his team. When he did, he could count on each member to perform their functions with a minimum of interference. If, then, the commander seemed to spend a great deal of time on the golf course, it was not a sign that he was not working but that the system he had created was working well.

In foreign affairs Eisenhower delegated much authority to his secretary of state, though given Eisenhower's character and managerial style it would be a mistake to attribute his foreign policy entirely to John Foster Dulles. The perception that Dulles was running American international policy, of course, deflected any possible criticism from Eisenhower. Dulles, the namesake of Benjamin Harrison's secretary of state, the nephew by marriage of Woodrow Wilson's secretary of state, had trained for his post since his youth. He had accompanied his uncle Robert Lansing to the Versailles Conference after World War I, and when he became secretary of state, his brother Allen was serving as head of the Central Intelligence Agency (CIA) and his sister Eleanor was running the State Department's Berlin Desk. In addition to Dulles, Eisenhower strengthened the National Security Council and created the position of national security adviser to the president. Eisenhower also created the White House chief of staff and organized the executive branch bureaucracy into the form it follows today.

Stephen Ambrose, Eisenhower's most recent, and in many ways most admiring, biographer, suggests that Eisenhower was the "best prepared man" in foreign affairs "ever elected President." As supreme allied commander in Europe, and as commander of the North Atlantic Treaty Organization (NATO) after the war, Eisenhower had already worked with European heads of state and political leaders. He had also come to an understanding of the Soviet Union that would influence his presidency. As a general Eisenhower understood both the bureaucratic infighting, which is often a characteristic of military organizations, and the limitations of different military forces. As a candidate for president, Eisenhower criticized the Truman administration's handling of foreign policy, particularly the futile war in Korea, and its policy of containment. His first task, he pledged just before the election, would be to "bring the Korean war to an early and honorable end." This would require "a personal trip to Korea," and he said, "I shall make that trip. . . . I shall go to Korea." Though candidate Eisenhower did not say what he would do when he got to Korea, after his overwhelming victory he did go to Korea, and shortly after he took office, the Americans and North Koreans agreed to a cease-fire.

Eisenhower, a Republican and a general, was able to do what Democrat Truman could not: agree to a cease-fire that acknowledged the partition of Korea, with half remaining under communist rule. After the cease-fire Eisenhower and Dulles devoted their attention to other areas. When the Soviet Union tested its hydrogen bomb in August 1953, Eisenhower became increasingly concerned about the prospect of a nuclear war. Such a war, he knew, would be a horrible thing. The fact that the leaders of the Soviet Union did not renounce the possibility that they might use nuclear weapons first, to Eisenhower, as an experienced military officer, meant that the Soviets were prepared to strike. In order to avert a nuclear catastrophe and reduce military spending, Eisenhower and Dulles changed American policy.

Under the Truman administration the United States had been committed to working with regional defense organizations and nations in containing the spread of communism. One powerful faction in the Republican Party saw any policy short of rolling back communism as appeasement and tantamount to treason. On the other hand, Eisenhower was committed to reducing the size of the American government and to limiting the power of what he later called the "military industrial complex." After learning of the Soviet hydrogen bomb, Eisenhower and Dulles devised the policy of massive retaliation. The United States would not commit ground troops to the defense of its allies but would be prepared to use its nuclear arsenal to retaliate against Soviet aggression. Eisenhower feared that the United States was vulnerable to a surprise attack, and rather than commit resources to troops, he diverted spending into missiles and jets that could bomb Soviet targets.

As a strategic policy massive retaliation had advantages for the United States. By 1955 the United States had 400 B-47 jet bombers and 1,350 airplanes capable of hitting Soviet targets, while the Soviets had fewer than 200 planes or jets capable of striking the U.S. mainland. On the other hand, the Soviets had more ground troops, and Eisenhower shared an American fear of standing armies as dangerous to a nation's liberty. Rather than raise a large permanent military force and have American soldiers strategically and permanently deployed around the world, Eisenhower reduced the size of the U.S. Army but increased the size and capability of the air force and missile program.

While Eisenhower delegated responsibility to his secretary of state in international affairs, and to his treasury secretary in economic affairs, he acted as his own secretary of defense. When Secretary of Defense Charles Wilson relayed to Eisenhower that the generals "required" more manpower, Eisenhower exploded, "You people never seem to learn whom you are supposed to be protecting. Not the generals, but the American people." If any general had the temerity to tell the president that the military needed more men or money, Eisenhower did not need to remind him that he had one more star on his shoulder than anyone at the Pentagon.

President Dwight D. Eisenhower answering questions at a press conference at the Paris Summit in May 1960

(Wide World Photos)

While massive retaliation was the threat used against the Soviet aggression, at the same time Eisenhower proposed the Atoms for Peace program, calling the Soviets to join the United States in turning over nuclear material to an independent international agency that could use the atom to generate power. It was a bold program and one which the Soviet Union did not hasten to join. At the Geneva Summit in 1955 Eisenhower proposed an Open Skies policy, in which the Americans and Soviets would allow one another to fly over and inspect each other's military installations and to exchange blueprints. The Soviets would not go along with this idea, and Eisenhower's only accomplishments in toning down the arms race were a unilateral American moratorium on nuclear testing in 1958 and a 1959 international accord putting Antarctica off limits to military use.

Eisenhower reduced the size of the military while increasing the capabilities of American missiles and bombers. His administration did not defuse Cold War tensions–in fact, some could blame increased tensions on the bellicose rhetoric and moralizing of Dulles. Nor did the United States end the Truman administration's support for local regimes–in fact, under Eisenhower the United States sponsored new regional defense initiatives, such as the South East Asia Treaty Organization (SEATO). And yet, the Eisenhower administration brought the war in Korea to an end–not a decisive or a glorious end, but an end–and did not commit American troops to any other wars. In the Suez Crisis, when the Soviets crushed the Hungarian freedom movement and when the People's Republic of China threatened Quemoy and Matsu, the United States did not commit troops, and though each of these cases seemed to threaten to begin a third, and final, world war, the Eisenhower administration avoided war while not betraying the national interest. American troops were sent to Lebanon in 1958, and at the end of his term American advisers were in Laos, but for the most part Eisenhower's administration did not use military force. During his tenure the CIA supported coups d'état in Guatemala and Iran and planned the botched Bay of Pigs invasion of Cuba. But under Eisenhower, at the height of the Cold War, the most notable use of American troops was not on any foreign battlefield but at Central High School in Little Rock, Arkansas, to enforce federal desegregation orders.

–ROBERT J. ALLISON, SUFFOLK UNIVERSITY

Viewpoint: Though President Eisenhower spoke often of the need for peace, his administration relied mainly on American military strength and preparedness to counter Soviet aggression.

Although Dwight D. Eisenhower is not generally remembered as an orator like John F. Kennedy or Franklin D. Roosevelt, few American presidents spoke as eloquently for the cause of peace. His presidency both began and ended with warnings of the perils of a prolonged arms race and the dangers of a military-industrial complex run amok. In addition to words of caution, Eisenhower also proposed several dramatic initiatives that appeared to signal his willingness to seek a form of peaceful cooperation with the Soviet Union. Many historians of the Eisenhower presidency have tended to take Eisenhower's words at face value, emphasizing his steadfast commitment to relaxing East-West tensions and to limiting the nuclear danger. According to one group of scholars, generally known as "revisionists," Eisenhower sought to brake the momentum on the nuclear-arms race through modest "trust-building" agreements. Steering away from comprehensive disarmament schemes, which he believed unworkable, Eisenhower instead put forth more-realistic plans for arms control, which would allow for incremental progress.

Eisenhower, however, did not view negotiations with the Soviet Union as a vehicle for Cold War cooperation. Instead, he used negotiations as public-relations exercises to unite the world under the American banner of "peace" and "freedom." He preferred to make stunning proposals designed less for their value at the bargaining table than for their impact on the resolve and allegiance of U.S. allies and neutral nations.

Eisenhower's approach to negotiation was decisively shaped by changes in Soviet foreign policy following the death of Soviet dictator Joseph Stalin in March 1953, two months after Eisenhower's inauguration. Under Stalin, Soviet foreign policy was reckless and confrontational–as witnessed by the Berlin blockade of 1948 and the officially sanctioned Korean invasion of 1950. Within days of Stalin's passing, his successors moved to abandon this approach for a "softer" line that emphasized peace, diplomacy, and accommodation. The new Soviet leadership moved quickly to bring the Korean War to a close; negotiated a peace treaty with Austria; pursued improved relations with such countries as Israel, Yugoslavia, and Greece; agreed to a summit with Western leaders; and, in general, emphasized peaceful coexistence over confrontation with the West.

Eisenhower did not see such gestures as evidence of a change of heart in the Kremlin but merely as a change in tactics. He feared that Soviet conciliatory measures would take the wind out of the sails of the American Cold War effort. According to Eisenhower, American allies and domestic audiences, eager for a relaxation of tensions, would press hard for a reduction in defense expenditures while the Soviets continued to build their military forces. American diplomacy, therefore, sought to expose Soviet maneuvering as fraudulent. Eisenhower wanted to score a propaganda victory over the Soviets by juxtaposing their intransigence with American flexibility.

Eisenhower's first four years in the White House included three spectacular presidential initiatives to boost American prestige as the superpower most committed to the cause of peace. The first of these occurred on April 1953, a month after Stalin's death. In his celebrated "Chance for Peace" speech Eisenhower warned that "every gun that is made, every warship launched, every rocket fired signifies, in the final sense, a theft from those who hunger and are not fed, those that are cold and are not clothed." Eisenhower called for a reduction in armaments and a relaxation of East-West tensions, apparently signaling his willingness to negotiate with the new Soviet leadership. However, was Eisenhower offering a realistic "chance for peace?" Since Eisenhower set the liberation of Eastern Europe and a unified, rearmed Germany as preconditions for negotiation, the answer appears to be no. He offered no concrete proposals for negotiation and deliberately ruled out a summit meeting with the new Soviet leadership until they adhered to his list of "deeds of good faith." While requesting proof of Soviet good faith, Eisenhower offered no concessions from the West. Eisenhower asked the Soviet leadership to alter its entire foreign policy in exchange for American goodwill. Despite his eloquence, the only chance for peace Eisenhower offered required Soviet capitulation to Western demands.

THE ROAD TO PEACE

Down the long lane of history yet to be written America knows that this world of ours, ever growing smaller, must avoid becoming a community of dreadful fear and hate, and be, instead, a proud confederation of mutual trust and respect.

Such a confederation must be one of equals. The weakest must come to the conference table with the same confidence as do we, protected as we are by our moral, economic, and military strength. That table, though scarred by many past frustrations, cannot be abandoned for the certain agony of the battlefield.

Disarmament, with mutual honor and confidence, is a continuing imperative. Together we must learn how to compose differences, not with arms, but with intellect and decent purpose. Because this need is so sharp and apparent I confess that I lay down my official responsibilities in this field with a definite sense of disappointment. As one who has witnessed the horror and the lingering sadness of war–as one who knows that another war could utterly destroy this civilization which has been so slowly and painfully built over thousands of years–I wish I could say tonight that lasting peace is in sight.

Happily, I can say that war has been avoided. Steady progress toward our ultimate goal has been made. But, so much remains to be done. As a private citizen, I shall never cease to do what little I can to help the world advance along that road.

Source: *Dwight D. Eisenhower, excerpt from his Farewell Address,* New York Times, *18 January 1961.*

Eisenhower made his second "peace" initiative later that year before the United Nations. In a dramatic speech he suggested that superpowers contribute nuclear materials from their weapons stockpiles to be applied to peaceful uses in agriculture, medicine, and electric-power production. The speech, dubbed "Atoms for Peace" by the media, received thunderous applause in the United Nations and was widely acclaimed in the press. Although it had no specific provisions for disarmament or arms control, Atoms for Peace appeared to offer a stepping-stone on the road to greater U.S.-Soviet cooperation.

Atoms for Peace, however, was neither a generous nor a practicable first step to enhance superpower trust. Viewed from any angle, the initiative overwhelmingly favored the United States. If the Soviet Union rejected the proposal, as it was expected they would, the United States stood to gain major propaganda points in the court of world opinion. If the Soviets accepted the proposal, the Americans would still come out ahead. The American stockpile of nuclear materials far exceeded that of the Soviet Union so that, as Eisenhower noted, "The United States could unquestionably afford to reduce its atomic stockpile by two to three times the amounts that the Russians might contribute . . . and still improve our relative position in the cold war." Atoms for Peace also promised espionage rewards, since the U.S.S.R. would have to open up its atomic facilities to international inspection.

Most ingeniously, the initiative actually promised to facilitate the buildup of nuclear weapons by distracting public attention from weapons testing and development. Utilizing the services of the United States Information Agency and enlisting the support of the private news media, Eisenhower flooded the airwaves with talk of the "friendly" atom. As one secret government memorandum explained, the Atoms for Peace campaign would cause people "to no longer think of mushroom clouds and mass destruction when hear[ing] the words atom, atomic, or atomic energy, but rather of the peaceful uses of atomic energy in the fields of industry, agriculture, and medicine." Eisenhower thus helped ease public fears of nuclear annihilation by presenting atomic energy as a boon to mankind. Rather than yield to public pressure for disarmament, therefore, Eisenhower sought to cut it off at the pass.

The third major peace initiative of Eisenhower's first term came two years later, in July 1955. By this time Eisenhower had agreed to a summit meeting with the new Soviet premier, Nikita Khrushchev, in the city of Geneva, Switzerland. It was to be the first meeting of Soviet and American heads of state since World War II. Eisenhower seized the summit as an opportunity to put forth another dramatic appeal for progress in arms control. He proposed a system of aerial inspection, whereby the United States and the Soviet Union would permit overflights of their territory to verify compliance with any arms control agreements that might be reached. Unlike his earlier initiatives, this one, known as "Open Skies," had real merit. It promised to overcome the most difficult hurdle in disarmament negotiations: inspection and verification of agreements. Quite reasonably, inspection was seen as a necessary condition for disarmament in order to prevent one side or the other from "cheating."

Rather than make his proposal in quiet negotiations to test Soviet intentions, Eisenhower preferred to use Open Skies as a propaganda stunt. Having informed the media that no new proposals were forthcoming, Eisenhower sprang Open Skies on the unsuspecting Soviet delegation at Geneva. In so doing he grabbed the headlines of newspapers around the world, but by offering it in such a public and propagandistic manner, Eisenhower virtually guaranteed Soviet rejection of the measure. As with Atoms for Peace, the United States had nothing to risk and everything to gain by making the proposal. Open Skies would pry open the "iron curtain" by legalizing reconnaissance flights over Soviet territory, but it offered no commensurate benefits for the U.S.S.R. For this reason officials in the Eisenhower administration never really expected the Soviets to accept Open Skies. Few were surprised when Soviet Premier Nikita Khrushchev denounced the scheme as a "bald espionage plot," and few tears were shed when he officially rejected Eisenhower's offer.

While the peace proposals of Eisenhower's first term seemed designed for Soviet rejection, the diplomacy of his next four years suggested that something had changed. In the last three years of his presidency Eisenhower worked hard to secure an agreement with the Soviet Union banning nuclear-weapons testing. In contrast to his earlier offers—which were given almost on a "take-it-or-leave-it" basis—Eisenhower and his advisers buckled down for protracted and highly technical negotiations with the Soviet leadership. This change in style and tone suggested to many observers (and historians) that, whatever Eisenhower's earlier tactics, he now endeavored to make genuine progress on arms control.

By the later 1950s some sort of agreement on the testing of nuclear weapons became a political necessity for both superpowers. Beginning in 1954, when the United States inadvertently drenched a Japanese fishing boat with radioactive fallout from a hydrogen-bomb test, world public opinion became increasingly critical of superpower nuclear-weapons tests. Foreshadowing the activism associated with the 1960s, popular protests of weapons tests grew in intensity around the world. In the United States the antitesting movement became even more critical in the late 1950s when reports that radioactive strontium-90 was seeping into dairy products and, through milk, poisoning the bloodstreams of America's children. As public pressure mounted, both sides faced isolation and condemnation if they refused to enter into discussions on nuclear testing.

Yet, Eisenhower's pursuit of a test ban should not be construed as an indication of his interest in bringing the Cold War to an early thaw. He continued to issue warnings that the Communists were waging "total cold war" and instructed the free world not to relax its vigilant challenge of the Soviet menace. He also continued to plan covert measures to challenge perceived elements of Soviet aggression. He instigated CIA planning of what would become, under Kennedy, the failed Bay of Pigs invasion of Cuba, and he sent military advisers to the Southeast Asian country of Laos to forestall a communist coup.

More significantly for his efforts to reach a test ban agreement with the Soviets, Eisenhower authorized provocative reconnaissance flights over Soviet territory using high-altitude U-2 spy planes. When one of these planes was shot down deep in Soviet territory, all hopes for a test-ban agreement were dashed. At first Eisenhower tried to deny the missions by issuing a cover story about a lost weather plane. Khrushchev blew the cover by producing the U-2 wreckage, pilot, and photographic spy equipment. When Eisenhower refused to apologize for the flights, Khrushchev called off the forthcoming summit conference.

The superpowers would have to wait until 1963 to reach an agreement on weapons testing. Even then the test ban did nothing to slow the arms race. In a curious twist of logic, partial measures such as the Limited Test Ban Treaty and failed measures such as Atoms for Peace and Open Skies actually facilitated the arms race more than they hindered it. By easing popular pressure for arms control and by providing apparent evidence of the other side's "intransigence," such measures made it easier for public opinion to accept massive expenditures for defense. Throughout the Eisenhower years, and quite possibly beyond, American foreign policy focused more on developing American military strength than on finding a means to bring the arms race to an end.

–KENNETH A. OSGOOD, UNIVERSITY OF CALIFORNIA, SANTA BARBARA

References

Stephen E. Ambrose, *Eisenhower: Soldier and President* (New York: Simon & Schuster, 1990);

Robert R. Bowie and Richard H. Immerman, *Waging Peace: How Eisenhower Shaped an Enduring Cold War Strategy* (New York: Oxford University Press, 1998);

Cecil V. Crabb Jr. and Kevin V. Mulcahy, *Presidents and Foreign Policy Making, From FDR to Reagan* (Baton Rouge: Louisiana State University Press, 1986);

Robert A. Divine, *Eisenhower and the Cold War* (New York: Oxford University Press, 1981);

Dwight D. Eisenhower, *Mandate for Change, 1953–1956: The White House Years* (Garden City, N.Y.: Doubleday, 1963);

Eisenhower, *Waging Peace, 1956–1961: The White House Years* (Garden City, N.Y.: Doubleday, 1965);

Eric F. Goldman, *The Crucial Decade–and After: America, 1945–1960* (New York: Vintage, 1960);

Fred I. Greenstein, *Hidden Hand Presidency: Eisenhower as Leader* (New York: BasicBooks, 1982);

Walter L. Hixson, *Parting the Curtain: Propaganda, Culture and the Cold War, 1945–1961* (New York: St. Martin's Press, 1997);

J. Michael Hogan, "Eisenhower and Open Skies: A Case Study in Psychological Warfare," in *Eisenhower's War of Words: Rhetoric and Leadership,* edited by Martin J. Medhurst (East Lansing: Michigan State University Press, 1994), pp. 137–156;

Klaus Larres, "Eisenhower and the First Forty Days after Stalin's Death: The Incompatibility of Détente and Political Warfare," *Diplomacy & Statecraft,* 6 (July 1995): 431–469;

Martin Medhurst, "Atoms for Peace and Nuclear Hegemony: The Rhetorical Structure of a Cold War Campaign," *Armed Forces and Society,* 24 (Summer 1997): 571–593;

Kenneth A. Osgood, "Form Before Substance: Eisenhower's Commitment to Psychological Warfare and Negotiations with the Enemy," *Diplomatic History* (forthcoming);

Chester J. Pach Jr. and Elmo Richardson, *The Presidency of Dwight D. Eisenhower* (Lawrence: University of Kansas Press, 1991);

David S. Patterson, "Pacifism and Arms Limitation," in *Encyclopedia of the United States in the Twentieth Century,* volume 2, *Global America,* edited by Stanley I. Kutler and others (New York: Scribners, 1996);

James T. Patterson, *Grand Expectations: The United States, 1945–1974* (New York: Oxford University Press, 1996);

Paul Peeters, *Massive Retaliation: The Policy and its Critics* (Chicago: Regnery, 1959).

END OF COLD WAR

Did Ronald Reagan win the Cold War?

Viewpoint: Yes, President Ronald Reagan's policies won the Cold War for the United States by overextending the financial resources of the Soviet Union.

Viewpoint: No, President Ronald Reagan can be credited only with helping end the Cold War because domestic problems within the Soviet Union were already putting a strain on their system.

Who won the Cold War? Clearly the United States did, as the Soviet Union failed to "bury the West" as Nikita Khrushchev had pledged to do in 1960. By the end of the 1980s it was clear that the Soviet Union could not destroy Western capitalist systems, and the communist regime collapsed.

However, why did the Soviet regime collapse? Was it because President Ronald Reagan reversed the policies of détente with the Soviet regime, which he called the "evil empire," and reignited the arms race, which forced the Soviets to strain their own system to the breaking point? Elizabeth Pugliese advances this argument, which credits Reagan with the collapse of the Soviet empire and the American victory in the Cold War.

On the other hand, Patrick Apel, a scholar whose special interest is Eastern Europe, argues that the Soviet regime probably would have collapsed with no help from the United States. The Soviet system was already stretched to the breaking point, and its chronic inability to deliver consumer goods, and even food, to its people weakened the state. Reagan and other more conservative Americans were right in their belief that communism was inherently inferior to capitalism in delivering goods to consumers. Apel argues that in this inability underlay a crisis in confidence in the Soviet regime, which was devastated by the misguided Afghanistan invasion in 1979. What Pugliese points to as Soviet expansion in the 1980s, in Afghanistan, Angola, and Nicaragua, which some in the United States took to be threats to American security, in the end destroyed the Soviet system.

Whichever way we look at this story, it is filled with ironies. Reagan and other Americans were right that the Soviet Union could not compete with the capitalist United States. Yet, the Soviet expansion in the late 1970s did not presage a communist triumph; instead it prepared the way for communism's utter collapse. Similarly, Mikhail Gorbachev's perestroika policies, designed to make socialism work, instead hastened the communist regime's collapse. Gorbachev, hailed as a reformer in the 1980s, would be scorned in the 1990s either for introducing the economic chaos that came with the end of a planned economy or as a throwback to the totalitarian past. A century earlier German economist Karl Marx, the intellectual father of communism, had predicted that capitalism, straining to produce maximum profits by pushing down wages and increasing production, would collapse of its own weight. Marx had seen this as an inevitable, inexorable process. Vladimir Lenin, the founder of the Soviet state, had argued that a communist party, led by correct-thinking revolutionaries, could advance this happy day and give history a push. By the end of the

1980s, Marx, Lenin, and Khrushchev seemed to have been proven wrong. Communism, not capitalism, collapsed of its own internal contradictions, and if history was given a push, it was not by the guiding hand of Leninists, but by the reformer Gorbachev and the conservative Republican Reagan.

Viewpoint:
Yes, President Ronald Reagan's policies won the Cold War for the United States by overextending the financial resources of the Soviet Union.

During the presidency of Jimmy Carter the political and military power of the United States decreased in relative terms to the Soviet Union. The bipolar system, the operative international view at the time, divided world power between two competing superpowers—the United States and the Soviet Union. The balance of power resulting from this division fluctuated throughout the Cold War period. The Soviets were gaining in influence, especially in Third World countries. During the Carter administration the Soviet Union extended its power. The era of détente manifest in the 1970s clearly was not working. It was time for a more confrontational style. President Ronald Reagan brought that style to U.S. relations with the Soviet Union.

Reagan was not interested in finding a way to live with the Soviets; he fundamentally believed that communism needed to be removed from the world scene. In fact, Reagan referred to the Soviet Union as the evil empire. There was no room for both democracy and communism; one system had to give way. Reagan was determined that communism would be the loser. By the end of his presidency the Cold War was essentially over and Reagan had won.

Realizing the old way of relating to the Soviets would not achieve his goal, Reagan looked for another solution. He detected a flaw in earlier relations with the Soviet Union. Previous administrations had dealt with the Soviets on the basis of matching them strength for strength: the Soviets got a missile and the Americans matched them; the Soviets upgraded a submarine or bomber design while the Americans did the same. He decided that rather than continue this method the United States would exploit Soviet weaknesses. One of these weaknesses was the truly bad shape of the Soviet economy. For years the Soviets had been faking their economic numbers to make their system appear healthy. Rather than rely on the official Soviet figures, William Casey, director of the Central Intelligence Agency (CIA), ordered a realistic assessment based on raw intelligence data. CIA analysts included such anecdotal evidence as the number of factories shutting down and the length of food lines. Evidence of the hard-currency shortages also received consideration. The CIA assessment revealed that the Soviet government proved barely able to provide basic necessities to its people.

The discovery played right into Reagan's plan. He wanted to strengthen the U.S. military and rebuild it from its post-Vietnam malaise. The Soviets would feel it necessary to match a massive military buildup by the United States in order to maintain equilibrium. Looking to the monies already budgeted for domestic purposes seemed the best option to finance the military expenditures. Unfortunately, the Soviet domestic budget was stretched to the limit—diverting money from domestic to military purposes would destabilize the entire system.

U.S. military spending rose to 27 percent of the federal budget under Reagan; just to stay even the Soviets needed to spend 60 percent of their budget. The fact that the Soviets had fallen behind U.S. technology partly contributed to this spending difference. Reagan knew of the disparities in development. Rather than an all-out military buildup of weaponry, he emphasized the development and deployment primarily of technologically advanced weapons. Although conventional weapons were not neglected, the B-1 bomber, M-1 Abrams tank, and F-15 fighter bombers received the majority of resources for development. New technologies needed to integrate these weapons into the command-and-reconnaissance structure demanded development. The president also ordered added restrictions on technology transfers to foreign countries, thereby increasing the cost for the Soviets to keep pace.

Reagan proudly announced in March of 1983 the military development that would cost the Soviets the most: the Strategic Defense Initiative (SDI), or Star Wars. SDI was to be a ground- and space-based system that would use lasers to shoot incoming nuclear missiles out of the sky, thereby providing a blanket of protection over the United States and rendering it invulnerable to nuclear attack. This system demanded new innovations in technology, the kind the Soviets did not have. The Soviets officially opposed SDI on the grounds that it would destabilize the nuclear balance and that it contravened the 1972 American-Soviet treaty on the Limitation of Anti-Ballistic Missile Systems. They argued the issue of destabilization because, in the age of nuclear parity, the nation with the

An East Berliner pickaxing the Berlin Wall on the night of 9 November 1989

(Dirk Heydemann)

best defense would be the safest. Therefore, in order to maintain parity the Soviets had to develop their own version of SDI, which would require diverting further funds from the domestic economy.

Not only did Reagan confront the Soviet Union in military matters directly, but he also challenged them through their respective client states. Reagan actively supported anticommunist insurgencies. After Vietnam the United States was reluctant to get involved in other nations' internal fights. Reagan was not afraid. He believed that democracy and freedom for all rated as matters of national interest to the United States and, therefore, were grounds for military intervention. He cast this belief as a crusade. Under the Reagan Doctrine, everywhere the communists attempted takeovers and people resisted, the United States would aid those fighting back. This was a change from the policy of containment that had prevailed since the end of World War II. Containment accepted the existence of communism; the Reagan Doctrine fought to destroy it.

Carter had authorized aid to the Afghan mujahideen but limited the amount and scope. In an effort to maintain U. S. deniability, third parties with no known U.S. connections, but supportive of the Muslims in Afghanistan, received money to purchase arms for the Afghan fighters. The intent was to harass, not defeat. Reagan immediately requested that Congress grant more money to purchase up-to-date arms to take the fight to Soviet forces in Afghanistan, and all the way into the Soviet Union, if possible. Stinger missiles, made in the United States, produced a war more costly for the Soviets in terms of both money and prestige.

In Central America communism had been making inroads for years. Reagan stopped aid to Nicaragua in retaliation for Managua's perceived support of the Sandinistas in El Salvador. The El Salvadoran government received a $25 million increase in aid. Reagan also authorized sending military advisors to El Salvador. To aid the Contras, who were fighting the government of Nicaragua, Reagan issued a directive in November 1981 that the United States would support them by forming and training action teams to gather intelligence and carry out paramilitary and political operations in Nicaragua. Not being done with the Caribbean region, Reagan authorized the invasion of Grenada to restore democracy after its prime minister was murdered by Stalinists. All these policies worked to diminish Soviet influence while adding to U.S. prestige and world standing.

The Reagan Doctrine worked with the military buildup to put further strain on the Soviet economy. Communists in the Latin American nations and Afghanistan received support from Moscow. Fighting against well-financed anticommunist insurgents became more expensive than the Soviets had originally planned. Maintaining its network of allies required the Soviet Union to reallocate more money from domestic programs to foreign policy. Its domestic economy could not afford such an additional diversion. No longer secure in its empire and failing at expansion, the Soviet Union had no choice but to withdraw its troops from abroad and retreat within its own borders. Unable to protect its satellites in both Eastern Europe and the Caribbean any longer, the Soviet Union abandoned and let fall the communist regimes in its former satellites. It could not stand up to Reagan's policy of active engagement.

Other factors also played a role in the demise of the Soviet Union, not least of which were the actions of Soviet general secretary Mikhail Gorbachev. However, it was Reagan's active confrontation of the Soviets that stood out as the main underlying cause. Gorbachev would not have had to liberalize his nation's economy through perestroika (restructuring) and glasnost (openness) if not for the strain on the Soviet economy of trying to keep pace with U.S. military strength. Gorbachev only attempted his reform programs in an endeavor to salvage a devastated Soviet economy.

The Soviets themselves acknowledged that U.S. policies led to the collapse of the Soviet Union. Former members of the Komitet gosudarstvennoy bezopasnosti (KGB), the senior staff, and the Central Committee all conceded that Reagan's active engagement of communism in the Third World and the new arms race destabilized the Soviet Union. Its economy could not afford the massive diversions necessary to keep up with the United States militarily. And with communism in the Soviet Union finished, the Cold War was over. It ended because one man believed there could be no accommodation with the communists. This one man believed that communism was wrong and that all people everywhere deserved to be free. He faced the Soviets, refused to back down, and, instead, forced the Soviet Union to retreat and then to collapse. The United States won the Cold War because of Ronald Reagan.

—ELIZABETH PUGLIESE, AUSTIN, TEXAS

Viewpoint: No, President Ronald Reagan can be credited only with helping end the Cold War because domestic problems within the Soviet Union were already putting a strain on their system.

Ask the question posed in this debate to Russians, and many might say the question should be turned around. They would rephrase it as, "Did Gorbachev lose the Cold War?" Many Russians have the opinion that it was Mikhail Gorbachev, not Ronald Reagan, who had more to do with the Soviet Union losing the Cold War than Reagan's policies winning it for the United States.

Since the end of the Cold War, intellectuals and academics have reviewed this subject. Attempts are made to lay blame, or declare victory, to the opposing sides in the conflict. Some scholars contend that Reagan was responsible for winning the Cold War for the United States. However, changes were well under way in the Soviet Union prior to Reagan's arrival at the White House. In addition, Gorbachev's policies of glasnost and perestroika were not done in reaction to Reagan's machinations but for reasons internal to the Soviet Union. There is little doubt that the arms race took a tremendous toll on the Soviet Union. However, it was the lack of a diversified economy, one that did not have the capacity to generate and assimilate independent technological innovations, aside from the military-industrial complex, that led to the implosion of the Soviet Union. To suggest that Reagan's policies were solely responsible for the U.S. claim of victory in the Cold War is shortsighted. The Soviet Union had dysfunctional political and economic institutions, lacked a civil society, and had a weakening intelligence service. These factors are at least equal in value to Reagan's foreign policy as it pertained to the U.S.S.R. What led the United States to victory is more accurately a combination of factors, many of which were far beyond the control of the White House.

The Cold War was a phrase first used in the late 1930s to describe Franco-German tensions. Journalist Walter Lippman is credited with popularizing the term in 1947 after writing a series of articles regarding international affairs. Although some scholars use the term in a narrow sense to describe severe tensions between the United States and the U.S.S.R. between 1947 and 1953, the most common usage refers to the ideological and military conflict between the two countries between 1946 and 1991.

Applying this most commonly used definition, it is hard to rationally argue that Reagan's policies were the primary impetus of the U.S. declaration of victory in the Cold War. This broad ideological and military conflict had several interrelated features. First, the United States and the Soviet Union each controlled opposing military and political alliances. Second, both factions depended on a combination of military and economic power. Much public attention is focused on the military power, but the economic power is more definitive. Also, both parties claimed superiority over political and economic values and kinds of societies. Each side tried exhaustively to promote their values. Finally, the United States and the Soviet Union battled for spheres of influence throughout the Third World.

Because of the interrelated factors involved in defining the Cold War, it is now clear to see the advantages the United States maintained during the conflict. Economically the United States proved to be the stronger combatant. Capitalism prevailed in Western Europe after World War II; free markets were opened up; and civil societies were built in conjunction with legitimate institutions designed to establish a stronger economy. The Soviet Union depleted Eastern Europe of its natural and economic resources. While capitalism flourished in the West, socialism in the East was failing. Soviet policies promoted dysfunctional and inefficient bureaucracies that stymied technological growth. Thus, the Soviet empire had inherent flaws in its economic system. Consequently, inefficient Soviet institutions directed the Warsaw Pact nations and the U.S.S.R. down an unproductive and damaging path.

In the beginning of the Cold War, American foreign policy as it related to the U.S.S.R. followed a policy of containment. The policy was based on the assumption that historic Russian insecurity was married to Marxist ideology, so that the country was committed to conflict with the United States and the Western way of life. U.S. diplomat George F. Kennan pushed this idea throughout the foreign-affairs community in Washington, saying, "Soviet expansionism must be contained by the adroit and vigilant application of counterforce at a series of constantly shifting geographical and political points." The idea was not to surrender any new territory to communism but to avoid an all-out conflict.

Later, foreign policy strategies between the United States and the U.S.S.R. were centered around the theme of détente: a period of peace that has every possibility of becoming permanent. However, détente implicitly assumes a deep ideological division, one that limited the degree to which cooperation was possible. Détente derives from a French word meaning "to relax." In foreign policy the term is more closely defined as the process of easing tensions between states whose interests are so radically divergent that reconciliation is inherently limited.

The Reagan administration did call for a much stronger stance against the Soviet Union and a crusade against communism. Reagan's foreign policy approach was based on philosophical notions that communism was simply wrong. It was no longer enough to contain the U.S.S.R. or just to coexist. The words "defeat" and "roll-back" described the new way of dealing with the Soviets. As a result the Reagan administration started a massive military buildup to create a force strong enough to deter and convince the U.S.S.R. that a war against the West could not be won. Politically, the rhetoric of getting tough with the Soviets drew support. Americans were left demoralized from the Iran hostage crisis and looked to the White House to reassert U.S. superpower.

Despite the perception of changing U.S. policy, evidence supports that even before Gorbachev came to power in 1985 high level talks occurred within the Soviet government on the need for reform. In 1982, when Yuri Andropov came to power, he stressed economic problems and the need to reform in a November speech to the Central Committee Plenum. Even prior to Andropov top political and military leaders recognized the need for a paradigm shift. In 1981 Marshal Nikolai Ogarkov, chief of the Soviet General Staff, called for a reorganization of the armed forces, as well as a restructuring of political and economic institutions. The physical illness of both Andropov and Konstantin Chernenko played a major role in the delay of real reform until Gorbachev assumed power. By that time many within the Soviet political and military hierarchy embraced a policy to enable change and reforms. Nevertheless, it is important to point out that there was no unanimity on what course of reform to follow.

One might argue that Reagan's military buildup led Soviet leaders to give up the arms race, make concessions to reduce nuclear stockpiles, and reform institutions that were encountering extreme difficulties in responding to massive increases in military spending. However, there is no verifiable data to suggest that the Soviet military budget increased in reaction to U.S. military spending. In fact, Gorbachev realized that the Soviet Union could not sustain an arms race. By the mid 1980s more than one quarter of the Soviet Gross National Product was being devoted to defense spending.

How then can we explain the diverse changes that took place at the end of the Cold War? With more than a decade of hindsight, there is no question that Gorbachev's dual policies of glasnost and perestroika were critical for many of the reforms, both internal and external. Glasnost was intended to bring greater self-criticism of Soviet society in an effort to root out inefficiencies and corruption that paralyzed government and industry. The press became freer; industries were made self-managing; and government bodies opened up to democratic-like voting. Thus, a proliferation of unofficial associations and journals began to arise. Although these organizations were under constant pressure, they expanded and began building what was the embryo of a civil society. By lifting the veil, fundamental and intrinsic socioeconomic problems within the entire communist system came to light.

Gorbachev called for perestroika, or "restructuring," to encourage better management, discipline, and the use of technology. The idea was to restore the Soviet Union to the original ideals of socialism. These two initiatives led to willingness on the part of the Soviet Union to make the political, military, and economic institutions more transparent and to embark on radical restructuring. Without Gorbachev's drive to execute these twin policies, it is highly unlikely the thaw in relations between the United States and the Soviet Union would have materialized.

Reforms executed through the ideas surrounding glasnost and perestroika escaped the control of Gorbachev in the late 1980s. Throughout Reagan's second term many Washington insiders were divided and uncertain as to what exactly was happening in the U.S.S.R. Many analysts saw Gorbachev's words as simply another ploy or deception. Although the Reykjavik Summit in October of 1986 did not resolve substantive disarmament issues, it was a turning point.

One of the major sticking points of the summit was the Strategic Defense Initiative (SDI), commonly known as "Star Wars." SDI was introduced by Reagan in March of 1983. Reagan proposed to develop "particle beam" and laser weapons to shoot down incoming nuclear weapons before they hit the United States. Although the concept was supported by Reagan's closest advisers, the initiative had not even been considered by the State or Defense Departments. In addition, Congress was totally unaware of the proposal as Reagan spoke about the project on national television. The Soviets argued that SDI broke the 1972 Anti-Ballistic Missile treaty and that it extended the arms race into space.

Although the United States found it impossible to develop an effective SDI system, the impact of the project was significant. SDI, whether proven or not, highlighted the growing technological gap between the United States and the U.S.S.R. The perceived threat of such a system was a factor complicating East-West arms-reduction talks, especially during the Reykjavik Summit. Despite their differences, it was clear from the summit that both Gorbachev and Reagan had made a strong political and personal commitment to the process of arms control, and each was prepared to think and act in radically different ways. In the end, however, it was Gorbachev who "delinked" arms-reduction talks from SDI; this eliminated a major obstacle to concluding future agreements.

In January 1986 Gorbachev effectively accepted the "zero option" for Europe (eliminating NATO intermediate and Soviet SS-20 missiles). This was a monumental agreement and one that highlighted the complexity of how decisions were really made. Sergei Tarasenko, chief foreign policy adviser to Foreign Minister Eduard Shevardnadze, spoke at a conference in 1998, revealing that he was the one who came up with the idea to abolish all nuclear weapons in April 1985. The idea surfaced as an official proposal from Marshal Sergei Akhromeyev, chief of the General Staff. Initially the idea was drawn up for propaganda purposes but was taken seriously by high-level officials on both sides. The final result was the "zero option" treaty.

In the final meeting between Reagan and Gorbachev, it was the latter who provided insight on the future of Eastern Europe and the Soviet Union. Addressing the United Nations Assembly in New York in December of 1988, Gorbachev called for the "deidolization" of super-power relations. He spoke of "the compelling necessity of the principle of freedom of choice as a 'universal principle.'" Gorbachev also announced a unilateral reduction of 10 percent in Soviet armed forces, with major cuts in European conventional deployments. Retired general Andrew J. Goodpaster, a former NATO commander, called the move "the most significant step since NATO was formed." By reducing the military conflict, along with retracting claims of ideological superiority, Gorbachev took away the two components that had given rise to the modern-day definition of the Cold War. One of the most compelling statements Gorbachev made during the speech was a declaration that "we in no way aspire to be the bearer of ultimate truth." In a single statement Gorbachev deactivated the ideological conflict between the United States and the U.S.S.R. that had existed since 1946, and he set the stage for self-determination in Eastern Europe.

U.S. policy did not shift necessarily based on Gorbachev's "new thinking" but waited for the implementation of this dramatic rhetoric. One example of Gorbachev's determination to follow through on his statements was the actual shift in power within the Warsaw Pact. A series of roundtable discussions took place in Poland by early 1989, leading the way for producing free elections that summer. By March 1989 multicandidate elections took place that included reformers and dissidents. Although the United States had worked hard to persuade the Soviet Union that self-determination could be achieved in Eastern Europe without impacting legitimate security concerns for the U.S.S.R., it was once again Gorbachev who steadfastly implemented change.

Clearly the Soviet Union was approaching an economic crisis by the beginning of the 1980s, and its sustained commitment of resources to military spending was breaking the Soviet economy. A primary factor facilitating the crisis was the massive expenditures in supporting Third World countries in an effort

GORBACHEV PROPOSES NEW LEADERSHIP

In a speech to the Central Committee of the Soviet Communist Party on 5 February 1990, President Mikhail Gorbachev proposed a major change in the political framework of the Soviet Union. He declared that the Communist Party should abandon its position as the only legal political party in the country and compete for power with other parties.

The main thing that now worries Communists and all citizens of the country is the fate of perestroika, the fate of the country and the role of the Soviet Communist Party at the current, probably most crucial, stage of revolutionary transformation.

. . .The party will only be able to fulfill the mission of political vanguard if it drastically restructures itself, masters the art of political work in the present conditions and succeeds in cooperating with forces committed to perestroika.

The crux of the party's renewal is the need to get rid of everything that tied it to the authoritarian-bureaucratic system, a system that left its mark not only on methods of work and inter-relationships within the party, but also on ideology, ways of thinking and notions of socialism.

The [newly proposed] platform says: our ideal is a humane, democratic socialism, expressing the interests of the working class and all working people; and relying on the great legacy of Marx, Engels and Lenin, the Soviet Communist Party is creatively, developing socialist ideals to match present-day realities and with due account for the entire experience of the 20th century.

The platform states clearly what we should abandon. We should abandon the ideological dogmatism that became ingrained during past decades, outdated stereotypes in domestic policy and outmoded views on the world revolutionary process and world development as a whole.

We should abandon everything that led to the isolation of socialist countries from the mainstream of world civilization. We should abandon the understanding of progress as a permanent confrontation with a socially different world. . . .

The party's renewal presupposes a fundamental change in its relations with state and economic bodies and the abandonment of the practice of commanding them and substituting for their functions.

The party in a renewing of society can exist and play its role as vanguard only as a democratically recognized force. This means that its status should not be imposed through constitutional endorsement.

The Soviet Communist Party, it goes without saying, intends to struggle for the status of the ruling party. But it will do so strictly within the framework of the democratic process by giving up any legal and political advantages, offering its program and defending it in discussions, cooperating with other social and political forces, always working amidst the masses, living by their interests and their needs.

Source: *Donald Kagan, Steven Ozment, and Frank M. Turner,* The Western Heritage *(Upper Saddle River, N.J.: Prentice Hall, 1998), p.1152.*

to gain influence throughout the world. Additionally, the impact of the military conflict in Afghanistan cannot be overlooked. In December 1979 the Soviet Union invaded Afghanistan, giving the justification that the new Afghan leadership invited the troops in. A decade-long war siphoned money away from other parts of the economy. The Gorbachev administration recognized that military means were counterproductive in influencing neighbors and Third World countries. Financially, these endeavors took a large toll. For instance, Ivan Head wrote in *Foreign Affairs* that the war in Afghanistan cost the Soviet Union approximately $1.7 million dollars a day. Domestically, the war was highly unpopular, with both a high human and financial cost. It was Gorbachev who realized that to modernize the fledgling economy, political consolidation and structural changes to the Soviet economy needed to take place. The "new thinking" with regard to Soviet foreign policy was more a result of domestic reforms than any action in response to U.S. policy.

The "Reagan victory" assumes that Reagan's squeeze and persistence forced Moscow to capitulate. Such an analysis suggests that Reagan had a unidirectional, monolithic strategy. American strategy, in fact, was at times inconsistent and contradictory. Policy was ultimately led by competing perceptions on force capabilities and power of the Soviets. In fact, by 1985 the Komitet gosudarstvennoy bezopasnosti (KGB) had planted a high-level mole inside the Central Intelligence Agency (CIA), who began to warp U.S. perceptions of political, military, and economic developments. In 1995 CIA Director John M. Deutch publicly acknowledged the deception, saying it "diminished our ability to understand what was really happening in Moscow." As a result the United States overestimated force capabilities of the U.S.S.R., and the deception led to justify massive investments in weapons programs.

Why would the Soviets want to inflate their military might? One answer might be that the government recognized its systems were failing. The military-industrial complex might be the only part of the economy Moscow could deceive the West into believing was an efficient, well-running machine.

Furthermore, the squeeze strategy was never consistently applied, and the economic aspects of détente were not completely dismantled. In addition, as Michael Cox notes: "What hurt the Soviet Union after 1980 was not economic pressure so much as the drop in the price of oil, the devaluation of the dollar, and the economic decision by western bankers not to lend any more money to Moscow's indebted Eastern European allies."

In the overall debate Reagan's policies in his first administration increased pressure on the Soviet leadership and encouraged new approaches beyond détente. However, to imply Reagan's strategy left no alternative for Gorbachev than to push for reforms that would eventually dismantle the Soviet empire is wrong. Gorbachev faced key decisions and was opposed by members of his own military. It appears that Gorbachev reevaluated both domestic and international strategies of the U.S.S.R. Little did anyone know, including Reagan, that these reforms would have such lasting implications and ultimately change the world.

–PATRICK APEL, BOSTON, MASSACHUSETTS

References

John Dumbrell, *American Foreign Policy: Carter to Clinton* (New York: St. Martin's Press, 1997);

John Feffer, *Beyond Détente: Soviet Foreign Policy and U.S. Options* (New York: Noonday Press, 1990);

Raymond L. Garthoff, *The Great Transition: American-Soviet Relations and the End of the Cold War* (Washington, D.C.: Brookings Institution, 1994);

Charles L. Glaser, *Analyzing Strategic Nuclear Policy* (Princeton: Princeton University Press, 1990);

Geoffrey Hosking, *The Awakening of the Soviet Union* (Cambridge, Mass.: Harvard University Press, 1990);

Jeff McMahan, *Reagan and the World: Imperial Policy in the New Cold War* (New York: Monthly Review Press, 1985);

Thomas H. Naylor, *The Cold War Legacy* (Lexington, Mass.: Lexington Books, 1991);

Peter Schweizer, *Victory: The Reagan Administration's Secret Strategy that Hastened the Collapse of the Soviet Union* (New York: Atlantic Monthly Press, 1994);

Strobe Talbott, *The Russians and Reagan* (New York: Vintage, 1984);

Robert A. Vitas and John Allen Williams, eds., *U.S. National Security Policy and Strategy, 1987–1994: Documents and Policy Proposals* (Westport, Conn.: Greenwood Press, 1996);

John W. Young, *The Longman Companion to America, Russia and the Cold War, 1941–1998* (London & New York: Longman, 1999).

FEAR OF ATTACK

Were American fears of Soviet technology exaggerated during the Cold War?

Viewpoint: American policymakers feared a sudden nuclear attack by the Soviet Union, but evidence shows that their fears were unfounded.

Viewpoint: Though the American race into space was prompted by fears of Soviet superiority, the Soviet space program was woefully incompetent.

On 7 December 1941 the Japanese had taken the Americans completely by surprise in launching their sudden attack on Pearl Harbor in Hawaii. Though the United States ultimately recovered sufficiently to fight back and win, the fear of a sudden attack haunted American military planners after the war, as the United States and the Soviet Union engaged in an undeclared cold war. Why did American planners believe the Soviets were capable of such an attack, and how did they respond?

Defense scholar Hanno W. Kirk argues that American fears of a Soviet surprise attack were greatly exaggerated. These fears, he suggests, did not come so much from the psychological residue of Pearl Harbor as from the real interests of what President Dwight D. Eisenhower called the "military-industrial complex." Eager to sell products to the American military, arms manufacturers promoted the idea of Soviet capabilities, and defense industry consultants, intent on proving their own value to American interests, presented studies that proved not only Soviet strengths, but also their perfidy.

How accurate were these assessments? Thomas H. Austin's essay on the Soviet space program, whose success with Sputnik spurred Americans to venture into space, suggests that while the Soviets may have had evil intentions, they were not capable of launching a devastating, or even a damaging, attack on the United States. Why, then, the fear of a sudden attack?

Hindsight is one of the great problems of history. We need to understand a period of time, or an issue, in the same way that the people who experienced it did, so that we can understand their reactions to it. At the same time, as Kirk and Austin show, we may have better information than they did.

In knowing more about Soviet capabilities, we run the risk of understanding less the Americans' reactions to it. Our role as historians is not to rewrite the past or to chastise those we study for not being as omniscient as we are. Our job is to understand why people acted in the way they did. In these two essays, Austin and Kirk look at the political and military leaders of the two nations, the Soviet Union and the United States, and imagine how each one looked at the other and how each one responded to the imagined threat of the other. Kirk and Austin both show that neither entirely, or even remotely, understood their opponent; each overestimated the other and reacted in ways we might consider reckless or ridiculous. While it may have been a tragedy of misunderstanding, it must also be a learning experience. Despite the fears, misapprehensions, paranoia, and jealousy, the United States and the U.S.S.R. did not, ultimately, go to war with each other, an outcome that all parties, with their limited knowledge, surely anticipated.

Viewpoint: American policymakers feared a sudden nuclear attack by the Soviet Union, but evidence shows that their fears were unfounded.

The idea that the United States was extremely vulnerable to a devastating Soviet surprise attack had its origin in a 1954 study of the vulnerability of Strategic Air Command (SAC) bases, conducted by RAND Corporation, the U.S. Air Force's strategic think tank. The leader of this study, Albert J. Wohlstetter, came to the alarming conclusion that SAC bombers were so highly concentrated that the Soviets could wipe out our whole fleet with a few dozen bombers in a surprise attack. From this thesis he argued that mere possession of nuclear weapons and delivery capability was not sufficient to create effective deterrence to attack. The Soviets had to know that our strategic forces could survive a sneak attack, be able to surmount the "barriers to retaliation," and deliver a "crushing" blow to them. In this view any sudden technological breakthrough—whether in antimissile defense or antisubmarine warfare—could upset a previously stable balance. This might then tempt the Soviets to launch a surprise attack.

The most important conclusion coming out of Wohlstetter's calculations was that the "balance of terror" would always be "delicate." Under this dynamic-vulnerability concept, no set number of nuclear forces could assure stable deterrence. The Americans always had to stay ahead of the Soviets, lest some breakthrough render their posture obsolete. Once this worst-case-scenario thinking, propagated by RAND civilian strategists, was accepted as strategic doctrine, it became the rationale for the strategic-arms race. Later, other worst-case scenarios, such as a sneak attack to destroy our command-and-control ability and a "decapitating" attack on our political leadership, were added. These fears were used to justify enormous expenditures to safeguard our retaliatory capability against a catastrophic Soviet surprise attack. The long-range impact of this type of reasoning was that most Americans came to accept that a Pearl Harbor–type Soviet surprise attack was not only possible but also quite likely.

Assertions of a Soviet attack out of the blue were unrealistic for several reasons. Strategists at RAND, up to mid 1961, had to rely on biased U.S. Air Force intelligence estimates of Soviet force capabilities. They did not have access to supersensitive intelligence-gathering resources developed by the United States. Through an extensive alliance system, the United States had managed to encircle the Soviet Union with highly sophisticated electronic installations, eavesdropping on Soviet communications and later their missile telemetry. Through microwave, and later laser, technology the National Security Agency (NSA) was able to listen in on conversations between the Soviet leadership and their strategic-forces commanders. When aerial reconnaissance of the U-2 spy planes was supplemented by satellite observation in 1961, the NSA attained the ability to monitor every square inch of Soviet territory.

Civilian strategists at RAND provided elegantly stated calculations that made it appear that the hypothetical worst-case scenario of a nuclear Pearl Harbor was not merely a remote theoretical possibility, but a near-certain probability. The sincerity of these assumptions must be questioned because they were so one-sided. For example, in his famous *Foreign Affairs* article, "The Delicate Balance of Terror," in 1959 Wohlstetter elaborated the many "barriers" to successful retaliation by American forces to prove the vulnerability of American retaliatory capacity. However, neither he nor other RAND strategists applied the same rigorous analysis to an examination of the even greater technical difficulties of the Soviets mounting a successful first strike.

Such an analysis would have revealed that coordinating a complicated simultaneous strike at close and far-flung targets required different launch times for planes and missiles. With our electronic eavesdropping and satellite observation, even the preparations for such an attack—without obtaining early warning—was next to impossible. There was no reason to assume that the Soviets were not aware of this point. Furthermore, Soviet strategic forces were never configured in a first-strike posture.

A Soviet knockout blow was no longer possible after U.S. Polaris submarines with sea-launched nuclear missiles (SSBNs) became operational in 1963. American seaborne strategic forces simply could not be located by the enemy, fixed upon, and destroyed with existing weaponry, or even with later advanced technology. The United States had achieved the ideal of a secure second-strike force, the essential prerequisite to successful deterrence in the nuclear age, as first stipulated by Bernard Brodie, the father of nuclear strategy, back in 1946. The Soviets understood this concept. They strove to protect themselves against American surprise attack by emulating our concept of an invulnerable submarine-based strategic-retaliatory force.

Another worst-case scenario—the surprise "decapitating" strike—was not only far-fetched but also highly unlikely. Invented after the invulnerability of our retaliatory force was assured, it stated that the Soviets might be tempted to crip-

Elementary-school children in Topeka, Kansas practice the "duck and cover" technique during civil defense drills, ca. 1960

(Popperfoto)

ple the U.S. ability to retaliate by launching a narrowly focused strike at national leadership and/or strategic command-and-control structures. Given the well-advertised "redundancy" of the U.S. command-and-control structure, such a disabling attack became technically impossible from the early 1960s on, and the Soviets knew it. This scenario also ignored the disastrous consequences for the attacker if they could not assure complete success in disabling the U.S. ability to retaliate.

Worst-case-scenario thinking also misconstrued Soviet intentions because it blithely assumed that the Communist leadership in their determined pursuit of world conquest would be indifferent to a death toll in a nuclear exchange equal to the twenty million Soviet citizens killed in World War II. There was never any evidence to support this assumption. Analysis of East-West confrontations during the Cold War shows that—contrary to the perception commonly held in the West—Moscow never went beyond taking limited and reversible risks. In addition, archival research on attitudes at the Kremlin reveals that avoidance of war with the West was the major foreign-policy goal of each successive Soviet leader. It also drew an unrealistic image of an irrational or foolhardy Soviet leadership willing to risk personal and national annihilation from a wounded, but angry, United States.

Given the Cold War atmosphere of East-West tensions, one can understand how the myth of surprise attack came into being. Nevertheless, how did it become an obsession, and why was it propagated with such zeal by RAND strategists and other key American policymakers even after accurate intelligence about Soviet strategic capabilities became available, or later after both sides had achieved assured-mutual-destruction capacity and had entered into an almost continuous arms-control dialogue with the Soviet Union? There were several reasons.

The research done by RAND was designed to please its employer, the U.S. Air Force. The concept of dynamic vulnerability became the basis for funneling almost unlimited funds into "airborne alerts" as well as purchases of more planes and missiles. RAND strategists went to elaborate lengths to maintain the myth of U.S. vulnerability and continued to do so after the U.S. capacity to retaliate and its superiority in nuclear weapons were no longer in question. The need to continue to attract government funding for their research clearly led to self-serving conclusions by this talented group. When Brodie challenged their continued emphasis on the delicacy of the balance-of-terror, he was pushed out of RAND in 1964.

The Pearl Harbor analogy propagated by RAND strategists was successful. Fear of surprise attack became real in America—witness the nuclear attack drills, where children had to hide under their school desks. Early postwar fears were fueled by a succession of Cold War events—the 1948 Berlin Blockade, wars in Korea and Indochina, Chinese offshore-island bombardments, Laos, the Berlin Wall, and the Cuban Missile Crisis. These events led Americans to accept the image of an aggressive monolithic Communist conspiracy aimed at world domination. For a few years it seemed personified by the volatile Nikita Khrushchev, who vowed to "bury" American capitalism and promised to support revolutionary movements around the world until the ultimate victory of Marxist socialism was achieved. All this activity created an atmosphere of imminent danger that made the American public ready to believe that a "nuclear Pearl Harbor" was entirely possible. Through sheer repetition, the "delicate balance" or "dynamic vulnerability" arguments—which rested on the various formulations of the surprise-attack myth—became an accepted axiom of all successive expressions of the American response to the "Soviet threat." The obsession led those who believed these definitions of threat to urge, without ceasing, that the United States had to protect itself against such a worst-case scenario through enlargement or technical improvement of strategic-force structures to close every "window of vulnerability."

The threat of a Soviet surprise attack also became a convenient political issue for both parties. RAND strategists had created the "missile gap" issue for John F. Kennedy's 1960 presidential campaign. Frustrated with the cool disdain for Wohlstetter's alarmist calculations by Dwight D. Eisenhower (who had much greater confidence in the U.S. ability to have ample warning), RAND found a ready listener in the less-experienced Kennedy. Their participation in the presidential campaign as security advisers to JFK gave them enormous visibility. A group of RAND civilians came to the Pentagon in 1961 to apply the principles of systems analysis, operations research, and statistical cost-benefit analysis to running the unwieldy defense establishment. Over time these "whiz kids," and their second- and third-generation disciples, became policymakers throughout the American security establishment. The way was paved for the apostles of surprise attack to become entrenched and promote their doctrine of dynamic vulnerability with successive administrations. They held sway over strategic thought and the design of nuclear-force structures for the next thirty-five years.

Not satisfied that simple nuclear parity or Mutual Assured Destruction was sufficient to prevent the Soviets from being tempted, the apostles of surprise attack also argued that American strategic forces must be so responsive that they could be launched on strategic warning alone. Starting at the end of the Carter administration and accelerating during the Reagan presidency, this doctrine led to the expensive pursuit of what many, including the Soviets, viewed as American preemptive-strike capability. These were the days of the "window of vulnerability" and "evil empire" labels, during which any increases in Soviet strategic capability were portrayed as efforts to gain surprise-attack capability.

The delicacy of the balance-of-terror argument long provided political cover for alliance among elected officials, the military, and major defense contractors. These arrangements are known to political scientists as "iron triangles." Each side stood to gain politically and economically from high levels of spending for strategic missiles, bombers, and missile-carrying submarines. Elected officials benefited from defense contracts going to companies in their home states or congressional districts. Defense-industry lobbyists enlisted the help of the military to convince elected leaders to keep money flowing for strategic systems. The military services and intelligence community played their role by producing estimates of "alarming" Soviet buildups—usually around defense-appropriations time. When various top decision makers, from Eisenhower on, showed "dovish" sentiments and tried to slow down defense spending and the arms race, these iron-triangle coalitions rallied to prevent cutbacks or downsizing. Often they enlisted the help of hawkish columnists and prominent persons to orchestrate concerted scare campaigns about "new" Soviet threats of surprise attack.

Did key American decision makers really believe in the myth and feel that increasing nuclear-missile arsenals could counter it? Psychologist Steven Kull explored these questions in *Minds At War: Nuclear Reality and the Inner Conflicts of Defense Policymakers* (1988). After hundreds of interviews, he concluded that most key policymakers were divided in their thinking on the vulnerability to surprise attack. On the one hand, many recognized that a nuclear war would be a disaster in which there could be no winners in the traditional sense. They could cognitively acknowledge that in the age of mutual-assured destruction, greater numbers of nuclear weapons conferred no military advantage and hence did not increase American security. However, as Kull pointed out, it seemed psychologically difficult for these men to let go of old military axioms. They wanted to believe that more was better in the nuclear age, just like in the good-old-days of conventional warfare. To reduce the discomfort of the cognitive dissonance in their own minds, they rationalized that nuclear weapons had not really changed the rules of war. They found it emotionally more satisfying to campaign for military superiority and create the "image" of American military security than to accept that a static force structure of finite numbers was sufficient in the nuclear era. The myth of a disarming surprise attack provided them with the perfect rationale for maintaining these beliefs and thus reduce the emotional discomfort of the realization that in a nuclear exchange there would be no "winners."

Kull found that the traditional American emphasis on winning was evident in the military training manuals as well as in official policy statements at the highest levels. For example, Ronald Reagan's secretary of defense, Casper Weinberger, insisted that the United States could create such overwhelming strategic superiority that it could not only neutralize a Soviet surprise attack through Strategic Defense Initiative, but that it could also win or "prevail" in a strategic nuclear exchange.

Many key decision makers were convinced that it was essential from a world public-opinion perspective that the United States, as the "leader of the Western World," must always be seen as having clear strategic superiority. Several presidents expressed the belief that if the United States were perceived as second-best to the Soviets, there would be major realignments of allegiance away from the American-led West toward the Soviet-led East. The assumption was that this shift would lead the Soviets to behave more aggressively in various trouble spots around the world and possibly launch a surprise attack.

Worst-case scenarios of a Soviet surprise attack were a myth, created by and reinforced by the Cold War. The persistence of the myth was a driving force behind the Soviet-American nuclear-arms race. When the Cold War ended, there was a need to rethink the reliance on nuclear weapons for deterring war. Some observers questioned the utility of nuclear weapons altogether, arguing that they have not been instrumental in preventing war. They point to their total irrelevance in all conventional conflicts in which any of the nuclear powers have been involved since World War II. The fact is that the United States now has overwhelming superiority in conventional weapons, and the ability to bring them to bear decisively in any part of the world. Thus, any potential aggressor who would wish to use any weapons of mass destruction (nuclear, chemical, or biological) would know that the United States could wreak selective or complete destruction of a nation's infrastructure in retaliation, even without resorting to nuclear weapons.

—HANNO W. KIRK, BLUEFIELD STATE COLLEGE

Viewpoint: Though the American race into space was prompted by fears of Soviet superiority, the Soviet space program was woefully incompetent.

During the Cold War the Russians could be perceived as arrogant, deceptive, egotistical, petty, dishonest, and, at times, annoying in their pursuit of the space race. Internal disputes and politics, however, frequently interfered with their plans and created disharmony and disaster. Yet, they were also inventive and made the best of what they had. Because they were basically an agrarian country, they should be applauded, because the Soviet Union achieved many firsts. They put the first satellite, *Sputnik I,* as well as the first man and woman, into space. Yet, these feats came at a terrible cost in money, livelihood, and human life. When entering an area about which little or nothing is known, risks are aplenty and caution should be taken. To take risks recklessly, or throw caution to the wind, questions the effort. When these endeavors also threaten world peace, they must be further queried. Nevertheless, American fears of Soviet superiority in space, and therefore possible attack from space, were misplaced because the Soviets had many serious problems with their space organization.

On 25 May 1961 U.S. president John F. Kennedy spoke of sending a man to the moon and returning him safely. Russia already had, and would continue to have, an active space program, led by Sergey Pavlovich Korolyov, who supervised and designed the Sputnik, Luna, Venera, Vostok, Voskhod, and Soyuz projects. *Vostok,* the first manned spacecraft to orbit the earth, carrying Yuri A. Gagarin, was actually a spy satellite—but the public was never offered this information in the 1960s. Yet Korolyov found the Soviet space program too diversified and proposed a major reform. He thought there should be a long-term centralized plan. Soviet premier Nikita Khrushchev, however, would have none of this, and the program remained in the hands of nonspecialized design bureaus, some working for different government ministries.

Vladimir Chelomei, who developed military missiles but had absolutely no experience with space vehicles, hired Khrushchev's son. Because of this family connection, Chelomei soon had the largest budget of all the design bureaus. Chelomei wanted to expand into territory controlled by Korolyov. To make matters worse, Valentin Petrovich Glushko, another top designer of rocket engines, entered the competition. Glushko and Korolyov were far from friends, their disagreements dating back to the 1930s when Glushko provided testimony that sent Korolyov to a gulag during a purge by Joseph Stalin. They had worked together on the R-7 rocket during the 1950s, but their mutual distaste stopped any other form of collaboration.

So three men vied for the attention and funds that the premier could provide. Rival bureaus not only designed but also built space hardware. Because of this situation it was not uncommon to have several parallel projects, a stumbling block to a coordinated plan to send cosmonauts to the moon.

Secrecy was another problem. For some reason, never fully explained, Vostok's flight configuration was not revealed until 1967. The reason there were only two manned Voskhod flights, although a third was planned, and their true objective were never revealed. The Soviets denied the existence of their moon rocket, the N-1. Although Americans served on the Russian space station *Mir* in the 1990s in a supposedly cooperative effort, Russian program managers did not inform their American counterparts of a planned docking test of the unmanned *Progress* ferry vehicle. Russian controllers also withheld information of the cause of a fire on *Mir* and were reluctant to discuss the aftereffects. Soviet controllers kept poor records, causing them to accidentally repeat procedures. This reluctance to offer any meaningful information was demonstrated on 18 August 1989 when the U.S.S.R. admitted the existence of a manned lunar landing program—a full twenty-eight years after Korolyov started work on it.

The monster lunar launcher, the N-1, was not immune to mistakes of the past. The first booster blasted off on 21 February 1969. It looked like a perfect launch; however, only sixty-six seconds after launch it became clear that all was not well. A leaking oxidizer pipe started a fire at the rear of the first stage. The N-1 booster was destroyed by the range safety officer. It was determined that excessive heat and vibrations from the thirty engines had damaged the rocket. The Soviets were running out of time if they were to beat the Americans to the moon.

After some alterations, a second N-1 launch attempt was made; again disaster struck. Only nine seconds after liftoff a chunk of debris entered the oxidizer pump of one engine, causing an explosion. The result was the complete loss of control over the engines and the control/thrust system. The launch escape system then activated, pulling the payload to safety, and the booster then fell backward toward the launch pad. The gigantic explosion that followed completely destroyed pad number 2 and did significant damage to pad number 1, as well as the N-1 mockup sitting on it. The Central Intelligence Agency discovered this accident through study of spy satellite photos of Baykonur Cosmodrome a few weeks later. After the explosion the Soviets realized that they had lost the race to the moon to the American *Apollo 11*.

Yet, the Soviets pressed on. To conceal its true purpose from the Americans they did not aim the third N-1, launched 27 June 1971, at the moon. At an altitude of approximately 250 meters an unplanned rotation tore apart support structures between the second and third stages. Seconds later the third stage collapsed near the pad and, as in test number two, damaged the launch pad. The remainder fell about twenty kilometers away. Some called for cancellation of the project, but the Soviet government decided to allow a fourth test.

The final N-1 rocket was radically redesigned: it was heavier, in an attempt to make it more reliable. On 23 November 1972 it rose majestically from the pad and looked as if all problems had been solved. Yet, ninety seconds into the flight an oxygen tank line failure caused a fire and the engines exploded, and then the entire first stage shut down. The launch escape tower pulled the payload away from the rocket, and the last N-1 was destroyed by the range safety officer.

These disasters did not halt the Soviet space program. *Buran* (Snowstorm), the only space shuttle of the Soviet Union, dates back to May 1960 and was part of Korolyov's plan. However, the government decided that he already had too much to do and gave the project to Chelomei. When the Khrushchev government fell, Chelomei lost the job. In the 1970s the Soviet government was informed that the Americans were working on a winged vehicle capable of changing its orbit and capable of flying over Moscow with a potentially lethal cargo. This information upset Premier Leonid Brezhnev. The space shuttle project was given to Glushko when the N-1 was canceled and Korolyov's deputy Vasilly Mishin was fired. In 1974 Buran was seen as a tool for the military, and in fact was ordered by the Kremlin. The Soviet shuttle was first seen by the West in 1978 at a secret Soviet test-flight facility. It was being carried atop a TU-95 Bear bomber for atmospheric tests.

Buran was designed by a group of engineers and designers who left the Mikoyan Design Bureau and instead formed NPO Molniya. The booster, designed by NPO Energia, was dubbed the Energia. Two small flyable versions of the orbiter were built to test specific aspects of Buran. The first was called BOR-4. Equipped with carbon on the wings and a thermal-protection system similar to that of the full-scale vehicle, it flew four orbital and one suborbital flights. The initial orbital flight, Cosmos 1374, was flown from Kapustin Yar, and the vehicle was recovered from the Indian Ocean.

The second vehicle, Cosmos 1445, was photographed by an Australian patrol plane. The second small-scale orbiter was called BOR-5. This test vehicle flew orbital missions simulating portions of the trajectory expected to be flown by Buran. BOR-5 provided valuable data since it closely resembled Buran, even though it was only one-eighth the size. To ready future pilots of the orbiter, a TU-154 was modified to become a mockup of the orbiter's flight deck. Later two Lyulka AL-31 engines were mounted on the aft fuselage shoulders, which allowed approach and landing tests.

Between 1985 and 1988 this configuration flew at least twenty-five times. The two engines also allowed the Soviets to check out the automatic landing system. Of the five vehicles ordered during the mid 1980s, only one was completed. In March 1988 an Energia booster was moved onto the launch pad at Baykonur. It was a rehearsal for the first shuttle flight. In May

SPUTNIK I

On 14 October 1957 a military affairs correspondent for Newsweek, *Richard J. Davis, submitted this assessment of American concerns following the Soviet launch of* Sputnik I *ten days earlier.*

. . . Nonetheless, whatever the confidence in Washington, it is inescapable that the Soviet satellite has been a stunning shock to the nation and is likely to bring heavy pressure on our military planners. The knowledge that a Soviet-made sphere is whirling over America many times a day will evoke a torrent of questions and there will have to be some solid answers.

Officials will parry as best they can, but behind the scenes they are surely going to work with greater dedication and speed to get the Atlas off on a good flight quickly. Economic and other restrictions on the missile programs will be lifted. Missilemen will now probably get what they want, even if their requests seem wasteful, or even if other parts of the defense program suffer.

The central fact that must be faced up to is this: As a scientific and engineering power, the Soviet Union has shown its mastery. The U.S. may have more cars and washing machines and toasters, but in terms of the stuff with which wars are won and ideologies imposed, the nation must now begin to view Russia as a power with a proven, frightening potential.

This is something our top scientists have known for some time, something the leaders of research and development have preached constantly within the military. They have urgently deplored the scarcity of youngsters going into science; they cry for more money for basic research; they cry for the kind of economic sacrifice that it takes to win an epic struggle in space.

But the Administration and Congress have been confronted with persistent demands for economy. Both will listen to the missilemen now. The harsh fact is that whatever we're doing is not enough.

Source: *Paul M. Angle,* The American Reader from Columbus to Today *(New York: Rand McNally, 1958), pp. 674–675.*

1988 TASS, the official Soviet news agency, announced that the second launch of Energia would carry the Soviet shuttle. In October 1986, before the first flight of *Buran, National Geographic* published an article titled "Soviets in Space: Are They Ahead?" In the article a Soviet general was quoted as saying "We see no need until the next century, when we want to transport more material between earth and space."

On 29 April 1988 the Soviet government announced that *Buran* would take its maiden flight by the end of the year. During the last week of September *Energia-Buran* was moved to its launch pad. Television coverage was planned, but not provided. The original launch date was 29 October; however, the countdown was halted at fifty-one seconds when the crew access arm failed to retract swiftly enough. A check revealed a flaw in the hinge mechanism, and modifications took two weeks.

The second launch attempt was announced for 15 November 1988. Again television coverage was promised; again it failed to materialize. A storm moved in from the Aral Sea, and making matters worse, it was only thirty-nine degrees Fahrenheit. The pad was cleared at midnight on 15 November to begin loading liquid hydrogen into *Energia.* During this time cosmonauts landed at the shuttle recovery runway. Liftoff occurred at 6:00 A.M. When the vehicle reached an altitude of 197,000 feet, the four strap-on boosters were jettisoned. At 6:47 the orbiter had an orbit of 156.6 by 159.1 miles.

As *Buran* descended, it was met by two chase planes. They relayed television pictures of the orbiter's final approach. Landing in a forty-mile-per-hour crosswind, *Buran* touched down at 9:25 A.M. at a speed of 207 mph. Three parachutes slowed the orbiter as it traveled almost one mile down a runway. Post-flight inspection showed that of thirty-eight thousand heat-shield tiles only five were lost during the flight.

The orbiter next appeared at the 1989 Paris Air Show atop an AN-225 carrier aircraft. In 1990, however, *Buran* was retired since it had reached the end of its ten-year lifetime: there would be no second flight. Another orbiter (OK-2K) was readied for flight in a mission to dock with space station *Mir,* but it was never launched. The Soviets did not know it, but that goal would only be attained after the fall of communism and by an American shuttle. A 25 May 1993 decision by the Council of Chief Designers ordered that the Buran project be placed in mothballs. The shuttle now decorates Gorky Park in Moscow; a company formed by NPO Molniya is using it as a new restaurant, offering one hundred varieties of space food at the cost of approximately seventy dollars.

Buran and the other projects were not the only problems for the Soviet space program. Field Marshall Mitrofan Nedelin, then chief of Cosmodrome, was in charge of a 24 October 1960 launch of an intercontinental ballistic missile. The signal for liftoff was given, but the missile simply sat on the launchpad. Nedelin sent a team to locate the problem, correct it, and return to the safety of the fireproof bunker. While the team investigated and moved about the scaffolding surrounding the missile, it exploded, killing almost one hundred men, including Nedelin. Apparently he had left the safety of the bunker to increase the speed of the investigation.

The explosion sent shock waves through the Soviet government, which made a series of contradictory statements and outright lies. First, it denied there had been any sort of accident and reported that Nedelin had perished in a plane crash. Later the government admitted that there was a small explosion and that only fifty-four men had died; it amended that by saying forty others had died "elsewhere."

A 1989 article in the journal *Ogonyok* briefly mentioned the Nedelin incident and took the government to task over the handling of the entire affair. In 1994, after the Soviet government had fallen, the Russians announced that there had been an explosion and that almost one hundred men had perished.

It would appear that Nedelin was under great pressure to launch the missile. The Soviet premier was at the United Nations, and he wanted a space spectacular to flaunt before the entire world–to show the superiority of communism. But the fact remains that a military missile exploded, and only if there had been a successful launch would it have become part of the space program. It appears that military and civilian applications of the space program were closely linked–too close for almost one hundred men. When Soviet space engineers did things too quickly, especially as a result of political pressure, the primary task failed and people died. When they took their time, things seemed to come out rather nicely. Fear replaced caution, and intelligence replaced fear.

The Soviet space program, especially its groundbreaking strides, pushed the Americans both scientifically and militarily. Many in the U.S. military feared that Soviet progress in the space program meant greater vulnerability from military, especially nuclear, applications. However, despite their astounding successes, there were many problems inherent in the Soviet space program.

–THOMAS H. AUSTIN, TORONTO, CANADA

References

Bernard Brodie, "The Development of Nuclear Strategy," *International Security,* 2 (Spring 1978): 65–83;

Thomas Y. Canby, "Soviets in Space: Are They Ahead?" *National Geographic* (October 1986): 420–459;

Owen Davies, ed., *The Omni Book of Space* (New York: Kensington, 1983);

James Digby, *Strategic Thought at RAND, 1948–1963: The Ideas, Their Origins, Their Fates* (Santa Monica, Cal.: RAND, 1990);

Anatoly Dobrynin, *In Confidence: Moscow's Ambassador to America's Six Cold War Presidents (1962–1986)* (New York: Random House, 1996);

Frederick S. Dunn and others, *The Absolute Weapon: Atomic Power and World Order,* edited by Brodie (New York: Harcourt, Brace, 1946);

Dennis R. Jenkins, *The History Of Developing the National Space Transportation System: the Beginning through STS-75* (Indian Harbour Beach, Fla.: D. R. Jenkins, 1996);

Fred Kaplan, *The Wizards of Armageddon* (New York: Simon & Schuster, 1983);

Steven Kull, *Minds At War: Nuclear Reality and the Inner Conflicts of Defense Policymakers* (New York: BasicBooks, 1988);

Richard Ned Lebow and Janice Gross Stein, *We All Lost the Cold War* (Princeton: Princeton University Press, 1994);

John E. Mueller, *Quiet Cataclysm: Reflections on the Recent Transformations of World Politics* (New York: HarperCollins, 1995);

James Oberg, "Spaceflight," *British Interplanetary Society Monthly,* 37 (August 1995): 254–255;

John Prados, *The Soviet Estimate: U.S. Intelligence Analysis & Russian Military Strength* (New York: Dial, 1982);

Peter Pringle and William Arkin, *SIOP: The Secret U.S. Plan for Nuclear War* (New York: Norton, 1983);

Marc Trachtenberg, ed., *The Development of Strategic Thought* (New York: Garland, 1988);

Stansfield Turner, *Caging the Nuclear Genie: An American Challenge for Global Security* (Boulder, Colo.: Westview Press, 1997);

Albert J. Wohlstetter, "The Delicate Balance of Terror," *Foreign Affairs,* 37 (January–February 1959): 211–234;

Wohlstetter and others, *Selection and Use of Strategic Air Bases: A Report Prepared For Air Force Project RAND* (Santa Monica, Cal.: RAND, 1963);

Roberta Wohlstetter, *Pearl Harbor: Warning and Decision* (Stanford, Cal.: Stanford University Press, 1962).

FEMINISM

Is feminism dead?

Viewpoint: Yes, feminism was killed by the excesses of its sponsors.

Viewpoint: No, the feminist movement is still alive, and its real achievement has been making its goals those of every woman.

The women's movement of the 1960s grew out of the antiwar and civil rights movements. Like those social movements, the feminist movement challenged the power structure and questioned the basic premises of society. However, unlike the antiwar or civil rights movements, the feminists did not just challenge men in power to change their ways of thinking. Feminists came to see all men as potentially part of the problem and believed that whatever their class, race, or nationality, all women were subjugated, in one way or another, to male oppression.

The women's movement represented a radical critique of society. While the antiwar and civil rights movements challenged the public actions of people, the feminists looked to private actions, arguing that the personal was in fact political. All aspects of one's life and behavior were scrutinized in order to root out either a man's tendency to oppress or a woman's to be complicit in her own oppression. Issues on which there had been relatively universal agreement, involving everything from child care to prostitution, came in for re-evaluation in light of feminist criticism.

Feminists, more than either civil-rights workers or antiwar protestors, had more than their share of criticism and ridicule. Men who agreed on nothing else could agree that feminists, or the "women's libbers" as they were known, sometimes overstated their cases and made what to men seemed ridiculous or exaggerated claims. Yet, in the quarter century since the Equal Rights Amendment failed, how have the basic tenets of feminism fared? In these two essays, two scholars make radically different appraisals of the feminist movement. Douglas Cooke, a scholar of twentieth-century literature and culture, argues that by exaggerating their case feminists ultimately discredited themselves and their movement. On the other hand, Pleun Bouricius, a scholar whose work focuses mainly on nineteenth-century women's fiction, argues that the feminist critique was less public and more pervasive than a study of its rhetoric would suggest. The feminist critique was a private one that did cause men and women to re-evaluate how they lived and how they treated one another. By its nature, then, its results are more difficult to quantify. If we look not to the public statements of controversial radicals but to the lives of ordinary women and men, we see a different story. Feminism may indeed have changed the way people live, and by forcing us to ask this question, it has forced us to think that the personal is political, and that would suggest its influence is more pervasive than its critics would like.

Viewpoint: Yes, feminism was killed by the excesses of its sponsors.

The fundamental tenet of feminism is the belief that throughout history men have sought to suppress women and that a ubiquitous male dominance, called patriarchy, pervades all art, culture, relationships, and aspects of daily life. Some feminists posit the need for an awakening through a "click" experience, the moment when a woman realizes the extent and power of the patriarchy that engulfs and oppresses her. The click experience can be sustained as "paranoia," a constant vigilance toward patriarchy, and is regarded as a necessary stage of feminist consciousness. Interpretations of the extent of patriarchy vary widely. Catharine MacKinnon claims in "Feminism, Marxism, Method, and the State: Towards Feminist Jurisprudence," in *Feminism and Methodology,* edited by Sandra Harding (1987), that patriarchy is so ubiquitous and insidious that the concept of consensual heterosexual sex is impossible. MacKinnon claims that no woman freely consents to heterosexual sex, because her powerlessness under patriarchy has conditioned her to submit to male domination. Her view is not widely accepted and is an embarrassment to many feminists.

A more moderate and commonly accepted view of patriarchy is that throughout history men have oppressed women, imprisoning them in the home and exploiting them as housecleaners, sex providers, and baby producers while men enjoyed all the freedoms and advantages of society. Although this view is widely accepted, it ignores that men have been burdened with oppressive work, competition in business, providing sustenance for their families, and military service–often resulting in the loss of life. The feminist view glamorizes the male laborer role as freedom rather than obligation and vilifies him as oppressor rather than provider. It claims that his participation in wars is a symptom of biologically determined male aggression rather than a socially imposed duty to protect wife, children, and country.

A more functional approach to traditional gender roles reveals that it is nature, not man, that imposed these roles: both males and females of all species are servants to the reproductive imperative of their genes. Historically, children were a necessity, not an option. In addition to providing needed labor, children were expected to care for their parents in sickness and old age. Before social security, only the wealthy could risk not having children. Furthermore, given the high rate of infant mortality, women often had to bear four or five children to have two healthy, surviving ones. With women spending so much of their lives in pregnancy and childrearing, the tasks of hunting and protection were left to men. Gradually men constructed hierarchical organization to develop strategies for hunting large animals. Eventually they applied hierarchy to other large-scale communal tasks, such as irrigation. With the rise of civilizations and commerce, men began to work for wages. Men protected and provided for women in exchange for intimacy and procreation. These roles developed over millennia because they worked, albeit imperfectly; however, for most humans, there were few alternatives. Institutions that men created, such as education and government, were not offered to women, who were

National Organization for Women (NOW) President Patricia Ireland under arrest outside the White House during a pro-choice demonstration in 1992

(Rueters)

needed at home. Furthermore, the majority of men were also deprived of education and participation in government. The history of inequity, brutal as it is, was not exclusively the plight of women.

The error of patriarchal theory lies in its assumption that all men are privileged and dominate women. This view ignores that millions of men throughout history were slaves, serfs, and laborers working under unimaginably wretched conditions. Both men and women of the working classes were powerless throughout most of history. Their conditions were improved through two ways only: when rights were wrested from the privileged or when technology that eased their labors was developed. Feminism arose either when political injustice was being questioned or when technology alleviated human burdens and made it possible for women to consider roles outside the home. Mary Wollstonecraft, author of *A Vindication of the Rights of Women* (1792), began her writing career by defending the French Revolution. Charles Fourier, Karl Marx, and John Stuart Mill also defended the rights of women. In England the Mine Act of 1842 forbade females to work in mines because of the harsh conditions and the nudity necessitated by the heat. Despite the claims of feminist historians, many women were happy to stay home from the mines, even if this led to the increased differentiation of masculine and feminine roles.

In the United States the first major wave of feminism arose during the abolitionist movement, and the second during the Civil Rights movement. American feminism began as humanist and egalitarian, supporting equal rights for all. Its leaders, such as Susan B. Anthony, were aware of their privileged status as middle-class, protected women and altruistically sought to protect the less fortunate.

However, second-wave feminism, though benefiting from the conscience-raising of the Civil Rights movement, was more directly a result of technology. The development of oral contraceptives–the pill was made commercially available in 1960–freed women from the enormous burdens of pregnancy and childrearing. Furthermore, a proliferation of electrical appliances–indoor plumbing and heating, refrigerators, washer, dryers, vacuum cleaners, and dishwashers–alleviated much of women's remaining labor. With more spare time, their thoughts turned from survival to fulfillment. Only when American women were living by the highest standards in the world did they have leisure to find oppression in their mechanized existence. Forgetting the severe conditions that necessitated their role in the home for millennia, some women began to blame men for their house-bound existence, believing that it was men, not nature, who demanded these roles.

The resentment was popularized by Betty Friedan in her influential book *The Feminine Mystique* (1963). Rebelling against the 1950s cult of the nuclear family, she described the traditional suburban home as a "comfortable concentration camp" and a "mass burial" comparable to "genocide." She stoked vague feelings of discontent in millions of women with her evocation of the problem "that has no name." Friedan claimed that childrearing, part-time work, or hobbies were inadequate for fulfillment: women had to have full-time jobs and remuneration to win back the self-esteem that she claimed they lacked. She believed that women should not even have the choice of staying home, fearing that "if there is such a choice, too many women will make that one." Many women began to blame men for their "imprisonment," calling it power and dominance when a man worked eight hours a day, perhaps taking orders from a callous boss, for the "privilege" of providing for his family. But only privileged women could believe such grotesque comparisons between the suburban household and the Nazi holocaust. Friedan's book displayed many characteristics that have plagued feminism: a self-centered concern for only women's issues; ignorance and disregard for the problems of other groups; provincialism; devaluation of the feminine role; resentment and hatred toward men; and a paranoid perception of ubiquitous male dominance, or "patriarchy," which they claim pervades all culture and society.

It is assumed that men were perfectly happy in the 1950s, as portrayed in the television series *Father Knows Best*. But dissatisfaction with suburban banality was no feminist epiphany. Stuck in dull office jobs and locked in bureaucracy, men recognized the hollowness of their commercialized existence. Playwright Arthur Miller ridiculed its emptiness in *Death of a Salesmen* (1949) and criticized the cult of the nuclear family in *All My Sons* (1947). William H. Whyte's classic sociological study, *The Organization Man* (1956), criticized how corporate conformism devastated the masculine spirit. Men too felt the dissatisfaction and wanderlust that Friedan acknowledged in women. They fantasized about life on the road in pursuit of adventure, as mythologized in the novels of Jack Kerouac. But men responded differently to their ennui. Entrenched in the workforce, they saw gender roles in a broader context, understood their limitations, and realized their functionality.

Men still had to work, not just for themselves but to provide for a family. Many women, on the other hand, envied their husband's careers and regarded their homes as prisons.

When women entered the workforce en masse in the seventies, they encountered work as their mothers had known during the Great Depression and World War II. The more vociferous women, instead of empathizing with men, began to blame them for job dissatisfaction. They began to complain about harsh conditions, harassment, and favoritism. Feminism taught women to vocalize their discontent, and they began to complain about unfair workplace practices many men had either combated or put up with in the name of good sportsmanship. Women made a positive contribution by enforcing increased sensitivity to employees, but they tended to assume that only women suffered from harassment or unfairness, thereby perpetuating the increasingly popular assumption that all men were oppressors and all women were victims.

This claim has always been a difficult one for men to dispute. First, men who contest feminist claims of victimization are accused either of being insensitive or complicit with the patriarchy. Second, it is more acceptable for a woman to envy the male role than for a man to envy the female role or to complain about obligations labeled as masculine: one must "take it like a man." It is difficult for men to discuss the myriad ways in which masculinity traps, confines, and controls their behavior.

Men's silence has allowed feminists to perpetuate increasingly distorted, alarmist views of women's oppression. For instance, radical feminists claim that patriarchal culture subtly encourages violence against women from childhood onward, but the truth is the opposite. Boys are taught not to hit girls: Warren Farrell, in *The Myth of Male Power: Why Men Are the Disposable Sex* (1993) reports that schoolgirls hit boys twenty times more often than the opposite. Feminists complain about an epidemic of violence against women, but Farrell asserts that men are twice as likely as women to be victims of violent crimes and three times more likely to be murdered. Feminists claim that patriarchy-controlled media delight in depicting violence against women in movies and television, but 95 percent of the characters killed in movies are men. Depictions of violence against females are rare and are almost always portrayed as an atrocity, but violence against males is often shown as humorous, inconsequential, or even edifying (the man is "put in his place"). Feminists argue that men join the military because they are ruthless killers, but studies of veterans suffering from post-traumatic stress report that their greatest trauma arose not from the fear of being killed but from the horror of killing. Feminists complain that men ignore women's problems, but in New York City there are only four social service centers dealing with veterans, while there are fifty agencies dealing with women's issues. More Vietnam War veterans have committed suicide than were killed in the conflict itself. Feminists contend that the patriarchy neglects female health issues, and yet the National Institutes of Health spend 10 percent of its research budget on women's health and only 5 percent on men's, according to Farrell, in spite of the fact that women live longer. American women's life expectancy rose 44 percent from 1920 to 1990, while men's rose only 34 percent. Feminists claim that society is designed to privilege men and subdue women, and yet males commit suicide four times more often than females. The American Association of University Women study, "How Schools Shortchange Girls," complained that boys were given more attention than girls in classrooms. Yet feminists ignored the explanation that boys require more discipline. Feminists also suppressed the facts that girls outperform boys in every subject except math and science; that girls are more active in all extracurricular activities except sports; that boys drop out of school more often, are likely to be victims of harrassment, use drugs and alcohol more frequently, and are less likely to go to college. In view of these facts, the theory of patriarchy—a society-wide conspiracy of men trying to subjugate women—is untenable.

Second-wave feminism began by devaluing the traditional feminine role in order to encourage women to pursue equality in male-dominated fields. The "women can be tough" ethos of Janis Joplin and other strong women downplayed gender differences in order to empower women. But as the movement grew increasingly radical and academic, many feminists began to reappropriate old sterotypes of femininity and masculinity; the only innovation to this redux was a reclassification of the feminine qualities as virtues and the masculine as vices. These "essentialist" feminists, emphasizing gender differences for the sake of promoting female superiority, rejected beliefs of equality and complementarity. They began to dichotomize the entire universe, creating the male oppressor/female victim dichotomy and arranging every imaginable human trait along the faultline of gender. Men were seen as hierarchical; women as egalitarian. Men were viewed as cold, competitive, and violent, while women were nurturing, cooperative, and peaceful. They argued that men were logical and women intuitive. Many of these stereotypes had been historically used to justify the exclusion of women from education and was lost on many feminists. The reinstatement of ancient prejudices for feminist purposes led to the devaluation of "masculine" values of abstraction, ambition, and achievement that are frequently credited with creating government, progress, technology, and even the universities in which feminists study and teach. The male oppressor/female victim dichotomy is the monster that hatches all the other canards of feminism.

Academic feminists have rejected logic, rigor, and abstraction as inferior, rather than complementary, to women's intuition. They claim that traditional standards of scholarship unfairly favor these qualities and that the scholarly requirement of proof is an unfair, patriarchal way of favoring men's quantitative thinking over women's qualitative thinking, which is less easily substantiated. This rejection of logic and rigor has led to an unprecedented morass of sophistry in academia, as feminists have appropriated postmodern theories of deconstructionism and social constructionism in order to reexamine and question all the accomplishments of mankind.

Sociological research also comes under feminist attack. Any study that does not support feminist claims is dismissed as having a patriarchal bias. For instance, a study on rape in *Ms.* magazine, conducted by Mary Koss, reported that 27.5 percent of college women have been victims of attempted or actual rape—the commonly cited "one in four" figure. When Neil Gilbert, professor at Berkeley's School of Social Welfare, questioned these alarmist figures and exposed what he believed was faulty methodology, he was accused of attempting to suppress women. Berkeley students protested, waving signs that read, "KILL NEIL GILBERT" and chanting, "Cut it out or cut it off!" In *Who Stole Feminism?: How Women Have Betrayed Women* (1994), Christina Hoff Sommers uncovers the shoddy methodology, dishonest suppression, and manipulation of data characteristic of feminist advocacy research. She argued that feminists sought to deliver the highest possible figures on the incidence of rape, spouse abuse, gender bias in the classroom, and other inequities in order to fuel women's fear of men and sustain the myth of patriarchy. Sommers shows that the figures for rape are an absurdity produced by a combination of biased sampling methods and loose definitions of rape that included unwelcome fondling on a date or consensual sex under the influence of alcohol that the woman later regretted. Although only 4.2 percent of women Koss interviewed stated that they had been raped, loose definitions served to inflate the figure to 27.5 percent, later vulgarized as "one in four."

Other research is appropriated and distorted by feminists. For instance, the American Anorexia and Bulimia Association reported that 150,000 U.S. women suffer from anorexia each year. Patriarchy theorist Naomi Wolf, author of *The Beauty Myth: How Images of Beauty Are Used Against Women* (1991), used this figure to claim that 150,000 women die each year, and further contends that they are "starved not by nature but by men," because patriarchy cultivates impossible standards of beauty in order to control women. In response, Camille Paglia in *Vamps & Tramps: New Essays* (1994) demands, "Let's get rid of Infirmary Feminism, with its bedlam of belly-achers, anorexics, bulimics, depressives, rape victims, and incest survivors. Feminism has become a catch-all vegetable drawer where bunches of clingy sob sisters can store their moldy neuroses."

Feminists often claim that men don't believe women who claim they were raped. Farrell argues that the opposite is true: men are too credulous of rape accusations, and male judges are more likely to believe false allegations. Farrell analyzes dozens of cases in which a woman falsely accused a man of rape, whether to explain an extramarital pregnancy, or to invent an alibi for breaking curfew, or simply for revenge. One study he cites reports that 27 percent of women who claimed to have been raped later admitted under polygraph tests that they were lying. The truth is that feminists don't believe women: Koss didn't believe the women in her study who said they weren't raped, and feminists often accuse women who don't regard themselves as victims of being brainwashed into complacency by patriarchy. Feminists have thus created a self-sealed, circular argument akin to religious fundamentalism.

There are two main branches of feminism: one based on principles of equality, the other on the paranoia of patriarchy. The first group believes that women can only gain independence by taking responsibility for their lives and actions, by meeting the same challenges that men do without getting special favors. It endorses equal rights and equal responsibility and advances arguments based on these principles. Farrell calls this group adult feminism.

Farrell labels the other branch adolescent feminism, made up of feminists who are concerned only with advancing quality of life for women, taking no interest in programs that might benefit both men and women. According to Farrell, they believe that women should be given equal or even extra rights, but not necessarily share the responsibilities. He argues that feminists employ revolutionary terms about overthrowing patriarchy that in fact perpetuate age-old habits of patronizing women by enlisting the government to be a surrogate husband/protector to shield women instead of encouraging them to fend for themselves in the competitive world. Adolescent feminists, he contends, believe that men subtly repel women from studying science by using offensive terms such as "big bang theory" to make them feel threatened. Farrell maintains that they push for imposing quotas for college admissions, scholarships, and employment for attractive jobs, but not for military combat or unattractive jobs, such as garbage collector, plumber, or roofer. He argues that they believe a man's history and character should be examined when he is accused of rape, but a woman's history, character, and identity should be protected. They characterize the traditional housewife as slave and vilify the traditional husband as oppressor rather than provider.

Many scholars have attempted to distance themselves from radical feminists, while retaining the term feminist: Paglia calls herself a dissident feminist; Sommers distinguishes between equity feminists and gender feminists. Others make distinctions between liberal and radical. All seek to dissociate themselves from the excesses of radicalism.

Among the general population about 33 percent of U.S. women considered themselves feminists, according to a 1992 poll in the *Washington Times.* But there is a growing awareness that radical feminism is largely the product of privileged, upper-class, white academics.

Women's Studies programs, which now number 670 in the United States, are not empowering women but rather debilitating them. Their students are culturally impoverished; they are not inspired by studying greatness in art, but rather soured by defeatist interpretations of patriarchy. Protected from male points of view that would be included in discussions were female students reintegrated into the broader curriculum, they are convinced that only women have, and are capable of uncovering and addressing, these problems. Paglia rejects Women's Studies as "institutionalized sexism" that silences men and dissenting women. She describes it as "a comfy, chummy morass of unchallenged groupthink . . . sunk in a cocoon of smug complacency." Paglia proposes instead an interdisciplinary program of sexology, which would welcome the findings of biology and other disciplines that feminists have tried to discredit and "would allow both men and women as well as heterosexuals and homosexuals to work together in the fruitful dialogue of dislike, disagreement, and debate, the tension, confrontation, and dialectic that lead to the truth." But this must be extended to all disciplines. History students, for instance, rather than studying the women's movement separately, should also study the Civil Rights movement and the cultural revolution as part of a continuum of profound social change. Students should read *The Organization Man* and Beat authors alongside Friedan to discover that both men and women strained against the confining sterility of the fifties.

Feminism has made significant contributions, but most of these advances were made by women who accepted the rigors of traditional education and the challenges of dealing with men in competition. Further progress in feminism will only come from women who tap their feminine strength and who join men in cooperation, rather than recede into resentment.

—DOUGLAS COOKE, BROOKLYN PUBLIC LIBRARY, NEW YORK

Viewpoint:
No, the feminist movement is still alive, and its real achievement has been making its goals those of every woman.

On 10 July 1999 the U.S. women's soccer team won the World Cup in Los Angeles, in the Rose Bowl jammed with ninety thousand screaming spectators. The tournament, played all over the country, experienced popular and media success that eluded the men's World Cup five years earlier. Commentators sighed wistfully that there was a real audience for women's sports. A professional women's soccer league was in the offing; young women bought posters featuring team members Mia Hamm and Michelle Akers.

The basis for this success was laid twenty-seven years previously. Title IX of the Education Amendments of 1972 "prohibits sex discrimination in all aspects of Federal educational programs." It became the law of the land that girls have the same access to sports in education as boys. Sex discrimination was banned in education just as it was in the workplace in Title VII of the Civil Rights Act of 1964, part of late-twentieth-century wholesale extension of civil rights, and policing of these acts fell to the Civil Rights Commission. The Equal Rights Amendment (ERA) was passed in 1972 in the House and the Senate and was endorsed by both major political parties. The ERA proposed that "equality of rights under the law shall not be denied or abridged by the United States or by any state on account of sex." After initial success, it expired in 1982, having fallen three states short of the two-thirds majority needed to amend the Constitution. Clearly, at the end of more than a decade of legal and political agitation, the public debate over women's rights had not been resolved. Started in the mid 1960s as an outgrowth of the Civil Rights movement by educated women who had felt pushed aside by the male protest establishment, the "women's rights movement," as it was called, was not nearly as self-evidently the right thing as its progenitor. Beyond an overdue extension of basic civil rights—women became obligated to sit on juries in 1970—Americans could not agree on what equality between men and women meant.

Early demands of third-wave feminism (the first wave occurred in the 1850s while the second was between 1900 and 1920) included political demands of "equal pay for equal work" and access to previously all-male sectors of the economy. In *The Feminine Mystique* (1963) sociologist Betty Friedan argued that women who fulfilled their potential would be much happier than women who submerged their identity into their families (this was a radical argument—women had been generally understood to be most completely fulfilled and happy by being submerged in their families). The rallying slogan of the National Organization for Women (NOW), organized in 1966, was "the personal is the political." Feminists did not invent that concept—it came straight out of the Civil Rights movement. However, "consciousness-raising," or becoming aware of the far-reaching presence of hierarchical (gender) differentiation, of one's own internalization of inferiority or powerlessness, became central to feminism in ways it had not been to other protest or liberalization movements. "Women's liberation is," wrote Robin Morgan in *Sisterhood is Powerful: An Anthology of Writing from the Women's Liberation Movement* (1970), "the first radical movement to . . . create its politics . . . out of concrete personal experiences."

Politicizing the question of whether nature or nurture shaped social organization, feminism unsettled the structure of the nuclear family that had been taken for granted. Should biology be destiny? Do men and women "naturally" operate in different spheres? Is motherhood women's life-fulfilling task? Is housework its logical extension? Feminists of all stripes answered these questions with a thundering "No" and added, moreover, that much of what had been seen as biology was socialization. All around the country women learned to dare "to be bad" and break the rules of womanhood. The New York Radical Women disrupted the Miss America pageant of 1968 and ran a sheep for the title; many women demonstrated on 26 August 1970, the fiftieth anniversary of the passage of the Nineteenth Amendment; and one woman refused to make coffee for her boss, got fired, but ultimately was re-hired. Thus, the women's "liberation" movement was born along with the less radical women's "rights" movement. By 1970 the spreading women's movement consisted of many groups that could not agree on the most basic goals: liberal feminists of NOW felt women needed to overcome their brainwashing to fulfill their potential; radical feminists believed women needed to fight the active oppression by all men; and separatist lesbian groups' answer to sexism was withdrawal from the playing field.

Despite the many crippling splits and differences among feminists, "mainstream" feminism increasingly complicated its early "simple" political goals of equity and equality in public life. As the women's liberation movement gained strength by the early 1970s, it began to take issues previously only privately discussed into the public arena. Feminists demanded freedom from the yoke of biology in the form of contraception, access to child care, wages for housework, and the right to decide whether to carry to term or not. Women, they argued, should not die from illegal back-alley abortions simply because they happened to be the ones who get pregnant. From 1969 to 1972 a Chicago underground collective performed safe, if still illegal, abortions, and women began to litigate for the right to rule their own bodies. In 1973 the Supreme Court decided in *Roe* v. *Wade* that the Constitution guarantees a right to privacy that extends to women's decisions regarding their own pregnancies in the first trimester.

However, the concept that women's personal experiences of disenfranchisement are a direct manifestation of the hierarchical power structures of society was, and continues to be, disturbing to many Americans. Feminists argued that women, of all classes and races, suffer from the same lack of social power. Thus, feminism was criticized and ridiculed from the beginning from all ends of the political spectrum. New Left and civil rights activists felt that women's "liberation" would come along with the liberation of the rest of humanity and that feminism would only dilute the power of dissent. "The only position women have in this movement," Stokely Carmichael remarked infamously, "is prone." By the mid 1970s the movement itself was driven by arguments over the middle-class white identity of many of its leading activists. Poor, lesbian, and nonwhite women felt they were excluded. At the same time an unlikely coalition of Republicans and the Christian Right began to argue that feminists undermined "family values."

With the failure of the ERA, the symbolic petering out of political feminism of the 1960s and 1970s, feminism began a period of social adjustment. Women's bodies became the most contentious political and social issue of the 1980s and into the 1990s. The conflict became most visible in the struggle over abortion rights on all levels of public discourse, including civil disobedience. Opposition against legal abortion stiffened into the Right-to-Life movement, and proponents of legal abortion united into the National Abortion Rights Action League. In the elections of the 1980s politicians had to pass a litmus test on their views on abortion. "Pro Life" activists chained themselves to clinic doors so as to close them temporarily, and in response "Pro Choice" groups tried to get there earlier to keep them away. Finally, after clinics had been bombed and abortion providers murdered, the Supreme Court upheld *Roe* v. *Wade* in the 1992 *Planned Parenthood of Southeastern Pennsylvania* v. *Casey* and decided in 1994 that activists on both sides had to keep their distance in *Madsen* v. *Women's Health Center*. The compromise has been made based on the principle that a woman cannot be presented with an "undue burden" in obtaining a legal abortion. To date, it is an uneasy truce at best.

FRIEDAN ON FEMINISM

The problem lay buried, unspoken, for many years in the minds of American women. It was a strange stirring, a sense of dissatisfaction, a yearning that women suffered in the middle of the twentieth century in the United States. Each suburban housewife struggled with it alone. As she made the bed, shopped for groceries, matched slipcover material, ate peanut butter sandwiches with her children, chauffeured Cub Scouts and Brownies, lay beside her husband at night—she was afraid to ask even of herself the silent question—"Is this all?"

For over fifteen years there was no word of this yearning in the millions of words written about women, for women, in all the columns, books and articles by experts telling women their role was to seek fulfillment as wives and mothers. Over and over women heard in voices of tradition and of Freudian sophistication that they could desire no greater destiny than to glory in their own femininity. . . . All they had to do was devote their lives from earliest girlhood to finding a husband and bearing children. . . .

If I am right, the problem that has no name stirring in the minds of so many American women today is not a matter of loss of femininity or too much education, or the demands of domesticity. It is far more important than anyone recognizes. It is the key to these other new and old problems which have been torturing women and their husbands and children, and puzzling their doctors and educators for years. It may well be the key to our future as a nation and a culture. We can no longer ignore that voice within women that says: "I want something more than my husband and my children and my home."

Source: *Betty Friedan,* The Feminine Mystique *(New York: Norton, 1963).*

Some experienced the period since 1980 as dominated by "backlash" against feminist ideas. Others, on the contrary, found it marked by far-reaching institutionalization of feminist social mores. Many men and women felt that feminists had gone too far in taking the private into the public eye, that the seriousness of "real" rape or sexual harassment in the workplace was being diluted. Camille Paglia gained national notoriety railing against those attempts to control the "messy biological business-as-usual that is going on within us and without us at every hour of every day." Society, she argued in *Sexual Personae: Art and Decadence from Nefertiti to Emily Dickinson* (1990), is our "frail barrier against Nature," protecting us from the darker imperatives of biology. Culture is our "defense against female nature," which is why women have been shifted "into the nether realm" in Western culture. Though "woman has a right to seize what she will and to vie with man on his own terms," she is limited in doing so by nature. Feminism, therefore, should not try to push beyond "its proper mission of seeking political equality." With a deterministic biological Freudianism that had all but been abandoned by most Americans, Paglia was putting the horse behind the cart. The extreme objectification of women's bodies in an increasingly consumption-driven culture had already created some interesting realignments. Phyllis Schlafly, as well as Andrea Dworkin, who called Schlafly "the Right's not-born-again philosopher of the absurd," both agitated against pornography. Feminist Naomi Wolf denounced the emphasis on beauty that cripples women's self-image in *The Beauty Myth: How Images of Beauty Are Used Against Women* (1991), and Wendy Shalit called for *A Return to Modesty: Discovering the Lost Virtue* (1999), both authors attempting to bolster women's self-esteem.

Despite political and social opposition, the feminist movement had pushed previously "private" issues into the public eye. Once there, however, the feminist concept that "sex is power" took on a life of its own in a world of competing media. "Sex" became the "power" to sell air time. Sexual harassment cases, as well as lurid scandals, garnered national publicity–and here the courts were busy, too. The wrangle over surrogate motherhood in the 1987–1988 Baby M case, the U.S. Navy's investigation of harassment of female officers at the 1991 Tailhook Association Conference, Senate hearings that pitted Anita Hill against Clarence Thomas, Paula Jones's charges against President William J. Clinton, and ultimately his affair with Monica Lewinksy–all resulted in the public airing of views on the legal aspects of the relationship between men and women. Neither feminists nor anti-feminists were happy–but the culture wanted, if not sensation, some clarity on questions ranging from the "war between the sexes" to issues of privacy, public accountability, and the normativeness of the nuclear family. "Women's lib" agitation, as well as the backlash against the ERA and legal abortion, tackled issues that were in flux in society and forced them out into the open. Domestic ideology of the 1950s posited women at the heart of a family that was ceasing to exist. Not only had women worked outside the home in increasing numbers since well before the turn of the century, children and husband were not gathered around the dining room table either. The period between the 1954 *Brown* v. *Board of Education of Topeka, Kansas* Supreme Court decision and the "losing" of the ERA saw de jure, if not de facto, extension of civil-rights legislation to all individuals. The issues discussed were and are large social developments and have to do with the changing nature of American social relations and structures in a postindustrial, extremely urban, and economically polarized world. This situation has become abundantly clear in the 1990s, when the "larger" legal issues of women's rights and duties have been replaced in public discourse by questions that tackle the limits of state involvement in the regulation of relationships between people. When Hill charged Thomas with sexual misconduct, she was not charging him for a crime committed (she did not go to the police), but she argued that he was not fit to be a Supreme Court Justice because he did not keep within limits of legal and social acceptance for conduct in the workplace.

Feminism is one manifestation of a two-hundred-year trend toward individualization–of a redefinition of society as made up of individuals rather than the eighteenth-century extended household that often included slaves or servants and the nineteenth- and twentieth-century nuclear families. The world looked much different in the everyday lives of women in 1760 or 1860 than it did in 1960. Poverty was not erased and was still a gender issue–and continues to be now more than ever. Rape has not been erased, but women have a way to name it and fight to obtain justice from their tormentors when it happens. Safe and legal abortion is more available than it was in the 1960s–though much less so than it was in the 1970s. The new chastity brought on by AIDS may have undone some of the more heinous aspects of the sexual revolution that divided feminists–without bringing back shame. Mothers who have ended up on government assistance are increasingly forced to work towards employment–no one, least of all the political right, would suggest that they ought to stay home with their children at all times. And "I am a feminist" has remained a militant statement; not surprisingly, many young women of the late 1990s refuse to be called feminists, even as they won the World Cup in soccer and embrace most of the ideas of the movement.

–PLEUN BOURICIUS, HARVARD UNIVERSITY

References

Eugene R. August, ed., *The New Men's Studies: A Selected and Annotated Interdisciplinary Bibliography* (Englewood, Colo.: Libraries Unlimited, 1985);

Johanna Brenner and Maria Rama, "Rethinking Women's Oppression," *New Left Review,* 144 (March–April 1984): 33–71;

Nicholas Davidson, *The Failure of Feminism* (Buffalo, N.Y.: Prometheus, 1988);

Rene Denfeld, *The New Victorians: A Young Woman's Challenge to the Old Feminist Order* (New York: Warner Books, 1995);

Andrea Dworkin, *Right-Wing Women* (New York: Coward, McCann, 1983);

Alice Echols, *Daring to be Bad: Radical Feminism in America, 1967–1975* (Minneapolis: University of Minnesota Press, 1989);

John M. Ellis, *Literature Lost: Social Agendas and the Corruption of the Humanities* (New Haven: Yale University Press, 1997);

Jean Bethke Elshtain, *Women and War* (New York: BasicBooks, 1987);

Sara Evans, *Personal Politics: The Roots of Women's Liberation in the Civil Rights Movement and the New Left* (New York: Knopf, 1979);

Susan Faludi, *Backlash: The Undeclared War Against American Women* (New York: Crown, 1991);

Sondra Farganis, *Situating Feminism: From Thought to Action* (Thousand Oaks, Cal.: Sage, 1994):

Warren Farrell, *The Myth of Male Power: Why Men Are the Disposable Sex* (New York: Simon & Schuster, 1993);

Shulamith Firestone, *The Dialectic of Sex: The Case for Feminist Revolution* (New York: Morrow, 1970);

Elizabeth Fox-Genovese, *Feminism is not the Story of My Life: How Today's Feminist Elite Has Lost Touch with the Real Concerns of Women* (New York: Nan A. Talese, 1996);

Betty Friedan, *The Feminine Mystique* (New York: Norton, 1963);

Friedan, *The Second Stage* (New York: Summit, 1981);

Friedan, "Sex, Society and the Female Dilemma: A Dialogue Between Simone de Beauvoir and Betty Friedan," *Saturday Review* (14 June 1975);

Sandra Harding, *The Science Question in Feminism* (Ithaca, N.Y.: Cornell University Press, 1986);

Bell Hooks, *Ain't I a Woman: Black Women and Feminism* (Boston: South End Press, 1981);

Angela Howard and Sasha Ranaé Adams Tarrant, eds., *Reaction to the Modern Women's Movement, 1963 to the Present* (New York: Garland, 1997);

Gloria T. Hull, Patricia Bell Scott, and Barbara Smith, eds., *All the Women are White, All the Blacks are Men, But Some of Us are Brave: Black Women's Studies* (Old Westbury, N.Y.: Feminist Press, 1982);

Cassandra L. Langer, *A Feminist Critique: How Feminism has Changed American Society, Culture, and How We Live from the 1940s to the Present* (New York: Icon, 1996);

Blanche Linden-Ward and Carol Hurd Green, *American Women in the 1960s: Changing the Future* (New York: Twayne, 1993);

Catharine MacKinnon, "Feminism, Marxism, Method, and the State: Towards Feminist Jurisprudence," in *Feminism and Methodology: Social Science Issues,* edited by Sandra Harding (Bloomington: Indiana University Press, 1987);

MacKinnon and Andrea Dworkin, eds., *In Harm's Way: The Pornography Civil Rights Hearings* (Cambridge, Mass.: Harvard University Press, 1997);

Jane J. Mansbridge, *Why We Lost the ERA* (Chicago: University of Chicago Press, 1986);

Susan McClary, *Feminine Endings: Music, Gender, and Sexuality* (Minneapolis: University of Minnesota, 1991);

Robin Morgan, *Sisterhood is Powerful: An Anthology of Writings From the Women's Liberation Movement* (New York: Random House, 1970);

Camille Paglia, *Sex, Art, and American Culture: Essays* (New York: Vintage, 1992);

Paglia, *Sexual Personae: Art and Decadence From Nefertiti to Emily Dickinson* (New Haven: Yale University Press, 1990);

Paglia, *Vamps & Tramps: New Essays* (New York: Vintage, 1994);

Daphne Patai and Noretta Koertge, *Professing Feminism: Cautionary Tales from the Strange World of Women's Studies* (New York: BasicBooks, 1994);

Katie Roiphe, *The Morning After: Sex, Fear, and Feminism on Campus* (Boston: Little, Brown, 1993);

Alice S. Rossi, ed., *The Feminist Papers: From Adams to de Beauvoir* (New York: Columbia University Press, 1973);

Phyllis Schlafly, *The Power of the Positive Woman* (New Rochelle, N.Y.: Arlington House, 1977);

Wendy Shalit, *A Return to Modesty: Discovering the Lost Virtue* (New York: Free Press, 1999);

Christina Hoff Sommers, *Who Stole Feminism?: How Women Have Betrayed Women* (New York: Simon & Schuster, 1994);

Naomi Wolf, *The Beauty Myth: How Images of Beauty Are Used Against Women* (New York: Morrow, 1991);

Judith P. Zinsser, *History and Feminism: A Glass Half Full* (New York: Twayne, 1993).

GENETIC ENGINEERING

Has genetic engineering benefited agriculture?

Viewpoint: Yes, scientific manipulation of genetic material in plants and animals has benefited agricultural yields and quality, enhancing the economy.

Viewpoint: No, genetic engineering has not benefited agriculture; it poses grave dangers to nature and civilization.

Will genetic engineering of plants and animals benefit agriculture? No scientific development offers more promise than genetic engineering, which is a major breakthrough of the twentieth century. By restructuring a plant or an animal's genetic code scientists can stimulate growth and eliminate either wasteful or problematic tendencies. Today farmers can grow pigs the size of bulls, ears of corn that are immune to pests, and sheep whose wool pulls off effortlessly.

Many things are possible. However, are they either likely or desirable? In these two essays, agricultural scholar Elizabeth D. Schafer points to the potential and realized benefits of genetic engineering, while Robert J. Allison looks at the potential problems with the entire project.

While genetic engineering of one kind or another has been practiced for centuries through selective breeding of cattle, horses, pigs, and sheep and cultivation, cross-fertilization, and hybridization of certain crops, the kind of intrusion Schafer and Allison discuss is a recent phenomenon. In the early twentieth century scientists discovered that all living things contained in their cells deoxyribonucleic acid (DNA), which determines their size, shape, and character. After World War II the Atomic Energy Commission commissioned scientists to study the effects nuclear radiation would have on all forms of life. In 1953 two of the scientists engaged in the study, James Watson and Francis Crick, discovered the structure of DNA as a double helix of two long strands intertwined. Each strand contains genetic information to create the living creature in whose cell we find the DNA. Over the next decades studies showed how the DNA replicates itself, creating new living creatures with characteristics similar to those of the parents. By the 1970s scientists were learning how to use DNA to create new life artificially, or how to combine DNA molecules to create even new forms of life.

That manipulating DNA is an amazing process is beyond question; that it has the potential to revolutionize life itself is obvious. It can do all that scientists say it can do. Yet, is it worth the risks? Schafer points to the potential benefits and argues that these outweigh the risks. Allison points to the risks, and argues that these outweigh the potential benefits. The dispute is not merely one between historians; it is between two competing views on the nature of life and on the trustworthiness of human beings. Readers such as you must make an informed decision.

Viewpoint: Yes, scientific manipulation of genetic material in plants and animals has benefited agricultural yields and quality, enhancing the economy.

Throughout the twentieth century agriculturists have used genetic engineering methods to improve plants and livestock. In the early 1900s selective breeding experiments resulted in the establishment of hybrid crops that were the foundation for the formation of lucrative seed companies and financial security for many farmers and agribusiness investors. By the 1980s more-sophisticated genetic engineering techniques created new types of plants and microbes, as well as altered traditional practices of livestock breeding. These developments were the catalyst for million-dollar agricultural genetic corporations that accelerated the transformation of agriculture from subsistence to commercial production. Few historians have addressed how the genetic engineering phenomenon has affected American agriculture.

The history of agricultural science has been limited by the reluctance of historians of science and technology and of agriculture to explore overlapping areas. Deborah Fitzgerald, a scholar who has breached this gap, explains that some historians consider the study of scientific applications to agriculture too practical and nonintellectual to be of scholarly interest. Fitzgerald's analysis of the development of hybrid corn in the early twentieth century examines early efforts to manipulate genetics to benefit agriculture. While many scholars, including Fitzgerald, criticize aspects of genetic engineering of agricultural crops and livestock as being potentially harmful to human consumers and the environment, several historians such as Fitzgerald also highlight the accomplishments of genetic engineering.

Because genes are the foundation of all living organisms, comprehension of genetic material and its behavior is essential to understand how animals and plants reproduce, grow, and function. During the nineteenth and early twentieth centuries, American farmers practically select the best plants and animals as breeding stock, carefully choosing matches between different breeds to reinforce strength and stamina in livestock and sturdiness and vigor in plants. Inferior livestock were slaughtered, sterilized, or used for nonbreeding tasks. Plants considered to have weaknesses and deficiencies were culled from fields. Through such selective measures, farmers developed herds and crops with valued qualities. In addition to selling increased amounts of enriched seed, meat, and milk, farmers earned money when neighbors used their male livestock for breeding.

Cloned corn plants raised from tissue samples

(Calgene, Inc.)

Around 1900, American scientists became aware of Austrian botanist Gregor Mendel's discoveries concerning the inheritance of traits in plant breeding. Botanists at agricultural colleges and scientific institutions began experimenting with corn to interpret how different qualities such as height, number of ears, and kernel size were passed from one generation to the next. Interested in scientific laws that regulated heredity, these scientists were not motivated to apply their results to solve agricultural problems. Farmers, on the other hand, eagerly reinforced their practical breeding plans with such knowledge in order to increase profits. Growing quickly and yielding more bushels per acre than regular corn, hybrid corn genetically improved every year because of scientists' and farmers' efforts. In 1908 corn was America's most valuable crop, adding $1,615,000,000 to the economy. U.S. Secretary of Agriculture James Wilson declared, "This wealth that has grown out of the soil in four months of rain and sunshine, and some drought, too, is enough to cancel the interest-bearing debt of the United States and to pay for the Panama Canal and fifty battle ships."

The United States has led other nations in bioengineering research and is the greatest producer of genetically altered crops. Most genetically engineered agriculture in America results from the recombination of a molecule of deoxyribonucleic acid (DNA). Cells contain chromosomes that each have a coil of DNA consisting of two strands chemically bonded to each other like a zipper. These DNA strands have thousands of genes that determine an organism's traits and functions. For example, genes regulate how much protein bread has and how much milk cows produce. They provide instructions for growth and biochemical activity in an organism. In a process called biotechnology, humans can modify these instructions with engineering methods to change the genetic composition of an organism. Individual genes can be removed from one DNA strand and spliced into another in a process geneticists refer to as recombination. Through controlled genetic manipulation of seeds and embryos, scientists can attempt to create plants and animals to meet consumer specifications.

In 1981 researchers employed by Monsanto, and its subsidiary Genentech, genetically developed a bovine growth hormone to increase the size of beef cattle that had more meat and ate less feed. That same year, United States Department of Agriculture (USDA) researchers genetically devised a vaccine for foot-and-mouth disease. Other USDA scientists successfully transferred a gene from a French bean plant to a sunflower cell, creating what was called a sunbean. These genetic agricultural innovations surpassed results from previous hybrid strains of plants and animals, suggesting unlimited combinations of genetic material to perform different functions and meet varied demands. With every new insight, the genetic base for further recombination was enhanced, and laboratory-designed agriculture introduced options previously unconsidered.

Researchers realized they could move genes between species and developed such crosses as broccolini from broccoli and Chinese kale, the pomato from potatoes and tomatoes, and the geep, a cross between a goat and a sheep. Genetically modified cotton is used in blue jeans. Special tomatoes are bred for spaghetti sauce, and altered corn is utilized for cereal, chips, and corn syrup for sodas. Cloning plants and animals allows a high-quality specimen to be replicated. Uniformity of genetically altered crops enables agricultural producers to meet demand for certain expectations and standards in foods. Consumers can purchase fruits, vegetables, meats, and other agricultural produce designed to be certain shapes, colors, sizes, sweetness, juiciness, firmness, and attractiveness. Genetically altered foods are common to Americans' diet, including corn, rice, oats, potatoes, pumpkins, tomatoes, black currants, and durum wheat. The fast-food restaurant chain McDonald's relies on the genetically designed Russet Burbank potato, which proportionally consists of more solids than water, resulting in crispy, flavorful fries. McDonald's has exported this potato worldwide for franchises to use.

Many organisms that are not closely related share genetic similarities, and scientists have learned how to transfer qualities such as disease resistance from one plant or animal to another and to remove undesirable traits from the genetic structure. These genes are then transmitted to future offspring. Genetics allows researchers to attempt to attain perfection of agricultural goods to be reproduced in great quantities. Seed banks preserve kernels and sperm banks store frozen semen of exceptional strains. The USDA estimates that genetic improvements are responsible for one billion dollars worth of crops harvested annually in the United States. Through increased yields, genetically engineered food provides not only an abundance of foodstuffs but also plenty of protein-rich nutrients to enhance diets. Biotechnology also has medicinal qualities, creating agriculturally based pharmaceuticals that offer new ways to combat diseases.

Historians stress the physical benefits of genetic engineering to agriculture. They explain that genetically engineered plants are more nutritional, tastier, and easier to process. Through genetically engineered biological controls, these plants can endure more environmental stresses such as drought, frost, and heat than nongenetically altered crops. Because of gene manipulation, plants can withstand extremes of salinity in soil, and some modified plants require minimal water to thrive. Genetically enhanced plant strains can resist diseases, viruses, bacteria, weeds, and insects, requiring less application of chemicals and pesticides harmful to the environment, humans, and livestock. These crops can be grown in many climates in addition to their native setting.

Biopesticides are transgenic plants with genetically programmed insecticides such as seeds that have poisons to kill pests that nibble on them. Corn has been genetically modified to produce a toxin in its tissues to protect it from insects. Known as Bt corn, one strain of pest-resistant corn introduced in 1996 accounts for almost twenty million acres of the nation's total eighty-million-acre corn crop. Bt corn has a gene from the bacterium *Bacillus thuringiensis* that kills corn borers that attempt to consume the plant. This internal, genetically designed regulation saves crops worth hundreds of millions of dollars each year, and researchers have also developed Bt potatoes and cotton. Instead of farmers spraying crops at specific times in the corn borers' life cycle, they can save time by planting corn that will automatically defend itself against predators when needed.

Similar achievements have been attained for livestock. Hybrid poultry, cattle, horses, sheep, and goats were developed by American farmers who culled their livestock in the same way they had carefully selected corn breeding stock. Scientists expanded these practical developments with more sophisticated laboratory procedures. Biotechnology allows researchers to breed some livestock resistant to diseases, which eliminates the need for costly vaccines and antibiotics. Also, genetically modified livestock eat less feed while producing more eggs, milk, and meat. Artificial insemination and implantation of genetically modified embryos allow livestock breeders to harvest the eggs of superior female livestock so they can produce multiple offspring per year instead of one or two babies. Frozen semen enables select stallions and bulls to father hundreds of offspring in an unlimited geographical area. Genetic engineering can be utilized to select the gender of these embryos. Implanted embryos also develop immunities to diseases to which the host mother has been exposed.

Scholars note the importance of genetically engineered agriculture as American farms become larger in size and fewer in number. As fewer people farm for a living, biotechnology eases labor requirements by eliminating the amount of time needed per acre or animal. Commercial farms consisting of hundreds and thousands of acres supporting thousands of hogs, chickens, and plants dominate American agriculture, thriving from profits from high-yielding, genetically altered crops. Some historians say that biotechnology has made farming more stable by ensuring continuity of uniform quality and quantity of produce. They also note that farming on such a large scale requires similarities of plants and animals in order to maintain everything equitably.

Ending starvation globally is perhaps the most convincing argument scholars stress to promote genetic engineering of crops in the United States. After World War II the global population increased rapidly, and Paul Erlich, an environmentalist, predicted that mass starvation would occur because the supply of food produced could not meet demand. Norman E. Borlaug, a plant pathologist from Iowa, used genetics to create a strain of high-yield dwarf spring wheat that he hoped would prevent starvation because it contained crucial calories and nutrients. Traveling to Third World nations including India in the 1960s, Borlaug distributed genetically modified seed and educated people about high-yield agricultural techniques. He defended high-yield agriculture, saying that growing more wheat on already available acreage would protect vulnerable habitats from slash-and-burn techniques traditionally used to clear additional farmland. During the first season, yields increased approximately 70 percent because of the genetically designed wheat. Pakistan became agriculturally self-sufficient by 1968, increasing its yields from 3.4 million tons of wheat in 1963 to 18 million tons by 1997. Yields in India soared from 11 million tons to 60 million tons, and that country exported surplus wheat for profit. Borlaug's genetically engineered expansion of food production saved hundreds of millions of people from starvation, and he won the Nobel Prize in 1970.

Biotechnology has provided wealth and power to agribusinesses and investors who profit from seed sales and exports worth millions of dollars, in addition to other genetically derived agricultural commodities. As the United States was transformed into an urban nation of consumers, commercial farms relying on biotechnology assured a high quality and quantity of food and clothing. Genetically engineered crops have also boosted the implement industry, which has developed special tools to process biotechnology. For example, tomato-harvesting machinery carefully pick tomatoes bred to mature at certain sizes. Colleges and research institutions have benefited from government and private funding for future agrigenetic projects, and corporations have become giants in the field, earning millions of dollars from patented genetically modified foodstuffs and techniques that are the intellectual property of industrial researchers. In 1998, 69.5 million acres internationally were cultivated with crops developed with recombinant DNA methods. These were primarily commercial crops of soybeans, cotton, corn, and oilseed rape and comprised 99 percent of global crops. As the amount of arable land dwindles and the world population continues to grow, genetic engineering offers innovative solutions to meet future challenges concerning agriculture and its consumers.

–ELIZABETH D. SCHAFER, LOACHAPOKA, ALABAMA

Viewpoint:
No, genetic engineering has not benefited agriculture; it poses grave dangers to nature and civilization.

Agricultural technology, the genetic engineering of plants and animals, promises much. It can increase the yields of crops, make them resistant to disease and drought, and make plants and animals grow bigger and faster. This technology can benefit farmers, who will be able to produce more without threatened destruction by forces of nature, and consumers, who will have a more abundant supply of food at a lower price. Globally, genetic engineering promises to end famine. It is a noble promise.

Perhaps genetic engineering can accomplish these things. We know that genetic manipulation–which has been going on ever since men and women began cultivating crops–can increase crop yields. The decision to plant one seed instead of another, crossbreeding of plants and animals, and other kinds of manipulation are all attempts by humans to change the balance of nature. Genetic engineering, though, as a scientific phenomenon, began in earnest after World War II; though its guiding principle is the same as Gregor Mendel's, its results can be much more dramatic and its implications more alarming.

There are four main arguments against genetic engineering. First is the moral argument: that tampering with genetic material, while it might be scientifically possible, is not morally responsible. It is taking into mortal hands a power men and women are not morally capable of exercising. This premise leads to the second argument, that people who wield a power they do not understand risk being destroyed by it. This message is conveyed to us by thousands of years of human experience, from the ancient stories of Adam and Eve, who ate of the tree that would make them like God and were punished for it; to the story of Daedalus and Icarus, who tried to fly; to Mary Shelley's *Frankenstein, or, the Modern Prometheus* (1818), a cautionary tale about trying to create life. These stories are instructive, but to scientific-minded proponents of genetic engineering they would seem like so many folktales. There are, however, additional reasons, economic and political, that should sway even the most staunch supporter of biological manipulation.

At the end of the nineteenth century, American farmers felt pressed by the new technological age. They depended on railroads to get their goods to market, and the owners of railroads wielded more political power than farmers, who had been at the center of the American political system. But by 1890 farmers were no longer central, and they reacted by forming the Populist Party. The technological revolution accelerated, and farmers lost more ground. By 1950, 25 percent of the American population lived in two thousand rural counties. By 1977, less than 4 percent of Americans lived in rural counties, and there were only 673 rural counties left. By 1988, fewer Americans lived on farms than had in 1820, when more than one-half of the American workforce was employed in agriculture. By 1988, 2 percent of the American people lived on farms. At every stage of development, advances in technology have meant good news for agriculture, bad news for farmers. The McCormick Reaper freed farmers from the backbreaking work of harvesting but also made it economically efficient to plant more acreage, and thus farmers who did not expand their holdings were crushed by their larger neighbors. It also meant that seasonal workers who might be able to find temporary day labor at peak times during the agricultural season were no longer needed. In good times these workers could migrate to cities and get manufacturing jobs; in bad times they, like other industrial workers, were unemployed. Railroads and mechanical harvesters made agriculture more efficient, but they squeezed out smaller farmers.

Improvements in agricultural technology have hurt farmers in a more fundamental way, by driving down the price of their crops. Being able to produce more at a lower cost meant that prices fell, so farmers found themselves producing more than had ever been achieved, and being paid less for it. This situation also had the effect of driving them off the farm, and the number of farmers as part of the general population fell precipitously from 1890 to 1930. The Great Depression, according to Herbert Hoover, was caused in part by this farm problem, and it accelerated the trend of forcing families off the farms. The Dust Bowl of the 1930s, the drought that destroyed much of the agricultural area of the Great Plains, was caused in part by overproduction, which depleted topsoil and eliminated the native grasses that had held the topsoil in place.

The history of agricultural improvements, which have all but eliminated farmers, should caution us about the claims of biotechnology. It is also important to remember that the promoters of biotechnology are often the same companies who have brought this economic havoc to America's farmland. Seed and pesticide companies have been at the forefront of biotechnological research. It is in their interest to sell products to farmers. The pesticide companies present an interesting example of innovation. The same companies who produced DDT and other deadly toxins, some of which were banned after driving some species of plants or animals to extinction, now are experimenting with genetic engineering to make plants resistant to insects. When DDT and other chemicals were first marketed, the promise was that these would eliminate insects that ate plants. Little was said at the time about the consequences for other forms of wildlife who might eat the poisoned insects, or about the consequences for humans who ingested DDT, or about the long-term damage to soils on which plants treated with DDT or other chemicals were grown. It was enough to promise higher yields, and the potential dangers were considered minimal, or the cost of progress. When enlightened and alarmed citizens protested, at first they were dismissed as naive cranks or know-nothing nature nuts. As evidence accumulated about how dangerous these chemicals are, it still took unrelenting public pressure to have the chemical companies remove them from the market.

This experience was similar to that which occurred with nuclear power, which promised to free humans from the hazards of coal, oil, or natural gas. The potential perils were considered negligible and unlikely until accidents at Three Mile Island (1979) and Chernobyl (1986) revealed how dangerous this fuel is. Genetic engineering, like DDT and nuclear power, is potentially fatal. The nuclear incidents, the Exxon Valdez oil spill (1989), and the deadly chemical release at Bhopal, India (1984), were big and ugly accidents. Every day, though, there are smaller accidents that release toxins into the environment. In New York State there were one thousand reported toxic accidents in 1987. Accidents involving chemicals can be cleaned up, the survivors treated and the dead buried. But what happens in a genetic accident? How long will it take us to understand the consequences, or even to know what all the consequences are?

As for the argument that genetic engineering can eliminate world hunger, history seems to suggest otherwise. Have the agricultural improvements of the past one hundred years abated world hunger? Or, by making it possible to grow certain crops in areas that were not meant for agriculture, and by increasing yields of crops, have these improvements not made hunger a more severe problem? It is instructive now to remember the gloomy caution of Robert Malthus, the British economist whose visit to India in the 1790s transformed his outlook on the ideas of progress. As agricultural yields increased, Malthus predicted, population would also increase. However, population would increase much more rapidly than agricultural production could, so the end result would be mass starvation. For example, in China the population had hovered at about 150 million until about 1650, when the introduction of new crops from the Americas, chiefly potatoes and corn, allowed greater yields of calories per acre, and the population began to increase, doubling by 1850, doubling again by 1950, and almost doubling again since 1950. This accelerating population growth shows the problem of expecting genetic technology to feed a population. Feeding existing populations is not the issue. A population will not remain stable; if fed it will grow. Malthus's dire predictions may upset notions of what is nice, but this reality must be taken into account: by further expanding the food supply greater population growth is encouraged, leaving future generations with the prospect of starvation.

In the 1990s there have been major famines in Africa and parts of Asia, where population growth has accelerated beyond the capacity of the area to produce food. Instead of producing more on less ground, the agricultural revolution so far has extended the sphere of cultivation, destroying the rain forest or other natural barriers to erosion and depleting levels of topsoil. These various problems reveal the disaster that awaits those who tamper with nature. Progressive thinkers in 1600 may have imagined that by introducing corn and potatoes into China they were going to alleviate hunger among that nation's 150 million people. They most likely did not foresee how their innovation would prompt a population explosion that would reach more than one billion. This change, too, involves merely taking a plant that grows in one place and planting it in another. Imagine the consequences of creating an entirely new species, whose long-term effects no one can predict.

The agricultural revolution of the past forty years has not ended hunger, but seems to have made the problem worse. It could be a natural phenomenon, or it could be a problem in distribution. Biotechnological products are not inexpensive: they are the result of tremendous research and experimentation. Thus they are controlled by corporations who can afford to manufacture them, and these corporations do not, as a rule, make things for the sake of satisfying either scientific curiosity or world hunger. An instructive example comes from the use of genetic technology to create vaccines. The World Health Organization (WHO) sponsored research into malaria vaccines at New York University, and after the development of a genetically engineered

THE USDA AND THE POTATO

In December 1994 the U.S. Department of Agriculture asked the public for comments on a petition for a determination of nonregulated status for potatoes that are genetically engineered for resistance to the Colorado potato beetle.

Monsanto Company, St. Louis, Mo., has asked to produce its genetically engineered potato without securing further USDA permits or acknowledged notifications, according to John Payne, acting director for biotechnology, biologics and environmental protection in USDA's Animal and Plant Health Inspection Service.

"After reviewing information submitted by Monsanto, as well as other relevant data and public comments, we'll determine whether it is appropriate to approve or deny the request that we no longer regulate this potato," Payne said.

The potato is currently regulated because it contains gene sequences derived from plant pathogenic sources. The potato was field tested at 34 locations under nine USDA permits issued between 1991 and 1993.

Payne said that USDA regulators have the responsibility to assure that in releasing any bioengineered plant, no plant pest risk is presented. APHIS reviewers focus on the biology, propagation and cultivation of the plant. The reviewers examine the source of the engineered genes, the method used to transfer them, and the stability of the genetic insertion.

In the process of reviewing applications for field tests with the potato, APHIS reviewers determined that the vectors and other elements used did not present a plant pest risk. In the current review process, USDA regulators will inspect all the data. . . .

Source: USDA Press Release No. 0929.94, *9 December 1994.*

product, the WHO approached Genentech to manufacture the vaccine. Genentech was not interested unless their company would have exclusive rights to market the vaccine. The WHO wanted the vaccine widely distributed to help eradicate the disease; Genentech, a private corporation, wanted to make a profit. The two organizations had different goals. WHO seeks to end diseases; Genentech, to sell products. A corporation such as Genentech, or any manufacturer of genetic materials, is not, and does not need to be, interested in the broader goals of ending hunger and disease or achieving world peace. As individuals the men and women in the company may wish for these things, but as corporate policy they are not mandated to work for them. Expecting, then, that the manufacturers of genetic products will use their resources to end hunger is naive at best.

Hunger has persisted despite the agricultural revolution. Either the problem is one of distribution, of corporate control of resources, or of climates favoring one area over another. It cannot be pretended, though, that genetic engineering, if the process is controlled by the same process that controls agriculture, will solve the problem of hunger.

–ROBERT J. ALLISON, SUFFOLK UNIVERSITY

References

Gigi M. Berardi and Charles C. Geisler, eds., *The Social Consequences and Challenges of New Agricultural Technologies* (Boulder, Colo.: Westview Press, 1984);

Robert H. Blank, *The Political Implications of Human Genetic Technology* (Boulder, Colo.: Westview Press, 1981);

Maarten J. Chrispeels and David E. Sadava, *Plants, Genes, and Agriculture* (Boston: Jones & Bartlett, 1994);

Alexander Richard Crabb, *The Hybrid-Corn Makers: Prophets of Plenty* (New Brunswick, N.J.: Rutgers University Press, 1947);

Jake Doyle, *Altered Harvest: Agriculture, Genetics, and the Fate of the World's Food Supply* (New York: Viking, 1985);

William Dudley, ed., *Genetic Engineering: Opposing Viewpoints* (San Diego: Greenhaven Press, 1990);

J. Warren Evans and Alexander Hollaender, eds., *Genetic Engineering of Animals: An Agricultural Perspective* (New York & London: Plenum Press, 1986);

Deborah Fitzgerald, *The Business of Breeding: Hybrid Corn in Illinois, 1890–1940* (Ithaca, N.Y.: Cornell University Press, 1990);

Bette Hileman, "Views Differ Sharply Over Benefits, Risks of Agricultural Biotechnology," *Chemical and Engineering News,* 73 (August 1995): 8–17;

Clive James, *Global Review of Commercialized Transgenic Crops,* ISAAA brief no. 8 (Ithaca, N.Y.: International Service for the Acquisition of Agri-biotech Applications, 1998);

Barbara A. Kimmelman, "The American Breeders' Association: Genetics and Eugenics in an Agricultural Context, 1903–1913," *Social Studies of Science,* 13 (1983): 163–204;

Jack Ralph Kloppenburg Jr., *First the Seed: The Political Economy of Plant Biotechnology, 1492–2000* (New York: Cambridge University Press, 1988);

Anatole F. Krattiger, *The Importance of Ag-biotech to Global Prosperity* (Ithaca, N.Y.: International Service for the Acquisition of Agri-biotech Applications, 1998);

Miles R. McCarry, "Doing What Comes Artificially," *Invention & Technology,* 15 (Summer 1999): 34–41;

Henry I. Miller, *Policy Controversy in Biotechnology: An Insider's View* (Austin, Texas: Landes, 1997);

Miller, "A Rational Approach to Labeling Biotech-Derived Foods," *Science,* 284 (28 May 1999): 1471–1472;

Joseph J. Molnar and Henry W. Kinnucan, eds., *Biotechnology and the New Agricultural Revolution* (Boulder, Colo.: Westview Press for the American Association for the Advancement of Science, Washington, D.C., 1989);

Meran R. L. Owen and Jan Pen, eds., *Transgenic Plants: A Production System for Industrial and Pharmaceutical Proteins* (New York: J. Wiley, 1996);

Kenneth O. Rachie and Judith M. Lyman, eds., *Genetic Engineering for Crop Improvement: A Rockefeller Conference, May 12–15, 1980* (New York: Rockefeller Foundation, 1981);

Paul Raeburn, *The Last Harvest: The Genetic Gamble That Threatens to Destroy American Agriculture* (New York: Simon & Schuster, 1995);

Jeremy Rifkin and Nicanor Perlas, *Algeny* (New York: Viking, 1983);

Rifkin, *Declaration of a Heretic* (Boston: Routledge & Kegan Paul, 1985);

Carol Kaesuk Yoon, "Pollen From Genetically Altered Corn Threatens Monarch Butterfly, Study Finds," *New York Times,* 20 May 1999.

GOALS OF CIVIL RIGHTS

What were the goals of the Civil Rights movement?

Viewpoint: The Civil Rights movement is justly celebrated for its attempt to integrate Americans into the promise of American society.

Viewpoint: Black nationalists offered a powerful critique not only of American society but also of African-American leaders, who attempted to bring their people into a society that would not treat them with respect.

What were the goals of the Civil Rights movement? "Black and white together" the marchers sang in their anthem, "We shall overcome." However, increasingly after 1964, leadership in the movement seemed to pass from the integrationist Baptist ministers to more-radical and, to white Americans, more-threatening figures, such as the Black Panthers or the Black Muslims. What had happened? Was this a betrayal of the movement?

Christopher W. Schmidt argues that it was indeed a betrayal. The key to the movement, as it progressed from Montgomery, Alabama, to Mississippi, was the creation of a beloved community, black and white, and ultimately integration of African Americans into the mainstream of American society. The black nationalists, by polarizing the debate and rejecting the benefits of the beloved community, damaged the enterprise.

Jeffrey Ogbar, on the other hand, argues that the black nationalists were a central part of the movement, that black-nationalist ideology was not outside the purview of the civil-rights discourse. The more-militant Panthers and Muslims did have a different perspective from Martin Luther King Jr. and the Baptist ministers, but both shared a fundamental sense of injustice in American society. King understood the critique the Muslims and Panthers offered of American society, though he did not share all their bitterness. Ogbar argues that the nationalist strain in black Americans runs deep, that it predates both the Panthers and the Civil Rights movement, and that it is in fact part of the American identity.

By understanding the goals of both King and the Southern Christian Leadership Conference (SCLC) and Malcolm X and the more-radical black nationalists, we can understand the kind of society they tried to change, as well as the society each hoped to create.

Viewpoint: The Civil Rights movement is justly celebrated for its attempt to integrate Americans into the promise of American society.

Much of the debate over the character of the Civil Rights movement derives from questions of definition. How one defines the movement itself–its major events, leaders and participants, and dates–affects one's understanding of the guiding philosophy of the movement. That is, whether it was at heart a movement for a more fully realized

A notice placed in an Atlanta store window in 1960

(Fred Powledge)

America based on the integration of all races or a movement of black nationalism and separatism based on the quest for a black existence set in opposition to the dominant American cultural and political institutions. Undoubtedly both of these strains were evident within the black community of the late 1950s and 1960s, yet what is commonly known as the Civil Rights movement for most of this period had a distinctively integrationist character that set it apart from other movements of black activism, such as Marcus Garvey's "Back to Africa" campaign of the 1920s or the Black Power movement of the later 1960s and early 1970s. To appreciate the accomplishments and failures of the Civil Rights movement, it must be viewed, in all its idealism, as a movement to change America, black and white.

Three events, more than any others, established the direction of the movement–and of the varying, oftentimes contesting, methods of achieving these goals: the 1954 Supreme Court decision *Brown* v. *Board of Education of Topeka, Kansas,* the Montgomery Bus Boycott of 1955–1956, and the 1960 student sit-in movement. Each of these events established a distinctive path toward the improvement of race relations; each developed out of diverse sources and would eventually splinter into diverging futures. For the period roughly between 1954 and 1965, however, the goals epitomized by these three events and their progeny found common ground in seeking integration through the Civil Rights movement. Similarly, two figures demonstrate the different approaches in attacking discrimination, but they both found common ground in their vision of an interracial nation. John L. Lewis, a leader of the student movement, was uncompromising in his faith in progress through nonviolent direct action and cooperation between races. Writer James Baldwin, while constantly probing the limitations of integration, always found the basis of his intellectual development in a vision of interracial possibility. These figures and events illustrate the diversity of views and methods that made up the movement, but they also represent the underlying unity of its goals.

With *Brown* the Supreme Court ended the system of state-sanctioned segregation in the South by overturning *Plessy* v. *Ferguson* (1896), which had first given the Court's approval of Jim Crow. Although Chief Justice Earl Warren carefully limited the language of the *Brown* decision to apply only to public education, it was clear that the days were numbered for legalized segregation of all forms, and the desperate, violent attempts of racist southerners to hold onto segregation only made this painfully clear to the rest of the nation. The wording of the decision clearly established the integrationist ideals of the Supreme Court. While reading the decision, Warren asked, "Does segregation of children in public schools solely on the basis of race, even though physical facilities and other 'tangible' factors may be equal, deprive the children of the minority group of equal education opportunities?" and answered to a hushed courtroom: "We believe it does." The decision marked the convergence of the efforts of the legal branch of the National Association for the Advancement of

Colored People (NAACP)—which was led by Thurgood Marshall, who would go on to be the first African American appointed to the Supreme Court—and an all-white Court willing to assert its moral authority to make a statement on racial equality. This event was a victory not only for African-American children, but also for the Constitution. The decision demonstrated that this document could still guide the nation: it demonstrated that the Constitution contained the flexibility necessary to deal with the social concerns of a diverse nation. *Brown* became a precedent for the use of the federal government to advance integrationist goals, not only in the courts but also in congressional legislation such as the Civil Rights Act of 1964 and the Voting Rights Act of 1965.

Like *Brown,* the Montgomery Bus Boycott demonstrated a faith in the possibility of reform in American society. This event initiated the direct-action phase of the movement when African-American activists, encouraged by the show of support by the Supreme Court, came together to demand their rights. The event demonstrated many of the defining characteristics of the movement: the use of powerful rhetoric to motivate and unite, the drama and inspiration of heroic action, and cooperative action between blacks and whites. The leader of this boycott was the young Martin Luther King Jr., who had recently returned to the South from his studies in the North. Here he, along with hundreds of participants in the boycott, put into action a philosophy of nonviolent protest to achieve the end of segregation on city buses. King set the tone for the movement in his address to protesters in the opening days of the boycott: "We are here in a general sense, because first and foremost—we are American citizens—and we are determined to apply our citizenship—to the fullness of its means." In the same speech King established the moral height the movement would assume: "And we are not wrong. We are not wrong in what we are doing. If we are wrong—the Supreme Court of this nation is wrong. If we are wrong—God Almighty is wrong!" Although a different approach from the legal one adopted by the NAACP, his vision of what America could be was similar to the ideals realized in the *Brown* decision. Indeed, along with the almost completely effective boycott, it was the Supreme Court that in late 1956 declared segregation in public transportation illegal and forced the authorities in Montgomery to accede to the demands of the protesters. King and others applied the techniques used in Montgomery to future civil-rights battles—the success in Birmingham in 1963 was based on unity and public spectacle, and the glorious vision of King's dream at the March on Washington touched people of all races and backgrounds.

Also inspired by the heroism of Montgomery were the participants of the student sit-in movement, which began with the attempt by four black students to eat at a segregated lunch counter in Greensboro, North Carolina, in February 1960. The students embraced King's faith in nonviolence, even integrating this belief into the name of their newly formed organization, the Student Nonviolent Coordinating Committee (SNCC). Although they adopted a less compromising position than the people behind *Brown* or the bus boycotts, their target, segregation, was the same. "Even as the scope of protest expanded to include targets other than lunch counters," writes Clayborne Carson in his *In Struggle: SNCC and the Black Awakening of the 1960s* (1981), "students continued to justify their actions by appealing to dominant political values." In the years following the sit-in movement, SNCC members became increasingly frustrated with what they viewed as the moderate approach of older civil-rights leaders, King included. Yet there is an important point in these early fissures in the unity of the movement—in the early 1960s, these were divisions of methods, not goals. Even as the students expressed their frustration with the tentativeness of established civil-rights organizations, they still worked toward realizing the dream of a new America based on the need for an integrated society. Eventually these differences expanded and this goal itself would be questioned, but not until the mid 1960s, when the Civil Rights movement had run its course.

In the countless cast of characters that made the movement, two men in particular, Lewis and Baldwin, help illustrate the dominant themes of the movement. They each expressed distinct views, often in opposition, but their ideas converged with their articulation of interracial ideals. Within the diversity of their experiences there was an underlying unity of vision, based on a basic faith in the doctrine of integration.

Lewis, in his recently published memoirs, *Walking with the Wind: A Memoir of the Movement* (1998), recounts his experiences, starting as a student activist in Nashville, Tennessee, to becoming a participant in the Freedom Rides, where he was beaten by racist southerners, to his time as chairman of SNCC. Although Lewis's commitment to nonviolence and "the Beloved Community" was exceptional in its fervor, it was by no means unusual. He was a quiet, uncompromising representative of the dominant strain of the movement in the early 1960s. At the age of twenty-three he stood on the steps of the Lincoln Memorial before two hundred thousand people, black and white, participating in the March on Washington. He had been at the center of a behind-the-scenes controversy in which leading figures of President John F. Kennedy's administration, along with other civil-rights leaders, criticized his proposed speech for being too critical of the president's civil-rights bill and too uncompromising in its language—he described the movement as a "revolution" and called for a march through the South, "the way Sherman did." Lewis eventually agreed to take out some of the most controversial language, yet even the original draft, for all the anger of its language, never wavered from the ideal of interracial cooperation. After all, the "scorched earth policy" was to be pursued "nonviolently," and the South would be broken "into a thousand pieces" only to be re-created "in the image of democracy." Lewis recalled, "Hope and harmony—that was the music of the day, that was the message."

While Lewis represented the certainties of the movement, probably the most representative voice of its complexities was Baldwin. Largely freed from the restraints of the civil-rights leaders who often had to negotiate carefully relations with other activists, both black and white, Baldwin was one of the most fiercely honest and insightful commentators on race relations in the early 1960s. He was in the unique position to comprehend the multiplicity of views permeating the intellectual climate and reflect them back to the nation in his essays and fiction. Although his later work revealed the powerful influence of black nationalist ideology, in the early 1960s he gave meaning and direction to the cacophony of ideas for racial progress through his articulations of the possibilities of interracial cooperation and of a nation with a real understanding of the meaning of love. Nowhere is this better illustrated than in his 1963 classic, *The Fire Next Time.* The essay opens with a letter to his nephew in which he states that the real meaning of "acceptance" and "integration" is not white acceptance of blacks; "The really terrible thing . . . is that *you* must accept *them.*" Baldwin's perceptive understanding of the potential attraction of black separatism never undermines his basic faith in his demanding vision of integration: "If we—and now I mean the relatively conscious whites and relatively conscious blacks, who must, like lovers, insist on, or create, the consciousness of the others—do not falter in our duty now, we may be able, handful that we are, to end the racial nightmare, and achieve our country, and change the history of the world." Although he closes with an apocalyptic vision of the costs of failure to deal with the race problem in the United States ("No more water, the fire next time!"), this language, like that of Lewis's original speech, was intended to add a sense of urgency to the need for interracial cooperation and understanding.

By understanding the central role of integration in the Civil Rights movement, one can better understand not only the unified vision contained within the significant internal tension over the way to achieve this goal but also the eventual fracturing of the movement when this unity was lost. Despite significant gains, by the mid 1960s there was an increasing sense of disillusionment with the direction of the movement. Even as the movement pointed the way to a new America, racist whites rejected any such ideas. Just two weeks after the March on Washington (1963), a bomb killed four black girls in the basement of a Birmingham church. As the beatings continued and as activists such as Medgar Evers, Michael Schwerner, Andrew Goodman, and James Chaney lost their lives for the cause, more and more people questioned the possibility of reforming American society—many questioned whether it was even worth reforming. The debate was no longer limited to discussion of means to a common end, but now the goal of an integrated American society came under increasing fire. With the solidification of these divisions, which began soon after the March on Washington and accelerated after 1965, the movement had run its course. The Black Power movement certainly owed much to its predecessor, but its underlying principles were in striking contrast to the ideals of the Beloved Community. The Civil Rights movement lived and died with the ideal of creating a new interracial America.

—CHRISTOPHER W. SCHMIDT,
HARVARD UNIVERSITY

Viewpoint: Black nationalists offered a powerful critique not only of American society but also of African-American leaders, who attempted to bring their people into a society that would not treat them with respect.

The Black Power movement was a direct outgrowth of the Civil Rights movement. The former found its inspiration in several sources and eventually developed into an important example of social, political, and cultural transformation. The effects of Black Power were profound and far-reaching in the United States. Black Power not only significantly influenced social, cultural, and political dynamics in the black community, it also affected the language, style, discourse, and activist symbolism of various ethnic groups, including Chicanos, Puerto Ricans, Native Americans, and Asian Americans, as well as whites. What emerged as a marginal and ridiculed slogan in 1966 eventually became supported by "mainstream" white and black leaders by the close of the decade, although its meaning remained contested. While some scholars and other observers have attempted to suggest that Black Power and/or black nationalism had no significant effect in the black freedom struggle, clearly Black Power not only played an important role but also became central to African American popular politics by the beginning of the 1970s. Moreover, the legacies of the Black Power movement have been ubiquitous in African-American institutional life since the 1970s.

While the Civil Rights movement unfolded primarily in the South, many African Americans in cities outside of the region had begun to gravitate to black nationalism in the early 1960s. The Nation of Islam had become the fastest growing major black organization by 1959, when its national spokesman, Minister Malcolm X, was highlighted on talk shows and news reports across the country. Its leader, Elijah Muhammad, had led the Nation from a small organization in the 1930s into a formidable national organization with name recognition in every major black community by 1960. Called the "Black Muslims" by the white press, the Nation of Islam disapproved of seeking integration with whites, instead arguing that African-American people should separate from their white oppressors and create their own nation. This was black nationalism in its purest form. Moreover, the Nation argued that it was foolish for black people to turn the other cheek to racists who beat, maimed, and terrorized black people.

By 1963 Malcolm X was the most frequently interviewed African American in the country. He was also one of the most often requested speakers on college campuses. The Nation of Islam launched its own newspaper, *Muhammad Speaks,* in 1960, which became in three years the most widely read black newspaper in the United States. By 1966 the Nation owned farms, supermarkets, cleaners, restaurants, and many other business enterprises, making it the richest African-American organization in U.S. history. It was clear that black nationalism was no marginal phenomenon, despite the fact that most African Americans were not willing to forfeit their American citizenship.

The Nation of Islam provided a two-fold contribution to the black-freedom struggle. On one front, it offered an alternative to the anti-direct action self-defense integrationists of the Civil Rights movement. Kennedy and other prominent politicians were aware that if white racists did not effectively deal with integrationists such as King, they were going to have to deal with blacks who were not convinced of the efficacy of nonviolence as King taught it. The platform, rhetoric, and tactics of pacifist civil-rights activists seemed much more attractive to white America than did the firebrand Nation of Islam and Malcolm X.

The Nation also helped lay a nationalist foundation upon which young radicals built the Black Power movement. The first major organization to argue that people of African descent were not Negroes but black people, the Nation promoted a narrow form of cultural nationalism, where blacks were inspired to abandon their European "slave" names. Moreover, the meteoric rise and popularity of Malcolm X provided young militants with an icon of resistance, courage, and radicalism that would become sacrosanct for the Black Power movement.

In June 1966, during the Meredith March Against Fear in Mississippi, civil-rights activists were beaten by police. Young militants from the Student Nonviolent Coordinating Committee (SNCC), Willie Ricks and Stokely Carmichael, explained to a crowd during the march that black people were fed up with being beaten and imprisoned by racists during attempts to achieve the justice and democracy promised by the Constitution. What blacks needed, they explained, was "black power." The term was not sufficiently defined. It meant different things to different people. But there were a few common denominators: self-definition, self-determination, and black pride. Moreover, it did not place integration at the cornerstone of black struggle, and it supported direct-action self-defense.

From the call for Black Power in June, nationalist fervor continued to grow throughout the country. Most civil-rights organizations denounced the call in the most virulent terms. Black Power was immediately criticized by King at the Meredith March and by other leaders who issued a statement titled "Crisis and Commitment" in *The New York Times,* where they declared that "we are committed to the attainment of racial justice by the democratic process." They assured the public that not all black organizations screamed such militant slogans. An outcry against Black Power also came from the largest black organization in the country, the National Baptist Convention, which issued a resolution in 1966 denouncing the slogan. President Lyndon B. Johnson lamented the new "extremism" found among advocates of Black Power and declared that "we are not interested in black power and we're not interested in white power, but we are interested in American democratic power, with a small d."

Despite the speed and vitriol with which opponents denounced Black Power, the slogan resonated throughout black America. A Black Power conference was held in the fall of 1966,

SNCC FOUNDING STATEMENT

In April 1960 at a Civil Rights conference being held in Raleigh, North Carolina, the younger members of that still-developing movement formed what was to become an important arm of their effort. Although the years would take their toll and more militant groups would pursue equality in their own ways, the founding statement of the Student Nonviolent Coordinating Committee (SNCC) remains one of the clearest summaries of the essential desire for social and political equality that served to define the Civil Rights movement as a whole.

We affirm the philosophical or religious ideal of nonviolence as the foundation of our purpose, the presupposition of our belief, and the manner of our action.

Nonviolence, as it grows from the Judeo-Christian tradition, seeks a social order of justice permeated by love. Integration of human endeavor represents the crucial first step towards such a society.

Through nonviolence, courage displaces fear. Love transcends hate. Acceptance dissipates prejudice; hope ends despair. Faith reconciles doubt. Peace dominates war. Mutual regards cancel enmity. Justice for all overthrows injustice. The redemptive community supersedes immoral social systems.

By appealing to conscience and standing on the moral nature of human existence, nonviolence nurtures the atmosphere in which reconciliation and justice become actual possibilities.

Although each local group in this movement must diligently work out the clear meaning of this statement of purpose, each act or phase of our corporate effort must reflect a genuine spirit of love and good-will.

and an organized body of clergymen broke with the National Baptist Convention, forming the National Council of Negro Churchmen (NCNC) in 1967. NCNC later issued an open letter of support for Black Power.

Because of the Civil Rights movement, historically white colleges that restricted enrollment of people of color experienced increased registration of black students after 1965. Beginning in 1967 at San Francisco State College, black students began demanding Black Power on college campuses. For them, Black Power meant increasing African-American faculty and students as well as obtaining programs for "black studies." King, Roy Wilkins of the National Association for the Advancement of Colored People (NAACP), and Whitney Young Jr. of the National Urban League all criticized the demands of student advocates of Black Power. Black studies offered no "practical" education or training, they insisted. Black student unions were attacked as "resegregation" and "Balkanization." Racially exclusive organizations and dorms turned back the clock of racial progress, claimed civil-rights leaders.

Black students did not heed the exhortations of integrationist leaders, taking over administration buildings and developing coalitions with other students of color. Soon black, Chicano, and Asian-American students in California formed the Third World Liberation Front and called for the creation of a School of Third World Studies. Profoundly affected by the militant example of Black Power advocates, Chicano and Asian-American students began demanding Chicano/Brown Power and Yellow Power, respectively.

The militant thrust of Black Power, however, was not confined to campuses. Scores of organizations claiming adherence to Black Power grabbed media attention after 1966, including the US Organization, founded by Maulana Karenga in 1965; the Black Panther Party for Self-Defense, formed by Bobby Seale and Huey P. Newton in 1966; and sundry other local organizations. Karenga founded Kwanzaa in 1966 as a cultural holiday that celebrated the fruits of a year's labor and an African-centered value system. The US Organization also provided a copious celebration of ancient African civilizations, languages, and clothing.

No Black Power organization generated more attention from the media, police, and federal government than the Black Panther Party. Founded in Oakland, California, their chief initial concern was to protect black people from the wrath of police brutality and terror. After the Panthers staged a demonstration at the California State Assembly in May 1967, people throughout the country became familiar with the militants in black berets, leather jackets, and sunglasses. The Panthers also created free breakfast, clothes, and medical-care programs in poor black communities.

By 1967 radicals outside of the black community created organizations modeled after the Panthers. In East Los Angeles, David Sanchez and other Chicano youth formed the Brown Berets. In Chicago, Cha Cha Jiminez politicized his Puerto Rican street gang, the Young Lords, into a revolutionary group after his association with the local Panthers. Young Lord chapters were established in several cities on the East Coast. Also, poor and working-class white gang members formed the Young Patriots, also modeled after the Panthers. In California, Asian-American radicals formed the Red Guard Party, Asian American Hardcore, and the Asian American Political Alliance. Richard Aoki, a Japanese American who was one of the first members of the Panthers, "went underground" into the nascent Asian movement to help develop an Asian-American version of the Black Panther Party. In Michigan whites formed the White Panther Party to assist in the struggle against racism, imperialism, and capitalism–the "three evils" identified by Panthers. In the Midwest the American Indian Movement (AIM) was founded and borrowed some of its militant symbolism from Black Power and the Black Panthers.

In November 1967 the NCNC, comprised of twelve Protestant denominations, announced its decision to work with advocates of Black Power. Others in Christian churches announced similar declarations of support for Black Power, if not a full-fledged declaration of black nationalism. As the Nation of Islam struck a chord with many who were disaffected with worshiping a Nordic-looking savior in the age of Black Power, black churches increasingly jettisoned their paintings of a white Jesus. By 1967 hundreds of Christian churches had developed programs and activities to complement the Black Power movement.

By the late 1960s black professionals, historically barred from joining white professional organizations, established African-American caucuses in their respective areas. For the first time by any significant measure, substantial numbers of black intellectuals supported either Black Power or black nationalism. In the arts a vibrant and dynamic movement emerged with playwrights and poets such as Amiri Baraka, Sonja Sanchez, Haki R. Madhubuti (Don L. Lee), Nikki Giovanni, and Larry Neal. In politics African Americans formed community-based organizations that sent hundreds of black people into public office. The most significant of these efforts were the Black Power Conferences (1966–1969), Congress of African People (1970), and National Black Political Convention (1972), where even the most ardent opponents of Black Power found themselves eager to participate.

Whitney Young Jr. and other moderates had to change their positions on Black Power if they hoped to maintain a following in African-American communities. Once a vehement opponent of Black Power, by mid 1968 Young recognized the popularity of the slogan in black communities. The white officials of the Urban League also voiced support of Young's pro–Black Power position. James A. Linen, president of Time, Inc., and national president of the Urban League, even declared that he was an advocate of Black Power. "Of course I'm for Black Power," he stated, "but not for black terrorist power." By 1970 President Richard M. Nixon, a consummate conservative, expressed his support of Black Power, in the form of black capitalism.

While it is possible that Young and other moderates came to believe in the genuine efficacy of Black Power, it is also probable that they were simply catching up with the spirit of black America, which had grown increasingly warm to nationalistic rhetoric since 1964. There was also an attempt by more-moderate elements to co-opt Black Power by "sanitizing" it and making it palatable to powerful whites, as well as to those white liberals who supported the civil-rights effort. While many advocates of Black Power were anticapitalist, corporate America was quick to market a wide range of goods from alcohol to underwear utilizing Black Power symbolism. Moderates were able to promote Black Power's racial pride without accepting its radical critique of society.

It is clear that Young and Nixon were not militants or fans of black nationalism, yet they and others embraced Black Power in an effort to bridge the growing chasm that separated them from the political mood of large sections of black people without fundamentally modifying their political platforms. This adoption of Black Power helped suffuse the slogan with a more innocuous meaning for many whites and moderate blacks. Black Power did not have to be antiwhite or violent. That Stokeley Carmichael and other Black Power advocates insisted so meant little for the new supporters. Young simply helped lead a process of de-radicalizing Black Power by ascribing conservative principles to a largely nebulous slogan. Indeed, Black Power often meant little more than an affirmation of the American tradition of ethnic politics. But its defiant style evoked a particular militancy that was hard to deny. It was this militant tone that attracted millions to the slogan as the decade progressed. Anti–Black Power moderates soon realized that they could embrace the slogan and imbue a more acceptable meaning to the term without fundamentally altering its essence. It was an effective attempt to defang white America's homegrown menace.

As historian Claude Andrew Clegg III explains in *An Original Man: The Life and Times of Elijah Muhammad* (1997), King and others were being displaced by radicals by 1966. Militants "began raising the new standard of revolt in the summer of 1966, the political center of the black community had shifted in a way that made King [and others] appear to be compromising moderate[s]." While integrationists such as King and Wilkins were reluctant to call people of African descent "black," the term was nearly universally used by 1970, as a replacement for Negro. From Afros, music, and fashion, the signs of Black Power were pervasive. Today the legacies of Black Power are ubiquitous.

Most major universities have African-American studies programs and departments, and have black student unions and/or black cultural centers, that are a direct outgrowth of the Black Power movement. In 1997 the United States Postal Service (USPS) unveiled its first Kwanzaa stamp, celebrating the holiday that emerged directly from the call for Black Power and cultural nationalism. Two years later the USPS issued a stamp commemorating the most popular African-American nationalist in U.S. history, Malcolm X. Black professionals spend hundreds of millions of dollars each year on conventions for organizations such as the National Association of Black Journalists, the Association of Black Psychologists, and scores of others that had their origins in the Black Power movement. Some of the most prominent intellectuals such as Cornel West, Henry Louis Gates, and Bell Hooks currently teach and procure impressive resources and status from black studies programs, providing a constant reminder of the widespread contributions of Black Power in many arenas of African-American life.

–JEFFREY OGBAR, UNIVERSITY OF CONNECTICUT

References

James Baldwin, *The Fire Next Time* (New York: Dell, 1963);

Baldwin, *The Price of the Ticket: Collected Nonfiction, 1948-1985* (New York: St. Martin's Press/Marek, 1985);

Taylor Branch, *Parting the Waters: America in the King Years, 1954–1963* (New York: Simon & Schuster, 1988);

Clayborne Carson, *In Struggle: SNCC and the Black Awakening of the 1960s* (Cambridge, Mass.: Harvard University Press, 1981);

William H. Chafe, *Civilities and Civil Rights: Greensboro, North Carolina, and the Black Struggle for Freedom* (New York: Oxford University Press, 1980);

Claude Andrew Clegg III, *An Original Man: The Life and Times of Elijah Muhammad* (New York: St. Martin's Press, 1997);

John Dittmer, *Local People: The Struggle for Civil Rights in Mississippi* (Urbana: University of Illinois Press, 1994);

Raymond L. Hall, *Black Separatism in the United States* (Hanover, N.H.: University Press of New England, 1978);

Charles E. Jones, ed., *The Black Panther Party Reconsidered* (Baltimore: Black Classic Press, 1997);

Richard Kluger, *Simple Justice: The History of* Brown *v.* Board of Education *and Black America's Struggle for Equality* (New York: Knopf, 1976);

John Lewis and Michael D'Orso, *Walking with the Wind: A Memoir of the Movement* (New York: Simon & Schuster, 1998);

Harvard Sitkoff, *The Struggle for Black Equality, 1954–1992* (New York: Hill & Wang, 1981);

William L. Van Deburg, *New Day in Babylon: The Black Power Movement and American Culture, 1965–1975* (Chicago: University of Chicago Press, 1992);

Van Deburg, ed., *Modern Black Nationalism: From Marcus Garvey to Louis Farrakhan* (New York: New York University Press, 1997);

Komozi Woodard, *A Nation Within a Nation: Amiri Baraka (LeRoi Jones) & Black Power Politics* (Chapel Hill: University of North Carolina Press, 1999).

HUMAN RIGHTS

Has the U.S. commitment to human rights been successful?

Viewpoint: The U.S. commitment to human rights has always been a cornerstone of American foreign policy and, in fact, defines the United States in the world.

Viewpoint: The U.S. commitment to human rights has undermined other aspects of American foreign policy.

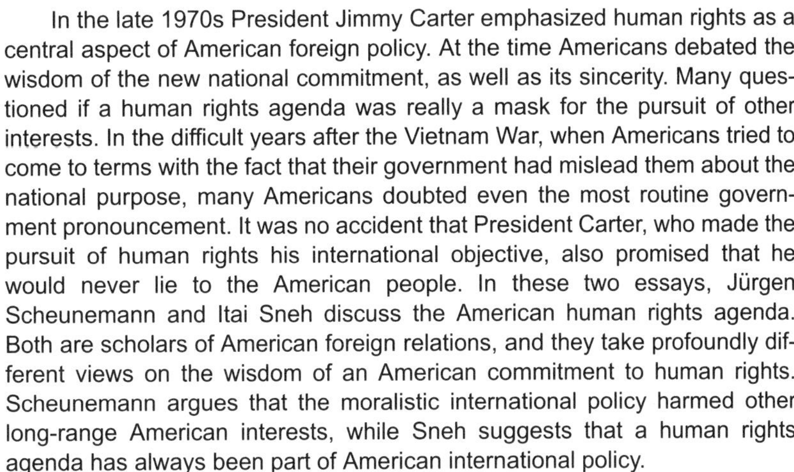

In the late 1970s President Jimmy Carter emphasized human rights as a central aspect of American foreign policy. At the time Americans debated the wisdom of the new national commitment, as well as its sincerity. Many questioned if a human rights agenda was really a mask for the pursuit of other interests. In the difficult years after the Vietnam War, when Americans tried to come to terms with the fact that their government had mislead them about the national purpose, many Americans doubted even the most routine government pronouncement. It was no accident that President Carter, who made the pursuit of human rights his international objective, also promised that he would never lie to the American people. In these two essays, Jürgen Scheunemann and Itai Sneh discuss the American human rights agenda. Both are scholars of American foreign relations, and they take profoundly different views on the wisdom of an American commitment to human rights. Scheunemann argues that the moralistic international policy harmed other long-range American interests, while Sneh suggests that a human rights agenda has always been part of American international policy.

Certainly the founders of the American republic believed that their new nation would be different from the nations of Europe. The Founding Fathers did not wish for the United States to engage in secret diplomacy or unnecessary wars to aggrandize its own rulers or subjugate other people. However, was this still true in the twentieth century? Or did this idea of a republican America end with the war against Mexico in 1846 or with the conquest of Cuba and the Philippines in 1898? After World War II, even if the United States did not copy the diplomatic style of Europe, it had replaced Europe as the protector of the world. How would a Pax Americana differ from the Pax Britannica?

These questions may seem new, and yet Americans have wrestled with them since 1783. With the advent of the Cold War, critics at home charged that U.S. campaigns to prevent Soviet domination in Asia, Europe, and Africa were mere covers for the protection of right-wing dictators. Were Francisco Franco of Spain, Mohammad Reza Pahlevi of Iran, Augusto Pinochet Ugarte of Chile, Ngo Dinh Diem of Vietnam, or the white government of South Africa preferable to socialist governments? This kind of questioning became even more acute after President Richard M. Nixon's breakthrough with the People's Republic of China. Nixon, a keen student of international affairs, sought rapprochement with China as a way of dividing the Communist world. Yet, if the United States could work with Mao Tse-tung, why could it not work with Chile's Salvador Allende or even Ho Chi Minh?

The rapprochement with China, the world's largest communist nation, at the same time as the United States was fighting against communism in Vietnam and in Chile made Americans question their national purpose. The war in Vietnam, ending with an American withdrawal and a communist victory, demoralized Americans. President Carter hoped to redirect American energies to a higher purpose than protecting favored regimes—to commit Americans to the protection of human rights. In so doing, was he following in the noblest tradition of American policymakers, or was he embarking on a naive and reckless path to national humiliation?

Viewpoint: The U.S. commitment to human rights has always been a cornerstone of American foreign policy and, in fact, defines the United States in the world.

The political culture in the United States has endured a perennial struggle. There has been a deep conviction that public policy requires an ethical meaning for materialistic success and even for the more mundane details of daily life and politics. The pattern hearkens back to the early settlements in the seventeenth century, notably to the Pilgrims and their Mayflower Compact, which guaranteed religious tolerance and some political liberties in an equitable form of government. The duality of agenda was already evident in the creation in 1776 of a polity based on "life, liberty, and the pursuit of happiness," displayed by the Founding Fathers in the lofty ideals embodied in the Declaration of Independence, Constitution, and Bill of Rights that translated into a guideline for creating a country and for operating a government. The interface of perfect ends with esoteric means was recast into the formulation and the execution of foreign policy.

As many Americans regarded themselves as chosen to lead the New World, they wanted to disavow the legacy of the Old World, especially that of Great Britain, which many of them had fled or fought against. Americans searched for words and for deeds to present a meaningful national agenda to foreigners, rather than merely bolstering parochial concerns. Following the warning of foreign entanglements in George Washington's Farewell Address (1796) and the Monroe Doctrine (1823), Americans opted to restrict as much as possible direct actions and diplomatic dealings to their neighbors in the Western Hemisphere.

Their self-perception as role models for the rest of humanity behooved Americans to conduct a foreign policy that espoused tolerance and self-reliance and that accorded protection to the weak from the abuse of power through observance of the fundamental principles of human rights. Major concerns focused on civic and political rights such as individual security and protection from arbitrary arrest, torture, and inhumane treatment by institutions and agents of the state; the safeguarding of due process and the rule of law in courts and in its enforcement; free, fair, and periodic elections, allowing full participation by the citizenry in government; self-determination and self-governance; freedom of conscience and religious practice; freedom from interference in private ownership and in the usage of property; and the freedom of movement within and between states. Some definitions also included the rights of children and women, but the legality of abortions and of the death penalty have been controversial.

The blend of protections accorded to collective freedoms and individual rights was endorsed by Americans for their public life and was consciously contrasted to the framework of realpolitik that had been the mainstay of European diplomacy. Traditionally, realpolitik viewed international relations as competitive rather than as cooperative and actions as driven solely by the preponderance of power. It was also based on a narrow definition of the national interest. Its purview was usually limited to securing economic benefits, addressing security concerns, and gaining political advantages. The national interest was thus devoid of any moral concern for official conduct and for its consequences, nor was it concerned with the welfare of others.

Concomitantly, however, influential American corporations and private individuals had tangible interests—commercial, strategic, and political—abroad, especially in Latin America. The interests were sanctioned and even advocated regularly by the U.S. government, although their pursuit frequently involved the oppression of the underprivileged classes in foreign societies. In addition, a history of slavery and discrimination against African Americans was highly problematic, as Americans could hardly preach to others about racial equality. The contradictions were often overlooked or justified as American leaders invoked the civilizing mission they felt they had in underdeveloped areas, ostensibly barely touched by the Reformation and by the Enlightenment, such as in Latin America.

Several matters combined to virtually preclude official, large-scale U.S. involvement in international affairs in places such as Asia and Europe until the late nineteenth century. The reasons included the continuous expansion of American boundaries through settlement at the expense of the British, French, Spanish, Mexican, and especially Native American tribes; internal discord over slavery coupled with a debate over federal sovereignty as opposed to states' rights; and isolationist, "America First" sentiments.

The pattern did change following American victory in the 1898 war with Spain. The conflict was largely caused by U.S. agitation over the gross violations of human rights in Cuba by Spanish soldiers' suppression of continuous local uprisings, and by a sense of American puissance. Thus, the United States became a recognized global power because of its subsequent conquest of the Philippines, Cuba, and Puerto Rico, as well as its overall economic might.

Shortly afterward, having entered Asia, American leaders addressed its conflicts. Beginning in 1899, the United States articulated an Open Door Policy in China, a country dismembered by foreigners. While demanding equal commercial access to ports held by powers such as the British, the French, the Russians, and the Japanese, it was couched in the protection of the right of the Chinese people to sovereignty and to self-government. According to its critiques, this policy set a new tradition of the abstract upholding of the rights of weak groups abroad while providing the United States with concrete benefits in the realm of trade or political domination. Nevertheless, American concern for the integrity of China did limit foreign encroachments until the 1930s, specifically affecting Japanese contact. It also directed international attention to the plight of the Chinese.

The United States thus began to develop a foreign policy addressing countries beyond the Western Hemisphere. The situation was coupled with the emergence of strong, worldly thinking presidents such as Theodore Roosevelt and Woodrow Wilson. They each won the Nobel Peace Prize for their international deeds in the first two decades of the twentieth century. Both were imbedded in the democratizing ideal and moral values of political and social reforms during the Progressive Era but were not averse to the use of economic and military force, especially in Latin America. Continual U.S. interventions in this region were mostly necessitated by the unstable political and financial situation of countries such as Cuba, the Dominican Republic, and Mexico.

American entrance into World War I facilitated a pioneering, albeit largely failed, attempt to reshape global diplomacy along U.S. patterns, as evident in Wilson's 1918 Fourteen Points. Wilson articulated American support for the principle of self-determination and for an international organization that would arbitrate conflicts between states. His subsequent advocacy for these principles in the Versailles Conference and at home, although it failed to fully implement his ideal, began a new era in American policy, giving rise to the term "Wilsonian" with respect to a conscientious, value-laden, humanitarian, progressive outlook on U.S. conduct abroad.

Sick and injured refugees awaiting treatment outside a clinic following the Soviet invasion of Afghanistan in 1979

Only a sense of American vulnerability forged by the 7 December 1941 Japanese attack on Pearl Harbor forced a more consistent agenda in the realm of foreign policy and a widespread domestic recognition for its need. Among the early policy formulations was President Franklin Delano Roosevelt's proclamation of the "Four Freedoms" in his State of the Union Address on 6 January 1941. Roosevelt stressed that these liberties (freedom of speech, expression, and worship as well as freedom from fear and want) should be guaranteed throughout the world as essential foundations for a secure, stable global community to follow the abyss of World War II. The concerns were reinforced by the Atlantic Charter several months later, before U.S. entrance into the war, thus articulating a blueprint for the American agenda in the postwar era that was founded on human rights. It was endorsed by other allies such as Britain and even the Soviet Union, serving as the basis for the 1945 creation of the United Nations (U.N.).

The implicit acknowledgment of a U.S. mission to help establish and aid existing regimes that uphold human rights was affirmed explicitly by the Truman Doctrine of March 1947. Congress also approved aid to be provided to "free peoples" whom the United States "must support" against "attempted subjugation or by armed minorities or by outside pressure" during the Cold War. While aimed primarily against Soviet subversion in the Near East, human rights were promoted as a model goal anywhere in the globe. Concomitantly, the Marshall Plan proffered financial support indiscriminately to post-Nazi Europe, but was accepted only by countries that largely followed market economies, political freedoms, and the formation of the North Atlantic Treaty Organization (NATO), which assured European countries of American protection from Soviet threats.

The policy blended strategic, commercial, political, and humanitarian concerns. It set the pattern for most of the Cold War, which lasted until 1989. That was a time when the United States often turned a blind eye toward regimes that regularly abused human rights–especially civic freedoms and political liberties–as long as they were loyal American allies in the conflict with the Soviet Union.

A major era of American activism concerning human rights was the 1977–1981 presidency of Jimmy Carter, who tried to negate the perception that American foreign policy subordinates humanitarian issues to other interests. His administration censured, reduced aid to, and imposed sanctions against U.S. allies who abused human rights in Latin America–including Argentina, Brazil, Chile, and Paraguay–and in the Philippines, although there were exceptions for "strategically placed states" such as South Korea and Indonesia. Carter also denounced the Apartheid regime in South Africa, a staunch American ally in the fight against Soviet interventions in its continent. Even the subsequent Reagan and Bush administrations, while repudiating Carter's policies, did not move far away from his positions.

Based on the need for urgent aid to distressed populations whose own governments were either oppressive, unwilling, or unable to help, humanitarian interventions were demanded by a public outraged over photos of starving children and sanctioned by the United Nations. These interventions have been repeated in American foreign policy since the Cold War came to an end, although they offered little advantage other than aiding the welfare of the affected population. Somalia in 1992, ravaged by famine until American marines escorted convoys of food and other supplies, was an example of that conduct.

Another successful example of American-led humanitarian intervention was the restoration of a popularly chosen leader to power–the Reverend Bertrand Aristide of Haiti. He was ousted by a military coup in September 1991, negating the results of an American-sponsored and -monitored democratic election. The new government, moreover, brutally persecuted Aristide's supporters, grossly and widely violating human rights. An uncharacteristic coalition assembled to support a military intervention to overthrow the illegal regime. It included Florida politicians, who feared an influx of refugees upon their shores if a civil war was to erupt in Haiti, and the Black Caucus in Congress, who supported their oppressed kin in Haiti.

Prudently, the United States joined forces with others, ensuring the legitimacy and enhancing the efficacy of the action. A concerted and multilateral effort led by the United States, the Security Council of the United Nations, and the Organization of American States combined diplomacy and a credible military threat to overthrow the junta. Interdenominational groups in the United States and private mediation by prominent figures such as former President Carter, General Colin Powell, and Senator Sam Nunn also helped resolve the issue. As a result Aristide reassumed the effective reigns of power in October 1994, stabilizing the country. Although there is still turmoil in Haiti, another set of free and fair democratic elections have been held.

Similarly, American involvement and mediation was crucial in the successful conclusion of the Dayton Accord, ending the war in the Balkans in the mid 1990s that was characterized by gross violations of human rights. It took American leadership to bring the fighting groups in this fierce conflict between the Greek-Orthodox Serbs, Catholic Croats, and Moslem Bosnian-Herzegovinians to the negotiating table. The United Nations and the European Union were also brought into the process. Only tenacious American leadership and the deployment of NATO and U.N. forces (led by contingents of U.S. troops) ended the most bloody war in Europe since World War II.

Significantly, the United States derived less advantages than liabilities in these actions. Similarly, the 1999 NATO's humanitarian intervention in Kosovo, where the Serbs grossly violated the human rights of the Albanians, who composed 90 percent of the population, was founded on humanitarian concerns much more than a display of other interests or tangible benefits. A lack of such preemptive and post-conflict reconstruction with respect to the conflict in

Rwanda and Burundi between Tutsis and Hutus in the mid 1990s has had tragic consequences, leading to mass killings of genocidal proportions, meriting more attention in the future by the United States to humanitarian needs in Africa. Thus, when the United States focused on its role as guardian and promoter of human rights, more security and prosperity prevailed. When merely commercial considerations were allowed to dominate policy making, the results were frequently less satisfactory for Americans and foreigners alike.

–ITAI SNEH, COLUMBIA UNIVERSITY

Viewpoint: The U.S. commitment to human rights has undermined other aspects of American foreign policy.

Human rights are an integral part of the U.S. national history and lie at the foundation of this nation. In fact, the Revolutionary War was fought over the issue of civil rights that the colonists felt were being denied them, indeed civil rights that are considered among the most important of human rights today. Closely tied to this period of early nationhood is the fundamental American idea of national exceptionalism in the community of nations. The notion is most clearly visible in U.S. foreign policy: Exceptionalism is born of the belief that the Declaration of Independence and the Constitution with the Bill of Rights promulgate a set of specific values, and of the deep conviction that these values are still unique in the international community. The sense of exceptionalism easily survived into the modern age, and–first in the framework of the Fourteen Points of President Woodrow Wilson–became one of the founding pillars of U.S. foreign policy. Exceptionalism also established human rights as a theme in foreign policy, which became moralistic, naive, and unilateral in character. Human rights, therefore, became damaging because the national interest of a country is mostly governed by more rational, economic, and security concerns and not so much by ideals and moralism.

There are four key problems related to human rights in foreign policy that explain the process. All of these issues emerged during the Carter presidency, the first U.S. administration that set out to formulate and execute a strong and viable human rights policy. Most of the following arguments were first proclaimed by President Carter's conservative critics. They began criticizing Carter in 1979 and 1981 with two famous magazine articles by political scientist Jeane J. Kirkpatrick denouncing the president's double standards, idealism, naiveté, and moralism. More precisely, Kirkpatrick accused Carter of not supporting right-wing dictators, even though they were close allies of the United States and therefore in support of our national interests. Instead, she charged, Carter's human rights policy favored left-wing, Communist regimes. In addition, according to Kirkpatrick, those left-wing regimes were much more likely to evolve into totalitarian systems with even worse human rights abuses, while right-wing regimes usually developed into democratic and more humane societies. Ultimately, Kirkpatrick and others claimed that the Carter administration's human rights policy did not serve its own cause well and was in itself a double standard.

Scholars such as Joshua Muravchik, Ernst Lefever, and Elliot Abrams, among others, later followed up this line of argumentation. In retrospect, most of their arguments seem to be too extreme and in almost all instances not supported by the evidence. However, the conservative criticism revealed some of the inherent problems of the juxtaposition of human rights policy and U.S. national interests. Many of their theories ultimately transformed U.S. human rights policy as conducted during the 1980s and 1990s. Moreover, during the Reagan administration Kirkpatrick and Abrams tried to implement their ideas in office, as U.S. ambassador to the United Nations and undersecretary for human rights at the State Department, respectively.

First of all, definition and inherent contradictions of human rights already give rise to several issues. Today there are three different sets of human rights: political, individual civil rights; economic collective rights; and developmental rights. Each new set of rights has been integrated into U.S. foreign policy. During the Carter administration political, individual civil rights were most important, even though the president had pledged to promote social "basic rights" as well. The problem of defining the idealism of human rights in an otherwise harshly realistic setting is one of the major obstacles toward incorporating human rights and the national interest. In addition, the unilateral U.S. definition of rights may be understood by other nations who do not share American cultural values as a threat of intervention and not as the promulgation of rights. The definition is one of the most powerful arguments even liberal critics of Carter's human rights policy, such as historian Stanley Hoffman, have used, namely the idea of "cultural relativism": it questions the proclaimed universality of human rights in the context of national foreign policy. The United States usually asserts that its unilateral definition of human

STATEMENT FROM FORMER U.S. PRESIDENT JIMMY CARTER ON THE 1980 OLYMPIC BOYCOTT

The decision about participation in the 1980 Olympics in Moscow was a very difficult one for me and for other political and sports leaders in America and in many other countries. When the Soviet Union, host for the games, crossed the borders of Afghanistan with a brutal invasion on December 27, 1979, the basic principles of the Olympics were violated.

In America, there was a remarkable consensus about what our response should be to the attack on the people of Afghanistan.

On January 4, I condemned this "callous violation of international law and the United Nations Charter" and added that the United States would prefer not to withdraw from the Olympic games. I pointed out, however, that continued aggressive actions by the Soviets would endanger the participation of athletes and travel to Moscow by spectators.

On January 20, I sent a message to the International Olympic Committee (IOC) suggesting that unless the Soviets withdrew within a month, the IOC should move the games from Moscow to an alternate site, preferably to Greece. The following day, the U.S. House of Representatives voted 386 to 12 to support this request to the IOC, and on January 29 the U.S. Senate affirmed the same position by a vote of 88 to 4.

Public opinion polls by the *Washington Star* and *New York Times* revealed that from 72% to 86% of the American public endorsed a boycott. Internationally, 104 nations supported a United Nations resolution condemning the invasion.

The U.S. Olympic Committee (USOC) voted 68 to 0 to ask the IOC to move, postpone, or cancel the games. When the IOC rejected this proposal, on April 12 the USOC decided by a two to one margin not to send a U.S. team to Moscow.

It should be remembered that in the United States and other free countries, the national Olympic committees were independent of government control. Of the more than 140 national Olympic committees, 118 were not part of the Communist bloc. Sixty-two elected not to send teams. In a few countries, including Great Britain, governments supported the boycott, but Olympic committees made the final decision about whether to send athletes to Moscow.

This was a sad episode in Olympic history, and its aftermath affected participation in the 1984 games in Los Angeles, which were still a great success. The most serious impact was on the thousands of athletes who were not given a chance to compete in either of the boycotted games.

The founders of the modern Olympic movement were concerned with more than sports. They believed the games would help bring about the reconciliation of warring nations. I think that the Olympic movement is now stronger than ever, with apparently unanimous participation in the Atlanta Games. I fervently hope that its exalted principles will prevail.

Source: *News release, 25 March 1996, Office of Public Information, The Carter Center, Atlanta, Georgia.*

rights is universal in the sense that it applies it whenever deciding on other nations' human rights records. However, the approach does not take into account that other countries have completely different values, historic traditions, and religious and cultural habits. U.S. human rights policy should, in fact, pay heed to the notion of cultural relativism, thus acknowledging different perspectives on human rights. During the Nixon and Reagan administrations, this position sometimes served as an excuse for non-intervention when human rights were violated abroad.

One can follow the insights and be confronted with another problem: the implementation of human rights can be construed as inherent intervention, albeit intervention in a presumably good cause. Smaller countries with a pronounced human rights foreign policy, such as Norway and the Netherlands, might be capable of pursuing a coherent human rights policy. The United States, however, is a superpower, and any of the means it might use to react to another country's bad human-rights record, such as quiet or open diplomacy and reduction or cancellation of financial or military aid, could be construed as slow or low-scale intervention in its internal affairs.

Secondly, the interrelation between human rights and national interest hangs in extremely fragile balance, which, in essence, makes it difficult to include human rights in the national foreign policy of a superpower that relies heavily on exact definitions and goals in order to succeed. Contrary to human rights, the national interest of the United States is usually defined as a set of economic, military, and political goals that ultimately ensure the safety and well-being of the American people. It is the oldest concept of foreign policy and serves primarily the national self-interest. Human rights, on the other hand, are a broad set of values and rights not even American foreign policymakers can agree on, and the international community even less. As sad and immoral as it often may seem, U.S. support of dictators throughout the 1970s and 1980s within the framework of the Cold War was often necessary to preserve the U.S. national interest in, for example, Latin America, Africa, the Persian Gulf, and Southeast Asia. Many of the regimes enjoying U.S. support exhibited widely publicized and gross human right violations but guaranteed the global presence of American power. Promotion of human rights was often directly opposed to the U.S. national interest because a viable human rights policy ultimately weakens a political dictatorship, even more so if it is voiced or executed by a major political ally such as the United States.

Third, as Stanley Hoffman once observed, human rights violations are always a sign of an unstable political system that eventually might collapse. In modern U.S. foreign policy, the first presidential administration to actually draw up a human rights agenda also had to face the collapse of the political systems of some of the most important and closest American allies: the Carter administration (and to a lesser extent the Reagan administration) had to cope with unrest, revolutions, and ultimately civil wars in Nicaragua, El Salvador, Iran, the Philippines, Zaire, Somalia, Indonesia, and South Africa. In all cases, the implementation of human rights ultimately did damage to U.S. national interest in many respects, especially during the Carter administration. Two of the best researched and most illustrative examples are Nicaragua and Iran. Both countries had been ruled by families (the Somoza dictators in Nicaragua and the Pahlavi family in Iran), and both had been militarily and economically supported by the United States and were therefore dependent on it. In addition, both countries had poor human rights records. In the global context of the Cold War, however, both countries also served crucial U.S. strategic interests in their respective regions. Nicaragua was viewed as an American stronghold in Latin America, whose countries (according to the Central Intelligence Agency) were increasingly turning toward Communism. Iran, on the other hand, was the closest U.S. ally in the Persian Gulf region and was surrounded by many Soviet-friendly countries (most notably Iraq, Syria, Yemen, and Egypt). The egregious human-rights situation in both Nicaragua and Iran was well known even during the Nixon administration, but was ultimately ignored for the sake of the political stability in both countries and because of their strategic value. The Carter administration, through public statements, quiet diplomacy, and, most importantly, the curtailment of U.S. foreign aid, military assistance, and arms exports to Nicaragua and Iran, set about changing the situation.

Beginning in 1978, the regimes of the Somoza family and the Shah started showing signs of political strain owing to growing domestic political opposition. The Carter administration tried to encourage both governments to continue and step up their improvements of human rights. The message was sent on the one hand through diplomatic channels, and on the other hand by the more punitive approach of curtailing foreign aid, as in Nicaragua, and weapons sales, as in Iran. The administration was sending mixed signals not only to Somoza and the Shah but also to their respective opposition movements and the Soviets: it looked as if the United States was no longer really committed to supporting the regimes, which, in turn, contributed to the escalation of political crises in both countries. The brutality of both political regimes was undeniable, so the human rights concerns of the American government were indeed noble, but also idealistic and ultimately counterproductive. At the same time, however, the United States did not balance the need for human rights improvements with the demands of the U.S. national interests. Worse yet, the Carter administration's preoccupation with human rights did not involve careful contact, encouragement, and guidance of the more moderate and liberal domestic opposition movements in Nicaragua and Iran. In the end the radical oppositions won the day, and the human rights record ultimately did not improve (at least during the first years of the Sandinista rule, though human rights violations are still now the order of the day in Iran). By the same token, U.S. national interests were also poorly served. The American approach to the Philippines and South Africa was similar, but in El Salvador and Guatemala the Reagan administration pursued a completely different policy.

Fourth, the day-to-day implementation of a viable human rights policy is often caught in the dichotomy of being either a tool or a goal in itself of U.S. foreign policy–an observation many neoliberal historians tend to forget. During the Carter administration, for instance, U.S. human rights policy often appeared arbitrary, because human rights sometimes served as a vehicle or leverage for different foreign-policy goals. However, human rights were also a genuine and sincere motivation for U.S. foreign-policy. As a result foreign nations, primarily those concerned, often regarded U.S. foreign policy as erratic and hypocritical. A good example of the conundrum was the Carter administration's early approach to the Soviet Union. During the first weeks of his presidency, Carter publicly criticized the Communist superpower for its poor human rights record, invited prominent Soviet dissidents to the White House, corresponded with Andrei Sakharov, and thus demonstrated to the world that the United States was fervently committed to the cause of human rights. The relationship between the two superpowers subsequently deteriorated. The Soviets responded to Carter's constant criticism by denouncing it as interference in their domestic politics. In this instance, human rights were being treated as a goal per se: the Carter administration hoped to actually move the Soviet leaders to improve their domestic human rights situation through public criticism.

Ever since Jimmy Carter proclaimed human rights to be a major element of his administration's foreign policy, the tools and strategies of U.S. foreign human rights policy have been fine-tuned and changed. The situation is the result of new insights into the nature of international human rights policy and a direct and positive outcome of the end of the Cold War and global ideological and military confrontation. Throughout the Reagan, Bush, and Clinton administrations the more punitive approach of Carter (for example, cutting foreign aid if a country has a poor human rights record) has evolved into policy tools that use encouragement. The close links between foreign and development aid, human rights, and democracy building are now all incorporated into a larger framework of national foreign policy. These developments are an indication of how the major actors have understood that the national interest and a human rights policy may ultimately converge in a new vision of a national interest in a post–Cold War world. Peace and stability, development aid, free trade, and human rights are closely interwoven issues that are ultimately all in the national interest of the United States.

–JÜRGEN SCHEUNEMANN, FOX FELLOW, YALE UNIVERSITY

References

David P. Forsythe, *Human Rights and U.S. Foreign Policy* (Gainesville: University of Florida Press, 1988);

Louis Henkin, *The Age of Rights* (New York: Columbia University Press, 1990);

Dilys M. Hill, ed., *Human Rights and Foreign Policy: Principles and Practices* (New York: St. Martin's Press, 1989);

Stanley Hoffman, *Duties Beyond Borders: On the Limits and Possibilities of Ethical International Politics* (Syracuse, N.Y.: Syracuse University Press, 1981);

Hoffman, *Primacy or World Order: American Foreign Policy Since the Cold War* (New York: McGraw-Hill, 1978);

Robert C. Johansen, *The National Interest and the Human Interest: An Analysis of U.S. Foreign Policy* (Princeton: Princeton University Press, 1980);

Robert O. Keohane and Joseph S. Nye, *Power and Interdependence: World Politics in Transition* (Boston & Toronto: Little, Brown, 1977);

Jeane J. Kirkpatrick, "Dictatorships and Double Standards," *Commentary,* 68 (1979): 34–45;

Kirkpatrick, "Establishing a Viable Human Rights Policy," *World Affairs,* 143 (April 1981): 323–334;

Seymour Martin Lipset, *American Exceptionalism: A Double-Edged Sword* (New York: Norton, 1996);

Hans J. Morgenthau, *In Defense of the National Interest: A Critical Examination of American Foreign Policy With a New Introduction by Kenneth W. Thompson* (Washington, D.C.: University Press of America, 1982);

Joshua Muravchik, *The Uncertain Crusade: Jimmy Carter and the Dilemmas of Human Rights* (New York: Hamilton Press, 1986);

J. Bruce Nichols and Gil Loescher, eds., *The Moral Nation: Humanitarianism and U.S. Foreign Policy Today* (Notre Dame, Ind. & London: University of Notre Dame Press, 1989);

Michael J. Smith, *Realist Thought From Weber to Kissinger* (Baton Rouge: Louisiana State University Press, 1986);

Tony Smith, *America's Mission: The United States and the Worldwide Struggle for Democracy* (Princeton: Princeton University Press, 1994);

William Appleman Williams, *The Tragedy of American Diplomacy* (Cleveland & New York: World, 1959).

INTERSTATE HIGHWAY ACT

Was the interstate highway system beneficial to the United States?

Viewpoint: Yes, the Interstate Highway Act strengthened the United States by linking urban areas, enabling economic development, and benefiting American culture.

Viewpoint: No, although the interstate highway system opened new areas for expansion and funded economic growth, it also hurt the inner cities by facilitating white flight to the suburbs.

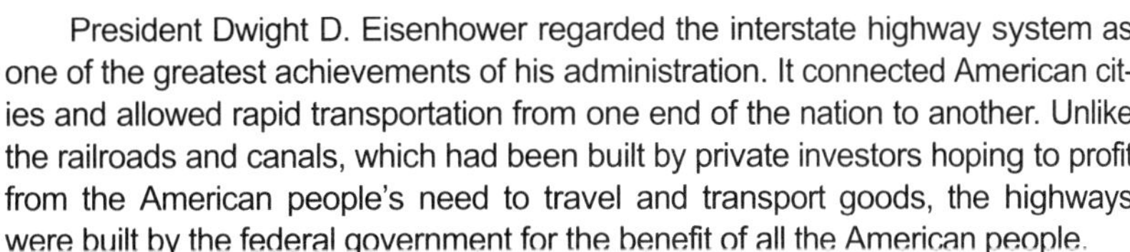

President Dwight D. Eisenhower regarded the interstate highway system as one of the greatest achievements of his administration. It connected American cities and allowed rapid transportation from one end of the nation to another. Unlike the railroads and canals, which had been built by private investors hoping to profit from the American people's need to travel and transport goods, the highways were built by the federal government for the benefit of all the American people.

However, did the highway system benefit all Americans? In these two essays Elizabeth D. Schafer, an independent scholar, and Michael Mezzano, an urban historian, take two different views of the interstate highway system. Schafer sees the benefits of this publicly financed highway network: the highways cut travel time between American cities and thus allowed easier transit by car and truck across the nation. The highways also allowed Americans to live outside crowded inner cities, moving instead to outlying suburbs, where they could enjoy fresh air and open space while still being within an easy drive of the city's cultural amenities.

Mezzano, on the other hand, argues that the interstate highway system reinforced American dependence on the automobile. The move to the suburbs had long-term consequences for those without the mobility to leave the cities, which have decayed since the 1950s. Furthermore, the construction of highways has caused the destruction of farmland and of inner-city neighborhoods—typically the neighborhoods of poorer and less politically powerful people were demolished to make way for highways and exit ramps in order to bring suburbanites into the city for work and pleasure. The highway system has made worse problems that may have been inevitable; it has created other problems its designers could not have imagined.

Viewpoint: Yes, the Interstate Highway Act strengthened the United States by linking urban areas, enabling economic development, and benefiting American culture.

When President Dwight D. Eisenhower signed the Interstate Highway Act in 1956, he implemented a transportation revolution that transformed the United States. Tom Lewis, in *Divided Highways: Building the Interstate Highways, Transforming American Life* (1997), praised the interstate highway system for initiating progressive reforms and advancing American technology. Lewis emphasizes that interstate highways improved the daily life of Americans. These highways influenced where people lived and worked and affected the location of consumer and recreational sites. By connecting urban areas throughout the United States with a network of accessible, well-designed roads, the federal government changed post–World War II culture and patterns of living. Interstate highways also offered defensive measures in case of military activity within the country.

Advocates of the interstate highway system believed that the roads would also enhance safety. Engineering and construction of interstates provided employment opportunities for war veterans and other laborers. Some scholars consider the interstate highway system to be the last New Deal project, rewarding Americans with varying engineering, architectural, and construction skills for applying their ingenuity to mold the country's landscape for efficient human mobility.

The history of American automobiles and highways explains the need for interstates. Since cars were first produced in the late nineteenth century, state and municipal governments were expected to maintain and upgrade roads. The federal government promoted the improvement of local roads for the rural free delivery mail system. Federal supervision and financial support of highway construction between states began in 1916 when the Federal Aid Road Act was passed. The Bureau of Public Roads oversaw construction of highways, including the Lincoln and Dixie Highways, as the number of automobiles increased in the 1920s. Yet, only several hundred miles of paved roads existed to convey several million automobiles. Americans began accepting the new transportation mode as a means for people and produce to reach other locations for commercial and personal reasons. Cars moved more quickly than traditional methods such as wagons and trains, and individuals had more control over when, where, and how they sent their goods to distant markets. Americans also embraced the freedom automobiles presented to travel beyond their community and experience other geographical regions. Highways promised easier, spontaneous, and often more affordable movement to enjoy these recreational adventures than did travel by boat and train. An automobile tourism industry emerged that offered food, shelter, fuel, repairs, and entertainment to travelers, financially benefiting businesses and local economies.

After the Great Depression stymied Americans' indulgence in automobiles, renewed interest expanded as people could once again afford to buy cars and learn to operate them. In the late 1930s more Americans demanded highways capable of supporting increased traffic across the continent. Automobile advocates envisioned multiple lanes to accommodate many cars simultaneously traveling at higher speeds and sufficient east-west and north-south highways for travelers to reach desired destinations from varied starting points using direct routes with minimal detours.

President Franklin D. Roosevelt had encouraged constructing toll highways across the United States to supply jobs and the Federal-Aid Highway Act of 1938 funded a study to determine if such a plan should be pursued. Although Congress was receptive to this highway idea, the beginning of World War II diverted attention and financial resources from road improvement, and fewer automobiles were produced as industry focused on wartime needs.

Legislators did pass the Federal-Aid Highway Act of 1944, which approved building 65,000 kilometers of interstate highways but did not legislate funding for construction. The Bureau of Public Roads, renamed the Public Roads Administration, began identifying routes that should be developed. The American Association of State Highway Officials and the Public Roads Administration determined design standards. States resisted construction plans because they wanted to use federal funds for other projects, and the Federal-Aid Highway Act of 1952 approved additional funds solely for building roads. By January 1953, when Eisenhower was inaugurated, state governments had improved 10,327 kilometers of highways, costing $955 million.

The federal government paid one-half of this amount. Less than one-fourth of the nation's highways, however, were prepared for the rigors of traffic. Eisenhower realized that adequate highways were essential for American economic success and national security. In 1919 he had joined the U.S. Army's transcontinental motor convoy from Washington, D.C., to San Francisco, observing impediments such as muddy roads and unstable bridges that plagued the motorists. He also noted how the German autobahn benefited both Axis and Allied troop mobility during World War II.

Industries accelerated production of luxury items such as cars in the 1950s. By this time more people could afford automobiles, and fuel prices also decreased. As additional Americans drove, the need for improved highways became urgent. Eisenhower declared that highways were one of his primary domestic concerns in his State of the Union Address on 7 January 1954. The Federal-Aid Highway Act of 1954 approved giving $175 million to states based on population figures and the distances highways covered in different geographical areas. Eisenhower praised

A sign celebrating the start of construction of highways provided by the Interstate Highway Bill

(American Highway Users Alliance)

the legislation but asserted that more measures be initiated to build interstates that would potentially lower accident rates; reduce traffic jams, detours, and automobile-related lawsuits; increase commercial transportation efficiency; and prepare for domestic defensive tactics in case of atomic war. Seeking financial cooperation between the federal government and states, Eisenhower promoted a modernized interstate system.

The National Defense and Interstate Highway Act of 1956 authorized sixty-six thousand kilometers of four-lane highways to be built over a thirteen-year period while considering the possible demands of future traffic. The Highway Revenue Act of 1956 assured ample funds to proceed with construction. Considered the largest public-works project in the United States and the world, the interstate highway system was begun with $1.1 billion distributed to states. Route markers and numbering for highways were specified. Interstates often followed the routes of previous highways that in many cases represented where pioneer settlers had traveled, and scholars noted that large truck stops sometimes were placed at sites near where frontier forts had served a similar purpose as trading centers for Pony Express riders, explorers, and overland immigrants.

Historians note the military motivation for construction of interstate highways. Proponents such as Eisenhower emphasized that the interstate would protect the country by insuring navigable roads to transport troops, supplies, and munitions across the country efficiently while encountering few road hazards. The Cold War heightened fear of an atomic attack and enemy invasion, and U.S. military strategists warned that inferior roads could render the country vulnerable and limit defenses. Interstates not only were capable of servicing large military vehicles and assuring direct routes to strategic locations, but they would also prove valuable to evacuate civilians from targeted areas. Regulations also required a straightaway in the interstate every five miles to enable emergency landings of military aircraft. Untried in war, American interstates designed for military evacuation have instead been designated for a similar purpose as emergency routes for residents fleeing coastal regions threatened by hurricanes.

The establishment of suburbs was perhaps the most significant cultural change caused by interstates. Many urban residents welcomed the opportunity to build homes in rural areas outside cities and to commute to work by using the interstate. Suburb settlers praised the large yards, unpolluted air, and safety while criticizing urban areas for their small spaces, filth, and crime. Censuses recorded the demographic shift of populations around metropolitan areas with the coming of interstate systems. Individuals identified with newly created suburban neighborhoods by organizing amateur sports teams, hosting barbecue parties, and interacting with other residents. Some people who already lived in rural areas used the interstates to seek new employment opportunities as well as access to educational and commercial offerings, linking rural and urban cultures. Interstates accelerated the modernization of rural regions and connected parts of the country that would have otherwise remained separated. Post–World War II housing shortages were alleviated as prefabricated homes were erected, often as quickly as in one day, filling pastures and establishing communities with clubhouses, pools, and symbolic decorations.

The suburbs represented the emergence of the American middle class and the enhanced prosperity of the 1950s. Historians also stress that interstates contributed to the economic growth of nonurban areas along interstates and near cities, extending the commercial borders of many metropolitan places into the countryside. Interstates daily brought nonresidential customers into areas where they invested money. Billboards advertised local entrepreneurial efforts such as diners, stores, drive-in movies, miniature golf courses, ice-cream stands, and motels (coined from the words "motorist" and "hotel" in the 1950s). Motel and restaurant franchises gradually displaced independently owned businesses that could not compete financially to provide the services that attracted clientele. Although some diners survived, many smaller restaurants closed because of nearby fast-food chains that appealed to motorists by quickly distributing food at drive-through windows. Motorists could have their cars repaired during their trips and fill up gasoline tanks at brand-name service stations. Standardized businesses assured motorists of an expected level of product quality whether it was a Big Mac hamburger or an oil change in Oregon or West Virginia. Malls and large retail stores such as K-Mart and Wal-Mart were located near interstates to attract motorists as well as provide easy access for residents. Factories also built outlet stores to sell brand-name stock at reduced prices to interstate users.

The interstate system expanded the role of trucking freight in the United States. Private businesses such as Federal Express and United Parcel Service were created to transport large amounts of packages and documents on interstate trucks in competition with the U.S. Postal Service, which also used interstate highways in an effort to achieve prompt delivery. Refrigerated trucks conveyed perishable produce indigenous to certain regions to consumers across the country. The interstates also aided industrial development in remote areas surrounding cities because employees, suppliers, and buyers could reach the factories by identifiable routes. Industrial parks were established so that trucks could easily deliver raw supplies and transport finished goods. Truck stops were built to provide drivers places to refuel, eat, and sleep; serve as rest areas for motorists; and offer other goods, from postcards and paraphernalia emblazoned with interstate logos to travel guides for specific interstates.

Driven on for pleasure as well as work, interstates encouraged the development of adjacent resorts. Car travel strengthened many families who enjoyed sharing time in a car while exploring America and discovering roadside attractions. Use of interstates minimized travel time and increased the number of accessible destinations, including national parks, beaches, mountains, and vacation spots such as Las Vegas and Atlantic City. Ball fields, amusement parks, and campgrounds were built near interstates to attract travelers. Some interstate engineers designed roadways to be compatible with regional environments, such as building passages beneath the interstate for panthers in the Everglades or erecting overpasses to assure continuity of the Appalachian Trail. Motorists utilized interstates to escape their routine lives and immerse themselves in intriguing activities. They had more possibilities for both work and play because of better roads. Interstates enabled Americans to seek the freedom of post–World War II indulgences, escaping the rigid wartime restraints and rationing that they had endured and that had been perpetuated to some degree in American cultural expectations.

Female and minority drivers welcomed the independence offered by interstates to lead them to parts of the country they believed promised fewer gender or racial restrictions. Interstates provided a vast transcontinental transportation network connecting the country internally, as well as externally to Canada and Mexico. The uniform design of interstate roads and signs across the country insured no significant surprises for motorists hurrying to reach destinations. Interstates, such as the Washington, D.C. Beltway, attempted to provide enough room for heavy traffic.

Begun in 1956, some sources indicate that the interstate system was finished in December 1977, with the final section of Interstate 75, while other references argue that interstate construction continued into the 1990s, which may actually refer to "3R" improvements–

"Resurfacing, Restoration, and Rehabilitation"—instead of new roads. Legislation has also established regulations since the initial interstate act was passed, requiring weight limits of vehicles. Despite statistics of interstate accidents and fatalities, enthusiasts stress that interstates have actually reduced the number of accidents that might have occurred on more congested, less improved roadways. They believe that motorists can maneuver their vehicles more defensively on wide, straight interstates than on smaller, meandering roads.

In his memoir *Mandate for Change, 1953–1956: The White House Years* (1963), Eisenhower stressed that the interstate highway system was his most significant domestic achievement. "More than any single action by the government since the end of the war, this one would change the face of America," he said. "Its impact on the American economy—the jobs it would produce in manufacturing and construction, the rural areas it would open up—was beyond calculation." In 1990 President George Bush signed an act approving the new name, the "Dwight D. Eisenhower System of Interstate and Defense Highways," which recognized Eisenhower's leadership in establishing the U.S. interstate highway system, an integral part of the quality of daily life of almost every American. The only made structure visible from space besides the Great Wall of China, the interstate highway system is considered historically significant for its political, cultural, and technological accomplishments that have modified the way Americans perceive and utilize their society.

—ELIZABETH D. SCHAFER,
LOACHAPOKA, ALABAMA

Viewpoint:
No, although the interstate highway system opened new areas for expansion and funded economic growth, it also hurt the inner cities by facilitating white flight to the suburbs.

The Federal Aid Highway Act, signed into law by President Dwight D. Eisenhower in 1956, completely redefined the way Americans viewed cities and transportation. It became the largest peacetime public-works program in history, and its sheer scope and design is rivaled perhaps only by the Great Wall of China. While America has always been a technologically driven society, few innovations have had such an intense and far-reaching impact on the lives of all Americans. The consequences, however, have not always been beneficial.

Technological change has always been embraced in the United States. The completion of the transcontinental railroad in 1869 opened up large areas of land for settlement. Industrial innovations such as Henry Ford's moving assembly line revolutionized the way work was performed. Urban areas were highly susceptible to these technological advances, witnessed by the growth of suburban areas concomitant with changes in transportation. As horse-drawn trolleys, omnibuses, elevated tracks, cable cars, and subways reached farther out of the cities, the ecology of surrounding areas was changed. The rapid growth of New York would not have been possible without the addition of more area to settle with the construction of the Interborough Rapid Transit system.

With the advent of the automobile there seemed no limit (other than the natural limitations of space) to how far Americans could go. The car opened vast new areas for settlement and allowed many people to take advantage of the "American Dream": owning a car and a house with a white picket fence. During the 1910s and 1920s states began to construct parkways and toll roads to increase land for settlement. Though the federal government assumed little of the cost of this construction, the Federal Bureau of Public Roads advocated drawing plans to connect the country with a large system of roads. During the Great Depression road construction became a public-works tool to curb unemployment, a theme that Eisenhower would later utilize when he signed the 1956 Highway Act.

American culture embraced the automobile like no other object. In Sinclair Lewis's *Babbitt* (1922), the protagonist, George Babbitt, expounds on the relative social standing of families based upon the cars they drive. The automobile culture was a symbol of ostentation and decadence in F. Scott Fitzgerald's *The Great Gatsby* (1925). During the Great Depression, John Steinbeck wrote his famous novel *The Grapes of Wrath* (1939), in which even the poorest farm families hopped into their auto to flee the Dust Bowl for sunny California. In the years after World War II, Jack Kerouac's *On the Road* (1957) became an expression of American affluence, consumption, and expansion across the West.

The economic importance of the automobile could be seen in the money it generated in ancillary industries. Cars needed rubber tires, mechanics, advertisements to sell them, fast-food restaurants to service hungry drivers, and gas stations for fuel-hungry cars. Road construction required enormous amounts of steel and concrete supports and employed construction workers, engineers, planners, and lawyers–the automobile was a veritable economy unto itself. Thus, when the federal government began funding 90 percent of the costs of highway construction in 1956, it seemed that no one would lose; how could something that produced so many benefits for so many people be bad?

The highway program was funded by an excise tax on gasoline, sent to the federal government and redistributed to the states for construction of the interstate system. New York City, led by Triborough Bridge and Tunnel Authority Commissioner Robert Moses, was building expressways and parkways well before 1956, but these were largely funded by tolls on the turnpikes and bridges. Moses alone spent $27 billion in New York City on bridge, tunnel, and highway construction. Other states had undertaken large highway construction projects before the government subsidized them, but with Washington picking up the tab, construction exploded throughout the country.

Now that money was flowing from Washington, states were able to begin constructing the highway plans that had been developed over the preceding years. Traffic patterns dictated the routes. By connecting urban areas to rural areas, the highways exposed enormous tracts of land to housing development. Along with federally guaranteed mortgages for veterans, housing construction and ownership skyrocketed. In all of these homes were placed the most modern appliances–the interstate highway system facilitated the growth of suburbia and the middle class like nothing else. Entire communities were planned, built, and filled in record numbers. Historians and sociologists both have marveled at the efficiency with which Abraham and William Levitt built entire subdivisions in a period of weeks–using prefabricated materials and a highly regimented work schedule so that dozens of houses could be built in a single day. Yet, within the housing contract that new buyers signed, the Levitts had a clause that dictated that units could not be resold to nonwhites, belying the notion that the interstate highway system put the "American Dream" within reach of all Americans.

Joel Garreau, in *Edge City: Life on the New Frontier* (1991), examined the formation of what he calls "edge cities," which are not concentrated cities but self-sufficient communities along the peripheries of highways. Like Levittowns, these are highly structured communities, planned from the top down. Edge cities provide places to work, shop, worship, learn, and play beyond the confines of crowded central cities. Like the subtle social control that operated within Levittowns, edge cities have what Garreau termed "shadow governments," which operate through homeowner associations to enforce normative behavior on their residents. Garreau wrote that "this is a place that is enforced, not just planned." Combined with highway construction, these enforced, homogenous communities have devastated urban economies and relegated racial minorities to the inner city.

If highway construction opened up new swaths of land for suburban settlement, they also reshaped urban environments. In 1948 the Commonwealth of Massachusetts designed its "Master Highway Plan" to combat costly traffic jams. It laid out a plan of two beltways to skirt Boston, a major north-south artery through downtown, and the extension of a western road to intersect with the beltways and the central artery. The construction of the John F. Fitzgerald Highway cut off from downtown a vibrant ethnic community. The extension of the Massachusetts Turnpike into the city gobbled up portions of Chinatown and South Boston. Though the growth of high-tech industry along Route 128–the outer beltway–gave rise to a literal "information superhighway," areas in the inner city were left to languish in the shadows of the elevated expressways. The planned paths of the expressways in Boston's master plan were inhabited, and as construction continued, residents rallied to save their neighborhoods and homes. It gradually dawned on citizens that the interstate-highway program put more emphasis on concrete than on people. The protests of residents in central Boston led Governor Francis Sargent to declare a moratorium on all highway construction in 1970. But the highway juggernaut had already sapped the city of industry, tax-paying residents, and businesses that contributed both jobs and taxes.

Similar events transpired in many of the other East Coast cities. In New York, Moses continued to hammer expressways through residential areas. His biographer has estimated that his road-construction programs displaced nearly half a million residents from their homes. While Moses defended his approach with pithy maxims such as "you can't make an omelet without breaking eggs" and believed that later generations who would use his highways would justify his approach, his biographer took a less sanguine view: "He had used the power of money to undermine the democratic processes of the largest city in the world, to plan and build its parks, bridges, highways and housing projects on the basis of his whim alone."

Mass transportation initiatives were starved for funds during this concrete bonanza. Because the interstate was built with a user tax–an added tax on gasoline sales–it was rationalized that the money should be used on highway construction alone. Thus more efficient and economical modes of transportation, such as subways, buses, and light rail systems, were starved of patrons and money. Few understood concepts such as "generated traffic" or "increased demand" when highways were being planned and built. The Sun Belt–areas of the South and Southwest–is largely a postwar construction, with highway construction underlying the expansion of urban areas in communities such as Phoenix, Dallas, and Los Angeles. By 1980 five of the ten largest urban areas in America were in the Sun Belt. These new settlements are largely auto-dependent and contain little open space. The air in Los Angeles is notoriously polluted. The costs of the highway are not measured simply in miles and dollars: there are ecological, social, and political costs as well.

The vast expansion of concrete has had deleterious environmental effects. Journalist Jane Holtz Kay in *Asphalt Nation: How the Automobile Took Over America, and How We Can Take it Back* (1997) has cogently captured the effects: "From the road slashed through a hill or gully to the coiling ribbon that rolls from sprawling house to house, the highway disrupts habitats and abets erosion. The polluting vehicle that travels its route channels a lethal runoff of antifreeze and oil of refrigerants from coolants and brake linings. . . ." Compound this problem with the eradication of open space and parks as suburban development creeps ever onward, and suddenly a nation of wall-to-wall concrete seems less appealing.

Devoted to serving the automobile, the interstate-highway program also fueled deindustrialization, white flight, and a terribly ill-conceived idea of "urban renewal." As a wartime expedient, the federal government had begun to build up industrial sites in the South and Southwest. The expansive areas of the Sun Belt were the chief beneficiaries of Cold War defense budgets as the availability of open land allowed plant designers to construct large, rolling factories that cost less than construction in already established urban areas of the Northeast and Midwest. The initiation of the Federal Highway Program sped up this process of industrial relocation, which had the effect of devastating the labor markets in certain areas. Tom J. Sugrue, in *The Origins of the Urban Crisis: Race and Inequality in Postwar Detroit* (1996), examined patterns of racial housing discrimination in central Detroit, demonstrating that even before the interstate highway system was begun, there was pervasive discrimination in housing and employment in the city. With the advent of the federal highway program and its attendant expansion of settlement areas, whites and jobs left the city en masse, leaving Detroit with no economic or tax base with which to generate revenue.

Accompanying white flight and deindustrialization was the process of urban renewal. Economically, it made sense to build highways through areas in which land values were lowest, even though most metropolitan governments used the process of "eminent domain" to expropriate lands below market rate anyway. Frequently however, properties with the least value were located in predominantly minority areas. Sugrue found that highway construction in Detroit devastated many prominent African American institutions in the city, while leaving

A PROUD MOMENT FOR AMERICA

On June 26, 1956 I signed [the Federal Aid Highway Act] into law. It was not only the most gigantic federal undertaking in road-building in the century and a half since the federal government got into this field by improving the National Pike between Cumberland, Maryland, and Wheeling, West Virginia—it was the biggest peacetime construction project of any description ever undertaken by the United States or any other country. . . . The big feature of the act was the amount it earmarked for the widening and improving of our interstate and defensive highway system, a forty-one thousand-mile network of roads linking nearly all major cities with a population of fifty thousand or more. . . .

The amount of concrete poured to form these roadways would build eighty Hoover Dams or six sidewalks to the moon. To build them, bulldozers and shovels would move enough dirt and rock to bury all of Connecticut two feet deep. More than any single action by the government since the end of the war, this one would change the face of America with straightways, cloverleaf turns, bridges, and elongated parkways. Its impact on the American economy—the jobs it would produce in manufacturing and construction, the rural areas it would open up—was beyond calculation.

Source: *Dwight David Eisenhower,* Mandate for Change 1953–1956 *(New York: Doubleday, 1963), pp. 548–549.*

suburban areas marginally impacted. Another scholar noted that in Osage, West Virginia, the right-of-way for Interstate 79 eliminated every black-owned dwelling in the town, a process that was duplicated in countless other cities.

Processes such as this led to a reappraisal in federal policy. The government gradually shifted to a policy of intermodal transportation, meaning that states can use the money for mass transit improvements, more road construction, or ideally, a combination of the two. In 1965 San Francisco succeeded in deleting its waterfront Embracadero Freeway from the interstate system, which stopped its construction. Milwaukee began to tear down one of its inner-city expressways, and Boston is burying its Central Artery underground. Portland, Oregon, has established an urban-growth boundary and instituted a light-rail system. Yet, the highway juggernaut creeps on, as witnessed in the construction of a massive new highway along the Great Salt Lake in Utah. Highway construction is big business. The debate over President Ronald Reagan's veto of the 1987 Highway Act (which was overridden) was telling: debate on both sides was couched in terms of jobs and economic stimulus. One senator went so far as to say "A year without a highway program would be like a year without summer."

Suburbia appears to be the ultimate benefactor of the interstate highway system. More Americans live in the suburbs than in central cities, and they have become key players in elections. The groups remaining in the cities—essentially trapped by inaccessibility to jobs and transportation—have lost most of their input in politics. The Department of Housing and Urban Development is starved of money. President Lyndon B. Johnson's War on Poverty policies for inner cities were left twisting in the breeze, forced to rely largely on their own funds to solve problems that suburbanites ignored and that were the result of poorly planned federal policy.

Eisenhower's interstate system accomplished a great deal of good. Into the reach of tens of millions of Americans it placed the ideal of a detached single-family house. Suburban developments and subdivisions stand largely in homage to the engineers and construction workers who built these roadways. An entire new social class had the opportunity to define itself. It is now possible to drive from coast to coast without stopping for a single stoplight. Like many other bureaucratic solutions, however, it was dangerously shortsighted. By fueling white flight and deindustrialization, the highway program exacerbated social and racial rifts. By the time the system was finally completed, many parts had already become obsolete. More highways bred more traffic and the need for more highways. Anyone who has been trapped in bumper-to-bumper traffic can relate to questioning the inherent wisdom of paving the entire country. The interstate highway system placed a premium on production, neglecting the more important processes of sound planning and community input. While it has truly reshaped the way Americans conceptualize community, transportation, and urban space, the interstate system has done so in not necessarily positive ways.

–MICHAEL MEZZANO, NORTHEASTERN UNIVERSITY

References

Warren J. Belasco, *Americans on the Road: From Autocamp to Motel, 1910–1945* (Cambridge: MIT Press, 1979);

Robert A. Caro, *The Power Broker: Robert Moses and the Fall of New York* (New York: Knopf, 1974);

Richard O. Davies, *The Age of Asphalt: The Automobile, the Freeway, and the Condition of Metropolitan America* (Philadelphia: Lippincott, 1975);

Dwight D. Eisenhower, *Mandate for Change, 1953–1956: The White House Years* (Garden City, N.Y.: Doubleday, 1963);

Robert Fishman, *Bourgeois Utopias: The Rise and Fall of Suburbia* (New York: BasicBooks, 1987);

James J. Flink, *The Automobile Age* (Cambridge: MIT Press, 1988);

Joel Garreau, *Edge City: Life on the New Frontier* (New York: Doubleday, 1991);

Clifton Hood, *722 Miles: The Building of the Subways and How They Transformed New York* (New York: Simon & Schuster, 1993);

John A. Jakle, *The Tourist: Travel in Twentieth-Century North America* (Lincoln: University of Nebraska Press, 1985);

Jakle and Keith A. Sculle, *The Gas Station in America* (Baltimore: Johns Hopkins University Press, 1994);

Jakle, Sculle, and Jefferson S. Rogers, *The Motel in America* (Baltimore: Johns Hopkins University Press, 1996);

Jan Jennings, ed., *Roadside America: The Automobile in Design and Culture* (Ames: Iowa State University Press, 1990);

Jane Holtz Kay, *Asphalt Nation: How the Automobile Took Over America, and How We Can Take it Back* (New York: Crown, 1997);

David L. Lewis and Laurence Goldstein, eds., *The Automobile and American Culture* (Ann Arbor: University of Michigan Press, 1980);

Tom Lewis, *Divided Highways: Building the Interstate Highways, Transforming American Life* (New York: Viking, 1997);

Chester H. Liebs, *Main Street to Miracle Mile: American Roadside Architecture* (Boston: Little, Brown, 1985);

John Margolies, *Home Away From Home: Motels in America* (Boston: Little, Brown, 1995);

Clay McShane, *The Automobile: A Chronology of its Antecedents, Development and Impact* (Westport, Conn.: Greenwood Press, 1997);

Henry Moon, *The Interstate Highway System* (Washington, D.C.: Association of American Geographers, 1994);

Lewis Mumford, *The Highway and the City* (New York: Harcourt, Brace & World, 1963);

Phil Patton, *Open Road: A Celebration of the American Highway* (New York: Simon & Schuster, 1986);

Yale Rabin, "The Roots of Segregation in the Eighties: The Role of Local Government Actions," in *Divided Neighborhoods: Changing Patterns of Racial Segregation,* edited by Gary A. Tobin (Newbury Park, Cal.: Sage, 1987), pp. 208–226;

John B. Rae, *The Road and the Car in American Life* (Cambridge: MIT Press, 1971);

Mark H. Rose, *Interstate: Express Highway Politics, 1939–1989,* revised edition (Knoxville: University of Tennessee Press, 1990);

Virginia Scharff, *Taking the Wheel: Women and the Coming of the Motor Age* (New York: Free Press, 1991);

Bruce E. Seely, *Building the American Highway System: Engineers as Policy Makers* (Philadelphia: Temple University Press, 1987);

Tom J. Sugrue, *The Origins of the Urban Crisis: Race and Inequality in Postwar Detroit* (Princeton: Princeton University Press, 1996);

Jon C. Teaford, *The Rough Road to Renaissance: Urban Revitalization in America, 1940–1985* (Baltimore: Johns Hopkins University Press, 1990);

G. Scott Thomas, *The United States of Suburbia: How the Suburbs Took Control of American and What they Plan to do with it* (Amherst, N.Y.: Prometheus, 1998);

United States, Federal Highway Administration, *America's Highways, 1776–1976* (Washington, D.C.: Government Printing Office, 1977);

R. F. Weingroff, "Federal-Aid Highway Act of 1956: Creating the Interstate System," *Public Roads,* 60 (Summer 1996): 10–17, 45–51.

KENNEDY

Was John F. Kennedy committed to international peace?

Viewpoint: Yes, President John F. Kennedy was a flexible and pragmatic leader who avoided direct conflict with the Soviet Union.

Viewpoint: No, John F. Kennedy's foreign policy contributed to the arms race and U.S. involvement in Vietnam.

No event has so traumatized Americans as the assassination of President John F. Kennedy. Americans were so shocked by his sudden, tragic death, that it was almost impossible in the late 1960s to recover what Americans had thought of him during his life. It was inevitable after his death that men and policies would be measured against both the standard he had set and the standard Americans imagined he had forged. As the United States became more involved in the Vietnam War, and as some of the late president's closest advisers broke with his successor, Lyndon B. Johnson, it was also inevitable that they would accuse Johnson of betraying Kennedy's legacy and policies and claim that had Kennedy lived, the United States would not have become so deeply involved in the war.

This view was relatively standard in the late 1960s. More than thirty years later, can historians come to a more objective decision? In these two essays, two scholars try to do so. Robert J. Allison assesses the Kennedy presidency, without the burden of grief, and determines that yes, President Kennedy was committed to international peace, and his policies offered reasonable and realistic ways to achieve this goal. Jürgen Scheunemann, on the other hand, believes that Kennedy was as much a Cold Warrior as any other American public figure of the day. By the end of the 1960s it may have been possible for prudent American statesmen to call for an end to the Cold War, but it was not possible in 1963, and Kennedy did not do so.

How will history judge John F. Kennedy? We should not forget as we evaluate his administration and legacy that the young Kennedy did not aspire to be a politician. He had hoped after graduating from college to be a journalist or an historian, and his first book, *Why England Slept* (1940), asks why the British failed to respond to Germany's military buildup in the 1930s. Kennedy did not shrink from asking tough questions of political leaders or of ourselves; nor should we. To be fair to his legacy we must examine it critically and thoughtfully. History, Kennedy said in his inaugural address, will be the final judge.

Viewpoint: Yes, President John F. Kennedy was a flexible and pragmatic leader who avoided direct conflict with the Soviet Union.

John F. Kennedy's legacy is not in specific policies or ideas, but rather in his ability to think things through and strive toward goals. Unlike two of his successors, Lyndon B. Johnson and Richard M. Nixon, Kennedy would not have allowed himself to have become so committed to a policy that he lost sight of what the policy was intended to do. Kennedy was flexible, pragmatic, and able to abandon policies that were not working without fearing that in doing so he would appear weak or indecisive. In this sense, Kennedy was the most able statesman to sit in the Oval Office since Franklin D. Roosevelt.

In a 1954 magazine article Senator Kennedy had tried to dispel dangerous Cold War myths, such as "the existence of inherently good, bad or backward nations," and throughout his public life Kennedy tried to redirect American policy to treat each nation as both a potential friend and a potential foe. This policy of informed neutrality sprang from the earliest period of American national existence and moved away from the close alliances the United States had developed during World War II. Kennedy was not swayed by arguments that some nations were permanent allies of the United States or that the same policies would work in all relationships. Instead, Kennedy wanted careful analysis of each situation so the United States could make an informed and wise policy choice.

On 13 March 1961 Kennedy met with ambassadors from Latin America to unveil his proposed Alliance for Progress. Kennedy had been thinking about American policy toward its Western Hemisphere neighbors for some time, and his Alliance for Progress called both for American aid to Latin American nations and for support to democratic governments in the hemisphere. The ten-year economic program was slow to start, but it was an important beginning to a new chapter in relations between the United States and other nations in the hemisphere.

The Alliance for Progress suffered a major setback in April, when the failed Bay of Pigs invasion tarnished the U.S. image throughout the hemisphere. The United States had become estranged from Fidel Castro's government shortly after the 1959 revolution. Under Dwight D. Eisenhower, the Central Intelligence Agency (CIA) had trained an army of anticommunist Cuban exiles to invade Cuba and overthrow Castro's regime. Kennedy at first thought this proposed action was exactly what the United States should do–support local insurgents against a communist government, rather than engage itself in a military action. While Kennedy countenanced the planned invasion, he insisted that the United States not have a direct military role–the planners of the operation believed either that the exiles could win without American aid, that they would stir the Cuban people to rebel against Castro, or that once the action started, the United States would have to step in to aid them.

The 17 April 1961 Bay of Pigs invasion was a complete fiasco. Castro's air force sank two freighters carrying supplies to the insurgents; the rebel troops, in their first combat, wasted ammunition; and within three days the rebellion was suppressed. Though the United States did not have a direct combat role, the blame arrived on the president's doorstep. Though Kennedy could easily have shifted blame for the disaster either to the CIA or to Eisenhower, instead he made clear it was his failure. He took complete responsibility for the disaster. It was the worst defeat of his political life, and Kennedy learned an important lesson: he would never again trust experts who claimed their plan was foolproof. This practical lesson served him well for the remainder of his administration. The disaster threatened American relations with its Alliance for Progress partners and with the Organization of American States (OAS), but it did not dampen Kennedy's enthusiasm for maintaining a peaceful American role in the hemisphere.

Kennedy also came to believe in a greater role for international organizations. When he took office the United Nations was in a state of crisis. Its intervention in the Congo had angered the Soviet Union, and the Soviets proposed replacing the single secretary general with three, one to represent the West, one to represent the Soviet bloc, and the third to represent the nonaligned nations. This change would effectively prevent any United Nations (U.N.) action. Secretary General Dag Hammarskjold had boldly led the United Nations into the Congo, maintaining the U.N.'s neutral role in the dispute between East and West. Nikita S. Khrushchev regarded Hammarskjold as a front man for the imperialist west, telling Kennedy that there could be neutral nations but not neutral men. The Soviet proposal for a troika seemed to isolate the United States against the Soviets, and also against the nonaligned nations of the world.

On 18 September 1961 Hammarskjold was killed in a plane crash in the Congo. The Soviets were going to seize the opportunity to force the United Nations to adopt its troika, vetoing any interim secretary general until the U.N. charter changed. Kennedy had already planned to address the United Nations when its General Assembly session opened on 25 September, and now he was challenged not only to open the session but also to help ensure the U.N.'s survival. Kennedy rose to the occasion, calling for a vital and active

President John F. Kennedy speaking in Berlin on 26 June 1963

(AKG)

United Nations, under the leadership of one secretary general, to preserve "world law, in the age of self-determination, to world war, in the age of mass extermination." An influx of new members, newly independent states, into the United Nations in the 1960s changed the nature of the institution, and since Kennedy's death it has become the peacekeeping force it was intended to be.

Two important American initiatives, the Peace Corps and the Food for Peace program, helped secure better relationships with the Third World. The Peace Corps was born of American idealism. It was modeled in many ways on the Mormon Church's missionary efforts, in which young Mormons are required to spend some time in spreading their religion throughout the world. The Peace Corps volunteers would not be spreading American values, but would be living and working among people around the world, helping to build schools and medical facilities to improve people's lives. By the end of his first year in office, Kennedy had sent five hundred Peace Corps volunteers to other countries; by March 1963 more than five thousand were engaged in good works; and by 1964 ten thousand idealistic young Americans were Peace Corps volunteers. This figure was one-half the number of American troops then in Vietnam, and it makes one wonder what might have happened had John F. Kennedy lived to rethink American policy in Southeast Asia.

Food for Peace was an imaginative use of the American farm surplus. The United States could help feed the world, and Food for Peace was the agency to do this. By the end of his term, Kennedy was also able to sell grain to the Soviet Union, which may have been the real beginning of the end of communism. Khrushchev had pledged to bury the capitalist West; by the mid 1960s the United States was feeding the Soviets.

In 1962 Kennedy had another challenge from Cuba. After the Bay of Pigs, Fidel Castro had come to rely on the Soviets for support and protection. In 1962 Castro allowed the Soviets to place missiles in Cuba, capable of reaching the U.S. mainland. For the first time the United States was within range of Soviet missiles. Kennedy reacted quickly, placing a quarantine around Cuba, mobilizing the American military, and threatening military action if the Soviets did not withdraw their weapons. These were the public steps–privately Kennedy and Khrushchev agreed that the Soviets would remove weapons from Cuba, and the United States would remove some of its weapons from Turkey and Greece. The two leaders also agreed to set up a hot line between their offices. Kennedy's response to the Cuban Missile Crisis was careful, reasonable, and effective.

While Kennedy did not end the Cold War, he did help to make a direct conflict with the Soviet Union less likely. Kennedy's greatest contribution to easing the arms race was the first Nuclear Test Ban Treaty, adopted by the United States and the Soviet Union in the summer of 1963. The treaty banned atmospheric testing of nuclear weapons and was aimed to slow the arms race between the Americans and Soviets and to prevent future nations from becoming nuclear powers. That it did not successfully complete all its objectives is clear. Equally clear is that without this crucial first step, the world would have continued to spiral toward nuclear catastrophe.

By the end of his administration Kennedy was speaking of making the world safe for diversity. A measure of his success in achieving peace can be found in the fact that he became president with the world divided between Communist and non-Communist states. The United States suspected all neutral powers of being in alliance with the Soviets; the Soviets suspected them of being American lackeys. By the end of his term, though, the United States had achieved stable relationships with Sekou Toure of Guinea, whom the Eisenhower administration had regarded as a Soviet stooge; Sukarno of Indonesia; Jawaharlal Nehru of India; and Gamal Abdel Nasser of Egypt. Kennedy's ability not to be blinded or constrained by ideology, or by the failed policies of the past, served him, and the nation, well.

–ROBERT J. ALLISON,
SUFFOLK UNIVERSITY

Viewpoint:
No, John F. Kennedy's foreign policy contributed to the arms race and U.S. involvement in Vietnam.

In the past few years, analysis of John F. Kennedy's foreign policy has undergone a dramatic change. Historians, supported by new evidence, now deliver a more accurate, sober, and neutral picture of the Kennedy presidency. From the first memoirs by Kennedy advisers Theodore C. Sorenson and Arthur M. Schlesinger Jr., who offer unequivocal appraisals of the White House as a distinct and brightly shining Camelot, to the harsh and at times biased accounts of Garry Wills and Thomas C. Reeves, historiography on Kennedy, and especially his foreign policy, has come a long way. The reinterpretation of these highly dramatic three years does not do damage to the myth surrounding the assassinated president, but it does introduce a note of normalcy shifting the history of the presidency back into the real context: the times and places of 1961 to 1963.

The portrait drawn by these new interpretations is certainly one of Kennedy as a Cold Warrior. Because of his foreign policy, the ideological, military, and political confrontation between the United States and Soviet Union not only intensified but also entailed considerable risks. Kennedy's foreign policy contributed to the arms race, to some of the most dangerous crises faced in modern history, and ultimately to U.S. involvement in counterinsurgency, which led to military commitments around the world, most tragically in Vietnam.

During the 1950s U.S. foreign policies had little opposition around the globe. The nuclear balance of power gave American cultural and political expansionism in Latin America, Africa, Asia, and Europe a safe cover and a certain stability. In foreign-policy terms, the latter Eisenhower years in particular seem to suggest interest in status-quo stability with the Soviet Union. The young up-and-coming Kennedy attacked this lack of mobility during his time in the U.S. Senate and then as a presidential candidate. By education and personal experience, Kennedy had been a Cold Warrior throughout his early political career. A sharp and critical analyst of British appeasement policy prior to World War II, and an outspoken opponent of his father's support for American isolationism, Kennedy supported a strong U.S. foreign policy.

Kennedy carried this attitude into the White House, remaining the Cold Warrior he was in the face of the strong-willed and able adversary Soviet premier Nikita S. Khrushchev, the rising power of communist China, and the creeping decline of American power. Compared to the Eisenhower foreign policy, many of Kennedy's initiatives appear to have signaled a new beginning, but their powerful rhetoric and style should not divert attention from their real essence. All of these measures were designed to make the Cold War a conflict the United States could ultimately win. In his foreign policy Kennedy hardly ever left out the psychological and political framework of global confrontation. He was a firm believer in American superiority and in the American obligation to protect the Free World, and he steered his administration on a course to defeat ideological and political antagonists. The flexibility Kennedy brought into the arena of international politics was not introduced by him and his advisers to end the Cold War, but rather to make it more manageable. Kennedy chose risky flexibility over stable gridlock.

The primary important step of the Kennedy administration was a blanket increase in defense spending, mainly in conventional arms, atomic weapons (both intercontinental ballistic missiles [ICBMs] and small-scale, tactical weapons with nuclear warheads). More money was ploughed into Pentagon counterinsurgency and CIA covert operations programs as well. In the first year of his administration alone, Kennedy managed to raise the defense budget by $6 billion. The Kennedy administration, however, knew all too well that the so-called missile gap—the presumed disparity in ICBMs with the Soviet Union and hence American inferiority—was a myth (one that Kennedy, as a candidate, skillfully exploited to defeat Nixon). In addition, Kennedy envisioned and implemented a new strategy: during the presidential race, and in the first weeks of his administration, he began to denounce publicly the doctrine of massive retaliation, the postwar strategy of a complete American nuclear counterattack if the Soviet Union were to attack the United States first. This doctrine certainly had disadvantages because it paralyzed American diplomacy and became increasingly ineffective in a changing international system. Overall, U.S. power was beginning to erode around the world, while the Soviet Union, with growing self-confidence, started a global ideological war and encouraged and supported "national liberation wars" around the world. Many African, Asian, and Latin American countries gained their independence and were hence the victims of both Soviet and U.S. interventions in order to draw them into the Eastern or Western bloc, respectively. In Europe the once-shattered Western nations, especially France and Germany, had regained some of their old strength and, in the process of uniting Europe, suddenly became difficult allies ready to use their new economic and diplomatic power to pursue their own foreign policy.

Massive retaliation policy was turned into "flexible response," a nuclear strategy that provided diversified instruments and several options of military responses to Soviet aggression. It admitted full-blown nuclear response only as a last resort, and envisioned more-limited alternatives, including conventional warfare and counterinsurgency. In doing so, Kennedy was motivated not only by his concern that a nuclear war would inevitably lead to global destruction, but also by his insight into the way times were changing. Kennedy was more interested in better controlling the arms race with the Soviet Union, and less in détente and disarmament itself. Two of the frequently cited examples of Kennedy's commitment to détente, his famous speech at the American University on 10 June 1963 and the Test Ban Treaty of 25 July 1963, actually support this view. He called for a new approach to the Cold War and simultaneously warned of the dangers of a nuclear exchange, thus appealing to the responsibility of both superpowers. At the same time he identified the Soviet Union as the sole responsible actor for global confrontation. Despite mentioning the Test Ban Treaty in this speech as an example of American-Soviet cooperation, the treaty, in reality, was not designed to ease tensions between the superpowers or to limit the arms race: it served primarily to uphold nuclear exclusivity of both superpowers. Again, this was an attempt to keep a changing international system manageable for the Western superpower. It was not aimed at changing the confrontational system.

Overall, Kennedy's defense policy did not constitute an effort at minimizing confrontation with the Soviet Union. Instead it was an attempt to make it more controllable: in effect to conduct "limited wars," to use a phrase of that era. The early 1960s was a time of intensified low-scale conflicts, primarily in Latin America, Africa, and Asia. The use of conventional forces and the perceivable use of short-range tactical nuclear weapons seemed to be a proper response to this development.

Another change in political style that further supports the perception of Kennedy as a Cold Warrior is of equal importance. Contrary to his predecessor, Kennedy chose to boast publicly in March 1962 of American superiority by claiming that the United States was winning the nuclear-arms race and that a first strike by the United States was therefore conceivable. The effects of this statement should not be underestimated, especially when considered in the context of U.S. arms. In retrospect, remarks such as these may appear to be negligible. Intense ideological warfare in which rhetoric played an integral part in the confrontation was common at the time. This rhetoric not only directly threatened the Soviet Union but also forced it to react if it did not want to lose face at a global level. But the Soviet reaction turned out to go beyond American control. Kennedy's hard-line statements certainly bore witness to his political beliefs in the legitimacy of global confrontation, but they also escalated the Cold War in theaters of small-scale conflict around the world. One of these places was Vietnam.

In 1963 American engagement in Vietnam still looked like a fairly ordinary low-scale intervention. By the time Kennedy became president, the United States had 685 military advisers in the small southeast Asian country to help the

South Vietnamese fight communist rebels, the so-called Vietcong. During his first year in office, Kennedy sharply increased the U.S. commitment in Vietnam by signing two pivotal strategy papers in May and November 1961, respectively: the National Security Action Memorandums (NSAM) 52 and 111. By elevating these documents to the rank of guideline for his administration's Vietnam policy, Kennedy not only increased American involvement but also sent a strong signal to China and the Soviet Union: the United States would continue to resist any communist threat in the world. By the summer of 1963 the number of military advisers had climbed to more than sixteen thousand, and their activities now included military involvement. Some historians have attempted to construct a counterfactual history, claiming that Kennedy would have withdrawn the troops from Vietnam, but the hard evidence does not support this reading of events. He had indeed endorsed–in general terms–a U.S. withdrawal, but this was a widely held assertion in the White House, State Department, and Department of Defense, and it was a plan only to be adopted if the military conflict in Vietnam was assessed to be under control, for example, if a victory was certain for the Vietnamese backed by U.S. support. The main source for this interpretation is NSAM 263, the last foreign-policy directive of the Kennedy administration regarding Vietnam.

In October 1963 Kennedy accordingly announced the withdrawal of one thousand men from Vietnam. This step was intended to counter the impression in the United States and abroad that the administration would ultimately send combat troops, thus escalating the conflict. Furthermore, it was announced with the thought that the war in Vietnam could be won within a few weeks. When the South Vietnamese military dictator's brother, Ngo Dinh Nhu, frustrated by the ongoing fight against the Vietcong, began holding secret talks with the Vietcong and the National Liberation Front (the Communist Party), he and his brother, Ngo Dinh Diem, were overthrown and killed by a group of generals on 1 November 1963. The coup d'état came at the right time: the Kennedy administration, far from having encouraged Nhu in his peace talks, later even admitted American involvement in the coup. In sum, the U.S. involvement in Vietnam showed a president who firmly believed in the Domino Theory, the idea that if even one country turns communist, its neighbors will inevitably follow. The first line of defense against communism therefore had to be held by all means necessary.

Another equally hawkish foreign policy stance came to light in April 1961, when the Kennedy administration approved of a (failed)

A CRISIS NEAR HOME

With the world on the brink of nuclear holocaust over the Cuban Missile Crisis, President John F. Kennedy wrote the following message to Soviet premier Nikita S. Khrushchev on 12 November 1962:

Dear Mr. Chairman:

I have read your letter of October 26th with great care and welcomed the statement of your desire to seek a prompt solution to the problem. The first thing that needs to be done, however, is for work to cease on offensive missile bases in Cuba and for all weapons systems in Cuba capable of offensive use to be rendered inoperable, under effective United Nations arrangements.

Assuming this is done promptly, I have given my representatives in New York instructions that will permit them to work out this weekend—in cooperation with the Acting Secretary General and your representative—an arrangement for a permanent solution to the Cuban problem along the lines suggested in your letter of October 26th. . . .

If you will give your representative similar instructions, there is no reason why we should not be able to complete these arrangements and announce them to the world in a couple of days. The effect of such a settlement on easing world tensions would enable us to work toward a more general arrangement regarding "other armaments," as proposed in your second letter which you made public. I would like to say again that the United States is very much interested in reducing tensions and halting the arms race; and if your letter signifies that you are prepared to discuss a detente affecting NATO and the Warsaw Pact, we are quite prepared to consider with our allies any useful proposals.

But the first ingredient, let me emphasize, is the cessation of work on missile sites in Cuba and measures to render such weapons inoperable, under effective international guarantees. The continuation of this threat, or a prolonging of this discussion concerning Cuba by linking these problems to the broader questions of European and world security, would surely lead to an intensification of the Cuban crisis and a grave risk to the peace of the world. For this reason I hope we can quickly agree along the lines outlined in this letter and in your letter of October 26th.

Source: Documents of American History, *2 volumes, edited by Henry Steele Commager (New York: Appleton-Century-Crofts, 1973), II: 674–675.*

invasion of Cuba by exiled Cubans and of an attempt to overthrow Fidel Castro, the leader of a communist, yet sovereign, state. Secondly, the administration faced and probably escalated the Cuban Missile Crisis from 22 October to 28 October 1962.

Communist Cuba was perceived as a direct threat to the national security of the United States and the Western Hemisphere. Not only was it a communist system, but in addition, Castro enjoyed wide popularity among the oppressed peoples of Latin America–even though Castro himself headed a strict dictatorship. In the early 1960s Cuban military advisers and troops supported communist and left-wing rebels around the world; the island was also closely tied to the Soviet Union, which, in turn, would later materialize as a major threat to the United States. Yet, even as late as August 1961, after the failed Bay of Pigs invasion on 17 April, the Cuban government was sending signals of its willingness to seek more peaceful, rational coexistence with the United States. Cuba faced serious domestic economic problems. The Kennedy administration did not acknowledge these tentative steps. Instead, Kennedy, bound by both his campaign promises to oust Castro and the public mood in the United States, chose to confront the Cuban leader directly, both in rhetoric and in action. It is arguable which of the two statesmen was ultimately responsible for the unfolding Cuban Missile Crisis. It is clear, however, that one of Premier Khrushchev's motives in deploying Soviet intermediate missiles on the island was in great part a reaction to the U.S. administration's repeated attempts to overthrow Castro or invade Cuba. The Kennedy administration had learned nothing from the failed coup. In November 1961 Kennedy ordered another secret CIA operation called "Mongoose," which was designed to weaken Castro and ultimately sabotage his regime. The operation was stepped up in late summer 1962. In addition, the United States tightened the political noose around the island. Under American pressure, the Organization of American States (OAS) expelled Cuba from its organization in early 1962, and the United States began an economic embargo and staged military maneuvers in the sea around Cuba. In sum, these steps were perceived by Cuba and the Soviet Union as a direct threat to the island state–the missile crisis ensued. This event undoubtedly changed Kennedy's outlook on the Cold War; in the months following, the president pursued a more cautious approach to Cuban affairs, but that approach was in fact the direct result of his policy of Cold War confrontation.

Ultimately, the question as to whether Kennedy was a prudent statesman or a Cold Warrior is difficult to answer. His sudden death has largely prevented a more-balanced analysis. Had Kennedy lived and completed a second term as president, the discussion probably would be nonexistent.

–JÜRGEN SCHEUNEMANN, FOX FELLOW, YALE UNIVERSITY

References

Michael R. Beschloss, *The Crisis Years: Kennedy and Khrushchev, 1960–1963* (New York: Edward Burlingame, 1991);

Montague Kern, Patricia W. Levering, and Ralph B. Levering, *The Kennedy Crises: The Press, the Presidency, and Foreign Policy* (Chapel Hill & London: University of North Carolina Press, 1983);

Diane B. Kunz, ed., *The Diplomacy of the Crucial Decade: American Foreign Relations During the 1960s* (New York: Columbia University Press, 1994);

Ernest R. May and Philip D. Zelikow, eds., *The Kennedy Tapes: Inside the White House During the Cuban Missile Crisis* (Cambridge, Mass.: Belknap Press of Harvard University Press, 1997);

Thomas G. Paterson, ed., *Kennedy's Quest for Victory: American Foreign Policy, 1961–1963* (New York: Oxford University Press, 1989);

Theodore C. Sorensen, *Kennedy* (New York: Harper & Row, 1965);

Richard J. Walton, *Cold War and Counter-Revolution: The Foreign Policy of John F. Kennedy* (New York: Viking, 1972);

Mark J. White, ed., *Kennedy: The New Frontier Revisited* (New York: New York University Press, 1998).

MASS MEDIA

What effect did mass media have on postwar America?

Viewpoint: Television and other media have fostered a new democratic sense of American identity.

Viewpoint: Television has narrowed and distorted Americans' understanding of the world.

What impact has television had on American society? On the one hand, it may be too soon to gauge its full impact, as it has been a social force for only fifty years. On the other hand, it is difficult to think of an invention that has so completely transformed our lives and our understanding of the world. Television brings people together, creating a community of viewers sharing a single experience. Yet, the television networks operate as businesses, seeking profits, and are not in the business of uplifting, enlightening, educating, or challenging the audience. Television can do great things, but has it?

In these two essays, scholars Tona J. Hangen and A. Bowdoin Van Riper take different views on the impact of television. Hangen, a cultural historian, sees television as one of several mass media that has transformed American life in the twentieth century. She argues that these media have in fact improved our society by creating grounds for national and international discussion, breaking down barriers, and bringing people together. On the other hand, Van Riper, also a cultural historian, sees television narrowing people's perceptions and distorting their views of reality. In this way, though television may have brought people together, it also damaged their views of the world.

Which is right? Is television, as Newton N. Minow once observed, a "vast wasteland," or is it something more? These questions occupy not only historians, but all citizens. How has television influenced or shaped political debate? How has television been part of social movements since the 1940s? Understanding how television, or other mass media, work is crucial to understanding how our world works. Knowing the difference between reality and television also seems to be a crucial skill, which may be lost in a world where the distinction is blurred.

Or perhaps critics of television look at the issue in the wrong way. It is wrong to say that television has the power to shape our ideas and perceptions of the world. The men and women who control television have this power; without them television is an empty box.

Viewpoint: Television and other media have fostered a new democratic sense of American identity.

The development of the media of mass communication is an inseparable component of the rise of modernity. Mass media's core characteristics have helped define and shape modern times since the introduction of print media and can be summed up in three broad generalizations. First, media dissociate the spatial and temporal dimensions of human experience. Events can be encountered or understood apart from the location and time of their actual occurrence. A second, related characteristic is the mass media's disruption of physical spaces in which people become socialized to group norms and behaviors, by introducing new or alternative "social locations" to audiences. Communication therefore has come to take precedence over transportation in helping people cross group boundaries. Thirdly, mass media also opens access to information beyond the control of ruling groups. Even the apparently simple process of some ordinary people in the late Middle Ages in western Europe becoming literate and having access to books, plays, tracts, and the Bible in their vernacular language had a profound effect on both the development of society and on conceptions of the self. Media, by changing the patterns of information flow among individuals and groups, create new social environments in which role definitions can be transformed.

All of these characteristics, already present in print, telegraphic, and photographic media before the twentieth century, have become more pronounced with the rapid rise of visual, broadcast, and electronic media in postwar America. When taken as a whole, the mass media since 1945 have fragmented the institutions of social and political authority and have served as important—and often deeply ambiguous—sites of cultural contest and struggle, as well as forums for the presentation of a national unifying narrative. Ultimately, although mass media foster a new sense of democratic connectedness, shift social norms toward inclusion and permissiveness, and undermine central control, they have left unfulfilled the promise of brokering genuine relationships among groups.

The revolution of print culture was an incomplete one, as print segmented and segregated its audience into "readers" and "non-readers," into those who could participate in the emerging public, literary sphere described by Jurgen Habermas and those who were excluded from participation. Print media culture enhanced hierarchical chains of power and created distances between women and men, young and old, ordinary people and those with access to education. Electronic media, which are accessible without particular skills, even to the young or uneducated, have gone a long way toward reuniting spheres of interaction that have been distinct for centuries, argues Joshua Meyrowitz in his book, *No Sense of Place: The Impact of Electronic Media on Social Behavior* (1985).

Yet, the breakdown of this older paradigm through the development of visual and electronic forms of media was driven in the United States by capitalist commercial success, not by inherently revolutionary new media content. Both radio and television were developed as "abstract technical systems" for the delivery of electronic signals before Americans had conceptualized what those signals would convey, but they were soon thoroughly commercialized. Furthermore, as television all but defined American mass media in the postwar period, it is helpful to keep in mind that even more than radio, out of which it evolved, television is a visual package for advertising messages. Television's simplified reality, stock characters, and idealized situations frame the "real" message of television, which is to sell products to viewers; or, more precisely, to sell vast numbers of viewers to the makers of products.

The technology of television had existed since the 1920s and was publicly unveiled during the 1939 New York World's Fair, but the entire industry was put on hold during World War II. In the immediate postwar period, both FM radio and television became available for private commercial development. Radio quickly evolved into a "format" industry (classical, Top 40, and so forth) and became more of a solitary, background, portable medium (first in cars, and also in handheld radios with the advent in the late 1940s of the transistor) than its prewar incarnation. Between 1948 and 1952 the numbers of television broadcast licenses were frozen at about one hundred, until the laying of a coast-to-coast coaxial cable in 1951 and the opening of the UHF band for television made nationwide TV saturation a technological possibility. Then licenses immediately exploded to more than 530 in just eight years.

Television programming began with most programs being sponsored by a single corporation—the "Philco Playhouse," for example, or Milton Berle's "Texaco Star Theater"—and broadcast live from New York City network studios. Anthologies and other vaudeville and theater-inspired genres predominated. In fact, all American media in the 1940s drew upon a surprisingly wide assortment of cultural categories and milieu for material. As with radio in its early years, immigrants, as well as ethnic and racial minorities, made strong contributions to movies (including, with segregated theaters, an entire industry devoted to making movies featuring black characters for black audiences) and to early television. Whole groups entered public discourse, which would prove critical in changing perceptions of their roles in American society—Catholics gained ground with the wildly successful run of Bishop Fulton J. Sheen's program *Life is Worth Living* (DuMont network, 1952–1955 and ABC, 1955–1957), and evangelicals moved toward the American mainstream with the televised revivals of Billy Graham and his weekly program *Hour of Decision* (beginning in 1950). Blacks and women who took on new and alternative roles in the mass media eventually transformed national norms regarding their participation in work, politics, and public life.

New Yorkers view the 1953 coronation of Queen Elizabeth II on a display television

(Range/Betman)

The decade after World War II was a volatile cultural moment, and media productions of the time reflect a discernible tension between the ideals of domesticity and security, on the one hand, and on the other, the impossibility of recapturing the prewar past. New suburban communities sprang up across the nation, row upon row of look-alike homes with TV aerials on every chimney. "Levittowns" such as the original built on Long Island, New York, housed one in two hundred American families, the vast majority of them white and middle class. The contradictory impulses of geographic mobility–more automobiles, highways, and suburban housing–joined with an intense privatization of America home life to create a cultural environment responsive to broadcasting. Suburbia symbolized both the affordable, attainable dream and the dark vision of arbitrary authority and mind-numbing sameness. The apparent self-sufficiency of these isolated, private homes was deceptive; they relied not only on the external economy to exist, but increasingly on external sources of news and cultural input from the broadcast media. Life in Cold War America seemed on the verge of coming unhinged, plagued by fears, and fragmented–a sense that suited television's fractured story lines and narratives.

By the late 1950s television had noticeably changed in several ways, all of which illustrate that the media served as a forum for cultural struggle. Unlike the early, live television shows, programs increasingly were filmed in Hollywood for later broadcast, featured continuing character series, and reflected the influence of feature movies: westerns, dramas, musical comedies, and the like. The television quiz show scandals, in which two of the most popular programs were shown to be fixed in the 1959–1960 season, reinforced a general sense among media critics that the quality of the medium was declining–though the American love affair with television continued, measured by rising rates of television purchases and of the number of hours watched per week. In 1961 Newton N. Minow, President John F. Kennedy's newly appointed Federal Communications Commission (FCC) chairman, marked a new cynicism about the commercialism and shrinking cultural prestige of television by declaring in a famous speech before the National Association of Broadcasters that TV was a "vast wasteland." By the early 1960s television clearly aimed for an aesthetic, political, and cultural middle ground to attract the greatest possible audience. As CBS president Frank Stanton acknowledged in 1962, television's "obligation to the majority" in occupying scarce channels meant the deliberate exclusion of "experimental or limited interest programs."

By 1960, 87 percent of American homes (representing more than 46 million households) owned a television set, an increase of 25 percent from 1956. During the Kennedy years television reached its zenith in presenting a common American culture. AT&T launched the satellite *Telstar* in 1962, offering global television coverage; additional channels were opened in the UHF band, and cable television was introduced in some urban markets. Perhaps nothing so signified the mediums' dominant hold on American cultural life than Kennedy's funeral, watched by nearly the entire nation and broadcast on every channel, mediating the grief of millions.

Kennedy's funeral, appropriately enough, also marked a gradual shift from television as a medium of pure entertainment to one that Americans relied on increasingly for their news and information. The Vietnam War, which homefront Americans experienced vicariously through live televised reporting, undid both Johnson's presidency and the ability of presidents in general to control the media's messages. By the time of the Watergate hearings, the line between politics and entertainment seemed nonexistent—as image took precedence over substance, political spectacle and entertainment events looked more and more alike. A significant part of the uprising of the late 1960s was the ability of the mass media, and especially television, to make national causes out of issues that had previously been interpreted as local, such as segregation, civil rights, and women's liberation. The social consciousness of the period (and its opposing resistance) was largely a conglomeration of mediated realities, born of the images and sounds brought so forcefully into every living room.

By the 1980s the demographics of the television population had shifted toward more educated viewers. A 1980 study comparing audience responses to television with those of viewers in 1960 found that people had less regard for television's quality or reliability, but they still watched it more often than had people in 1960—an average of seven hours a day by 1982. Whereas a hardcover best-seller at the time might have drawn 115,000 in sales (or about one-twentieth of 1 percent of the population), each episode of a successful television program was seen by 25 to 40 million viewers, or between 11 and 18 percent of the population. Although still much larger than the audience for books, magazines, and radio, television programs have seen their viewer counts decline since the 1980s, when VCR sales and cable began to undermine the hegemony of the three major networks; this trend has accelerated in the 1990s.

As David Marc put it in *Demographic Vistas: Television in American Culture* (1984), "watching television is an act of citizenship, participation in culture." Today it may be even more that being seen on television is an act of citizenship—hence the democratization of television production through local access cable, programs featuring home videos or amateur footage, and on radio with call-in talk shows across the dial. The populist strain in broadcast media in the 1990s is, however, also a form of cultural containment—the ordinary American is not the intelligent hero but merely the buffoon in *America's Funniest Home Videos,* or the utterly dysfunctional and combative victim in daytime talk shows and "real courtroom" series such as *The People's Court,* or the pursued criminal in the *Cops* genre. One of the deep ironies of television is that it succeeded in demystifying the people who were disproportionately represented on its flickering screen—that is, middle-class white Americans—by showing them to be banal (*Leave It to Beaver*), boorish (*All in the Family* and *Married with Children*), or completely self-absorbed (*Seinfeld* and MTV's *Real World*).

Each medium of mass communication is a product of opposing impulses, explains Daniel J. Czitrom in *Media and the American Mind: From Morse to McLuhan* (1982), holding progressive, utopian visions of unity and connection in creative tension with dystopian visions of domination and exploitation. Scholars have studied mass media in a variety of ways, including audience research, textual analysis of films and broadcast programs, and historical studies of broadcast technology. Often whether a particular scholar emphasizes the progressive impulses of mass media (for example, the way it can unite Americans and celebrate diversity) or the exploitative ones (media's isolation of the individual or the tendency to marginalize minority points of view) depends a great deal on his or her theoretical perspective and choice of method.

In the second half of the twentieth century social change has been deep and swift, and much of that change has been portrayed on or intimately linked to the growing channels of mass media. At century's end, many contend that the mass media have eroded community and social trust, or that by its celebration of the capitalist white middle class it has systematically excluded others from public dialogue. However, the enormous range of media in America, and the ever-changing access of various groups to the means to use those media, will continue to permit (and display) transformations in the roles certain groups play in society. Whether the media are blamed for inculcating antisocial values and behavior or whether they are celebrated for their potential to increase people's sense of collective responsibility and awareness has more to do with the way that individuals selectively accept certain messages in the media and reject others than with anything inherent in the structure of the media themselves.

In other words, in a world of increasing sources of information and the introduction of new, mediated, social locations, people have greater control over the self they fashion and the world they perceive. The move toward interactive media and "narrowcasting" rather than broadcasting has the power to further segment the American population and isolate groups or individuals within it, but it also invites people to imagine, inhabit, and create alternative realities that acknowledge and embrace others. The mass media's legacy in the latter half of the twentieth century remains ambiguous because they have been a key location for cultural struggle without fully wresting away from people the tools to forge genuine connections in society and effect meaningful change. For better or worse, that responsibility and opportunity still belongs to each person.

–TONA J. HANGEN, BRANDEIS UNIVERSITY

Viewpoint: Television has narrowed and distorted Americans' understanding of the world.

Television plays a dual role in American society: it entertains and it informs. It has often been criticized, as entertainment, for immersing audiences in mediocre, formulaic programming and for pandering to their interest in sex and violence. These criticisms, though valid to an extent, could be leveled equally well against other branches of American popular culture. Entertainment television has maintained levels of artistic quality and social engagement similar to those of motion pictures and popular music. Critics who portray it as a uniquely potent threat to the nation's aesthetic and moral sensibilities are, therefore, on shaky ground. Informational television occupies, by contrast, a unique position in American culture. The images and sounds it provides have become most Americans' principal source of information about people, places, and events beyond their firsthand experience. Its failures are less commented on than those of entertainment television, but far more significant because the stakes are higher.

A democratic society can function neither efficiently nor justly if its citizens are ignorant of the world around them. Information about elected officials' ideas and actions alters the outcomes of elections; news about the intentions of foreign governments shapes relations with them; and knowledge about domestic conditions determines public support (or lack of support) for policy initiatives. The idea that the free flow of information will strengthen democracy is reflected in the First Amendment, in the Freedom of Information Act, and in financial-disclosure and open-meeting laws. American democracy operates on the principle that more information is better than less.

Judging by the quantity of information to them available at the touch of a remote-control button, Americans should be well informed. Those who watch television regularly should be conversant with the issues and events of the day, both at home and abroad. Unfortunately, the opposite is true. Television's coverage of the world is, as a whole, neither broad nor deep. It is, in its way, as shallow and formulaic as the much-derided comedies and action dramas offered as entertainment. Americans' reliance on television as their sole or principal source of information has impoverished their understanding of the world they live in. It has led many to mistake television's systematically biased view of reality for reality itself and therefore diminished their ability to be informed, responsible citizens.

The emergence of television substantially increased Americans' access to information about the world around them. It brought viewers both images and sound in real time, allowing them to witness events they could never have seen in person. Though invented in the 1930s and put into wide commercial use in the 1950s, television matured as an information source in the 1960s. Television coverage of the assassination of President John F. Kennedy in 1963 showed the new medium's power. Its sense of immediacy and ability to respond to rapidly changing events allowed it to supplant print media as the source of information about the assassination and its aftermath. The remainder of the 1960s brought a string of events that confirmed television's preeminence in covering breaking news. The assassinations of Robert Kennedy and Martin Luther King Jr., the escalating war in Vietnam, and the first manned landing on the moon all highlighted television's strengths as an information source. No other medium could show a political assasination, napalm-fed flames consuming a jungle, or an astronaut's low-gravity lope across the surface of a new world.

Television steadily consolidated its position as Americans' preferred information source after 1970. The expansion of the noncommercial Public Broadcasting System (PBS) brought a fourth "network" newscast to most major American cities beginning in the mid 1980s. The consolidation of the Fox Network added a fourth local newscast to many markets by the mid 1990s. The growth of cable television, with its multitude of new channels, created both space and demand for new programming. Most significantly, it established a venue for round-the-clock broadcasts by the Cable News Network (CNN), developed by Atlanta entrepreneur Ted Turner.

Television's rise took place alongside the slow decline of other information sources. The newsreel, once a standard part of movie theater programs, was dead by the mid 1960s. The narrowly specialized radio stations of the dawning FM era reduced news programming to headlines read at the top of the hour. Afternoon newspapers had been in decline since the end of World War II, hurt by television but also by changing work and commuting patterns. Americans were, by the end of the 1960s, turning to television not only for updates on breaking news but also for routine summaries of the state of the world around them.

The amount of information-oriented programming has grown steadily since 1970. Current events are now covered on local and national programs, news magazines such as CBS's *60 Minutes,* interview shows such as NBC's *Meet the Press,* and panel discussions such as PBS's *The McLaughlin Group.* Aspects of contemporary society other than breaking news are covered by an even wider range of programming. The Discovery Channel and the Learning Channel fill much of their airtime with series and specials covering contemporary aspects of science, medicine, law enforcement, engineering, and military affairs. The Lifetime Network, as well as the Arts and Entertainment Network, do so to a lesser degree, as do Fox and PBS. The average television viewer has access, in the course of an average week, to a staggering amount of information. If most Americans get their news from television, as surveys routinely report, it is not difficult to see how.

Television's limitations as an information source lie in the quality, not the quantity, of information it presents. The picture of the world that it offers viewers is systematically biased—not by any political agenda, but by the nature of the medium. Television coverage represents reality in much the same way that the fossil record represents the history of life on Earth. We know much about dinosaurs and little about jellyfish from the same era because dinosaurs fossilize better than jellyfish. Television's coverage of the contemporary world emphasizes bipolar conflicts and visual spectacles because they are far easier to present on television than other kinds of human experience.

American television typically presents information in brief segments. A lead story of a newscast (whether local or network) seldom runs more than a few minutes. Lesser stories frequently receive less than one minute of airtime. Even CNN, freed from time constraints by its round-the-clock broadcasting, packages its stories in bite-sized chunks. Network news magazines such as CBS's *60 Minutes,* ABC's *20/20,* or NBC's *Dateline* generally offer three segments in an hour. After time for commercials, introductions, viewers' letters, and credits are subtracted, less than fifteen minutes are available for each segment. Full-hour documentaries on serious subjects, a regular feature on the (then) three major networks in the 1950s and 1960s, have now been relegated to PBS series such as *Frontline* and *P.O.V.* Current-events programs longer than an hour are, except for events such as the State of the Union Address, virtually nonexistent.

The need to tell a complete story in less than twelve (or, more often, less than three) minutes limits the kind of stories that can be told well. Simple stories work better in television's hypercompressed world than complex ones. Stories with strong visual elements work better than nonvisual stories because images can efficiently replace exposition. Stories revolving around familiar individuals (President William J. Clinton) or archetypes (heroic rescuer, grieving family member, and other human-interest stories) work better than ones whose principal figures (the King of Morocco) need introductions. The same preference for the familiar over the exotic also applies to setting and content. It is easier, within the limits imposed by television, to explain a new war than a new religious schism and simpler to explain a story in a West European context rather than in a Southeast Asian one. Events and trends that fall on the wrong sides of these preferences tend to appear less often on television than those that fall on the right sides. When they do appear, they tend to receive briefer and less comprehensive coverage, and to fade away more quickly.

Overt conflicts—war, revolution, crime, and strikes—play well on television. Strife lends itself to the brief, streamlined summaries that television requires. It is reducible (for purposes of a three-minute story) to one of a series of "plots" already familiar to most audience members: A invades B; A murders B; or, A defrauds B. The story of an overt conflict can be summed up, efficiently if not meaningfully, by identifying A and B and specifying the details of what, when, and where. Overt conflict also generates the kind of vivid images that television thrives on: burning buildings, angry crowds, and crumpled bodies. Not surprisingly, conflict is well represented in television's information-oriented programming. Wars, strikes, and revolutions feature prominently on network newscasts when they are available. The prominence of crime on local newscasts is sardonically summed up in the famous slogan "If it bleeds, it leads." Series and specials based on video clips of police officers in action, such as Fox's *Cops,* offer similar content. On cable, A & E's *Justice Files* and the Discovery Channel's *Medical Detectives* feature reenactments, interviews, and re-created crime scenes.

The partisan aspects of domestic politics—elections, inter-party squabbles, diplomatic standoffs—also loom large on television. They, too, are easily reducible to formula: A smears B's character; A denounces B's policies; or, A vows no concessions to B. They, too, can be efficiently if not meaningfully summed up in the space of a few minutes. Media-conscious politicians, recognizing television's preference for striking images and simple, conflict-driven stories, routinely accommodate it. They appear at "photo opportunities" where they dispense "sound bites," knowing that snappy lines delivered in visually interesting settings attract television coverage. They emphasize the differences between their positions and those of their opponents, knowing that issues painted in black-and-white are more striking on television than those in shades of gray. Presidents Ronald Reagan, George Bush, and Clinton have all been masters of these tactics, as have many leading members of Congress. News and commentary programs alike now frequently cover domestic politics as if it were a sporting event, focusing more on tactics and poll-based "scorekeeping" than on the issues of the day.

The complex and the abstract are, by contrast, ill-suited to television's self-imposed limitations. The behavior of complex systems cannot be dealt with coherently in three-minute snippets. It tends, therefore, not to be dealt with at all on television. Stories about social, economic, and environmental change are comparatively rare on informational television. Those that do appear tend to be narrowly focused in ways that conform to the people-in-conflict formulas. A typical news story on the environment juxtaposes loggers and forest-preservation groups, legislators for and against stricter pollution controls, or scientists with divergent views on the reality of global warming. The environment itself, like the theories and models on which our understanding of it rests, receives scant attention. The same is true of stories on the economy: many are about pay-hike and minimum-wage disputes; few are about inflation-adjusted trends in wages over the last few decades. Others stories are about social trends: much concern about teenage pregnancy; little mention about the dropping age of puberty and rising age of first marriages.

Stories involving foreign societies are particularly ill served by television's simplified, formulaic coverage. The internal workings of any society, Western or non-Western, are enormously complex and difficult to summarize briefly. No two societies, no matter how superficially similar, are precisely identical, and the differences can be crucial in understanding their behavior. Television coverage of non-U.S. societies falls at the extreme ends of a spectrum, leaving a vast gulf between them. Western societies tend to appear on American television as analogues of the United States, using different languages and money, but essentially similar in outlook. Non-Western societies, on the other hand, tend to appear on informational television as collections of exotic behaviors and alien beliefs. The process reduces Western societies into Americans-with-accents, ignoring significant cultural differences. It reduces non-Western societies to caricatures while implying that their motives–rooted in their alien beliefs–are ultimately incomprehensible to Westerners.

Americans who rely on television as an information source thus absorb a limited, distorted view of the world around them. The world that television shows them each night is not a pleasant one. It is a world rife with conflict and division, violence and argument, destruction and pain. It is a world in which leaders' public statements on the issues of the day are sharply worded and deeply polarized. It is a world in which all problems appear to be simple ones, presumably amenable to simple solutions, and yet, one in which the same problems (taxes, pollution, border disputes, for example) seem to drag on endlessly without hope of resolution. It is a world divided starkly into two camps: the familiar, Western "us" and the alien, non-Western "them." Such a worldview is not, of course, the necessary and inevitable product of watching the evening news. Personal experience, information from other

NEWTON N. MINOW AND THE VAST WASTELAND (1961)

When television is good, nothing—not the theatre, not the magazines or newspapers—nothing is better.

But when television is bad, nothing is worse. I invite you to sit down in front of your television set when your station goes on the air and stay there without a book, magazine, profit and loss sheet or rating book to distract you—and keep your eyes glued to that set until the station signs off. I can assure you that you will observe a vast wasteland.

You will see a procession of game shows, violence, audience participation shows, formula comedies about totally unbelievable families, blood and thunder, mayhem, violence, sadism, murder, western badmen, western good men, private eyes, gangsters, more violence, and cartoons. And, endlessly, commercials—many screaming, cajoling, and offending. And most of all, boredom.

True, you will see a few things you will enjoy. But they will be very, very few. And if you think I exaggerate, try it. . . . do not accept the idea that the present over-all programming is aimed accurately at public taste. . . . I believe in the people's good sense and good taste, and I am not convinced that the people's taste is as low as some of you assume.

Source: *James R. Andrews and David Zarefsky, eds.,* Contemporary American Voices *(New York: Longman, 1992), pp. 405–412.*

sources, and active engagement with (rather than passive absorption of) television may all undermine it. Still, for viewers who use television as their sole or principal information source, this worldview is reality.

Widespread belief in a worldview such as the one that television promotes is a matter of more than academic interest. Living in an interdependent world, we cannot afford to divide our neighbors into lists headed "just like us" and "not at all like us." Living in an age when social, economic, and diplomatic problems are more complex than ever, we cannot afford to view every one of them in terms of simple bipolar conflict. Residing in a country where popular cynicism about government is at an all-time high, we cannot afford to see politics as a game to be won rather than a means of creating solutions. Americans have, for nearly forty years, relied on television as their principal window to the world. It has not served them well, either as individuals or as citizens of history's most powerful democracy.

–A. BOWDOIN VAN RIPER, SOUTHERN POLYTECHNIC STATE UNIVERSITY

References

William F. Baker and George Dessart, *Down the Tube: An Inside Account of the Failure of American Television* (New York: BasicBooks, 1998);

William Boddy, *Fifties Television: The Industry and Its Critics* (Urbana: University of Illinois Press, 1990);

Robert T. Bower, *The Changing Television Audience in America* (New York: Columbia University Press, 1985);

Robert Campbell, *Media and Culture: An Introduction to Mass Communication* (New York: St. Martin's Press, 1998);

Timothy Corrigan, *A Cinema Without Walls: Movies and Culture After Vietnam* (New Brunswick, N.J.: Rutgers University Press, 1991);

Daniel J. Czitrom, *Media and the American Mind: From Morse to McLuhan* (Chapel Hill: University of North Carolina Press, 1982);

Michael Emery, Edwin Emery, and Nancy L. Roberts, *The Press in America: An Interpretive History of the Mass Media* (New York: Allyn & Bacon, 1996);

James Fallows, *Breaking the News: How the Media Undermine American Democracy* (New York: Pantheon, 1996);

Jürgen Habermas, *Communication and the Evolution of Society*, translated by Thomas McCarthy (Boston: Beacon, 1979);

Edward S. Herman and Noam Chomsky, *Manufacturing Consent: The Political Economy of Mass Media* (New York: Pantheon, 1988);

Donald Lazere, ed., *American Media and Mass Culture: Left Perspectives* (Berkeley: University of California Press, 1987);

Anthony Lewis, "TV Erodes a Sense of Community," *New York Times*, 21 December 1995;

David Marc, *Demographic Vistas: Television in American Culture* (Philadelphia: University of Pennsylvania Press, 1984);

Joel W. Martin and Conrad E. Ostwalt Jr., *Screening the Sacred: Religion, Myth and Ideology in Popular American Film* (Boulder, Colo.: Westview Press, 1995);

Joshua Meyrowitz, *No Sense of Place: The Impact of Electronic Media on Social Behavior* (New York: Oxford University Press, 1985);

John E. O'Connor, ed., *American Television: Interpreting the Video Past* (New York: Ungar, 1983);

Dana Polan, *Power and Paranoia: History, Narrative and the American Cinema, 1940–1950* (New York: Columbia University Press, 1986);

Neil Postman, *Amusing Ourselves to Death: Public Discourse in the Age of Show Business* (New York: Penguin, 1985);

Robert Putnam, "Bowling Alone: American's Declining Social Capital," *Journal of Democracy*, 6 (1995): 65;

Robert P. Snow, *Creating Media Culture* (Beverly Hills, Cal.: Sage, 1983);

Robert Sobel, *The Manipulators: America in the Media Age* (Garden City, N.Y.: Anchor Press, 1976);

Frank Nicholas Stanton, *Mass Media and Mass Culture* (New York: Columbia Broadcasting System, 1962);

John B. Thompson, *The Media and Modernity: A Social Theory of the Media* (Stanford, Cal.: Stanford University Press, 1995);

Mary Ann Watson, *The Expanding Vista: American Television in the Kennedy Years* (New York: Oxford University Press, 1990);

Raymond Williams, *Television: Technology and Cultural Form* (New York: Schocken Books, 1975).

MCCARTHYISM

Was McCarthyism caused by global events or internal radicalism?

Viewpoint: McCarthyism was a response to global communism, not domestic radicalism.

Viewpoint: McCarthyism was an attempt by conservatives to overturn the perceived radicalism of the New Deal.

Republican senator Joseph R. McCarthy of Wisconsin was hoping to make some headlines and get reelected when he announced in 1950 that he had a list of State Department employees who were members of the Communist Party. We can understand McCarthy's motives, and historians have generally regarded McCarthy as both a scoundrel and a drunk. However, attributing the entire phenomenon of McCarthyism to one man, particularly one as repellent as McCarthy, is difficult. Why did so many people come to believe that there was a communist menace on the scale McCarthy imagined? Why did the federal government spend so much time and energy looking for conspiracies and disloyalty? McCarthy and other Republicans hoped to use the communism issue against the Democrats; yet, the Democratic Party also moved against communists and other subversives, and while today historians regard the whole episode with shame and horror, they must ask why well-intentioned men and women were so caught up in this hysteria.

In these two essays, Margaret Mary Barrett and Robert J. Flynn approach the McCarthy phenomenon from different angles. Barrett sees the McCarthy phenomenon as part of a general concern with Soviet expansion. Perhaps Americans overreacted, but McCarthyism was generally a response to Soviet threats. Flynn, on the other hand, views McCarthyism as an attempt by Republicans and conservatives to overturn domestic progressive measures.

Whichever way scholars analyze the phenomenon, they can now understand it somewhat better. Even if McCarthyism was an attempt to overturn the New Deal, perhaps historians can understand that well-intentioned people might have been party to it.

Nevertheless, this approach hardly seems satisfying. As in the case of other profound events, the final judgment of McCarthyism does not belong to politicians or historians, but to a harsher and less forgiving judge. Playwright Arthur Miller, to whom the U.S. government once refused to grant a passport (he was to attend a performance of one of his plays in Belgium), looked back into history during the McCarthy years and wrote *The Crucible,* about the Salem witch trials of 1692. How had well-meaning men and women in Salem turned on their neighbors to accuse them of being witches? In an artistic masterpiece, Miller shows the range of individual jealousy and ambition and personal and ideological conflicts that could fuel the mass hysteria of 1692 and of the early 1950s. After a production in Shanghai in the 1980s, one audience member, a survivor of China's cultural revolution, was incredulous that the play had been written by a non-Chinese; the interrogation scenes were so much like what she had endured under the Red Guard's terror. For Miller, perhaps the most telling moment was during a London production in the 1960s. He sat in the audience behind an English couple and heard the wife whisper, "I think this has something to do with that American senator. What was his name?"

Viewpoint: McCarthyism was a response to global communism, not domestic radicalism.

In the years following World War II, the United States and the Soviet Union each sought to promote their form of government. What soon erupted into a fierce global struggle between democracy and communism led many legislators, the media, and politically influential individuals in Washington to make exacting demands to ensure a loyal populace. The cleansing project they embarked on—championed by Sen. Joseph R. McCarthy (R-Wisconsin) and several other legislators—was an attempt to expel communists, communist sympathizers, and suspected communists from the United States. Characterized by excessive trials, antiradical legislation and anticommunist propaganda, McCarthyism was instigated by the fear of Soviet aggression. It was a paranoid reaction to Soviet advances in technology, espionage, and the political conversion of other nations in the postwar period. It was, in essence, a drastic domestic response to growing Soviet power.

The seeds of McCarthyism were planted in Congress on 12 March 1947 when President Harry S Truman asked Americans to join in a global commitment against communism. The Truman Doctrine was a response to Soviet ambitions in Europe and in Asia. In his speech Truman warned Congress that the world must now "choose between alternate ways of life," an admonishment that initiated an ideological war between democracy and communism. The Truman Doctrine was both a response to communism abroad and the basis for domestic legislation against communists. Just nine days after his speech, Truman announced a loyalty program to dismiss communists from government.

With Truman's loyalty order, many legislators were well on their way to seeking out communists. In 1948 the House Un-American Activities Committee (HUAC) began investigating communists in union leadership, as well as in the motion-picture industry. Truman's call for a global war against communism had initiated more-intensive investigations, but additional events would create the full-blown frenzy of McCarthyism. The transformation was an expression of what has been called a "crisis of confidence" among many members of Congress and the Truman administration. The crisis was, more appropriately, a collective feeling of disbelief and then fear that resulted from Soviet advances.

As World War II ended in 1945, Soviet authorities moved in behind the Red Army in Eastern Europe to establish control of the political processes. In February 1948 communists took over Czechoslovakia. This event was followed the same year by the blockade of Berlin. In August 1949 Chinese communists took over China. Soviet troops installed a communist regime in North Korea, and local communist groups made serious bids for power in Vietnam, Burma, and Malaysia. The outbreak of the Korean War in June 1950 confirmed the extent to which communism had infiltrated Asia. These developments, although complex political movements, were viewed simplistically by the media and many leaders as ideological victories for the Soviet Union. Even worse, they were overtly called ideological "losses" by many in Washington, a summation of their collected feelings of angst and paranoia.

Soviet nuclear capability was another shock. Just four years after the United States dropped the first atomic bomb on Japan to end World War II, the Soviet Union exploded their first nuclear device in August 1949. This unexpected advance frightened many in Washington, who immediately suggested that the United States build up their nuclear arsenal, a move that rapidly propelled both nations into an arms race, which was the most expensive and potentially dangerous exhibition of U.S. paranoia.

Perhaps the Soviet advance that most damaged the morale of McCarthy and his counterparts was that of espionage. During World War II and in the postwar period, the Soviets developed an intricate global spy network. The existence of espionage, in itself an element of unknown power or size, exacerbated fears in Washington about the spread of communism. On 30 July 1948 Whittaker Chambers claimed that communists had infiltrated the State Department and accused Alger Hiss of being a party agent. The Hiss-Chambers hearings were held by HUAC and signaled the beginning of a brutal hunt for communists in government. Amid allegations of spies throughout the Truman administration, Hiss was convicted and sentenced to prison in January 1950. Just weeks later, the British government announced the arrest of Klaus Fuchs, a communist spy who operated in Canada during the war. Fuchs's confessions led FBI investigators to a group of American spies who helped him transport atomic secrets to the Soviets.

Soviet espionage committed on American soil enraged the American people, the media, and many congressmen and intensified their pursuit of communists. Reacting to five years of Soviet victories in technology, ideology, and espionage, McCarthy gave a speech in Wheeling, West Virginia, just six days after Fuchs's arrest was announced. McCarthy alleged that he held proof that the State Department was filled with communist spies. McCarthy then accused the Truman administration of employing more than two hundred communist agents in influential government positions.

The infamous speech that ignited McCarthyism was an expression of omnipresent insecurities. McCarthy recounted the communist victories and American defeats in the Cold War, citing the "loss" of China and the marked increase of global populations under the "absolute domination of Soviet Russia" as grave concerns. His words echoed the powerlessness that many influential people in Washington felt over postwar Soviet progression and the simplistic terms to which the imagined war between communism and democracy had been reduced. McCarthy depicted America as the last stronghold in an ideological war. The only justified response, according to McCarthy, was to step up investigations and ferret out communist spies who threatened to tear down democracy. Many followed his lead.

Global communist conflict not only ignited McCarthyism but also permitted it to burn at full force through the early 1950s. Suspected spies during the Korean War, for example, were treated harshly. Viewed by their accusers as accomplices to the atrocities U.S. soldiers were experiencing in Korea, defendants were convicted and imprisoned as scapegoats for the Cold War. The most memorable example was the sentencing of Julius and Ethel Rosenberg, who were executed in June 1953 for espionage. Judge Irving R. Kaufman called their crime "worse than murder" and suggested that their conduct had "caused the Communist aggression in Korea."

Throughout the Korean War, HUAC was a forum used to pursue anticommunist concerns. The 1951 creation of the Senate Internal Security Subcommittee provided additional support for communist hearings. As U.S. soldiers fought communism abroad, McCarthyism raged on at home.

Evidence of Korea's impact on McCarthyism was apparent in the frequency of congressional investigations following McCarthy's 1950 speech. There were four investigations from 1945 to 1947, twenty-two from 1947 to 1949, twenty-four from 1949 to 1951, thirty-four from 1951 to 1953, and fifty-one from 1953 to 1955. The Korean War also led to increased anticommunist legislation. The Internal Security Act of 1950, which was sponsored by Richard M. Nixon (R-California) and Karl E. Mundt (R-South Dakota) and supported by many in Congress, prohibited members of Communist-front organizations from employment in the federal government. The Truman administration, which McCarthy had accused of being "soft" on communism, issued Executive Order 10241 in 1951, which tightened the standards of the existing loyalty-review program for federal employees. In addition, in 1950 and 1951 there was an increase in the proposal of anticommunist bills. Included among these were bills that proposed "emer-

CARD-CARRYING COMMUNISTS

The reason why we find ourselves in a position of impotency is not because our only powerful potential enemy has sent men to invade our shores, but rather because of the traitorous actions of those who have been treated so well by this Nation. It has not been the less fortunate or members of minority groups who have been selling this Nation out, but rather those who have had all the benefits that the wealthiest nation on earth has had to offer—the finest homes, the finest college education, and the finest jobs in Government we can give.

This is glaringly true in the State Department. There the bright young men who are born with silver spoons in their mouths are the ones who have been worst. . . .

In my opinion the State Department, which is one of the most important government departments, is thoroughly infested with Communists.

I have in my hand fifty-seven cases of individuals who would appear to be either card carrying members or certainly loyal to the Communist Party, but who nevertheless are still helping to shape our foreign policy.

One thing to remember in discussing the Communists in our Government is that we are not dealing with spies who get thirty pieces of silver to steal the blueprints of a new weapon. We are dealing with a far more sinister type of activity because it permits the enemy to guide and shape our policy. . . .

Source: *"Senator Joseph McCarthy's Speech at Wheeling, West Virginia, February 9, 1950," in* The Age of McCarthyism: A Brief History with Documents, *edited by Ellen Schrecker (Boston & New York: Bedford Books of St. Martin's Press, 1994), pp. 211–214.*

gency" concentration camps and the death penalty for peacetime spying.

Thus, McCarthyism, which began as a result of global communist events, raged on as long as that fear persisted. A series of events in 1953, including the death of Joseph Stalin in March, the execution of the Rosenbergs in June, and the end of the Korean War in July, brought the hysteria into question. In December 1954 the Senate censured McCarthy, denouncing his frenzied attacks for their irresponsibility, irrationality, and utter abuse. Anticommunism did not end, however; it persisted as long as the perception of a global Soviet threat existed, a trend that would continue for thirty-five years after the censure of McCarthy.

–MARGARET MARY BARRETT, ANN ARBOR, MICHIGAN

Viewpoint: McCarthyism was an attempt by conservatives to overturn the perceived radicalism of the New Deal.

McCarthyism–the movement to uncover communist subversives in the federal government and in other parts of society–was not a response to the external threat to the United States posed by the Soviet Union. Events abroad played an important role in triggering the movement, in lending it credence, and in creating the atmosphere necessary for it to achieve broad popular support. America's perception and handling of foreign affairs, moreover, changed dramatically as a consequence of McCarthyism. Fundamentally, however, McCarthyism was a response to perceived domestic radicalism. It enjoyed a brief ascendancy because it offered a compelling explanation of America's apparent lack of success in the Cold War.

McCarthyism predated both the Cold War and Sen. Joseph R. McCarthy's appropriation of the issue. From the beginning its core adherents consisted of midwestern isolationists; America's older, declining, small-town elites; members of reactionary organizations, such as the American Legion and the Daughters of the American Revolution; and opportunistic congressional conservatives such as McCarthy (R-Wisconsin), Kenneth Wherry (R-Nebraska), and Henry Styles Bridges (R-New Hampshire). These groups were bound together by their shared hatred of the New Deal and communism. The New Deal, they believed, was in the process of morally, politically, and economically destroying American society through its replacement of fiscal solvency with deficit spending; individual rights with an expanded, centralized bureaucracy; and open shops with powerful trade unions. Worse, the New Deal constituted a vehicle through which communist subversives and fellow travelers had infiltrated the federal government. Episodes such as the *Amerasia* case–in which a liberal diplomat had leaked classified documents to a leftist journal in 1946–appeared to confirm these fears.

Adherents to McCarthyism, moreover, did not believe that the Soviet Union constituted a legitimate threat to the United States. Following World War II, the Soviet Union was an economically devastated nation that lacked the naval and air strength necessary to project power in the Western Hemisphere. America, on the other hand, enjoyed unchallenged might through its potent air force, atomic monopoly, and unprecedented economic dominance. Only with the assistance of fifth columnists, saboteurs, and subversives working to rot America from within, the McCarthyites concluded, could the Kremlin redress the balance of power and challenge the United States.

Such views about the New Deal and assumptions regarding the extent and nature of the Soviet threat led grassroots McCarthyites to focus on combating domestic radicalism in the late 1940s. Growing fears of potential communist subversion fueled popular agitation that led Alabama to outlaw the Communist Party and Indiana to implement a loyalty oath for professional wrestlers. Other states demanded that teachers affirm their allegiance, and New York vowed to fire any who took the Fifth Amendment to avoid self-incrimination. American Legion members, meanwhile, picketed leftist meetings and organized boycotts of plays that employed suspected communists. Three former FBI agents founded a newsletter called *Counterattack* that compiled lists of names and cleared suspected subversives for a fee.

The same views of the New Deal and the Soviet menace that spurred such local actions also shaped the McCarthyites' focus and agenda at the national level. Believing that the greatest danger to national security came from within, congressional conservatives such as Sen. William E. Jenner (R-Indiana) saw little to gain and much to lose in the Truman administration's increasingly hard-line–and expensive–approach toward the Soviet Union. They thus backed the Truman Doctrine only reluctantly, dragged their feet in authorizing funds to rebuild Europe through the Marshall Plan, offered objections to universal military training, and invoked long-standing traditions against foreign alliances in opposing the North Atlantic Treaty. National security would be better insured, they felt, by exposing

Sen. Joseph McCarthy posing with mail his office received during his committee hearings, March 1950

(Wide World Photos)

suspected domestic subversives and by discrediting the New Deal political system that was responsible for communist infiltration of government and other key institutions. Many thus backed the successful effort by Sen. Robert A. Taft (R-Ohio) to limit the power of unions and to assure that they remained free of communist influence through the Taft-Hartley Act of 1947. Members of the House Un-American Activities Committee (HUAC), meanwhile, moved to expose and blacklist communists in Hollywood and issued reports claiming that subversives had infiltrated the New Deal. Most notably, Congressman Richard M. Nixon (R-California) worked to discredit the New Deal by doggedly pursuing suspected subversives and New Deal symbol Alger Hiss on charges that he had served as a Soviet agent while employed at the State Department. Though the statute of limitations prevented Hiss from being charged with treason, he was eventually convicted of perjury in January 1950.

Foreign affairs did play an important role in the developing Red Scare by establishing the proper conditions for McCarthyism's full flowering in the early 1950s. Concerns about external events had grown steadily since the end of World War II. Joseph Stalin's belligerent and ideologically charged election speech in early 1946 had rekindled fears that the Soviet Union sought to impose communism across the globe. The Soviet-engineered Czech coup in February 1948 increased those anxieties dramatically, as did the Berlin Blockade that began in June. More ominous events followed in 1949. Mao Tse-tung's victory in the Chinese Civil War that year led many to conclude that the balance of power was tilting away from the United States and lent credence to charges that the administration had done little to help Chiang Kai-shek's Nationalist government resist the communists. More important, the Soviet detonation of an atomic bomb in September 1949 heightened the already tense atmosphere by suggesting that America was no longer safe from external attack. In conjunction with the revelation of an atomic spy ring and Hiss's perjury conviction, these shocking international events made credible the McCarthyites' charges and set the stage for the most intense part of the Red Scare.

McCarthy formally initiated that period during a Lincoln Day address to the Ohio County Women's Republican Club in Wheeling, West Virginia, on 9 February 1950. In his speech the opportunistic senator advanced a simple and compelling explanation of why America was losing the Cold War despite its enormous military and economic advantage over the communist bloc. "The reason why we find ourselves in a position of impotency," the senator exclaimed, "is not because our only powerful potential enemy has sent men to invade our shores, but rather because of the traitorous actions of those . . . who have had all the benefits that the wealthiest nation on earth has to offer." Honeycombed throughout the State Department, these subversives, liberal dupes, and fellow travelers had handed China to the communists and permitted the Kremlin to take Eastern Europe and incorporate it into the communist bloc. "Communists within our borders have been more responsible for the success of Communism abroad," he asserted, "than Soviet Russia." In short, the real threat to America emanated not from the Soviet Union but from traitors and subversives working from within.

A political opportunist with little attraction to anticommunism beyond the publicity it afforded, McCarthy stuck with this theme throughout his brief political ascendancy. In June 1951 he attacked General George C. Marshall by claiming that he conspired with other high government officials to sabotage American foreign policy and thereby make possible communism's drive for global dominance. As chair of the Permanent Subcommittee on Investigations, he held hearings in 1953 in which he accused the Voice of America radio broadcasts of undermining America by broadcasting procommunist material and the Overseas Library Program of shelving books by communist authors. Later that year he investigated accusations of lax internal security at the U.S. Army Signal Corps facility at Monmouth, New Jersey. All the while, he attacked the State Department, which he claimed had a "small but dominant percentage of disloyal, twisted, and, in some cases, perverted thinkers who were rendering futile the Herculean efforts of the vast majority of Americans." At no time, however, did McCarthy center his efforts squarely on foreign policy.

Many of McCarthy's allies did temporarily focus on the international threat to American security after the outbreak of the Korean War in June 1950. Keen to resolve the conflict decisively and to score political points at the administration's expense, many backed General Douglas A. MacArthur's call for a wider war against communism in Asia. For the most part, however, they exploited the heightened sense of crisis caused by the war to intensify their accusations that communists and liberals in government were the principal threat to American security. "I charge that this country today is in the hands of a secret inner coterie," Jenner declared after Truman sacked MacArthur in 1951, "which is directed by agents of the Soviet Union." The Senate Internal Security Subcommittee (SISS), chaired by Patrick A. McCarran (R-Nevada), concluded later that year that communist sympathizers in the State Department including "Owen Lattimore and John Carter Vincent were influential in bringing about a change in United States policy . . . favorable to the Chinese Communists." Recalling Secretary of State Dean Acheson's speech in January 1950 in which he declared that South Korea lay outside of the American defense perimeter in Asia, meanwhile, other congressional conservatives maintained that Acheson had all but invited the North Korean attack. His hands, Wherry viciously asserted, were thus "stained with 'the blood of our boys in Korea.'"

McCarthy's allies also took advantage of the war-inspired crisis atmosphere to broaden their efforts to expose subversives in government and other key institutions. McCarran, for instance, exploited the war to secure passage of the Internal Security Act in September 1950 over Truman's veto. Of dubious constitutionality, the act required communist groups to register with the government, provided for the detention of communists during times of emergency, and added muscle to existing espionage laws. In 1952 and 1953 the SISS held hearings to investigate suspected fellow travelers in secondary and higher education; many who invoked the Fifth Amendment subsequently lost their jobs. Continuing its earlier efforts to roll back the New Deal, meanwhile, HUAC held hearings to investigate communist penetration of America's labor unions. At the grassroots level, American Legionnaires held mock communist uprisings in local communities to highlight the dangers posed by subversives and joined Daughters of the American Revolution in pressuring public libraries to remove allegedly subversive materials, including magazines such as *The Nation* and *The New Republic*. Throughout the depths of the Red Scare, in short, the McCarthyites centered their efforts principally on exposing alleged communists in government, on trumpeting the dangers of domestic subversion, and on discrediting the New Deal rather than on dealing with explicitly international threats.

McCarthyism did, however, have important consequences for America's subsequent response to international events. Ceaseless charges by McCarthy and his allies demoralized State Department employees and led President Dwight D. Eisenhower's secretary of state, John Foster Dulles, to purge many qualified and loyal Foreign Service Officers, especially in the department's Far Eastern Bureau. More important, the success of McCarthy's reckless attacks taught future administrations that the loss of any further territory to communism would come at a steep political price. McCarthyism thus played an important part in setting the stage for America's military intervention in Vietnam in the 1960s.

McCarthyism, in sum, was not principally a response to international threats. Events abroad such as the Chinese Civil War, the Soviet detonation of an atomic bomb, and the outbreak of fighting in Korea proved important because they helped foster the crisis environment necessary for the movement to thrive and made the McCarthyists' shrill accusations appear credible. As its predominantly internal focus makes clear, though, McCarthyism was primarily a response to domestic radicalism and an effort to discredit and overturn the New Deal.

–ROBERT J. FLYNN, UNIVERSITY OF KENTUCKY

References

David Caute, *The Great Fear: The Anti-Communist Purge under Truman and Eisenhower* (New York: Simon & Schuster, 1978);

Richard M. Freeland, *The Truman Doctrine and the Origins of McCarthyism: Foreign Policy, Domestic Politics, and Internal Security, 1946–1948* (New York: Knopf, 1972);

Albert Fried, ed., *McCarthyism: The Great American Red Scare: A Documentary History* (New York: Oxford University Press, 1997);

Richard M. Fried, *Nightmare in Red: The McCarthy Era in Perspective* (New York: Oxford University Press, 1990);

John Lewis Gaddis, *We Now Know: Rethinking Cold War History* (New York: Oxford University Press, 1997);

Robert Griffith, *The Politics of Fear: Joseph R. McCarthy and the Senate* (Lexington: University Press of Kentucky, 1970);

Griffith and Athan Theoharis, *The Specter: Original Essays on the Cold War and the Origins of McCarthyism* (New York: New Viewpoints, 1974);

John Earl Haynes, *Red Scare or Red Menace?: American Communism and Anticommunism in the Cold War Era* (Chicago: Ivan R. Dee, 1996);

Kenneth O'Reilly, *Hoover and the Un-Americans: The FBI, HUAC, and the Red Menace* (Philadelphia: Temple University Press, 1983);

David M. Oshinsky, *A Conspiracy So Immense: The World of Joe McCarthy* (New York: Free Press, 1983);

Richard Gid Powers, *Not Without Honor: The History of American Anticommunism* (New York: Free Press, 1995);

Ellen Schrecker, *Many Are The Crimes: McCarthyism in America* (Boston: Little, Brown, 1998);

Schrecker, ed., *The Age of McCarthyism: A Brief History with Documents* (Boston & New York: Bedford Books of St. Martin's Press, 1994).

MEANING OF *BROWN*

What was the significance of the *Brown* v. *Board of Education* decision?

Viewpoint: The *Brown* decision, highpoint of the NAACP Legal Defense Fund campaign against segregation, brought African-Americans into the mainstream of American political life.

Viewpoint: In the short term *Brown* did not help African-Americans achieve true equality, and in the long term it has become implicated in the reaction against affirmative action.

On Monday, 17 May 1954, the United States Supreme Court unanimously ruled that segregated schools were in violation of the Constitution. Chief Justice Earl Warren led the Court in what would prove one of the most significant decisions of the twentieth century. With their ruling in *Brown* v. *Board of Education of Topeka, Kansas,* the Court opened the doors of change and helped fuel the civil-rights struggles of the next two decades. Ramifications of the verdict still reverberate to this day.

The Warren Court overturned *Plessy* v. *Ferguson* (1896), in which it had been ruled that separate accommodations were legal as long as they were equal. In *Plessy* a man who was one-eighth black was removed from a rail coach and told to sit in one with people of his own race. He refused and was jailed in Louisiana. Justice Henry Billings Brown wrote in the majority opinion: "The object of the amendment was undoubtedly to enforce the absolute equality of the two races before the law, but in the nature of things it could not have been intended to abolish distinctions based upon color, or to enforce social, as distinguished from political equality, or a commingling of the two races upon terms unsatisfactory to either." Justice Brown argued that the most common instance of a necessary separation based on color was "the establishment of separate schools for white and colored children. . . ."

The Supreme Court of 1954 ruled that separate accommodations were inherently unequal. *Brown* was actually five cases brought together under one name. Nominally, the Court's only legal directive was that states could no longer segregate the races in schools. In fact, however, the decision destroyed the edifice of legitimacy *Plessy* had given segregation, laid the foundation for the Civil Rights movement, and revolutionized what courts, lawyers, and the law might do to expand racial justice.

In the North the decision was lauded in liberal circles and by most blacks, but there were those who believed it was a step in the wrong direction. In the South the decision was met, unsurprisingly, with mixed reviews. Some southerners believed that integration was inevitable and that this judgment was just another step in the dismantling of a way of life; others felt it was their duty to fight to preserve that way of life. Overall *Brown* helped bring about a series of changes in the social fabric of the United States.

During World War II blacks began to make substantive advances in American society. The war effort required a massive mobilization of labor, and many jobs filtered down to blacks. Blacks were not, on the whole, satisfied with the opportunities offered during the war. In most cases they were confined to the dirtiest, most dangerous, least prestigious positions in manufacturing. Leaders such as A. Philip Randolph pressed hard to gain more opportunities. The black community was energized and moved forward, attempting to secure that which the Constitution guaranteed.

In 1934 Charles Hamilton Houston, a Harvard-educated black attorney, became a part-time counsel for the National Association for the Advancement of Colored People (NAACP) and special counsel in 1935. Houston was determined to challenge the system through the courts and believed that the Constitution was on his side. In the mid 1930s Houston began a systematic attack on segregation in professional schools. He believed that law schools were a good place to begin because judges might be more sympathetic to a young student trying to get a legal education in his home state. Another positive to this strategy was that few women were enrolled in these schools, this would keep Houston from having to deal with the explosive issue of white women and black men sitting next to each other in classes.

These cases became the foundation for the strategy the Legal Defense Fund (LDF) pursued over the next twenty years. Houston brought one of his top students from Howard University onto the LDF team. Thurgood Marshall joined Houston in New York in 1936 and took charge of the operation when Houston left in 1938. Houston was working in Washington, D.C., on *Bolling* v. *Sharpe,* one of the cases that would make up *Brown,* when he died in 1950.

The LDF worked hard, using Houston's blueprint, to eradicate segregation in public schools. A talented group of lawyers, they began to win cases centered around graduate and professional schools in the late 1940s and early 1950s. These successes helped drive LDF to expand their work to undergraduate students, high schools, and elementary schools. At the same time the Supreme Court was moving in the same direction. Discussions among the justices in the 1950s showed that they were ready to reexamine the "separate but equal" doctrine if the right case was brought. When the *Brown* cases were presented, the Court finally had its opportunity. These cases directly questioned the doctrine of "separate but equal" with regard to public education. The Court still needed time to figure out what remedy should be used: immediate desegregation nationwide, prompt desegregation with minor adjustments for peculiar local conditions, or gradual desegregation to take account of anticipated resistance.

In the wake of the ruling, school boards throughout the South took one of two options: prepare for integration or dig in and fight. The attitude of many segregationists was typified by Mel Bailey, sheriff of Birmingham, Alabama, when he expressed his feelings after *Brown:* ". . . go to school with my little daughter? That is why . . . resistance." In the *Jackson Daily News,* the major newspaper of the capital of Mississippi, an editorial on *Brown* declared: "It means racial strife of the bitterest sort. Mississippi cannot and will not try to abide by such a decision." Statements in southern papers, such as this one, were contrasted by those of northern papers. In the *New York Daily News,* for example, the tone was much different. "We'll join in the applause for the U.S. Supreme Court's unanimous decision that race segregation in the nation's public schools must start getting out."

As for the black community, there were differing opinions on the meaning of *Brown*. Zora Neale Hurston rejected the logic of the *Brown* decision as self-defeating at best and antiblack at worst. She believed in the strength of all-black institutions. W. E. B. Du Bois did not disagree with the decision itself but was concerned that it might be shortsighted with regard to the potential for mistreatment of black students in integrated schools. Like Hurston, Du Bois believed that black culture would not be taught in integrated schools.

Brown was not the end of segregation of course, and the Court understood that the process would be a difficult one. Years of deeply entrenched segregation were built on an even longer standing belief in the inferiority of the black race and would not be changed simply by a court ruling. Just as segregationists were digging in for a fight, so were blacks. In a way, the Supreme Court was as well. When the Court rejected the "separate but equal" doctrine in 1954, it scheduled dates for arguments on the issue of remedy for the following fall. By deferring the question, the Court opened up a different phase in the litigation campaign and in the nation's experience with the issue of race.

What came next was a series of challenges across the South. Possibly the most famous of these was in Little Rock, Arkansas, in 1957, where black students were prepared to integrate Central High School, touching off a clash between Governor Orval Faubus and President Dwight D. Eisenhower. Little Rock was considered a liberal southern city. The University had already integrated, as had the city buses, without serious incident. In an effort to comply with *Brown* the Little Rock school board launched a plan to integrate the high school. Nine black students were selected, based on their academic performance, and it was decided that they would attend Central in the fall. When the school year began, Little Rock became a battleground.

Viewpoint: The *Brown* decision, highpoint of the NAACP Legal Defense Fund campaign against segregation, brought African-Americans into the mainstream of American political life.

The 17 May 1954 Supreme Court decision in *Brown* v. *Board of Education of Topeka, Kansas,* which ordered the desegregation of public schools, was one of the most important judicial decisions in American history. Although the decision is often remembered for the resistance it sparked in much of the South and the slow path to implementation, its accomplishments are undeniable. Its contribution to the struggle for racial justice took place not only in the courtrooms but also on the battlefields of the Civil Rights movement. *Brown* provided a legal precedent that helped define a new era of judicial activism. *Brown* also offered African-Americans a sign that the federal government, while oftentimes painfully slow to act, was not blind to the racial inequities of the segregated South. It was on these two levels of legal precedent and motivational symbol that the *Brown* decision made its attack on racial injustice.

On behalf of a unanimous court, Chief Justice Earl Warren articulated the basic principle of *Brown* in clear, blunt terms: "We conclude that in the field of public education the doctrine of 'separate but equal' has no place. Separate education facilities are inherently unequal." With these words the Court overturned *Plessy* v. *Ferguson* (1896), which had given the judicial stamp of approval on the segregation system that defined southern race relations since Reconstruction. In the years leading up to *Brown,* the Legal Defense Fund branch of the National Association for the Advancement of Colored People (NAACP), led by brilliant lawyers such as Charles Hamilton Houston and Thurgood Marshall, won a number of crucial decisions undermining the legitimacy of segregation. The culmination of these efforts in the 1954 decision was initially greeted enthusiastically by the blacks and liberal whites. Yet, its implementation posed serious difficulties because of the entrenched nature of segregation in the South and the unwillingness of the federal government to assert itself. The Supreme Court itself contributed to the confusion with its 31 May 1955 implementation decision (referred to as *Brown II*), in which it ruled that the desegregation of schools must be accomplished with "all deliberate speed," leaving the interpretation of this phrase to local communities and lower courts. It would be many years before *Brown* would be put into effect throughout the South.

Despite the trials of implementation, the impact of *Brown* as a legal precedent should not be underappreciated. Legal historian Morton J. Horwitz, in *The Warren Court and the Pursuit of Justice* (1998), described the decision as "a nuclear event in American constitutional law." It was the first momentous step away from a court dedicated to judicial restraint (for example, an appearance of neutrality and nonintervention with regard to social issues), and led to a series of groundbreaking civil-rights decisions. While judicial restraint tended to benefit the most powerful segments of society, this decision addressed the needs of, in Horwitz's words, "the weak and the powerless, the marginal and the socially scorned." The belief gained legitimacy that the Constitution was a "living" document that could be interpreted to deal with pressing societal needs. In his decision Warren pushed aside the need to interpret the Fourteenth Amendment solely in the context of its original framing: "In approaching this problem, we cannot turn the clock back to 1868 when the Amendment was adopted, or even to 1896 when *Plessy* v. *Ferguson* was written. We must consider public education in the light of its full development and its present place in American life throughout the Nation." The faith in a living Constitution was accomplished in large part by the Court's use of the Equal Protection Clause of the Fourteenth Amendment. It would act as a precedent to support the rights of minorities and women in many future court decisions.

Although the Court limited the language of *Brown* to apply only to segregation in public schools, it soon became apparent that its impact went well beyond this into all forms of state-sanctioned segregation. In the years following the decision, the Supreme Court struck down segregation of transportation, public buildings, housing, recreational facilities, and restaurants. For the most part, desegregation of such public facilities took place much more quickly and smoothly than the integration of public schools, although there were notable exceptions such as the brutal attacks on the 1961 Freedom Riders, who were testing the ruling desegregating interstate transportation carriers and facilities. In *Johnson* v. *Virginia,* the 1963 decision desegregating public buildings, the Court demonstrated the natural expansion of the scope of *Brown* with the broad assertion, "[I]t is no longer open to question that a State may not constitutionally require segregation of public facilities."

Some of the most important decisions to grow out of *Brown* were in reapportionment.

With shifting demographics resulting from the urbanization of African-Americans during the twentieth century, government officials who feared the strengthening of the black vote allowed the distribution of voting districts to become skewed. Thus, a minority of voters, usually representing rural interests, effectively controlled state legislatures; the granting of benefits to the cities by these legislatures was chronically inadequate. A major hurdle for the Supreme Court was simply deciding whether this issue was one on which they had the right to decide. The 1962 *Baker* v. *Carr* decision, in which the Court decided it had the right to intervene on the reapportionment issue, was, like *Brown,* a major move away from the doctrine of judicial restraint. It was followed in 1963 by *Gray* v. *Sanders,* in which the Court held that there must be equal apportionment ("one person, one vote") in elections for U.S. senators and statewide officials, and in 1964 *Reynolds* v. *Sims* held that the Equal Protection Clause of the Fourteenth Amendment (the same clause used as the basis for *Brown*) required equal distribution for state legislatures. These reapportionment cases were born from the atmosphere created by *Brown* in which the Supreme Court decided to get involved with such "political" issues and assert its authority, especially on behalf of African-Americans.

Another important decision that *Brown* made possible was *Loving* v. *Virginia* (1967), in which the Court struck down a Virginia law prohibiting interracial marriages. This ruling dealt directly with the southern fears of miscegenation that underlay much of the initial motivation for segregation–many whites defended Jim Crow laws and customs as necessary to protect white women from black men, thousands of whom were lynched as a result of these fears. Yet, just thirteen years after *Brown,* the *Loving* ruling was issued to relatively little reaction. Even if the *Brown* decision had a tortuous road to implementation, it had initiated a reevaluation of cultural assumptions that, by 1967, had changed the way the courts and many in the South viewed the interaction of blacks and whites. The Supreme Court had established itself as a powerful antidote to obvious inequities of racism.

In addition to its role as a legal precedent, *Brown* had an important impact on the burgeoning Civil Rights movement. This is not to say that *Brown* began the movement–its heritage in the black community was largely separate from the doings of the Supreme Court. But the decision left an indelible mark on the direction and shape of the movement, especially in its early stages. It not only acted as a legal precedent instrumental in achieving legal and legislative victories, it also became a symbol to activists of the potential for change in the white-dominated power structure–it represented, as Richard Kluger wrote in *Simple Justice: The History of Brown* v. *Board of Education and Black America's Struggle for Equality* (1975), "nothing short of a reconsecration of American ideals." It demonstrated that the government was not blind to the injustices of racism, and the symbolic importance of this gesture should not be overlooked when examining the optimistic, interracial approach of the Civil Rights movement between 1954 and 1965. One elated black remembered his reaction to the decision: "My inner emotions must have been approximate to the Negro slaves' when they first heard about the Emancipation proclamation. . . . I felt that at last the government was willing to assert itself on behalf of first-class citizenship, even for Negroes. I experienced a sense of loyalty that I had never felt before. I was sure that this was the beginning of a new era of American democracy." This

A NEW LAW FOR A NEW LAND

. . . In approaching this problem, we cannot turn the clock back to 1868 when the Amendment was adopted, or even to 1896 when *Plessy* v. *Ferguson* was written. We must consider public education in the light of its full development and its present place in American life throughout the Nation. Only in this way can it be determined if segregation in public schools deprives these plaintiffs of the equal protection of the laws.

Today, education is perhaps the most important function of the state and local governments. Compulsory school attendance laws and the great expenditures for education both demonstrate our recognition of the importance of education to our democratic society. It is required in the performance of our most basic public responsibilities, even service in the armed forces. It is the very foundation of good citizenship. Today it is a principal instrument in awakening the child to cultural values, in preparing him for later professional training, and in helping him to adjust normally to his environment. In these days, it is doubtful that any child may reasonably be expected to succeed in life if he is denied the opportunity of an education. Such an opportunity, where the state has undertaken to provide it, is a right which must be made available to all on equal terms. . . .

We conclude that in the field of public education the doctrine of "separate but equal" has no place. Separate educational facilities are inherently unequal. Therefore, we hold that the plaintiffs and others similarly situated for whom the actions have been brought are, by reason of the segregation complained of, deprived of the equal protection of the laws guaranteed by the Fourteenth Amendment. . . .

Source: Brown v. the Board of Education of Topeka, Kansas, *347 U.S. 483, 1954, Appeal from the U.S. District Court, District of Kansas.*

kind of unqualified optimism was not uniformly felt in the black community–the government had let them down too many times. Yet, many saw this as a victory of at least a crucial battle within the struggle for equality.

Brown served as a rallying point for many of the leaders of the early Civil Rights movement. In the year following the first decision and preceding the implementation decision there was a period of hope and action in much of the South that is often overshadowed by the repression and violence of white supremacists in their campaign of "massive resistance" against the integration orders. In Mississippi, for example, it was during this period that the NAACP established itself as a significant organization. It was, as John Dittmer wrote in *Local People: The Struggle for Civil Rights in Mississippi* (1994), "an exhilarating time for NAACP activists. After years of frustrating, mostly unsuccessful efforts to register voters (or even sign up NAACP members), here was an opportunity to confront the state on a Constitutional issue where the U.S. Supreme Court has spoken directly." Although this initial optimism would be undermined by the resistance of the South to abide by the Court's decision, along with the government's inability to enforce it, essential organizational growth took place as a result of *Brown.* It gave many civil-rights leaders a clear objective, and it helped increase membership in the organizations. *Brown*-motivated activism was not limited to school segregation. The decision helped spark drives to desegregate public facilities and increase African-American voter registration. It was only six months after *Brown II* that Rosa Parks refused to give up her seat on a bus in Montgomery, Alabama, setting in motion the bus boycott that would mark the beginning of the direct-action phase of the Civil Rights movement.

Even in the darkest moments of conflict resulting from *Brown,* the importance of the decision was evident. Following *Brown,* opposition to changes in the Jim Crow system in the South coalesced into massive resistance, resulting in delays in implementing the Court's decision. In the spring of 1956 more than one hundred southern members of Congress signed what came to be know as the "Southern Manifesto," declaring *Brown* unconstitutional and demanding that it be ignored. Through the efforts of southern governors, mayors, judges, and others in power, only a fraction of the schools in the South had begun to desegregate when in September 1957 the situation became focused on a dramatic confrontation in Little Rock, Arkansas. President Dwight D. Eisenhower had been wary of directly involving executive power in the issue of school desegregation–he had commented that he did not believe one could change people's beliefs with laws or court decisions–but here was a situation where the governor was openly defying the power of the federal government. A lower court ordered Central High School to desegregate, but implementation was thwarted by the threat of violence when a white mob surrounded the school. Segregationist governor Orval Faubus did nothing. Eisenhower responded by federalizing the Arkansas National Guard and sending in troops; only then were the black children able to enter the doors of the school. Whether this was a victory for the Civil Rights movement is up for debate. The president had acted only reluctantly, and Faubus eventually shut down the schools rather than abide by the decision. Yet, from a broader perspective the importance is apparent. The movement gained much-needed publicity: the nation saw the confrontation between the law, as defined by *Brown,* and open rebellion. The lines of the movement were being drawn, and the power and authority of the Constitution and federal government–even if divided and more often than not reluctant to act–was on the side of the activists.

The student sit-in movement of the early 1960s also revealed the influence of *Brown.* In the city where the movement began, Greensboro, North Carolina, black parents had been trying unsuccessfully to force the school board to integrate the school system. Integration throughout the South had been discouraging: by 1960 one-sixth of 1 percent of black children attended integrated schools. It was largely as a result of the racist attitude of many whites in Greensboro, coupled with the knowledge that they had not only the moral high-ground but also the legal one, that four black college students decided to stage a sit-in at the local segregated Woolworth's lunch counter. This sparked similar acts of resistance around the South. The frustration of undelivered promises, most prominent of which was the inability to accomplish what *Brown* so clearly demanded, contributed to the heroic activism of the students and countless others. The decision heightened aspirations, and when these were not met, blacks took to the streets. Even as *Brown* demonstrated the potential for institutional change, it also revealed its limitations, and this was a necessary precondition for the success of the philosophy of civil disobedience that dominated the movement of the late 1950s and early 1960s.

On the two fronts of legal precedent and symbol of federal support *Brown* made its essential contribution to the movement. Both showed the limitations of the decision: legally, the color-blind ideal behind *Brown* has been used to attack more-recent attempts to address racial inequality, most notably in affirmative-action cases; symbolically, the decision was often noted for its ineffectual implementation as much as for its far-reaching statement on racial justice. Yet, despite these difficulties, the decision had a monumental impact on American law and society. For all its flaws and weaknesses, *Brown* is one of a handful of Supreme Court decisions that has significantly and irreversibly moved the United States closer to its true ideals.

–CHRISTOPHER W. SCHMIDT, HARVARD UNIVERSITY

Viewpoint: In the short term Brown did not help African-Americans achieve true equality, and in the long term it has become implicated in the reaction against affirmative action.

Brown v. *Board of Education of Topeka, Kansas* (1954) was the result of a long-standing legal campaign waged by the National Association for the Advancement of Colored People (NAACP), and its legal arm, the Legal Defense Fund (LDF), to remedy the effects of Jim Crow laws, which segregated public facilities along racial lines throughout many southern states. Starting in the 1930s, the NAACP, led by Thurgood Marshall and Charles Hamilton Houston, sued state and local governments using the Supreme Court's decision in *Plessy* v. *Ferguson* (1896), which had held that Jim Crow laws did not inherently violate the Equal Protection Clause of the Fourteenth Amendment. *Plessy*'s doctrine–known as "separate but equal"–helped to legitimate poor physical maintenance of black public institutions, low pay for black public workers, and dismal employment prospects for blacks. At first Marshall and the NAACP tried to enforce the "separate but equal" doctrine by bringing suits against governments to make them equally support segregated public facilities. This strategy of enforcing *Plessy*, however, increasingly seemed impractical. Therefore, NAACP lawyers began focusing on overturning *Plessy* itself.

By the late 1940s, following a series of legal victories for the NAACP in which the Supreme Court ruled that racial segregation related to election primaries (*Smith* v. *Allwright* in 1944), housing (*Shelley* v. *Kraemer* in 1948), and law school admissions (*Sweatt* v. *Painter* in 1950) was unconstitutional, Marshall turned his attention to public schools. At the time few public schools were integrated in many of the districts straddling the Ohio River and Mason-Dixon Line. In states further south, almost all public schools were racially segregated by law. By taking *Brown* to the Supreme Court, Marshall presented to the justices the heroic opportunity to overrule *Plessy* and steer the country on a course toward racial equality under the law. In 1954 the Court embraced the opportunity and made an attempt at ending segregation. Despite good intentions, *Brown* did not meet its authors' expectations.

First, it failed in the short term, because for ten years most public schools in the South remained radically segregated. In North Carolina and Virginia, for instance, less than one-tenth of 1 percent of black children attended desegregated schools seven years after *Brown*. In South Carolina, Alabama, and Mississippi not one black child attended an integrated public grade school in the 1962–1963 school year. One historian, Michael Klarman, characterized the results of *Brown:* "For ten years, 1954–1964, virtually nothing happened."

Part of the reason for *Brown*'s ineffectiveness was that it failed to offer lower courts bold legal remedies to achieve its objectives. Brown, in fact, consisted of two separate opinions, referred to as "*Brown I*" and "*Brown II.*" *Brown I* provided the legal, moral, and social-scientific justifications for racial integration of public schools, and, in a much criticized ruling, *Brown II* set forth vague remedies to achieve *Brown I* by declaring that desegregation be pursued "with all deliberate speed." This rhetoric signaled the justice's hope that school districts would develop their own timetables for desegregation that would be consistent with *Brown*. Instead, most school districts did nothing, and in some cases local politicians, most infamously Governor Orval Faubus, cynically stymied the integration of public schools by blaming the Supreme Court for illegitimately interfering in southern institutions. Thus, rather than supplementing the high-minded principles of *Brown I* with detailed legal rules, *Brown II* failed to give lawyers and judges any legal weapons to wield in concrete cases as local school boards and politicans flouted constitutional laws.

Though it may be accurate to say that *Brown* eventually contributed to desegregation of public schools by the late 1960s and early 1970s, it is also true that such change was not directly the result of the action of the Court, and, in fact, largely resulted from grassroots efforts. In particular, the Civil Rights movement fostered dozens of confrontations involving students, demonstrators, troublemakers, police, lawyers, and federal troops. Rather than *Brown*, it was these confrontations that drew the attention of television cameras, thereby shocking moderate white voters, most of whom were otherwise deeply indifferent to issues concerning racial justice. Only after President Lyndon B. Johnson signed the 1964 Civil Rights Act, in response to the organized pressure of the leaders of the Civil Rights movement, most prominently Martin Luther King Jr., can one observe a clear change in the reporting of the racial make-up of formerly segregated schools. In this light, *Brown*'s beneficial consequences appear unintended, as the decision helped to foster the dramatic, and often brutal, conflicts from which eventually emerged

Supreme Court Justice Thurgood Marshall (center) and two African-American leaders following the historic *Brown* decision of 1954

(U.P.)

political support for the desegregation of public schools.

Second, *Brown* failed because it helped focus Northern attention away from itself and toward the South, thereby obscuring how suburban development in the North fostered its own patterns of racial segregation. By changing property, zoning, and tax laws, northern voters intensified school segregation in the late 1960s through the 1970s and 1980s–at the same time politicians devised a vocabulary to name urban spaces inhabited by African Americans as the "inner city." Though achieved without Jim Crow laws, Northern segregation was indistinguishable from its southern counterpart, except that *Brown,* by itself, provided little equipment to name it as such.

Finally, *Brown* represents a failed decision in the long term, because it helped shape certain ideas about racial identity that proved to be ultimately self-defeating. Though intended to accomplish many things, the decision helped portray blacks as powerless and victimized. As argued by historian Daryl Michael Scott, in *Contempt and Pity: Social Policy and the Image of the Damaged Black Psyche, 1880–1996* (1997), *Brown* represented the black mind as "damaged" by racism and racial segregation. Indeed, among Chief Justice Warren's stated reasons for ending segregation was his view that public education helped a child "to adjust normally to his environment." According to Warren, since black schools were legally segregated, and thereby rendered inferior, the law failed to mainstream and normalize black children to American society. According to Scott, "Warren had crafted a psychiatric appeal that subtly but effectively conveyed the plight of the victim without censuring the guilty."

Warren's nod to psychology in his opinion was related to the Supreme Court's intellectual commitment to individualism in the 1950s and 1960s. By talking about racial justice in psychological terms, the Court made it appear that racism mainly resulted in individual pain and suffering rather than collective struggle. Failing to call attention to the shared history of African-Americans resisting slavery and struggling both within and against segregation, Warren caricatured African-Americans as individuals victimized by law. Thus, their difference from whites was judicially rendered as a simple legal difference, the erasure of which promised to effect a liberation of all individual Americans.

By eliding the history of black public institutions and achievements of African-Americans in the name of normalizing individuals through constitutional law, the Supreme Court helped reinforce a broader consensus about individual happiness then dominating postwar American culture. An important and overlooked consequence of this post-*Brown* valorization of the normal and happy individual has been an inability for judges in the last two decades to provide an intellectual bulwark supporting affirmative action against its critics.

Affirmative action represents a conscious attempt to consider race in the redistribution of public resources, but, as its critics readily complain, race-conscious remedies often perpetuate collective racial identities that appear to contradict the goal of rewarding and promoting individual talent. At their worst, critics of affirmative action argue, with *Brown* in mind, that the law should neither discriminate according to race nor acknowledge its political relevance at all. Often they uphold the vision of a "color-blind" Constitution, as Harlan expressed in *Plessy.* They also argue that race hardly matters any longer, or they argue that it has been transformed into something of a collective national identity, which all Americans supposedly share. Supreme Court Justice Antonin Scalia has written in a recent Supreme Court opinion that limited affirmative action: "In the eyes of the government, we are just one race here. It is American." By celebrating American identity in racially explicit terms, critics of affirmative action such as Scalia cynically appropriate *Brown*'s vision of an integrated society. At the same time, however, Scalia's reading of *Brown* is not tortured. His bad-faith appropriations can be read as ironically consistent with *Brown*'s promotion of equality under the Constitution, since the decision elevates as one of its goals the education of normal, individual Americans enjoying the fruits of affluence.

Brown is viewed today as a fixed star in the constellation of American rights. If viewed from another perspective, the most important Supreme Court decision of the twentieth century appears to have had little social effect as intended. It also appears to have disserved African-Americans by hampering the struggle against ways of thinking in racist terms. Therefore, the promotion of racial justice may require going back to *Brown,* reconsidering first principles, and reaching for something deeper than normalizing people into the affluence of an imagined American race.

–LOUIS ANTHES, NEW YORK UNIVERSITY

References

Taylor Branch, *Parting the Waters: America in the King Years, 1954–1963* (New York: Simon & Schuster, 1988);

William H. Chafe, *Civilities and Civil Rights: Greensboro, North Carolina, and the Black Struggle for Freedom* (New York: Oxford University Press, 1980);

John Dittmer, *Local People: The Struggle for Civil Rights in Mississippi* (Urbana: University of Illinois Press, 1994);

W. E. Burghardt Du Bois, "Does the Negro Need Separate Schools," *Journal of Negro Education* (July 1935): 328–335;

Jack Greenberg, *Crusaders in the Courts: How a Delicate Band of Lawyers Fought For the Civil Rights Revolution* (New York: BasicBooks, 1994);

Morton J. Horwitz, *The Transformation of American Law, 1870–1960* (New York: Oxford University Press, 1977);

Horwitz, *The Warren Court and the Pursuit of Justice: A Critical Issue* (New York: Hill & Wang, 1998);

Michael Klarman, "How *Brown* Changed Race Relations: The Backlash Thesis," *Journal of American History,* 81 (June 1994): 81–118;

Richard Kluger, *Simple Justice: The History of Brown* v. *Board of Education and Black America's Struggle for Equality* (New York: Knopf, 1975);

Gerald N. Rosenberg, *The Hollow Hope: Can Courts Bring about Social Change?* (Chicago: University of Chicago Press, 1991);

Austin Sarat, ed., *Race, Law, and Culture: Reflections on Brown* v. *Board of Education* (New York: Oxford University Press, 1997);

Daryl Michael Scott, *Contempt and Pity: Social Policy and the Image of the Damaged Black Psyche, 1880–1996* (Chapel Hill: University of North Carolina Press, 1997);

Harvard Sitkoff, *The Struggle for Black Equality, 1954–1992,* revised edition (New York: Hill & Wang, 1993);

Mark V. Tushnet, *Making Civil Rights Law: Thurgood Marshall and the Supreme Court, 1936–1961* (New York: Oxford University Press, 1994);

Tushnet, *The NAACP's Legal Strategy Against Segregated Education, 1925–1950* (Chapel Hill: University of North Carolina Press, 1987);

Tom Wicker, *Tragic Failure: Racial Integration in America* (New York: Morrow, 1996);

Patricia Williams, "*Metro Broadcasting, Inc.* v. *FCC:* Regrouping in Singular Times," *Harvard Law Review,* 104 (1990): 525.

MIDDLE EAST POLICY

Why did the United States find itself in an antagonistic relationship with Egypt?

Viewpoint: The antagonism between the United States and Egypt arose from the American view of Gamal Abdel Nasser as a Soviet puppet.

Viewpoint: The failure of the United States and Egypt to respect one another's interests led to tension and hostility.

The Middle East is, and for centuries has been, a complicated region. Its climate is generally harsh and arid, yet its people have produced the world's greatest civilizations. It is the home to three of the world's most influential religions: Islam, Christianity, and Judaism, all of which worship the same God. Yet, practitioners of these three faiths have fought over territory and belief for much of their history. The Arab states, historically the poorest of the region, isolated and barren, since 1945 have become the wealthiest societies on earth as they have tapped the oil and natural gas reserves beneath the Arabian Desert and the Persian Gulf.

The term *Middle East* was actually coined by American admiral Alfred Thayer Mahan, architect of American international policy at the end of the nineteenth century. Previously the area had been known by many different names, and parts of what we now call the Middle East were included in various other regions: the Near East, North Africa, the Levant, Asia Minor, and the Ottoman Empire. The region itself is defined loosely, encompassing much of North Africa, the Arabian peninsula, Palestine, Turkey, Iraq, and Iran. Before World War I much of this territory was under the loose hegemony of the Ottoman Empire, though the British and French had both established colonial power throughout the region. After the war, with the dismemberment of the Ottoman state, new boundary lines were drawn.

Americans have had varied interests in the region over the course of many years. In his essay, Itai Sneh, a scholar of American foreign relations, traces American interests in the region and argues that the American failure to achieve universal respect and peace stemmed from the complications of Middle Eastern affairs. Americans saw the Middle East through the prism of the Cold War. Salim Yaqub, also a specialist in American foreign policy, sees the American failure in a more specific way: the United States failed to achieve a working relationship with the region's most charismatic statesman, Egyptian president Gamal Abdel Nasser.

How has the United States responded to the challenges of this region? As Sneh and Yaqub show, the American reaction has not been effective. Could the United States have responded differently? What shaped American policies in the Middle East? These questions will continue to trouble American policymakers and the people of the Middle East.

Viewpoint: The antagonism between the United States and Egypt arose from the American view of Gamal Abdel Nasser as a Soviet puppet.

The United States has concerned itself with the Middle East since its early history. Often misunderstood by locals who equated its actions with intentions to dominate, American leaders asserted U.S. prominence and fought other powers who possessed spheres of influence or wished to establish them. Having regard to conflicting domestic constituencies and to foreign interests, Americans tried to conduct themselves as honest brokers and as custodians of the collective welfare of the region's residents.

Viewing themselves as the new Israelites, chosen for a mission in the New World, some Americans displayed strong interest in the development of the religious and political identity of the Middle East during the reign of the Ottoman Empire in the nineteenth century. As a result, American interests came into competition with the British domination in Egypt and involvement in Palestine and with French influence in the Levant (Lebanon and Syria). Realizations of American sentiment were embodied in the establishment of prestigious educational institutions such as Robert College in Turkey, the Syrian Protestant College (now renamed the American University in Beirut, Lebanon), and the American University in Cairo, Egypt.

Having taught many local leaders, possessing significant Jewish constituencies, devoid of any imperial designs in contrast to the British or the French, buffeted by support for the principle of self-determination in President Woodrow Wilson's Fourteen Points, and by commitment to their implementation in the Versailles Conference, American statesmen gained the trust of the Arabs as well as the Jews in the negotiations that followed the collapse of the Ottoman Empire in World War I. An American team toured Palestine and the Levant. The King-Crane Commission investigated the desires of the local inhabitants. Perhaps not surprisingly, many of them opted for American control. Isolationist pressures at home and preagreements between Britain and France did not change the predicted outcome–the League of Nations appointed mandate powers to the two European nations. Nevertheless, the Americans enjoyed a favorable reputation in the Middle East.

Oil concerns, especially in Saudi Arabia, and the Zionist aspirations for a Jewish homeland in Palestine kept a degree of American interest in the region during the interwar period. As is the global case with American foreign policy, World War II and the Cold War brought a more permanent U.S. presence in the Middle East. The decline of the colonial Western powers, Britain and France; the intensity of the Arab-Israeli conflict (including the demand for a sovereign Jewish state articulated in the 1942 Biltmore Conference held in New York City); the rising importance and accessibility of oil; and geostrategic concerns arising out of growing Soviet encroachments, compelled American policymakers to pay closer attention to developments in the region.

A pattern for U.S. foreign policy was set in 1947. In March, President Harry S Truman pronounced his doctrine, promising American support to regimes that counter Soviet intervention, such as Iran and Turkey, effectively inheriting the mantle of protecting Western interests in the Middle East. The previous year, the United States was actively involved in the discussions over the plight of Jewish refugees who survived the Holocaust in Europe and over the future of Palestine. Known as the Anglo-American Investigative Commission, which was apppointed by the British government in conjunction with the Truman administration, its recommendations included permitting one hundred thousand Jewish survivors from Europe to immigrate to Palestine. President Truman enthusiastically supported this proposal. The Jews in Palestine, including the radical underground organizations, were willing to forego the armed struggle against the British. The British, however, refused. This process culminated with American support for the United Nations' decision in November to terminate the British mandate and to partition Palestine into two separate countries–one Jewish and the other Arab, which was accepted by the former, but rejected by the latter, leading to war. Oil exploration, moreover, was emerging as the mainstay of the regional economy, with companies such as Arab-American Corporation (ARAMCO) at the helm, forging a foundation for a strong relationship with petrol-producing countries, especially Saudi Arabia.

The United States was officially neutral in the war that ensued after Israel's independence in 1948. Arab perceptions, however, were different. They were caused by the speedy American recognition of the Jewish state (resulting largely from the mobilization of effective pressure by the Jewish Lobby, as the votes that it could muster were crucial for Truman's reelection later that year), the financial help given by private individuals and by Jewish communities to Israel, and by the visible participation of English-speaking volunteers in the successful Israeli war effort. Active diplomatic Soviet support to Israel, and the provision of arms through Czechoslovakia, intended primarily to weaken the British standing in the region, were not as widely known.

The 1950–1953 Korean War, although geographically distant, greatly affected the Middle East, opening a turbulent decade. Turkey fought on the American side, gaining an invitation to join the North Atlantic Treaty Organization (NATO) in 1952 (alongside Greece), which it happily accepted. As a result of a strengthening ideological bond with the democratic United States, facilitated by active interaction with its Jewish communities, Israel, initially neutral and still implementing a Socialist-style economy, officially supported the U.S. position. The transition was aided by stern Soviet opposition to Israeli contacts with its own Jewish population and improved relations with Arab countries such as Egypt and Syria, where military coups ousted conservative regimes. Frequent skirmishes with Israel, often triggered by Palestinian refugees and many times supported and organized by Arab countries, caused more Arabs to turn to the Soviets for military equipment and training, while Israel relied primarily on its own nascent industry and on considerable Western support.

While Syria endured frequent military coups (until 1970 when Hafiz El Assad took the reigns of power for more than a generation), the situation in Egypt did stabilize following the 1952 ouster of the pro-Western King Farouk by the Free Officers and the 1954 consolidation of powers by Gamal Abdel Nasser. The Western powers counteracted with the 1955 formation of the Baghdad Pact—including Iraq, Turkey, Iran, Pakistan, and Britain, with subsequent U.S. participation, but no actual membership—which was similar in its construction to NATO as it guaranteed mutual support in case of an external attack.

In Iran, in 1952–1953, American agents secured the overthrow of the popular prime minister, Mohammed Mossadegh, who opposed the predominance of the Western oil interest, restoring the authority of the pro-American Shah, Mohammed Rezh Pahlavi, although tarnishing his credibility as an independent ruler. Concomitantly, in 1953–1954 an American representative, Eric Johnston, arbitrated over sharing the waters of the Jordan River between Israel, Jordan, Lebanon, and Syria, trying to diffuse a growing conflict over the allocation of this precious, scarce resource, positioning the United States as an honest broker between these countries who were mostly Western-leaning.

Egypt secured a British promise to evacuate the Suez Canal Zone, the source as well as a remnant of a long colonial domination, by September 1956. Simultaneously, however, Egypt moved closer to the Soviet bloc. In September 1955 it signed a deal to sell rice and cotton in exchange for $86 million in arms from Czechoslovakia. Nasser wanted to balance the strategic disparity with Israel and to signal a shift from the Western sphere to the independent, nonaligned movement. In February 1956 the United States announced a suspension of all arms shipments to the Arabs and the Israelis, with an immediate partial exemption only for Saudi Arabia. Three months later Egypt signed another agreement with Soviet satellite, Poland, for the purchase of military equipment. Egypt also recognized the (Communist) People's Republic of China as the legitimate regime (as opposed to the Western-backed Nationalist regime based in Taiwan).

The British relinquished control over the Suez Canal in June 1956. However, in July the United States and Britain withdrew their offers to Egypt to assist in the construction of the Aswan Dam to control the Nile River. Nasser viewed its realization as crucial for the future of Egypt—its economic independence, agricultural development, and energy supply—and as the personal hallmark of his regime. The Soviets, in contrast, were eager to extend technological and financial help to the Aswan Dam. Their aim was to enhance their own influence in Egypt in particular and in the Arab world in general through Nasser's patronage. A week later Nasser ordered the immediate nationalization of the Suez Canal, claiming that the proceeds were needed to pay for the Aswan Dam, causing the ire of Britain, France and the United States. This event lead to a series of futile diplomatic maneuvers.

In October 1956 Britain (humiliated by the nationalization of the canal), France (concerned about Nasser's support to the Algerian independence movement), and Israel (worried about Egypt's forthcoming arms supplies and agitated over constant Palestinian attacks encouraged by Egypt), joined forces in a surprise attack on Egypt, triggering the Suez Crisis. While the Americans and the Soviets collaborated to denounce and to counter what was largely viewed as a gross violation of Egyptian sovereignty by colonial powers, their motives were quite different. The Americans felt betrayed by their allies. President Dwight D. Eisenhower was particularly incensed with the timing on the eve of the vote for his reelection and during the Hungarian crisis but wanted to preserve Western influence and to maintain Israel's security. Thus, the proximity of interests between the United States and Nasser's pretense to lead the Arabs and display

Bullet holes in a window at Port Said, Egypt, entrance to the Suez Canal, November 1956

(A. H. Swann)

"positive neutrality" in the Cold War was temporary.

Already in January 1957 Eisenhower articulated his own doctrine, promising U.S. economic assistance, military support, and even armed intervention to sustain regimes opposed to "international Communism." Egypt, a recipient of Soviet aid, was thus presumed to be an antagonist. Indeed, Nasser's leadership and vision of centralized economy and distribution of lands to peasants caused considerable domestic turmoil among the Arab masses against pro-Western regimes, especially in Iraq, Jordan, and Lebanon. In February 1958 Egypt and Syria joined a short-lived United Arab Republic. The following July the Iraqi monarchy was toppled, triggering American intervention in Lebanon, in concert with the British deployment of forces to aid King Hussein of Jordan in the face of mass demonstrations across the region.

The actions, and the strengthening American support to Israel, especially after the Democrats, traditionally more friendly toward Israel, returned to power when Kennedy took office in 1961, further polarized U.S. relations with the Arabs. Although Nasser's relationship with the Soviet Union was not without its difficulties, and his controversial intervention in Yemen caused erosion in his own stature, two camps emerged in the Middle East in the early 1960s: those who sided with Nasser (most of the Arab people, and several regimes such as Syria and Iraq) and those who rallied with the Americans (Israel and the conservative regimes, including Jordan, Saudi Arabia, Turkey, and Iran). While these groupings were not cohesive, they reflected the general Cold War competition between American interests and Soviet clients (and, to a lesser extent in the Middle East, divergent economic systems). Israel's victory in the 1967 Six Days War further binded the United States and Israel and strategic allies. Israel received considerable American military and financial aid, and the Johnson administration supported Israel consistently in the diplomatic arena. In contrast, U.S. relations with Egypt deteriorated while Soviet assistance brought Egypt and the U.S.S.R. closely together. A recast of this paradigm had to await Nasser's death in 1970, with American negotiations in the Arab-Israeli peace process playing a decisive role.

–ITAI SNEH, COLUMBIA UNIVERSITY

Viewpoint: The failure of the United States and Egypt to respect one another's interests led to tension and hostility.

In seeking to account for the antagonistic relationship between the United States and Nasserist Egypt, one should first note that relations between the two parties were not invariably hostile. In the early years of the Free Officers' regime, the United States had generally good relations with Gamal Abdel Nasser, whom it hoped to cultivate as a pro-West, anticommunist leader in the Middle East. During the Suez War of 1956, the United States vigorously opposed the combined British-French-Israeli military attack on Egypt, briefly winning Nassar's gratitude. Moreover, in the late 1950s and early 1960s the United States and Egypt enjoyed a more extended rapprochement.

Apart from these instances, however, relations between the United States and Nasserist Egypt were severely strained. At the heart of the problem was a series of disagreements between the two states over how to treat third parties. Each state had bitter enemies it wanted the other to shun, and each became angry when the other refused to do so. Conversely, each state had close allies it wanted the other to refrain from harassing; this wish, too, was often disregarded. The disagreements over third parties were exacerbated by personal factors. Nasser was a deeply suspicious man who often ascribed base motives to U.S. policy, which he harshly attacked in public speeches. Though irritated by Nasser's invective, Presidents Dwight D. Eisenhower and John F. Kennedy were, on the whole, sufficiently detached and self-confident to avoid taking the attacks personally. Thin-skinned Lyndon B. Johnson was not. American-Egyptian relations drastically deteriorated during the Johnson years, culminating in a formal rupture following the Arab-Israeli war of 1967. Full diplomatic ties were not restored until after Nasser's death in 1970.

Among the third parties over which the United States and Nasser disagreed, the most important were the Sino-Soviet bloc, Britain, France, and Israel. Throughout the Nasser period, but especially in the 1950s, the United States pressured Nasser to limit his dealings with communist states. However, Nasser believed that Egyptian and Arab interests would best be served by a policy of "positive neutrality," or nonalignment, in the Cold War, whereby the Arab states profited from cordial relations with both Cold War blocs. In 1955 Egypt purchased some $86 million in arms from the Soviet Union via Czechoslovakia, and began using propaganda and subversion to pressure other Arab countries to adopt neutralist policies. In 1956 Egypt opened diplomatic relations with the People's Republic of China. That same year, angered by Nasser's continued dealings with the Sino-Soviet bloc, the United States withdrew its offer of financial assistance for construction of the Aswan Dam, an ambitious Egyptian project aimed at regulating the Nile's flow for agricultural and hydroelectrical purposes. The U.S. action backfired in two ways. First, it led directly to the Suez Crisis, which, while allowing the United States to demonstrate its support for Egyptian sovereignty (and thus increase its prestige in the Arab world), enabled the Soviet Union to do the same thing far more ostentatiously. Second, the U.S. reaction prompted Nasser to turn to the Soviets for funding of the Aswan Dam.

Just as the United States tried to limit Nasser's dealings with the communist world, so Nasser hoped to limit U.S. support for Britain, France, and Israel. Yet, he too was largely disappointed. U.S. support for Egypt during the Suez war delighted Egyptian and Arab observers, raising expectations throughout the region that the United States would henceforth pursue an independent Middle East policy, free of association with Britain, France, and Israel. Actually, the Eisenhower administration had opposed the attack on Egypt because it believed such a move would inflame the Arab world against the West, not because it favored the rapid elimination of British or French power in the region. Nor did the administration intend to lessen its support for Israel's existence and security, or even, for that matter, to push Israel to make substantial territorial or political concessions in exchange for peace with the Arabs. As these realities became clearer, Nasser's gratitude toward the United States evaporated.

Things went downhill from there. Having failed to get Nasser to shun the Soviets, the United States pressured other Arab leaders to shun Nasser. In early 1957, in a declaration known as the Eisenhower Doctrine, Eisenhower promised increased military and economic aid and direct U.S. military protection to Middle Eastern states willing to recognize the threat of "international communism." Implicitly, the Eisenhower Doctrine was an invitation to the other Arab states to repudiate Nasser and "positive neutrality." Nasser, not surprisingly, strongly opposed the new U.S. policy. The next two years were a period of intense American-Egyptian rivalry. While avoiding direct confrontation, the United States and Egypt repeatedly harassed each other's allies: U.S. operatives sought the overthrow of Syria's leftist government; Egyptian agents subverted pro-West regimes in Jordan, Lebanon, and Libya.

By late 1958 it had become clear that Egypt, which had since merged with Syria to form the United Arab Republic (UAR), was too politically

THE MANDATE SYSTEM

The Treaty of Versailles (1919) addressed the issue of how to deal with the prewar colonies of the defeated nations. Although the principle of self-determination was a major consideration, the victorious powers were unwilling to grant immediate independence to many of the former colonies. The treaty decreed certain regions as mandated territories under the tutelage of the great powers. As a result, a strong British and French presence was permitted in the Middle East. The former Ottoman territories of Palestine and Iraq came under British control while France supervised Syria and Lebanon. Nevertheless, independence came slowly. In fact, twenty years after the signing of the treaty, none of the mandates in the Middle East had achieved full independence. Not until after World War II was the problem of colonialism in the Middle East solved.

An excerpt from Article 22 of the treaty, establishing the mandate system, appears below:

To those colonies and territories which as a consequence of the late war have ceased to be under the sovereignty of the States which formerly governed them and which are inhabited by peoples not yet able to stand by themselves under the strenuous conditions of the modern world, there should be applied the principle that the well-being and development of such peoples form a sacred trust of civilization and that securities for the performance of this trust should be embodied in this Covenant.

The best method of giving practical effect to this principle is that the tutelage of such peoples should be entrusted to advanced nations who by reason of their resources, their experience or their geographical position can best undertake this responsibility, and who were willing to accept it, and that this tutelage should be exercised by them as Mandatories on behalf of the League.

The character of the mandate must differ according to the stage of the development of the people, the geographical situation of the territory, its economic conditions, and other similar circumstances.

Certain communities formerly belonging to the Turkish Empire have reached a stage of development where their existence as independent nations can be provisionally recognized subject to the rendering of administrative advice and assistance by a Mandatory until such time as they are able to stand alone. The wishes of these communities must be a principal consideration in the selection of the Mandatory. . . .

In every case of mandate, the Mandatory shall render to the Council an annual report in reference to the territory committed to its charge.

The degree of authority, control, or administration to be exercised by the Mandatory shall, if not previously agreed upon by the Members of the League, be explicitly defined in each case by the Council.

A permanent commission shall be constituted to receive and examine the annual reports of the Mandatories and to advise the Council on all matters relating to the observance of the mandates.

Source: *Donald Kagan, Steven Ozment, and Frank M. Turner,* The Western Heritage *(Upper Saddle River, N.J.: Prentice Hall, 1998), pp. 953–954.*

powerful in the region to be safely opposed by other Arab states, and Eisenhower had to moderate his anti-Nasser stance. Fortunately, in early 1959 Nasser's relations with the Soviet Union soured, permitting a modest improvement in UAR-American relations that lasted into the Kennedy years. Although the UAR continued to receive considerable military and economic aid from the Soviet Union, and although Washington kept trying to hold UAR-Soviet ties to a minimum, the United States was no longer so fearful that Nasser would become an outright ally of the Soviet bloc.

As for Nasser's view of U.S. policy, by the early 1960s his critique centered mainly on the role of Israel. In part the change of emphasis reflected a decrease in British and French power in the Middle East, but mostly it resulted from a steady improvement in U.S.-Israeli relations. In the final years of its tenure, even as it had sought better relations with Nasser, the Eisenhower administration had begun to recognize Israel's potential as a strategic ally of the United States, capable of defending the region's oil installations from disruption by radical nationalists. This attitude became more pronounced under Kennedy, who began supplying Israel with anti-aircraft missiles, much to Nasser's chagrin.

There were other third parties over whom the United States and the UAR disagreed during this period. In the Congo crisis of 1960–1961, the UAR and the United States were at odds over Congolese prime minister Patrice Lumumba, whom Nasser supported and the Americans opposed. Nasser was outraged when U.S.-supported Congolese officers arrested and murdered Lumumba. In late 1962 Yemen erupted in civil war, pitting Yemen's newly established republican government against ousted Yemeni monarchists. Nasser sent troops to protect the republican government, while the United States, less wholeheartedly, supported Saudi Arabia, which in turn aided the monarchists.

By the time President Kennedy was assassinated in late 1963, the cumulative effect of these disputes was a significant erosion of the UAR-American rapprochement that had begun in the late 1950s. The erosion drastically accelerated after Johnson became president. Nasser took an immediate dislike to the "cowboy" in the White House, whom he saw as a determined foe of nonaligned nations in general and of the UAR in particular. The Egyptian leader was angered by Johnson's escalation of the Vietnam War and by his continued support for anti-Lumumba forces in the Congo. Nasser also saw Johnson's hand in the overthrow of Ghanaian president Kwame Nkrumah and the political defeat of Indonesian president Ahmed Sukarno, both prominent figures in the nonaligned movement. Closer to home, Nasser was alarmed by increased U.S. support for Israel and Saudi Arabia and offended by U.S. attempts to regulate UAR behavior through the granting and withholding of food aid. At the same time, Nasser was under growing pressure from radical leaders in Iraq and Syria (the latter having seceded from the UAR in 1961) to take a harder line against Israel and the West. To mollify such critics and to express his own outrage over U.S. policies, Nasser directed a stream of public invective toward Johnson and his administration.

Johnson, for his part, was at a loss over how to deal with Nasser, oscillating between clumsy efforts to charm the Egyptian leader and equally clumsy efforts to intimidate him. Stung by Nasser's verbal attacks and under increasing pressure from anti-Nasser forces in Congress, by 1967 Johnson had largely given up on conducting fruitful relations with the UAR.

Dealing the most devastating blow to UAR-American relations was the Arab-Israeli war of June 1967. Ironically, the war was the product of inter-Arab rivalry. In the spring of 1967 Nasser was taunted by Arab critics for his alleged timidity in the face of Israeli power. To silence the criticism, Nasser made a series of menacing gestures against Israel: he ousted United Nations peacekeeping forces from UAR territory, imposed a blockade on Israeli shipping through the Strait of Tiran (leading into the Gulf of Aqaba), and signed military pacts with Syria and Jordan. Although Nasser had no intention of starting a war with Israel–much of his army was tied down in Yemen–his public posture was sufficiently belligerent to give Israel grounds for claiming an Arab attack was imminent. On 5 June, Israel launched a "preemptive" strike against Egypt, destroying its air force on the ground. Over the next several days Israel routed the combined forces of Egypt, Syria, and Jordan, seizing major territories from each. It was a humiliating defeat for the Arab world and for Nasser personally.

The 1967 war caused a rupture in UAR-American relations. Unwilling to admit that Israel had destroyed his air force single-handedly, Nasser publicly charged that the United States had taken part in the attack. The claim was false, but the Johnson administration showed its partiality to Israel in other ways. Instead of demanding an immediate withdrawal of Israeli forces to their prewar positions–as Eisenhower had done following Israel's attack on Egypt in 1956–Johnson called for a simple cease-fire, allowing Israeli forces to remain indefinitely in the territories they had seized. Johnson also supported Israel's view that any return of Arab territories must await a comprehensive settlement of the Arab-Israeli dispute. In retaliation for such partiality, the UAR severed diplomatic relations with the United States.

From 1967 until Nasser's death in 1970, the UAR drew closer to the Soviet Union while the United States, under Presidents Johnson and Richard M. Nixon, cemented its strategic partnership with Israel. However, Nasser was never fully satisfied with the amount of Soviet military support he received, and in his final months he seemed increasingly receptive to the view that the United States, because of its influence with Israel, held the key to an acceptable settlement of the Arab-Israeli dispute, entailing the return of Arab territories seized in 1967. It is impossible to know how far Nasser might have acted on this perception had he lived, but over the next decade his successor, Anwar Sadat, ended Egypt's strategic relationship with the Soviet Union, restored diplomatic relations with the United States, and concluded a U.S.-brokered peace settlement with Israel.

To some extent, given the political, moral, and strategic needs of each country, it was inevitable that American and Egyptian interests would clash during the Nasser years. The United States could not repudiate its alliance with Britain and France if it hoped to remain competitive in the Cold War. Nor could American administrations renounce their basic support for Israel's existence and security, lest they lose political and moral standing at home and abroad. It was equally unreasonable to expect Egypt to align itself with the West in the Cold War. Not only would such a move deny Egypt the resources of the communist world, it would place a stamp of moral approval on Egypt's former imperial masters and on Israel's current supporters.

At the same time, both parties made the situation much worse than it had to be. Each country refused to respect the other's basic geopolitical interests, striking out in anger when it failed to get its way. Each violated the sovereignty of the other's Middle Eastern allies, further exacerbating the bilateral conflict.

There were additional failings that were peculiar to each party. The United States was excessively partial to Britain, France, and Israel, an attitude that fueled Nasser's anger. While the United States could not disavow Britain and France as Cold War allies, it could have done more to distance itself from their Middle East policies. Likewise, having played a crucial role in Israel's creation, the United States had a special responsibility to help solve the problems caused by this act. It should not have allowed itself to become Israel's primary benefactor without insisting on some Israeli concessions, such as relinquishment of territory or repatriation and compensation of Palestinian refugees, to address legitimate Arab grievances. The Johnson administration was especially culpable on this score, since it tacitly supported Israel's seizure of additional Arab territory.

Nasser, too, deserves a good deal of blame. Nasser was an intelligent, dedicated, and courageous leader who did much to consolidate Egyptian independence and instill pride in the Egyptian people. However, he was a deeply suspicious and contentious man, obsessed with his personal dignity and prone to react fiercely to any perceived slight. It was not uncommon for Nasser to deliver anti-American tirades in retaliation for supposed affronts that turned out, once more reliable reports were in, to have been greatly exaggerated or even nonexistent. Nasser defended such practices by claiming that, in his struggles against powers possessing vastly greater military and economic resources, the mobilization of Egyptian and Arab opinion was one of the few weapons at his disposal. His argument does have some force. Yet, even a weak nation's weapons should be used with precision and restraint. Nasser's careless rhetorical attacks needlessly embittered U.S.-Egyptian relations and, to the extent that they made it easier for the United States to relax its restraints on Israeli action, eventually damaged Nasser himself.

In the Nasser era the United States and Egypt had non-negotiable commitments–attachments and aversions to third parties–that placed them at odds with one another. This built-in rivalry was exacerbated by poor judgment and bad faith on both sides. It is doubtful that the two countries ever could have been allies in this period. Still, had they been a little more respectful of each other's interests, they could have avoided much of the enmity that plagued their relationship.

–SALIM YAQUB, UNIVERSITY OF CHICAGO

References

John A. DeNovo, *American Interests and Policies in the Middle East, 1900–1939* (Minneapolis: University of Minnesota Press, 1963);

Irene Gendzier, *Notes from the Minefield: United States Interventions in Lebanon and the Middle East, 1945–1958* (New York: Columbia University Press, 1997);

Fawaz A. Gerges, *The Superpowers and the Middle East: Regional and International Politics, 1955–1967* (Boulder, Colo.: Westview Press, 1994);

Mohamed Hassanein Heikal, *The Cairo Documents: The Inside Story of Nasser and His Relationship With World Leaders, Rebels, and Statesmen* (Garden City, N.Y.: Doubleday, 1973);

Matthew F. Holland, *America and Egypt: From Roosevelt to Eisenhower* (Westport, Conn.: Praeger, 1996);

Burton I. Kaufman, *The Arab Middle East and the United States: Inter-Arab Rivalry and Superpower Diplomacy* (New York: Twayne, 1996);

Malcolm H. Kerr, *The Arab Cold War: Gamal 'Abd al-Nasir and His Rivals, 1958–1970* (London & New York: Oxford University Press, 1971);

George Lenczowski, *American Presidents and the Middle East* (Durham, N.C.: Duke University Press, 1990);

Malik Mufti, "The United States and Nasserist Pan-Arabism" *The Middle East and the United States: A Historical and Political Reassessment,* edited by David W. Lesch (Boulder, Colo.: Westview Press, 1996), pp. 167–186;

Anne Murray, *The United States, Great Britain, and the Middle East: Discourse and Dissidents* (Boulder, Colo.: Social Sciences Monograph / New York: Columbia University Press, 1999);

Anthony Nutting, *Nasser* (London: Constable, 1972);

Robert Stephens, *Nasser: A Political Biography* (London: Allen Lane, 1971);

Peter Woodward, *Nasser* (London & New York: Longman, 1992).

NEW WORLD ORDER

Was the Bush administration's vision of a New World Order a triumph for American diplomacy?

Viewpoint: Yes, the New World Order promulgated by President George Bush has been a success because it gave the United States a framework in which to confront major crises.

Viewpoint: No, the grand design of the Bush administration for a New World Order ultimately failed because its goals were too ambitious for changing global conditions.

Few men have come into the presidency with more international experience than George H. W. Bush: the son of a U.S. senator, Bush served as American ambassador to the United Nations, first American envoy to the People's Republic of China, director of the Central Intelligence Agency (CIA), and vice president for eight years. Though he self-deprecatingly said he was fuzzy on "the vision thing," Bush did have a clear view of America's role in the world. His father had been one of the internationalist Republicans who had helped shape a bipartisan post–World War II American foreign policy, and George Bush was a consistent advocate of a prudent, disciplined, and consistent American role in the world.

With the collapse of international communism and the Soviet Union, the United States needed to rethink its role. Bush ambitiously proclaimed the beginning of a New World Order, based not on the conflict between the United States and the U.S.S.R. but rather on the protection of sovereignty and the curbing of international aggression. It was the most ambitious American pronouncement, perhaps, since Woodrow Wilson unveiled his Fourteen Points in 1918. The United States would lead through international agencies such as the United Nations (UN), the Organization of American States (OAS), and the North Atlantic Treaty Organization (NATO), continuing to protect its allies, but more and more leaving the protection of sovereignty and the resolution of international problems to these agencies. The United States would maintain its military strength not to combat Soviet aggression but to support peace-keeping efforts around the world.

Has it worked? In these two essays, Jürgen Scheunemann and Robert J. Allison disagree. Scheunemann argues that the New World Order was an impossibly ambitious project, doomed by its conflicting and poorly articulated goals. Allison, pointing to the Gulf War and the Bosnian and Kosovar crises, argues that the New World Order has been a relative success. It may be too soon for history to deliver its verdict on the New World Order. Nonetheless, an informed understanding of its objectives, and of American intentions, will be crucial to its future success or failure.

Viewpoint:
Yes, the New World Order promulgated by President George Bush has been a success because it gave the United States a framework in which to confront major crises.

After World War II the United States became the de facto leader of the free world in its contest with the communist world. Yet, with the collapse of communism and the Soviet empire, the United States now could be the leader of the entire world. Under the administrations of presidents George H. W. Bush and William J. Clinton, the United States was able to create what President Bush called a "New World Order," coalitions of nations, in some cases former enemies, who could protect peace and human rights anywhere in the world.

This development is a dramatic change. In the nineteenth century international diplomacy was dominated by the major imperial powers–England, France, Germany, and Russia. These nations used power for their own ends–establishing colonies in Africa and Asia and extracting trading privileges from rulers they allowed to remain in power. With the development of sophisticated weapons and military technology, the imperial powers were able to keep peace roughly from 1815 to 1914. The system collapsed in 1914, leading to two devastating world wars which utterly destroyed the economies of these former powers.

The United States then had an opportunity not only to fill the power vacuum but also to do it in a different way. The United States would not be an imperial power, but instead would show Europe the proper way to maintain peace in the rest of the world, by granting and protecting the autonomy of all the world's peoples. Since World War II the United States had maintained the largest military in the world, but its purpose was not to extend American territory or power but to protect its allies against communist aggression. The collapse of communism meant that all nations of the world were potential allies of the United States. The United Nations no longer would be driven by tension between Soviets and Americans but instead could be a deliberative body where all the world's people could meet as equals.

The first real test of the New World Order came in the Persian Gulf. Kuwait, a small but wealthy oil-producing state on the Persian Gulf, had lent financial support to Iraq during the nine-year war between Iraq and Iran in the 1980s. Kuwait demanded repayment from Iraq, and the two nations also quarreled about oil production and export. In July 1990 talks between the two nations broke down, and on 2 August, Iraqi troops seized Kuwait, which Iraqi president Saddam Hussein proclaimed a province of Iraq.

Bush immediately mobilized, moving through the United Nations to assemble an international alliance opposed to Iraq's invasion. The United States was joined in denouncing the invasion by both Middle Eastern nations (Egypt, Saudi Arabia, Qatar, the United Arab Emirates, and Turkey) and European nations (England, France, and Germany) as well as some of the former members of the Soviet bloc (Russia, Poland, and Bulgaria). It was a remarkable achievement to have so many former enemies on the same side. American troops led the international forces that assembled in Saudi Arabia to protect it from a potential Iraqi invasion. In the United Nations the international community condemned Iraq and ordered Hussein to remove his forces from Kuwait.

When Iraq failed to withdraw from Kuwait by 15 January 1991, President Bush ordered massive air strikes into Iraq and Kuwait, pounding military targets in both countries. When this attempt to move Iraqis out of Kuwait failed, on 24 February the combined allied forces invaded Kuwait, routing the Iraqis and driving them well into Iraq in four days of fighting. Three days later, with Iraq prepared to agree to all the allied terms, President Bush ordered a cease-fire.

It was a brief war, with a clearly stated objective. Not only did the New World Order succeed in its first real test, but it also achieved another of President Bush's stated objectives, to help the American people overcome the legacy of Vietnam. That war had not only divided the American people but had divided American allies, and the failure to have a reasonable goal had complicated the war beyond comprehension. In Kuwait, the United States and the international community had moved quickly, with a simply stated objective, and had quickly defeated Hussein.

Some critics subsequently argued that the war was not fought to free Kuwait but to protect oil resources, or that in the final analysis the Gulf War failed because it did not dislodge Hussein from power. In the 1990s Hussein was able to trick U.N. arms inspectors who needed to verify that he was not producing chemical weapons. However, if the allied forces had continued on to Baghdad and turned the war's goal from the liberation of

President George Bush conferring with his military and diplomatic advisers during the crisis with Iraq in 1991

(R. D. Ward–DOD)

Kuwait to the overthrow of Hussein, it would have hopelessly complicated the situation. Aside from the logistical problems of overthrowing Hussein, had the international community engaged in this kind of internal political struggle, it would have tainted the entire operation and all subsequent operations. By moving only to liberate Kuwait, the international community made it clear its goal was the protection of national sovereignty. Had it moved against Hussein in Iraq, it would have violated Iraq's sovereignty.

In the former Yugoslavia the international community has been less able to resolve the ancient conflicts between Muslims and Christians, between Serbs and Bosnians or Croats or Albanians. The crisis in the Balkans differs from the crisis in the Persian Gulf, and the fact that the international community approached it differently actually reflects well on their grasp that different crises require different solutions. Yugoslavia, a socialist nation that had maintained its distance from the Soviet Union during the 1950s and 1960s, was a federation of six republics. Its people were of varied religions (Muslims, Orthodox Christians, Catholics, and Protestants) and cultural or ethnic identities (Bosnian, Serbian, and Albanian). Resistance to the Germans during World War II and the creative leadership of Marshall Josip Broz Tito held all these diverse people together. After Tito's death in 1980, tensions between people of the different republics escalated. In March 1992 Bosnia and Herzegovina declared independence. The Yugoslav army, mainly Serbian, supported the Serbian minority in Bosnia, which wanted to remain part of Yugoslavia (now reduced to the Republics of Serbia and Montenegro). Complicating the issue were the traditional Russian support for Serbians (support that had helped trigger World War I, as a Serbian nationalist assassinated the Austro-Hungarian crown prince in Sarajevo) and the fact that over centuries of living together, there were few clear-cut "Serbian" or "Bosnian" areas in Bosnia-Herzegovina. Instead, Bosnians and Serbs lived next to one another and frequently intermarried. Between 1992 and 1995 Serbs and Bosnians brutalized one another, as the Serbs and their allies tried to suppress Bosnian independence.

In 1994 Russia convinced the Serbs to halt their siege of Sarajevo, and the following year President Clinton convened peace talks between the factions in Dayton, Ohio. The Dayton Accords created a Bosnian federation, with a three-member executive council, whose presidency would rotate between a Croat, a Bosnian, and a Serb. Sixty thousand NATO troops were sent to supervise the disarmament of Bosnia and the orderly elections that followed years of bloody fighting. The process was stymied by resistance from some Bosnian Serbs, who ignored the call to disarm. Instead, these Bosnian enclaves remained hostile to the idea of Bosnian independence, hoping instead to maintain a "greater Serbia" in the ruins of Yugoslavia.

While Bosnia and Herzegovina were left to pick up the pieces, in other parts of the former Yugoslavia more violence ensued. Kosovo, an important province of Serbia, has an overwhelmingly Muslim population (90 percent of Kosovars are Muslims, while Muslims make up only 19 percent of Serbia's total population). In February 1998 the Serbian police force and Yugoslavian army attacked Kosovo, which wanted independence from Serbia. Massacres of civilians and other atrocities, similar to those reported in Bosnia earlier in the decade, ultimately triggered NATO air strikes at Belgrade. Unlike Bosnia and Kuwait, Kosovo is not a sovereign nation.

Is the purpose of the New World Order to protect national sovereignty or to protect human rights? In this case there seems no ready solution. In other cases of genocide or of bloody ethnic conflict such as in Rwanda and Burundi, Somalia, and Kashmir, the international community has been equally slow to act, because in contrast to the Persian Gulf, there is no apparent solution. How does one prevent people from killing one another? If this is the goal of the New World Order, few will dispute that it is a worthy one. On the other hand, few will be able to propose either an effortless or an effective way to achieve it.

The New World Order is an experiment whose success or failure cannot yet be determined. President Bush, nonetheless, did not shrink from his vision of the United States leading a peaceful world. The New World Order requires American aid, military and economic, to other nations who will on the whole be left to resolve their own problems. International diplomacy is rarely dramatic; it requires patience and a keen understanding of history, culture, and local economic and political conditions. For the United States to be a leader in seeking international peace, Americans must be ready not only to launch smart bombs and pick up anti-aircraft guns but also to learn the languages, cultures, and histories of other people.

—ROBERT J. ALLISON, SUFFOLK UNIVERSITY

Viewpoint: No, the grand design of the Bush administration for a New World Order ultimately failed because its goals were too ambitious for changing global conditions.

From 1989 to 1991, as the Cold War drew to a close, the future of the international system looked promising. With the imminent demise of the Soviet Union, the global adversary of almost fifty years, the United States and its Western allies finally seemed free to turn away from the arms race, ideological warfare, and theaters of small-scale wars in developing nations. Throughout the world democracy, human rights, and free trade appeared to be on the rise. Thus, it was in a spirit of idealism and hope that President George Bush repeatedly spoke of a New World Order:

> We stand today at a unique and extraordinary moment. . . . Out of these troubled times . . . a New World Order can emerge. . . . Today, that New World Order is struggling to be born, a world quite different from the one we have known, a world where the rule of law supplants the rule of the jungle, a world in which nations recognize the shared responsibility for freedom and justice, a world where the strong respect the weak.

Despite the generally successful foreign policy of the Bush administration, this vision was soon proven erroneous by the test of reality. Its failure was the result both of basic foreign policy miscalculations and of U.S. responses to threats to the New World Order.

The New World Order that the Bush administration envisioned was perceived as a system of interdependent states. This approach, long established in scholarly writings on foreign policy, claims that modern states have come to accept the various economic, political, cultural, and ecological dependencies among themselves and will therefore act accordingly, preferring cooperation over confrontation. However, even with the fall of the Soviet Union, the international system has remained ruled by a balance of power.

The Bush administration made a concerted attempt to avoid boasting about having won the Cold War, so as to not hurt the Soviet Union's standing in the world and to reassure the international community that the New World Order would not entirely be a Pax Americana, a system dominated by American power. Nevertheless, it assumed a leading, guardian-type role for the United States, the only surviving global superpower. Upholding such a system, however, creates two major problems for the guardian state. First, it requires full commitment on the part of the leading nation and its allies when it comes to actually implementing and upholding the principles of that world order. Secondly, there needs to be a basic and mutual understanding among all states regarding these principles. Bush did quite the contrary—he stressed the flexibility of the New World Order:

> In the complex world we are entering there can be no single or simple set of fixed rules for using force. . . . Using force makes sense as a policy where the stakes warrant, where and when force can be effective, where no other policies are likely to prove effective, where its application can be limited in scope and time, and where the potential benefits justify the potential costs and sacrifice.

So when the Cold War came to an end, the U.S. perception of the international system, as expressed in several speeches by Bush, was not congruent with the reality of international politics. In fact, as the subsequent crises such as the Panama intervention, the civil war in Somalia, and unrest in former Yugoslavia showed, the U.S. view of the international system was not shared by many other nations.

Historically, the United States has tried more than once to unilaterally formulate and implement its vision of the world, mostly with mixed results. Among the first was the Monroe Doctrine of 1823, which tried to organize the spheres of influence between the major European powers and the emerging new power, the United States. Later, American involvement in World War I and the subsequent diplomacy of Woodrow Wilson–resulting most notably in the League of Nations–showed that without American involvement the international system would collapse. American participation in World War II from 1941 to 1945, Franklin D. Roosevelt's "Four Freedoms," and the "Atlantic Charter," which led to the founding of the United Nations, revealed that only prolonged American commitment could restore the original order. The New World Order offered by Bush was one of the last of these attempted grand designs for a unilateral U.S. foreign-policy program. In addition, it demanded considerable U.S. commitment. This New World Order therefore gave rise to an even more interventionist policy than the Cold War, because governing a multitude of independent states is much more difficult than organizing a world divided into two power blocs. Historian John Lewis Gaddis once called the Cold War the "long peace" because all international conflicts were superseded, and therefore contained, by the superpowers' overall interests. This "long peace" had now come to an end.

Finally, the vision of a new world proved to be highly idealistic as it also neglected the national interest of the key actor, the very guardian of the New World Order. Quite naturally, the United States, being a nation-state and a superpower, has a strong sense of national interest, which does not necessarily correspond to those of the international system or other major powers. The United States faces a constant quandary between weighing its own national interests against those of the world at large.

The U.S. commitment to successfully upholding a New World Order should have been absolute, continuous, and coherent. A good example of how the system first worked, but then failed, is the Persian Gulf War (1991), also known as Operation Desert Storm–the war between the (mostly) Western alliance and Iraq. Many historians consider this conflict one of the few triumphs of the international community against an expansionist, aggressive, and brutal dictator who is often compared to Adolf Hitler and Joseph Stalin. The Gulf War, in fact, brought to light all the flaws of the New World Order.

First of all, the single most important prerequisite for upholding a world order under U.S. leadership–which was the objective of the Gulf War–was namely maintaining the morale of the American people, who would only support the war as long as it generated no American casualties. Even sixteen years after the end of the Vietnam War, the American public was still haunted by the "Vietnam Syndrome," the fear of getting involved in a war with no clear goals, and the possibility of a heavy American death toll. Bush accurately spotted the dangers of the Vietnam Syndrome and pushed for a heavy military buildup and a prolonged five-week aerial bombardment before actually sending in American ground troops. This strategy turned out to be highly successful in the case of the Iraq war. Most conflicts between states, or even worse, between factions in the same society, however, are low-key and long-term conflicts where other means are necessary, as the United States was to learn in Somalia in 1991 and again in 1992 in Yugoslavia.

Secondly, the Gulf War seemed to begin with a clear goal, namely to liberate Iraq-occupied Kuwait, to punish the aggressor, and to reestablish the balance of power in one of the most important regions because it contains some of the most important oil reserves. In addition, the Iraqi invasion had also threatened the Middle East peace process between Israel and the Palestinians. In the course of the Gulf War, however, these aims became blurred as the administration considered actually shifting the original objective to make it an attempt to remove Saddam Hussein from power and thus to liberate the Iraqi people from tyranny. Basically, this situation demonstrated the question of how far American intervention should go when it came to upholding the principles of a New World Order. Subsequently, Hussein was not removed, even though it would have been fairly easy for American forces. Instead, a truce was negotiated and severe economic sanctions and limitations (such as the no-fly zones) were implemented against Iraq. The main reason for U.S. reluctance to go all the way became clear soon after: the United States was well aware of the absence of international support for an overthrow of Hussein, and it understood that Iraq without its dictator would need political guidance and support to reorganize the country. The United States only tried to back the Kurds and Shiites–two large and suppressed ethnic minorities in Iraq and Turkey–in their fight against Hussein. However, their rebellions were crushed by the still-intact Iraqi army.

This example illustrates that a New World Order could function only if the leading member of the international system, the United States, was willing not only to solve a conflict using the necessary military means but also to draw up and implement political solutions. In the case of the single most important conflict in the 1990s, the United States was not prepared to do so. It therefore did not demonstrate the necessary determination to uphold the New World Order it had just proclaimed. Hence it undermined both the credibility of its national foreign policy as well as the strength of the New World Order.

Thirdly, difficulties and obstacles arise when trying to orchestrate the world community. In the case of the Gulf War, the United States succeeded in making "Desert Storm" an official United Nations mission that had full support of the international community and the tacit agreement of Russia and China. Other conflicts at the time involving the United States, however, most notably the intervention in Panama in 1989, did not find any international support, even though the Bush administration viewed these conflicts as genuine threats to international peace and stability. And despite the joint effort of the United States and its allies in defeating Hussein, the Desert Storm alliance was wracked by internal divisions. Even during the Gulf War it was difficult for the United States to find the military and financial support of its Western allies. This, in turn, was also a result of growing European self-confidence and strength. The European Union was about to launch its monetary union. European nations were no longer willing to simply tag along with United States diplomacy. This independence put even more limits on a New World Order and the American governance of it: it showed that even a superpower could easily reach its financial limits. A world of interdependent states, however, is likely to suffer from several simultaneous military conflicts. It would be literally impossible for the United States to solve all of them or even commit itself in all of them.

Fourthly, the New World Order is limited to the moment nations that are larger and more powerful than Iraq, nations that are simply not willing to back down under international pressure, become involved. The crushing of the human-rights and student movement in China in 1989, for example, could not be stopped by the United States and the Western allies despite economic sanctions and diplomatic pressure. In addition, these same nations, primarily Germany and the United States, made peace with China for economic purposes. A New World Order inherently subscribes to a double standard: as long as conflicts remain domestic and do not directly threaten the international system, or economic and security interests of the United States, these conflicts are neglected. This problem was in full evidence when war broke out among the former Yugoslav republics. Even though the leading European powers scrambled to find a diplomatic solution, the United States remained passive and did not threaten intervention because southeastern Europe was of no strategic significance to the United States. The principles of the New World Order were repeatedly violated during the war; nevertheless, the United States limited its intervention to indirect military support in the form of arms sales. To the interna-

A THOUSAND POINTS OF LIGHT

In George H. W. Bush's acceptance speech of the Republican nomination for president of the United States (18 August 1988), he stated:

. . . Look at the world on this bright August night. The spirit of democracy is sweeping the Pacific rim. China feels the winds of change. New democracies assert themselves in South America. One by one the unfree places fall, not to the force of arms but to the force of an idea: freedom works.

We have a new relationship with the Soviet Union—the I.N.F. treaty, the beginning of the Soviet withdrawal from Afghanistan, the beginning of the end of the Soviet proxy war in Angola, and with it the independence of Namibia. Iran and Iraq move toward peace.

It is a watershed. It is no accident.

It happened when we acted on the ancient knowledge that strength and clarity lead to peace; weakness and ambivalence lead to war. Weakness tempts aggressors. Strength stops them. I will not allow this country to be made weak again.

The tremors in the Soviet world continue. The hard earth there has not yet settled. Perhaps what is happening will change our world forever. Perhaps not. A prudent skepticism is in order. And so is hope. Either way, we're in an unprecedented position to change the nature of our relationship. Not by pre-emptive concession, but by keeping our strength. Not by yielding up defense systems with nothing won in return, but by hard, cool engagement in the tug and pull of diplomacy. . . .

I will keep America moving forward, always forward—for a better America, for an endless, enduring dream and a thousand points of light.

That is my mission. And I will complete it.

Source: *James R. Andrews and David Zarefsky,* Contemporary American Voices: Significant Speeches in American History, 1945–Present *(White Plains, N.Y.: Longman, 1992), pp. 385–391.*

tional community it became clear that the United States would only act as a guardian of the New World Order if it involved U.S. national interests—a development that in turn undermined the authority of the New World Order.

The few successes and many failures of ruling a New World Order since 1989 show that this grand U.S. design has failed. In many low-conflict regions such as Panama, Haiti, North and South Korea, Rwanda, the Middle East, Indonesia, Somalia, and former Yugoslavia, the United States has militarily or politically intervened and then left the conflict parties to their own devices. The results were mixed at best.

—JÜRGEN SCHEUNEMANN, FOX FELLOW, YALE UNIVERSITY

References

Michael R. Beschloss and Strobe Talbott, *At the Highest Levels: The Inside Story of the End of the Cold War* (Boston: Little, Brown, 1993);

George Bush, *Public Papers of the Presidents of the United States, George Bush: 1989–1993* (Washington, D.C.: Government Printing Office, 1990–1993);

Michael J. Hogan, ed., *The End of the Cold War: Its Meaning and Implications* (Cambridge & New York: Cambridge University Press, 1992);

Kenneth A. Oye, Robert J. Lieber, and Donald Rothchild, eds., *Eagle in a New World: American Grand Strategy in the Post–Cold War Era* (New York: HarperCollins, 1992);

Brad Roberts, ed., *The New Democracies: Global Change and U.S. Policy* (Cambridge: MIT Press, 1990);

James N. Rosenau and Hylke Tromp, eds., *Interdependence and Conflict in World Politics* (Aldershot, U.K. & Brookfield, Vt.: Avebury, 1989).

1960s PROGRESSIVE MOVEMENT

Were the movements of the 1960s responsible for progressive change or were they lessons in destruction?

Viewpoint: The youthful idealism of the 1960s sparked the mass movements against racial injustice and the Vietnam war.

Viewpoint: The tactics of the New Left inspired a vigorous debate and energized communities across the nation to seek social improvement.

Viewpoint: The progressive movements of the 1960s liberated only those who had no need of it—the well educated, elite, and politically powerful—while it created a new culture that disparaged the values of hard work.

The political movements of the 1960s, particularly the Civil Rights and the anti–Vietnam War movements, were different from earlier political movements. These movements were as much cultural as political. They sought not only immediate political goals (changes in the law, and end to a war) but ultimately cultural and social goals (equality of all, not only before the law but in everyday life; changes in the way people lived and worked). The movements seemed to emanate from younger people, from the generation born after World War II, which came of age in the 1960s. The lunch counter sit-ins of 1960, the "Freedom Rides" of the early part of the decade, led to the Free Speech movement at Berkeley, California, and the National Mobilization against the War in the late 1960s. By the end of the decade, college students were speaking out not only against segregation and the war, but against narrow curricula and rules in colleges; calling for the creation of programs to study African American and women's history; and for a more active social involvement of colleges and universities in redressing social wrongs.

In these three essays, David Steigerwald and Bryn Upton take differing views on the effectiveness of the political movements that originated among the students of the 1960s known as the "New Left." Upton sees the 1960s movements as part of a youthful, idealistic culture which achieved worthy ends. His essay is a concise narrative of events and ideas, putting the 1960s into historical context. David Steigerwald gives two analytical critiques of the movements. Steigerwald's first essay takes a longer view of the 1960s, and looks more at the tactics fo the New Left than at the agenda. Steigerwald sees that even the New Left's staunchest opponents learned something from the movement's strategy, and conservatives have used New Left tactics to energize their own counter-revolution. In his last essay, Steigerwald shows how a scholar looking at the same material can come to a completely different conclusion. The New Left, he argues, was a sham. Rather than seeking the equality of all and the creation of a new world, the New Left really sought more privileges for an already spoiled generation, which had grown up in prosperous times never knowing the hardships of the Great Depression or the mass sacrifices required during World War II.

Which is the correct interpretation? All three essays contain part of the truth. All three have definite points of view. It is essential to remember that all history contains the historian's own perspective, even if it claims objectivity.

Read the three essays critically and try to understand how scholars looking at the same set of facts can interpret them in such different ways.

Viewpoint: The youthful idealism of the 1960s sparked the mass movements against racial injustice and the Vietnam War.

The promise of the New Left was that of youthful idealism. It was a movement based on the truly American ideas of liberty, self-determination, and rule of the people. Yet, the lofty goals of participatory democracy did not take hold in the American political scene, and at the end of the 1960s the New Left, and most of the counterculture revolution, had dissolved. The decade that produced the most significant civil-rights legislation in U.S. history also buried its most visible and powerful supporters. The generation that saw the collapse of legalized segregation also supported the presidential candidacy of a confirmed segregationist. The near decade-long cry for new politics ended in the nominations of two former vice presidents. In the end, the New Left helped initiate changes that stood the test of time, but the movement also failed to achieve many goals.

The 1950s was a time of change. After years of economic depression and wartime rationing, the United States experienced a time of unprecedented growth and consumer spending. A population explosion was another postwar phenomenon. These children, especially those of the middle class, grew up in a new world. They were free from many of the difficulties and responsibilities their parents had known, free from the effects of the Great Depression, and free from World War II. At the same time, they grew up in a world that seemed to have two clear sides, democracy and communism, locked in ideological combat.

The new generation was in many ways more privileged than previous ones. Their parents and grandparents had fought in wars on foreign lands, were convinced of the rightness of democracy and the American way, and had sacrificed during the 1930s and 1940s. Middle-class youths in the 1950s came of age in suburban developments with new schools, in families with enough food for all, and surrounded by material abundance. Cars, televisions, refrigerators, and dishwashers became normal possessions.

Members of the New Left tended to come from middle-class families, with educated, liberal parents. These young activists frequently attended top-tier universities such as Berkeley, Michigan, Wisconsin, Harvard, and Columbia. Ideologically, the New Left was influenced by the writings of Allen Ginsberg, Jack Kerouac, C. Wright Mills, and Herbert Marcuse.

The New Left emerged from this climate, free from want, at the end of the 1950s and the beginning of the turbulent 1960s. There were leftist organizations in the early 1950s, and indeed throughout American history, but leftist student groups of the early 1950s were constrained by the fervor of McCarthyism. One example was the Student League for Industrial Democracy (SLID), which had to define its position within the emerging ideological dichotomy. In 1951 SLID released a statement drawing a clear line between their brand of liberalism and socialism and that practiced in the Soviet Union, which they branded as imperialistic. However, a series of events awakened middle-class America to the realities of life outside their experience. This awakening had more to do with creating the New Left than with organizations such as SLID.

In 1959 the revolution in Cuba, led by intellectual radicals Ernesto "Che" Guevara and Fidel Castro, awakened in the American intellectual community a greater sense of the excesses of capitalism. C. Wright Mills praised Castro's revolution in *Listen, Yankee: The Revolution in Cuba* (1960). This work brought into view, for the first time for most Americans, the harsher side of the capitalist system. Exploitation abroad was only the first part of the awakening.

Growing tensions over the struggle for equal rights for blacks in the South started to gain national attention. In 1960 groups of black students began sit-ins at lunch counters throughout the South. These protesters were in many ways similar to the white middle-class students of the New Left who were frustrated by the slow pace of change. The young activists not only generated sympathy for their cause, but also energized the New Left.

At the end of 1960 a ray of hope emerged for the New Left. The election of John Fitzgerald Kennedy to the presidency in November gave hope to many black, as well as New Left, activists. Kennedy was the first president born in the twentieth century; he was young and vibrant, spoke of the future, and represented hope. As 1961 began, the revolution in Cuba, the sit-ins in the South, and the election of Kennedy were much in the minds of a group of students at the University of Michigan. There they had founded the Students for a Democratic Society (SDS) in 1960. The organization called for new politics and participatory democracy (eventually they

THE MAY 2nd MOVEMENT

On 2 May 1964 the first major student demonstrations against the war in Vietnam occurred in the United States. Students marched and held rallies in Boston, New York City, San Francisco, Seattle, and other cities. The May 2nd Movement denounced the war as a product of an imperialistic system.

We, as students in the richest but most brutally confused country in the world, cannot understand that world and our part in it with the ahistorical education we receive in our universities. In order to make ourselves into effective social beings and in order to discover, sharpen, and use the power of our knowledge, we should organize ourselves in the broadest possible way to combat that lack of education. For it is a lack, a vacuum, that leads to political degeneration and default. The May 2nd Movement was formed to fight against a politics of default, specifically by organizing student protest and revolt against our government's savage war on the people of Vietnam. . . .

The university offers no explanation of what's wrong, of what's happening in a world principally marked by revolution. Instead, it grooms us for places as technicians, managers and clerks within the giant corporations, or to be professional apologists for the status quo within the giant multiversities, or to fit some other cog-space that needs the special "sensitivity" that only the polish of factory education can bring. . . . The university is doing its job, supplying the system with loyal, well-trained, intelligent servants—who are moral, cultural and social morons. Lest this job prove too much of a burden for overstrained college administrators, it is shared with other institutions, from the moves to the Peace Corps. . . .

When the student protest movement refers to "the establishment," we are not kidding. That which we are out to change—be it a university or a government—is built on a tremendously powerful structure of material and organization. The money and resources available to it are immense. We will change nothing unless we organize ourselves, forge ourselves into a united and disciplined force and match the strength of the establishment in confrontations. We can do so because our strength is based on people, not cash. May 2nd Movement is building an organization of students that recognizes, and works to satisfy, our needs as students and as men and women. These needs are inseparable from the worldwide struggle for liberation. One can choose to oppose this struggle, or to join it. To oppose it is to be a murderer. To join together and fight to change this murderous society is the only way for any of us to live with decency and dignity. We will succeed when large numbers of students have the insight, the dedication and the will to organize themselves, to join the struggle with their sections of the popluation, and to see it through.

Source: *"What is the May 2nd Movement?," in* The Sixties Project *(University of Virginia: Institute of Advanced Technology in the Humanities, 1993), internet web page.*

would also become the voice of the antiwar movement). At the same time James Lawson and a group of students in the Nashville area (including Diane Nash, Marion Barry, and John Lewis) formed the Student Nonviolent Coordinating Committee (SNCC). SDS formalized the ideology of the New Left, while SNCC advocated many of the same ideas in a more direct format. Many groups formed over the next several years with similar goals, but not always the same means.

Throughout the early 1960s SDS worked alongside groups like SNCC and the Congress of Racial Equality (CORE) in efforts at voter registration throughout the South. SNCC and CORE organized the Freedom Rides of 1961, in which some white students, who were proponents of the New Left ideology, took part. During Freedom Summer (1964) white students from the North and West traveled to Mississippi to teach at Freedom Schools and to learn firsthand the ways of nonviolent struggle in the South. At the same time a smaller project was undertaken by SDS in Northern urban ghettoes. These years were the apex of cooperation between different groups on the Left, as well as the peak period of success for the New Left. The goals of participatory democracy were taking hold as evidenced by the Mississippi Freedom Democratic Party and their protest at the 1964 Democratic National Convention. The voice of the people was being heard by President Lyndon

B. Johnson. Civil-rights and voting-rights legislation were passed in 1964 and 1965.

With these successes and spirit of cooperation new groups began to pop up in attempts to add more voices to the movement. The hippies, yippies, and counterculture seekers of the mid-to-late 1960s had many of the same beliefs and desires, yet they did not always see eye-to-eye. New Left organizers did not like the hippies, who were more interested in sex and drugs than in community organization and participatory democracy. The yippies, brainchild of Abbie Hoffman and Jerry Rubin, were formed specifically to shock the world, and in order to do that they concentrated on creating media-ready events. Yippie activities were staged and drew press attention away from serious issues addressed by the New Left.

In 1968, at the Democratic National Convention in Chicago, the New Left and counterculture came head-to-head with the Democratic Party power structure and Mayor Richard Daly. The year had begun with the Tet Offensive, and for the first time it seemed that the general public was turning away from supporting the war in Vietnam and beginning to side with the New Left in its opposition to the conflict. When Johnson announced, on 31 March, that he would not run for reelection, the New Left had, perhaps, its greatest victory. Johnson had become the symbol of the war and the old politics, and now he was gone. Just four days later, however, Martin Luther King Jr. was shot and killed in Memphis. King's assassination was a serious blow to the black community, the Civil Rights movement, and the New Left. Hope faded but it did not disappear. Robert Kennedy entered the race for the presidency and in his candidacy the New Left saw much of the promise they had seen in John F. Kennedy just a few years earlier. Blacks and Hispanics saw a compassionate friend; peace activists saw a man who wanted to end the war; and blue-collar workers believed the young senator heard their voices. The flames of hope were extinguished in June when, after winning the California primary, Robert Kennedy was killed.

At the convention in Chicago there was violence in the streets between protesters and police. There, the yippies nominated a pig for president, SDS members denounced the war, and the police tried to keep protesters from the convention. The resulting violence was broadcast around the nation during the nightly television coverage of the convention. Hubert H. Humphrey was nominated by the Democrats in Chicago. Meanwhile, Richard M. Nixon secured the Republican nomination amid racial violence in Miami. A third candidate, former governor George C. Wallace from Alabama, emerged to make it a three-way race. All these developments represented serious blows to the New Left.

Many things that the New Left had been fighting for were in jeopardy. The idea of new politics was gone; the candidates consisted of two former vice presidents and an avowed segregationist. The antiwar movement seemed to be in trouble as well, and with Kennedy assassinated and peace candidate Eugene McCarthy out of the race, no candidate took a firm stance on ending the war. Participatory democracy suffered hits as many voters stayed home.

Although both Nixon and Humphrey had tried to identify themselves with the new politics, their nominations, and the election of the former, showed the tenacity of old politics. A study of the voting behavior of 1968 showed that the people most likely not to vote were young, poor, and black. Those most likely to vote were wholly unsympathetic to youthful radicalism and tended to identify the New Left and counterculture with ingratitude. By the end of the year the New Left and counterculture were beaten. They had failed.

The war in Vietnam would last for seven more years; student protests became more violent and were more often met with violence by police or troops. Nixon was reelected in 1972 with the lowest percentage of voter participation since 1948. The social policies of Johnson's Great Society were gutted. The hippies and yippies faded away. Black Power replaced the direct nonviolent protests of the early 1960s. While the age of protest was not over, 1968 represented a change in radicalism and in the response to radicalism in the United States. The New Left hung on, but was never the same. New movements emerged, most notably the Women's movement, but there was never the kind of cooperative effort that had existed between organizations just a few years earlier.

The New Left did have a lasting impact on the political and social fabric of America, but in the final analysis it failed in what it was trying to do in the 1960s.

—BRYN UPTON, BRANDEIS UNIVERSITY

Viewpoint: The tactics of the New Left inspired a vigorous debate and energized communities across the nation to seek social improvement.

The progressive movements of the 1960s changed America forever. By empowering several groups who had been previously oppressed or unrepresented, and destroying many of the stifling moral demands that were holdovers from the nineteenth century, they made America a much better society. Their main themes of group empowerment and personal liberation have become the fundamental propositions of American life.

The movements transformed American political institutions. The African American freedom struggle altered national politics more profoundly than any other force. Taking it upon themselves to throw off the shackles of racism, which were locked in place by widespread disenfranchisement of African Americans in the South, the Civil Rights movement permanently destroyed Jim Crow segregation, not through court decisions so much as through gaining access to the ballot. Through grassroots voter-registration drives, movement activists not only forced the Johnson Administration to pass the Voting Rights Act of 1965 but taught powerless people how to take power for themselves. After the Voting Rights Act was passed, African American voting in the South dramatically increased, which led in turn to the election of African American representatives on the local, state, and national level.

The incorporation of African Americans into the national political system served as an impetus for other previously marginalized groups to demand representation. Hispanics and Native Americans pressed for inclusion; feminists and gay-rights activists took their place in the system. The scope of change can be easily measured by looking at the dramatic transformation of the Democrats. At the 1964 national convention, the party refused to seat a delegation of Mississippians composed of African Americans as an alternative to the white-dominated state party; by 1972, racial and ethnic minorities, feminists, and gay-rights activists not only had infiltrated the convention delegations, but they were virtually writing the rules of representation.

Political parties and government at every level have never been the same. Both parties eagerly court activist groups, and neither can afford to snub the concerns of the newly empowered. Republicans might shun what they see as "extremists" among feminists and gays, but they try to promote conservative representatives of these groups while having "extremists" among their own activists. It is testimony to how successful the progressive movements of the 1960s were that the concerns of groups that were so recently oppressed or ignored have become mainstream, which the whole system is geared to addressing. As Terry H. Anderson has written in *The Movement and the 1960s* (1996), "the long era of white men exclusively controlling the body politic was over."

More widely, the progressive movements forced the nation to give up the Cold War politics of fear and conformity and to accept dissent as the healthy, indeed, vital, circulation of ideas. Whereas the Cold War made even the most critical citizens circumspect and cautious, a refreshing expectation of vigorous self-assertion into political practice emerged in the 1960s. The practice of vigorous dissent crossed party and ideological lines. Even conservatives began to see it as their duty to organize and express their interests zealously. There is no better example of this than Phyllis Schlafly's Eagle Forum, which was organized to counter the movement toward passage of the Equal Rights Amendment, the main cause of liberal feminism in the late 1960s and early 1970s.

Along with the demand for group empowerment and the assumption that vigorous dissent is a necessary part of a healthy society, progressive politics of the 1960s changed the basic disposition of Americans toward government in the abstract. Whereas the World War II and Cold War generations had been raised on the obligations of citizens to accept governmental control because of national emergency, the 1960s generation recognized that what should be temporary obligations had calcified into blind obedience and acceptance of the status quo for its own sake. Activists insisted that government should be responsive to the immediate needs of people, whether in the form of economic assistance or improving the quality of life through such measures as environmental regulations. Part of this new disposition toward government bred an intense desire for decentralized, community control of resources, and face-to-face discussion and debate. James J. Farrell, in *The Spirit of the 1960s: Making Postwar Radicalism* (1971), described this sensibility as "personalism," the expectation that people can govern themselves. As with the drive toward activism, this sensibility informed conservatism as much as it did liberalism. One can argue, in fact, that the anti-Washington impetus that appeared in the conservative Ronald Reagan years and the liberal William J. Clinton years was a direct result of the 1960s.

The new disposition was not just directed at national politics or government. It was an essential part of the spirit of the day and informed how progressive-minded people addressed all the institutions in their lives. It was a constant theme of student activists, for example, that institutions should be run by the people for whom they were built–in the case of the university, that meant students. It is too easily forgotten just how deadening and unresponsive American institutions had become. Almost all universities exercised the duties of in loco parentis and dictated the personal habits of students. Dormitories were segregated by gender (not by race because so few minorities attended colleges); male visits to women's rooms were strictly regulated; and women often had curfews. Customary dress had men in coats and ties and women in knee-length dresses. Professors lectured; students dutifully wrote notes; and the two rarely interacted otherwise—a discussion group was a rare thing. The uprising of the 1960s blew the old educational system apart.

What can be said about the universities holds true, to some extent, for most other institutions, including one important example, the Catholic Church. Roughly one-quarter of all Americans identified themselves as Catholic in the 1960s. At the beginning of the decade, the Church exercised censorship power over the movie industry through the Legion of Decency; its lobbying was powerful enough to prevent distribution of birth-control information between doctors and their patients in some states; and the liturgy was still said in Latin, with the priest's back to the congregation throughout the mass. Responding to the winds of change, the Second Vatican Council unleashed an institutional revolution in 1963 that transformed the role and inner workings of the Catholic Church.

More than any other institution, the family was dramatically altered. Restrictive divorce laws were replaced, making it possible for women, who saw their economic prospects expanding, to escape abusive or unhappy marriages. The myth of the happy, patriarchal suburban family of the 1950s gave way to an image of shared burdens and roles (even if the reality was that women bore more of the household burdens). Alternative living arrangements, including heterosexual cohabitation and homosexual unions, became more common.

As important as their political legacy was, the progressive movements of the 1960s had an important effect on private life, forcing change in several areas—moral, familial, and sexual—where change is difficult and most directly felt on an individual level. Obviously this personal revolution expressed itself in the dramatic alterations in sexual attitudes. In fact, there were two sexual revolutions during the decade, which overlapped but were at odds in some ways. The first, the Playboy revolution (the name is derived from the adult magazine *Playboy*), aimed mostly at loosening heterosexual conduct, especially for men, by equating high living with beautiful women. The second, more democratic and important, rejected the dominance of heterosexual standards and called for the liberation of all sexual impulses. It was this revolution, of course, from which the gay-rights movement emerged, especially when relaxed taboos combined with political activism.

Nonetheless, the revolution in personal life was perhaps most important for women. "The personal is the political" was the feminist battle cry, and women worked from that slogan to publicize all restrictions and forms of discrimination against them. The 1964 Civil Rights Act prohibited discrimination based on gender, along with race, but its inclusion was something of a legislative mistake. Women, however, made the most of the opportunity to call attention to the great discrepancies in pay. Before its passage, women were rarely hired as university professors, business executives, or for other prestigious occupations; in some professions they were not permitted to join male colleagues in essential meetings. Women struggled to break down these barriers and also endeavored to assert their private concerns with domestic abuse, child support, women's health issues, and other long-ignored issues.

When people criticize the 1960s as an age of extremism, they forget just how stifling American society was at the time. None but the most conservative Americans would ever want to return. All Americans, whether they admit it or not, are better off because of the energy and commitment of 1960s progressives, who by no means won all their battles or were flawless. However, they expanded the definition of what it means to be an American and broadened the chances for gaining the American dream in the bargain.

—DAVID STEIGERWALD,
OHIO STATE UNIVERSITY

Viewpoint:
The progressive movements of the 1960s liberated only those who had no need of it—the well educated, elite, and politically powerful—while it created a new culture that disparaged the values of hard work.

The progressive movements of the 1960s—the New Left, radical feminism, gay and lesbian rights, and ethnic and racial advocacy—

often are credited with forcing America to broaden its idea of citizenship in important ways, especially in the case of women and African Americans. Yet, any accurate historical assessment of the women's and African-American movements reveals that the 1960s cannot genuinely claim either movement. The women's movement reached back to the pre–Civil War era, and the renewal of female activism was only one of the several waves that rose and fell in the larger history of the United States. The Civil Rights movement, meanwhile, contained many parts, but its most dynamic aspect, that which groups in the 1960s claimed as their own, was actually part of the grassroots movement of working people who began protesting against racial oppression in the mid 1950s. That grassroots movement, made up as it was of mostly poor and working-class Southern blacks, was far removed from the high-blown media acts that made up much of the radical politics of the 1960s. These other movements merely tried to appropriate the moral authority that the Civil Rights movement rightly accumulated by imitating its strategies of protest and by claiming to work in its image.

When the young activists actually got hold of the women's and Civil Rights movements, they did considerable damage to both. Indeed, the Civil Rights movement ended, for all intents and purposes, in 1965, when the Voting Rights Act was passed. In the shadow of that great victory, the movement fell apart. The main student wing expelled white members that year, Stokely Carmichael introduced the Black Panthers to the movement while disavowing the long commitment to nonviolence, and Martin Luther King Jr. was forced to adjust to the radicalization of the movement by moving his operations from Atlanta to Chicago, where he met nothing but frustrating failures. As the movement squandered its moral authority, radical black nationalists emerged who could deliver little by way of tangible improvements to African Americans, but they cleverly manipulated guilt-ridden whites and convinced fellow blacks that they were victims who deserved government programs and protection.

The real political legacy of the progressive movements of the 1960s was not the liberation of once-marginalized people but rather the refinement of the politics of splinter groups. Self-proclaimed representatives of allegedly victimized groups stepped forward to demand recognition and some form of compensation, while at the same time declaring America a morally bankrupt and hopelessly bigoted society.

Police and antiwar protestors clash outside the 1968 Democratic National Convention in Chicago

(Jerry Lieberman)

The eruption of narrow-minded, interest-group politics can hardly be called a success. Practitioners of the so-called New Politics took over the Democratic Party but only succeeded in destroying it as the majority coalition. Since President Franklin D. Roosevelt, the Democrats had joined ethnic and working-class Americans to liberal intellectuals and Southern conservatives, and in this form the party dominated mid-century political life. But once New Politics activists got hold of the party, the majority status was quickly destroyed. Contemptuous of working people in general, the New Politics treated union leaders with particular scorn. By 1972, the year Republican Richard M. Nixon trounced the Democratic candidate, George S. McGovern, the activists had seized control of the party, driving out not only union leaders but the bulk of working-class, ethnic voters as well. Although they considered this a success, they failed to realize that now they only represented splinter groups that could never be formed into any meaningful coalition. Most Americans, one wag pointed out, were "unpoor, unblack, and unyoung," a truth admirers of 1960s politics never understood.

Once in position to influence government policy, progressives constructed a web of bureaucratic programs that greatly increased the scope of federal power and hamstrung economic growth. Most of the bureaucracy emerged out of the War on Poverty, which was designed to uplift the poor, especially urban blacks. In spite of their self-righteous talk of "participatory democracy" and "community control," in the 1960s progressives were quick to rely on government bureaucracy to achieve their ends. Far from empowering America's poor, the War on Poverty really benefitted local activists and unelected federal officials, leaving the poor more dependent than ever.

Just as the supposed antibureaucrats took control of the most powerful bureaucracy, so too did those who derided many of the nation's institutions gain control of some of the most important ones. Progressives assumed control of public schools, as universities churned out professional pedagogues schooled less in particular subjects than in popular teaching methods. They emphasized self-esteem enhancement at the expense of educational basics and the result has been a steady decline in academic performance, easily quantified in any transnational assessment of student achievement. Meanwhile, these progressives also dominated American law. University law schools focused overwhelmingly on two causes: furthering minority rights, including the rights of criminals and the mentally unstable, and the radical application of the First Amendment to include nearly all forms of expression, from pornography to flag burning. Moreover, the radicals who were dedicated to tearing down the universities became esteemed tenured professors who merely reshaped those institutions in their own image, hiding their power behind anti-institutional rhetoric.

What of the claims of liberation made on behalf of the 1960s activists? This liberation was conducted entirely in the cultural sphere. Radicals had ridiculed the nuclear family, commitment to work, the idea of deferring gratification for the sake of long-term goals, patriotism, religious faith, and other bulwarks of traditional American life. They insisted that these beliefs were false, hypocritical values that imposed conformity, stifled creativity, and excused the social domination of white, heterosexual males. They called for individual freedom, claimed the right to "do your own thing," and announced the end of "shame-and-guilt culture."

The counterculture became mainstream, with its core values diffused throughout society. What was supposed to become utopia, however, produced a nightmare. The sexual revolution brought skyrocketing divorce rates and pummeled family structure; mass media was saturated with sexual messages, and the promiscuity it fostered led to two decades of rampant illegitimate births and the explosion of AIDS. The demand for "expanded consciousness" led to a succession of drug epidemics, including the terribly destructive crack cocaine epidemic that scourged American cities in the 1980s and 1990s. The demand for personal freedom, especially when enacted in a political climate geared to advance grievances, destroyed the sense of community obligations and created a society-wide sense of victimization that devalued personal responsibility.

Of all the social destruction wrought by 1960s progressives, its worst consequences were felt by the groups that were supposed to benefit most from emancipation: women and poor minorities. The collapse of family structure, heralded as an historic liberation from the patriarchal male, has thrown more women than ever into poverty. Single-parent families, overwhelmingly female-headed, became increasingly common and financially worse off. In 1990, for example, these households had a median income totaling only 42 percent of that of two-parent families.

In 1965 Daniel Patrick Moynihan raised progressive hackles by releasing a Labor Department report on the black family that deplored the frequency of out-of-wedlock births. Illegitimacy not only fractured the family, Moynihan argued, but also increased child poverty, heightened the chances of children turning to crime, and fostered the "cycle of poverty" where young girls became pregnant though economically and emotionally unfit to raise children. Moynihan was appalled in 1965 that 25 percent of African American children were born out-of-wedlock. By the early 1990s nearly two-thirds of African American children were born to single mothers, and they have experienced all the social repercussions—higher crime rates, lower educational performance, and cyclical poverty.

While many would argue that the rise of female-centered poverty was a function of an unjust economy, this widespread dysfunction is actually a cultural aspect of America. After all, the national economy since the recession of the 1980s generated tens of millions of new jobs. It cannot be said that economic opportunities have been lacking. How otherwise to explain the great waves of immigration during the last two decades?

The values of the counterculture seeped down from progressive elites through Hollywood, television, and pulp magazines and eroded values that are essential for self-help. In a culture that devalued hard work and self-sacrifice, there was no encouragement for those at the bottom to undertake the struggle to raise themselves up. In a culture that ceaselessly claimed that sex without consequences was the key to happiness, there was no reason to expect a young unmarried girl to avoid pregnancy, particularly when her mother did the same thing and the government was willing to pay her for doing so.

Of course, the 1960s progressives, who were mostly social elites to begin with, enjoyed the benefits of the social changes they pushed. Well-to-do women benefited from loosened marital obligation, while poor and working-class women were "liberated" into a world of male irresponsibility and economic hardship. Upper-class minorities benefited from affirmative-action programs, but the programs did little for individuals whose background made them unlikely candidates for admission to Harvard or Yale.

Richard Hofstadter, esteemed Columbia University historian, reputedly called the 1960s "the age of rubbish." The progressive elites pushed their way into power and reshaped America to suit themselves. However, they left the rest of the nation to live, as Hofstadter suggested, in their trash.

–DAVID STEIGERWALD,
OHIO STATE UNIVERSITY

References

Terry H. Anderson, *The Movement and the 1960s* (New York: Oxford University Press, 1996);

Edward J. Bacciocco Jr., *The New Left in America: Reform to Revolution, 1956 to 1970* (Stanford, Cal.: Hoover Institution Press, 1974);

Peter Collier and David Horowitz, *The Destructive Generation: Second Thoughts About the 1960s* (New York: Summit, 1989);

John Patrick Diggins, *The Rise and Fall of the American Left* (New York: Norton, 1992);

David Farber, *Chicago '68* (Chicago: University of Chicago Press, 1988);

James J. Farrell, *The Spirit of the 1960s: Making Postwar Radicalism* (New York: Routledge, 1997);

Todd Gitlin, *The Whole World Is Watching: Mass Media In the Making & Unmaking of the New Left* (Berkeley: University of California Press, 1980);

Myron Magnet, *The Dream and the Nightmare: The 1960s Legacy to the Underclass* (New York: Morrow, 1993);

C. Wright Mills, *Listen, Yankee: The Revolution in Cuba* (New York: Ballantine, 1960);

Norman L. and Emily S. Rosenberg, *In Our Times: America Since World War II* (Engelwood Cliffs, N.J.: Prentice Hall, 1999);

Sohnya Sayres and others, eds., *The 60s Without Apology* (Minneapolis: University of Minnesota Press, 1984);

David Steigerwald, *The 1960s and the End of Modern America* (New York: St. Martins's Press, 1995);

George R. Vickers, *The Formation of the New Left: The Early Years* (Lexington, Mass.: Lexington Books, 1975).

NIXON'S FOREIGN POLICY

Was Richard M. Nixon's foreign policy toward China a success or a failure?

Viewpoint: President Richard M. Nixon's foreign policy was a success, because by opening relations with China, it actually improved U.S. relations with the Soviet Union.

Viewpoint: Nixon's foreign policy was a failure, because it alienated important U.S. allies and failed to implement a lasting period of détente.

It was the most dramatic diplomatic breakthrough of the twentieth century. Richard M. Nixon, who had launched his political career by castigating Harry S Truman's administration for "losing China," allowing the world's most populous nation to become communist, now stepped off a plane in Beijing to shake hands with Chou En-lai, the People's Republic's foreign minister, in 1972. Only eighteen years earlier, in Geneva, American secretary of state John Foster Dulles had refused to shake Chou's hand, and the United States had resolutely refused to acknowledge that the government in Beijing was in fact the legitimate government of China. In one handshake, however, Nixon brought the United States and China back together again. It was so dramatic that American composer John Adams based an opera, "Nixon in China," on the momentous event.

In these two essays, scholars Elizabeth Pugliese and Robert J. Flynn examine the opening with China. Pugliese sees Nixon's trip, and the subsequent reestablishment of relations with China, as a major breakthrough in international diplomacy, which improved the American position in its steady campaign against the Soviet Union. Nixon recognized that the Soviets and the Chinese, though they shared a common Marxist ideology, had many differences, which he adroitly exploited. Nixon justly deserves praise for his imaginative foreign policy.

Flynn, on the other hand, argues that the Chinese opening was important, but not as important as Nixon and Secretary of State Henry Kissinger wanted to make it. It also resulted less from Nixon and Kissinger's brilliant grasp of foreign relations than from necessity within China and the United States to break the twenty-three-year isolation. China had been sending signals to the United States since the late 1960s that its leaders were ready to talk. How much credit should go to individuals—Nixon, Kissinger, or Chou En-Lai? Is history made by individuals, or is it shaped by forces of markets, geopolitics, or iron laws? These two essays point to different ways to interpret this important event.

Viewpoint: President Richard M. Nixon's foreign policy was a success, because by opening relations with China, it actually improved U.S. relations with the Soviet Union.

After the revolution of 1918, the Soviet Union viewed itself as the sole source of communist dogma. In the 1930s and 1940s Joseph Stalin tried to build an international communist monolith directed from Moscow. After 1949, China, a nation too large and populous to treat as a mere satellite, as were the nations of Eastern Europe, eclipsed the Soviet Union as the largest communist nation. Mao Tse-tung of China often clashed with Moscow. Beginning in the 1950s, the Soviets and Chinese constantly confronted each other, often massing troops on their common border. Each country's leader accused the other of excesses and betrayals of communism. An alliance of the United States with one of these countries should, by all conventional views of international politics, have turned the other against the United States. The alliance turned out not to be the case: in the world of realpolitik things are accepted as they are, not as they theoretically should be. Opening relations with China did not harm U.S. relations with the Soviet Union–it improved them.

The antagonism between the Soviet Union and China increased in the 1960s with the two nations fighting several border skirmishes. The worst clash–skirmishes along the Ussuri River–came in March 1969. In the United States, President Richard M. Nixon had been elected and inaugurated. To some of his advisers, it appeared the war might spread and grow into a global war. The Soviets sent diplomatic feelers to the United States to see how it would react if the U.S.S.R. launched an all-out war against China. The Ussuri River War, and subsequent actions taken by Soviet diplomats in the United States, showed Nixon the insecure, hostile attitudes the Chinese and Soviets had toward one another. He recognized the opportunities for the United States in the Sino-Soviet split. The emerging strategic triangle helped ease U.S. relations with the Soviet Union because the Soviets feared a powerful China allying with the United States against them.

The idea of taking advantage of the animosity between the two major communist nations was hardly new. President Charles de Gaulle of France in the early 1960s perceived the advantages of exploiting Soviet fears regarding the Chinese. He believed that problems with the Chinese would guarantee that the Soviets would adopt a more cooperative attitude with the West. The international position of France, however, did not allow de Gaulle to put his belief into action. Nixon, being in a better diplomatic position, also appreciated this analysis of diplomatic relations in a competitive world system. Henry Kissinger, Assistant to the president for National Security Affairs at the time of the opening of relations with China, likened diplomacy to a game of chess. The more options one side has, the fewer the other side will have and the more careful one must be in pursuing its objectives. Kissinger persuaded Nixon that increasing America's foreign-policy options through opening relations with China would soften rigid Soviet positions at the bargaining table.

In order to discover what these expanded options might be, Kissinger ordered a special National Security Council study on Sino-Soviet relations. Incorporating this study into his first foreign-policy report, completed in February 1970, Nixon made clear that his overall foreign-policy objective was pursuing closer relations with both major communist nations. The United States would conduct practical negotiations with China and would not collude with the Soviet Union against China. Later foreign-policy reports stressed that Washington would not conspire with either country to the detriment of the third. His foreign-policy team advised that the state of relations between the U.S.S.R. and China would have a direct bearing on each nation's relations with the United States. Nixon acknowledged the rivalry between the two communist nations as a factor that would force each to improve its relations with the United States. Therefore, improved Sino-American relations became key to the Nixon administration's Soviet strategy.

Not everyone supported this strategy. Leading Soviet scholars in the United States, following the accepted theory of the day that friendship with either the U.S.S.R. or China meant making an enemy of the other nation, feared that opening relations with China would exacerbate tensions between the Americans and Soviets. Therefore, they argued any exploitation of the wedge between China and the Soviet Union was an unacceptable risk that could lead to war. Relations with the Soviet Union were especially tense at this time. For months General Secretary Leonid Brezhnev had been stalling on a summit meeting with Nixon. Arms-control negotiations were at a standstill because of intransigent demands for

NIXON ON CHINA, 15 JULY 1971

. . . As I have pointed out on a number of occasions over the past three years, there can be no stable and enduring peace without the participation of the People's Republic of China and its 750 million people. That is why I have undertaken initiatives in several areas to open the door for more normal relations between our two countries.

In pursuance of that goal, I sent Dr. Kissinger, my Assistant for National Security Affairs, to Peking during his recent world tour for the purpose of having talks with Premier Chou En-lai.

The announcement I shall now read is being issued simultaneously in Peking and in the United States:

"Premier Chou En-lai and Dr. Henry Kissinger, President Nixon's Assistant for National Security Affairs, held talks in Peking from July 9 to 11, 1971. Knowing of President Nixon's expressed desire to visit the People's Republic of China, Premier Chou En-lai on behalf of the Government of the People's Republic of China has extended an invitation to President Nixon to visit China at an appropriate date before May, 1972.

"President Nixon has accepted the invitation with pleasure.

"The meeting between the leaders of China and the United States is to seek the normalization of relations between the two countries and also to exchange views on questions of concern to the two sides."

Source: Documents of American History, *2 volumes, edited by Henry Steele Commager (New York: Appleton-Century-Crofts, 1973), II: 752–753.*

unilateral U.S. concessions made by the Soviet team. These scholars argued this was not the time to introduce any uncertainty into the already fragile balance between the two superpowers by changing the American relationship with China.

Nixon paid no heed to these negative assessments. He went ahead with his own version of détente, which consisted of an overall plan of easing strained relations. He meant to improve relations with all communist nations, not just the Soviet Union. His main goal was winding down American foreign commitments. Improved relations with communist countries would best achieve this goal. Nixon aimed for a balance of power in the international system that would contain both China and the Soviet Union, thereby making the system as a whole more stable. Opening relations with China was, therefore, carefully calculated to balance or play off the Chinese against the Soviets.

The president's plan succeeded mainly because of Soviet insecurities and fears. Massing of Chinese troops on their border had already made the Soviets nervous. The prospect of enemies on both their eastern and western flanks made the Soviet government even more uneasy. The Soviet Union faced the possibility of a two-front conflict if the United States should ally with China. Normalization of relations between China and the United States would keep Moscow worried about Washington's intentions. By taking advantage of this worry, the United States could pit the two communist antagonists against each other. Nixon gambled that the Soviets would eagerly oblige the United States and attempt to edge out China as America's best communist friend.

No longer able to count on Sino-U.S. antagonism, a situation that had prevailed since 1949, Soviet options narrowed. This situation forced a more conciliatory attitude on the part of the Soviets, because anything less might lead to greater Chinese-American cooperation—up to the frightening possibility of the two militarily strong nations uniting against the Soviet Union in a war. One of the outcomes of Kissinger's secret mission to China in July 1971 was the Chinese government inviting Nixon to visit Beijing. The president's trip to China was announced on 15 July and caught the Soviets by surprise. The results of this announcement were instantaneous. The Soviets immediately moved forward with arms negotiations. Opposition to a summit between Nixon and Brezhnev ended, on 10 August 1971, less than one month after the announcement of the China trip, and the Soviets invited Nixon to visit the Soviet Union. The United States and U.S.S.R. signed agreements that reduced the risk of the outbreak of nuclear war on 30 September 1971.

Nixon's visit to Beijing in February 1972 added to Soviet concerns and increased American diplomatic leverage with them. Apparently, rather than harming détente, opening relations with China helped U.S. relations with the Soviet Union. The Soviets seemed willing to accommodate the United States on almost anything. The Brezhnev-Nixon summit was set for 22–30 May 1972. Less than two weeks before the summit, on 8 May 1972, Nixon announced the mining of North Vietnamese ports. Some in the United States expected this move to scuttle the summit. When relations between two superpowers were delicate, summits were routinely canceled over such incidents, or even lesser ones. However,

Moscow surprised Washington by allowing the summit to go forward as scheduled. The products of the summit were amazing. Brezhnev and Nixon signed both the American-Soviet Treaty on the Limitation of Anti-Ballistic Missile Systems (ABM) and the first Strategic Arms Limitation Treaty (SALT I), as well as the Soviet-American Agreement on cooperation in space. Diplomatic negotiations move notoriously slow, yet, less than one year after negotiations seemed hopelessly stalled over impossible demands, the signing of the final treaties took place. This speedy resolution was almost unheard-of. The opening of relations with China marked an improvement of Soviet-American relations. By understanding, and being willing to exploit, the Sino-Soviet split, Nixon was able to maintain détente and to prevent the Cold War from heating up.

–ELIZABETH PUGLIESE, AUSTIN, TEXAS

Viewpoint: Nixon's foreign policy was a failure, because it alienated important U.S. allies and failed to implement a lasting period of détente.

"In one giant step," former Secretary of State and National Security Advisor Henry Kissinger wrote in his memoirs, the opening he and President Richard M. Nixon engineered to the People's Republic of China (PRC) in 1972 "had transformed our diplomacy. We had brought flexibility to our foreign policy. We had captured the initiative and also the imagination of our own people. We had much farther to go, of course. But we had made a new departure and traveled some distance down the road."

The opening to China had indeed fundamentally altered the geostrategic balance. By ending America's twenty-year-old, Cold War-inspired refusal to deal directly with the world's most populous state, Nixon and Kissinger transformed the prevailing bipolar diplomatic order into a triangular one between the United States, the Soviet Union, and China. That system appeared to make a more stable world possible and to enhance American security by making the U.S.S.R.–then mired in an ideological, diplomatic, and occasional military conflict with China–more willing to negotiate meaningful strategic arms control agreements with the United States, more inclined to work to resolve outstanding issues such as the status of Berlin, and, in general, more disposed to shift its relationship with America from one rooted in confrontation to one based upon limited cooperation. The opening to China also promised to yield a face-saving solution to America's decade-old embroilment in Vietnam and, by easing tensions in the Western Pacific, allowed the relatively weakened United States to reduce its global commitments to a level consistent with its diminished capabilities. It permitted the United States, in short, to uphold effectively its global interests during a period of relative decline.

Rapprochement with China was, however, neither the unqualified success nor the example of heroic risk taking that Kissinger and Nixon have described in their memoirs. Determined to conduct negotiations in secret and to exploit the opening for maximum political gain, the president and his national security adviser alienated the foreign-policy bureaucracy, upset relations with important non-aligned states and critical allies, and put key government agencies at odds with one another. The opening to Beijing, moreover, could not attain the lofty results that the president's inflated rhetoric suggested: it failed to yield a breakthrough in America's drawn-out negotiations with North Vietnam and proved unable to prevent the collapse of détente between the United States and the U.S.S.R. at the end of the 1970s. Rapprochement with China, finally, was the product less of political bravery and farsightedness than of changing geostrategic considerations.

By the late 1960s, both the United States and the People's Republic of China confronted mounting strategic difficulties that made possible their dramatic reconciliation. Long at odds with the U.S.S.R., China found itself engaged in border skirmishes in 1969 with superior Soviet forces along their shared, four-thousand-mile frontier. Already in relative decline, meanwhile, the United States faced growing economic, political, and diplomatic problems as a result of its continuing involvement in the Vietnam War. Believing that China had the power to help the United States find a face-saving way out of Indochina and sensing correctly that tensions with Moscow would leave Beijing receptive to American overtures, Nixon and Kissinger worked to arrange high-level contacts with the Chinese government during the summer of 1969.

Initially, the two governments continued the decade-old practice of conducting these talks between their respective embassies in Poland. Fearing opposition on the part of the State Department bureaucracy and desiring to keep the secretary of state from sharing the credit for any

Richard M. Nixon, his wife, Pat, and Chinese delegates at the Great Wall of China during the president's historic 1972 visit to China

(R. David King Collection)

breakthrough, however, Nixon and Kissinger moved to create several back channels–secret links to Beijing that excluded the State Department–through intermediary governments such as Norway, Romania, and, most importantly, Pakistan. After the administration signaled its flexibility regarding the contentious issue of Taiwan by conveying its intention to reduce American forces stationed on the island, the two nations made rapid progress towards high-level contacts. Using Pakistani President Yahya Khan as an intermediary, the Chinese government invited Kissinger to visit China secretly so as to arrange for a later presidential trip. Traveling to Thailand, India, and Pakistan as cover, the national security adviser secretly flew from Islamabad to Beijing for several days of meetings with Chinese Premier Chou En-lai in early July 1971. Kissinger and Chou quickly reached an agreement for a presidential visit. A few days later on 15 July 1971 Nixon shocked and electrified the country by announcing on national television that Kissinger had visited China in preparation for a presidential trip to Beijing in the spring of 1972.

The pace quickened after Nixon's announcement. Coincidental with the State Department's failed effort to retain Taiwan's seat in the United Nations, Kissinger returned to Beijing in October 1971 to complete the broad, preliminary negotiations necessary to insure a successful presidential visit. Enjoying near-continuous television coverage carefully orchestrated to improve his standing in the upcoming presidential election, Nixon spent a triumphal week in Beijing in February 1972 that included a dramatic tour of the Great Wall and an historic meeting with Chinese leader Mao Tse-tung (from which Secretary of State William Rogers was excluded). At the conclusion of his visit the two states issued the Shanghai Communiqué, which affirmed their opposition to Soviet "hegemony" and which smoothed over their differences regarding Taiwan. After three years, Nixon and Kissinger had achieved the diplomatic breakthrough they had most sought: they could now count on China to help balance and contain the U.S.S.R., to aid America indirectly in extricating itself from Vietnam, and to permit the United States to reduce its commitments in the Western Pacific to a level consistent with its capabilities. By pursuing the China opening in secret and by exploiting it for domestic-political advantage, moreover, they had pulled off a major political coup during an election year.

The resort to secrecy, however, and the relentless, scripted televised coverage of Nixon's visit created almost as many problems as the opening to China solved. The dramatic nature of Nixon's trip to Beijing and the administration's assertions that triangular diplomacy would make possible breakthroughs in relations with the U.S.S.R., for example, heightened expectations among the American public that the superpowers were entering a period of meaningful and lasting détente. The predictable failure of Washington and Moscow to live up to such unrealistic expectations, in turn, contributed to the intensification of the Cold War in the late 1970s. Nixon and Kissinger's end run around the diplomatic bureaucracy also created problems for the administration. In the long run, their exclusion of foreign-policy experts from the decision-making process undermined support for the president's initiatives in the executive branch, contributed to serious morale problems, and helped further a backlash against Nixon's policies among the professional diplomats. In the short run, the refusal to bring the bureaucracy on board adversely affected the negotiations with Beijing and created damaging internal conflicts within the executive branch. Kissinger's second trip to Beijing in October 1971, for instance, coincided with and sabotaged the State Department's effort to prevent Taiwan's expulsion from the United Nations. Unwilling to consult with the State Department's foreign-policy experts during the negotiation of the Shanghai Communiqué, meanwhile, Kissinger failed to make certain that the document contained language noting the United States' treaty obligation to defend Taiwan. The communiqué thus called into question not only America's assurances to Taipei but its commitment to defend its many other treaty partners.

The administration's resort to secrecy and efforts to make the most political benefit out of the China opening also strained America's relations with several important allies and key non-aligned states. This tension was most evident regarding Japan, the United States' second-most-important ally. Lacking input from State Department experts and keen to maximize the potential domestic political benefit of the rapprochement with China, Nixon failed to inform Tokyo of the American initiative to Beijing prior to his 15 July 1971 televised announcement to the nation. Referred to by the Japanese as the first "Nixon Shock," the president's sudden announcement and refusal to offer prior consultation stunned the Japanese government and undermined its confidence in Washington. As the journalist Walter Isaacson later wrote, "there were certainly less shabby ways to treat such an important ally."

The administration's secret approach to China also led it to pursue regional policies that greatly destabilized the Indian subcontinent and that further alienated New Delhi. Seeking to demonstrate to Beijing that the United States was a reliable and credible partner, Nixon and Kissinger opted to support the Pakistani president Khan—a longtime ally of the United States—when he brutally cracked down on secessionist-minded East Pakistan in 1971. After Khan sought to resolve the crisis through a failed invasion of India in December of that year, the administration brazenly signaled American support for Pakistan by ordering the aircraft carrier USS *Enterprise* into the Indian Ocean. Nixon and Kissinger's effort to prove American reliability thus angered the Indian government—which signed a treaty of friendship with the U.S.S.R. during the crisis—left the administration open to charges that it put little stock in human rights, and ultimately proved counterproductive because American support failed to prevent Pakistan from suffering a substantial defeat at the hands of India. The decision to signal American support for Pakistan by sending the nuclear-weapons-equipped *Enterprise* into the region also influenced India to go forward with a nuclear-weapons program. Kissinger and Nixon's desire to impress American credibility upon Beijing—despite China's showing little doubt in Washington's reliability—thus played a part in undermining stability in South Asia, in angering New Delhi, and in adding nuclear weapons to the already intense ethnic conflict between India and Pakistan.

While the opening to China set in motion a series of decisions that would strain ties between India and the United States, it did play an important role in improving American relations with the U.S.S.R. Nixon's 15 July 1971 announcement that he would visit Beijing—and the implications that a rapprochement between China and the United States would have on superpower relations—spurred the Kremlin to agree quickly to a summit meeting in May 1972. In the fall of 1971, meanwhile, the United States and the U.S.S.R. concluded an accord regarding the status of Berlin and signed the Agreement on Measures to Reduce Accidental Outbreak of Nuclear War. At the same time, though, the opening to China and the consequent development of triangular diplomacy failed to produce a lasting détente; by the late 1970s, the superpowers had returned to a confrontational relationship that ended only with the demise of the Soviet Union.

The opening to China produced similarly mixed results regarding America's embroilment in Vietnam. Rapprochement with Beijing doubtless undercut Hanoi's international position and helped the administration finally conclude an agreement that permitted the United States to withdraw from Vietnam without complete loss of face. At the same time, the opening to China left the North Vietnamese less tractable than either Nixon or Kissinger had hoped. For instance, the opening failed to prevent Hanoi from launching a massive offensive into South Vietnam just a month after Nixon's visit. While the agreement with North Vietnam that made possible the American withdrawal likely benefited from China's reduced diplomatic and material support following Nixon's visit, moreover, it ultimately proved little better than the agreement the administration could have secured in 1969.

The opening to China in the early 1970s was thus an important diplomatic event, but one that fell well short of the heightened expectations its dramatic, televised presentation raised. It helped produce a temporary thaw in the Cold War between the United States and the U.S.S.R., permitted the United States to scale back its global commitments, contributed to the American withdrawal from

Vietnam, and ended twenty years of Sino-American hostility. At the same time, it alienated key allies, adversely affected American policy toward South Asia, and proved unable to foster a lasting period of détente. Rapprochement was an important achievement, in short, but one that failed to live up to the billing it received in either Nixon's or Kissinger's memoirs.

–ROBERT J. FLYNN, UNIVERSITY OF KENTUCKY

References

Stephen E. Ambrose, *Nixon: The Triumph of a Politician, 1962–1972* (New York: Simon & Schuster, 1989);

Dan Caldwell, *American-Soviet Relations: From 1947 to the Nixon-Kissinger Grand Design* (Westport, Conn.: Greenwood Press, 1981);

Foster Rhea Dulles, *American Policy Toward Communist China: 1949–1969* (New York: Crowell, 1972);

Raymond L. Garthoff, *Détente and Confrontation: American-Soviet Relations from Nixon to Reagan* (Washington, D.C.: Brookings Institute, 1985);

Seymour M. Hersh, *The Price of Power: Kissinger in the Nixon White House* (New York: Summit Books, 1983);

Walter Isaacson, *Kissinger: A Biography* (New York: Simon & Schuster, 1992);

Henry Kissinger, *Diplomacy* (New York: Simon & Schuster, 1994);

Kissinger, *White House Years* (Boston: Little, Brown, 1979);

Richard M. Nixon, *RN: The Memoirs of Richard Nixon* (New York: Grossett & Dunlap, 1978);

Robert D. Schulzinger, *Henry Kissinger: Doctor of Diplomacy* (New York: Columbia University Press, 1989);

Franz Schurmann, *The Foreign Politics of Richard Nixon: The Grand Design* (Berkeley: Institute of International Studies, University of California, 1987);

Tad Szulc, *The Illusion of Peace: Foreign Policy in the Nixon Years* (New York: Viking, 1978).

NIXON'S REPUTATION

How will Richard M. Nixon's presidency be regarded by history?

Viewpoint: President Richard M. Nixon will be remembered as an unstable personality whose paranoia was the catalyst for Watergate.

Viewpoint: Although Nixon hoped his legacy would be in international affairs, he will be remembered for his notable domestic policies, including food stamps and Head Start.

How will history remember Richard M. Nixon? No president has been more concerned with his place in history. And yet when he left office, his place seemed certain—he was the only president in U.S. history to resign. Facing certain impeachment if he remained, Nixon avoided a trial and possibly prison (the fate of many of his aides) thanks only to his resignation and the merciful pardon granted by his successor, Gerald R. Ford. Nixon seemed doomed to historical disgrace.

How did this happen? Many scholars have sought in his personality clues to the riddle of who Nixon was. His fall coincided with the vogue of psychohistory, using the tools of psychoanalysis to explain the personalities of historical figures. In her essay scholar Elizabeth D. Schafer shows how various historians have analyzed the Watergate affair as part of Nixon's paranoid style and have shown how his entire administration emanated from his character flaws.

Though this form of historical analysis has its merits, it also has limits. How did the American people come to elect such a man? Political historian Judith A. Barrett, who has long experience working in government, takes a different approach. Rather than beginning with his personality, Barrett looks at his accomplishments. Nixon, she finds, accomplished many notable things, and rather than being the power-mad megalomaniac his critics and some historians have described, he used power in imaginative and wise ways. He curbed some of the excesses of Lyndon B. Johnson's Great Society, but maintained, or even improved, other key features—food stamps, Head Start, and affirmative action were all strengthened by Nixon—and in some areas he blazed his own trail. Environmental protection, Native American rights, and a power shift from the federal government to states in handling local problems were all central features of Nixon's domestic agenda.

Where should we look to understand historical figures? At their personalities, or at their public accomplishments? We need to understand both, but also recognize the limitations inherent in either method, to discern the truth.

Viewpoint: President Richard M. Nixon will be remembered as an unstable personality whose paranoia was the catalyst for Watergate.

Scholars have examined Richard M. Nixon's personality development as a child and psychological state while an adult to consider how his psychoses may have contributed to his political decline and the tragedy of Watergate. Historians such as Stanley Kutler, in *Abuse of Power: The New Nixon Tapes* (1997), argue that Nixon's paranoid behavior was the catalyst for Watergate. Journalists Garry Wills, in *Nixon Agonistes: The Crisis of the Self-Made Man* (1970) and Fred Emery, in *Watergate: The Corruption of American Politics and the Fall of Richard Nixon* (1994) dissect Nixon's political career, depicting him as a flawed individual who lacked control of his reactions and fears. Vamik D. Volkan, a psychiatry professor and co-author of *Richard Nixon: A Psychobiography* (1997), and physicians, including Nixon's psychiatrist, examine Nixon's mental condition in psychobiographies that offer clinical explanations for Nixon's personality patterns displayed in office and his personal life. Roger Morris analyzed the first decades of Nixon's life in *Richard Milhous Nixon: The Rise of an American Politician* (1990), commenting on how his family, friends, and acquaintances perceived him. All of these authors depict Nixon as a self-absorbed loner who lacked confidence in himself and distrusted everyone, questioning individuals' motivations and actions toward him. They stress that Nixon's obsession for power, need to control people and situations, paranoid ideas about alleged enemies, refusal to stop self-destructive behavior, and lack of fulfillment despite his successes contributed to the events that caused his political demise as the first U.S. president to resign from office.

Illness permeated Nixon's life from childhood to adulthood and helped establish a mindset of apprehension. He and his four brothers suffered different ailments. Nixon's younger brother, Arthur, suddenly died in 1925, and their mother, Hannah Nixon, née Milhous, recalled how Richard "sat staring into space, silent and dry-eyed in the undemonstrative way in which, because of his choked, deep feeling, he was always to face tragedy." When his brother Harold died from tuberculosis in 1933, Richard fretted that he would also succumb to that disease. Throughout his life, Nixon was sickly and often hospitalized, enduring pneumonia and phlebitis, and he even sought psychosomatic healing techniques from one physician.

Nixon biographers try to understand how his parents influenced his emotional development. Hannah was patient, supportive, and empathetic, while his father, Frank, was temperamental, demeaning, and impulsive. After Arthur's death, Frank became intensely religious and was described as almost fanatical. Frank was Hannah's social inferior, and her family disapproved of their relationship. When they married the unsophisticated Frank controlled Hannah, who tolerated his outbursts and abuse. Although not impoverished, the Nixon family lacked material items that other Quaker families in the area took for granted. Frank expected his wife and sons to work diligently, punishing them when they did not meet his demands. Relatives justified Frank's shouting at Hannah and his sons by explaining that it was his way of demonstrating his affection in a family whose members repressed their emotions. Frank was possessive of his wife and children, allowing them few freedoms. These actions reinforced his son's inferiority complex and affected how he interacted with people.

Scholars also are interested in how non-family members assessed Nixon. His childhood peers summarized his personality as odd and perplexing, and were confused by his contradictory behavior, such as when he sometimes reacted bizarrely to normal situations. Some high-school classmates admired Nixon's academic achievements and leadership, yet commented that he was aloof, cold, and intense. Often preoccupied, Nixon was also known for being volatile, exploding emotionally at perceived slights. His hot temper caused him to be combative. Keenly competitive, Nixon studied industriously but sometimes acted impetuously, to the dismay of others. He disregarded people's feelings: he callously ignored his longtime sweetheart, then became appalled and felt victimized when she started dating someone else.

At Duke University Law School, Nixon's classmates considered him amoral and unethical, saying that he lacked convictions and was only interested in self-advancement. Like his high-school companions, they also recognized two paradoxical sides of his personality: vengeful versus compassionate. Some students remembered acts of kindness Nixon performed, such as carrying a disabled classmate up the law-school steps. Socially inept, Nixon did not encourage friendships and acted hostilely, alienating almost everyone. His classmates labeled him a sullen, paranoid loner. Filled with self-doubt, Nixon resented criticism. He often thought of quitting law school and returning home where he thought he would be appreciated. Through self-analysis, Nixon was somewhat aware of his character deficiencies, calling himself "antisocial" in a letter to Patricia Ryan, his future wife.

His biographers note that Nixon perpetuated his teenage psychological patterns in his political career. He relied on attacking the character of his opponents by depicting them as dangerous and subversive instead of emphasizing his own strengths. He tried to intimidate rivals who threatened his power, and believed he was justified to discredit and accuse them of treason if that assisted his election. In 1946, Nixon won a seat in the U.S. House of Representatives by exaggeratedly casting incumbent Horace Jeremiah "Jerry" Voorhis as being too liberal. This victory enabled Nixon to participate in the Committee on Un-American Activities and the investigation of Alger Hiss as a communist spy, reinforcing Nixon's dependence on smear tactics. During the 1950 U.S. Senate race against Congresswoman Helen Gahagan Douglas, Nixon campaigned that she was a communist sympathizer. Although he won the election, Nixon was criticized for his malicious tactics. After serving two terms as President Dwight D. Eisenhower's vice president, Nixon lost a close presidential election to John F. Kennedy in 1960. This defeat enraged him and incited self-contempt that he directed against future political opponents through vindictive behavior. Two years later he lost in the California gubernatorial contest against Edmund G. "Pat" Brown and reverted to his coping mechanism of quitting. At an emotional press conference, he declared, "You won't have Nixon to kick around anymore." After this, Nixon wrote a book, *Six Crises* (1962), revealing insights about his emotional responses to difficulties.

Dwelling in self-pity, Nixon ignored his self-declared political farewell and remained active in the Republican Party, while developing a New York City law practice. In 1968 he was nominated again to run for president and won, defeating Democrat Hubert H. Humphrey. Selfishly pursuing his interests, Nixon delegated authority to his aides H. R. Haldeman, John D. Ehrlichman, and Charles W. Colson, so he could focus on international politics. Those closest to Nixon were aware of his erratic behavior as his moods shifted quickly from melancholy to elation. Staffers described Nixon's countenance as dark and brooding. He used anger to punish aides by glaring at them. Nixon also acted mute and displayed other unnatural reactions to express his dissatisfaction. One example of Nixon's inconsistency was his visit to the Lincoln Memorial in an effort to convince Vietnam War protesters to embrace his point of view. He was aghast that others did not endorse his opinions, arrogantly thinking that his approach was the best for everyone.

According to his biographers, Nixon became more paranoid as he felt besieged by the antiwar movement. Fearful of losing the Vietnam War, he also worried about not being reelected in 1972. When reports of secret bombing missions in Cambodia were leaked, Nixon implemented what he called "counter-government" measures. He ordered his aides to tap phones and compile information to malign designated enemies such as Democrats and counterculture leaders. Nixon was infuriated when the front page of *The New York Times* (13 June 1971) printed an article about the Pentagon Papers adjacent to coverage of his daughter Tricia's wedding to Edward Cox Jr. The Pentagon Papers were classified documents that chronicled U.S. involvement in Vietnam. Daniel Ellsberg, who had been employed by the Defense Department when Lyndon B. Johnson was president, leaked the documents to the *Times.* Nixon considered Ellsberg's action treasonable and sought to vilify him. In September 1971 he directed agents to break into the office of Dr. Lewis J. Fielding, Ellsberg's psychiatrist. Nixon justified this action as a means to locate evidence crucial to national security. Although he despised Ellsberg, the inconsistent Nixon also respected his intellectual abilities and wished he had someone equivalent to Ellsberg on his staff.

As further evidence of his paranoid actions, scholars stress how Nixon designated operatives, known as "plumbers," to locate and stop leaks such as the Pentagon Papers, and also to attack foes. In 1972 these plumbers were arrested at the Watergate Hotel, where they had installed electronic surveillance devices at the Democratic National Committee headquarters. Although Nixon believed he could defeat Democratic opponent George S. McGovern in the 1972 election, he egotistically wanted to win by a larger margin than the 1 percent he had achieved in 1968. Nixon became fixated on retaining his power and was obsessed with winning. He feared being a one-term president. The Committee to Re-Elect the President (CREEP) zealously guarded Nixon's efforts, shredding documents and posting security guards at strategic locations. Using precious gems as code names, Nixon and his aides devised plans to sabotage the Democrats, such as hiring unruly demonstrators and damaging the air conditioning at their convention. They also covertly schemed to plant radical leftist pamphlets in the apartment of Arthur Bremer, who had shot Democratic presidential candidate George C. Wallace, so that Americans would not think Bremer was a Nixon supporter. A network of people cased places that Nixon wanted bur-

Richard M. Nixon campaigning in Philadelphia in 1968

(Dick Halstead/United Press International)

glarized to obtain influential documents and also posed as reporters to acquire information to use against opponents.

Nixon's biographers reveal how his anxieties about reelection culminated in the Watergate affair. After the plumbers were arrested, Nixon secretly asked the Central Intelligence Agency (CIA) to hinder the Federal Bureau of Investigation's inquiry into the break-in. Witnesses whom he could not manipulate divulged information about the Nixon administration such as corruption, illegal campaign contributions, and income-tax fraud. One source revealed that Nixon had voice-activated tape recorders in the White House and at Camp David. Nixon made scapegoats of individuals whom he felt threatened his authority. In what is known as the "Saturday Night Massacre," he dismissed special prosecutor Archibald Cox who pressured him to release the tapes. This action aggravated speculation of Nixon's knowledge of Watergate and the subsequent cover-up. Nixon worried about declining public support, and showed his strain at press conferences by publicly shoving an aide, mispronouncing words, and providing rambling complex answers to simple questions. Elizabeth Drew wrote in *The New Yorker* that "The President's demeanor changed when he dealt with the questions about Watergate and his property. He became tense, and he breathed hard." Other reporters described Nixon as "off his rocker."

As the Watergate investigation intensified, Nixon acted oblivious to reality. Denying culpability and exhibiting no remorse, he continued his official duties, traveling to the Soviet Union and Middle East to divert attention, as if he were untouchable. In June 1974, Nixon refused to provide documents and tapes to the House Judiciary Committee. He commanded his lawyer, James St. Clair, to inform the Judiciary Committee that he had not known about the Watergate break-in before it occurred and had not implemented a cover-up. Nixon did not acknowledge the seriousness of the charges against him. When the Judiciary Committee passed the first article of impeachment regarding obstruction of justice in July, Nixon was swimming in the Pacific Ocean. He predictably refused to resign despite counsel from friends about the inevitability of impeachment.

Feeling falsely persecuted, the depressed Nixon seemingly lacked a conscience and convinced himself he was morally right, lying to his family and advisors, who defended him and unknowingly committed perjury while risking their happiness and careers. Alone, Nixon struggled with anxiety attacks and sleeplessness, which he had dealt with before every major crisis in his life. The publication of *The Washington Post* investigative reporters Carl Bernstein's and Bob Woodward's *The Final Days* (1976) and premiere of the movie, *All The President's Men* (1976) infuriated Nixon, who was portrayed as being unstable, drinking to excess, confiding to White House portraits, and sobbing and praying on his knees with Secretary of State Henry Kissinger. Nixon declared both depictions as fabrications and felt betrayed that Americans accepted them as truth.

Nixon's psychological instability was common knowledge in the White House where aides monitored Nixon during suicide watches as his guilt became evident. Staffers also worried that he might impulsively place the country militarily at risk and disabled the red phone so that he could not contact the Soviet Union. Dr. Arnold A. Hutschnecker, Nixon's New York City psychiatrist, called Nixon's secretary, Rose Mary Woods, who told Nixon on 14 May 1973 that "he's thinking of you all the time" and asking "if there is anything on God's earth that he can do." Nixon confided in Woods that "They may kill me in the press, but they will never kill me in [my] mind. I'm going to fight these bastards to the end." Talking about the stress and turmoil he endured, he told her a month later, "It's almost a miracle that I've survived this. . . and then to have this brutal assault, brutal, brutal, brutal assault–day after day after day after day–no let up." He considered himself a martyr, responding to Wood's comment, "[Y]ou're killing yourself with the job," with "I don't mind killing myself, what I mean is, but I would expect to kill myself and I would do it."

Before he left the White House, Nixon hypocritically advised his staff: "Never be petty. Always remember others may hate you, but those who hate you don't win unless you hate them, and then you destroy yourself." Both Kissinger and Chief of Staff Alexander M. Haig commented in their memoirs that Nixon acted psychologically "deeply unsettled" at the time of his resignation. In his televised farewell speech Nixon remarked that he had exercised poor judgment. "I would have preferred to carry through to the finish whatever the personal agony it would have involved," he stressed. "I have never been a quitter. To leave office before my term is completed is opposed to every instinct in my body." His aides who had been imprisoned for assisting Nixon's crimes angrily complained that Nixon refused to admit his guilt. Nixon dramatically presented himself as a wronged victim: his tearful family surrounded him, and then he stoically walked toward the helicopter for his final farewell as president. Kissinger observed, "It was as if having kept himself in check all these years he had to put on display all the demons and dreams that had driven him." Accepting President Gerald R. Ford's pardon, Nixon admitted he was confused about what had happened. He did not express any accountability for his abuse of executive power.

Almost twenty-five years after Watergate, Volkan, director of the Center for the Study of Mind and Human Interaction, and his co-authors psychoanalyzed Nixon to understand how his psychological dynamics influenced his leadership. Consulting primary sources and interviewing individuals who knew Nixon, the authors diagnose him as suffering from narcissistic personality disorder. Narcissists, they explain, often create their own fantasy worlds starring themselves as powerful people whose rules are not to be questioned and reacting with extreme anger if challenged. They emphasize that Nixon's unconscious directed many of his political decisions, both positive and negative. This psychobiography stresses that Nixon's conflicted psyche was the source of his self-destruction. He reflected his own low self-esteem toward others–whom he demonized and tried to either destroy or manipulate. His inability to overcome this obsessive mistrust of people ultimately annihilated him politically. The authors cite three significant aspects of Nixon's personality. The grandiose persona enabled him to pursue almost unattainable goals such as relations with China. The peacemaker secured resolutions like détente and desegregation. The paranoid president degraded entities–institutions, organizations, and people–whom Nixon believed had shamed and thwarted him, and was displayed in behavior that endorsed the Watergate break-in, denied complicity, and defended his irrational motives.

Understanding why Nixon's personality contributed to his downfall can shape future scholarly studies determining how American politics can be manipulated by the unconscious needs, fears, and desires of its leaders. Nixon's narcissistic personality initiated Watergate and sustained it, focusing the nation's attention and energy on him to the detriment of the country and the presidency. Defending himself despite his guilt, Nixon "was the ultimate 'me' person." In his final years an angst-ridden Nixon vigilantly protested public access to his tapes as an invasion of his privacy, while he tried to rehabilitate his historical reputation by controlling how he would be portrayed. The Nixon tapes offer insights into a tormented personality, unable to reconcile reality and fantasy, as he directed domestic and international policy. The tapes also humanize a man who could have remained an elusive, mythical figurehead in the American imagination, instead of the embittered, rancorous blasphemer whose curses invite Freudian interpretations of who really ruled the United States during the Nixon presidency and how pathological fears and lies implemented a constitutional crisis.

–ELIZABETH D. SCHAFER, LOACHAPOKA, ALABAMA

Viewpoint: Although Nixon hoped his legacy would be in international affairs, he will be remembered for his notable domestic policies, including food stamps and Head Start.

By the time he left the White House in August 1974, Richard M. Nixon's first presidential victory six years earlier was a distant, bitter memory for American voters, the Washington power establishment, and the press. A comeback campaigner who yearned for the nation's highest office despite two early blows to his political career, Nixon helped unite the fractured Republican Party during the 1960s and claimed a narrow majority at the polls when widespread dissatisfaction with the Vietnam War toppled the hopes of the rudderless Democratic Party in 1968. Sworn into office in January 1969 by Chief Justice Earl Warren, a Nixon adversary, the newly inaugurated president told Americans:

> The greatest honor history can bestow is the title of peacemaker. This honor now beckons America–the chance to help lead the world at last out of the valley of turmoil, and onto that high ground of peace that man has dreamed of since the dawn of civilization.

In fact, Nixon's election came at the heels of a highly tumultuous year in modern American history, one that called for peacemaking at home and abroad. Seemingly overnight the January 1968 Tet Offensive had turned American public opinion against the Vietnam War and decimated Lyndon B. Johnson's reelection odds. The 1968 assassinations of Martin Luther King Jr. and Robert F. Kennedy fueled deep, broadly held concerns that the nation was unraveling at the seams. Urban riots proved that America's too-little-too-late Civil Rights movement was no match for centuries of pent-up rage toward racism; together, demands for racial equality, women's liberation, and an end to the Vietnam War supplied the platform for student protests on college campuses nationwide between 1968 and 1969. In keeping with the country's violent mood during the latter half of the 1960s, the 1968 Democratic Party convention in Chicago exploded when riots pitted antiwar demonstrators against city police and the National Guard. Americans watched the television news in horror as Chicago police officers beat the demonstrators with clubs, no doubt inspiring this Arlo Guthrie refrain: "Why do police guys beat on peace guys?" Meanwhile, campaigning in the reactionary margins of American politics was former Alabama governor George C. Wallace, who stumped for states' rights and law-and-order as the American Independent Party's presidential candidate.

This mosaic of political turbulence was all but foreshadowed by the 1963 assassination of President John F. Kennedy, and it formed the backdrop for Nixon's ascension to the White House. The same political upheaval made Nixon electable despite his reputation as an impersonal right-wing politician who, according to journalist Tom Wicker in *One of Us: Richard Nixon and the American Dream* (1991), triggered "the instinct of many Americans that he was not what he seemed." Nixon's close victory suggests Americans were hardly persuaded that the well-known, but not well-liked, Republican candidate could restore peace or bring about public unity. Ambivalence toward Nixon was particularly prominent among "doves," liberals, intellectuals, and the young, but they were not alone in questioning Nixon's motives, his politics, or the extent to which his anticommunist beliefs might spawn a new wave of suppressed "free" speech. If anything, election day 1968 revealed as much about the weakened state of the Democratic Party as it did about Republican loyalties Nixon had assembled while fund-raising and campaigning for party allies in federal and state elections during the 1960s. The political conditions surrounding Nixon's victory are important, for they show that the thirty-seventh president entered office without a clear public mandate. Notwithstanding the problems this electoral ambiguity created for both Nixon and Congress, between 1969–1974 he scored several important achievements that were later submerged by the infamous Watergate scandal.

Anti-Nixon books rolled off the presses for more than two decades after his resignation and many made the best-seller lists. They differ in form, style, and quality, but each seems to have addressed two purposes. First, by the early 1970s Americans were becoming fluent in "psycho-speak," owing to the widespread popularity that psychology had begun to obtain at least a decade earlier. B. F. Skinner's earlier pioneering work in operant behavior, Carl Ransom Roger's humanistic psychology, the self-actualization and hierarchy-of-needs theories of Abraham H. Maslow, Harry Stack Sullivan's interpersonal relations school, and Fritz Perls's Gestalt therapy transformed the entire field, pervading U.S. culture much as the "New Psychology" did a half-century before. If the birth of *Psychology Today* in 1967 remains an obvious barometer of psychology's public appeal, the endless flow of "Nixon personality" books before, and for many years after, his presidency also indicate that the new language of psychology was being appropriated by intellectuals, popular writers, political leaders, and journalists for a wide variety of agendas and audiences.

A second feature of these earlier Nixon works is that as a group they met the public's need for reassurance that political problems are caused by individuals–demagogues, radicals, and criminals–not by the American system of government. Indeed, the common story line in Nixon-bashing literature proffers that Watergate was the tip of the iceberg, not an isolated incident of pathology in an otherwise stellar political career. Writers from across the ideological spectrum took aim at the fallen president, variously describing him as a megalomaniac, a fervent anticommunist who distrusted all forms of dissent, a hopeless paranoiac, and a self-absorbed, calculating vote seeker who put his own interests ahead of the country's throughout his thirty years in politics. Nixon's resignation was characterized as a last-gasp effort to spare himself the nightmare of impeachment, the act of a liar who refused to own up to his abuse of presidential power. To paraphrase the polemics of the day, Tricky Dick was nixed.

Poets, essayists, political commentators and cartoonists, Nixon's former loyalists, a career's worth of enemies, real and would-be psychologists, and reporters who achieved stardom during the Watergate investigation joined in the public battering of an intensely private, undoubtedly wounded man. A handful of scholars tried their hand at explaining Nixon to the world inside the academy, a world he often condemned even though he ranked third in his graduating class at the esteemed Duke University Law School. Whether the eulogists of good government correctly analyzed Nixon's conduct on a continuum of evil to deranged, they unfairly dismissed the former president's record in affirmative action, environmental protection, and urban development, and failed to make a nonpartisan assessment of his New Federalism. Indeed, for many years the only positive recognition given to Nixon owed to his foreign-policy achievements, most notably the normalization of U.S. relations with the People's Republic of China in 1972.

Because Nixon vacated the White House with the specter of Watergate and three articles of impeachment in the foreground, his legacy has been memorialized almost exclusively in Watergate terms: he remains, after all, the only U.S. president to resign. To understand his presidency may require, as so many have argued, that one also understand Nixon's personality and paranoia, yet clearly his tenure produced more than a cover-up of the 1972 reelection committee's break-ins at Democratic National Committee's Watergate Hotel headquarters. Since Nixon's death in 1994 scholarly and popular writers have begun to extract Nixon from Watergate, reexamining old evidence and mining the past for the forgotten or ignored record of his work. Their findings and conclusions vary, but recent reviewers of Nixon's presidency have argued that his domestic agenda was strikingly moderate to liberal and his political philosophy was remarkably consistent.

Concerns about his psyche persist, yet this first wave of revisionism is invested less in Nixon's unhappy childhood than in the man whom Joan Hoff calls "aprincipled," in *Nixon Reconsidered* (1994) or whom Wicker characterizes as "an introverted intellectual. . . brutally distorted [by] the calculated (however necessary) presentation of a public persona." These reconstructed images may offend generations that recall Nixon as a singularly Draconian, unprincipled politician, but these evaluations represent a broader effort to understand Nixon as president–as a figure who possessed, according to Richard Neustadt in *Presidential Power and the Modern Presidents: The Politics of Leadership from Roosevelt to Reagan* (1991), "the personal capacity to influence the conduct of the men who make up government. . . . Power means influence." Significantly, one of the earliest post-Watergate volumes on Nixon, *Before the Fall: An Inside View of the Pre-Watergate White House* (1975), was written by speechwriter-columnist William Safire, who argued that:

> Nobody who wants to understand what happened in Nixon's presidency will succeed by becoming transfixed by Watergate's subsequent impeachment drama. A great deal more was going on at the time; Nixon and his men were trying to shape great events, not to seize dictatorial power. Perhaps historians will revise the angriest judgments of the mid-Seventies.

It took twenty years for scholars and veterans of U.S. politics to answer Safire's call. Those seeking to study the Nixon presidency should consider at least two questions: what is Nixon's enduring legacy, and how did he exercise presidential power to achieve his policy aims?

Common portrayals of Nixon as a conservative, corporate-loving politician have led many Americans to believe that he brought Johnson's

NIXON'S WELFARE REFORM SPEECH, 8 AUGUST 1969

Since taking office, one of my first priorities has been to repair the machinery of government, to put it in shape for the 1970s. I have made many changes designed to improve the functioning of the executive branch. And I have asked Congress for a number of important structural reforms; among others, a wide-ranging postal reform, a comprehensive reform of the draft, a reform of unemployment insurance, a reform of our hunger programs, a reform of the present confusing hodgepodge of Federal grants-in-aid.

Last April 21, I sent Congress a message asking for a package of major tax reforms, including both a closing of loopholes and the removal of more than 2 million low-income families from the tax rolls altogether. I am glad that Congress is now acting on tax reform, and I hope the Congress will begin to act on the other reforms that I have requested.

The purpose of all these reforms is to eliminate unfairness; to make the government more effective as well as more efficient; and to bring an end to its chronic failure to deliver the service that it promises. . . .

Abolishing poverty, putting an end to dependency—like reaching the moon a generation ago—may seem to be impossible. But in the spirit of Apollo, we can lift our sights and marshal our best efforts. We can resolve to make this the year not that we reached the goal, but that we turned the corner—turned the corner from a dismal cycle of dependency toward a new birth of independence; from despair toward hope; from an ominously mounting impotence of government toward a new effectiveness of government, and toward a full opportunity for every American to share the bounty of this rich land.

Source: Contemporary American Voices: Significant Speeches in American History, 1945–Present, *edited by James R. Andrews and David Zarefsky (New York & London: Longman, 1992), pp. 186–193.*

Great Society initiatives to a halt and turned the federal government's back on racial minorities. In fact, Nixon pressed for and ultimately formalized affirmative action as a central feature of federal domestic policy. By doing so he edged the nation toward measuring race relations by "equality of results" rather than "equality of opportunity," the model on which the Great Society was based. During Nixon's early years in the White House, the federal government instituted "hiring goals"–a concept that bordered on quotas–in order to guarantee minorities access to jobs created by federally funded construction contracts. Nixon was not the first president to confront discrimination against black labor by the large-scale general contractors and unions that benefited from federal public-works and urban-renewal projects. Presidents Dwight D. Eisenhower, Kennedy, and Johnson had made mild efforts to increase minority participation in public contracts, yet each stopped short of imposing sanctions against biased contractors that failed to comply with antidiscrimination policies and executive orders.

Nixon's success where his predecessors failed can be attributed to several factors, including a practical one: the severe shortage of skilled trade workers at a time of record-high residential construction costs. In addition, however, Secretary of Labor George P. Schultz, with Nixon's backing, directed the U.S. Labor Department to dust off and revamp what Johnson administration officials had called the Philadelphia Plan, and required federal contractors to make a "good faith effort" to hire enough minority workers to meet numerical workforce goals. In a classic case of the curious alliances that single-cause political disputes can generate, labor unions joined conservative Democrats and Republicans to oppose the Nixon-Schultz version of the Philadelphia Plan, just as they had united against earlier attempts to impose nondiscrimination standards on federal construction contracts. Assistant Secretary of Labor Arthur A. Fletcher, one of Nixon's policy-level African American appointees, countered the opposition in an August 1969 press conference: "We must set goals, targets and timetables. The way we put a man on the moon in less than ten years was with goals, targets and timetables."

Nixon took considerable heat for reinvigorating the Philadelphia Plan, and at times his commitment to economic benefits for minorities seemed to waiver, especially during his second term. Nonetheless, he managed to defend his affirmative-action agenda against an attempted end run by the Senate in late 1969. He also lowered the dollar threshold that triggered hiring-goals compliance and broadened the reach of his policy umbrella to include both minority and women workers–a move that was thematically consistent with Supreme Court rulings on gender discrimination under Chief Justice Warren E. Burger, a Nixon appointee. In addition, at Nixon's direction the Labor Department worked with local government officials to establish a program of "mini" Philadelphia Plans that were designed and carried out by fifty-six communities across the country. Finally, Nixon successfully urged Congress in 1972 to authorize the Equal Employment Opportunity Commission (EEOC) to sue private employers against whom there was evidence of bias against women and minorities. As affirmative action slowly became nationalized, terms such as goals, timetables, proportional representation, and quotas entered the lexicon of private industry.

In a related endeavor, Nixon's issuance of Executive Order 11458 launched the federal Office of Minority Business Enterprise (OMBE) in 1969. As Dean Kotlowski explains in *The Historian,* the president favored "black capitalism" in part to "promote minority economic development and thus allay urban unrest." Since his program guaranteed few political rewards, however, it is important to consider that Nixon may have "genuinely believed in minority business enterprise" and wanted to open "the full range of business opportunity to all by removing the inherited and institutional barriers to entry." Seen this way, OMBE may have been "practical and political," but also it fit with Nixon's belief that, "Aiding small entrepreneurs advanced equal opportunity, social mobility and economic independence—ideas associated with moderate Republicans."

A second policy area for which Nixon has been credited recently is environmental protection. Although not one of his favorite issues, the environment became a 1960s cause célèbre primarily because of water pollution and Rachel Carson's widely read *The Silent Spring* (1963). Persuaded by some of his top advisers to put the environment on the administration's priority list, Nixon appointed a special environmental task force that reported back to him in November 1969. He then experimented with bureaucratic restructuring because he saw the maze of overlapping agency jurisdictions as a barrier to policy implementation. Further, Nixon generally distrusted career bureaucrats and believed that reorganization supplied the means for gaining control over federal agencies. Significantly, however, Nixon won congressional support for several pieces of environmental legislation, even though many others were defeated. Among the proposals introduced or supported by the Nixon administration were the Environmental Protection Agency (EPA), the National Environmental Policy Act (NEPA) and Endangered Species Conservation Act, the Clean Air Act Amendments of 1970, the Water Quality Improvement Act, the state-administered Coastal Zone Management Act, the Marine Mammal Protection Act, and the Federal Pesticide Control Act. During the Nixon presidency two environmental figures—William D. Ruckelshaus and Russell Train—became responsible for major federal environmental-protection initiatives and the formation of federal environmental policy.

It is true that at times Nixon locked horns with his own environmental appointees and tried to veto measures that were dear to Congress, particularly to Senator Edmund S. Muskie (D-Maine), who had his own eye on the White House. Nonetheless, vetoes based on fiscal policies or philosophy and programmatic concerns are different: the former reflects a disagreement over how much money should be spent; the latter over the merits or necessity of a program. Watergate negativity had a significant impact on later interpretations of Nixon's use of the veto power, for sometimes he sought to reduce spending on programs that he otherwise supported. A case in point were the Federal Water Pollution Control Act Amendments of 1972. Nixon's decision to impound water-pollution control funds appropriated by Congress that year created a serious constitutional conflict, one that remains distorted by contradictory Supreme Court rulings in 1975 and 1985. Nixon was more probusiness than proenvironment, but the 1972 struggle over the control of water pollution had nothing to do with bowing to corporate allies and everything to do with spending limits. To dismiss all of Nixon's environmental initiatives as ineffective, insincere, or another example of two-faced political leadership is to read only part of the Nixon presidential record—and to read it selectively through the lens of Watergate.

In addition to such major achievements as establishing the EPA and the sewage-plant-construction subsidies that became popular among local government officials, the Nixon administration put whales on the endangered-species list and implemented oil-spill protection programs (although they were faulted for not going far enough). Despite his probusiness beliefs, Nixon proposed or agreed to proposals that placed significant compliance costs on private industry. In a 1998 article in *Presidential Studies Quarterly,* John Barkdull points out that if Nixon were as enmeshed with private-sector interests as critics have claimed, one would expect to find evidence in an area that customarily gives presidents great latitude with little congressional interference: foreign policy. Instead of showing disinterest, Nixon championed the Marine Polution Convention (MARPOL), the 1973 international treaty on oil pollution at sea—an action foreshadowed by his call for a NATO Committee on the Challenges of Modern Society (CCMS) in 1969. Although Nixon became wary of environmental policymaking after numerous feuds with Congress, he remain committed even when he "could have resisted popular and congressional pressures most easily—the making of foreign environmental policy. . . Nixon's was the environmental presidency."

A third aspect of Nixon's presidency that demands reconsideration is the New Federalism, which reflected Nixon's approach to federal/state relations and his attempt to grapple with international responsibilities as well. Hoff argues that the New Federalism "was based on ascertaining where the responsibilities logically lay and then determining the level of domestic or international power that should handle a specific function or activity." Generally, the New Federalism model would classify such functions as environmental protection as a national government duty while education would fall squarely under state control. Nixon's objective was not to reduce federal domestic spending, but to reallocate power from the federal bureaucracy to states and communities whenever it made sense to do so. At the same time he saw national unity and local diversity as complementary, not incongruous, political conditions—or what Safire described as "national localism." What began as revenue sharing—a formula method for distributing federal revenues to states with few strings attached—led to eliminating "categorical" or competitive grants and creating the most flexible grant system in the United States, the Community Development Block Grant (CDBG) program. In purely statutory terms the 1972 State and Local Fiscal Assistance Act authorized revenue sharing, and the Housing and Community Development Act of 1974 gave birth to CDBG. President Ronald W. Reagan later dismantled revenue sharing, but CDBG was, and remains, so popular among states and a large network of "entitlement" cities that it enjoys unusually strong (some would say impenetrable) political support. It is not surprising that Reagan's efforts to reduce CDBG spending were met with enormous opposition from the program's long-standing base of major cities and its newer contingent of recipients, state governments—which obtained control over a share of the annual CDBG appropriation because of Reagan's own view of New Federalism.

It is important to note that the concept of revenue sharing was hardly a Nixon invention. Democrats in Congress had pressed for a similar plan, but their arguments held no sway with Johnson. By the time Nixon took occupancy of the Oval Office, the idea had gained popularity and seemed to square with Nixon's larger interest in reducing the power of federal agencies to restrict or regulate state and local government activities. Neustadt bluntly suggests, though, that Nixon's overriding goal was to "circumvent the bureaucracy" by reducing overall federal power while increasing White House control. In theory revenue sharing offered possibilities for scaling back the scope of bureaucratic authority because distributing federal funds on a formula basis made the assistance nondiscretionary. At the same time, receiving steady support from the federal government without red tape would build state and local loyalties to the president, for example, to Nixon.

By the time Reagan did away with revenue sharing in his second term, State and Local Fiscal Assistance Act authorizations had put $83 billion into the hands of states and communities nationwide. During its fourteen-year lifetime, however, the act produced mixed outcomes and never delivered on the structural changes Nixon had predicted. For instance, he envisioned more public participation in state and local government as a direct result of federal financial assistance, yet the fact that many New Federalism initiatives cut red tape also meant considerable local discretion, thereby reinforcing the power of traditional constituencies to influence how the funds were used. Thus the concept of "targeting" (directing federal dollars to the neediest areas) became a mainstay of federal domestic policy, but in practice the targeted communities did not necessarily apply their new funds to accomplish national goals. On this point Johnson had more foresight than Nixon; Johnson's concerns with inequality no doubt made him suspicious of such federalist ideas as revenue sharing. Nixon believed federal funds could reduce economic inequality and facilitate a condition known euphemistically as "empowerment."

Once reelected, Nixon partially reorganized the bureaucracy and made the Department of Housing and Urban Development (HUD) the locus of community development oversight at the federal level. (The Department of Health, Education, and Welfare administered a related block-grant system, the Comprehensive Employment and Training Act.) According to Michael J. Rich, in *Federal Policymaking and the Poor: National Goals, Local Choices and Distributional Outcomes* (1993), the combined total of New Federalism allocations reached $13 billion in 1978, or about one-seventh of all national payments to state and local governments. Successive presidents tried to shape CDBG as an agent of national policy, and in so doing they made HUD's administrative role much stronger than Nixon intended. Additionally, Congress reacted when incidents of local discretion seemed incompatible with the purposes of the Housing and Community Development Act, but ideological differences and partisan politics have made it difficult for congressional leaders to agree on the intent of CDBG, let alone to share a president's opinion about the desirability of spending choices made by cities and towns.

The resulting confusion made HUD seem capricious and inconsistent as it changed in response to presidential and congressional pendulum swings. Moreover, the same tensions made local community-development practices vary significantly across regions and over time. As recalled by Safire, what Nixon's advisors originally anticipated—"a greater respect for national conscience by individuals, and more respect for local concerns in the application of that conscience"—either was unattainable from the start or became distorted by ever-shifting federal expectations and requirements, especially through red tape. A compelling argument can be made that once national authorities de-emphasized the "hands-off" message of Nixon's New Federalism and magnified their interest in federal-policy consistency, local recipients of CDBG and other block-grant programs became highly creative at subverting the 1974 act and HUD's massive regulations. When the rules and their enforcement are unpredictable, implementation is also erratic. Such outcomes have little to do with Nixon, who left office too soon to witness the evolution of CDBG, yet the benefits that it has produced in many of the country's poorest cities are linked inextricably to the New Federalism agenda and hence, to Nixon.

Wicker encourages contemporary analysts to understand that Nixon was more like "one of us" than Watergate historians have argued in the past. Historians including Kotlowski and Barkdull have tried to excavate information that remained lodged beneath the composite of Watergate facts, fiction, and fear, principally by posing questions in non-Watergate language. Hoff goes so far as to assert that a generalized "misreading of the impact of Watergate reflects the determination of certain scholars to exaggerate its importance in order to ensure that nothing connected with Nixon's presidency be positively interpreted." Whether intellectuals have conspired against Nixon or intentionally blinded themselves to the whole of his presidential record, and whether popular psychology helped to demonize Nixon by supplying the analytical framework for "pathological president" theories, the real danger in extreme Nixon negativity lies in this subtext: Watergate, and hence Nixon, represent an aberration in a sound, legitimate system of government. In fact, however, Watergate bespeaks a system that was (and is) in shambles, a system too tolerant of abuse of power and official misconduct–evidenced by congressional reluctance to intercede or investigate Watergate allegations until daily disclosures in *The Washington Post* and other major newspapers made further delays politically untenable. Hoff summarizes it this way, and her conclusion is chilling: "Watergate is more than Nixon because the potential for future Watergates is as great as ever."

–JUDITH A. BARRETT, DUXBURY, MASSACHUSETTS

References

David Abrahamsen, *Nixon Vs. Nixon: An Emotional Tragedy* (New York: Farrar, Straus & Giroux, 1977);

Jonathan Aitken, *Nixon, A Life* (London: Weidenfeld & Nicholson, 1993);

Stephen E. Ambrose, *Nixon,* 3 volumes (New York: Simon & Schuster, 1987–1991)–comprises volume 1, *The Education of a Politician 1913–1962* (1987); volume 2, *The Triumph of a Politician 1962–1972* (1989); volume 3, *Ruin and Recovery 1973–1990* (1991);

Robert Sam Anson, *Exile: The Unquiet Oblivion of Richard M. Nixon* (New York: Simon & Schuster, 1984);

John Barkdull, "Nixon and the Environment," *Presidential Studies Quarterly,* 28 (Summer 1998): 587–602;

Fawn M. Brodie, *Richard M. Nixon: The Shaping of His Character* (New York: Norton, 1981);

Eli S. Chesen, *President Nixon's Psychiatric Profile: A Psychodynamic-Genetic Interpretation* (New York: Wyden, 1973);

Fred Emery, *Watergate: The Corruption of American Politics and the Fall of Richard Nixon* (New York: Times Books, 1994);

J. Brooks Flippen, "Pests, Pollution and Politics: the Nixon Administration's Pesticide Policy," *Agricultural History,* 71 (Fall 1997): 442–457;

Joan Hoff, *Nixon Reconsidered* (New York: BasicBooks, 1994);

Arnold A. Hutschnecker, *Drive for Power* (New York: M. Evans, 1974);

Joseph Nathan Kane, *Presidential Fact Book* (New York: Random House, 1998);

Dean Kotlowski, "Black Power–Nixon Style: The Nixon Administration and Minority Business Enterprise," *Business History Review,* 72 (Autumn 1988): 409–412;

Kotlowski, "Richard Nixon and the Origins of Affirmative Action," *Historian,* 60 (Spring 1998): 523–541;

Stanley Kutler, *The Wars of Watergate: The Last Crisis of Richard Nixon* (New York: Knopf, 1990);

Kutler, ed., *Abuse of Power: The New Nixon Tapes* (New York: Free Press, 1997);

J. Anthony Lukas, *Nightmare: The Underside of the Nixon Years* (New York: Viking, 1976);

Lawrence J. McAndrews, "The Politics of Principle: Richard Nixon and School Desegregation," *Journal of Negro History,* 83 (Summer 1998): 187–215;

Christopher Matthews, *Kennedy & Nixon: The Rivalry That Shaped Postwar America* (New York: Simon & Schuster, 1996);

Bruce Mazlish, *In Search of Nixon: A Psychohistorical Inquiry* (New York: BasicBooks, 1972);

Roger Morris, *Richard Milhous Nixon: The Rise of an American Politician* (New York: Holt, 1990);

Richard P. Nathan, "A Retrospective on Richard M. Nixon's Domestic Policies," *Presidential Studies Quarterly,* 26 (Winter 1996): 155–165;

Richard E. Neustadt, *Presidential Power and the Modern Presidents: The Politics of Leadership from Roosevelt to Reagan* (New York: Free Press, 1991);

Richard M. Nixon, *Six Crises* (Garden City, N.Y.: Doubleday, 1962);

Herbert S. Parmet, *Richard Nixon and His America* (Boston: Little, Brown, 1990);

Leo Rangell, *The Mind of Watergate: An Exploration of the Compromise of Integrity* (New York: Norton, 1980);

Michael J. Rich, *Federal Policymaking and the Poor: National Goals, Local Choices and Distributional Outcomes* (Princeton: Princeton University Press, 1993);

Margaret C. Rung, "Richard Nixon, State and Party: Democracy and Bureaucracy in the Postwar Era," *Presidential Studies Quarterly,* 29 (June 1999): 421–444;

William Safire, *Before the Fall: An Inside View of the Pre-Watergate White House* (Garden City, N.Y.: Doubleday, 1975);

Maurice Stans, "Richard Nixon and His Bridges to Human Dignity," *Presidential Studies Quarterly,* 26 (Winter 1996): 179–184;

Gerald S. and Deborah H. Strober, *Nixon: An Oral History of His Presidency* (New York: HarperCollins, 1994);

Vamik D. Volkan, Norman Itzkowitz, and Andrew W. Dod, *Richard Nixon: A Psychobiography* (New York: Columbia University Press, 1997);

Jerry Voorhis, *The Strange Case of Richard Milhous Nixon* (New York: Eriksson, 1972);

John C. Whitaker, "Nixon's Domestic Policy: Both Liberal and Bold in Retrospect," *Presidential Studies Quarterly,* 26 (Winter 1996): 131–154;

Theodore H. White, *Breach of Faith: The Fall of Richard Nixon* (New York: Atheneum, 1975);

Tom Wicker, *One of Us: Richard Nixon and the American Dream* (New York: Random House, 1991);

Garry Wills, *Nixon Agonistes: The Crisis of the Self-Made Man* (Boston: Houghton Mifflin, 1970);

Bob Woodward and Carl Bernstein, *All the President's Men* (New York: Simon & Schuster, 1974);

Woodward, *Shadow: Five Presidents and the Legacy of Watergate* (New York: Simon & Schuster, 1999);

Woodward and Bernstein, *The Final Days* (New York: Simon & Schuster, 1976);

Arthur Woodstone, *Nixon's Head* (New York: St. Martin's Press, 1972).

ORGANIZED LABOR

Did the American labor movement decline in the postwar era?

Viewpoint: American labor declined in power after World War II because the unions pursued benefits for their members rather than a broader political agenda.

Viewpoint: American labor did not decline in power after World War II, but rather the labor movement evolved to meet changing economic conditions.

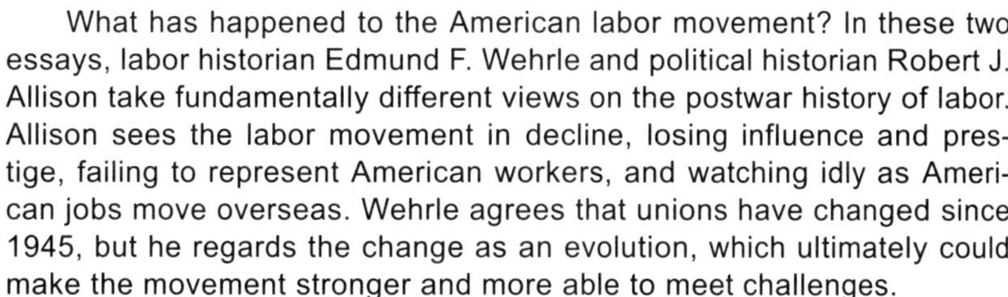

What has happened to the American labor movement? In these two essays, labor historian Edmund F. Wehrle and political historian Robert J. Allison take fundamentally different views on the postwar history of labor. Allison sees the labor movement in decline, losing influence and prestige, failing to represent American workers, and watching idly as American jobs move overseas. Wehrle agrees that unions have changed since 1945, but he regards the change as an evolution, which ultimately could make the movement stronger and more able to meet challenges.

Who is right? Labor unions certainly are different in the 1990s than in the 1930s or even the 1950s. Is this decline or evolution? Was the attachment labor made with the Democratic Party in the 1930s a grave mistake or Faustian bargain, as Allison suggests, or has this resulted in substantial gains for all Americans? For example, Allison points to the G.I. Bill and Social Security as gains for all Americans that made labor unions unnecessary, while Wehrle points out that labor unions supported these acts, as well as Medicare and other Great Society programs. These laws probably would not have passed without labor support, and this suggests a greater political role for labor than Allison sees.

On the other hand, labor unions have not prevented American jobs from moving overseas. Yet, was this movement caused by unreasonable American wages, or was it a natural economic change in which wages were but one part? Can the American labor movement, or can an international labor movement, revive to organize workers in the Philippines, Singapore, or Korea? Certainly the conditions in South East Asian or Latin American factories would not shock the men and women who organized American workers in the 1880s and 1890s. Will the labor movement evolve to encompass all workers of the world? Or will American unions continue to content themselves with the self-interest of their own members? Working men and women will decide the answers to these questions, and based upon their actions we can see the judgment of history.

Viewpoint: American labor declined in power after World War II because the unions pursued benefits for their members rather than a broader political agenda.

After World War II the American labor movement went into a period of decline from which it has never rebounded. Once a vigorous and important voice of the American worker, contributing ideas and energy to the political process, the labor movement became smaller and less consequential after 1945. Most of the blame for this development must be placed on the movement itself. As unions stopped addressing issues that did not meet the immediate needs of union members, focusing instead solely on raising wages for members, the unions became less important players in the political system. Moreover, as the economy boomed, raising wages without intercession from union members, the unions themselves seemed less important, and membership declined.

We can attribute the decline of unions to other factors, notably the political changes of the late 1940s. During the Depression years organized labor had tied its fortunes to the Democratic Party rather than using the opportunity to create a labor-based political movement. Instead, the unions became just another constituency in the Democratic coalition, and the Democrats delivered, with the Wagner Act (1935) creating the National Labor Relations Board, with minimum-wage laws, guarantees of union shops, and other benefits to union members during the war.

After the war, as the Republicans looked for issues with which to challenge the Democrats, they seized on the Democratic attachment to organized labor. In 1947 the Republicans regained control of Congress for the first time since 1931. In June the Congress passed the Taft-Hartley Act, the most antilabor bill Congress had passed since the 1920s. Taft-Hartley forbade the closed shop (in which only union members could be employed), prohibited unions from making political contributions (most of their contributions went to the Democrats), required unions to file financial reports, made unions liable for breaches of contract, and required union leaders to take oaths that they were not communists. Though President Harry S Truman vetoed the bill, Congress overrode his veto, and Taft-Hartley became law. While union leaders saw this as severely restraining their ability to organize (as it was intended to) and attributed the subsequent decline of unions to this pernicious bill, in reality Taft-Hartley was less important in weakening their position than actions the unions themselves had already taken.

American labor had already taken the wrong path toward becoming an important feature in American life. Early in the twentieth century American working men and women had two choices for organization. One path led to the American Federation of Labor (AFL), a collection of craft unions, each of which organized workers in a certain craft, such as plumbers, cigar makers, or train engineers. A second led to trade unions, in which men or women employed in a certain industry, such as the garment industry, the textiles, railroads, or later the automobile industry, would join one union no matter what job each member had. A related form of union, represented by the Industrial Workers of the World (IWW), sought to organize all workers, skilled or unskilled, into one big union that would be a political as well as an economic organization.

For the craft unions, the first priority was to improve conditions for their own members. The guiding force behind the American Federation of Labor, Samuel Gompers, believed that to be successful, unions would have to be able to deliver to their own members and should avoid political agitation that could only make enemies for labor. When Gompers was asked what American working men wanted, he was blunt: "More!" Working men and women represented by the AFL would get more, as their unions focused on higher wages for union members. Trade unions and the IWW would try to agitate on political questions, or improve working conditions for all workers, but the AFL realized that these kinds of crusades would not have an immediate or direct impact on the fortunes of AFL members. During the first decades of the century the IWW was suppressed by government action, leaving the AFL and the trade unions, who organized into the Congress of Industrial Organizations (CIO), as the primary organizers of working people.

American labor, then, had virtually renounced political activity by the 1930s, focusing instead on trying to improve the incomes of union members. During the Depression labor had found allies in the Roosevelt administration, and sometimes violent union activity, such as the San Francisco general strike launched by the longshoremen or the CIO's organization of the auto workers, proceeded without counter-violence from the state. Having an ally in the White House prevented labor from becoming an underground or revolutionary movement, but it also meant labor would not push for social change. Instead, the American system worked through compromise, and labor did not need to appeal to a broader constituency. Some attempts to do so, such as the organization of the Southern Tenant Farmers Unions, in which white and black farmers were organized by the Communist Party, had a brief success until racism and anticommunism did them in.

The mainstream American labor movement had decided to settle for improved wages over economic and political change. While this improved the livelihoods of American union members, it did little to guarantee continued improvement for all workers. Had labor made its goal the organization of all workers, the labor movement would have had a more pronounced political role in the United States. Yet, labor did not do this, and the consequences after World War II were profound for labor. By accepting the system as it was, and by ceding labor's political role to the Democratic Party, labor's political fortunes depended on the fortunes of the Democrats. As we have seen, when the Democrats lost control of Congress in 1947, the Republicans took their first opportunity to punish the labor movement.

The Taft-Hartley Act was only one facet of a political campaign against labor. Taft-Hartley required union leaders to take an oath that they were not members of the Communist Party. Labor suffered more than any other segment of the American polity from the anticommunist hysteria, since communists had been active organizers of working people. In fact, the whole communist philosophy rests on organizing the men and women who work into a political force. Yet, after the war, unions were required to bar communists from positions of power, and labor lost some of its most important voices, who happened to be communists, such as Harry Bridges. In a better publicized case, the Screen Actors Guild, a union of Hollywood actors, voluntarily purged communists from its ranks, under the leadership of union president Ronald Reagan. By purging communists, the unions lost some of their most active and farsighted organizers and leaders.

The purge of communists was the culmination of labor's movement away from political activity. Unions did not stand for political action but for more benefits for members. However, after the war, it would be the government, not the unions, which delivered for American workers. The G.I. Bill of Rights, guaranteeing a college education for all veterans, guaranteeing low-cost housing loans for veterans, and implementing the Social Security system, did more for American workers than unions had ever been able to deliver. The G.I. Bill transformed the American workforce from a blue-collar manufacturing force into a white-collar managerial force. American workers, who might have been encouraged to join unions to improve their conditions, now instead could join the army. The goal was not necessarily better wages or working conditions in a particular occupation, but to move out of that occupation altogether into management. Mobility became possible, not because unions organized, but thanks to the policies of Washington.

Jimmy Hoffa (left) at a 1959 Teamsters rally in New Jersey

The unions themselves resolutely avoided politics, with one or two important exceptions. The United Auto Workers (UAW), under the leadership of Walter Reuther, engaged in imaginative political activity. The UAW, along with the Brotherhood of Sleeping Car Porters, founded by the socialist activist A. Philip Randolph among African American railroad porters, were leaders in the Civil Rights movement (Randolph in 1941 had threatened President Franklin D. Roosevelt with a massive march on Washington to demand more jobs for blacks in defense industries). However, on the whole the unions, which were dedicated to keeping wages high for their own members, did not want to see blacks or anyone else entering the skilled trades and threatening their wages.

With Washington serving the one remaining purpose unions had, improving the lives of members, what was left for unions to do? That was not clear, and unfortunately the union leaders since World War II have not been able to create a new role for their organizations. It became clear that some unions wielded great power over their industries and members, who were required to pay dues to a union that did little. In 1954 Elia Kazan's *On the Waterfront* depicted corruption in New York's longshoremen's union, which, the movie charged, had connections with organized crime. The union bosses had power to decide who would work and who would not, and the union boss single-handedly could shut down the New York waterfront. This public image of union leaders, who had begun as interested in the welfare of their own union's members and had become merely interested in their own well-being, derived from the fact that unions had undergone this evolution. At the end of the 1950s Massachusetts senator John F. Kennedy made a national reputation by taking on Teamster union leader Jimmy Hoffa, using Hoffa's corruption as a way to advance Kennedy's political career. Attorney General Robert F. Kennedy's book, *The Enemy Within* (1960), revealed the Teamster's corruption.

Unions tried to police themselves, with the AFL-CIO (the two had joined in 1955) purging Hoffa and the Teamsters, as well as any unions tainted with communism. During the 1960s and 1970s union leaders did little to advance labor's cause. In 1970 United Mine Workers president Tony Boyle had challenger Joseph Yablonsky and his family murdered. In the early 1970s Albert Shanker and New York's chapter of the American Federation of Teachers shut down the city's school system rather than surrender power to New York parents, particularly minority parents who wanted more African American and Hispanic teachers and administrators hired. The unions seemed interested only in the welfare of their own members, not in the broader interests of the American public. Having surrendered their political and social roles, unions had to care only for their own members.

A further irony developed from this situation. By driving up wages for union members, the unions had made American workers among the highest paid in the world. The high salaries have had two major implications. One, American union members do not typically see a common bond between themselves and other struggling members of society. Little empathy or shared sense of belonging has developed that would make all Americans see labor's agenda as their agenda. Second, American employers, desperate to make money, have found cheaper sources of labor in Mexico, Latin America, and Southeast Asia. As wages in American manufacturing jobs have increased, those jobs have been shipped to Singapore, Korea, Mexico, and Brazil. The unions, which had shunned any political role for so long, had no tools with which to prevent the loss of manufacturing jobs, and Americans who did not have the good fortune to belong to these unions had little sympathy for the newfound plight of the unions. When the Air Traffic Controllers Union went on strike in 1981, President Reagan, the only union president who has ever been elected president of the United States, quickly moved to break both the strike and the union.

The only unions of any consequence as the twentieth century ends are those in occupations that cannot be shipped out of the country. The American Federation of State, County, and Municipal Employees (AFSCME) represents government workers; the American Federation of Teachers and National Education Association represent classroom teachers; and baseball players have their own powerful union. While these unions are able to achieve high wages for their own members, doing so has made them appear self-interested and opposed to the public interest. By taking more for their members and shunning a political role that would make the unions represent all working people, the American labor movement has brought its collapse on itself. "Sundown for the unions," Bob Dylan sang in the 1980s, "was made in the U.S.A.," created by the selfishness of union leaders, who wanted more for themselves and their members, not a change in the American economy.

–ROBERT J. ALLISON,
SUFFOLK UNIVERSITY

Viewpoint:
American labor did not decline in power after World War II, but rather the labor movement evolved to meet changing economic conditions.

The death of organized labor in the postwar period has been greatly exaggerated. Economic historians understand that situations perpetually evolve–resulting in social, political, and cultural changes. Labor historians, however, seem to insist that the intense activism of the 1930s, the outgrowth of a unique moment in history, should remain the ideal of the labor movement. Economic, political, cultural, and social circumstances, in fact, have changed drastically, and the labor movement has changed with them. The postwar period represents yet another period of transition, posing grave challenges for labor unions. Yet, in response, organized labor set new standards for employer-employee relations, remained politically active, and began (although not as quickly as some would have liked) to address the needs of a new, more diverse workforce in a challenging and often hostile work environment.

Historically, worker movements have enjoyed great periods of successes as well as times of near-extinction. In the early nineteenth century the rise of a market economy and early manufacturing shattered the world of the small craftsmen, anchored in republican dignity. Later in the century, as industry grew larger and more mechanized, skilled workers, indispensable to early factories, found themselves increasingly replaced by the unskilled wave of immigrant laborers pouring into the country. Many unions suffered. Naturally, older unions, such as the Chandelier Workers Union, the Carriage Workers, and the Broom and Whisk Makers, found themselves losing membership and ultimately succumbing to extinction. In the 1930s, just when it seemed that the American economy was embarking on a new nonunionized period, organized labor staged a dramatic comeback in the face of the Great Depression. The resurgence of the 1930s managed to incorporate many of the less-skilled, industrial workers—the sons and daughters of immigrants—previously thought unorganizable.

Following the gains of the 1930s, which were solidified during World War II, growth appeared slower for American unions. Detractors argued that labor's leadership had grown soft; that unions had entered into a corporate partnership with American business—a pact that sold out American workers. Yet, these critics often give short shrift to both the historical anomaly represented by the Great Depression and the economic changes overtaking the American economy in the postwar period. The tremendous growth experienced by unions, particularly industrial unions, in the 1930s was the product of a desperate workforce with nothing to lose. In the more prosperous postwar period, enjoying tremendous material gains, American workers had little reason to resort to militant tactics such as had been practiced in the 1930s.

Likewise, far from selling out workers, American unions negotiated a groundbreaking series of contracts in the late 1940s that gave workers an unprecedented security. In the auto industry, for instance, workers won health insurance, automatic cost-of-living raises, and pension programs. Nothing of the like had been offered workers on a large scale before. Over the course of the second half of the twentieth century, these pathbreaking gains set the standard for American workers. As labor historian Alan Dawley explained, as a result of these contracts, providing workers a share of postwar prosperity, "a generation of children grew up beyond the clutches of the terrible insecurity their parents and grandparents had always known." These watershed developments either have been ignored by historians, or when treated, depicted as a sellout, compromising the true radical desires of workers. Of course, anyone who knows Americans understands that they, especially working people, are hardly radical militants but rather individuals focused on security for themselves and their families.

The breakthroughs achieved by organized labor in the 1930s and World War II period came at a time when industry—especially the automotive and steel sectors—dominated the American economy. However, as early as the late 1950s, the economy began shifting away from its powerful industrial base. International competition picked up, and a new information-based economy began taking hold. By the 1970s one surveying the economic landscape could not help but be shocked at the changes. The older industrial order was in full-scale retreat, while a new service sector and information-based economy struggled to take hold. In the same way that the Industrial Revolution presented challenges to American workers, so too would the arrival of the information age force the working class to adapt. Meanwhile, the nature of the workforce also was changing. More women (particularly married women) took jobs. In addition, spurred by the 1965 immigration act, a new wave of immigrants from Asia and Latin America further crowded the job market.

Naturally, as large-scale American industry declined, so too did the unions associated with these former behemoths. However, in their place other unions rose, addressing the needs of the changing workforce. The Service Employees International Union (SEIU), growing to include 1.3 million members by 1999, developed into one of the strongest, most active unions in the labor movement by organizing workers in the burgeoning service sector. Its "Justice for Janitors" campaign, begun in the 1980s, specifically aimed at energizing a new, diverse workforce by reviving many of the aggressive organizing techniques of the New Deal period. Likewise, aided by President John F. Kennedy's executive order in 1962, supporting the right of federal employees to organize and bargain collectively, public employees' unions have also seen enormous growth. The American Federation of State, County, and Municipal Employees (AFSCME), for instance, grew from a mere 99,000 members in 1955 to nearly 1.2 million in 1995. No sector has enjoyed greater growth in the postwar era than that of education. By the 1980s the National Education Association (representing nearly 2 million teachers) was the largest union in the country. This public and service sector growth

PREAMBLE TO THE AFL-CIO CONSTITUTION (1955)

The establishment of this Federation through the merger of the American Federation of Labor and the Congress of Industrial Organizations is an expression of the hopes and aspirations of the working people of America.

We seek the fulfillment of these hopes and aspirations through democratic processes within the framework of our constitutional government and consistent with our institutions and traditions.

At the collective bargaining table, in the community, in the exercise of the rights and responsibilities of citizenship, we shall responsibly serve the interests of the American people.

We pledge ourselves to the more effective organization of working men and women; to the securing to them of full recognition and enjoyment of the rights to which they are justly entitled; to the achievement of ever higher standards of living and working conditions; to the attainment of security for all the people; to the enjoyment of the leisure which their skills make possible; and to the strengthening and extension of our way of life and the fundamental freedoms which are the basis of our democratic society.

We shall combat resolutely the forces which seek to undermine the democratic institutions of our nation and to enslave the human soul. We shall strive always to win full respect for the dignity of the human individual whom our unions serve.

With Divine guidance, grateful for the fine traditions of our past, confident of meeting the challenge of the future, we proclaim this constitution. . . .

Source: Documents of American History, *2 volumes, edited by Henry Steele Commager (New York: Appleton-Century-Crofts, 1973), 2: 609–613.*

has led some scholars to speak of the emergence of a "new unionism," replacing the older, industrial-based unions, which represented increasingly obsolete economic areas. The 1995 election of John J. Sweeny, president of the SEIU, to the presidency of the AFL-CIO in many ways symbolized the coming-of-age of this new unionism.

While the postwar period has been a time of readjustment, organized labor can claim real gains, especially in the political arena. Much of the labor movement carefully avoided politics before the New Deal period, when labor's effective working relationship with President Franklin D. Roosevelt suggested that fundamental gains could be achieved through a labor-state alliance. While detractors might focus on the setbacks, in particular the Taft-Hartley and Landrum-Griffin Acts, labor has played a central role in the passage of the most important pieces of social legislation of the postwar period. Labor unions, for instance, both helped draft and lobbied aggressively for the 1963 Equal Pay Act, forbidding pay differentials between men and women. Strong labor support also resulted in the 1965 passage of the Medicare and Medicaid Acts, providing health insurance for the elderly and poor. In another arena, organized labor also solidified a strong relationship with the emerging Civil Rights movement. The United Auto Workers were among the sponsors of the 1963 March on Washington, culminating in Dr. Martin Luther King Jr.'s "I Have a Dream" speech. Likewise, labor lobbyists pressed hard for passage of the 1964 Civil Rights Act, forbidding discrimination in the workplace. King neatly summed up the security-centered aims of both the Civil Rights and the labor movements: "Our needs are identical with labor's needs: decent wages, fair working conditions, livable housing, old age security, heath and welfare measures, conditions in which families can grow, have education for their children and respect in the community."

Most of labor's legislative achievements, of course, were made in cooperation with the Democratic Party and Democratic presidents. Indeed, labor's symbiotic relationship with the Democrats grew significantly in the postwar period, facilitating the Civil Rights movement and helping to give birth to the Women's movement. Far from the "barren marriage" depicted by one historian, the relationship has born significant fruit. Even without a Democrat in the White House, however, organized labor's legislative agenda, while hardly flourishing, survived and even advanced. In 1970, for instance, the AFL-CIO in cooperation with the Republican administration of President Richard M. Nixon managed to pass the seminal Federal Occupational Safety and Health Act, creating a federal agency to oversee the health and safety concerns of American workers.

The leadership of American organized labor has been less in step with its liberal allies in consistently promoting an anticommunist international agenda. Many of the leaders of organized labor in the postwar era were themselves veterans of battles against communist infiltration of American unions in the 1920s. They carried with them deep animosity toward communists that only grew when, under orders from Soviet premier Joseph Stalin, American communists attempted to disrupt mobilization for World War II, during the brief period of the Stalin-Hitler nonaggression pact between 1939 and 1941. In the postwar period American labor leaders such as George Meany, David Dubinsky, and Walter Reuther–all vehement anticommunists who had fought communists for control of their unions–began focusing increasing attention on thwarting the designs of communists on "free trade unions," first in Western Europe, then in the Third World. This international work–at times in cooperation with the Central Intelligence Agency–was controversial. The intense anticommunism of many in the labor movement led them to support the Vietnam War, even after it appeared that the war would be costly, divisive, and probably end in defeat for the Americans. Although often shrill in tone, American labor leaders tempered their vehement anticommunism with a commitment to human rights. By the early 1980s the first real fruit of the labor's anticommunist crusade could be seen in the rise of the Solidarity Union in Poland, to which the AFL-CIO had strong links. Organized labor may then take some credit for the collapse of communism in the late 1980s.

The frequent reports of the demise or imminent death of organized labor, then, appear to have been circulated by those with no understanding of either the historical context of the issue nor the inevitable changes constantly reshaping the course of American history. American labor unions have had to endure revolutionary economic and social changes and yet have emerged with a solid strategy for keeping the needs and interests of American workers at the forefront of the nation's agenda. In the late 1940s, through a series of path-breaking contracts, organized labor established a new precedent in which employers were required to place the security of workers at the forefront of their concerns. Through active political organizing, lobbying, and its relationship with the Democratic Party, labor helped many, including minorities, the poor, and the elderly, stake their claim to security and betterment. Today, organized labor, baring little resemblance to the movement of the 1930s, remains a vital and active force in economic, social, and cultural times that likewise bare little resemblance to the 1930s.

–EDMUND F. WEHRLE, U.S. COAST GUARD ACADEMY

References

Kevin Boyle, *The UAW and the Heyday of American Liberalism, 1945–1968* (Ithaca, N.Y.: Cornell University Press, 1995);

Gordon L. Clark, *Union and Communities Under Siege: American Community in the Crisis of Organized Labor* (New York: Cambridge University Press, 1989);

Taylor E. Dark, *The Unions and the Democrats: An Enduring Alliance* (Ithaca, N.Y.: Cornell University Press, 1999);

Michael Davis, *Prisoners of the American Dream: Politics and Economy in the History of the US Working Class* (London: Verso, 1986);

Melvyn DuBofsky, *The State and Labor in Modern America* (Chapel Hill: University of North Carolina Press, 1994);

Michael Goldfield, *The Decline of Organized Labor in the United States* (Chicago: University of Chicago Press, 1987);

Seymour Martin Lipset, ed., *Unions in Transition: Entering the Second Century* (San Francisco: Institute for Contemporary Studies, 1986);

Kiim Moody, *Workers in a Lean World: Unionism in International Economy* (London: Verso, 1997);

Christopher L. Tomlins, *The State and the Unions: Labor Relations, Law, and the Organized Labor Movement in America, 1880–1960* (New York: Cambridge University Press, 1986);

Robert Zieger, *American Workers, American Unions, 1920–1985* (Baltimore: Johns Hopkins University Press, 1986).

PEROT

Was the reform movement of H. Ross Perot in 1992 a continuation of earlier independent political movements or was it a unique phenomenon?

Viewpoint: The Perot movement sought political redress through an electoral vehicle outside the Democratic and Republican parties: it also challenged the ideologically driven organization of the two major parties.

Viewpoint: H. Ross Perot's candidacy reveals more about the role of money in politics than about any reform impulse.

Did the 1992 presidential election represent the beginning of the end of the two-party hegemony in American politics? It is too soon to answer that question. In these two essays, historians Omar Ali and Robert J. Allison take close looks at the 1992 election and speculate as to its long-term significance.

Ali sees the candidacy of billionaire H. Ross Perot as a significant event, not because Perot had enough money with which to convey his message, but because Perot was able to attract significant support from millions of men and women anxious to break the power of the two major parties. Perot offered an alternative, and Americans were eager to hear alternative voices. Ali traces the independent political movement on its twentieth-century history, looking to the 1948 election, the 1960s movements among blacks in the South, and the local elections in New York State (where Liberals, Conservatives, and antiabortion advocates were all on the ballot) as laying the foundation for Perot's independent challenge in 1992.

Allison, on the other hand, argues that Perot's relative success owed more to Perot's wealth than his message. The American political system, he argues, is now firmly controlled not only by Democrats and Republicans but also by a national press that ignores local issues in pursuit of big stories.

However one analyzes the 1992 election, these two essays must make us reconsider the health of the political system. Can democratic government survive in America? That is a question history cannot answer.

Viewpoint: The Perot movement sought political redress through an electoral vehicle outside the Democratic and Republican parties: it also challenged the ideologically driven organization of the two major parties.

In 1992 a new movement shattered the conventional categories of American politics when nearly 20 million people voted for the independent candidacy of H. Ross Perot. With 19 percent of the national vote, he received the highest percentage of votes cast for an independent presidential candidate since 1912, when Theodore Roosevelt ran as an independent in the Progressive Party and garnered the largest popular vote for an independent in the history of the United States. Perot's campaign exposed how politicized and dysfunctional the American government had become, as manifest in corruption, an unfathomable debt, and a deep distrust in both the Democratic and Republican parties to solve the nation's problems. While not running on a third-party ticket, Perot ran to win the White House by galvanizing the American electorate into taking back control of the country. Most journalists, political scientists, and historians have overidentified this independent movement with Perot, its best known and wealthiest proponent. (In 1992 he reputedly spent a record $72.6 million of his personal fortune on the campaign.) However, the analysts have also undervalued the grassroots movement out of which the Perot campaign had grown and the impact that this movement would have in shaping a new politic based not on political ideology but on democracy and political reform instead.

The 1992 electoral revolt that made Perot synonymous with independent politics may be correctly located within the independent electoral traditions that have spanned the century. At the same time, the revolt was fundamentally new in its focus on political process, as opposed to concentrating on programmatics or social issues (such as welfare, housing, and the death penalty), as the method through which a healthier economy, society, and polity could be achieved. In 1992 Americans set in motion a populist process of reshaping the traditional contours of ideologically driven bipartisan American politics. The political impact of the Perot campaign was nothing less than a relative shift away from the dominant left/center/right paradigm of electoral politics to a top/down populist model, uniting diverse constituencies around the shared experience of being excluded from the electoral, legislative, and policy-making processes. The challenge to the constraints placed upon the American people's inclusion into the political process appealed to a broad section of Americans with an accompanying broad range of political ideologies and political party affiliations. Voters not only came out to the polls in larger numbers in 1992 (more than thirteen million additional voters came to the polls than in the 1988 general election) but, more significantly, broke with the two major parties in record numbers across the United States.

The populism that emerged out of the 1992 campaign was a model of party-building, as seen in the Patriot Party in 1994 and in the Reform Party in 1996, that was more vertical–more bottom (the American people) versus top (the two parties of the government)–than a horizontal model based on the left/center/right paradigm. Most Americans consider themselves moderates who do not agree with the extreme positions taken by either the ideological right-wing of the Republican Party or the ideological left-wing of the Democratic Party. The populism that developed in 1992 was both inclusive and tolerant of divergent views, differing from centrism–which tends to include only those ideologically "at the center." Centrism, however, is not an ideological position. It is more closely akin to a political compass than an ideology. Hence, the equation often made between "centrist" and "moderate" confuses the matter; for most people who voted Democrat or Republican were also moderates. Polls taken during the 1992 campaign indicated that the majority of Americans were dissatisfied with the ineffectiveness of the two parties–which had to do not with the failure to be moderate but with the emphasis in the bipartisan political culture of America on winning even at the cost of effective government, an example of centrism.

The dissatisfaction with the two-party system has its most recent roots in the restructuring of U.S. politics that occurred in the 1930s. Faced with massive economic collapse, the government intervened into the mounting chaos to create a safety net not just for the poor but for the free-enterprise system itself. Democrats and Republicans closed ranks behind this approach, out of which developed what has become known as the welfare state, the transformation of the federal government from a kind of coordinating body to an extremely centralized regulatory body that provides welfare both for the poor and for corporate America. The federal government had become far more extensive, intrusive, and powerful than even the most ardent Federalist could have imagined.

The change to a highly regulated system of government created profound changes in the economic and political makeup of the country.

PEROT ON WASHINGTON

Nobody takes responsibility for anything in Washington. Who was in charge of deregulation all through the '80s? Vice President George Bush. Has the press ever said how did you let the banking and Savings and Loan mess occur? No. Has the press ever said in 1984, when you were officially told that the Savings and Loan mess was a $50 billion mess, you waited until the day after the election in 1988, the PAC money poured in, and then when it was a several hundred billion dollar mess, you tried to fix it? No.

Then, has anyone ever said who was in charge of anti-terrorism during the '80s? Who created Saddam Hussein with billions of dollars and whose personal fingerprints are all over it for ten years? The President of the United States. No. If I ever get stuck up there, and I do something really stupid, and I probably will, I will step before the American people and say, I did that. I shouldn't have done that. Here is why I did it, but hold me accountable, because I did it.

Source: Ross Perot Speaks Out, *edited by James W. Robinson (Rocklin, Cal.: Prima Publishing, 1992), pp. 54–55.*

With regulation becoming a key avenue for business to improve its competitive edge, corporate boards began to transform from assemblies of manufacturing and industrial magnates to pools of lawyers expert in navigating government regulations for the profitability of the company. Political influence over the two major parties became more key than ever, since elected officials (invariably from the two major parties) were the ones who promulgated the regulations. The revolving door between the government and the private sector began to spin, as special interests acquired greater influence over the legislative process. The legislature, which in the earliest stages of American history had been the most populist, democratic, and responsive to the American people, became one of the most top-down controlled institutions of American government.

Throughout the rise of this "regulatoryism," the two major parties were taking measures to ensure their control of the governmental process. Ballot access regulations, designed to protect the incumbency of the two parties and restrict independent politics, were enacted in state legislatures across the country. (In the 1912 general election the average election ballot had 4.1 candidates for Congress. By 1984 there were only 2.3 candidates for Congress on the typical general election ballot, and one-ninth of the districts—49 out of 435—had only one candidate on the ballot). Campaign finance laws were written and rewritten, largely as a function of two-party rivalry, but always with an eye toward repressing the rise of a third party. Reapportionment and redistricting were implemented by bipartisan legislatures so that it became the case that legislators often picked their districts before the districts picked their legislators. Bipartisanism, as opposed to nonpartisanism, in the conduct of elections was institutionalized in the Federal Election Commission in 1974 and the pseudo-governmental Commission on Presidential Debates in 1987.

The 1992 independent electoral movement challenged the two major parties' tight reign over the elective, legislative, and policy-making processes, all of which had been customized by the two parties over the previous sixty years to suit the needs of special interests. And while this movement distinguished itself both qualitatively and quantitatively from previous independent and third-party challenges, it was well within the tradition of independent movements dating back to the Republican Party's displacement of the Whig Party in the late 1850s as the main opposition to the Democrats concerning the issue of the expansion of slavery into the free territories. Other challenges to the two major parties, which now included the Republicans, followed soon thereafter.

In the 1890s the People's Party (also known as the Populist Party) elected 38 people to Congress, gained control of the state legislature in Georgia and North Carolina (in a successful fusion effort with the Republicans in that state), and elected two governors. In 1892 James B. Weaver, the Populist presidential candidate, won nearly 9 percent of the vote. Building on the momentum created by earlier Greenback Party efforts, the People's Party forced the major political parties to pass significant antimonopoly legislation and important labor legislation. Nearly one generation after the People's Party called for the direct election of U.S. senators, Congress enacted the Seventeenth Amendment to the Constitution, guaranteeing this democratic reform.

The twentieth century saw a flurry of independent party campaigns. In the two decades before World War I, the Socialist Party elected 1,200 people to office, including 79 mayors and two congressmen (one from Milwaukee, the other from New York City). Socialist Eugene V. Debs ran for president from jail in 1920 and received more than one million votes. Four years later, Senator Robert LaFollette of Wisconsin ran for president as the candidate of the independent Progressive Party and received almost five million votes—more than 16 percent of the total.

During the Great Depression that was touched off by the 1929 stock market crash, mass social action–which took organizational form in councils of unemployed workers, the Congress of Industrial Organizations (CIO), and the Black Sharecroppers Union–fueled support for independent political parties. The Farmer Labor Party became the most powerful party in Minnesota; LaFollette's Progressive Party reemerged as a significant force in Wisconsin politics; and the American Labor Party helped to elect three eminent congressmen from New York City by placing them on their ticket: Vito Marcantonio, Adam Clayton Powell Jr., and Fiorello LaGuardia.

Threatened by the unrest and growing support for these independent parties, the Democrats and Republicans were forced to make concessions to poor and working-class people. In 1935 President Franklin D. Roosevelt and Congress enacted laws that gave labor unions the right to organize, limited the work day to eight hours, established a minimum wage, protected child labor, and guaranteed social security and unemployment insurance. In turn, the African American electorate broke with the party of Abraham Lincoln and came over to the Democrats; together with organized labor they would become the backbone of the "New Deal" coalition. The coalition ended half a century of national Republican hegemony, giving the Democratic Party control over the White House for the next twenty years, and further secured Democratic control of Congress for all but four of the next sixty years.

In 1948 Henry Wallace, one of Roosevelt's former vice presidents, ran for president under the banner of the Progressive Party (not the same as LaFollette's organization); the Wallace candidacy was a product of the deep-running tensions within the New Deal coalition that also produced an independent presidential run to the right of the Democratic Party standard-bearer, Harry S Truman, by "Dixiecrat" segregationist J. Strom Thurmond. Although Wallace (like Thurmond) got one million votes in that election, the Progressives–bowing to the winner-take-all mentality promoted by the bipartisan political monopoly–considered the campaign a failure and never ran a candidate for president again.

During the campaign, Truman, like FDR before him, was forced to adopt many of the positions taken by Wallace, his independent opponent. But once in office the new president and the right-wing Republican senator from Wisconsin, Joseph R. McCarthy, launched a bipartisan attack against progressives and independents designed to root them out of American political life. Part of that all-out assault was an attack on fair elections. By the end of the 1950s a convoluted maze of state laws concocted to keep "outsiders" off the ballot virtually prevented independents from participating in elections (California, for instance, had raised the new party petition from 1 percent of the last gubernatorial vote to 10 percent, and Ohio raised the new party petition from 1 percent to 15 percent). Nonetheless, in 1964 the Mississippi Freedom Democratic Party, a grassroots phenomenon that came directly out of the Civil Rights movement, arose to challenge the seating of the regular, "whites only," state party at the national nominating convention. They were eventually awarded two at-large delegates in a compromise orchestrated by Minnesota's senior senator, Hubert H. Humphrey.

Humphrey won both the Democratic Party's nomination in 1964 for vice president and then won the vice presidency under Lyndon B. Johnson. However, four years later Humphrey lost the presidential election to Richard M. Nixon when segregationist George C. Wallace, running on the American Independent line, siphoned off the votes of six million Southern Democrats. Nevertheless, the coming period would be one of independent parties and campaigns helping to define the era as one of progressive challenges to the status quo.

The late 1960s witnessed the flowering of several independent statewide parties rooted in the antiwar movement, such as the Liberty Union Party in Vermont (where Congressman Bernie Sanders, the only independent in the U.S. House of Representatives, began his political career), California's Peace and Freedom Party, and the Wisconsin Alliance (later the Wisconsin Labor Farm Party). Other independent parties were inspired by the Civil Rights movement, such as La Raza Unida in the Southwest, the Puerto Rican Young Lords (which originated in Chicago but established itself most firmly in New York City), and the Black Panther Party (which began organizing in Oakland, California, but soon had a powerful presence in every major Northern city). With the exception of Peace and Freedom, one of only two progressive parties in the country with permanent ballot status (the other being the Workers World Party in Michigan), the rest either died violent deaths at the hands of the police (the Young Lords and the Panthers), disappeared into local obscurity (Vermont's Liberty Union and Wisconsin's Labor Farm), or became a vehicle for a handful of former militants to drive the Chicano vote into the Democratic Party (La Raza).

Dr. Martin Luther King Jr., who was considering an independent presidential run before his murder in 1968, and Malcolm X, in his "the ballot or the bullet" speech a few years earlier, recognized the problematic overreliance of African Americans on the Democratic Party to solve its problems. A strategy for the exercise of black empowerment therefore required examining African American loyalty to the Democratic Party (or the Republican Party for that matter). However, like white middle-class America, communities of color have been conflicted about breaking with the two major parties. African Americans, for instance, who throughout American history had been on the cutting edge of political reform and participated in several independent political efforts involving majority white parties (from the participation of delegates of the Colored Farmers' Alliance in the founding of the People's Party in 1891 to Eldridge Cleaver's run as a Black Panther in the Peace and Freedom Party in 1968), made a decisive turn away from independent politics at the 1972 National Black Political Convention in Gary, Indiana.

Exactly twenty years before the voter revolt of 1992, a cross-section of religious, cultural, and political leaders in the African American community met in Indiana to chart an electoral course for the empowerment of their communities. The mayor of Gary, Richard Hatcher, who hosted the 1972 convention, spoke about a day in the future when African Americans would "cross the Rubicon" (that is, form an independent multiracial party) and take with them not only a "kaleidoscope" of people of color but "the best of white America." Despite such appeals, the convention opted to invest the only political wealth the black community as a whole possessed–its vote–in electing more African Americans to office under the banner of the Democratic Party. The strategy (analogous to those taken by the women's movement and gay rights' movement to increase female and gay representation) significantly increased the number of black Democratic Party–elected officials at the municipal, county, state, and national level and reached its pinnacle, and perhaps its limit, in the Reverend Jesse Jackson's two bids for the Democratic nomination for the presidency. The strategy, however, left the black community (along with the rest of the American people) more vulnerable to both major parties by not making the Democrats or Republicans accountable to an independent force.

The ensuing twenty years prior to Perot's entrance onto the national independent electoral stage marked a gradual estrangement for much of America from the electoral, legislative, and policy-making processes. In 1976 Eugene McCarthy got on the ballot in twenty-nine states and polled 756,691 votes. Four years later former Republican John Anderson ran for president as an independent and received six million votes, while environmental activist Barry Commoner also ran as an independent in 1980, receiving a quarter of a million votes. However, few believed that the impulse toward independent voting could evolve into an actual independent party, especially an independent party that could capture the imagination of diverse Americans.

In 1988 a left-of-center independent party, the New Alliance Party, achieved what many believed to be impossible. A political/legal barrier had been broken that would help set a precedent for Perot's run in 1992 when Dr. Lenora Fulani ran for president with the New Alliance Party and became the first woman and the first African American ever to appear on the ballot in all fifty states (most independent presidential candidates have appeared on only a fraction of all fifty states' ballots). She also qualified for nearly $1 million in primary matching funds, which fueled her campaign for political reform. Fulani's campaign challenged the loyalty of most African-American voters to the Democratic Party, which was in the process of abandoning its most loyal constituency. Although she received only a quarter of a million votes, her accomplishment did not go unnoticed when four years later Fulani's legal team was called upon by Ross Perot for counsel on how to get on the ballot in every state in his bid for the presidency.

Prior to Perot's 1992 campaign, independent politics had been relegated by political analysts and the media to the fringes of American politics. Perot's name, money, and message of political reform placed not only independent politics squarely on the map of American electoral politics but, in the process, shook the foundations of the two-party system. While Perot had concerned himself with the issue of the mounting national debt, his appeal was primarily based on a cross-section of Americans wanting to be included in the decisions that affected their lives. In the wake of the 1992 campaign, the development of a national third party based on the restructuring of the political process seemed within the realm of possibility.

In 1994, 110 delegates from more than twenty states gathered in Arlington, Virginia, to found the Patriot Party. Among those who founded the new party were grassroots Perot, leader Nicholas Sabatine III, African American independent Fulani, and gay-rights activist Jim Mangia. The Patriot Party lasted a little more than three years and served as a transitional organization that both stimulated and acted as a bridge between the 1992 Perot experience (and preexisting elements of the independent movement) and the founding of the Reform Party in 1996. The Patriot Party was, in effect, an experiment in creating a post-ideological populist alliance based on principles rather than programmatics. It made political reform and fiscal responsibility the focal point of its prescription for the political crisis in America and projected the third-party alternative, in a small way, to the American public and in a more-substantial way to the Perot movement. Patriot was less of a bona fide third party than a "pre-party"–a political tactic designed to generate a bigger, broader party with greater presence on the political scene. That broader party, the Reform Party, came about as a result of Perot's decision to establish a national third party with his presidential bid in 1996. Despite his exclusion from the national debates by the bipartisan Commission on Presidential Debates and the refusal of several networks to run his campaign advertisements, he received 8.4 percent of the popular vote, thus automatically securing for the Reform Party future ballot status in more than twenty-five states and $12.6 million in federal matching funds for the 2000 presidential election.

The Reform Party, which grew directly out of the Patriot Party and the broader Perot movement, has achieved modest success. In Minnesota, Governor Jesse Ventura became the Reform Party's first elected statewide officeholder. In New York the state affiliate to the national Reform Party, the Independence Party, holds the third line on the ballot and has a duly elected state committee of 269 members that is running the party and fielding its own grassroots candidates. Significantly, a quarter of the Independence Party's state committee, the leadership body of the party, is made up of members under the age of thirty. The evidence suggests that the youngest generation of voters is rapidly moving away from the Democrats and Republicans and toward independent politics. In 1996 more than 72 percent of all voters under thirty years of age said they would support an independent candidate for president, and in 1997 a Gallup Poll revealed that 44 percent of African Americans between the ages of 18 and 35 identified themselves as independents.

The indicators of growing independent support notwithstanding, it remains an open question whether or not the Reform Party, or any other independent party, will be able to successfully capture this wave of support and serve as a political vehicle for the American people to transform the way politics is conducted in the United States. Whatever the immediate outcome may be, what continues is the underground independent sentiment that was partially unleashed by the Perot movement in 1992.

—OMAR ALI, COLUMBIA UNIVERSITY

Viewpoint: H. Ross Perot's candidacy reveals more about the role of money in politics than about any reform impulse.

Historians are nearly infallible when explaining the past but, like other mortals, cannot predict the future. One can interpret the election of 1992 in a variety of ways but cannot predict whether the relative success of H. Ross Perot's Reform Party is the harbinger of a political realignment away from the Democrats and Republicans. Historians can look at other events of the 1990s and make predictions, and they can trace the Reform Party impulse to other political challenges to two-party hegemony, but they cannot say whether this was a fluke or whether Americans really are looking for political alternatives.

No successful new party has emerged in the United States since 1856. The Republicans captured the White House in their second national campaign in 1860, and since then Democrats and Republicans have been the two major national parties. Other minor parties have flourished at various times and in various places; the Greenbacks, Populists, Prohibitionists, Progressives, and Socialists all have elected members of Congress, state legislatures, and municipal governments. Though independent candidates have contested for the presidency, none has come close to winning, and only a few have garnered any electoral votes: Theodore Roosevelt in 1912, Robert LaFollette in 1924, J. Strom Thurmond in 1948, Harry Byrd in 1960, and George C. Wallace in 1968. Roosevelt, a Progressive candidate and an extremely popular former president, finished second to Woodrow Wilson, leaving incumbent William Howard Taft in a distant third place. LaFollette, also a Progressive, carried only his home state of Wisconsin, finishing third behind incumbent Republican Calvin Coolidge and Democrat John W. Davis. Thurmond, Byrd, and Wallace all ran as disaffected Democrats, breaking with the party after it embraced a civil-rights agenda. Their independent movements prefigured the political shift of the white South from the Democrats to the Republicans, and the electoral votes they attracted came mainly from former Democrats in the Southern states.

Two important third-party candidates, Henry Wallace in 1948 and Illinois congressman John Anderson in 1980, may have influenced the election results but did not lead to any long-term political role for the parties they launched. Wallace's Progressives may have taken votes from President Harry S Truman, but Truman still won the election (despite losing the white South to Thurmond). In 1980 Anderson's moderate-to-liberal challenge probably took votes from Democrat Jimmy Carter and helped elect Republican Ronald W. Reagan.

Perot is something of an anomaly. He apparently entered the 1992 campaign not because of a sincere desire to reform American politics but because he had for some reason developed an intense dislike of President George Bush. He suspended his candidacy early in the summer but resumed it later on, leaving his sup-

Vice President Al Gore and H. Ross Perot debate the issue of free trade with Mexico on a 9 November 1993 broadcast of *Larry King Live*

(AP/World Wide Photos)

porters somewhat confused. His ability to spend huge amounts of money allowed him to attract more attention than any third-party candidate since Theodore Roosevelt and also allowed him to bankroll the Reform Party, which dutifully nominated him again in 1996. Perot received the votes of more than 19 million Americans in 1992; four years later he received just more than 7 million. This decrease does not bode well for the Reform Party's chances in 2000.

The 1994 election suggests that the American people, if they want to protest, are more comfortable acting through the existing political parties. In 1994 a Republican Congress was elected for the first time since 1952. This change seemed to indicate that the Republicans could regain the White House in 1996, but instead, the American people reelected William J. Clinton and a Republican Congress. First, one must ask why the Reform Party did not work on the local level to run candidates in the 435 Congressional districts, or even for the Senate seats up for election. Instead, in 1994 the challenge to the status quo came from Republican insurgents on Capitol Hill, not from the Reform Party. Second, one must wonder why the American people voted both for Republicans and a Democrat, and why the politicians then set up the whole impeachment drama of 1998 and 1999.

These events may seem anomalous unless we look at the structure of American government and conclude that the American people in fact know what they are doing. In 1988, Vice President Bush raised "gridlock" as a campaign issue. He wanted the American people to elect a president and a Congress of the same party. Otherwise, he argued, policies would be stalemated, or gridlocked; necessary measures would be blocked by one branch of government or the other. President Reagan had been constricted by a Congress of the other party, as had every Republican president since Dwight D. Eisenhower's first term. Bush was elected president, but apparently the American people did not buy his line of reasoning, as they also reelected a Democratic Congress. Running for reelection in 1992, Bush again called for an end to gridlock, and this time the people listened. They reelected the Democratic Congress and replaced Bush with Clinton. This shift seemed to restore unity to government, but in 1994 Congress changed again.

The American people had a keener understanding of the national government, it seems, than did President Bush. One of the architects of the American government, John Adams, had argued that it would be dangerous for the legislative and the executive branches to agree on everything. The two, Adams said, were necessarily antagonistic—otherwise, they would be able to trample on people's liberties. When Adams designed the Constitution for the Commonwealth of Massachusetts in 1779, he had separated the powers of government, so the executive and the legislature could not have the same functions but would, in fact, check each other. When Bush complained about gridlock, he was actually complaining about checks and balances, and the American people seem fond of these. Thus, in the 1980s most Americans supported Reagan's reforms of the federal government, but they would not have supported a general Republican assault on Medicare and Social Security or gutting the Occupational Safety and Health Administration. Having a Democratic Congress check a Republican president was valuable, as it would be essential in the 1990s to have a Republican Congress check a Democratic president.

Though the framers of the Constitution did not envision a two-party system, the system has almost always worked with two parties, and it seems impossible that there will be a successful third-party movement. There have been in the 1990s several successful independent candidates on the state level—Connecticut's governor is independent Lowell Weicker, a former Republican senator, and Minnesota's governor is former professional wrestler Jesse Ventura. However, both these men achieved office based more on their name-recognition than on their platforms. In Vermont, independent socialist Bernard Sanders has been elected to Congress. While Vermont, Connecticut, and Minnesota have found independent candidates appealing, it is difficult to see Ventura, Weicker, and Sanders cooperating with Perot to form a national independent movement. They contend that the Democrats and Republicans are not appealing, but it would probably be impossible for them to agree on a palatable alternative.

The American political system is structured currently to allow some success for independent candidates on the local level, but it will be almost impossible to create any kind of national independent movement. One major reason for this is the nationalization of the media. Independent newspapers, radio stations, and television stations have gone the way of the paper ballot and the smoke-filled room. Local newspapers are more and more owned by chains, or by larger papers in other cities. The media since the 1970s have focused more and more on big national stories, spending millions of dollars extracting every ounce of material out of sensational events such as the O.J. Simpson trial, the death of Princess Diana, or the Monica Lewinsky scandal. Less attention is paid to issues, candidates, and elections on the local level. It is harder, then, for local voices to be heard and for issues to be discussed. Candidates for office need to spend enormous amounts of money on advertising, as media coverage is almost nonexistent for any but the highest-profile elections.

The vestiges of local politics on the national scale, the political primaries to choose candidates for national office, have also become less local and more national. Once upon a time, candidates could go to New Hampshire or Iowa, relatively small states, and meet with individual voters in living rooms and coffee shops. Voters in these states would then get a chance to evaluate candidates directly, noticing who looked them in the eye and who could talk intelligently about issues. However, by the 1970s these primaries and caucuses had been taken over by the national press, and candidates went to these places not to meet voters but to be seen by the national press. Candidates went to Iowa, New Hampshire, Wisconsin, or any other state, followed by reporters from the national press. Once the voters of these places had spoken, the press then expected other states to ratify their choice.

Political campaigns are incredibly expensive, given the limitations of press coverage. In the 1970s, as a way to clean up elections and free them from the baneful influence of big money, Congress created a presidential campaign fund, paid out of a contribution check-off box on federal income tax forms. Candidates in both parties would qualify for this money once they had raised a certain amount on their own, and if they agreed to certain limits. The fund guaranteed money to Democrats and Republicans, but left potential minor-party challengers empty-handed. The system also did not address the real cause for high campaign costs—the price of television or radio advertising. In the early days of the republic, vigorous newspapers with their own political agenda guaranteed a clear and colorful discussion of ideas and issues. One need only look at the newspaper articles written on the Constitution, the issue of slavery, the Mexican-American War, or the Civil War to see how far the popular media have descended over the past century and a half. Now the press both charges candidates to have their voices heard and then condemns candidates for having to raise incredible amounts of money for the privilege.

Perot had his own money to pour into the campaign. Other third-party candidates, Libertarians, Socialists, and Right-to-Lifers, do not have his resources. Even in the major-party primary elections, the press focuses on how much money a candidate has and speculates on a candidate's chances to win based upon how much money the candidate has been able to raise. If the press says a candidate has not raised sufficient funds, then it becomes almost certain the candidate will not be able to raise enough money.

The alternative method of winning elections, by meeting with people face-to-face and getting their support, has also vanished, thanks to the progressive reforms of the early twentieth century. In those distant days, people participated in the political process, handing out flyers, getting people to the polls, explaining the issues, and then after the election, if their candidate was successful, they could expect to be rewarded with a job in the new administration. However, the civil-service law eliminated most of these patronage jobs, and the press, which is always on the hunt for a scandal, regards the rare instances of this kind of reward as somehow corrupt. There are indeed selfless men and women who work on political campaigns, making phone calls, handing out flyers, and doing the unglamorous work of electing people to office. Yet, these democratic heroes are not as plentiful as one would hope or have reason to expect.

Perot's candidacy was a fluke as far as independent campaigns go, in that he was able both to have his voice heard and to receive the votes of nineteen million men and women. However, it was less of a fluke than it might appear, since Perot came into the campaign armed not with any particularly notable ideas, but with millions of his own dollars with which to convey his message.

–ROBERT J. ALLISON,
SUFFOLK UNIVERSITY

References

Pat Choate, *Agents of Influence* (New York: Knopf, 1990);

Fred Newman and Lois Holzman, "Deliberately Unsystematic Thoughts on a New Way of Running a Country," in *The End of Knowing: A New Developmental Way of Learning* (London & New York: Routledge, 1997);

Joseph S. Nye Jr., Philip Zelikow, and David King, *Why People Don't Trust Government* (Cambridge, Mass.: Harvard University Press, 1997);

Kevin Phillips, *Arrogant Capital: Washington, Wall Street, and the Frustration of American Politics* (Boston: Little, Brown, 1994);

Robert B. Reich, *Tales of a New America* (New York: Times Books, 1987);

Jacqueline Salit, *Reforming America: An Insider's View of the Independent Political Movement* (forthcoming);

Michael J. Sandel, *Democracy's Discontent: America in Search of a Public Philosophy* (Cambridge, Mass.: Belknap Press of Harvard University Press, 1996);

Richard Winger, "How Ballot Access Laws Affect the U.S. Party System," *American Review of Politics*, 3 (Winter 1995): 321–350.

POLITICAL CONSENSUS

Was there a political consensus on foreign policy in the United States in the early years of the Cold War?

Viewpoint: Yes, a foreign-policy consensus based on the issue of anticommunism did emerge in the early years of the Cold War.

Viewpoint: No, any notion of bipartisanship in the face of a perceived Soviet threat was undermined by clear ideological differences between political leaders in America.

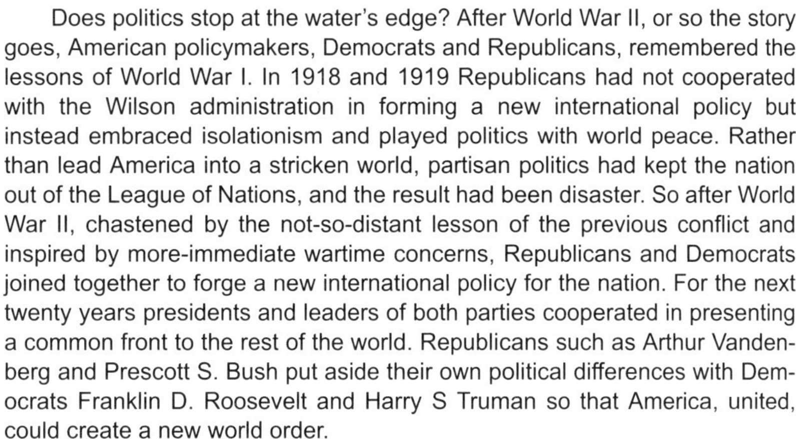

Does politics stop at the water's edge? After World War II, or so the story goes, American policymakers, Democrats and Republicans, remembered the lessons of World War I. In 1918 and 1919 Republicans had not cooperated with the Wilson administration in forming a new international policy but instead embraced isolationism and played politics with world peace. Rather than lead America into a stricken world, partisan politics had kept the nation out of the League of Nations, and the result had been disaster. So after World War II, chastened by the not-so-distant lesson of the previous conflict and inspired by more-immediate wartime concerns, Republicans and Democrats joined together to forge a new international policy for the nation. For the next twenty years presidents and leaders of both parties cooperated in presenting a common front to the rest of the world. Republicans such as Arthur Vandenberg and Prescott S. Bush put aside their own political differences with Democrats Franklin D. Roosevelt and Harry S Truman so that America, united, could create a new world order.

Both of these essays challenge this view. Jonathan Bell, a British scholar, and thus a more neutral observer of the American political scene, is convinced that the idea of bipartisanship does not explain American policy after the war. In fact, he argues, Republicans and Democrats still had quite different approaches to America's role in the world and were prepared to follow their own agenda rather than compromise it for some phantom national good. On the other hand, Andrew Johns draws a distinction between consensus, which he argues did actually exist, and bipartisanship, which suggests constant agreement. American leaders, Johns contends, shared some fundamental ideas and attitudes, and even a common ideology, despite their different political affiliations. All were committed to containing the spread of communism and, for the most part, favored national military strength. In this sense, the American leaders of 1945–1950 had learned a lesson from the mistakes of 1918–1920.

President Harry S Truman signing the Economic Cooperation Act, which authorized the Marshall Plan, 3 April 1948

(Truman Library)

Viewpoint:
Yes, a foreign-policy consensus based on the issue of anticommunism did emerge in the early years of the Cold War.

In his classic study on the American policy of containment during the Cold War, *Strategies of Containment* (1982), John Lewis Gaddis discusses the different approaches to foreign policy employed during seven successive administrations. Gaddis describes the varying tactics used by presidents from Harry S Truman to Jimmy Carter, but contends that overall the strategy remained the same—to contain the Soviet Union. The fact that a single overarching foreign policy endured during this period has been attributed to an underlying consensus among policymakers in the executive branch, Congress, the press, and public opinion concerning the fundamental goals of American foreign policy. While political battles might erupt over the means employed, the ends remained constant. Although the strength of this agreement waxed and waned, a consensus based on the twin pillars of institutional and partisan agreement on the issue of anti-communism did emerge from 1945 to 1947.

Consensus should be understood not as full agreement on principles or details but rather as an adherence to a broad compromise on political procedures and policies. In the case of the Cold War, it means that agreement existed on the main themes of foreign policy—resistance to communist expansion by using economic, diplomatic, propagandistic, and (if necessary) military means, as well as the establishment of a peaceful and legal international order in which American material and security interests would be protected.

Consensus, however, must also be considered on another level. Consensus and bipartisanship have been used interchangeably in discussing American postwar foreign policy. Yet, it would be a mistake to equate the two concepts. The elementary difference between them lies in who is included in each idea. Whereas consensus consists of a general agreement on fundamental attitudes and ideology between both the executive and legislative branches—an institutional entente—and the normally partisan political parties, bipartisanship simply requires the president to bring responsible members of the opposition party into the making of foreign policy. Bipartisanship does not include the executive-legislative accord, exclusive of party affiliation, that consensus implies. Conversely, consensus cannot develop without bipartisanship. Both the institutional and partisan components must be present to have true consensus.

A consensus on foreign policy did emerge during the first two years following the end of World War II. Anti-communism not only became the holy writ of American foreign policy, but it also crossed partisan and institutional boundaries. One of the central figures in the development of the consensus was Sen. Arthur Vandenberg (R-Michigan). As the principal spokesman for congressional Republicans in matters of foreign policy, and a well-respected member (and later chairman) of the Senate Foreign Relations Committee, he negotiated the terms of Republican support for Truman-administration foreign policy and sought to shape that policy in conformity with both his objectives and those of his party. Yet, he also realized that new postwar geopolitical circumstances required increased American participation in world affairs, both for American interests and for international peace and stability. By involving himself, his party, and Congress in the decisions that would affect the direction of American foreign policy after the World War II, Vandenberg can be considered the architect of consensus.

A convergence of forces and events combined to produce an important shift in American policy. Upon assuming the presidency in April 1945, Truman had initially hoped to continue the policy of cooperation with the Soviet Union that had begun under his predecessor, Franklin D. Roosevelt. Most of Truman's military and foreign-policy advisers, however, urged him to adopt a more uncompromising stance toward Moscow, and over time he became converted to their way of thinking. In addition, increased congressional assertiveness in foreign affairs, prompted by its resentment at having been left out of the loop by Roosevelt during the war; Soviet intransigence in negotiations, particularly over atomic energy; and an aggressive British stance toward Moscow led the administration to take a harder line in its Soviet policy. This policy shift was underscored in February 1946 when Joseph Stalin made his "election" speech. The Soviet leader warned of the potential for war in the future as a result of the contradictions in capitalism and implicitly recognized that the wartime alliance with Washington was no longer viable. Stalin's rhetoric hardened feelings in the United States even further toward the Soviet Union and contributed to the growing sentiment for a more rigid stance.

The new paradigm was articulated in a series of progressive moves toward an overall policy of containment. The first step was the "Long Telegram," written by the chargé d'affaires at the American embassy in Moscow, George F. Kennan, whose eight-thousand-word dispatch became the rationale for much of the Cold War. The Soviets, Kennan wrote, were "a political force committed fanatically to the belief that with [the] U.S. there can be no permanent modus vivendi, that it is desirable and necessary that the internal harmony of our society be broken, if Soviet power is to be secure." The only options available to the United States were to resist communist attempts to overthrow Western institutions and to wait for internal changes within the Soviet Union to produce alterations in Moscow's foreign policy. Kennan's cable prompted a reconsideration of the status quo policy and arrived at an opportune time. As Kennan noted in his memoirs, "Six months earlier this message would probably have been received in the Department of State with raised eyebrows. . . . Six months later, it would probably have sounded redundant, a sort of preaching to the convinced."

Kennan's telegram laid the foundation for a review of American policy. During a staff meeting on 12 July 1946, Truman discussed his growing frustration over Soviet behavior. He complained that the Soviets were trying to chisel away at the Tehran, Yalta, and Potsdam agreements, and if the ongoing Paris conference broke up, he wanted to be ready to reveal what he considered to be the Russian failure to honor agreements. He then instructed White House special counsel Clark Clifford to prepare a report of Soviet violations of international agreements for this purpose. Clifford, a relative newcomer to the White House staff, solicited the assistance of George Elsey, another White House aide, in compiling the memorandum. As they discussed the issue, they decided to recommend to the president an alternative approach. Elsey suggested they use Kennan's analysis of Soviet-American relations as the basis for a comprehensive policy review "to see what *consensus,* if any, existed" within the administration. Truman authorized the revised focus of the project and ordered them to proceed as quickly as possible.

Two months later the Clifford-Elsey report, titled "American Relations with the Soviet Union," reached the president's desk.

Armed then with Truman's authority, they solicited the views of senior officials within the government, including Secretary of State James F. Byrnes, Undersecretary of State Dean Acheson, Secretary of the Navy James V. Forrestal, and Kennan, who had just returned from Moscow. Their inquiries forced policymakers to reformulate and articulate their basic ideas on the nature of American foreign policy, something they might not have otherwise done in a systematic way. The final report—including extensive comments by Kennan in consultation with Elsey—revealed virtually unanimous acceptance of the Long Telegram as the basis for American foreign policy.

Nevertheless, the timing of the report and its contents were critical. Not only did it come halfway (chronologically) between the Long Telegram and the later announcement of the Truman Doctrine (the American policy of providing support to European countries to thwart communist insurgents), but it also made a significant new point. Clifford and Elsey argued that as a matter of national security the United States needed to create an integrated policy and a coherent strategy to resist the Soviet Union. Much of the analysis mirrored Kennan's Long Telegram, but the prescriptive section went further. The memorandum outlined a policy similar to that which Kennan proposed in his "Sources of Soviet Conduct" article in the July 1947 issue of *Foreign Affairs.* Writing as "Mr. X," he detailed the policy of containment. Clifford and Elsey wrote that the primary objective of United States policy was to convince Soviet leaders that it was in the Soviet interest to participate in a system of world cooperation. If the Kremlin did not abandon its aggressive policies, they argued, the United States must assume that the U.S.S.R. might at any time embark on a course of expansion. As a result the United States needed to maintain sufficient military strength to restrain the Soviet Union. As Clifford noted in his memoirs, this was something new. While others had warned of the Soviet threat previously, no one had proposed such a comprehensive American response to the Soviet challenge. The Clifford-Elsey report, and its focus on restraining the Soviet Union, clearly foreshadowed Kennan's containment policy, the Truman Doctrine, and the fundamental propositions of U.S. Cold War strategy as encapsulated in National Security Council memorandum 68 (NSC 68).

Further, the report also carried a special authority because it showed, for the first time, that consensus on Soviet relations among the president's senior policy advisers existed. As Clifford said in his cover letter to Truman,

> I believe that the simultaneous definition by so many government officials of the problem with which we are confronted is in itself a forward step toward its solution. There is remarkable agreement among the officials with whom I have talked and whose reports I have studied concerning the need for a continuous review of our relations with the Soviet Union.

If it served no other purpose, the report provided the president with a clear indication of what senior officials thought about Soviet-American relations—most of whom supported a comprehensive policy of resistance to Soviet expansionism.

Some scholars contend that political controversy and divisive partisan struggles that arose during this period render the claim that consensus existed to be "almost pure fantasy." They argue that the postwar years were characterized by a "bitter, partisan, and utterly consensus-free debate." Admittedly, politics always played a role in the debates over foreign policy during the early years of the Cold War. The actions of Vandenberg did not spring entirely from altruistic motives. He could be as partisan and institutionally biased as any politician, and he certainly wanted Republican ideals imprinted on American foreign policy. Yet, he and other members of Congress willingly sublimated these tendencies to help construct a foreign policy that projected unity and commitment to the rest of the world, particularly toward Moscow. Indeed, even those scholars who argue that politics did not stop "at the water's edge" recognize that a near-consensus in elite opinion existed.

Did critics exist? If so, would they represent evidence to refute the authenticity of this consensus? Recall that consensus does not require full agreement on all of the details of foreign policy. Unilateral reservations, special emphases, as well as actual and potential conflict over ideology could exist within a consensual framework. For example, Senator Robert A. Taft (R-Ohio) believed that the duty of the opposition party was to attack and expose and that when it collaborated in making foreign policy, it failed to discharge its proper role. However, consensus implies neither unanimity nor fixed ideas; unlike pregnancy, consensus is not a dichotomous condition. The agreement on fundamental attitudes and ideology did not preclude honest disagreements over policy and allowed for a measure of partisan bickering. Still, for all of the difficulties inherent in dealing with the cacophony of opinion in a democratic government, the basic tenets of anti-communism remained virtually unchallenged among the policymaking elite. The fear of Soviet expansionism became the catalyst for the anti-communist consensus.

Yet, the argument can be made that consensus existed because no serious dissent existed—or was tolerated—within policymaking circles. Does this imply an artificial consensus? Can consensus be authentic if contrary opinions are either purged or repressed? Certainly challenges to administration policy arose, for in a complex and pluralistic society such as the United States, consensus does not imply an absence of critics. Historian Thomas G. Paterson has argued, however, that most of those who seriously challenged the consensus in Washington "found themselves at the receiving end of calculated distortion and charges ranging from idiocy to conspiracy." Moreover, by 1946 the anti-communist mentality that pervaded Washington had created deep fissures on the political Left, which was the most likely source of dissent. Indeed, the most likely focal point for dissent, former vice president and Secretary of Commerce Henry A. Wallace, had been forced to resign by Truman in September 1946 for publicly disagreeing with the administration's foreign-policy goals and assumptions, which Truman believed were shared by the majority of the American public. By the time the Truman Doctrine was announced in 1947, liberals were either unwilling to support any organization that openly accepted communist membership or were nervous about being labeled procommunist. This attitude further restricted contrarian ideas from surfacing. The negative connotations associated with communism during this period not only marginalized critics of the emerging consensus but, perhaps more importantly, led to the activities of Senator Joseph R. McCarthy (R-Wisconsin) and the House Un-American Activities Committee. Magnification of the Soviet threat, combined with the tendency to reduce foreign policy to a simple black-and-white issue, helped to create the anti-communist consensus. Concurrently those who subscribed to the shared mind-set grew increasingly uncomfortable with conflict both within and outside policymaking circles.

The foreign-policy consensus did allow for debate over the means of implementation of various policies, within the broad framework of anti-communism. That fact tended to limit the locus of feasible options. Policy statements made by Truman and his surrogates were designed to preclude change, rather than adapt to it, and to maintain a united front against the Soviet Union. As agreement on fundamental attitudes and ideology emerged, the nature of the foreign policy debate changed. Certainly discussion would continue over issues of specific policy implementation. What ceased to exist, however, was the debate over the underlying ideological outlook—the ends. The assumptions that shaped the foreign-policy goals of the administration were continually reaffirmed.

It is clear that the consensus was, to a degree, artificial. Yet, it would be a mistake to totally disregard the authenticity and sincerity of the agreement between both the institutional and partisan components of government. A real sense of anxiety about the Kremlin's intransigence at the conference table and their apparent desire to expand militarily, territorially, and ideologically helped to create the anti-communist mentality. However, perhaps the most important catalyst for consensus among the decision makers of 1945–1947 was their pervasive fear of history repeating itself. The use of historical analogies in dealing with the foreign-policy issues of the postwar period helped to shape the nature and direction of debate and policymaking in Washington. Truman, Vandenberg, and other members of the foreign-policy elite had lived through and experienced the dashed hopes of the League of Nations in 1919–1920 and the appeasement of Adolf Hitler in the 1930s. These men feared that if the United States lacked a strong policy toward the Soviet Union, backed by some sort of international organization that promoted peace, the hard-fought victory in World War II could easily give way under the assault from another totalitarian regime. This fear of Soviet expansionism, represented by historical analogy to Versailles and Munich, solidified and broadened the anti-communist consensus and allowed a coherent Cold War strategy to emerge between 1945 and 1947.

In March 1947 Truman announced American support for anti-communist activities in Greece and Turkey in a speech before Congress. The Truman Doctrine represents a landmark in American history. Not only did it publicly redefine his administration's view of the geopolitical situation, but it also led to a global military commitment by the United States and greatly augmented presidential power. In addition, it solidified the broad American consensus on the need to fight the Cold War aggressively. The support the proposal received in Congress represented a high point of the postwar consensus so painstakingly constructed by Vandenberg, Truman, and others. Although a response to a specific problem, the Truman Doctrine derived from thinking that existed in relatively specific form as early as the summer of 1946, as exemplified by the Clifford-Elsey memorandum. Historian Melvyn Leffler correctly points out that by this time,

> there was general agreement in the United States that the Kremlin was an ideological enemy with no legitimate fears or grievances. Most people were willing to follow the administration in the direction that it wanted to lead. So long as the Truman administration practiced containment and deterrence, so long as it rejected a policy of reassurance and accommodation, it could do pretty much as it liked. The Cold War had begun.

The Truman Doctrine served to bring into focus a general attitude that was sufficiently widespread in both parties and the executive and legislative branches of government to facilitate the emergence of consensus. In the years to come, however, foreign-policy consensus would not continue unchallenged. The "loss" of China in 1949 and dissension over American policy in Asia severely tested and virtually destroyed consensus. The Eisenhower administration revived consensus—notably with its use of joint resolutions granting the president authority in crisis situations—but even this respite proved temporary. Disagreements over American actions in Latin America, the Caribbean, and other regions eroded support for consensus in the long term. Ultimately the war in Vietnam would shatter the remaining fragments of foreign-policy consensus. The American strategy of containing the Soviet Union and communism remained unchanged during the period from 1945 to 1965. What did change was the coalition of institutional and partisan forces that supported that strategy. Nevertheless, consensus did emerge during the early years of the Cold War. It resulted in large measure from both a pervasive fear of Soviet expansionism and from a recognition that the United States, because of its preponderant military and economic power, had a dominant role to play in international politics.

—ANDREW L. JOHNS, UNIVERSITY OF CALIFORNIA, SANTA BARBARA

Viewpoint:
No, any notion of bipartisanship in the face of a perceived Soviet threat was undermined by clear ideological differences between political leaders in America.

Bipartisanship, a term frequently used by certain members of Congress and the Truman administration in the late 1940s to describe a united approach toward questions of foreign policy, masked deep divisions in the United States concerning America's postwar role in the world. It is often argued that there was some sort of anti-communist consensus as the Soviet Union undertook a policy of geopolitical expansion in Eastern Europe. While it is possible to argue that such a consensus existed on a superficial level, Americans were by no means united over the practical direction of U.S. foreign policy. Political groups saw foreign-policy debates in the same ideological terms as they did domestic issues, and ideological warfare over the aims and methods of American policy overseas would persist as a perennial source of political conflict. The Cold War altered the dynamics of debates over foreign affairs but did not create any sort of sustainable consensus.

It is true that some American politicians attempted to build consensus in certain areas of foreign policy. The Roosevelt and Truman administrations were mindful of the internecine battles over foreign affairs that had characterized the period leading up to the early 1940s and were determined that the hands of the executive branch not be tied again in the same manner. Thus, during the creation of the United Nations and the building of the postwar political settlement among nations, the Democratic administration in Washington was careful to include members of both main political parties, and various factions therein, in the negotiations. A foreign-policy elite grew out of this decision. Senators Arthur Vandenberg (R-Michigan), Tom Connally (D-Texas), Howard Alexander Smith (R-New Jersey), and Henry Cabot Lodge Jr. (R-Massachusetts) were examples of this group, and Truman also consulted House members, governors, and foreign-policy advisors to the administration, such as John Foster Dulles. What joined people of different political persuasions together was the realization of the threat of Soviet foreign policy to American interests after 1945, and the idea that noncommunist countries, notably in western Europe, were essential allies in containing Soviet expansion. Phrases such as bipartisanship and politics "stopping at the water's edge" were commonly used in debates in Congress and in private memos to Truman from his foreign-policy advisors. The growth of a professional congressional staff in the wake of the Congressional Reorganization Act of 1946 encouraged this trend. Francis O. Wilcox, the first chief of staff of the Senate Foreign Relations Committee in 1947, argued in an interview, "I think there was a consensus in our country about what we needed to do in the world." When one sees the consultation process between the branches of government over policies such as the Truman Doctrine and Marshall Plan, which provided financial assistance to European countries for postwar economic development, it is easy to see where notions of consensus originate.

To argue from this, however, that American foreign policy was somehow free of conflict in the 1940s is to ignore vast sections of the American political scene, not to mention the electoral influences that shaped that political activity. Isolationism, the idea that America should not undertake any diplomatic or military activity outside its own borders, was certainly moribund after the experience of the recent world war. Discord over the nature of the new internationalism certainly was not. Truman's foreign policy was by its very nature linked to a particular domestic ideology, provoking dissent from American political figures on both the Right and the Left. As Michael Hogan has argued convincingly, the Marshall Plan was conceived around liberal principles of government intervention in the economy and free trade between nations. The Truman Doctrine assumed that whatever governments existed in Greece and Turkey, they were far superior to any administration formed by communist guerrillas. The program of interim aid to Italy, Austria, and France in late 1947, as well as the loan of $3.75 billion to Great Britain in 1946, assumed that the governments of those nations required American financial assistance not only for their own economic well-being but also for reasons of American security. All these foreign-policy projects had a direct impact on the domestic-political scene.

In the Republican Party, which had won a majority in the eightieth Congress, there was considerable concern that overseas programs could have an adverse effect on their domestic political agenda. Partisanship over questions of foreign policy was made all but inevitable by the fact that the political elite was exactly that: an elite, from which many on the political Right felt excluded. A young Congressman named Richard M. Nixon (R-California) confronted administration loyalist Representative Lawrence Brooks Hays (D-Arkansas) in July 1947 on this issue, arguing that bipartisanship could only be meaningful if it was "bipartisan in its inception and creation as well as in its execution." How could it be if the policy was at odds with stated Republican goals? Many Republicans saw lavish foreign-spending programs as inconsistent with promises to the electorate of reduced spending, tax cuts, and the demobilization of U.S. forces abroad. The war had not only cost the United States billions of dollars but also raised the tax burden to its highest level in history and had forced the encroachment of government into the affairs of the body social in ways not envisaged even by the New Deal. An assertive response to the specter of the Cold War would possibly crush any hopes Republicans had of a return to their antistatist principles of government.

Senator George Wilson Malone (R-Nevada), at a dinner of the Colorado Mining Congress in Denver in February 1948, announced that the "so-called Marshall Plan is the most amazingly brazen and preposterous scheme . . . that has yet been proposed, even by the socialistic European governments, to level our living standard down to their own." During debate on the Marshall Plan in the Senate, a group of senators led by Homer Earl Capehart (R-Indiana) attempted to rewrite the bill to make it conform to Republican ideological standards. Capehart proposed an international Reconstruction and Finance Corporation, like the one created by President Herbert Hoover during the Great Depression, to reflate the U.S. economy without direct governmental control which would handle international aid. Capehart argued that this scheme would use "American means[,] . . . the free enterprise system. . . . Let us not imitate state socialism and communism in fighting Mr. Stalin." Many on the political Right also expressed unease at the administration's sponsorship of undemocratic governments, such as those of Greece and Spain. The Republicans succeeded in challenging an integral part of the administration program in 1948. Congress changed the original 1934 Reciprocal Trade Act to override the program when any American industries were threatened by foreign imports. It was simply impossible to divorce foreign policy from domestic ideology in the 1940s, and this fact resulted in serious divisions within the federal government over how to lead as a great superpower. Although most of the old isolationists, such as Senators Henrik Shipstead (R-Minnesota) and Burton K. Wheeler (D-Montana), had departed from the political scene by 1947, a majority of Republicans still argued that political power was useless if it could not be exercised in domestic policy and, by extension, foreign policy.

The political Right was not alone in expressing serious reservations about the direction of American foreign policy. In 1948 Henry A. Wallace, Truman's former Commerce Secretary and, prior to that, Franklin D. Roosevelt's vice president from 1941 to 1945, challenged Truman for the presidency on a Progressive Party platform. Wallace represented the most progressive face of the New Deal, was deeply committed to governmental

THE TRUMAN DOCTRINE

Harry S Truman's proposal to underwrite the defense of Greece and Turkey was viewed as the global equivalent of the Monroe Doctrine. (Moscow, meanwhile, held it to be an open threat to Soviet expansion.) Truman requested $400 million in aid to both countries and in his address to a joint session of Congress delineated the reasons behind his proposal. In order to convey the urgency of the situation to the Republican majority in both houses, he made an impassioned plea, describing the situation as one of democracy versus tyranny.

One of the primary objectives of the foreign policy of the United States is the creation of conditions in which we and other nations will be able to work out a way of life free from coercion. This was a fundamental issue in the war with Germany and Japan. Our victory was won over countries which sought to impose their will, and their way of life, upon other nations. . . .

I believe that it must be the policy of the United States to support free peoples who are resisting attempted subjugation by armed minorities or by outside pressures.

I believe that we must assist free peoples to work out their own destinies in their own way.

I believe that our help should be primarily through economic and financial aid which is essential to economic stability and orderly political processes. . . .

The seeds of totalitarian regimes are nurtured by misery and want. They spread and grow in the evil soil of poverty and strife. They reach their full growth when the hope of a people for a better life has died. We must keep that hope alive. The free peoples of the world look to us for support in maintaining their freedoms.

If we falter in our leadership, we may endanger the peace of the world—and we shall surely endanger the welfare of this nation.

Great responsibilities have been placed upon us by the swift movement of events. I am confident that the Congress will face these responsibilities squarely.

Source: Documents of American History, *2 volumes, edited by Henry Steele Commager (New York: Appleton-Century-Crofts, 1973), II: 525–528.*

action to improve social conditions, and was one of a large number on the Left increasingly critical of America's role in establishing the Cold War. Other notable members of this group were Senators Claude D. Pepper (D-Florida), Glen H. Taylor (D-Idaho), and economist Rexford G. Tugwell, a former member of Roosevelt's "Brain Trust" and now professor at the University of Chicago. Their opposition to the course of American foreign policy after 1945 stemmed from their collective experience of foreign policy under Roosevelt. FDR had brought the U.S.S.R. into the diplomatic arena during the war; and he had assumed Russia would form an important part of the world geopolitical settlement after the cessation of hostilities; he had gone to great lengths to convince Joseph Stalin that his country would be safe from further invasion if he would help create a lasting peace. There had never been any doubt in Roosevelt's mind that the Soviet Union was a communist country and that its people lacked certain basic liberties. For the sake of peace and cooperation among nations, however, that had to be overlooked. Contrary to popular belief, Roosevelt was not a utopian in foreign affairs; rather, he was a pragmatist where Russia was concerned. Breaking off effective communication with a powerful state such as the Soviet Union would only make a viable world settlement less likely. The progressive group, led by Wallace, simply continued this line after Roosevelt's successor had long since abandoned it.

Whether Roosevelt himself would have continued his policy of attempting to find common ground with Stalin will never be known. However, Wallace took up this refrain in spectacular style in September 1946 in a speech at Madison Square Garden: he argued that America's aggressive approach to the Soviet Union was an invitation to war and that America had to take the lead in establishing a foreign policy in which there would be no favorites and no implacable foes. He joined other progressives in condemning the inconsistency of U.S. foreign policy, supporting as it did British imperialism and fascist dictatorships while attacking the Soviet equivalent. Truman's response to this challenge to the notion of consensus was to fire Wallace. Interestingly enough, many on the Right shared some of Wallace's concerns, particularly those about supporting imperialism. Where the Left deviated entirely from the rest of educated political opinion was in its priorities in foreign policy. To the progressive left, the great enemy in 1945 was Nazism, not communism. Germany was still seen by the Left as a far more likely cause of any future international conflagration than the Soviet Union. In a 1946 Senate speech, Pepper vociferously condemned the sudden desire by the administration to rehabilitate Germany, an ideal shared by many Republicans who had always seen the Soviet Union as more dangerous than Germany. Pepper's speech came only two years after Treasury Secretary Henry Morgenthau had put forward the Morgenthau Plan to de-industrialize Germany after the war; not all in the Democratic Party had abandoned the worries and concerns of that time. Taylor, who in 1948 was

Wallace's running mate, wrote to Harold Ickes, fellow progressive from the Roosevelt years, in November 1947 that he had planned a ride on horseback from coast to coast to protest Truman's foreign policy, a ride that had to be somewhat shortened by time constraints. Taylor wrote that "this country should refrain from baiting Russia both domestically and abroad at every opportunity. . . . I believe that Communism and free enterprise capitalism can exist in the same world." This statement again suggests the link between domestic ideology and foreign policy: the political Left could always see some possibility of redemption for the Soviet system. The stance would cause them much trouble at the hands of the violently anti-communist mainstream of American society. Wallace was trounced in the 1948 presidential race; Pepper and Taylor were deposed from the Senate in 1950 by anticommunist elements of their own party; and Helen Gahagan Douglas (D-California) was defeated in her bid for the Senate by Nixon, who successfully tied her liberalism to communism. Nevertheless, the concerns of this group are vital to an understanding of the dynamics of foreign policy debates in this period.

Even if in a general sense anticommunism was an all-embracing mantra in the United States in the late 1940s and early 1950s, this did not mean that a commitment to the general principle would translate into an interest in foreign affairs. It is extremely important when discussing consensus to differentiate between domestic anti-communism and a commitment to an anti-communist foreign policy. It would be a mistake to argue that the most prominent examples of anti-communist zealots in the United States, such as Senators Joseph R. McCarthy (R-Wisconsin) and Karl Mundt (R-South Dakota) and Rep. John E. Rankin (D-Mississippi), were just as assiduous in supporting the waging of cold war as in ferreting out subversives. Domestic anti-communism was for the most part simply another example of the merging of ideology and domestic politics; the American right was committed to liberty and freedom in its own eyes, and so any deviation from social norms as defined by the Right was liable for labeling and control. McCarthy represented not an aspect of the consensus on foreign policy but rather a political desire by one group to make their political and social credo representative of the entire nation. As McCarthy argued: "When I talk about fighting Communists, I don't mean fighting Communism. . . . You can condemn Communism in general terms, in the Acheson manner with a lace handkerchief, a silk glove, and a Harvard accent if you please. But you can't fight Communists in that fashion." This attack on the elite appearance of Secretary of State Dean Acheson in June 1950 hardly suggests much accord on U.S. foreign policy; there was no agreement between the administration and the McCarthyites over what American society should look like, let alone the rest of the world.

Any consensus that may have been reached over foreign policy in the 1940s was shattered, in any case, by events in Asia in 1949 and 1950. The idea that the administration had let China "fall" into the hands of the communists by its policy of concentrating entirely on Europe and entrusting its Far Eastern policy to leftist sympathizers almost allowed a rare moment of unity for the Republican Party. Finding someone in the House or Senate to espouse this line was not difficult. Many in the president's own party shared Republican misgivings over the trends in U.S. foreign policy after the Yalta Agreement of 1945. The Asia debate is important because it had the contradictory effect of pushing the Republican party further toward the bellicose internationalism that would later characterize the majority of its membership while at the same time heightening the sense that any bipartisanship that had ever existed was now dead. The Korean War demonstrated this dilemma well. In the 1952 campaign both candidates, Republican Dwight D. Eisenhower and Democrat Adlai Stevenson, supported American action in the Far East but assailed each other for belonging to the party that had led to the extensive American casualties there. The Democrats were accused of losing Asia by refusing to support the Nationalist leader Chiang Kai-shek, and the Republicans, in failing to support the administration efforts, had talked about China without taking any action to support their words. Far from marking a new high point in bipartisan relations, the dawn of the 1950s saw a new low in inter-party agreement on foreign affairs, a trial run of the bitter ideological divisions that characterized American politics in the 1960s.

In the wake of World War II, American politicians had to decide how they would relate the changed domestic conditions of postwar America to the American electorate. At the same time, a coherent American response to events overseas had to be forged. The overlapping of these two concerns precluded any real consensus-based approach to any policy, overseas or domestic. In the final analysis, foreign-policy debates formed an important forum in which struggles over the nature of America as defined by differing ideologies were played out. The broad term anti-communism was certainly a consensus builder in this period, even for many on the progressive left who wanted no part of a Marxist dictatorship, but the actual policies that were pursued, and the goals defined, would rarely engender anything other than discord. Such a realization helps to put into perspective any notion of a singular American interest in world affairs.

–JONATHAN BELL, UNIVERSITY OF CAMBRIDGE AND UNIVERSITY OF MARYLAND, COLLEGE PARK

References

Gabriel A. Almond, *The American People and Foreign Policy* (New York: Harcourt, Brace, 1950);

Barton J. Bernstein and Allen J. Matusow, eds., *The Truman Administration: A Documentary History* (New York: Harper & Row, 1966);

Howard Bliss and M. Glen Johnson, *Beyond the Water's Edge: America's Foreign Policies* (Philadelphia: Lippincott, 1975);

Clark Clifford, *Counsel to the President: A Memoir* (New York: Random House, 1991);

I. M. Destler, Leslie H. Gelb, and Anthony Lake, *Our Own Worst Enemy: The Unmaking of American Foreign Policy* (New York: Simon & Schuster, 1984);

Justus D. Doenecke, *Not to the Swift: The Old Isolationists in the Cold War Era* (Lewisburg, Pa.: Bucknell University Press, 1979);

John Lewis Gaddis, *Strategies of Containment: A Critical Appraisal of Postwar American National Security Policy* (New York: Oxford University Press, 1982);

Gaddis, *The United States and the Origins of the Cold War, 1941–1947* (New York: Columbia University Press, 1972);

Thomas Michael Hill, "Senator Arthur H. Vandenberg, the Politics of Bipartisanship, and the Origins of the Anti-Soviet Consensus, 1941–1946," *World Affairs,* 138 (1975–1976): 219–241;

Jerome L. Himmelstein, *To the Right: The Transformation of American Conservatism* (Berkeley: University of California Press, 1990);

Michael J. Hogan, *The Marshall Plan: America, Britain, and the Reconstruction of Western Europe, 1947–1952* (Cambridge: Cambridge University Press, 1987);

Michael H. Hunt, *Ideology and U.S. Foreign Policy* (New Haven: Yale University Press, 1987);

George F. Kennan, *Memoirs,* 2 volumes (Boston: Little, Brown, 1967–1972);

Kennan, as "X," "The Sources of Soviet Conduct," *Foreign Affairs,* 25 (July 1947): 566–582;

David R. Kepley, *Collapse of the Middle Way: Senate Republicans and the Bipartisan Foreign Policy, 1948–1952* (New York: Greenwood Press, 1988);

Melvyn P. Leffler, *A Preponderance of Power: National Security, the Truman Administration, and the Cold War* (Stanford, Cal.: Stanford University Press, 1992);

George Wilson Malone, *Mainline* (New Canaan, Conn.: Long House, 1958);

Thomas J. McCormick, *America's Half-Century: United States Foreign Policy in the Cold War and After,* second edition (Baltimore: Johns Hopkins University Press, 1995);

Richard E. Neustadt and Ernest R. May, *Thinking in Time: The Uses of History for Decision Makers* (New York: Free Press; London: Collier-Macmillan, 1986);

Thomas G. Paterson, *Meeting the Communist Threat: Truman to Reagan* (New York: Oxford University Press, 1988);

Paterson, ed., *Cold War Critics: Alternatives to American Foreign Policy in the Truman Years* (Chicago: Quadrangle Books, 1971);

Robert A. Taft, *A Foreign Policy for Americans* (Garden City, N.Y.: Doubleday, 1951);

Adam B. Ulam, *The Rivals: America and Russia Since World War II* (New York: Viking, 1971);

U.S. Department of State, *Foreign Relations of the United States,* volume b, *Eastern Europe; The Soviet Union* (Washington, D.C.: U.S. Government Printing Office, 1969);

John Kenneth White, *Still Seeing Red: How the Cold War Shapes the New American Politics* (Boulder, Col.: Westview Press, 1997).

ROCK AND ROLL

Was rock-and-roll music a spontaneous eruption of youth culture or a contrived marketing ploy?

Viewpoint: Rock and roll is an American art form that broke down social barriers and liberated a generation.

Viewpoint: Rock and roll was a mass-marketing tool whose main purpose was to profit record companies and radio stations from the income of the baby-boom generation.

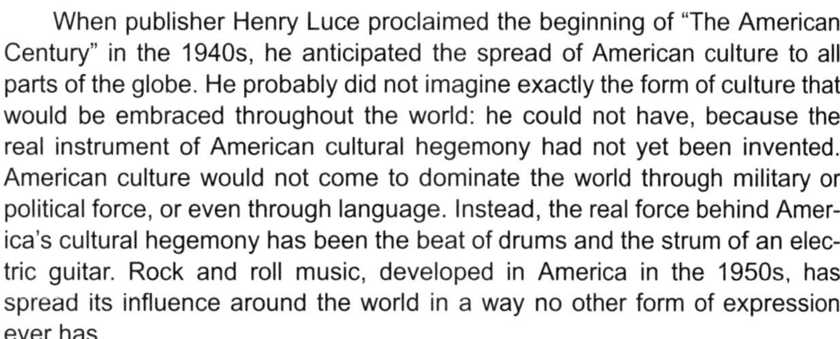

When publisher Henry Luce proclaimed the beginning of "The American Century" in the 1940s, he anticipated the spread of American culture to all parts of the globe. He probably did not imagine exactly the form of culture that would be embraced throughout the world: he could not have, because the real instrument of American cultural hegemony had not yet been invented. American culture would not come to dominate the world through military or political force, or even through language. Instead, the real force behind America's cultural hegemony has been the beat of drums and the strum of an electric guitar. Rock and roll music, developed in America in the 1950s, has spread its influence around the world in a way no other form of expression ever has.

How and why was rock and roll so successful? In these essays two different explanations are given. In the first, social critic Lonna Douglass, a fan of rock and roll, argues that the music presented a way of liberation for young people in the 1950s and 1960s, and its underlying, sometimes unspoken, message continues to resonate throughout the world. In the second, historian Robert J. Allison argues that from its inception rock and roll was a carefully contrived scam by recording and radio executives to make profits. Douglass's argument is that rock and roll came about because a public demanded it; Allison suggests rock and roll was foisted upon them in one of the most successful mass-marketing campaigns ever conceived.

Which is the truth? Which is the better explanation for the phenomenon of rock and roll, or have these two scholars missed the point? In writing about elusive feelings or sensations, scholars are at a disadvantage. These are phenomena best captured by artists. Once an historian can get a handle on a feeling, it has usually vanished. Why did rock and roll flourish? It is like asking why people fall in love. Yet, to understand the history of our time, we must investigate what people were thinking and how their ideas were shaped. Certainly rock and roll music played a part in this era. Yet, was it a cause for the 1960s revolution, as Douglass would suggest? Or is it more of a piece with the general trend toward American consumerism and cultural imperialism, as Allison argues? How did ordinary men and women react to this new sound in the 1950s? How do people react to the same songs today? What do these songs tell people about the world in which they were made? What will a person's favorite song tell their grandchildren about their world and life?

Viewpoint: Rock and roll is an American art form that broke down social barriers and liberated a generation.

Rock and roll is a quintessentially American art form. Not only does it incorporate musical influences and traditions from all who have become American, but it also speaks to the American sense of youth and freedom. For these reasons it has endured longer at the forefront of American culture than any other musical style.

One Saturday afternoon in July 1953, Elvis Presley went to the Memphis Recording Service to make a record as a gift for his mother. Marion Keisker, the receptionist, tried to calm down the nervous young man before he took his turn in the studio. When she asked why he was visiting the studio, he said he was a singer. She asked what kind of songs he sang, and he replied, "I sing all kinds." "Who do you sound like?" she asked. Elvis responded: "I don't sound like nobody."

He was right. Elvis Presley had grown up singing in the Assembly of God Church but sought spiritual and musical solace in Memphis's black churches as well. He also heard the popular music of the day, ballads sung by Dean Martin and Frank Sinatra, and the two songs he sang that afternoon in Memphis had been recorded by the black a cappella group, the Ink Spots. The rest, as they say, is history—Presley's seemingly effortless embodiment of these varied musical forms made him a sensation, accomplishing what record producer Sam Phillips had thought an impossible dream. "If I could find a white man who had the Negro sound and the Negro feel, I could make a billion dollars."

American music in 1953 was almost as rigidly segregated as other aspects of American life. Though jazz had broken down many barriers, it was the white stars—Tommy Dorsey, Glenn Miller, and Benny Goodman—who made hits, not black artists, such as Duke Ellington and Count Basie. Though Goodman had integrated his orchestra, the color line still cut through American music. The *Billboard* charts that tracked sales of records and sheet music were separated into classifications that included "Race" and "Folk"—in the 1940s the two labels meant songs popular among African Americans or those popular among whites—though "Race" later was changed to "Rhythm and Blues," and "Folk" to "Country and Western."

Elvis transcended the color line, erasing the barrier between white and black. Other young whites more self-consciously tried to cross the color line, as Jerry Lieber, the son of Jewish immigrants, recalled, "Actually, I think we wanted to be black. Black people had a better time." Lieber joined with fellow alienated white youth Mike Stoller to write songs embodying what they thought were the free and unrestrained ideals of the black community, such as "Kansas City," first recorded by Little Willie Littlefield and later by Richard "Little Richard" Penniman, and "Hound Dog," which, sung by Willie Mae "Big Mama" Thornton, became a No. 1 song on the rhythm-and-blues charts. Lieber and Stoller wrote these songs not because they hoped to get rich (both were radical members of a Marxist commune in Los Angeles), but because they saw music as a revolutionary force.

Though Elvis seemed to defy politics, the fact of his singing African-American songs was a potentially revolutionary act. Rock and roll, as concerned adults who saw the movie *Blackboard Jungle* (1955) understood, had the potential to undermine American society. The music forced a change in attitudes and blasted away hypocrisy. For the young people listening, rock and roll offered liberation and an end to the stultifying sameness of American society. For adults it posed a challenge to the foundations of the social order. The term *rock and roll* came from the black vernacular for sex, and when Wynonie Harris first sang "Have you heard the news? There's good rockin' tonight!" (1948), everyone knew what he meant. That the term later was taken to mean "a good time" owes to its slang origins. Without having to take a political stand, the music by itself was a rebuke to an uptight and puritanical American society. This music, by being loud and different, as well as by being performed by artists with brightly colored Fender electric guitars or outlandish costumes, also made a statement. Little Richard made a career with his flamboyant style and noticed that the more outrageous he acted, the whiter his audience became. Black audiences did not respond to his song "Tutti Frutti" the way white audiences did.

Music as a political force was nothing new. In the 1930s Woodrow "Woody" Guthrie and Huddie "Leadbelly" Ledbetter sang political songs, and in the 1948 election Pete Seeger and the Weavers offered lyrical support to Henry Wallace's presidential campaign. But the rock-and-roll craze offered something a bit different—a music that in itself was a form of rebellion. In the 1960s the "folk revival" spawned many protest singers—including Bob Dylan, Buffy St. Marie, Phil Ochs, and Tom Paxton. Though all self-consciously drew inspiration from the radical songbook of Guthrie and the career of the Weavers, they were also influenced by the rock-and-roll sound of the 1950s. Part of the folk mystique of the 1960s was a rejection of the vapid

Cover of the first LP (1956) by one of rock and roll's most influential performers

complacency of rock and roll, but still it acknowledged the potential power of the medium. Ochs declared that if there was any hope for revolution in America, it was in having Elvis become an Ernesto "Che" Guevara (the Argentinian revolutionary). Disappointed that Elvis refused to do this, Ochs appeared at a Carnegie Hall concert dressed in a gold lamé suit and sang songs made popular by Elvis, Buddy Holly, and Conway Twitty.

Dylan's revolutionary nature was both more successful and more subtle. Hailed by the folk community as its purest writer, Dylan had been deeply influenced by the blues, rhythm and blues, and rock and roll (he had been in a rock-and-roll band during his high school days in Minnesota). Though Dylan shocked the folk world in July 1965 by performing with an electric band at the Newport Folk Festival, he had already met with the Beatles during their American tour (he introduced them to marijuana), and his musical and personal influence helped shape their *Rubber Soul* album. Dylan was more of a protest singer than Elvis would ever dream of being but also more of an artist than any other musician of the 1960s. Dylan's music brought together the disparate elements of the American canon, and his lyrics are of alienation and despair, intermingled with ironic hope.

Unlike jazz or classical music, rock and roll did not require technical proficiency. Instead, it was about self-expression and the dream that anyone could succeed. Spontaneity and naturalness were its hallmarks, though both were accomplished with great technological effort. The recording studio was essential to the success of rock and roll, and perhaps the revolution would not have been possible without it. As Andy Warhol put it in the 1960s, "The Pop idea was that anybody could do anything, so naturally we are all trying to do it all." People were looking for new sounds and sensations, and rock and roll offered both. One could be a performer and a participant—concerts and musical festivals were opportunities for the audience, as well as the performers, to express themselves. In fact, John Lennon and Paul McCartney noted they could not hear each other during their concerts, drowned out as they were by the audience's screams. The idea of a concert was not just to enjoy the music, as one would at a jazz or symphony concert, but to feel a part of something. Dancing was no longer a connection between two people, but an effort of thousands of individuals acting and moving together. Rock and roll changed the music and dance experience and by its influence transformed society.

Rock and roll has been a tremendous liberating force. It is, as Walt Whitman might have said, our barbaric yawp above the rooftops of the world. Even though its moment of triumph—when the Beatles arrived in February 1964 and took America by storm—suggests a foreign influence (it was called the "British invasion" as the Beatles were followed by such bands as the Rolling Stones and the Who), the music itself began here. The Beatles filled out their repertoire with what by 1964 were rock-and-roll standards—"Kansas City," "Matchbox," "Twist and Shout," "A Taste of Honey,"—and the Rolling Stones were billed as playing "unrepressed rhythm and blues." The Beatles took their name from Holly's group, The Crickets, and the Rolling Stones took their moniker from a Muddy Waters song. The music connected young people throughout the world, and as the generation that created it matured, the music has grown along with them. Rock and roll was a force of liberation: in Czechoslovakia the resistance to communist rule called itself the "Velvet Underground," an homage to Lou Reed's 1960s group, and an underground Czech rock group called itself the "Plastic People," after a Frank Zappa song. While the words might not be translatable, the feeling certainly was—as surely as the feeling of Ludwig van Beethoven's symphonies unites all hearts in freedom.

At the same time as it has been a unifying force, rock and roll has also offered a paradoxical sense of detachment. Irony and alienation have been central to its message, and these have prevented rock and roll from being used for totalitarian ends the way Beethoven and Richard Wagner were used by the Nazis. Implicit in rock and roll is a distrust of authority and an insistence on trusting in instinct and nature. "Don't follow leaders," Dylan sang, and told his listeners that "propaganda all is phony." The Rolling Stones's "Sympathy for the Devil" points to the evil within all ("I shouted out 'Who killed the Kennedys?' When after all it was you and me"). This ironic detachment, the posturing or attitude, has fed into other rock-and-roll trends, such as punk, which reject all received wisdom and authoritarian control.

Rock and roll is a complex and sophisticated medium. It can be interpreted on many levels; it drew its influence from many sources. In addition to its subversive influence, origins in black and white vernacular culture, and achievements in the 1960s, the most important cultural contribution of rock and roll may have been to make people sing, in the words of James Brown, "I feel good!"

—LONNA DOUGLASS, BOSTON, MASSACHUSETTS

Viewpoint: Rock and roll was a mass-marketing tool whose main purpose was to profit record companies and radio stations from the income of the baby-boom generation.

No music form in history has been as contrived or promoted as rock and roll. Presented to a gullible public as rebellious free expression, rock and roll from its inception has been the creation of studio engineers, radio stations, and record company executives with the single aim of making money. Dick Clark, who made a career for himself as host of the television show *American Bandstand* (which premiered on 5 August 1957) noted that "The music industry is the only business . . . where a man can invest less than $500 and profit by as much as $50,000 to $100,000 for a single record." With profits like this, it is no wonder that businessmen lined up to invest.

Why was there so much to be made in the business? One can speculate on three possible causes for the boom. During the Great Depression in the 1930s and World War II in the early 1940s, Americans had fewer children. After the war, from 1946 until about 1960, years of prosperity and the promise of wealth, there was a tremendous increase in the annual birthrate. This situation meant that from the late 1950s until the early 1970s, at least, there would be large numbers of teenagers and adolescents in the American population. During the 1950s the problems of adolescents and teenagers became the focus of much debate and public discussion.

What was not discussed was that most teenagers actually had a great deal of discretionary income. In 1956 *Scholastic* magazine reported that thirteen million American teenagers had $7 billion to spend every year. Unlike their parents, who had learned the lesson of hard times in the 1930s, these teenagers had known only prosperity and had no worries that banks might fail or the economy might collapse. They could spend freely, and records became the purchase of choice. *Billboard,* the trade paper of the music industry, reported in 1956 that more money was being spent on records than at any other time in history.

This discretionary spending marked a change in the music business, a change driven by technology. Before the war, records were relatively expensive and cumbersome. Heavy wax plates, which would spin at 78 revolutions per minute (rpm), could only hold one song or one movement of a symphony. The brevity of most recordings was a good thing, as the phonograph had developed before widespread use of electricity, and early phonographs had to be cranked by hand. A person who had purchased a Victrola in 1900 could still use the same equipment to listen to recordings in 1945. But after World War II two important technological changes made the Victrola obsolete: the development of vinyl meant that records could be produced more cheaply and mass marketed more successfully; and less expensive turntables and records meant more people would have access to phonograph equipment. Also, the inventions of the 45 rpm and 33 rpm record players had a significant impact on the recording industry.

Before World War II, the music industry had not been too interested in selling recordings. Instead, it concentrated on publishing sheet music for Americans who played musical instruments. While radio provided an alternative form of entertainment, it still only complemented the entertainment of people in their homes. They could hear a song on the radio, buy the sheet music, and then play it for themselves. The radio, too, featured live programming, including variety shows modeled on vaudeville, which would feature singers or musicians performing popular songs. The song was important, not the singer; one would likely hear many different arrangements or interpretations of a song, rather than a single version identified closely with a particular voice. In their own homes Americans could then interpret the song for themselves or merely sing it to be entertained.

The record industry changed this perception of entertainment, and rock and roll ultimately demolished any inkling of creativity. Americans, able to buy all the records they could possibly listen to, had no need to play any instruments for themselves, and by the 1980s most American schools no longer offered music instruction. For live musical entertainment, American rock-and-roll audiences have two major choices: either pay a tremendous amount of money to go to a large arena with tens of thousands of others to see and hear a famous band giving a faithful, note-by-note rendition of its hits, or, for the more adventurous, go to a small

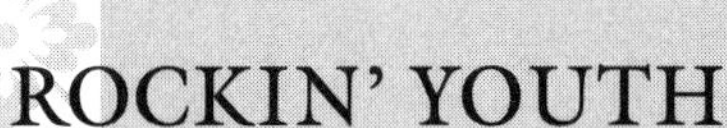

ROCKIN' YOUTH

Gertrude Samuels, a staff writer for The New York Times *in the late 1950s, wrote this article on rock and roll. As a parent and a student of music trends, she voiced some concerns over the behavior associated with the new brand of music.*

. . . For some understanding of the rock 'n' roll behavior which has aroused a great deal of controversy, at least in adult circles, one must go to the sources.

An important source, of course, is the music itself. Technically, rock 'n' roll derives from the blues. But rock 'n' roll is an extension of what was known as Rhythm and Blues, a music of the Thirties and Forties that aimed primarily at the Negro market; that music emphasized the second and fourth beats of each measure. Rock 'n' roll exploits this same heavy beat—by making it heavier, lustier and transforming it into what has become known as The Big Beat. It is a tense, monotone beat that often gives rock 'n'roll music a jungle-like persistence. . . .

Another rich field for research is found among the children themselves. They come from all economic classes and neighborhoods, sometimes lone-wolfing it, but mostly with their pals, dates, clubs and gangs. Outside the theatre they seem to become one class—rocking the neighborhood with wild and emotional behavior as they break through the wooden police barriers to improve their positions in line or fight toward the box office and their heroes inside. . . .

Enthusiasm, hysteria, misguided hero worship? On one thing all experts agree: rock 'n'roll will surely be with us for a while longer. For apprehensive adults who think nothing as alarming as The Big Beat has ever existed, there may be comfort in a college joke of some years back. An Englishman, watching some contorting American dancers in fascination and disbelief, turned to his friend, murmuring, 'I say, old boy, they get married afterwards, don't they?'

And that was in the foxtrot and shimmy days, long before rock 'n' roll appeared, amid commotion, on the scene.

Source: *Gertrude Samuels, "Why They Rock 'n' Roll—And Should They?,"* New York Times, *12 January 1958.*

club and hear a local band "paying tribute" to the more famous band, giving a faithful, note-by-note rendition of its hits. Blues singer Billie Holiday once said that she could not perform the same song the same way twice. If she could, she said, she was not sure what it would be, but she was sure it would not be music.

The change in the nature of popular music came about through the economic and technological innovations of the late 1940s and 1950s. Radio in the 1930s and 1940s featured programs, not programming. On a given day one could hear a variety of programs and musical styles on a radio frequency. Classical music and jazz had become the real centerpieces of American radio, though listeners could also hear other genres. *Billboard* kept track of the sales of recordings and sheet music and every week published a chart showing how many copies, in print or on record, of various songs had been sold. The chart was divided into categories: Classical, Jazz, Popular, Folk, and Race. In 1949 *Billboard* changed the last two categories to Country and Western and Rhythm and Blues.

When television developed in the late 1940s, the large networks, NBC, CBS, and ABC, devoted less time and energy to their radio stations and also removed from radio the soap operas, dramatic programs, and comedies that had given real diversity to the airwaves. Music and news were left, and most radio stations continued offering a variety of music. In Omaha, Nebraska, station KOWH consistently finished dead last in listener surveys, drawing about 5 percent of the local listening audience. A small audience meant meager advertising revenues, and a diminished budget meant the station was hard-pressed to increase its audience. The station hired two consultants to improve its market share. The two men, Todd Stortz and Bill Stewart, repaired to a local tavern to discuss the station's dilemma. As they sat and drank, they noticed a curious phenomenon on the jukebox. Though patrons had a wide variety of choices, they continually selected only one song. It happened to be one of *Billboard*'s most popular songs of the week, and the patrons individually chose to hear it again and again. Even the waitress, after most of the customers had left, would stoke the jukebox to hear the song one more time. Further study over subsequent weeks, as the popular song changed, revealed that this sample audience preferred hearing one or two songs repeated endlessly to being offered a variety.

Top 40 radio was born as a result. KOWH, instead of offering many different programs with varied genres of music, supplied its audience *Billboard*'s Top 40 songs and repeated them over and over. From less than 5 percent of the Omaha market, KOWH soon attracted 44 percent of local listeners; its revenues grew and its format was eagerly copied throughout the nation. The format has obvious advantages to radio stations as businesses. Previously, a station would have to hire disc jockeys who knew something about music, whose job it was to put together programs appealing to listeners. Stations also had to acquire large record libraries in many different genres or have disc jockeys with big collections of records. Now the station only needed the top forty songs in a given month, which it could repeat endlessly. The disc jockey's role changed, from being an emcee to being a personality, spinning out a set list of popular tunes, controlled by the station executives, but using various sound effects and gimmicks to create what one rock-and-roll historian calls a "carefully contrived atmosphere of frenzy." Record companies, of course, were only too happy to provide records to stations, knowing the broadcast would encourage listeners to buy the record so they could hear it at home. Owning a record became a mark of status among teenagers, who had a great deal of disposable income.

Could the radio stations and record companies have mass marketed another musical genre in the same way? Why rock and roll? Part of the answer to the first question is "Yes," as among the singers of top hits in the 1960s were Dean Martin, Frank Sinatra, and Louis Armstrong (jazz singers of an earlier era); Belgian nun Sister Luc-Gabrielle, who recorded under the name Soeur Sourire, or Sister Smile (her song "Dominique," spent four weeks at No. 1 and twelve weeks on chart, from November 1963 to January 1964); and Republican Senator Everett Dirksen (his "Gallant Men" spent three weeks on the *Billboard* chart in January 1967). Yet, to become a rock-and-roll star, one did not need to serve the kind of apprenticeship that Martin, Sinatra, or Armstrong had or that was necessary in virtually any other kind of music. One needed a publicity machine. When Beatles' manager Brian Epstein arranged his group's first American tour, he was concerned that American fans would not whip themselves into the same kind of frenzy that British audiences had, creating the phenomenon of "Beatlemania." Epstein cleverly hired fans to storm the airport on the Beatles' arrival in February 1964 and create the impression of mass hysteria. If the passion would not happen spontaneously, it could be created artificially. The phenomenon itself came as a surprise to the musicians, who conceded they were rather modestly talented, or as George Harrison put it, "We're rather crummy musicians." Paul McCartney added, "We can't sing; we can't do anything, but we're having a great laugh." The success of this foursome of modestly talented but presentable young men inspired television executives to create *The Monkees* program in 1966, in which four young men who answered an advertisement in *Variety* were used to create a show based on the life and adventures of a musical group.

Why rock and roll? Why not rhythm and blues or country and western, or traditional pop songs? Was there something different about this form of music that made it appealing to such a mass audience? Rock and roll was a musical hybrid, blending the aforementioned musical forms and incorporating other genres. Sam Phillips, whose Sun Records in Memphis recorded local blues artists B.B. King and Chester "Howlin' Wolf" Burnett and sent their songs to national distributors of "race" records, often said, "If I could find a white man who had the Negro sound and the Negro feel, I could make a billion dollars." Elvis Presley accomplished this for Sun Records. Part of rock and roll's appeal is its bridging of this cultural gap.

A more important facet of its success must be its tapping into a youth market, as opposed to a racial market. Rock and roll appealed to teenagers by presenting itself as a form of rebellion. Symptomatic of this was the movie *Blackboard Jungle*, released in 1955, showing juvenile delinquents turning "a school into a jungle!" The film opens with a man in a suit approaching a schoolyard full of juvenile delinquents, while blaring from the sound system is Bill Haley's "Rock around the Clock." The film joined images of youthful nihilistic rebellion with Haley's song, and theaters around the world were trashed by young audiences eagerly embracing the chance to rebel. *Blackboard Jungle* touched off an international debate about youthful disorders, but more importantly for its makers it sold a lot of records. Tapping into this market, Hollywood produced a sequel, *Rock Around the Clock* (1956), featuring more music by Haley and disc jockey Alan Freed, who sanctimoniously argued that rock and roll was really harmless. This was followed by another sequel, *Don't Knock the Rock* (1956), featuring, among others, Little Richard. These films were targeted at a teenage audience, as *Variety* noted in a headline: "Film Future: GI Baby Boom."

By presenting teenagers with something they could buy that symbolized their own rebellion, mass marketers performed an amazing feat. Millions of copies of the same album or 45 rpm record would be purchased by individuals who each thought it made them distinct or rebellious. Yet, by doing something that everyone else was doing, teenagers were also reassured that they were fitting in. Rock and roll performed this function of allowing youth to rebel and conform at the same time, beginning in the 1950s. Some features of rock and roll, which connoisseurs criticized–its being driven by a record industry hungry for profits, its mindlessness and banality, and its crass commercialism–were present at the start. Chet Helms, an organizer of the 1967 Monterey International Pop Festival, a crowning moment for rock and roll as a countercultural phenomenon, commented that "There are only three significant pieces of data in the world today. The first is, God died last year and was obited by the press. The second is, fifty percent of the population is or will be under twenty-five. . . . The third is that they got twenty billion irresponsible dollars to spend."

While perhaps the fifty thousand or so fans who came to hear the Grateful Dead, Janis Joplin, and Jimi Hendrix at Monterey tuned in more to the first of these three points and saw themselves and their music as somehow creating a substitute for the faith of their fathers, points two and three were clearly in the minds of record-company executives who had come to the San Francisco area not to, as the song said, wear flowers in their hair, but to sign up hot new acts. Executives from Columbia attended and signed Big Brother and the Holding Company; Warner Brothers came to see its new acquisition, the Grateful Dead; and Atlantic saw Monterey as a good venue to increase Otis Redding's visibility. The revolution, to paraphrase Gil Scot-Heron, would not be televised, but that would only increase the value of recording rights.

Occasionally, a real artist can both transcend the mindless commercialism of the medium, succeeding both on the artist's and the industry's terms–one thinks of Stevie Wonder, Diana Ross, Bruce Springsteen, or Bob Dylan–but these are exceptions. Rock and roll began as a commercial venture, meant to tap into a ready market. Unlike virtually every other form of music ever created, its purpose was not to inspire or even entertain, but to make money. Far from being a symptom of rebelliousness, it has instead been the most mainstream and American of ventures.

–ROBERT J. ALLISON,
SUFFOLK UNIVERSITY

References

Marc Eliot, *Death of a Rebel* (Garden City, N.Y.: Anchor, 1979);

James Miller, *Flowers in the Dustbin: The Rise of Rock and Roll, 1947–1977* (New York: Simon & Schuster, 1999);

Michael Schumacher, *There but for Fortune: The Life of Phil Ochs* (New York: Hyperion, 1996);

Robert Shelton, *No Direction Home: The Life and Music of Bob Dylan* (New York: Beech Tree Books, 1986);

Joel Whitburn, *The Billboard Book of Top 40 Hits* (New York: Billboard Books, 1992).

ROE V. WADE

Was the Supreme Court *Roe* v. *Wade* decision the correct one?

Viewpoint: The *Roe* v. *Wade* decision protected the rights of women to have control over their own bodies.

Viewpoint: *Roe* v. *Wade* ignored the fundamental fact that abortion kills the innocent.

No political question has been more violently debated than the legality of abortion. Proponents of opposing views cannot even agree on the terms of debate: those opposed to abortion maintain that they are pro-life, while their opponents maintain they are pro-choice. No one wants to be against either life or choice. Yet, this debate forces men and women either to favor life and deny an individual woman's freedom of choice, or to favor choice and deny the state's responsibility to protect life.

History is not neutral. One must, as Abraham Lincoln said of the debate over slavery, be on one side or the other. In one essay legal scholar Heidi Jo Blair-Esteves and attorney Alexander M. Esteves examine the history of both *Roe* v. *Wade* and subsequent Supreme Court decisions emanating from it. They agree with the Court that the right to choose is protected by the U.S. Constitution. However, Margaret Carroll-Bergman, an independent scholar and writer, takes a fundamentally different view, arguing that *Roe* v. *Wade* was not a victory for liberty but a violation of liberty.

Who is right? It may be too early for history to judge the full consequences of *Roe* v. *Wade,* but time and conscience do not allow one to suspend judgment and await history's verdict.

Viewpoint: The *Roe* v. *Wade* decision protected the rights of women to have control over their own bodies.

Seldom, if ever, has a single U.S. Supreme Court decision so decisively transformed American constitutional history or altered the relationship between law and morals, both public and private, than the decision in *Roe* v. *Wade* (1973). *Roe* legitimized what had previously been almost universally condemned: the practice of abortion. The Supreme Court, by a seven-to-two vote, struck down all state laws that restricted a woman's right to an abortion during the first trimester of pregnancy and granted to the states only very limited regulatory rights during the second trimester (the state must have a compelling interest in order to infringe upon a woman's right to an abortion during the second trimester). This decision was heralded by an editorial in *The New York Times* as "a major contribution to the preservation of individual liberties." The euphoria was short-lived, however, as the religious right and other abortion opponents quickly mobilized to overturn *Roe* or, at least, limit its impact.

Although illegal in the nineteenth century, the numbers of abortions increased dramatically by century's end. The makeup of women seeking abortions also changed from primarily single, poor black women to rich, married, white women. In addition, unlike many present-day arguments, the debate on abortion was more about the health and safety of the mother than about morality. Supported by the American Medical Association (AMA) after the Civil War, about forty state legislatures passed antiabortion laws that remained on the books until the 1960s. At this time new views on individual freedom and equality, as well as civil rights, and particularly the activism of feminists, helped influence the medical profession, state legislatures, and popular consciousness to repeal abortion laws in many states.

Roe v. *Wade* was based on persuasive precedent, opinion, and the root of the Supreme Court's decision that abortion is a fundamental right established within the meaning of the Constitution. In *Roe* the Court debated a challenge to a Texas antiabortion statute. Although the Court held that a fetus is not a "person" under the Fourteenth Amendment and thus is not protected thereby, it declared the statute unconstitutional on the grounds that it did not strike the proper balance between the mother's protected right to privacy and the state's interests. The Fourteenth Amendment defines a person as being protected by the Equal Protection Clause against discriminatory state action. Furthermore, the amendment provides that all persons born or naturalized in the United States, and subject to the jurisdiction thereof, are citizens of the United States and of the state wherein they reside.

The Court prohibited any antiabortion statutes that were aimed at stopping procedures carried out in the first trimester and permitted restrictions on abortions sought during pregnancies in the third trimester. Statutes dealing with the second trimester had to be carefully drafted so that any infringements on the mother's rights had to demonstrate compelling state interests.

The penultimate justification for the *Roe* opinion, which galvanized the seven members of the Court, was that the right to privacy be given a constitutional foundation in a major opinion. Essentially the Court determined that the "Constitution does not explicitly mention any right of privacy . . . [but] the Court has recognized that a right of personal privacy, or a guarantee of certain areas or zones of privacy, does exist under the Constitution. . . . These decisions make it clear that only personal rights that can be deemed 'fundamental' or 'implicit in the concept of ordered liberty' are included in this guaranty of personal privacy." The Court found that the underpinnings of the right to privacy were anchored in the Constitution and based their decision on the Equal Protection Clause of the Fourteenth Amendment. The clause prohibits a state from denying to any person within its jurisdiction the equal protection of the law. According to Sylvia Law, in a *University of Pennsylvania Law Review* article, "sex equality concerns are implicated when laws outlawing abortion impose upon women burdens of unwanted pregnancy that men do not bear."

The Court, however, had no delusions about the tenuous foundation upon which one of the ingredients of *Roe* rested, namely the issue of "viability." In one of Justice Harry Andrew Blackmun's initial drafts of the *Roe* opinion, states would be prohibited from regulating abortions until the third trimester, that period when the fetus becomes viable. Justice William Joseph Brennan Jr. spotted the weakness in this argument after the draft had been circulated to the various chambers and suggested that the linkage between state intervention and viability was risky. Indeed, Blackmun himself acknowledged that advances in medical technology increased the chances that fetuses would become viable sooner after conception than was then possible and that improvements in medicine could undermine the linchpin of the opinion. Other critics of Blackmun's draft maintained that the rights of women had been relegated to a backseat role behind those of the doctor and state. Subsequent opinions of the Court underscored the fragile viability basis for *Roe* and its collision course with technology, while others have focused on the fetus's rights (for example, the right to life) and the role that the doctor and state play in the abortion process.

Roe did not sanction abortion "by demand," as many of its critics maintain. In fact, Chief Justice Warren Earl Burger's concurring opinion stated that, "Plainly, the Court today rejects any claim that the Constitution requires abortion on demand." In addition, Blackmun carefully articulated that privacy, not abortion, was a "fundamental right." In any event, as with other fundamental rights, they were subject to regulation on proof of "compelling state interest."

This concept meant that a state could seek to regulate abortion by insisting that any rights that a woman might have are overridden by the need to save human lives. Under the Fourteenth Amendment, laws that impinge on protected personal rights will be sustained only if they are suitably tailored to serve a "compelling state interest." Once it is shown that a law impinges upon a right, the burden is on the state to demonstrate that its interest is "compelling," leaving the Court to resolve the issue of whether the interest supersedes that right.

Demonstrators outside the U.S. Supreme Court in 1973

(Betty Lane)

Arguably, due process and equality are preserved even when a fundamental right is impinged upon or a disadvantaged group is discriminated against, so long as a compelling state interest is shown. Although *Roe* may have had its weaknesses, the Court correctly concluded that Texas had not met its burden in showing a compelling state interest.

Millions of abortions have been performed since *Roe* was decided, and the United States ranks third in the world in the number of abortions carried out. There has also been a reduction of morbidity and mortality rates among women. Undoubtedly the Court's decision has resulted in the prevention of many unwanted births and the legalization of abortion has also improved the techniques used. Some advocates also fear that if *Roe* is overturned, U.S. society will revert to the period when "back-alley abortions" were performed, as they often were from the Civil War to the 1960s.

Therefore, state regulations that have a purportedly valid, independent purpose–that incidentally make it more difficult or expensive for a woman to obtain an abortion–are not necessarily considered unconstitutional. An example is *Planned Parenthood of Missouri* v. *Danforth* (1976), requiring preabortion and physician counseling, a twenty-four-hour delay after preabortion consultations, and accurate record keeping. However, the state may not require that all midstage abortions be performed in a hospital, as decided in *Akron* v. *Akron Center for Reproductive Health* (1983), nor may the state require spousal consent or notification. The Court also precluded parents from vetoing a minor's seeking an abortion in *Bellotti* v. *Baird* (1979), by creating the so-called judicial bypass; thus, statutes containing such a provision have been deemed constitutional.

Postviability abortions, except those that endanger the mother's health, may require that two physicians be present–one for the woman and the other for the fetus, on the chance that the fetus may be delivered alive. But the viability of the fetus must be left to the attending physician. Equally important, *Colautti* v. *Franklin* (1979) held that the state cannot question a physician's decision that the health of a woman requires that she have an abortion nor decide whether a particular fetus is viable. However, the state may require a physician to conduct viability tests on the fetus, as decided in *Webster* v. *Reproductive Health Services* (1989), but may not dictate an abortion procedure that is less dangerous to the fetus but more dangerous to the mother. Thus the *Roe* decision does not confer the right of a woman to have an abortion; rather, that the state may not unduly interfere with a woman's decision in that regard before the fetus becomes viable. Oddly, the government's refusal to fund abortions, even medically necessary ones, is not unconstitutional, nor is the government under a duty to provide abortion counseling.

In *Planned Parenthood of Southeastern Pennsylvania* v. *Casey* (1992), a bare majority reaffirmed *Roe* as it applied to the interests concerning the health of the mother, the potential new life, and the interests of third parties. However, *Casey* overturned the unstable trimester framework by holding that the state had an important interest in potential life throughout a pregnancy, which undervalued the woman's right to decide when she could have an abortion. Thus, post-*Casey* decisions posed the essential question of whether the woman's decision to abort was overshadowed by the state imposing an "undue burden" on the abortion process. *Casey* replaced the trimester framework with a "strict scrutiny" standard of review. In other words, a state may regulate abortions only to the extent that "its purpose and effect [does not] place a substantial obstacle in the path of a woman seeking an abortion before the fetus retains 'viability,'" striking down a Pennsylvania statute imposing spousal notification prior to abortion.

Unsatisfied with the fact that women can still have abortions, some antiabortion activists have turned to more-violent protests. The Freedom of Access to Clinic Entrances (FACE) Act has not stopped antiabortion terrorism or the accompanying bloodletting. Dr. David Gunn was murdered on 10 March 1993 by "right-to-life" activist Michael Griffin. On 29 July 1994, Paul J. Hill used a twelve-gauge shotgun to kill Dr. John Bayard Britton and his volunteer driver, retired U.S. Air Force lieutenant colonel James H. Barrett, outside a Pensacola, Florida, abortion clinic. Barrett's wife was also wounded in the incident. Subsequent to these murders, John C. Salvi III killed two receptionists and wounded five others at separate abortion clinics in Brookline, Massachusetts. Thereafter, the American Coalition of Life Activists (ACLA) distributed a "hit list" of twelve abortion doctors which it labeled the "Deadly Dozen."

In response to this senseless carnage the Supreme Court upheld in *National Organization for Women* v. *Joseph Scheidler* (1994) the right of pro-choice groups to use the federal Racketeering Influenced Corrupt Organization (RICO) statute to pursue civil damages. In addition, FACE legislation empowered pro-choice groups with both criminal and civil sanctions against violent opponents. President William J. Clinton also forced states to abide by newly liberalized federal statutory language by providing for Medicaid coverage of abortions occasioned by rape or incest.

Despite these actions to protect women seeking abortions, operators acknowledge that antiabortion protesters were less of an impediment to services than the "profusion of regulatory obstacles thrown up by right-to-life dominated legislatures" in an increasing number of states. Essentially, segregation and ostracization of abortion services away from hospitals and into freestanding clinics has resulted in the virtual disappearance of organized medicine from the "front ranks of the abortion rights movement." This dilemma notwithstanding, the medical profession's ambivalence about abortion may be significantly altered once RU-486–a birth control pill approved in France–becomes fully available in the United States. The advent of syringe-administered techniques for early "surgical" abortions may also hasten the shift toward early abortions, even without the universal availability of RU-486.

Undoubtedly, the abortion debate is far from over. Antiabortion activists continue to step up their campaign throughout the country. To deny that there will always be a conflict between those in favor and those opposed to abortion seems not only naive but disingenuous. The abortion issue has been a critical issue for many voters in local and national elections for more than twenty years. Many Christian evangelists and their followers have contributed to the realignment of the social and political landscape by using the abortion issue since the 1980s. Financial support to pro-life Republicans is sizable, and in an age of weak campaign-finance laws and television sound bites, the religious right was a major source of the Republican reclamation of Congress in 1992.

Despite the physical siege of violent demonstrators, American courts have drawn clear lines on the limits of antiabortion protests and excessively restrictive state statutes. The election of pro-choice Clinton as president in 1992 and his subsequent appointments of Ruth Bader Ginsberg, a feminist judge, and Stephen G. Breyer to the Supreme Court has temporarily receded the threat to *Roe*. Moreover, the Supreme Court's steadfast commitment to its holding in *Casey*, as well as Congress's willingness to provide safeguards for women seeking abortions and enact new laws to combat domestic terrorism, accurately reflect the strength and stability of American public opinion concerning abortion and hence its continued viability into the next millennium.

–ALEXANDER M. ESTEVES, NEW ENGLAND SCHOOL OF LAW; HEIDI JO BLAIR-ESTEVES, UNIVERSITY OF MASSACHUSETTS, BOSTON

Viewpoint: *Roe* v. *Wade* ignored the fundamental fact that abortion kills the innocent.

Roe v. *Wade*, the 1973 Supreme Court decision to legalize abortion, was a knee-jerk reaction to the feminist era that heralded in a new code of sexual conduct–one that even feminists themselves came to reject when they saw that sexual liberation chiefly benefited men. In the last twenty-six years there has occurred great social change, advancements in medical technology, and a crime called "feticide"–the murder of the unborn–giving way to thinking that further underscores the barbaric and medieval nature of abortion. While it is America's contraception of "choice," it remains at the end of a long list of poor choices for women.

In the mid 1970s, at the height of the sexual revolution, a woman would rather be held up at gunpoint than find herself alone, unwed, and pregnant. There was no "choice" in a society where "good girls don't" get pregnant. The sexual revolution may have been in full swing, yet unwed motherhood was the last social taboo: a woman usually had to drop out of school, leave town, or marry someone she did not love. In the 1970s middle-class Americans were still hotly debating whether married women, let alone teenage girls, should use contraception. In the 1980s teenage pregnancy was on the rise; inner-city problems of the late 1970s, such as alcohol and drug abuse, burst into the suburbs; and not only was birth control taught in health class, but some public schools had birth-control clinics and onsite nurseries. Not to teach birth control was considered backward and inhumane. Abstinence was outdated: it was a fact of life that teens would use drugs, drink alcohol, and get pregnant. Abstinence is now taught in public schools again and is strongly encouraged by the church and media. Young adults are urged to remain virgins; if they decide to have sexual relations they are reminded to be responsible and practice "safe" sex. The new morality was the answer to problems created by the old morality. The sexual revolution of the 1970s ushered in an unprecedented teenage-pregnancy rate and widespread sexually transmitted diseases, including acquired immunodeficiency syndrome (AIDS). Many people learned that unplanned sex could result in AIDS, and the disease killed thousands of men, women, and babies. The new canon preaches that it is un-American and socially irresponsible not to use a condom while having sex. For the first time, the onus of "birth control," albeit under the name of "safe sex," is placed squarely on the shoulders of both men and women. It took a plague spread by a sexual disease–a medical and social emergency–for Americans to rethink their attitudes about sex.

In *Roe* v. *Wade* the Supreme Court was faced with new realities–women were entering the workforce and demanding equal rights. The country was not ready to give women equal rights or equal access to power. (As the end of the century approaches, women still do not receive equal pay for equal work; there is no government-sponsored day care; the Equal Rights Amendment failed; and there never has been a female president of the United States.) The Supreme Court invented a theoretical right to privacy–interpreted as the right to exercise control over one's body (as well as a bogus right to sexual privacy)–in an effort to appease a splinter group of abortion-rights activists. "Right or wrong, *Roe* v. *Wade* had all the effect of a law without emerging from the popular consensus that ought to go into a law," wrote abortion-issues expert Roger Rosenblatt in *Life Itself: Abortion in the American Mind* (1992). "I do not think I am alone among liberals in feeling that one of the troubles wrought by *Roe* v. *Wade* was the misidentification of abortion as purely a rights issue."

So shaky was the Court's interpretation of the word *liberty* to include the right to destroy human fetuses, that Justice William H. Rehnquist, in his dissenting *Roe* v. *Wade* opinion, wrote, "To reach its result the Court necessarily has had to find within the scope of the Fourteenth Amendment a right that was apparently completely unknown to the drafters of the Amendment." While the Court was granting a new constitutional right to exercise "control over one's body," another segment of the population, eighteen-year-old boys, was being drafted and sent to fight in the Vietnam War. Society has certain expectations: young men will go to war and return either alive, maimed, or dead; a mother will not willingly kill her unborn. In a democratic society everyone does their part for the greater good.

The idea of having control over one's body is new. "The right to abort, we are told, inheres in 'liberty' because it is among 'a person's most basic decisions'. . . it involves a 'most intimate and personal choice,'" wrote Justice Anton Scalia in his 1992 *Planned Parenthood of Southeastern Pennsylvania* v. *Casey* decision. "The same adjectives can be applied to many forms of conduct that this Court has held are not entitled to constitutional protection–because, like abortion, they are forms of conduct that have been long criminalized in American society. Those adjectives might be applied, for example, to homosexual sodomy, polygamy, adult incest, and suicide, all of which are equally 'intimate' and 'deeply personal' decisions involving 'personal autonomy and bodily integrity.'"

Many abortion-rights activists believe morality cannot be legislated and that changing the law will not end abortion. "What is forgotten, however, is that law is the great teacher," wrote Catholic archbishop John O'Connor. "Children grow up believing that if a practice is legal, it must be moral." At one time slavery was legal in the United States and African Americans were thought to be less-than-fully human. The economic integrity of the South depended on slavery. It took the Civil War and a constitutional amendment to end slavery and this, immoral treatment of African Americans. "Slavery was no less intrinsically wrong when it was legal and widespread than it is to us today," wrote pro-life activist Nancy E. Myers. "And, so it is with abortion. Killing another human being . . . has always been, and will always be wrong."

There are two problems with abortion. First, the woman who considers an abortion is a friend, roommate, boss, wife, sister, or neighbor to someone. She finds herself in a desperate, untenable situation where it seems the only solution is to have an abortion. Second, no matter how much one empathizes with her, abortion is not a "choice"; it is the killing of an unborn human life. Since it is immoral to own another human being and to act as if some humans are not fully human because it serves some economic purpose, abortion runs contrary to democratic principles, which protect equality and human life. "Most Americans are both for the choice of abortion as a principle and against abortion itself–for themselves," wrote Rosenblatt. Therefore Americans know instinctively that abortion is wrong and have structured the debate from a painful one of preservation of life to one of a woman's choice.

Many feminists view abortion as a non-choice. "We should protect the women who are being victimized because they are the accepters of abortion. What I cannot bear is to have access to an invasive procedure to end a pregnancy . . . be presented to women as a privilege for which they should be grateful," said feminist Germaine Greer. "Abortion functions as an equalizer," claims feminist Kathy Rudy in *Beyond Pro-Life and Pro-Choice: Moral Diversity in the Abortion Debate* (1996), "The choice women face today is to be like men and not be pregnant or to be unlike men and be pregnant. The idea that pregnant women might desire more choices than 'being pregnant' and 'not being pregnant' such as adequate child care or larger systems of kinship in which the cost and burden of raising a child is spread among many is beyond the limits of the liberal imagination."

When *Roe* v. *Wade* made women's reproductive issues a private matter, the decision dismantled church and community services that helped women "choose" to have a baby. Before 1973 choice meant adoption: adoptive parents chose to have a child. After 1973 "choice" meant abortion. "By the mid 1970s, a significant number of feminists began to assert that having sex with more men more often only forced more women to go to clinics more frequently," wrote Rudy. "Any woman who is truly liberated would never need an abortion."

Prior to *Roe* v. *Wade* abortion was not illegal in this country. Most of the fifty states had statutes that permitted a physician to make the medical decision to perform an abortion when the mother's physical or mental health was in jeopardy. To most people these situations would include the cases of pregnancy resulting from rape or incest. *Roe* v. *Wade* went beyond the parameters of mother's health and allowed for abortions if the child was "unwanted for anyone or more of a variety of reasons–convenience, family planning, economics, dislike of children, the embarrassment of illegitimacy . . . for any reason or for no reason at all . . . any woman is entitled to an abortion," contended Justice Byron R. White in his opinion.

THE MAJORITY OPINION

Justice Harry Andrew Blackmun helped write the majority opinion for Roe v. Wade *in 1973. In it, he expressed the need to resolve the abortion issue by "constitutional measurement free of emotion and of predilection."*

. . . This right of privacy, whether it be founded in the Fourteenth Amendment's concept of personal liberty and restrictions upon state action, as we feel it is, or, as the District Court determined, in the Ninth Amendment's reservation of the rights to the people, is broad enough to encompass a woman's decision whether or not to terminate her pregnancy. The detriment that the State would impose on the pregnant woman by denying this choice altogether is apparent. Specific and direct harm medically diagnosable even in early pregnancy may be involved. Maternity, or additional offspring, may force upon the woman a distressful life and future. Psychological harm may be imminent. Mental and physical health may be taxed by child care. There is also the distress, for all concerned, associated with the unwanted child, and there is the problem of bringing a child into a family already unable, psychologically and otherwise, to care for it. In other cases, as in this one, the additional difficulties and continuing stigma of unwed motherhood may be involved. . . .

On the basis of elements such as these, appellants and some *amici* argue that the woman's right is absolute and that she is entitled to terminate her pregnancy at whatever time, in whatever way, and for whatever reason she alone chooses. With this we do not agree. . . . [A] state may properly assert important interests in safeguarding health, in maintaining medical standards, and in protecting potential life. At some point in pregnancy, these respective interests become sufficiently compelling to sustain regulation of the factors that govern the abortion decision. The privacy right involved, therefore, cannot be said to be absolute. . . .

We therefore conclude that the right of personal privacy includes the abortion decision, but that this right is not unqualified and must be considered against important state interest in regulation. . . .

Source: Documents of American History, *2 volumes, edited by Henry Steele Commager (New York: Appleton-Century-Crofts, 1973), II: 798–801.*

Roe v. *Wade* broke down pregnancy into three stages or trimesters. Before 1973 life was considered to begin at the moment of conception. Either a woman was pregnant or she was not. There were no degrees of pregnancy: no one was a "little" pregnant, as no one person is a "little" dead. The life the mother was carrying was small, but growing. The Court ruled that as long as the unborn baby was not viable, that is, it could not live outside the mother's womb, it was okay to abort. "To pick any moment other than that of conception as the starting point of human life is artificial and arbitrary," wrote legal historian John T. Noonan Jr. in *The Morality of Abortion* (1970). According to the landmark decision, any abortion in the first three months was at the sole discretion of the woman, who did not have to consult her partner.

However, abortion on demand does occur well into the fourth month of pregnancy. Women over the age of thirty-five are often encouraged by their doctors to undergo the invasive procedure of amniocentesis, in which a needle is stuck into the womb to extract amniotic fluid to determine if the child will be mentally or physically handicapped. Down's syndrome, Turner's syndrome, Tay-Sachs disease, and sickle-cell anemia are tested for during the eighteenth to twentieth week of pregnancy. Although advancements have been made in teaching children with Down's syndrome (most learn to read, go on to college, get jobs, and live on their own), it is considered a mother's duty to abort if she is carrying a Down's syndrome child. Before 1973 mothers accepted whatever child they got, regardless of intelligence or physical abilities.

Advancements in medical science, such as 3-D ultrasound, give people a miraculous window on the womb. DNA research since *Roe* v. *Wade* shows that "biological man is the product of the forty-six chromosomes that combine to confer a unique entity at the time the egg is fertilized by a sperm," according to Landrum B. Shettles, pioneer of in vitro fertilization. He argues that, "I accept what is biologically manifest–that human life commences at the time of conception." Recent research performed in England and Germany on fetal pain reveals that the fetus has a heightened sense of pain and feels it in the womb more deeply than an older baby. In vitro fertilization, test-tube babies, surrogate mothers, custody battles over frozen embryos, and the long, almost two-year wait to adopt babies, are all reproductive issues born after *Roe* v. *Wade*. There are simply not enough babies to go around: couples often go through heroic measures to conceive or to adopt, contradicting what was considered true in 1973.

As society shifts away from accepting the *Roe* v. *Wade* decision, a growing field of criminal prosecution has emerged. "Feticide" treats third-party abortions (performed by others than the mother) as a homicide, crime punishable by a life sentence in some states. Almost half of the U.S. states have feticide statutes. Minnesota's statute protects the fetus from conception and has gradations for degrees of murder, manslaughter, and assault. In Massachusetts feticide laws also protect the nonviable fetus, as does California, where the law applies from seven weeks of conception. In addition to these laws, fourteen states have a twenty-four-hour waiting period before an abortion can be performed, except in pregnancies resulting from rape and incest. The intent of the law is to allow time to provide women with information about alternatives to abortion to ensure they give voluntary consent for the procedure.

Perhaps the most dramatic turnaround in the post-*Roe* era is that of Jane Roe (Norma McCorvey). McCorvey had been approached at an adoption agency by two lawyers who wanted to test the Texas abortion law in the 1970s. In 1995 McCorvey converted to Catholicism, regrets her role in the Supreme Court's decision to legalize abortion, and now works for a pro-life organization.

–MARGARET CARROLL-BERGMAN,
PROVINCETOWN, MASSACHUSETTS

References

Edward L. Barrett Jr., William Cohen, and Jonathan D. Varat, *Constitutional Law: Cases and Materials*, eighth edition (Westbury, New York: Foundation Press, 1991);

Charles P. Cozic and Stacey L. Tripp, eds., *Abortion: Opposing Viewpoints* (San Diego: Greenhaven Press, 1991);

David J. Garrow, *Liberty and Sexuality: The Right to Privacy and the Making of Roe v. Wade*, revised edition (Berkeley: University of California Press, 1994);

Sylvia Law, "Rethinking Sex and the Constitution," *University of Pennsylvania Law Review*, 132 (1984): 955–1016;

James C. Mohr, *Abortion in America: The Origins of and Evolution of National Policy, 1800–1900* (New York: Oxford University Press, 1978);

John T. Noonan Jr., ed., *The Morality of Abortion: Legal and Historical Perspectives* (Cambridge, Mass.: Harvard University Press, 1970);

Roger Rosenblatt, *Life Itself: Abortion in the American Mind* (New York: Random House, 1992);

Kathy Rudy, *Beyond Pro-Life and Pro-Choice: Moral Diversity in the Abortion Debate* (Boston: Beacon, 1996);

Miriam Schneir, "Jane Roe v. Henry Wade" in *Feminism in Our Time: The Essential Writings, World War II to the Present*, edited by Schneir (New York: Vintage, 1994);

Bob Woodward and Scott Armstrong, *The Brethren: Inside the Supreme Court* (New York: Simon & Schuster, 1979).

ROSENBERGS

Were Julius and Ethel Rosenberg guilty or innocent of spying, and should they have been executed?

Viewpoint: The Rosenbergs were rightfully convicted of passing nuclear secrets to the Soviets, a capital offense.

Viewpoint: The Rosenbergs were executed because they refused to cooperate with the government and inform on other spies.

Were Ethel and Julius Rosenberg guilty of passing atomic secrets to the Soviet Union, or were they victims of anti-Communist hysteria and anti-Semitism? The Rosenberg's fate, their trial and execution, divided Americans at the time and for years afterward.

In these two essays, scholars Margaret Mary Barrett and Elizabeth D. Schafer evalutate the Rosenbergs, asking essentially if Julius and Ethel Rosenberg were guilty as charged. Barrett argues that the U.S. government prosecuted the Rosenbergs during the height of the McCarthy period because the two refused to name other Communists involved in their circle. This was the standard leftist interpretation of the Rosenberg case at the time and since. Schafer, on the other hand, argues that the Rosenbergs were spies for the Soviet Union and that they were rightfully convicted of treason.

What evidence does each scholar present to inform her decision? Is there room here for reasonable doubt? In any historical debate, we must ask these questions, as carefully as if we were in a court of law. Unlike a courtroom, historians do not always deal with real people, but have the luxury of working with abstract concepts and issues. The Rosenberg case reminds us that history is made by men and women, and in order to understand history, we cannot forget this fact.

Viewpoint: The Rosenbergs were rightfully convicted of passing nuclear secrets to the Soviets, a capital offense.

On 29 March 1951 a U.S. District Court jury found Julius and Ethel Rosenberg guilty of violating the 1917 Espionage Act. During the trial the federal prosecutor outlined how the couple had conspired to commit espionage, and witnesses substantiated his evidence. The Rosenbergs were charged with providing information and sketches of classified U.S. defense technology, primarily of aeronautics, radar, and electronics associated with the atomic bomb, to the Union of Soviet Socialist Republics (U.S.S.R.), with the knowledge that the Soviets could possibly use that information in attacks against Americans. The government argued that the Rosenbergs' actions had ended the U.S. monopoly of nuclear-weapons production. Denying involvement, the Rosenbergs proclaimed their innocence and refused to answer questions about their affiliation with the Communist Party in the United States. Receiving a death sentence, they were electrocuted on 19 June 1953.

Scholars and writers have been divided over this case, arguing the couple's guilt or innocence. Ronald Radosh and Joyce Milton, in *The Rosenberg File* (1997), present irrefutable historical analysis and primary proof that the conviction was justified. They base their argument on a variety of documents, including Federal Bureau of Investigation (FBI) files for which the Rosenbergs' sons, Michael and Robert Meeropol, had sued the government for access in 1975. The National Committee to Re-Open the Rosenberg Case thought the files would prove the Rosenbergs' innocence and vindicate them, but the 250,000 pages obtained through the Freedom of Information Act only condemned the couple more. Radosh and Milton also examined federal files and interviewed key participants and witnesses who admitted that some communists would publicly say the Rosenbergs were not guilty or would justify that the couple acted rightfully if they had spied because of ideological motivations.

In their book Radosh and Milton describe Julius Rosenberg's radical political activities as a teenager in New York City and student at the City College of New York. The Communist Party of the United States had been established in 1929, and Rosenberg joined the Young Communist League. He publicly protested what he perceived to be governmental abuses, such as the Scottsboro case of 1931 in which nine African American youths in Alabama were convicted of rape. Julius met Ethel Greenglass, a labor organizer, at a union fundraiser, and they were married while he was still in school. Graduating with an electrical engineering degree, Julius accepted employment with the U.S. Army Signal Corps in 1942. During the next year the Rosenbergs stopped being actively affiliated with the Communist Party, including canceling their subscription to *The Daily Worker*.

Using court documents, eyewitness accounts, and FBI files, Radosh and Milton reveal exactly how the Rosenbergs spied and transmitted American defense secrets to the Soviets by retracing the couple's activities. In 1943, Aleksandr Semyonovich Feklisov, a *Komitet gosudarstvennoy bezopasnosti* (KGB), or Committee for State Security, officer affiliated with the New York Russian Consulate during World War II, recruited Julius to spy. Feklisov told Rosenberg what to do and expected frequent status reports. As a member of the Federation of Architects, Engineers, Chemists and Technicians, a front for the Communist Party, Rosenberg began to recruit spies for the KGB but wanted also to direct the spies, causing conflicts with his superiors.

Rosenberg targeted Max Elitcher, an engineer for the U.S. Navy, to procure secrets about American anti-aircraft and fire-control technology. He also identified his brother-in-law, David Greenglass, a machinist employed at Los Alamos, New Mexico, as a source of information about the Manhattan Project, in which scientists were developing an atomic bomb. In November 1944, Julius convinced Greenglass's wife, Ruth, to encourage him to prepare sketches of technology, describe the laboratory's physical layout and security systems, and list significant scientists researching there who might cooperate with the Soviets. She was to memorize information to convey to Rosenberg when she returned home. Initially reluctant, Greenglass acquiesced to his brother-in-law's incessant demands.

In January 1945, the Greenglasses traveled to New York on furlough and gave Rosenberg design notes for a high-explosive lens mold developed for the Manhattan Project. Rosenberg cut a Jello boxtop in two, telling the Greenglasses that their contact would present them with the matching piece. Ethel confided in her brother and sister-in-law that she frequently typed handwritten espionage notes for her husband. Julius also invited a Russian man to meet the couple and quiz Greenglass about details of the atomic bomb.

Harry Gold, another spy, traveled to Albuquerque in June 1945 to contact Greenglass, showing half of the Jello boxtop as proof of his identity. Greenglass cooperated with Gold, suggested possible recruits, provided more sketches of the lens mold, and explained how implosion, or the movement of energy toward the center, was incorporated into the atomic bomb's design. Gold also met with British spy Klaus Fuchs, who worked at Los Alamos. The spies carefully monitored development of the atomic bomb. One month after Gold's visit the first American atomic bomb was exploded in a secret test at Alamogordo, New Mexico, and several weeks later a second atomic bomb was detonated over Hiroshima, Japan, to force the Japanese surrender in World War II. The Americans' possession of nuclear-warfare technology became publicly known.

Radosh and Milton also note another technology theft Rosenberg performed during this time to benefit the Soviets. Discharged by the Signal Corps in February 1945 because he had concealed his Communist membership, Rosenberg smuggled a proximity fuse from his new workplace, the Emerson Radio Corporation, in a bag of garbage to give to the Soviets. This fuse, innovated during World War II, expanded the range of anti-aircraft missiles so that they could damage an object without striking it. The Soviets later used a proximity fuse to shoot down an

Ethel and Julius Rosenberg during their 1951 espionage trial

(International)

American U-2 spy plane flown by Major Francis Gary Powers above Soviet territory in 1960. As a result a summit between President Dwight D. Eisenhower and Soviet Premier Nikita Khrushchev was canceled, and Rosenberg was posthumously honored with KGB medals.

Before his spying was detected, Rosenberg established a machine shop, the G & R Engineering Company, in New York City with his brothers-in-law. He offered Greenglass financial support, provided by the Soviets, to pursue nuclear-physics studies at the Massachusetts Institute of Technology, hoping Greenglass would have access to more classified projects and scientists willing to collaborate with the Soviets. Greenglass refused to enroll. Rosenberg continued his spying activities in the post–World War II era, bragging to Greenglass that he used microfilm to transmit information and that the Soviets gave him gifts such as watches and cash as rewards.

Rosenberg met with Feklisov a final time in 1946. During that same year U.S. cryptanalysts deciphered the Venona Code, used to translate messages transmitted between Soviet consulates in the United States and Moscow, that would be crucial to identify and convict spies. Three years later, on 28 August 1949, the U.S.S.R. detonated an atomic bomb that historians believe was developed more quickly than would have been possible without the information stolen by Rosenberg and his spies. Rosenberg's transmissions not only revealed crucial details but also helped Soviet physicists envision new methods to resolve problems.

In February 1950, soon after communist spy Alger Hiss was convicted of perjury, Fuchs was arrested based on incriminating evidence found in Venona messages. He admitted that he had spied, and he led federal authorities to Gold, who also confessed and was arrested. Rosenberg, fearing that the prisoners would divulge their names to authorities, warned Greenglass to consider leaving the United States with the Rosenbergs and gave him $4,000. The Rosenbergs posed for passport photographs and contacted a physician regarding necessary immunizations for international travel. About the same time, Sen. Joseph R. McCarthy (R-Wisconsin) announced that more than two hundred communists worked for the U.S. State Department, provoking public antagonism against promoters of anti-American activities, especially communists. Politicians initiated a frenzied agenda of identifying and blackballing American Communists.

On 15 June 1950 federal agents arrested Greenglass, who named Julius as the initiator and director of his espionage activity. FBI agents interviewed Rosenberg the next day and charged him with treason one month later. Ethel was imprisoned in August. The co-conspirators were indicted by a grand jury in January 1951. At the trial in March, Irving Saypol, who had prosecuted Hiss, represented the government against the Rosenbergs. According to Radosh and Milton, especially damning evidence included Greenglass's revelations about his brother-in-law and Elitcher's testimony about transporting microfilm to Rosenberg with Morton Sobell, who was the third defendant in the Rosenberg trial imprisoned for spying. A convincing statement by Walter Koski, an Atomic Energy Commission physicist, also underscored the detrimental results that could have occurred if more of Greenglass's sketches had been obtained by political and military enemies.

Rosenberg's prison chess partner and confidante, Jerome Eugene Tartakow, provided officials information that the egotistical and talkative Rosenberg had alluded to, thus unintentionally identifying potential prosecution sources, such as the passport photographer, Ben Schneider, who was a surprise witness on the last trial day. Other indisputable evidence included Rosenberg's leasing two apartments for microfilming, a fine console table used for microfilming that his maid Evelyn Cox described, and gold watches. The expenses for these luxurious items exceeded the Rosenbergs' income, reinforcing the claim that the Soviets had supplied them.

The Rosenbergs' supporters said that the couple had been framed and were victims of a capitalist government that persecuted liberals. They called them martyrs of Cold War McCarthyism waged against communists. They vilified Greenglass as being disloyal to his family by testifying against them, claiming that he was jealously engaging in a vendetta. Rosenberg advocates also alleged that the prosecution's evidence was fraudulent and that witnesses had not told the truth in order to support a conspiracy against American communists. These friends stressed that the Rosenbergs were not scientifically competent to comprehend atomic-bomb designs and were incapable of the crimes of which they had been accused. Radosh and Milton discredit these Rosenberg defenders, showing how they manipulated evidence and facts in an effort to corroborate their statements.

Judge Irving R. Kaufman declared that the Rosenbergs had exposed American citizens to the risk of atomic weapons domestically and in South Korea, where an anticommunist war was being waged by Allied troops versus Soviet-supported Chinese and North Korean forces. He stretched historical accuracy by blaming them for enabling the Korean invasion and assigning them guilt for any future deaths suffered by noncommunists from Soviet atomic weapons. Kaufman concluded, "We have evidence of your treachery all around us every day—for the civilian defense activities throughout the nation are aimed at preparing us for an atom bomb attack."

Radosh and Milton supplement their discussion of contemporary events with recently released revelations that further implicate the Rosenbergs. Khrushchev recalled in his memoirs that he heard aide Vyacheslav Molotov tell Joseph Stalin that the Rosenbergs had assisted the Soviets to acquire the atomic bomb. On 11 July 1995 the National Security Agency (NSA) and Central Intelligence Agency (CIA) released the decoded Venona cables that noted the Rosenberg's espionage roles. Initially, monitors only read messages about routine issues such as Lend Lease funding. In 1947 one cryptanalyst recognized a comment about KGB work in the United States. The message referred to an American called "Lib" and "Atenko" (for "Liberal" and "Antenna") whose wife was named Ethel, proving that Julius was an active agent. Because the Soviets were unaware that their transmissions were insecure, they often listed the non-coded names of spies and their activities. NSA scholar David Kahn wrote in *The Codebreakers: The Story of Secret Writing* (1996) that, "The Venona intercepts show one thing beyond doubt, that the Rosenbergs spied for the Soviet Union against the United States."

Radosh and Milton also discovered that two of Rosenberg's spies, Joel Barr and Alfred Sarant, had disappeared to develop microelectronics in a KGB laboratory near Leningrad, where they were known as Joseph Berg and Philip Staros. In 1997 Soviet spy Anatoli Yatskov told *Washington Post* journalist Michael Dobbs that an American communist named Morris Cohen had recommended Julius to the Soviets as a potential spy. And in a 1997 Discovery Channel documentary, "The Rosenberg File: Case Closed," Feklisov admitted his nefarious interactions with Rosenberg. The authors defend sources such as Tartakow, arguing that his testimony was accurate because he did not profit from sharing his information and was unknown until the FBI files were opened in 1975. When critics suggested that documents such as communist-agent Elizabeth Bentley's 1945 statement about telephone calls from Julius asking her to contact Soviet spy Jacob Golos had been forged in 1975, Radosh and Milton countered that it would have been impossible for agents to manufacture documents with authentic serial numbers from the 1950s and to cross reference those folders with all existing field-office files and printed excerpts. Updating their book with information from the NSA and Soviet files, the authors also cite the changed opinions of former Rosenberg supporters Walter and Miriam Schneir, who admitted in an August 1995 article in *The Nation* that Julius was in charge of a spy ring to obtain defense secrets, but they insisted that data about the atomic bomb was "relatively minor."

Some historians admit that capital punishment was an extreme verdict and that life imprisonment would have been an acceptable alternative. They note that in the early 1940s the Soviet Union was a wartime ally and that no other spies were executed for committing similar crimes. Other scholars contend that government agents utilized the Rosenberg trial not just to punish them, but as an effort to learn the names of more spies and to intimidate others from becoming spies in the future. They believe that Ethel's arrest and imprisonment was primarily an unsuccessful attempt to manipulate her husband into cooperating with federal authorities. Radosh and Milton also stress that FBI files are incomplete because of the destruction of some documents, as well as omissions of the names of informants or information crucial to national defense. They say the Rosenberg case encouraged the distortion and withholding of facts, necessitating verification of federal files with other reliable sources. Future historians may interpret new or more complete documentation to confirm or refute the Rosenbergs' guilt and complicity with the Soviets to steal American atomic secrets during World War II.

–ELIZABETH D. SCHAFER,
LOACHAPOKA, ALABAMA

Viewpoint: The Rosenbergs were executed because they refused to cooperate with the government and inform on other spies.

Coerced confessions and plea bargains characterized the trials and sentencing of the espionage suspects in the alleged Rosenberg spy ring. Almost all of the spies admitted their guilt and provided the FBI with the names of additional members. In exchange for their cooperation, suspects who cooperated were given shorter prison sentences and preferential treatment in prison. The only exceptions, Julius and Ethel Rosenberg, who maintained their innocence and refused to provide names for the sake of appeasing the FBI, were given the harshest sentence of all: the death penalty. They pleaded innocent, were found guilty, and were sentenced to death by electrocution. They were the only spies in American history executed for espionage. They were executed not because of guilt but because they refused to cooperate. Their lives might have been spared if they had provided their inquisitors with the names of other alleged spies. There were, in fact, many offers from the FBI and the courts to commute their sentence if the couple had "informed."

As was a characteristic of many espionage investigations and subsequent trials during the Red Scare of the early 1950s, the Rosenbergs were uncovered after a series of confessions from other alleged spies. An initial confession had led the FBI to its first suspect, and a series of coerced confessions and plea bargains had convinced other suspects to inform. It was a system that rewarded those who cooperated and punished those who refused.

The informing began in May of 1950 when Klaus Fuchs, a British national and admitted wartime spy, confessed to the FBI that in 1942, after being sent as a British delegate to participate in the Manhattan Project at Los Alamos, New Mexico, he passed atomic-bomb data to the Soviets through connections he had made in Canada. Fuchs was arrested in early 1950. After a one-day trial, in which he pleaded guilty and willingly confessed his crimes, Fuchs was sentenced to fourteen years in prison. When the FBI sent delegates to visit Fuchs in a London prison, he provided the name of Harry Gold, a Philadelphia chemist who allegedly assisted Fuchs in his espionage activities at the Los Alamos facility.

The FBI next pursued Gold, who had allegedly served as a courier between Fuchs and another member of the espionage ring. When the FBI first questioned Gold, he denied ever having been near the testing site in New Mexico, let alone any involvement in the Fuchs spy ring. However, the FBI convinced Gold to confess, and they subsequently arrested him. The degree to which Gold cooperated with the FBI was enigmatic. Emotionless, he admitted his guilt, named several other co-conspirators, and provided authorities with the name of David Greenglass.

Coerced confessions, by this time, had become a forte for the FBI. On 15 June 1950 the FBI arrested Greenglass, a New York machinist and former GI who had been stationed at the Los Alamos atomic testing site during World War II. Greenglass was accused of giving atomic-bomb information to Gold in Albuquerque during the summer of 1945. Like Gold, Greenglass initially denied involvement and then complied with FBI questioning, providing the name of an additional "co-conspirator." On 17 July the FBI announced the arrest of Greenglass's brother-in-law, Julius Rosenberg.

Rosenberg had been employed by the Army Signal Corps during World War II. During this time, according to Greenglass, Rosenberg was reportedly recruited by an official with the Soviet consulate in New York to provide the Soviet government with information about atomic research being done at Los Alamos. It was said that Rosenberg called upon his brother-in-law, Greenglass, who worked at Los Alamos, to provide assistance.

Rosenberg was the first uncooperative suspect in the string of arrests. His refusal to inform or even confess became the subject of public controversy. It frustrated the FBI's swift attempts to round up more "spies" and was an insult to the American government and their plans to banish domestic communism. Like many other influential politicians at the time, FBI director J. Edgar Hoover was on a fierce hunt to round up and punish communists. A large part of this drive was dependent on confessions and the process of "naming names." Suspects who refused to cooperate were often coerced into confessions or offered special consideration for providing information to the authorities.

Rosenberg was an obstacle to the system. Even after grueling questioning and repeated attempts to break down his composure, his inquisitors were at a frustrating standstill. It took more than three additional weeks for the FBI to apprehend another member of the alleged spy ring. On 11 August 1950 Ethel Greenglass Rosenberg was arrested and also charged with conspiracy to commit espionage. Six days later Julius and Ethel Rosenberg were indicted and charged with conspiring with Gold and Greenglass to obtain national defense information for the Soviet Union. The Rosenbergs stood out among the accused. They maintained their innocence under intense questioning and refused to help the FBI uncover more spies. It was a move that infuriated the prosecution and led them to threaten the Rosenbergs with the death penalty. The Rosenbergs were indeed tried, found guilty, and sentenced to death. They were executed at Sing Sing Prison in New York on 19 June 1953.

What has struck many critics of this case was the execution of both Julius and Ethel, and the subsequent abandonment of their two young sons. When Julius refused to inform, the government threatened him with the execution of his wife, who played a much smaller role in the spy ring. Ethel's arrest and trial were driven by the prosecution's desire to pressure Julius into a confession. They desperately wanted the names of additional spies. While evidence suggested that Ethel knew about her husband's activities, her role was not as central. The prosecution, however, treated her as a full partner in the espionage ring and pursued the death penalty for both, with the expectation that this threat would induce Julius to inform on other spies.

Examples of informers who had saved their lives were apparent to the Rosenbergs. Gold shone as a cooperator and informer, providing information during more than sixty hours of questioning by the FBI, and serving as a key witness in two trials in addition to the Rosenberg trial. In return for his services Gold was sentenced to thirty years in prison instead of the death penalty. His time spent in prison was rumored to be pleasant: he allegedly received a daily ration of cigars and various other amenities. However, the stigma of having assisted the FBI in their brutal tactics never left Gold, who was frequently called a "snitch" and "songbird" for having informed.

Ethel's brother, Greenglass, also informed and pleaded guilty to espionage. Having allegedly played a role equal to that of the Rosenbergs, he was sentenced to fifteen years in prison. At the time of their sentencing it was apparent that the Rosenbergs were being punished specifically for their refusal to inform. Judge Irving R. Kaufman denounced the Rosenbergs and declared "neither defendant has seen fit to follow the course of David Greenglass and Harry Gold. Their lips have remained sealed and they prefer the glory which they believe will be theirs by the martyrdom."

The fate of the Rosenbergs rested in their willingness to cooperate with the FBI. They maintained their innocence and refused to invent names and lies to save their own lives. They set out on a course to prove their innocence. During the twenty-seven months that followed their trial, the Rosenbergs wrote press releases and letters to their sentencing judge and to President Dwight D. Eisenhower, as well as letters to the American public that were published in the *Daily Worker,* a Communist newspaper. They also worked diligently with their attorney, exhausting every possible avenue to attain clemency through a grueling series of petitions and attempted appeals. Despite all of their pleas, clemency was denied.

In the era of informing and naming names, the only action that could save the Rosenbergs from death was a confession accompanied by names of "co-conspirators." As they awaited death, the pressure to inform continued to be impressed upon the couple, applied from all sides including the government, the media, and even their families. Newspapers predicted that only a confession could save them. Ethel's mother visited her in prison, urging her to confess. The FBI tried to strike an agreement where a lesser sentence would be given if they cooperated. Despite this relentless pressure the Rosenbergs refused to confess.

The media amplified the consensus that a confession would be the only salvation for the Rosenbergs. Just a few weeks before their scheduled execution, *The New York Times* reported ". . . the Rosenbergs may escape the death penalty if they decide to talk. They have maintained throughout the two years of trial and appeal that they were innocent. . . . If they now decide to talk, that action might influence the President to grant executive clemency." On 25 May 1953 a headline in *The New York Times* echoed this sentiment: "Rosenberg Appeal Denied for 3D Time By Supreme Court–Stay of Execution for Spies Vacated–Mercy for Couple Hinges on Their Talking."

As the Rosenbergs moved closer to their deaths, the government continued to pursue a confession. On 3 June 1953, just sixteen days before their scheduled execution, the government presented the Rosenbergs an offer to cooperate and reduce their prison sentence. Within hours they flatly rejected the proposal and published their response in a press release: "Yesterday we were offered a deal by the Attorney General of the United States. We were told that if we cooperated with the Government, our lives would be spared. By asking us to repudiate the truth of our innocence, the Government admits its own doubts concerning our guilt. . . We solemnly declare, now and forever more, that we will not be coerced, even under pain of death, to bear false witness and to yield up to tyranny our rights as free Americans. Our respect for truth, conscience and human dignity is not for sale."

Even as the Rosenbergs approached the electric chair, the authorities were prepared for a last-minute confession. On the night of the executions, FBI agents sat in offices on death row. Both Julius and Ethel were asked separately by a rabbi if they were willing to confess. Even if one of the prisoners was strapped into the chair and indicated a willingness to talk, the execution was to be halted. A system of signals had even been arranged for the benefit of FBI agents waiting down the hall. In addition, there were reports of a wire directly connected to the White House from the prison. In the event that the Rosenbergs should decide to break their silence, the news was to be flashed to the president.

In the end the Rosenbergs refused to inform. They maintained their innocence and were executed because they declined to provide the government with the names of other spies. By refusing to invent information or incriminate others, they paid for their silence with their lives and were electrocuted as scapegoats.

–MARGARET MARY BARRETT

SPY OR DEVOTED WIFE?

The Rosenbergs' convictions were upheld by the U.S. Circuit Court of Appeals on 25 February 1952. The next day, Ethel penned this poignant letter to her husband.

7:30 AM Feb. 26

My dear one,

Last night at 10:00 o'clock, I heard the shocking news. At the present moment, with little or no detail to hand, it is difficult for me to make any comment, beyond an expression of horror at the shameless haste with which the government appears to be pressing for our liquidation. Certainly, it proves that all our contributions in the past regarding the political nature of our case, have been amazingly correct.

My heart aches for the children, unfortunately they are old enough to have heard for themselves, and no matter what amount of control I am able to exercise, my brain reels, picturing their terror. It is for them I am most concerned and it is of their reaction I am anxiously awaiting some word. Of course, Manny [Bloch] will get here just as soon as he puts in motion proper legal procedure for our continued defense, but meanwhile, my emotions are in storm, as your own must be.

Sweetheart, if only I could truly comfort you, I love you so very dearly. . . . Courage, darling, there's much to be done.

Your devoted wife,

Ethel

Source: *Ellen Schrecker,* The Age of McCarthyism: A Brief History with Documents *(Boston & New York: Bedford Books of St. Martin's Press, 1994), pp. 147–148.*

References

Roger M. Anders, "The Rosenberg Case Revisited: The Greenglass Testimony and the Protection of Atomic Secrets," *American Historical Review,* 83 (April 1978): 388–400;

David Caute, *The Great Fear: The Anti-Communist Purges Under Truman and Eisenhower* (New York: Simon & Schuster, 1978);

Ralph De Toledano, *The Greatest Plot in History* (New York: Duell, Sloan & Pearce, 1963);

Michael Dobbs, "Julius Rosenberg Spied, Russian Says; Agent's Handler Contradicts Moscow in Controversial '50s Case," *Washington Post,* 16 March 1997;

S. Andhil Fineberg, *The Rosenberg Case: Fact and Fiction* (New York: Oceana, 1953);

Marjorie Garber and Rebecca L. Walkowitz, eds., *Secret Agents: The Rosenberg Case, McCarthyism, and Fifties America* (New York: Routledge, 1995);

Virginia Gardner, *The Rosenberg Story* (New York: Masses & Mainstream, 1954);

Alvin H. Goldstein, *The Unquiet Death of Julius and Ethel Rosenberg* (New York: Lawrence Hill, 1975);

H. Montgomery Hyde, *The Atom Bomb Spies* (New York: Atheneum, 1980);

David Kahn, *The Codebreakers: The Story of Secret Writing* (New York: Scribners, 1996);

Robert J. Lamphere and Tom Shachtman, *The FBI–KGB War: A Special Agent's Story* (New York: Random House, 1986);

Michael Meeropol, ed., *The Rosenberg Letters: A Complete Edition of the Prison Correspondence of Julius and Ethel Rosenberg* (New York: Garland, 1994);

Robert and Michael Meeropol, *We Are Your Sons: The Legacy of Ethel and Julius Rosenberg* (Boston: Houghton, Mifflin, 1975);

Victor S. Navasky, *Naming Names* (New York: Viking, 1980);

John F. Neville, *The Press, the Rosenbergs, and the Cold War* (Westport, Conn.: Praeger, 1995);

Louis Nizer, *The Implosion Conspiracy* (New York: Doubleday, 1973);

Michael E. Parrish, "Cold War Justice: The Supreme Court and the Rosenbergs," *American Historical Review,* 82 (October 1977): 805–842;

Oliver Pilat, *The Atom Spies* (New York: Putnam, 1952);

Ronald Radosh and Joyce Milton, *The Rosenberg File* (New Haven: Yale University Press, 1997);

William A. Reuben, *The Atom Spy Hoax* (New York: Action Books, 1955);

Richard Rhodes, *Dark Sun: The Making of the Hydrogen Bomb* (New York: Simon & Schuster, 1995);

Jonathan Root, *The Betrayers: The Rosenberg Case–A Reappraisal of an American Crisis* (New York: Coward-McCann, 1963);

Walter and Miriam Schneir, *Invitation to an Inquest* (Garden City, N.Y.: Doubleday, 1965);

Malcolm P. Sharp, *Was Justice Done?: The Rosenberg-Sobell Case* (New York: Monthly Review Press, 1956);

Morton Sobell, *On Doing Time* (New York: Scribners, 1974);

United States Congress, House Committee on Un-American Activities, *Investigation of Communist Activities (The Committee to Secure Justice in the Rosenberg Case and Affiliates) Hearings Before the Committee on Un-American Activities, House of Representatives, Eighty-fourth Congress, First Session, on Aug. 2, 3, 1955* (Washington, D.C.: United States Government Printing Office, 1955);

Allen Weinstein, *Perjury: The Hiss-Chambers Case* (New York: Knopf, 1978);

John Wexley, *The Judgment of Julius and Ethel Rosenberg* (New York: Cameron & Kahn, 1955).

SEXUAL REVOLUTION

What kind of impact did the birth control pill have on American sexual mores?

Viewpoint: The pill caused the sexual revolution.

Viewpoint: The sexual revolution was not caused by the pill, which was only part of a broader cultural empowerment of women.

What caused the sexual revolution? Few cultural changes have had as great an impact on the United States, and few are as cloaked in mystery. Americans' favorite television shows in the early 1950s could not show married couples sharing the same bed, and some bolder movie directors used images of the wind gently wafting through bedroom curtains to signify that sexual intercourse had taken place. By the 1990s, though, sexual imagery was inescapable, and an entire session of Congress was occupied in discussing President William J. Clinton's sexual practices. Something clearly had changed. Not only was sex openly and frankly discussed, but apparently sexual activity was now practiced and condoned outside of marriage. Some American high schools distribute condoms to students, who are bombarded with sexual messages every day.

What caused all of this? When did this change begin? In the two essays that follow, Daniel Lednicer and Lonna Douglass offer different explanations. Lednicer argues that the birth control pill, which gave women the option of engaging in sexual activity without suffering the consequences of an unwanted pregnancy, made women more active sexually. Lednicer takes a somewhat biological approach to the question. Feminist scholar Lonna Douglass, on the other hand, argues that the sexual revolution was the culmination of a series of cultural changes. Women had won the right to vote by the 1920s and by the 1940s had entered the workforce in growing numbers. Having gained control of their political and economic lives, women by the 1960s took control of their sexual lives as well.

Neither essay addresses all of the ramifications of the sexual revolution. Why has the discussion of sex become so pervasive in American culture? The answer to that may be deceptively simple. Sex sells, and the purveyors of mass media know it.

Viewpoint: The pill caused the sexual revolution.

Societal mores that prevailed well into the 1960s maintained that women were passive participants in sexual activity and only went along to please their male partners. Women also had to consider the possibility of becoming pregnant. In 1960 there became available to women a method for avoiding pregnancy that was close to 100 percent effective, safe, and convenient. Oral contraceptive

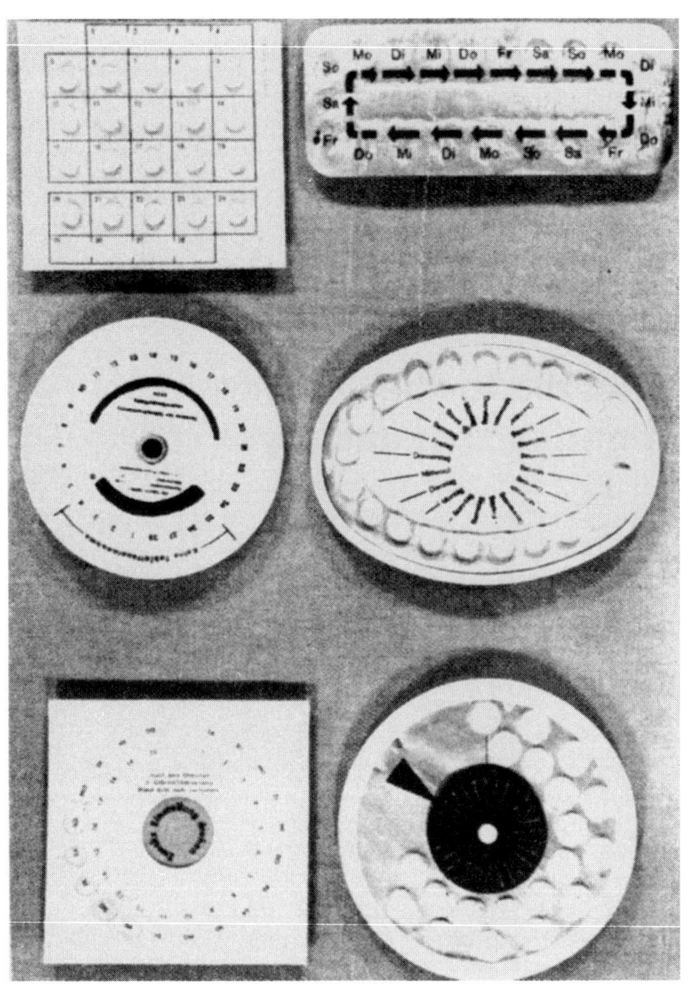

Six examples of contraceptive dispensors, all designed to facilitate proper dosage

drugs, quickly dubbed "the pill," arguably allowed many women to assert a previously repressed interest in sex. Women now could separate the recreational aspects of sex from procreation.

Women asserted a sexual equality that has led to a marked change in the code that ruled relations between the sexes for centuries. The new ethic rejected the traditional dominant/subservient relationship between men and women. These changes, often referred to as the sexual revolution, started precipitously toward the end of the 1960s as use of the pill became widespread; they have continued on a more gradual, but almost inexorable, pace. They have gone beyond the sexual ethic and extended the overall role of woman in society. The more open recognition of sex in popular culture is also traceable to the same event. Graphic descriptions of sexual encounters, for example, in literature and movies would have scandalized the public within living memory; this is to say nothing of easier access to hardcore pornography.

Societal attitudes that prevailed up until the 1960s can be traced to the drive for survival that characterized all living species and was reflected by society at large. One of the prime requirements for survival is stability. A group cannot easily persist as such in the absence of defined and stable relationships among its members. The family grouping of one male, one female, and their direct offspring is the basic unit found in most stable human societies. Perpetuation of the species constitutes an equally important drive for survival. This situation, however, places real strains on the desire for stability because it calls on the strong mating instinct present in all vertebrates, especially mammals. An additional complication was introduced when, at some undefined point in evolution, the act of mating became supplemented by stimulation of the pleasure centers in the brain. Sexual play seen in monkeys and apes shows that this antedates the arrival of homo sapiens.

It takes considerable effort to provide nourishment and shelter for a typical family group. Humans have been liberated from a literal hand-to-mouth existence for only the last few millennia. No paterfamilias, or for that matter his spouse, it can be inferred, would gladly support offspring that did not clearly derive from their union. This is arguably one of the main driving forces toward monogamy. Additional impetus almost certainly comes from the strong emotions that surround sex. Sexual exclusivity can only serve to reinforce the attachment of the couple. Monogamy bolsters stability of the family, clan, and even society. Strictures for enforcing monogamy have as a consequence been codified by most of the major religions that arose as societies developed. Note, however, that these strictures fly in the face of the mythically innate desire of males to mate with more than one female. Ostracism, eternal damnation, and even incarceration provided incentives for following societal dictates. An equally strong, or arguably stronger, motivation for following the Sixth Commandment (for Judeo-Christians) comes from the not infrequent consequence of sex: pregnancy. Here was incontrovertible evidence that someone had strayed.

In the late 1940s societal attitudes in Western societies still condemned sex outside marriage. Yet several so-called barrier methods for avoiding conception were available. Diaphragms were more or less restricted to married women since their purchase required a doctor's prescription: the loss of spontaneity occasioned by this method limited its widespread acceptance. Though condoms were more widely available, they were kept under the counter by druggists. They also obviously involved premeditation and were regarded as unreliable and unsatisfactory. The potential for conception was ever present as a deterrent for casual sexual encounters. The invention of a magical pill that would prevent pregnancy was a subject for much talk among women.

Enormous strides were made in the physical sciences by the 1930s. Organic chemistry had developed to the point where its practitioners could, and did, study the hormones involved in mammalian reproduction. They were able to isolate in pure form minute amounts of these substances present in blood and to determine their chemical structures. Detailed experiments with pure samples of these steroid hormones confirmed that they were involved in the regulation of the reproductive cycle of the female. Data from these experiments also hinted that it might be possible to interrupt that cycle by administering chemically modified steroids related to the sex hormones. Further progress was postponed for a time by the scarcity of steroid starting materials: complex structures ruled out synthesis from simpler chemicals with methods then available. The advent of World War II also delayed progress for close to a decade. By the mid 1940s Russell Marker had identified the presence in the rhizomes of a Mexican yam, Barbasco, a plentiful source of the plant steroid, diosgenin. This steroid could be converted by a series of chemical transformations to starting materials for modified sex hormones. The availability of these compounds in kilogram amounts led to the synthesis of modified steroids in several pharmaceutical company laboratories. Two labs, apparently unknowingly, pursued parallel programs and synthesized a pair of closely related molecules. A group at G. D. Searle & Company, led by Frank B. Colton, synthesized a compound that came to be know as norethynodrel; a group at Syntex, under the leadership of Carl Djerassi, prepared norethindrone. Pharmacological testing revealed that these compounds inhibited ovulation in the mammalian female. After extensive animal-safety tests, clinical trials confirmed that the compounds had the same effect on women. Norethynodrel was approved by the U.S. Food and Drug Administration in 1960 and went on sale as an oral contraceptive under the name of Enovid®; norethindrone was made available slightly later as Norlutin®. Several other chemically related steroids, known generically to the public as "the pill," have been launched in the intervening years. Most advances in the area have focused on lowering the doses of these potent drugs in order to improve on an already good safety record.

The pill actually comprises a series of tablets ingested by a woman once daily over the best part of each month. (Some products are taken daily month-round.) The contraceptive efficacy of the pill is generally estimated to run well above 95 percent when used according to directions. Ease of use and convenience has led to the pill becoming the mainstay for contraception in Western society. Reports that appear periodically claiming that long-term use may be associated with a low incidence of cancer seem to have an only minor effect on usage. A survey by the Kinsey Institute led to the projection that 93 million women worldwide were using the pill in 1990; the same survey led to the estimate that 80 percent of U.S. women (in certain demographic groups) had used this contraceptive method at some time in their lives. An impressive number of women clearly take advantage of the fact that sex need not involve the chance of becoming pregnant.

–DAN LEDNICER, NORTH BETHESDA, MARYLAND

Viewpoint: The sexual revolution was not caused by the pill, which was only part of a broader cultural empowerment of women.

The real sexual revolution was not about sex. It was, and is, about power. The birth control pill may have made sexual relations possible without the consequences of pregnancy, but it has not changed the nature of sexual relationships between men and women. What has changed in the sexual revolution is that women have been able to take control of their lives, rejecting centuries of dominance by men, but it is a mistake to see female sexuality as dependent upon the birth control pill. The rejection has been cultural, economic, and political.

Nineteenth-century psychoanalyst Sigmund Freud believed that anatomy is destiny. Biology, according to Freud, determines our actions. Freud's ideas about sex codified what many in the West took to be natural law. Men were the sexual aggressors; women were passive and masochistic sexual creatures. Freud also held that a vaginal orgasm was a sign of a woman's sexual maturity, and that a central fact of a woman's self-identity was her not having a penis. Freud believed this created "penis-envy" in women. This "scientific" explanation for sexual differences relegated women to a passive sexual role.

Feminist theorist Kate Millett has observed in *Sexual Politics* (1970), "Coitus can scarcely be said to take place in a vacuum;

A RESPONSE TO THE PILL

In Mount Vernon, New York, a group of African-American housewives, grandmothers, welfare recipients, and a psychotherapist signed the following statement (11 September 1968) concerning the use of the birth-control pill among minorities. A previous statement issued by African-American males denounced the pill as a means of contributing to the genocide of black people in America.

Dear Brothers:

Poor black sisters decide for themselves whether to have a baby or not to have a baby. If we take the pills or practice birth control in other ways, it's because of poor black men.

Now here's how it is. Poor black men won't support their families, won't stick by their women—all they think about is the street, dope and liquor, women, a piece of ass, and their cars. That's all that counts. Poor black women would be fools to sit up in the house with a whole lot of children and eventually go crazy, sick, heartbroken, no place to go, no sign of affection—nothing. Middle class white men have always done this to their women—only more sophisticated like.

So when whitey put out the pill and poor black sisters spread the word, we saw how simple it was not to be a fool for men any more (politically we would say men could no longer exploit us sexually or for money and leave the babies with us to bring up). That was the first step in our waking up!. . . .

Poor black women in the U.S. have to fight back out of our own experience of oppression. Having too many babies stops us from supporting our children, teaching them the truth or stopping the brainwashing as you say, and fighting black men who still want to use and exploit us.

Source: *Judith Clavir Albert and Stewart Edward Albert,* The Sixties Papers: Documents of a Rebellious Decade *(New York: Praeger, 1984), pp. 478–480.*

although of itself it appears a biological and physical activity, it is set so deeply within the larger context of human affairs that it serves as a charged microcosm of the variety of attitudes and values to which culture subscribes." Freudian theory and other attitudes toward sexual activity were part of a general cultural tradition, which had been seriously undermined in the 1960s. Most students of American or Western culture see the sexual revolution as beginning in the 1920s, when women achieved the right to vote and thus became independent political players. Women also entered the work force in larger numbers in the 1920s, achieving a degree of economic independence. Though the 1930s were lean times for all, women reentered the work force in the 1940s in unprecedented numbers, taking manufacturing jobs that had traditionally gone to men. Though after World War II there was a push by some to have women return to their "traditional" roles, women remained at work. In 1947 a million more women were working than had been in 1940. Despite the widespread notion in the 1950s that women returned to the home, by 1960 twice as many women were working as in 1940. The median age of working women in 1960 was forty-one, an increase over previous years when most women would only work while they were young and single. In 1960, 30 percent of all working women were married, and 39 percent of women with school-aged children (ages six to seventeen) were employed. Women were expanding their economic and political roles (President John F. Kennedy appointed the Commission on the Status of Women in 1961) and taking positions previously reserved to men.

Women were challenging their traditional economic and political roles in society. It is not surprising that women questioned traditional sexual roles as well. Freud's idea that women should be passive and men aggressive came under scrutiny, as did his ideas about vaginal orgasms. Alfred Kinsey, Wardell B. Pomeroy, and Paul H. Gebbard's *Sexual Behavior in the Human Female* (1953) demonstrated that the vagina was not a particularly sensitive organ and that women were more likely to achieve sexual satisfaction from stimulation of the clitoris, not through penetration of the vagina. This argument undermined Freudian theory, as well as many male assumptions about sexual practice. As scholar Anne Koedt wrote in "The Myth of the Vaginal Orgasm" in *Liberation Now! Writings from the Women's Liberation Movement* (1971), "Men fear that they will become sexually expendable if the clitoris is substituted for the vagina as the center of pleasure for women. Actually, this has a great deal of validity if one considers *only* the anatomy." Women by the 1960s could achieve political power and economic control of their lives without the assistance of men. By this time, too, women began questioning their need for men as sexual partners.

By the 1960s feminists and more clear-headed sociological thinkers had turned the discussion of gender relations and sex around. Freudian theory had maintained that men were biologically driven, that women were their passive but willing partners, and that the roles of both were determined by anatomy. Feminists, engaging in the same kind of critical inquiry that engaged others in the 1960s, argued that male and female roles were determined by society, not genetics. Men and women were socialized to treat sex in gender-specific ways. For example, sociologists John Gagnon and William Simon observed that adolescent boys and girls reacted differently to sexual activity during courtship. "When girls are in love they increase their sexual activity and are more likely than boys to want premarital coitus. When boys are in love they tend to avoid sexual relations with their girls." Freud and his followers had analyzed this anomalous activity as part of the male dichotomization of females as either "good girls" who did not have sex or "bad girls" who did. Gagnon and Simon, however, regard this activity as part of a complicated socialization. Girls were socialized to bring together sex and romance, while boys were socialized to keep the two separate.

The fact that a scholar could write about sexual activity in this way is a stunning confirmation of the success of the sexual revolution. What in 1900 had been considered scandalously obscene was by the 1940s the subject of scientific, or pseudoscientific, research. By the 1960s it was the subject of best-selling books, and by the 1990s it was a staple of major media talk shows and movies. This pervasiveness of sex in American popular culture, which is part of the general sexual revolution, did not emanate from the pill but was part of a broader phenomenon.

To a cultural historian the real change began with the development of novels in the eighteenth century, which focused on emotions and inner lives rather than on the moral or pietistic values of virtuous men and women. In the eighteenthth-century seduction novel, the wages of sin still were death. But in Gustave Flaubert's *Madame Bovary* (1857) the protagonist's sensuality is not condemned, and in Theodore Dreiser's *Sister Carrie* (1900) the "fallen woman" is not punished. These slightly scandalous literary breakthroughs were signs of things to come. Movies and radio, which emerged in the 1910s and 1920s, respectively, further undermined the moral authority of church and family, enshrining in their place ideas of individual liberty in pursuit of pleasure. Traditional front-porch courtships, under the watchful eyes of family and neighbors, had prevented young lovers from going too far. Now the automobile and movie theater both encouraged, or at least permitted, clandestine sexual encounters.

Since the 1950s, mass media has increasingly bombarded young men and women with ideas about sex and sexuality, undermining constraints that earlier prevented sexual activity. The birth control pill further undermined constraints against sexual activity, but most cultural restrictions had already been knocked away by mass media. Women may have been given more of a choice, but while freed from one consequence of coitus, pregnancy, they were still faced with many others.

Though the pill may have given women a guarantee against unwanted pregnancy, it was not a magical elixir that liberated women to pursue their own sexual freedom. Men and women, as Gagnon and Simon and others have argued, have different ideas about the nature of sexual activity and the relationship between love and sex. The pill, in fact, liberated men from feeling any responsibility to controlling their own tendency to procreate. It is no accident that the scientists devising birth control methods have focused on women rather than men. It is true that the sexual revolution fostered greater sexual independence in women. It is not true, though, that the pill had anything to do with this development. The pill reinforces a woman's responsibility to control her pregnancies, just as society has expected the mother to care for the newborn child.

If the pill did liberate women, one would have to ask why then have legalized abortions become necessary, and why has "date rape" become a social problem? If the pill caused the sexual revolution, then why do sexually active women get pregnant and seek abortions? The "date rape" problem suggests that while birth control frees women from possible pregnancies, and while access to legal abortions permits women to terminate them, the truly liberated ones are men. Now that men know women do not necessarily become pregnant as a result of sex, there is one less constraint upon men who want to engage in sex with women. Men expect that women will take care of preventing pregnancy, or terminate unwanted pregnancies. The birth control pill, far from liberating women, has instead increased pressure on women to have sex.

The sexual revolution began with the political and economic transformation of women's role in society. It promised to liberate women from the final vestiges of sexual oppression. Yet, of the many ironies implicit in the story, the greatest may be that instead of liberating women, the birth control pill has increased the sexualization of women. The sexual revolution clearly has not gone far enough. The birth control pill may have been a weapon in this revolution, but it was not the weapon used by revolutionaries.

–LONNA DOUGLASS, BOSTON, MASSACHUSETTS

References

Bernard Asbell, *The Pill: A Biography of the Drug that Changed the World* (New York: Random House, 1995);

Deborah Babcox and Madeline Belkin, comp., *Liberation Now! Writings from the Women's Liberation Movement* (New York: Dell, 1971);

Carl Djerassi, *The Politics of Contraception* (New York: Norton, 1980);

Lucile Duberman, *Gender and Sex in Society* (New York: Praeger, 1975);

Betty Friedan, *The Feminine Mystique* (New York: Norton, 1963);

Alfred C. Kinsey, Wardell B. Pomeroy, and Paul H. Gebbard *Sexual Behavior in the Human Female* (Philadelphia: Saunders, 1953);

Daniel Lednicer, ed., *Contraception: The Chemical Control of Fertility* (New York: Marcel Dekker, 1969);

Robert T. Michael and others, *Sex in America: A Definitive Survey* (New York: Little, Brown, 1994);

Kate Millett, *Sexual Politics* (Garden City, New York: Doubleday, 1970);

Jean O'Barr and Mary Wyer, eds., *Engaging Feminism: Students Speak Up & Speak Out* (Charlottesville: University Press of Virginia, 1992);

Hal D. Sears, *The Sex Radicals: Free Love in High Victorian America* (Lawrence: Regents Press of Kansas, 1977);

Rickie Solinger, *Wake Up Little Susie: Single Pregnancy and Race before Roe* v. *Wade* (New York: Routledge, 1992);

Timothy Taylor, *The Prehistory of Sex: Four Million Years of Human Sexual Culture* (New York: Bantam, 1996);

Elizabeth Siegal Watkins, *On the Pill: A Social History of Oral Contraceptives, 1950–1970* (Baltimore: Johns Hopkins University Press, 1998).

SPACE RACE

What prompted the United States to venture into space?

Viewpoint: While the Cold War directly induced the United States to develop a national space program, earlier efforts in science provided the critical foundation that enabled the American space program's initiation in the 1950s.

Viewpoint: Although the timing of the space program was the result of Cold War considerations, the U.S. drive into space grew out of Americans' fascination with the frontier.

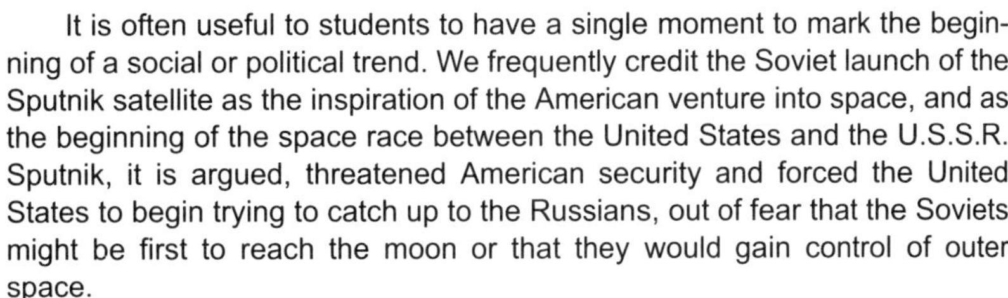

It is often useful to students to have a single moment to mark the beginning of a social or political trend. We frequently credit the Soviet launch of the Sputnik satellite as the inspiration of the American venture into space, and as the beginning of the space race between the United States and the U.S.S.R. Sputnik, it is argued, threatened American security and forced the United States to begin trying to catch up to the Russians, out of fear that the Soviets might be first to reach the moon or that they would gain control of outer space.

There is some merit to this argument and to using the launch of Sputnik to mark the beginning of the space race. Some historians even see the space race as driven by Cold War fears. In these two essays, however, Amy Paige Snyder and Susan Landrum Mangus offer somewhat different perspectives. Neither would deny that the Cold War may have influenced the course of the space program, but both see much more important cultural elements at work. Snyder looks at the history of American interest in space and rocketry, seeing both as part of general human curiosity and scientific inquiry. Curiosity, not fear, motivated scientists to begin thinking of ways to conquer space.

Mangus has another approach. The frontier has long defined America, at least according to historians such as Frederick Jackson Turner. Space was "the final frontier" (to quote from a popular 1960s television show) and conquest of the frontier was central to the American tradition. Scholars, as well as ordinary citizens, will argue, she says, whether or not a frontier ever actually existed, and what it meant if it did exist. Yet, the myth of the frontier sustained three centuries of American development and secured Americans in the belief that they were, in fact, different from other nations of the world.

Snyder and Mangus both take a creative, cultural approach to the historic phenomenon of the space race. What motivated it? It seems far too simplistic to blame (or praise) Sputnik for sending Americans to the moon. Such an ambitious and costly enterprise needed more than fear to launch it. In the 1960s, as American society was torn apart by urban rioting, the sexual revolution, youth rebellion, and the Vietnam War, the space program offered Americans their few moments of hope and glory. Congress may have paid for the space program partly out of a fear of the Soviets' technological advance, but the benefits came not in making the United States the masters of space, but in proving to all Americans, once again, that their nation could accomplish great things.

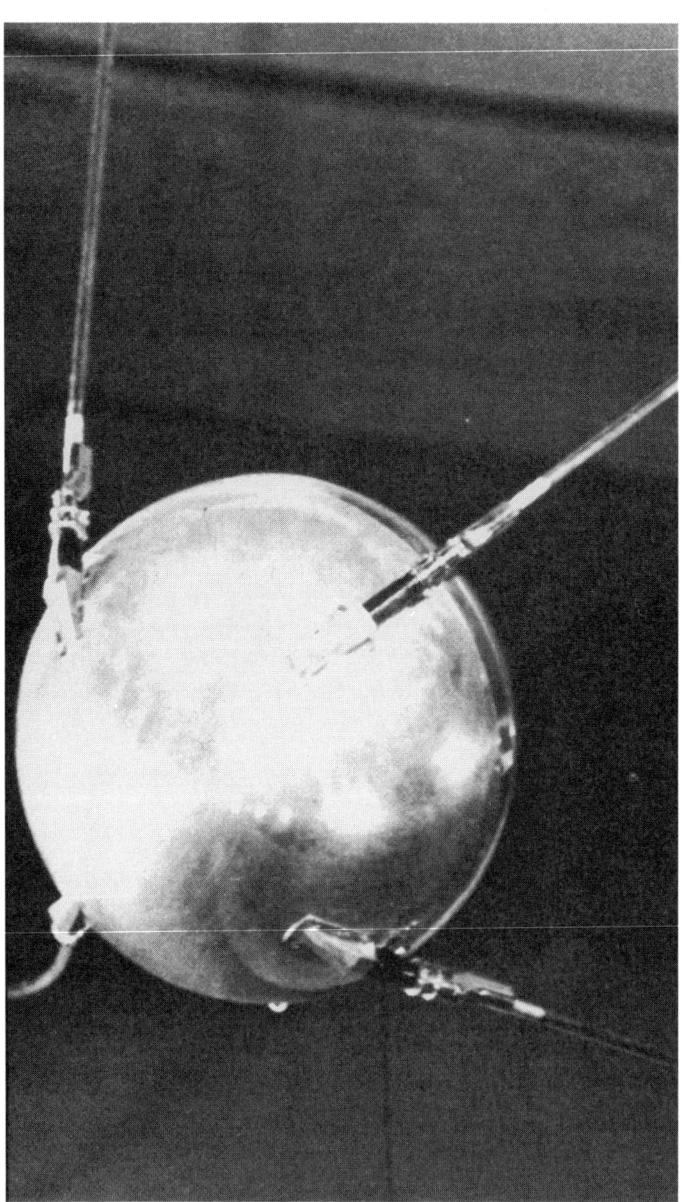

Sputnik, the first man-made satellite in space, was launched by the Soviet Union in October 1957

Viewpoint: While the Cold War directly induced the United States to develop a national space program, earlier efforts in science provided the critical foundation that enabled the American space program's initiation in the 1950s.

The vast majority of federal documents and historical literature on the origins of the U.S. space program suggests that the American people never would have approved the infusion of billions of public dollars into a program to build rocket boosters and send humans and satellites into space without the perceived need to ensure national security and to outdo the Soviet Union in technological capabilities. Indeed, only after World War II, when relations between the two superpowers soured and the Cold War ensued, did U.S. government officials realize the military and intelligence merits space offered the nation. During this time, military and civilian groups embarked on the development of rockets that could both deploy Earth-orbiting satellites and serve as missiles for national defense. Prospects of observing missile-building activities in the Soviet Union without infringing on Soviet airspace convinced the U.S. Army Air Forces to study the feasibility of developing a spy satellite starting in the late 1940s. President Dwight D. Eisenhower even approved the development and launch of a scientific Earth satellite to precede any intelligence satellites in order to first peacefully establish freedom of space, or the right of nations to fly satellites over any other country. When the Soviets beat the United States by putting the satellite Sputnik into orbit in 1957, the United States quickly passed legislation to create a permanent government space agency—the National Aeronautics and Space Administration (NASA)—and soon increased efforts to develop rocket technology.

While the Cold War most certainly precipitated U.S. involvement in space activities that eventually led to the space race with the Soviet Union in the 1950s, it is inaccurate to credit the Cold War alone with bringing about the nation's achievements in space starting at this time. Although the U.S. government's willingness to provide major funding for space activities, and ultimately a permanent space program, derived from the desire to eclipse the Soviet Union in technological prowess, in truth American interest in space began to grow well before the Cold War began. The first federally funded space pursuits trace their origins to the labors of scientists, engineers, writers, and other visionaries who lived and worked both in the United States and abroad. Recognizing the efforts of those who pondered and experimented with space travel and exploration before the start of the U.S.-Soviet conflict forms the basis for a true appreciation of the Space Age: without the earlier dreams and endeavors of space enthusiasts to open up the space frontier, the U.S. space program may well never have commenced in response to tensions with the Soviet Union. In essence, pre–Cold War efforts in three arenas—rocket science and technology, space science, and popular culture—provided the foundation from which the U.S space program of the 1950s was able to rise and earn public approval.

Marveling about the tendency of humans to pursue means of reaching higher and higher altitudes, NASA's first space-science administrator, Homer E. Newell, pointed out that "when men could leave the earth they would do so." By

1783 Joseph-Michel and Jacques-Etienne Montgolfier of France confirmed this propensity when they successfully tested the first-ever hot-air balloon. Flight capability progressed, resulting in the development of balloons that attained greater heights and lofted scientific, and then human, payloads. Just as powered balloon flight became reality, Americans Orville and Wilbur Wright proved the ability of humans to leave the earth with a set of wings by flying the first airplane in 1903. In 1915 the U.S. government expressed its interest in keeping up in aviation technology by establishing a small federal agency, the National Advisory Committee for Aeronautics, to perform aeronautics research.

Other inventors were not content making trips several kilometers off the ground, but aspired to reach the heights of space in rockets. First developed as firecrackers and military weapons by the Chinese in the twelfth century and then used later in European military efforts, rockets captivated the attention of amateurs worldwide who dreamed of making spaceflight reality starting around the turn of the twentieth century. These pioneering rocketeers laid developmental groundwork without which the U.S. government never could have initiated a space program in the short time it did. Inspired by the writing of Jules Verne, Russian Konstantin Tsiolkovsky is credited as the world's first theoretical rocket scientist. Self-educated in mathematics, physics, and astronomy, Tsiolkovsky published a paper in 1903 in which he put forth the basic theory of rocket propulsion. In later years he wrote about reaching outer space with multistage rockets and using artificial satellites as way stations for interplanetary flight. In Germany, Hermann Oberth considered the applications of rocket propulsion to spaceflight in his 1923 work, *Die Rakete zu den Planetenräumen* (The Rocket into Interplanetary Space), garnering German interest in rocketry for military purposes. It was an American, Robert Goddard, who not only theorized about rocketry but actually built a working booster. After writing papers on the subject, Goddard succeeded in launching a homemade liquid-fueled rocket to fifty-six meters in 1926. While Goddard continued to develop even more powerful rockets, he never put many of his most ambitious ideas into practice because he refused to share his ideas with groups such as the American Rocket Society, one of the world's recently emergent rocket enthusiast organizations, which could have helped him find the financial support his ideas required. That in 1960 the U.S. government awarded the Goddard estate $1 million for the use of his patented rocket inventions emphasizes the significance of his contributions to rocket technology.

Though rocketry in the United States lagged in comparison to efforts in Germany and the Soviet Union because of the government's lack of interest, World War II presented the nation with a cogent reason to increase rocket research and development. In 1939 the government funded the California Institute of Technology's (Caltech) Guggenheim Aeronautical Laboratory (which became the Jet Propulsion Laboratory in 1944) to study the feasibility of using small rockets to assist the takeoff of heavily loaded planes from short runways. In 1945 the Caltech group developed the first American rocket for upper-atmosphere research, the WAC Corporal. National rocketry capabilities made enormous strides when at the end of the war the U.S. Army captured remaining German V-2 rockets—the liquid-fueled, ballistic missiles that had caused carnage in England and elsewhere. The army also brought rocket mastermind Wernher von Braun, along with other German rocketeers, to the country to work on advanced weapons development. While the army had commissioned von Braun to focus primarily on ballistic missiles and not space rockets, the work that the army rocket team did—based on years of pioneering rocket studies worldwide—served as a ready source of technology to make spaceflight possible when the government made the decision to go. In addition, recognizing the extent of pre–Cold War rocketry work gave government leaders the confidence they needed to go ahead with funding a large-scale space program.

With a history even older than that of rocketry studies, human interest in astronomical science also paved the way for the U.S. space program in the 1950s. Since antiquity, civilizations around the globe have attempted to chart and study the nature of the Sun, Moon, planets, and stars for scientific, practical, religious, and philosophical reasons. Many peoples erected great observatories for studying the cosmos. In the seventeenth century Galileo Galilei of Italy brought the heavens into closer view with his telescope. Well into the twentieth century astronomers have endeavored to make the skies more accessible, building telescopes with increasing magnifying and resolving power. By 1946 a Yale astronomer named Lyman Spitzer suggested that many scientific benefits would stem from putting a large optical telescope into Earth-orbiting space.

Around the time that Spitzer put forth his vision, army officials offered scientists interested in studying the upper atmosphere an opportunity to place experiments aboard the V-2 rockets they had brought home from Germany and planned to test fire. Having begun to send experiments into the atmosphere on balloons at the turn of the century, researchers jumped at the chance to loft scientific instruments even higher. Over several years a tightly knit group of civilian and military scientists routinely selected experiments to be placed on the rockets to study upper-atmospheric characteristics, as well as solar radiation, the Earth's magnetic field at high altitudes, and cosmic rays.

By the mid 1950s, scientists involved in upper atmosphere and astronomy studies suggested and received the opportunity to launch a scientific earth satellite into orbit—and at the same time significantly helped the government establish a permanent presence in space. The International Council of Scientific Unions had designated 1 July 1957 through 31 December 1958 an International Geophysical Year (IGY), in which scientists worldwide would initiate many studies of geophysical and atmospheric phenomena. In 1954 a group of researchers proposed that nations launch artificial satellites to study the earth. The international committee planning IGY approved the proposal, and the Soviet Union quickly announced its intention to deploy an IGY satellite. Eisenhower responded by formally committing the United States to scientific exploration of space. By first launching a scientific satellite, the United States, which had a reconnaissance satellite in the works during the mid 1950s, could establish freedom of space under peaceful auspices. Although the Soviet Union trumped the United States in achieving this precedent, it is important to recognize that without the IGY scientific satellite opportunity—which stemmed from the interests, determination, and previous work of space researchers—the nation might have faced difficulty in moving ahead with a large space program. The scientific pretext gave the budding national space program the peaceful and benevolent image Eisenhower felt was necessary for public approval at home and abroad of the U.S. presence in space before it moved on to pursuing military space activities. The early years of scientific work also provided the nation with the capability to make a scientific satellite a physical reality.

While prior technological and scientific efforts provided the knowledge and a publicly pleasing motive to establish a strong space program, the popular imagination also played a tremendous role in bringing the American space efforts to fruition. Literature on space travel dates to the seventeenth century, composed then of imaginary tales of traveling to the Moon by astronomer Johannes Kepler in 1634 and by writer Cyrano de Bergerac in 1649. Though the early works about space travel consisted of fictional accounts and often were scientifically implausible, they made the important contribution of expressing in words for the first time a fantastic and romantic vision of spaceflight. Later writers such as Verne and H. G. Wells combined this vision with scientifically valid considerations of the problems of spaceflight and the nature of other worlds in works that inspired Tsiolkovsky, Oberth, and Goddard. As if the writers were challenging them to validate their literary claims, rocketry pioneers labored to turn classics such as Verne's *From the Earth to the Moon* (1865), Edward Everett Hale's *The Brick Moon* (1869), and Wells's *First Men on the Moon* (1901) into physical existence.

In the years following World War II, popular works on space exploration began to surge to the point that one could hardly browse in a bookstore or magazine shop, take in a movie on the big screen, or turn on the television without seeing space-related images. Creative works of this period portrayed space in multiple ways. Many writers, artists, and filmmakers depicted space as the next frontier for human exploration as well as a venue for wars of the future, while others reflected the postwar fear of nuclear holocaust in works about alien invasions from space and international struggles for control of the Moon. Writers such as Isaac Asimov and Arthur C. Clarke built bridges between science and fiction in their accounts of space travel. Newell considered Clarke's *The Exploration of Space* (1951) so technically valid that he called it the "blueprint of the space program to come." In the 1950s, Walt Disney populated the "Tomorrowland" region of his new theme park with simulated rocket and space-station rides to reflect and educate visitors about the coming Space Age. Wanting to convince the American people of the imminent reality of spaceflight and win their support for national space endeavors, von Braun and other scientists and engineers explained principles of spaceflight and shared their visions of space exploration in television appearances, public lectures, and articles in popular magazines.

Thanks to the public-relations efforts of so many innovators and visionaries, space exploration was becoming part of American culture well before the federal government announced its plans to launch a satellite during IGY. No matter how the popular media depicted space—as a frontier to explore, a place for scientific experimentation, or a battleground for war—the public, as well as government officials, received the impression that space activities could serve the national interest. Although imagination alone did not serve as a justification for massive government spending on space activities, popular culture proved essential in preparing an otherwise uninformed American public to accept and encourage the government's decision to move ahead with feats in space.

Howard McCurdy points out in *Space and the American Imagination* (1997) that space enthusiasts who in the early 1950s pressed for a space program based on scientific and commercial merits could not convince the government to fund their idea. In the absence of a clear and vital national need, the United States simply was not prepared to embrace a program of space exploration. When the Cold War began to escalate and the federal government recognized a compelling reason to go into space, rockets and satellites and human flights to the Moon suddenly became a high national priority. However, just as the United States would not have embarked on a space program without the Cold War motive, the nation could not have successfully reached space had it not been for countless individuals so passionate about space exploration that they devoted their careers to sharing their visions with others and striving to make their dreams technically feasible. Indeed, political impetus represented only part of the formula leading to the creation of a formal U.S. space program: vision, incrementally improved technological capabilities, growing scientific interest, and creative expression comprised the other elements. Had these rudiments not developed and converged by the 1950s to provide such a strong foundation, it is quite unlikely that the United States would have possessed the ability at that time, as well as the drive, to rush headlong into space.

–AMY PAIGE SNYDER, GEORGE WASHINGTON UNIVERSITY

Viewpoint: Although the timing of the space program was the result of Cold War considerations, the U.S. drive into space grew out of Americans' fascination with the frontier.

In the late 1950s and 1960s, the United States committed to a national effort to explore space. The timing and sense of urgency of the space program were directly linked to the Soviet Union's early space achievements, but Cold War considerations failed to account for most Americans' enthusiasm for space exploration. Manned space flight, and particularly the goal of landing a man on the moon, captured American imaginations. Space exploration was an extension of the nation's frontier heritage, with all of the economic, political, and social benefits of past American frontiers.

Americans defined the frontier broadly. It included much more than popular frontier symbols such as Daniel Boone, Conestoga wagons, cowboys and Indians, and pioneers. The frontier encompassed the whole experience of European expansion into North America, beginning with the first explorers to the New World (most often personified by Christopher Columbus), and continuing with English colonization and settlement starting in the seventeenth century. Exploration of the frontier was an "adventure," a feat performed by "courageous" men and women. At the same time, moreover, the frontier imagery that Americans used to describe the space program was a reflection of the continuing influence of Frederick Jackson Turner's frontier thesis: the exploration of the space frontier could work as a safety valve to ameliorate economic and social problems within the United States. In short, the frontier had allowed Americans to develop a distinct identity, one that colored their perspective of the world. Space could serve the same purpose as had earlier American frontiers, rejuvenating the nation and safeguarding democracy for future generations.

Americans did not suddenly invent the concept of the frontier in the 1950s and 1960s to justify space exploration. Both popular and intellectual interpretations of the frontier myth evolved slowly over decades, reflecting the influence of literature, popular culture, and historical events. Since the frontier identity developed in such a slow manner, most Americans had come to believe in the myth without question–it had taken root in their subconsciousnesses. Turner's theories about the importance of the frontier put into words what many Americans had already come to believe. The frontier, as defined by Turner, has had a powerful grasp on the American imagination and cultural identity, especially its sense of exceptionalism. Speaking in 1893, Turner argued that the frontier "experience has been fundamental in the economic, political, and social characteristics of the American people and in the conceptions of their destiny." Frontier exploration had renewed and reinvented Americans, through its promotion of democracy, opportunity, and individuality. These beliefs made it easy for Americans to apply the frontier myth to space exploration.

There was already a tradition of using the frontier myth to justify American policies in the past. Turner's thesis proved to be a useful justification for Progressive actions in the late nineteenth and early twentieth centuries. Assimilation of the massive numbers of immigrants was essential to prevent societal conflict and threats to democracy, especially if the "free land" that the nation was based on had disappeared, as Turner had claimed. In the 1930s New Deal reformers also used frontier arguments to validate their programs. By the 1950s and 1960s new challenges, such as the Civil Rights movement and domestic turmoil over the U.S. role in Vietnam, seemingly threatened traditional American life once again. Many Americans welcomed space exploration as the new safety valve that would safeguard democratic ideals and hold society together.

Historians of the American West have since challenged Turner's explanation of the nation's history, but few Americans beyond the academy have ever questioned its validity. Americans were exposed to the frontier myth as they went to school and through literature, television, and movies. Having accepted the premise of Turner's thesis, most Americans believed that the space frontier would rejuvenate the nation, economically, politically, and socially. It is unsurprising in this climate that the National Aeronautics and Space Administration (NASA), the presidents, Congress, and popular sources such as the media all utilized frontier language in justifications of the space program. In fact, it would have been more astonishing if they had not done so. While American perceptions of the frontier past were often inaccurate, sometimes what people believed to be true is as important as the truth itself. After all, it is those beliefs that influenced the way in which Americans viewed their present and future–particularly with regard to space exploration.

NASA quickly incorporated frontier language into its discussions of the American space program. As the agency entrusted with carrying out the civilian space program, NASA faced several pressures. On the one hand, the agency had to develop the scientific and technical capabilities to explore space. On the other hand, NASA administrators also had to justify their spending and persuade their audience of the necessity of space exploration. It is in this second category that frontier rhetoric was prominent.

Just as the majority of Americans connected the importance of the frontier past to national character, NASA leadership also believed that the frontier had molded national identity in a special way, making the United States distinct within the world. This belief permeated agency discussions of its mission. Administrators introduced a version of Turner's frontier thesis to describe the benefits of investigating the new space "frontier" and employed popular frontier images to make the space program more exciting for their audience. They compared astronauts to frontiersmen, pioneers, and Columbus. They described space exploration as a "challenging adventure," something done by a "curious" and "courageous" people. At the same time, NASA leadership also argued that space would have an impact similar to that of earlier American frontiers, rejuvenating the American spirit, encouraging economic and technological growth, and protecting democratic values for future generations. Presidents, the Congress, and the majority of American citizens agreed and were convinced that space was the new frontier. Despite growing opposition to the amount of money spent on space exploration by the late 1960s and 1970s, most Americans still accepted NASA's view of America's legacy and its connections to space.

From the onset of the space program, presidents have also had a major impact on how Americans have viewed space. As a key figure in the creation of space policy, the president influenced not only the way in which NASA administrators referred to their mission but also the manner in which other Americans, from congressmen to journalists and the general public, perceived space exploration. Presidents brought their own historical assumptions to their office, which also clearly influenced the way they viewed space. As a result, their views of the American space program were varied, and they prioritized space differently. With Dwight D. Eisenhower as the only exception, presidents since the 1940s have had one common aspect in their discussions of space exploration: the connection of space to the frontier past. The goals varied through the decades, space competition with the Soviet Union declined and eventually disappeared altogether, and NASA's popularity fluctuated; despite these changes, the one theme that remained constant was the comparison of space to the nineteenth-century frontier. Some presidents utilized this rhetoric more than others, but it never disappeared entirely.

John F. Kennedy was the first president to connect space and the frontier past. Running for president in 1960 on the slogan "The New Frontier," Kennedy used the word *frontier* to describe American ventures on all fronts: science, technology, the economy, politics, and even social change. He charged Americans to follow the examples of their pioneer ancestors in tackling the challenges of the second half of the twentieth century. While his definition was based mostly on Turner's model, Kennedy also used popular frontier symbolism to support his points. He carried this rhetoric from his campaign into his presidency, making it the theme for all he tried to accomplish. It is no coincidence that space exploration became synonymous with the frontier during his presidency, since Kennedy instigated the major push for space exploration, with the specific goal of putting Americans on the Moon. His success with the frontier metaphor encouraged future presidents to follow his example.

From Kennedy onward, all of the presidents understood the connection between the frontier and space. As have most Americans, presidents looked to the exploration of space to help safeguard important aspects of the American character, especially in eras when domestic and political events had the potential to tear the nation apart. Although presidents prioritized space differently, they never ceased to describe the benefits of space exploration. The frequency of such references declined somewhat in the 1970s. Since frontier language was exciting, Kennedy, Lyndon B. Johnson, and Richard M. Nixon used it to validate their space goals. Presidents in the 1970s downplayed the frontier element in their space discussions, significantly reducing the money spent on exploration, but in the 1980s Ronald Reagan focused American attention once again on the space frontier as part of his larger rhetorical strategy to increase national confidence.

As the guardian of the national budget, the U.S. Congress has also had a significant impact upon the direction and scope of the American space program. At the same time, a variety of people influenced the way legislators thought about space. Often these groups used frontier references in their discussions of space exploration. NASA lobbied Congress, consistently utilizing frontier rhetoric in an attempt to gain maximum financial support for its missions. Journalists, scientists, and aerospace-industry experts also employed frontier imagery in justifying space exploration. Even many congressmen used frontier rhetoric to describe space policies, reflecting their own historical assumptions as well as other influences.

There were limitations to the influence of frontier language on Congress. The widespread use of this discourse did not necessarily translate into more congressional support for NASA. Congress viewed space exploration as an important national venture, especially in the late 1950s and early 1960s, when the Soviet Union seemed superior to the United States in space technology. The 1960s and 1970s proved to be a much more difficult climate for NASA's ambitious goals. As the Vietnam War and Great Society programs required increasing amounts of funding, some legislators targeted NASA's budget for reduction. Congressmen cited polls of constituents who placed space much lower than most other national priorities. Increasingly, congressional space enthusiasts were in the minority, as critics wondered why so much money should be spent exploring the space frontier when so many problems needed to be solved back on Earth. Legislators and their constituents did not dispute the validity of the frontier analogy, but the space program seemed frivolous in comparison to these other concerns. Even American elation at the accomplishment of major space feats, such as the first moon landing, was not able to overcome the larger trend of reducing NASA's budget.

The Cold War provided a nurturing environment for the American space program in the 1950s and 1960s, but U.S. competition with the Soviet Union cannot fully explain why Americans chose to explore space. The nation faced many challenges during this period, not only from the Soviet Union but also as a result of domestic changes, such as

THE LAUNCH OF EXPLORER

On 31 January 1958 at Cape Canaveral, Florida, the United States successfully sent Explorer, *its first satellite, into orbit. It was a proud moment for the American people, as the attempt in December to launch a satellite aboard a* Vanguard *missile had proven to be an embarrassing failure. An Associated Press dispatch described the launching of* Explorer *as follows:*

The army fired a satellite into an orbit around the earth last night.

It completed its first orbit around the earth in 106 minutes.

A 70-foot long Jupiter-C launching vehicle sent a six-foot long tube of metal more than 200 miles into space and clusters of smaller rockets pushed it to orbital velocity of 19,400 miles an hour.

The Jupiter-C roared away from its launching pad into a starry sky at 8:48 P.M.

Two hours later President Eisenhower announced that America's first satellite was in orbit around the earth. . . .

The missile took off in a beautiful launching. It rose slowly at first in a huge splash of flame with a roar that could be heard for miles. . . .

Newsmen watching the launching shouted and cheered as though at some exciting sports game. . . .

At the moment the rocket engine was started, there was a sharp flash of fire. Almost immediately this expanded to a huge orange balloon of flame accompanied by an earthshaking roar.

The thunder of the rocket engine was so terrific that observers had to shout at each other, and even then could not make themselves understood. Watchers waved their arms and pounded each other on the back as the missile surged skyward.

Source: Paul M. Angle, The American Reader: From Columbus to Today *(New York: Rand McNally, 1958), pp. 675–677.*

the Civil Rights movement and the Women's movement. In many respects, Americans faced an identity crisis. Just as earlier generations had relied on the frontier myth to reinforce national character in times of crisis, Americans in the 1950s and 1960s looked to the space frontier as the solution to their problems, revitalizing the nation by strengthening the economy, society, and political system.

–SUSAN LANDRUM MANGUS, OHIO STATE UNIVERSITY

References

Wernher von Braun, "Crossing the Last Frontier," *Collier's* (22 March 1952): 25–29, 72–73;

Arthur C. Clarke, *The Exploration of Space* (New York: Harper, 1951);

Robert H. Goddard, "A Method of Reaching Extreme Altitudes," *Smithsonian Miscellaneous Collections* 71 (1919): 54;

Edward Everett Hale, "The Brick Moon," *Atlantic Monthly* (October 1869): 451–460; (November 1869): 603–611; (December 1869): 679–688; (February 1870): 215–222;

James L. Kauffman, *Selling Outer Space: Kennedy, the Media, and Funding for Project Apollo, 1961–1963* (Tuscaloosa: University of Alabama Press, 1994);

Johannes Kepler, *Somnium: The Dream, or Posthumous Work on Lunar Astronomy,* translated by Edward Rosen (Madison: University of Wisconsin Press, 1967);

Linda T. Krug, *Presidential Perspectives on Space Exploration: Guiding Metaphors from Eisenhower to Bush* (Westport, Conn.: Praeger, 1991);

John M. Logsdon and others, eds., *Exploring the Unknown: Selected Documents in the History of the U.S. Civil Space Program,* volume 1, *Organizing for Exploration* (Washington, D.C.: National Aeronautics and Space Administration, 1995);

Howard E. McCurdy, *Space and the American Imagination* (Washington: Smithsonian Institution Press, 1997);

Walter A. McDougall, *The Heavens and the Earth: A Political History of the Space Age* (New York: BasicBooks, 1985);

Homer E. Newell, *Beyond the Atmosphere: Early Years of Space Science* (Washington, D.C.: National Aeronautics and Space Administration, 1980);

Hermann Oberth, *Die Rakete zu den Planetenräumen* (Munich: Oldenbourg, 1923), translated as *Rockets into Interplanetary Space* (Washington, D.C.: National Aeronautics and Space Administration, 1964);

Richard Slotkin, *Gunfighter Nation: The Myth of the Frontier in Twentieth-Century America* (New York: Atheneum, 1992);

Lyman Spitzer, "Astronomical Advantages of an Extra-Terrestrial Observatory, September 1, 1946" reprinted in *Astronomy Quarterly,* 7 (1990): 131–142;

Konstantin Tsiolkovsky, "Exploration of the Universe with Reaction Machines," in *Sobraniye Sochineniy,* Tom II: *Reaktivnyye Letatal'nyye Apparaty* (Moscow: Izdatel'stvo Akademii Nauk SSSR, 1954), translated as *Collected Works of K. E. Tsiolkovskii,* volume 2, *Reactive Flying Machines,* edited by A. A. Blagonravov (Washington, D.C.: National Aeronautics and Space Administration, 1965), pp. 72–117;

Frederick Jackson Turner, *The Frontier in American History* (New York: Holt, 1920);

Jules Verne, *De la terre à la lune; trajet direct en 97 heures* (Paris: Hetzel, 1865) translated by Edward Roth as *From the Earth to the Moon: All Around the Moon* (New York: Dover, 1962);

H. G. Wells, *First Men on the Moon* (London: G. Newnes, 1901);

Richard White and Patricia Nelson Limerick, *The Frontier in American Culture: An Exhibition at the Newberry Library, August 26, 1994–January 7, 1995,* edited by James R. Grossman (Berkeley: University of California Press, 1994).

SUBURBIA

Was the rise of suburbia an American dream or nightmare?

Viewpoint: The rise of suburbia after World War II contributed to many problems, including the decline of cities, a spoiled natural environment, dependence on automobiles, and enforced social conformity.

Viewpoint: The postwar emergence of suburbia completed the American dream by increasing individual home ownership and freeing people from decaying urban environments.

By 1950 America's social environment was clearly in need of far-reaching renovation. After roughly three generations of urbanization, reaching back into the mid nineteenth century, the cities were overcrowded; their infrastructures were badly in need of updating; and much of the housing stock was inadequate. These problems were to be expected as the predictable results of aging and growth, but several coincidental developments made them particularly acute. Demand for wartime labor and the mechanization of cotton production ignited the great migration of rural African Americans and white Appalachians to Northern cities, straining already overburdened housing and public services. The end of the war in 1945 meant that millions of men would return home and seek to rebuild normal private lives and start families.

Americans met these needs in characteristic fashion: partly through private initiative and government programs and by muddling along without much planning. Private builders who had gained experience in mass-producing housing for the military during the war naturally turned their expertise to the peacetime housing market. Just as naturally they began to build on the edges of cities, where land was inexpensive but demand was high. New suburban communities of mass-produced homes sprang up, beginning with the first Levittown, in New York in 1947. Wealthy Americans always had moved outward into suburbs to get away from the crunch and inconveniences of city life, but with planned communities such as Levittowns, Americans of modest means could enjoy suburban living for the first time.

The expansion of metropolitan areas outward into the suburbs gained much from governmental housing policy. Federal home-loan programs favored new housing, because it more easily met construction codes than renovated dwellings. The GI Bill and veterans loans encouraged millions of returning soldiers to move into new homes. Finally, the 1956 National Defense Highway Act approved federal funding for the interstate highway system, which tied these suburbs to urban cores and opened up the countryside to further development.

Together, private initiative and government programs drove the great suburban boom of the 1950s, a boom that never has stopped. Between 1945 and 1950, five million new homes were built, making it possible for more than half of Americans to own their own homes. The vast majority of this construction was undertaken around urban peripheries of cities; from 1950 to 1960,

75 percent of metropolitan growth took place in suburban areas, which increased their population five times faster than the urban areas they surrounded.

Even as the wave of suburbanization began, critics denounced the new lifestyle. They argued that the suburbs were hideous places of social regimentation and conformity, with none of the organic diversity that cities accommodated. They were nothing more than extensions into private life of the corporate blandness that had turned most work into dull and uninteresting office labor. The boring public life of the "organization man" or "man in the grey flannel suit" was reenforced in a setting where all houses were the same: people all had the same socioeconomic status, and petty materialism reigned. Because it made true community life impossible, the suburb became the breeding ground of middle-class alienation.

The critics also began to add up other social costs of suburbanization. By the mid 1960s it had become clear that suburbanization was convoluted with the nation's race problem. Those millions of people fleeing the cities for suburban homes were overwhelmingly middle-class whites, and at least part of the motivation was to escape the rising numbers of urban African Americans or, in the Southwest, Latino immigrants. Even when it was not overtly racist, so-called white flight deepened urban problems by lowering property values in cities and thereby diminishing the tax base, which had ripple effects on urban schools, police and fire protection, and trash collection. America's postwar cities became more segregated by race and class than its small southern villages ever were. Add to these deep social ills the accumulating environmental problems that come with dependence on the automobile, to say nothing of the destruction of the countryside, and suburbanization has to rank, so the critics contend, as among the most pernicious social developments in American history.

Through the 1950s suburbia had far more critics than friends. However, beginning with sociologist Herbert Gans in the mid 1960s, some observers began to defend the new arrangements. First, there were good reasons for people to get out of the increasingly dirty and crime-ridden cities. Many wanted a decent place to raise their children. The critics of the suburbs overrated the amenities of urban life. Considered snobbish intellectuals, they valued the museums, opera houses, and orchestras, while common folks mostly just endured growing inconvenience and decay.

What looked at first glance like homogenous places, moreover, were on closer inspection more diverse than urban neighborhoods. America's cities, composites of ethnic enclaves, were built on ethnic and racial segregation; the suburbs were virtually the only place where a Lithuanian Jew might live next to an Irish Catholic or an Anglo-Protestant. To say that the suburbs were somehow not true communities, moreover, was to forget that they were new and that communities take time to build. Whatever else the intellectuals wanted to think, the suburbs' defenders noted, Americans themselves have always flocked to the suburbs. They vote with their feet, and suburbs have always won over urban living.

Viewpoint: The rise of suburbia after World War II contributed to many problems, including the decline of cities, a spoiled natural environment, dependence on automobiles, and enforced social conformity.

In order to appreciate just how badly suburbanization deformed humane living, it is necessary to remind ourselves that the two great virtues of city life, its cultural dynamism and human diversity, are integral to meaningful social existence. The city as a social environment is essential to culture. In its free cultural institutions, its museums, galleries, libraries, and parks—some would say even in its "palaces of consumption," department stores—the city brings together a complex assortment of people whose interaction is the stuff of human creativity. Often these institutions are the philanthropic creations of urban elites who care about their cities and self-consciously seek to bring some measure of refinement to the lives of less fortunate residents. Yet, even its less exalted places are scenes of a healthy intercourse. City parks, where the poorest can mingle with the wealthiest, have always been living expressions of democratic ideals. In the modern American city, the baseball stadium was always an important location for regular civic unity. In the days before personal seat licenses, skyboxes, and private lounges, the baseball stadium lent itself to a fairly well-enclosed mixing of people across race and class lines.

At the very time they promoted the democratic mixing of people, American cities accommodated enormous human diversity. Immigrants into American cities did what immigrants always tend to do: they sought out their own kind. To mitigate the difficulties that resettlement always brings, immigrants understandably gravitated to those urban neighborhoods where familiar people lived who could be both welcoming and

A view of one of the first planned residential subdivisions in the United States, on Long Island, New York, circa 1950

helpful. Thus emerged the ethnic neighborhoods found in every American city by World War I, and with this self-segregation cultural diversity flourished. Collected among their own, immigrants could engage in traditional rituals without self-consciousness. Local peddlers sold traditional foods and other commodities. Traditional religious practices were transplanted and local languages preserved. Extended family ties and the practices that preserved kin networks–arranged marriages and taboos against interethnic and interreligious marriage–often remained intact. The solidarity within ethnic groups located in physical proximity gave rise to mutually reinforcing institutions. Burial societies, invariably organized according to national origins, were common and typically provided insurance so that members could be assured of proper burial regardless of earthly poverty, or in the case of Chicano immigrants, assured that their remains would be taken back to Mexico. Most groups had fraternal organizations; many had credit unions or other cooperative means of raising capital, something still practiced among Korean immigrants. The larger and more coherent the particular immigrant community, the more successful the survival of old-country folkways. It is a staple fact in the history of immigration that new arrivals into a neighborhood constantly replenished the energy that cultural sustenance required in a radically different setting.

None of these conditions prevail in the suburbs. Instead of mixing, the classes are clearly separated, even as ethnic assimilation breaks down the genuine cultural diversity of the urban mosaic. It is true that suburbia was opened to people of modest means, but the sort of housing they were offered was nothing to boast of. Abraham Levitt established the basic elements of the suburban design: houses with similar designs, if not outright copies; streets that went nowhere; peripheral shopping centers accessible only by automobile; and all laid out in what had initially been the country. The basic Levitt house was 720 square feet, had a standard interior layout with little external variation, and was sold under race-restrictive deed covenants. Such suburban houses are typical American responses to real human needs. They show that mass production is more important than quality and that private greed outweighs more humane values such as architectural originality. Indeed, the modern development invariably was built by reducing the natural variations of the landscape. Trees were uprooted, hills flattened and valleys raised, all to make it easier to put down the standardized house.

The only thing that could emerge from such a mass-produced environment was the mass-produced American. It is hardly any wonder that the *Father Knows Best* image of the average American prevailed in the 1950s. Stuck in identical homes and compelled into almost compulsive relationships with neighbors who were themselves interchangeable, the suburbanites were archetypes of social conformity, just as in television. John Keats, in order to emphasize this condition, named the protagonists of his 1956 novel on suburbia, *The Crack in the Picture Window*, John and Mary Drone. They had moved into "a house that could never be a home, . . . into a neighborhood that could never be a community." It was a strange new America they had entered, Keats wrote, a kind of "communism," for suburban existence "was made possible by destruction of the individual," which "began with the obliteration of the individualistic house and self-sufficient neighborhood, and from there on, the creation of mass-produced human beings followed as the night the day."

In reducing the physical environment to homogeneity, suburbia revealed itself to be a mere extension of the whole American system of cultural mass production. Life itself became a commodity, the family an instrument of consumption. Analyzing one of the earliest comprehensive studies of suburbia, social critic Maurice Robert Stein noted that everything from career motivation, social life, and child rearing in suburbia seemed to revolve around the acquisition of consumer goods. The father saw his work as a means to sustaining or increasing fashionable goods, which had to be thrown out and replaced as fashion dictated, and the child therefore saw getting new things "as a source of ego-enhancement." Because the family's schedule was shaped around activities related to buying or disposing of goods, Stein concluded in *The Eclipse of Community: An Interpretation of American Studies* (1960), time itself "is transformed into a disposable commodity."

Bad enough for those stuck in such places, the movement of home owners out of the city spelled disaster for new migrants into American cities, the African Americans, Appalachian whites, and Latinos. More than 2.75 million African Americans moved from the rural South into Northern and Western cities between 1940 and 1960; probably as many Appalachian whites and Latinos did as well. In any event, these new immigrants hoped to follow the same course that eastern and southern Europeans had taken early in the twentieth century. They came to the cities to work hard, raise families, and succeed. Unlike their urban predecessors, however, they came into cities that were already falling apart, as middle-class whites fled for suburbia, taking with them many of the jobs the new immigrants had hoped to obtain. The economic and social separation was surely made more intense by white racism.

It is true that more and more minorities have scratched their way up the social ladder and also have moved into suburbia in the last twenty years. Yet, even this change has an important downside, for it drained minority communities of their most successful members, leaving urban communities with even fewer resources and role models whom struggling young people might imitate.

Leaving aside how suburbanization worsened America's already depressing history of racial injustice, the spewing of unplanned construction across the national landscape resulted in a foolish dependence on the automobile as the only common form of transportation. By 1960 some 75 million cars ran across the American landscape, and the numbers steadily increased thereafter. There were more new cars sold in America during the 1980s than there were babies born. Just as important was the number of miles driven, which dramatically increased in the 1990s. This transportation revolution furthered the national dependence on foreign oil, dramatically elevated levels of air pollution, and increased traffic congestion and the destruction of countryside–to say nothing of the tens of thousands of deaths each year from traffic accidents. With the momentary exception of Portland, Oregon, every major city in America has experienced an astonishing sprawl outward. It got to the point that the original motivation for living in a suburb–the desire to renew one's contact with nature and to find some open space to breath–turned into a nightmare in which it was no longer possible to tell the difference between city and country. The whole environment became homogenized into one extended strip of asphalt.

–DAVID STEIGERWALD, OHIO STATE UNIVERSITY, MARION

SUBURBIA: A MAR ON THE LAND

The following selection is from an essay titled "The Suburban Dislocation" in sociologist David Riesman's Abundance for What? and Other Essays *(1964). It represents a typical 1960s condemnation of suburbia and its negative impact on American society.*

Where the husband goes off with the car to work (and often, in the vicious circle created by the car, there is no other way for him to travel), the wife is frequently either privatized at home or must herself, to escape isolation, take a job which will help support her own car, as well as the baby-sitter.

The children themselves, in fact, before they get access to a car, are captives of their suburb, save for those families where the housewives surrender continuity in their own lives to chauffeur their children to lessons, doctors, and other services which could be reached via public transport in the city. In the suburban public schools, the young are captives, too, dependent on whatever art and science and general liveliness their particular school happens to have. . . .

. . . the suburban kaffee-klatsch is proverbial in which the women sit around and discuss their children—the main "surrogates" they have in common. Their husbands, working downtown or in a nearby plant, have some opportunity to meet people on an occupational basis who are of different backgrounds, different ages, and different life-chances than they themselves; but the wives, falling into or forced into a neighborly gregariousness, tend to see others of similar age, setting, and TV exposure . . . cross-sex friendships are ruled out by lack of sophistication in such relations and by the lack of privacy. And the husbands, if not the tired businessmen of legend, are less eager than some of their wives to drive long distances at night for out-of-suburb contacts, . . . In this situation, many women of college education feel trapped, aware of falling behind their own ideals and their husbands' in breadth of view and nourishing experience. The various leisure-time activities they undertake do not seem to fill this void. . . .

Source: *Charles M. Dollar and Gary W. Reichard, eds.,* American Issues: A Documentary Reader *(New York: Random House, 1988), pp. 437–439.*

Viewpoint:
The postwar emergence of suburbia completed the American dream by increasing individual home ownership and freeing people from decaying urban environments.

It is hard to think of any part of American life that has been so vilified by intellectuals and experts, while so eagerly accepted by Americans themselves, as suburban living. The usual charges begin with criticism of the physical environment, particularly the house architecture. It was obvious that builders such as Abraham Levitt mass-produced identical homes, but criticizing him invariably ignored two things. First, against what standard should Levitt's homes be compared? Middle- and working-class people who moved into the new suburbs after 1950 were not choosing between a mass-produced home and a home in the city. Their real choice was between a Levitt home or city apartment, which was even more dull and regimenting than the suburban tract home. Intellectuals might concoct many reasons why that city apartment was superior, but for young families trying to raise children safely, the suburban home was clearly preferable.

Second, suburbia's critics complained about tract housing well before suburban communities had a chance to mature. When Herbert J. Gans moved into one of the original Levittowns in the 1960s, after the tract was more than a decade old, he discovered and reported in *The Levittowners: Ways of Life and Politics in a New Suburban Community* (1967) that people had a way of turning the homogenous into the distinct and personal. Original deed restrictions–including those that excluded people of color–had worn away, and people put their own stamps on their homes with different colors of paint, new gardens and shrubs, and additions of various sorts. What had seemed so artificial when it was first constructed, Gans found, was becoming more organically diverse, as people expressed themselves.

Similarly, the social homogeneity of the suburbs was grossly exaggerated. Even Levittown contained a variety of different neighborhoods within its boundaries, and was ethnically and religiously diverse. Gans found everyone from unskilled blue-collar workers to doctors and lawyers during his two-year residence there. This class diversity mirrored religious and ethnic diversity. Among his neighbors were two WASP engineers, one agnostic and a Methodist; a Baptist married to a Polish-American Catholic; "an Italian-American tractor operator (whose ambition was to own a junkyard) and his upwardly mobile wife"; a Southern fundamentalist couple; and a Viennese Jew who had converted to Catholicism.

It was true, Gans conceded, that the Levittown in which he lived was economically homogenous, which also meant that it was home to few African Americans, but he argued that one ought to distinguish between people searching for "compatibility" as against homogeneity. Most Levittowners wanted to live among people of similar age and income, which may or may not have been regrettable but was a far cry from a socially destructive hostility to human diversity. At the least, suburbia should not be the "whipping boy" for the problems that beset all of American culture. If suburban neighborhoods reflected increasing economic homogeneity, Gans argued, they reflected "the breakdown of rigid class and caste systems in which low-status people 'knew their place,' and which made residential segregation unnecessary." One could argue, in other words, that economic homogeneity resulted from the upward mobility of urban ethnics who previously had been confined to their respective ghettos.

The antisuburban critique revealed a pervasive snobbishness and upper-class bias, as Gans put it, that "reflects the critics' disappointment that the new suburbs do not satisfy their particular tourist requirements: that they are not places for wandering, that they lack the charm of a medieval village, the excitement of the metropolis, or the architectural variety of an upper-income suburb." Those social critics who lamented the physical drawbacks of suburbia ignored much of the most farsighted work of architects and planners of their own time. The fact was that modern city centers, whether in London, New York, or Chicago, had gotten so densely populated that they could scarcely accommodate life on a human scale any longer. In response, many of the best minds in the field of urban planning began to consider the prospects for decentralized living. Among the trends that emerged was the so-called Garden City movement, which swept the imagination of British and American experts in the mid twentieth century and resembled in many ways the sorts of communities that were springing up in more informal forms in the United States. Indeed, one of the greatest American architects of the century, Frank Lloyd Wright, spent much of his creative energy imagining and planning a development he called Broadacre. While he envisioned Broadacre as a largely self-sufficient community, even Wright saw the necessity of the automobile as the essential means of transportation for decentralized living.

For all the criticism that suburbia attracted, it was Wright, in *The Living City* (1958), who appears the most prophetic of writers in the 1950s. The so-called postsuburban age of the 1990s saw the rise of "edge cities," areas of planned development that are within metropolitan areas but that are physically, economically, and culturally independent of the city itself. Every major city in the nation–and around the world–now boasts of just such developments. Los Angeles might even be described as made up entirely of edge cities.

Far from being unplanned blobs of toxic development oozing outward, these developments are planned down to the square foot. Their developers know exactly how much retail and office space, how many parking spaces, and how many workers and residents an area needs to succeed. Their formulas are so precise that they can guarantee investors not only that enough businesses and office workers will relocate to edge-city property but also that there will be enough density to attract full-time residents as well. Edge cities are virtually crime-free because their public spaces have become privatized. Their security is particularly helpful for women, who make up a good part of the labor force and consumers. The combination of density and desirability encourages sociability as well.

No one could walk through an edge city, moreover, without being deeply impressed by its cultural and ethnic diversity. The great wave of immigrants who came to the United States in the last two decades has washed through these newly developing areas. Edge cities are now home to an incredible array of ethnic businesses–especially restaurants–and communities of Asians, Middle Easterners, Latinos, and Eastern Europeans; they are global communities in microcosm. Far from the dull homogenized world of Levittown, edge cities have blossomed, as architectural critic Christopher Jencks recently wrote of Los Angeles, into an "urban bouillabaisse" in which people live pretty much however they see fit.

Most remarkably, edge cities established lessons in planning and development that have been applied to central cities as well, and as a consequence an urban renaissance has developed. This welcome paradox, in which the extremes of suburban development showed the way toward urban revival, was possible because edge cities showed how technological development could be mixed with shopping and residential districts to create well-defined environments that appealed to a diverse collection of people. In the new social environment, the development in which early suburbia was only the first stage, everyone could find their niche.

Here is the key difference between the social environment of city and suburb: suburban living has always been based on individual choice, not social obligations, desperation, or legal segregation. Suburbia reflected the freely expressed desire of people to live a certain way. And given the way cities worldwide are imitating American metropolises, it looks as if the American dream, which forty years ago was barely born among Americans themselves, is becoming an international dream. What Gans noted of Americans thirty years ago was becoming increasingly true of people from Tokyo to Paris to Sao Paulo: "If suburban life was as undesirable and unhealthy as the critics charged," Gans wrote, "the suburbanites themselves were blissfully unaware of it; they were happy in their new homes and communities, much happier than they had been in the city."

–DAVID STEIGERWALD, OHIO STATE UNIVERSITY, MARION

References

Herbert J. Gans, *The Levittowners: Ways of Life and Politics in a New Suburban Community* (New York: Pantheon, 1967);

Joel Garreau, *Edge City: Life on the New Frontier* (New York: Doubleday, 1991);

Kenneth T. Jackson, *Crabgrass Frontier: The Suburbanization of the United States* (New York: Oxford University Press, 1985);

Christopher Jencks, "Hetero-Architecture and the L.A. School," in *The City: Los Angeles and Urban Theory at the End of the Twentieth Century,* edited by Allen J. Scott and Edward W. Soja (Berkeley: University of California Press, 1996), pp. 47–75;

John Keats, *The Crack in the Picture Window* (Boston: Houghton Mifflin, 1956);

James Howard Kunstler, *The Geography of Nowhere: The Rise and Decline of America's Man-Made Landscape* (New York: Simon & Schuster, 1993);

Maurice Robert Stein, *The Eclipse of Community: An Interpretation of American Studies* (Princeton: Princeton University Press, 1960);

Frank Lloyd Wright, *The Living City* (New York: Horizon, 1958).

U.S. SPACE PROGRAM

What was the importance of the space program to the United States?

Viewpoint: The space program, especially the moon landing, reaffirmed American confidence.

Viewpoint: Despite the publicity generated by the race to the Moon, the real benefit of the U.S. space program was in satellite technology.

Sending men to the Moon and returning them to Earth, long the dream of science-fiction fantasies, was accomplished in July 1969. President Richard M. Nixon said it was the most significant week in the history of the world since its creation. The Apollo program, beset by tragedy early on, had overcome terrific obstacles to achieve its promised goal.

Yet, was the moon landing the most significant part of the space program? How important was the moon landing to the advance of science, or even to the space program? Historian A. Bowdoin Van Riper argues that the lunar landing was the central feature of the space program, and that without the National Aeronautics and Space Administration (NASA) would not have been able to generate public enthusiasm, and consequently congressional support, for its other programs.

On the other hand, Robert N. Wold argues that while the Apollo program was the main public component of the space program, it was much less significant. After NASA stopped sending men to the Moon, its real public and scientific service began, with the less glamorous but, in the long run, more important work of launching satellites. While moon exploration may have advanced scientific knowledge, satellites, Wold argues, have brought advances to many more people. Cellular phones allow communication around the world; the Global Positioning System allows us to pinpoint our location anywhere; and weather satellites give accurate and immediate pictures of hurricanes and typhoons, saving millions of lives by warning people of these deadly storms. While the moon landing may have inspired those able to watch it, the less glamorous work of launching satellites has transformed our world.

Should NASA have focused its attention on satellites, and not spent so much time and energy sending men to the Moon? Without the public excitement generated by the race to the Moon, would Americans have supported NASA's satellite program? How we ask the question often determines our answer.

Viewpoint: The space program, especially the moon landing, reaffirmed American confidence.

Grand-scale building projects that test the limits of the possible and reshape the human relationship to nature are as old as urban civilization. They are especially prominent in American history: the transcontinental railroad in the 1860s, the Panama Canal in the 1910s, and the Hoover Dam in the 1930s. Such projects often have symbolic functions, as well as practical ones. The Panama Canal, for example, proclaimed President Theodore Roosevelt's renewal of the Monroe Doctrine and America's emergence as a player in world affairs. Project Apollo, created in response to President John F. Kennedy's 1961 call for a manned landing on the Moon by the end of the decade, is unique among such endeavors. Its practical functions–gathering scientific data, for example–took a distant back seat to its symbolic ones. Created to project a carefully crafted image of America, it did so, brilliantly.

The moon-landing program took place amid the social and political tumult of the 1960s and early 1970s. It entered the public consciousness through a presidential speech delivered during the sour aftermath of the Bay of Pigs debacle and its early stages unfolded alongside the Cuban Missile Crisis and the Watts Riots. Its greatest technical achievement came at the end of 1968–a year that fractured the Democratic Party, the Civil Rights movement, and any hope of a national consensus in favor of the Vietnam War. The summer of 1969, when Neil Armstrong became the first human to set foot on another world, was also the summer of Woodstock. The final flight of the program, an Earth-orbit rendezvous with a Soviet spacecraft, took place in 1975 as communist forces overran South Vietnam and leading figures in the Watergate scandal received their jail sentences.

These events shook long-held beliefs about America's place in the world and unsettled long-held assumptions about American values. Project Apollo's significance lay in its ability to reinforce those beliefs and assumptions. The moon-landing program became a cultural icon for those Americans that Richard M. Nixon dubbed the "great, silent majority." It showed them people recognizably like themselves–clean-cut, conservatively dressed white men–working as a team in pursuit of a common goal. The program displayed, proudly and without apology, core American values of patriotism and piety. Most of all it reinforced their faith that, despite setbacks abroad and division at home, America remained capable of great things. Project Apollo did for the moderate-to-conservative middle classes what Woodstock did for the counterculture. It gave them the opportunity to say, to themselves and others, "*This* is what we are all about."

The early years of the American manned space program were also among the coldest of the Cold War. The program was shaped, therefore, by intense competition between the United States and the Soviet Union. Technologically speaking, the three-orbit flight of John Glenn's Mercury spacecraft *Friendship 7* in February 1962 was not a milestone in that competition. Soviet cosmonaut Yuri Gagarin, the first human in space, had made an orbital flight in April 1961. Symbolically, however, the flight of *Friendship 7* was a triumph.

The United States entered the "space race" in second place. The Soviet Union had launched the first artificial satellite, *Sputnik I,* in 1957. Hampered by inadequate, unreliable booster rockets, the United States had remained behind the Soviets. The space race was widely seen as a surrogate for the arms race, and since rocket technology was central to both, second-place status raised serious concerns about military preparedness. Glenn's flight did not erase those concerns, but it did ease them. The United States now looked like a serious contender in the space race.

Glenn himself fit perfectly into the roles that Kennedy had defined for astronauts: champions of freedom and symbols of the American people. A clear-eyed, crewcut U.S. Marine combat veteran, Glenn looked like a picture of "the average American" that had been improved by a Madison Avenue ad agency. Relentlessly serious and unswervingly moral, he projected a public persona defined by his devotion to job and wife. He even had the perfect, humanizing touch of frivolity in his background: he had appeared on the television game show *Name That Tune.* For three orbits aboard *Friendship 7,* Glenn *was* America, rising to do symbolic battle with the Soviet Union. "Thank you from the bottom of my heart for what you have done for America!" began one of the quarter-million letters Glenn received after his flight. "You have awakened the hearts and minds of all of us to what America and the word 'American' really stands for: Faith–Courage–Humility–Love of God and Country."

The successful flight of *Friendship 7* brought fulfillment of Kennedy's challenge within the realm of possibility. The equally successful flight of *Apollo 8,* in December 1968, transformed it into a virtual certainty. *Apollo 8* also marked a symbolic transition: it

A Redstone military rocket carrying the *Mercury* spacecraft during a test launch, circa 1961

(Associated Press)

was the last act in the decade-long U.S.-Soviet space race. American intelligence agencies alerted National Aeronautics and Space Administration (NASA), in mid 1968, that the Soviet *Zond* program would be capable of placing a cosmonaut in lunar orbit by December 1968 or January 1969. The Soviets had no lunar-landing capability, but a lunar orbit flight would allow them to claim the title "First to the Moon" and so dilute at the last minute the long-planned-for American triumph. Appalled at this possibility, NASA managers took an unusually bold step. Even before the first manned test flight of the new Apollo spacecraft, they rewrote the flight plan of the second test flight. Originally designed as a shakedown cruise in Earth orbit, *Apollo 8* became a half-million-mile round trip to the Moon.

The gamble paid off handsomely. Convinced that they had time to spare, Soviet mission planners overrode the wishes of their flight crews and delayed the launch of a manned *Zond* mission. The crew of *Apollo 8*, meanwhile, turned in a flawless performance. They became, at a stroke, the first humans to escape Earth's gravity, to reach and orbit the Moon, and to see its features firsthand. NASA had a triumph as significant as *Sputnik I* and a green light for a landing attempt in 1969. The space race that had begun in 1957 was, for all practical purposes, over. *Apollo 8* mission commander Frank Borman retired from NASA after his return to Earth, satisfied that any future mission–even the first landing–would be anticlimactic.

Many Americans' most potent memories of the triumphant mission focused, significantly, on one of its quietest moments. Broadcasting from lunar orbit on Christmas Eve, the crew of *Apollo 8* took turns reading the first verses of Genesis, ending with the Creation of the Earth and the words "God saw that it was good." With the spacecraft about to pass out of radio contact, Borman signed off: "Good night, good luck, a Merry Christmas, and God bless all of you, all of you on the *good earth*." The impromptu reading was a gesture of extraordinary power. It provided a gentle coda to the most turbulent year in American history and suggested that the ideological tensions of the Cold War might be fading. The crew's words "expressed their deep humility and abiding good will. They had been given this glorious opportunity to brag, and instead chose to pray, finding words that would include as many people as possible in the message." When the U. S. Postal Service issued an *Apollo 8* stamp in 1969, it bore the words "In the beginning . . ." and a picture of Earth seen from lunar orbit: a blue and white ball, alone in the deep black emptiness of space.

Six months later, the crew of *Apollo 11* took the first human steps on another world and the final steps in fulfilling Kennedy's 1961 challenge. They flew a well-tested spacecraft on a mission whose key elements–up to the final descent to the lunar surface–had been rehearsed by earlier crews. Consistent with NASA's plan for the entire moon-landing program, the crew of *Apollo 11* "pushed the envelope" in a crucial but narrowly defined area. They demonstrated that a pair of astronauts could land on the surface, do useful work there, and then take off again. Technologically and operationally, it was an impressive step, though not as bold as the flights of *Friendship 7* or *Apollo 8*. Thanks to its status as the first lunar landing, however, *Apollo 11* carried more symbolic weight than any mission before it. Conscious that the world was watching, NASA and mission commander Armstrong chose this mission's symbols carefully.

The ceremonial aspects of the *Apollo 11* landing struck a balance between nationalism and internationalism. The astronauts acknowledged that the moon-landing program had been an American enterprise, but also portrayed it as a *human* enterprise in which all the world's population symbolically shared. They raised an American flag, carrying out the explorer's traditional act of "claiming" a newly discovered territory for their nation, and smaller flags adorned their spacesuits and lander. Armstrong's first words from the lunar surface offered a more inclusive vision: "one small step for [a] man, one giant leap for mankind." In his public announcement, if not in his private thoughts, Armstrong was not an American but simply a man, acting not for his tribe but for his species. An engraved plaque left behind on the discarded lower half of the lander struck a similar note. Though it bore an image of the American flag and the signature of then-President Nixon, these words dominated: "Here men from the planet Earth first set foot upon the moon. We came in peace, for all mankind."

The safe return of *Apollo 11* and its crew officially concluded the moon-landing program that Kennedy had proposed in 1961. Doubts that had then existed about American resolve and technological prowess were gone. Concerns about Soviet domination of outer space that loomed large in Kennedy's speech were gone as well. The moon-landing program continued, but its complexion changed. The successful flight of *Apollo 12* in November 1969 expanded the limits of flight operations one last time, by demonstrating that pinpoint landings at predetermined sites were possible. Beginning in 1970, the focus of Apollo missions slowly shifted from physical exploration to scientific data gathering. The act of getting to the Moon and back, though never a trivial proposition, receded into the background as activities on the lunar surface took center stage.

Public interest in NASA's moon landings faded quickly as exploration gave way to science. The fulfillment of Kennedy's challenge and the absence of Soviet competition left the space agency unable to create the sense of drama that had prevailed throughout the 1960s. Faced with a steadily declining budget, NASA scrapped the last three planned *Apollo* missions in order to guarantee the survival of its next project: the Earth-orbiting research station *Skylab*. One more *Apollo* spacecraft remained, and in 1975 it was used to write a final, ironic postscript to the enterprise that Kennedy had set in motion.

The *Apollo-Soyuz* rendezvous flight generated no scientific data and served no real engineering purpose. It was political theater, pure and simple: a meeting of former rivals in Earth's orbit for shared meals, exchanged gifts, and a symbolic handshake in the adapter joining the two spacecraft. Soviet and American leaders alike hailed the rendezvous flight as a sign that the Cold War was over (premature) or at least on hold for a time (accurate). The presence of Alexei Leonov aboard the Soviet spacecraft and Deke Slayton aboard the American counterpart completed the image that *Apollo-Soyuz* had been designed to project. Both men were veterans of the earliest, most intense days of the space race. Their meeting in orbit provided a fitting sense of closure to a moon-landing program that had begun in the heat of that race and ultimately helped to end it.

The moon-landing program unfolded in a time characterized both by tension abroad and by turmoil at home. Its confident, seemingly unstoppable progress toward a distant goal reassured middle America that, at some level at least, the country still worked. The public, human face of the program—white men with crew cuts, shirts, and ties—silently endorsed traditional values. Throughout its history, the program offered Americans a grand, heroic vision of themselves and their role in the wider world. Like the experience of Vietnam, it pervaded the culture of the 1960s and early 1970s, leaving its mark on the worldview of everyone old enough to have witnessed it.

—A. BOWDOIN VAN RIPER, SOUTHERN POLYTECHNIC STATE UNIVERSITY

Viewpoint: Despite the publicity generated by the race to the Moon, the real benefit of the U.S. space program was in satellite technology.

Thirty years after the flight of *Apollo 11*, it is hard to find public complaints about the many taxpayer dollars that were spent on human tours to the Moon instead of trying to find solutions to America's exasperating terra firma social problems. No longer, at least on prime-time television, do we hear Archie Bunker's refrain: "Ain't we got anything more important to do with twenty billion dollars than send a guy up on the moon to hit a few golf balls?" or "Those guys go on this trip and all they bring back is a bag full of rocks?"

Andrew Chaikin, a respected historian and the author of *A Man on the Moon* (1994), recently described the manned lunar-trip package that John F. Kennedy sold to Congress in

May 1961, four months after he had become president. Said Chaikin, "We didn't go to the moon for science; we didn't go to the moon for the love of exploration; we went to the moon to beat the Russians."

Kennedy had opposed the space program, first as a senator from Massachusetts and later in early 1961 as our nation's new president. Two months after his inauguration, he had told James Webb–the new chief of the National Aeronautics and Space Administration (NASA)–that he would veto funding for Apollo, the agency's ambitious program to explore the moon. Assuredly, Kennedy was not a diehard advocate for the space program, but he was, like his father, a politician.

What was it that completely turned him around for his 21 May address to Congress, titled "Urgent National Needs"? He passionately asked Congress and the public to approve Project Apollo, a manned expedition to the Moon, plus developmental projects: communications satellites, weather satellites, and nuclear rocketry.

Kennedy had found himself in a difficult situation: losing public stature. U.S. involvement in Laos, a precursor to the Vietnam War, had become a disaster. An attempt by Cuban mercenaries hired by the Central Intelligence Agency (CIA) to invade Cuba and assassinate Fidel Castro was another disaster. In addition, the Soviets had just succeeded in orbiting the first human being, cosmonaut Yuri Gagarin. The problems in Laos and Cuba were troublesome but, even more so, the Gagarin flight was a powerful blow to the political prestige of both the United States and its young president.

In Kennedy's election campaign against the Republicans–won by a slim margin–he had disparaged Dwight D. Eisenhower and Richard M. Nixon as "do nothings" who had enabled the Soviet Union to develop a massive technological superiority over the United States. Kennedy dwelled repeatedly on a "missile gap" in which the Soviets had alleged superiority. When he became president in late January 1961, however, he was privy to the nation's most significant secrets, including revelations that American photo reconnaissance of the entire Soviet Union landmass–begun years ago in 1956 by Eisenhower and employing highly confidential assets of the CIA and air force–proved there was no so-called missile gap. The United States had utilized high-flying U-2 spy aircraft until one was shot down on 1 May 1960, but by then aviation tactics had been superseded by more-efficient Corona (code name "Discoverer") spy satellites. The Soviets' propaganda bluster had succeeded in misleading Kennedy while Eisenhower was forced to keep the truth from the public.

Engulfed in the swirl of these developments and revelations, Kennedy asked Jerome Wiesner, head of the President's Science Advisory Committee (PSAC) and also president of the Massachusetts Institute of Technology (MIT), whether he would recommend manned flights to the Moon. Wiesner argued strongly that using robots and instruments exclusively would be far less expensive and much more productive. (Other scientists generally shared his belief.) Nevertheless, Kennedy ignored his scientific advice and decided to go for manned flights. Being a public-relations evangelist by nature, he had admired NASA's selection of its first seven astronauts and the use of their photographs by many publications. He just knew that real people would be better propaganda symbols than mechanical robots and instruments.

Wiesner, in effect, had been in agreement on the manned/unmanned issue with Eisenhower. The former president and previously supreme commander of the Allied forces in World War II had not been shocked by *Sputnik* in 1957. Knowing the missile gap did not exist, he had not changed his mind. As president he repeatedly asked Americans not to worry about attacks from space, yet the generally liberal press of the time chose to characterize him as either on a golf course or asleep. The facts were that he had a close rein on the Soviets from his first day in office in January 1953, and had steered a tight financial ship during his eight years as president. He kept tight control on military spending and wanted to be certain that the NASA civil agency spent wisely too. When he learned in December 1960–as a lame-duck president–that NASA was considering manned lunar expeditions, and the cost would be somewhere between \$26 to \$58 billion compared to an estimated \$8 billion for a "fly-around" circumlunar voyage, he said that he would not be willing to "hock his jewels" (as in financing Christopher Columbus) to send people to the Moon. In his retirement, Eisenhower stated that "Anyone who would spend \$40 billion in a race to the Moon for national prestige is nuts."

New vice president Lyndon B. Johnson also had much to say about the space program. As the Senate's chairman of space matters during Eisenhower's second term, "Mr. Texas" was an unabashed space enthusiast. In addition to becoming vice president in 1961, he was named chairman of the National Space Council. Johnson had been startled, along with many others, by the Soviets' Sputnik program and had worked with Eisenhower's team to establish NASA as the nation's civil space arm. While the extensive military efforts were being consolidated in a central Department of Defense space program, Johnson responded to congressional naysayers, "Would you rather have us be a second-rate nation or should we spend a little money?" It was understood this proposal included a major NASA facility at Houston.

On 20 April 1961 President Kennedy asked Johnson, "Do we have a chance of beating the Soviets by putting a laboratory in space, or by a trip round the moon, or by a rocket to land on the moon, or by a rocket to go to the moon and back with a man? Is there any other space program which promises dramatic results in which we could win?" Johnson had earlier advised Kennedy, and the latter had not forgotten, that "being first in space is now to be the world's best everything." The central idea was prestige, called "winning." Science and military defense were secondary. On 28 April the vice president responded in detail: on the main subject regarding circumnavigation of the Moon or a manned trip to the Moon, he wrote, "With a strong effort, the United States could conceivably be first in those two accomplishments by 1966 or 1967."

Kennedy's speechwriters, headed by Richard Goodwin–the husband of historian Doris Kearns Goodwin–provided the president with his message to Congress. Most everyone has forgotten this address included his recommendations to fund research and development of communications satellites, weather satellites, and nuclear rocketry. The eloquence remembered includes

> If we are to win the battle that is now going on around the world between freedom and tyranny, the dramatic achievements in space which occurred in recent weeks should have made clear to us all, as did the Sputnik in 1957, the impact of this adventure on the minds of men everywhere, who are attempting to make a determination of which road they should take. . . . I believe that this nation should commit itself to achieving the goal, before this decade is out, of landing a man on the moon and returning him safely to the earth.

He asked for and received an additional $531 million for fiscal year 1962, and an estimated $7 billion to $9 billion "additional" over the subsequent five years. (The fiscal year 1998 equivalent was about $32 billion to $40 billion.) Kennedy's proposal was approved.

Between 1962 and the program's final year in 1973, NASA has reported that Apollo cost 19.4 billion in real-year dollars, which would be equivalent to 82.2 billion in 1998 inflated dollars. These figures do not reflect NASA's costs for the Mercury and Gemini programs required to precede Apollo. We cannot place an accountant's value on the elusive "prestige" President Kennedy pursued so diligently, nor is it possible to determine a "return on investment."

SPACE EXPLORATION

James A. Michener, a popular novelist and winner of the Pulitzer Prize, addressed the Senate Subcommittee on Science, Technology, and Space on 1 February 1979. As an advocate of the space program, Michener warned that a nation must not ignore "the foundations on which it can build the future." He maintained that the United States was "obligated to pursue its adventure in space."

. . . There are moments in history when challenges occur of such a compelling nature that to miss them is to miss the whole meaning of an epoch. Space is such a challenge. It is the kind of challenge William Shakespeare sensed nearly four hundred years ago when he wrote:

> There is a tide in the affairs of men,
> Which, taken at the flood, leads on to fortune;
> Omitted, all the voyage of their life
> Is bound in shallows and in miseries.
> On such a full sea are we now afloat,
> And we must take the current when it serves,
> Or lose our ventures.

We risk great peril if we kill off this spirit of adventure, for we cannot predict how and in what seemingly unrelated fields it will manifest itself. A nation which loses its forward thrust is in danger, and one of the most effective ways to retain that thrust is to keep exploring possibilities. The sense of exploration is intimately bound up with human resolve, and for a nation to believe that it is still committed to forward motion is to ensure its continuance. . . .

Therefore we should be most careful about retreating from the specific challenge of our age. We should be reluctant to turn our back upon the frontier of this epoch. Space is indifferent to what we do; it has no feeling, no design, no interest in whether we grapple with it or not. But we cannot be indifferent to space, because the grand slow march of our intelligence has brought us, in our generation, to a point from which we can explore and understand and utilize it. To turn back now would be to deny our history, our capabilities.

Source: Contemporary American Voices: Significant Speeches in American History, 1945–Present, *edited by James R. Andrews and David Zarefsky (White Plains, N.Y.: Longman, 1992), pp. 413–417.*

In the area of communications satellites, on the other hand, NASA's investment has been entirely for research and development. During the first twenty years leading into the late 1980s, expenditures were less than $250 million in real-year dollars. But private industry had stepped into the picture early and—in those first twenty years—invested at least $13 billion in real-year dollars, according to a 1987 estimate by Albert Wheelon, former chairman and chief executive of Hughes Aircraft Company.

Today, NASA sustains a relatively modest research and development effort with its Advanced Communications Technology Satellite program while the commercial industry it helped spawn enjoys dramatic growth: $45 billion in 1996 worldwide revenues, $56 billion in 1997, and $66 billion in 1998, according to the Satellite Industry Association. During NASA's first forty years, in 1998 dollars, it invested $520 billion, of which $82 billion went into the politically driven Apollo program, compared to about $1 billion for satellite development. Patriotism aside, it is easy to determine which of these projects produced the best return on investment.

—ROBERT N. WOLD, LAGUNA NIGUEL, CALIFORNIA

References

Cynthia Boeke and Robustiano Fernandez, "Global Satellite Survey," *Via Satellite,* 14 (July 1999): 28–44;

Andrew Chaikin, *A Man on the Moon: The Voyages of the Apollo Astronauts* (New York: Viking, 1994);

John Glenn, *Letters to John Glenn* (Houston: World Book Encyclopedia Science Service, 1964);

Roger D. Launius, *NASA: A History of the U.S. Civil Space Program* (Malabar, Fla.: Krieger, 1994);

Launius and Bertram Ulrich, *NASA & The Exploration of Space* (New York: Stewart, Tabori & Chang, 1998);

Richard S. Lewis, *Appointment on the Moon: The Inside Story of America's Space Venture* (New York: Viking, 1968);

John Logsdon, *The Decision to Go to the Moon: Project Apollo and the National Interest* (Cambridge, Mass.: MIT Press, 1970);

Walter A. McDougall, *The Heavens and the Earth: A Political History of the Space Age* (New York: BasicBooks, 1985);

Charles Murray and Catherine Bly Cox, *Apollo: The Race to the Moon* (New York: Simon & Schuster, 1989);

Richard Reeves, *President Kennedy: Profile of Power* (New York: Touchstone, 1993);

Robert Zimmerman, *Genesis: The Story of Apollo 8: The First Manned Flight to Another World* (New York: Four Walls Eight Windows, 1998).

VIETNAM CAUSES

How did the United States get involved in the Vietnam War?

Viewpoint: The Vietnam War was a logical consequence of American post-war policy in the struggle to contain communism.

Viewpoint: The United States entered into a costly war in Vietnam because of an aggressive economic policy.

Robert Wilensky and James Carter offer differing interpretations of how the United States became involved in the Vietnam War. Wilensky sees the Vietnam conflict as an inevitable outgrowth of American postwar fears of Communist expansion. The conflict, he says, was inevitable, though it did not have to happen in Vietnam. Carter, on the other hand, argues that American interests in Asia, particularly in Japan, which predated World War II, led to the American conflict in Vietnam.

Which is true? The Vietnam War is rife with tragic ironies and misunderstandings. Some scholarship has been tinged with its author's ideological positions, and students of the war need to remember that at the time it raged, all Americans took strong positions on it. Some believed that the United States should win at all costs since it had never lost a war. They believed the war was not only against Ho Chi Minh or the National Liberation Front (NLF) but was against a global effort by totalitarian communists to extend their sphere of tyranny. Other Americans believed that the government of South Vietnam, America's ally, was a corrupt and tyrannical force, and that this government was only sustaining itself thanks to generous military and economic aid from the United States.

Americans took sides. Those who supported the war believed that those against it were disloyal, that they were interested in a Communist takeover, and that their opposition presented a grave danger to American troops in Southeast Asia. If we did not support our South Vietnamese allies, they reasoned, why would any other American ally respect the United States?

On the other hand, opponents of the war came to see the war's supporters as naively and blindly following an American policy which did not seem to promise success. "We are fighting in a war we lost before the war began," folksinger Phil Ochs sang. Americans did not understand Vietnam, its history or culture. The United States had become involved in the war for all the wrong reasons, and once in, could not find a plausible reason for getting out.

The tremendous hostility between "hawks" and "doves," always bitter and often violent, further clouded the issue at home. The war became less about Vietnam and more about the American purpose or the national honor. For supporters of the American war effort, these ideals became the essential objectives. For opponents of the war, purpose and honor seemed empty and meaningless words used to justify an impossible policy. The American withdrawal and ultimate triumph of the North Vietnamese and NLF left all Americans feeling betrayed.

In these two essays Carter and Wilensky are not trying to assess blame, which hawks and doves had done quite liberally in the 1960s and 1970s.

Instead, they try to analyze why an American policy that seemed to have the noblest intentions produced the worst possible outcome: Vietnam bombed and ravaged by American air power; South Vietnam conquered by the NLF; twenty years of political terror and recriminations against former supporters of the pro-U.S. government; and an America bitterly divided and cynically demoralized, unwilling to accept the legitimacy or integrity of any government pronouncement.

Viewpoint:
The Vietnam War was a logical consequence of American postwar policy in the struggle to contain communism.

At the end of World War II, the world was a new place. Great Britain, France, and Japan sustained major war damage in World War II, and Germany was divided. The Soviet attempt to close off allied access to West Berlin in 1948 resulted in the Berlin Airlift, which lasted until the lifting of the blockade the following year. China was engaged in a civil war, won by the Communists led by Mao Tse-tung in 1949. Two great powers remained: the United States with its industrial might at a peak of production, and the Soviet Union, with millions dead and great expanses of the country in shambles, but with the largest standing army in the world. The Marshall Plan was America's response to rebuild war-torn Europe, making it capable of resisting the U.S.S.R.

George F. Kennan became an aide to Ambassador W. Averell Harriman at the U.S. Embassy in Moscow in July 1944. He advocated abandonment of any inclination toward postwar cooperation with the Soviets and the adoption of a sphere-of-influence approach to Europe. Kennan's 22 February 1946 "Long Telegram" to the secretary of state outlined his views of the pending struggle. He amplified his views, first in "The Sources of Soviet Conflict," published anonymously under the pseudonym "X" in July 1947, and then in "America and the Russian Future," in 1951. In both articles Kennan advocated encirclement of the Soviets and decried any concept of peaceful coexistence with the regime. American-led alliances such as the North Atlantic Treaty Organization (NATO) and the Southeast Asia Treaty Organization (SEATO) formed a ring of anti-Communist states around the U.S.S.R.

The political turmoil in Europe had far-reaching effects elsewhere in the world. The United States desperately needed France as an active member in the center of NATO, founded in 1949. France desired security but also wished to regain control of its Southeast Asian empire. Ho Chi Minh and the Communists were able to seize the nationalist banner in Vietnam. They had filled the void left by the retreating Japanese and proclaimed a republic in September 1945. France requested and received American aid in order to rebuild domestically and to thwart Communist insurgents in Vietnam, but the United States would not provide direct military assistance. President Dwight D. Eisenhower refused to be drawn into the fighting without at least British support. The British were unwilling to take any action while the Geneva negotiations were still under way. After the end of the fighting in Korea, the United States did not wish to become embroiled in another Asian land war.

Nationalist movements arose around the world. The desires for independence in North Africa, Southeast Asia, India, and Eastern Europe came into conflict with the desires of colonial powers to reassert their control and of the Soviet Union to both establish a buffer zone around Russia and to spread the Communist doctrine. Echoes of post–World War I nationalism received the same negligible hearings and had similar results in the post–World War II era, bowing to Great Power desires. Ho Chi Minh had unsuccessfully sought an audience with President Woodrow Wilson at the Paris Peace Conference in 1919 to plead the case for Vietnamese independence.

As the fighting of World War II ended, especially in Europe, the seeds of future conflict arose. General George S. Patton Jr. advocated continuing the war against the United States wartime Soviet allies, implying that it was better to fight them now while the United States had an army in Europe. Both the United States and the Soviet Union foresaw future friction between their respective systems of government and economics.

Counterfactual hypotheses are ahistorical. A perfect world would have totally reasonable national leaders and politicians able to resolve disputes in a reasoned, calm, and equitable manner. However, this ideal was not the reality at the end of World War II. Confrontation between the world powers with contesting systems of government and economics was to a degree inevitable. The confrontation did not have to occur in Southeast Asia, but that was actually as likely a place as any and more likely than most other possible locations. With the confluence of circumstances in Vietnam of a French colonial history, raw materials of rice and rubber, location on the border of China, and the fate of all of Southeast Asia at stake, Vietnam was a prime location for

JOHNSON REFLECTS ON VIETNAM

The following excerpt is from a speech President Lyndon B. Johnson gave at Johns Hopkins University on 7 April 1965. At the time, many Americans believed that only North Vietnamese intransigence prevented a negotiated settlement to the conflict in Southeast Asia. Later, it became apparent that the Johnson administration, still hoping for a decisive military victory, shunned several opportunities to negotiate a peaceful conclusion to the struggle.

Our objective is the independence of South Vietnam, and its freedom from attack. We want nothing for ourselves, only that the people of South Vietnam be allowed to guide their own country in their own way.

We will do everything necessary to reach that objective. And we will do only what is absolutely necessary.

In recent months, attacks on South Vietnam were stepped up. Thus it became necessary to increase our response and to make attacks by air. This is not a change of purpose. It is a change in what we believe that purpose requires.

We do this in order to slow down aggression.

We do this to increase the confidence of the brave people of South Vietnam who have bravely borne this brutal battle for so many years and with so many casualties.

And we do this to convince the leaders of North Vietnam, and all who seek to share their conquest, of a very simple fact:

We will not be defeated.

We will not grow tired.

We will not withdraw, either openly or under the cloak of a meaningless agreement. . . .

Once this is clear, then it should also be clear that the only path for reasonable men is the path of peaceful settlement.

Such peace demands an independent South Vietnam securely guaranteed and able to shape its own relationships to all others, free from outside interference, tied to no alliance, a military base for no other country.

These are the essentials of any final settlement.

We will never be second in the search for such a peaceful settlement in Vietnam.

There may be many ways to this kind of peace: in discussion or negotiation with the governments concerned; in large groups or in small ones; in the reaffirmation of old agreements or their strengthening with new ones.

We have stated this position over and over again fifty times and more, to friend and foe alike. And we remain ready, with this purpose, for unconditional discussions.

Source: *Documents of American History, 2 volumes, edited by Henry Steele Commager (New York: Appleton-Century-Crofts, 1973), 2: 698–700.*

the showdown. There it could be played out without a face-to-face battle between the major world military powers, with a potential for a massive conflagration.

The problem with encirclement, which Kennan did not address, is that each protagonist can view it as either encircling or being encircled. The resulting opposition of forces creates a state of steady confrontation, either in one locale or in many. If world leaders strive to avoid worldwide conflict (the outbreak of World War III), smaller wars develop at these points of contact or where either side (or a proxy) attempts to expand, with the potential to involve the great powers. This situation occurred in Korea in 1950. The potential for further conflicts in Southern Africa, Cuba, or along the Pacific Rim in Southeast Asia was great. Unless, or until, one system of government, society, and economics emerged as superior, these areas of friction would persist. Ultimately American involvement in Vietnam became the logical extension of the containment policy begun by the Truman administration.

In a world of two superpowers with the nuclear capability of annihilating not only each other but potentially the entire world, limiting the confrontations to small wars or proxy wars was both an aim and a success in and of itself. Neither side undertook actions that would have forced the other into a major response. The Cuban Missile Crisis (1962) illustrated how potentially dangerous direct confrontations between the two major powers were. Historian Arthur M. Schlesinger Jr. recalls that President John F. Kennedy pointed out that escalation did not occur in Cuba because the United States had clear local conventional superiority, Soviet national security was not directly engaged, and the Russians lacked a case they could convincingly sustain before the world. However, the confrontation was not a scenario to be repeated. The United States carefully limited the bombing in North Vietnam in order not to involve China or the Soviet Union, despite the realization that this meant there could be no limitation on the resupplying of North Vietnam. Historian Michael A. Hennessy described the resulting air campaign as "tentative" in nature.

Following the May 1954 defeat at Dien Bien Phu, the French withdrew from Vietnam. An end to the fighting was concluded with the Geneva Accords two months later, which the United States refused to sign. In October 1955 Ngo Dinh Diem won a controlled referendum in South Vietnam and replaced Emperor Bao Dai, refusing to hold an election on reunification of the country (which he would have lost).

Meanwhile in the Western Hemisphere, Fidel Castro landed in Cuba to begin his fight against Fulgencio Batista in 1956. In 1959 Castro toppled the regime, and the following year confiscated U.S. property in Cuba. The United States responded by instituting an embargo, labeling Cuba a Soviet satellite. President Kennedy approved a CIA-supported attempt to overthrow the Castro regime (which Eisenhower had refused to authorize) with about 1,500 Cuban exiles. The attempt failed miserably at the Bay of Pigs in 1961.

The Cold War was in full bloom in the early 1960s. To "Cold Warriors" in both American political parties it appeared that Communism was on the advance all around the globe. Communism reigned over Eastern Europe and the Soviet Union, China (including Tibet), Cuba, and in North Vietnam. Both sides carried out above-ground nuclear weapons testing. China invaded India. The Viet Cong under the direction of North Vietnam established the National Liberation Front (NLF) to reunify the country. South Vietnam, under Diem, was in turmoil with no popular support for the government.

In 1963 the United States had 16,000 advisers in Vietnam. The war to prevent a Communist takeover was going badly. In November of that year, President Kennedy finally agreed to permit a coup, which overthrew Diem. Kennedy was reportedly devastated by the accompanying assassinations: when he learned of them "he turned ashen and rushed from the room."

When Lyndon Baines Johnson became president following the November 1963 assassination of Kennedy, he retained the Kennedy administration personnel and attempted to maintain continuity with the slain leader's programs. Nevertheless, many Kennedy supporters viewed Johnson as a usurper. His main area of interest was in domestic policy, and he achieved major successes in passing legislation dealing with civil rights and medical care. Vietnam, however, became a problem he could neither solve nor make go away.

With the American-backed overthrow of Diem, the United States became more responsible for the survival of South Vietnam as an independent state than had previously been true. Politically, President Johnson could not disavow the policy of the slain Kennedy. The Republican Party had attacked the Democrats for losing China. Johnson did not want to give them another opportunity for this type of attack by losing South Vietnam to the Communists. Under a Democratic President, the Bay of Pigs fiasco had already resulted in a Communist regime remaining ninety miles off the U.S. coastline. Johnson adhered to the domino theory in Southeast Asia. He believed that if Vietnam fell to the Communists, so would Laos, Cambodia, Thailand, Burma, and perhaps even India. He did not want to withdraw from Vietnam and be the first American president to lose a war. A president by accident, Johnson wished to win the presidency on his own merit in 1964 in order to legitimize his claim to power. A defeat in Vietnam would not help him politically.

The American need for French support in Europe coupled with French inability to hold Vietnam, the belief in the domino theory that if Vietnam went Communist all of Southern Asia was at risk, and the domestic American political scene all made withdrawal from Vietnam difficult, if not impossible. President Johnson needed to maintain the policies of his predecessor while striving for his own election. He dared not appear weak on Communism. A momentum developed for increasing American participation in the war in order to protect U.S. personnel and interests that made withdrawal increasingly difficult. Johnson could not win the war, could not withdraw from it, and would not lose it.

–ROBERT J. WILENSKY,
AMERICAN UNIVERSITY

Viewpoint:
The United States entered into a costly war in Vietnam because of an aggressive economic policy.

To Ho Chi Minh and the Vietnamese people in 1954, the long struggle to end colonial oppression in Vietnam appeared to be rapidly coming to a close. The French had just been soundly defeated at the tiny outpost of Dien Bien Phu, concluding the First Indochina War. A conference on East-West relations convening at Geneva in the spring of 1954 promised to resolve the decades-old conflict through the removal, once and for all, of the French imperialists. Colonialism, as many had recognized, was in fact collapsing all over the world. Ho Chi Minh had now only to proclaim Vietnamese independence, as he had done in 1945 with U.S. acquiescence, if not aid. With France willing to cut its own losses, surely the result would be Vietnamese independence. However, independence did not follow in 1954 for reasons having less to do with Vietnam and more to do with American power and global aims in the post–World War II period.

At the close of the World War II, the United States found itself in an unprecedented position of power and prestige. Europe had been ravaged by six years of intense and devastating war. A motley corridor of war-torn regions through Eastern Europe separated the West from Soviet Russia. The Soviets also suffered unbelievable losses during the war. Russian sacrifices totaled 20 million dead, the destruction of 1,700 towns and 70,000 villages, and 25 million homeless. The United States, to an extent no other belligerent experienced, avoided this level of destruction. Knowing this outcome would be the case, American policymakers began during the war to formulate a sophisticated agenda for the establishment of a "capitalist world framework."

The postwar agenda of the United States did not necessarily involve Vietnam. The Americans considered the problems of Europe first and then the problems of the rest of the world insofar as it contributed to or ameliorated the situation in Europe. One of the chief goals of the United States at the cessation of hostilities was the rebuilding of Western Europe, namely France and Germany, but several other Western European countries as well. Powerful communist and leftist political movements had flourished during the 1930s and later during the war. In many cases, these leftist groups formed bands of resistance and had been important in opposing the German onslaught in Western Europe. By the end of the war, however, their power would have to be curtailed, as the Americans saw it, in order to maintain the status quo antebellum. France was needed as a partner in a mutual defense pact, later the North Atlantic Treaty Organization (NATO), designed to stymie Soviet moves in Eastern Europe. Consequently, the Americans quickly moved to support France and aid in the rebuilding of its economy. An understanding of this background is crucial for understanding not only why the United States became involved in the effort to restore France's colony in Vietnam, but also to explain American policy in many other countries for the one-half century after World War II.

The French fought, with substantial American aid, to retake Vietnam from 1946 until their defeat in the spring of 1954. By that time the United States had underwritten about 80 percent of the French effort. Starting in 1950 with $150 million in aid and another $785 million in 1953 alone, the United States ended up pumping $1.2 billion in monetary and military aid into Vietnam by 1954. This level of U.S. involvement stemmed from three interrelated objectives of the Americans.

First, the reestablishment of France's hold on Vietnam would help restore the French economy and, at the same time, foster political stability for a west European ally (and NATO member). France had relied on its Indochinese colonies for tin, rubber, rice, coal, iron ore, and other raw materials. The Vietnamese people had provided cheap labor for the removal of these materials during the decades leading up to World War II. Additionally, the restoration of the French colonial system would enhance the prestige of Charles De Gaulle and of France generally at a time when the parties of the Left had made serious inroads into the political process. European containment, the brainchild of diplomat George F. Kennan, depended in no small part on the strength, both political and economic, of the Western European nations.

After the Vietnamese compelled the French to abandon their claims to Vietnam, the United States stayed on for a second reason. The idea of containment quickly spilled beyond the European context to envelop the world. By 1954 the threat of Soviet expansion into Western Europe was minimal. Now, American policymakers applied the concept of containing communism in several places, including Vietnam. According to the Geneva Accords, Vietnam existed in two pieces, divided at the seventeenth parallel. The agreements called for national elections within two years to determine the government of the country. Recognizing the immense popularity of Ho Chi Minh, sometimes referred to as the George Washington of Vietnam, the United States quickly moved to solidify its hold on the southern half of Vietnam by imposing and paying for its own government under Ngo Dinh Diem. Despite Ho Chi Minh's earlier overtures to the Americans and appeals for aid and recognition, the United States sought to undermine the communist leader at all costs. In this context, the triumph of the Communists in China in 1949 had indeed been a bitter pill. Maintaining a hold on Vietnam became a critical element in stemming the tide of communism that, according to U.S. policymakers, threatened to sweep all of Southeast Asia like dominoes collapsing under the weight of the most recent fallen.

United States policymakers considered Asia important for a variety of reasons. Since the nineteenth century, American businessmen attempted to break into the China market with the Open Door policy first declared by Secretary of State John Hay in 1899. After the Communist victory in

Battle gear of U.S. Marine casualties during Operation Harvest Moon outside Da Nang, South Vietnam, December 1965

(Francois Sully-Newsweek)

China in 1949, the region quickly assumed greater importance. With the immediate threat of Soviet Russia spreading into Europe gone, the larger threat of incipient communist puppets cropping up around the world all owing allegiance to the U.S.S.R. seemed real to American policymakers, despite evidence to the contrary. In the years after World War II, the domino theory gained broad acceptance as an appropriate framework for considering the development of communism. The theory postulated that when one country fell to communism, it became exponentially more likely that its immediate neighbors and others in the region would soon fall. In the case of Asia, with China under communist rule, its smaller neighbors were sure to succumb in short order. The critical country for the United States within this context was, of course, Japan.

In 1945 the United States became the first nation to employ an atomic device in warfare. Only days before the Soviet Union had agreed to declare war on Japan to help end the fighting in that theater, the United States exploded two atomic bombs one each over the Japanese cities of Hiroshima and Nagasaki, killing between 150,000 and 200,000 people and effectively ending the war. In the aftermath, the Americans demanded and obtained sole occupation of Japan. The objectives from the outset were clear.

The United States intended to rebuild Japan along capitalist lines and to quickly reintegrate the country into "an economically vigorous . . . system of non-Communist, multilateral trading nations." Obviously, a communist sweep of southeast Asia would leave Japan relatively isolated in terms of trade. During the years prior to World War II, Japan sent more than 60 percent of its exports to Far Eastern countries and received 50 percent of its imports from those same nations. The United States intended all along that China would provide the crucial economic link with an industrialized Japan. After 1949, the objective of global containment of communism essentially removed China from the equation. The nations of Southeast Asia–Indochina, Burma, British Malaya, and Indonesia–now began to come into focus. By 1954 these factors dovetailed and compelled America's entry into what was in reality a French colonial problem. Even though the French themselves were prepared to leave Vietnam, the United States and certain key policymakers had found reasons to remain, reasons that clearly had little to do with Vietnam itself.

After 1949, rebuilding France and stamping out the various leftist groups had effectively been accomplished, largely through American aid. The United States embarked on a much more ambitious program of global containment as outlined by Kennan and others within the American state department. Global containment, particularly following the success of Mao Tse-tung's Communists, ensured American interest and perhaps direct involvement in Asia. In addition, the United States, since at least the early 1940s, had begun to piece together its own version of a new postwar world order, a new global economy based on trade liberalism. In this context, liberalism meant reduced international trade barriers such as tariffs, anticommunism, and antinationalism where its adherents sought control of their country's resources, and piecemeal reform measures designed to enhance the global economy. These factors combined to define American objectives in the Pacific. The effort to carve out a permanent, lucrative, and stable niche in Asia led the United States on a search for outlets for sustaining trade relationships for a reconstructed Japan. The search led ultimately to Vietnam.

In brief, America's global objectives in the post–World War II period led to massive military involvement in Vietnam and several other places around the globe as well. The United States became heavily involved in Iran, Greece, Turkey, Korea, Guatemala, Indonesia, Chile, and various other spots where the Cold War turned hot during the 1950s, 1960s, and 1970s. The factors setting Vietnam apart from the others are many. Certainly among the most important was the glaring contradiction between the rhetoric of liberalism at home and the mayhem in Vietnam. In defining its new role in the years immediately following World War II, the United States did not recognize the limitations of its own power. In many ways, the tragic experiment in Vietnam defined those limits.

—JAMES CARTER, UNIVERSITY OF HOUSTON

References

Kai Bird, "Cries and Whispers," *Washingtonian*, 21 (October 1998): 41–48;

Robert Buzzanco, *Vietnam and the Transformation of American Life* (Oxford: Blackwell, 1999);

Carlo D'Este, *Patton: A Genius for War* (New York: HarperCollins, 1995);

John L. Gaddis, *The Long Peace* (New York: Oxford University Press, 1987);

Michael A. Hennessy, *Strategy in Vietnam: The Marines and Revolutionary Warfare in I Corps, 1965–1972* (Westport, Conn.: Praeger, 1997);

George C. Herring, *America's Longest War: The United States and Vietnam, 1945–1975* (New York: McGraw-Hill, 1986);

George McTurnan Kahin, *Intervention: How America Became Involved in Vietnam* (New York: Anchor, 1987);

George F. Kennan, "America and the Russian Future," *Foreign Affairs*, 29 (April 1951): 351–370;

Kennan, "The Sources of Soviet Conduct," By X, *Foreign Affairs*, 25 (July 1947): 566–582;

Gabriel Kolko, *Anatomy of a War: Vietnam, The United States, and The Modern Historical Experience* (New York: New Press, 1984);

Walter LaFeber, *America, Russia and the Cold War 1945–1992* (New York: McGraw-Hill, 1992);

Wilson D. Miscamble, *George F. Kennan and the Making of American Foreign Policy, 1947–1950* (Princeton: Princeton University Press, 1992);

James A. Nathan, ed., *The Cuban Missile Crisis Revisited* (New York: St. Martin's Press, 1992);

Andrew Rotter, *The Path to Vietnam: Origins of the American Commitment to Southeast Asia* (Ithaca, N.Y.: Cornell University Press, 1987);

Arthur M. Schlesinger Jr., *The Bitter Heritage: Vietnam and American Democracy 1941–1966* (London: Deutsch, 1967);

Robert Scigliano, *South Vietnam: Nation Under Stress* (Boston: Houghton Mifflin, 1963);

Howard R. Simpson, *Dien Bien Phu: The Epic Battle America Forgot* (Washington, D.C.: Brassey's, 1994);

Marilyn B. Young, *The Vietnam Wars, 1945–1990* (New York: HarperCollins, 1991).

WAR ON POVERTY

Why did Lyndon B. Johnson's War on Poverty fail?

Viewpoint: The War on Poverty failed because the war in Vietnam drained resources, and the Republicans, particularly after the election of Richard M. Nixon, hindered the program.

Viewpoint: The War on Poverty failed because it did not focus on the one sure way to eliminate poverty: creating jobs.

Lyndon B. Johnson believed his Great Society program would complete the work of Franklin D. Roosevelt's administration in ensuring a decent living and an opportunity to succeed for all Americans. Instead, by the end of his administration the Great Society was in ruins, and twenty years later conservative scholars actually blamed the Great Society for perpetuating the cycle of poverty Johnson hoped to break.

What happened? How did a program launched with such noble motives come to such an ignominious end? Most historians attribute the Great Society's failure to the simultaneous drain of the Vietnam War, which eliminated the budget surpluses that Johnson had hoped to spend in lifting Americans out of poverty. Others see the failure to produce jobs as the crucial element. Economists might argue that the kind of poverty Johnson hoped to combat was structural, endemic to the system. The Heritage Foundation and other conservative groups attribute poverty to the failure of an individual, and would argue that no government program could change these unworthy poor.

There are two related questions at work here. One is the historical question, what happened to the Great Society? The other is a public policy question, was the Great Society a good idea? Both of the scholars represented here, Judith A. Barrett and Robert J. Allison, think the Great Society was a good idea, and both lament its failure. However, as historians, they differ on why it failed. Barrett, with long experience in state government, looks to the failure of Johnson and his advisers to understand the nature of poverty and to their naive belief that the United States was different from other nations and that it was possible, with a few minor changes in policy, to eliminate poverty. She argues that the failure to provide jobs, the failure to grapple with the idea that maybe as an industrial society the United States was not different from other nations, ultimately forced Johnson's failure to achieve the Great Society. Allison, on the other hand, sees the failure in more mundane terms, that the Office of Economic Opportunity (OEO) created in 1964 was fatally flawed and that political circumstances combined to destroy the plan of such great promise.

In addition, while both scholars see the War on Poverty and the Great Society as failures, each one also points to some notable successes. Barrett notes that the War on Poverty actually did ease poverty in many cases, and the Nixon administration, which dismantled the OEO, actually stabilized and extended other facets of the Great Society. Allison, too, sees in the most controversial feature of the War on Poverty, the Community Action Programs, not only the seeds of the Great Society's defeat but also the seeds of its greatest triumph. Johnson is, as Barrett says, a tragic figure, and his failure, his tragedy, is one of contradiction and irony. Perhaps it is a tragedy inherent in our nature as human beings, and as Americans, to pursue a goal with means that make it impossible to achieve.

Viewpoint: The War on Poverty failed because the war in Vietnam drained resources, and the Republicans, particularly after the election of Richard M. Nixon, hindered the program.

The War on Poverty failed for two major reasons: one, because resources that would have gone to fighting poverty instead were absorbed into the Vietnam War. In 1964, when President Lyndon B. Johnson declared an "unconditional war on poverty," the U.S. government had a financial surplus, and projections promised that it would grow into the early 1970s. Daniel Patrick Moynihan, one of the planners of the War on Poverty, said that Johnson did not launch the program because it was necessary, but because it was possible. With this much extra money coming in, Johnson had the opportunity to spend it on an ambitious legislative agenda. But by 1967 the surplus had been absorbed into the military, and the United States was going into debt. Second, while the War on Poverty began with the promise of collaboration between different government agencies and with private institutions (notably the Ford Foundation), what ensued was fierce bureaucratic infighting. There were also fundamental disagreements over basic strategy and philosophy at different levels of government and among the poor themselves.

By 1963 four major areas of concern, in which the federal government could provide leadership, came to the attention of the White House. These problems involved the urban poor, who lived in blighted housing and were being displaced by urban renewal, which often involved simply tearing down slum neighborhoods without providing for the displaced residents; juvenile delinquents, who were the subject of an Eisenhower administration study completed in 1960; growing welfare rolls, which indicated that the rising economy was not lifting all Americans out of poverty; and adult illiteracy. President John F. Kennedy had asked Walter Heller, his chief economic adviser, to prepare a legislative agenda for 1964 focusing on these problems, trying to imagine ways the federal government could address poverty. To prepare this agenda Heller convened a committee of individuals drawn from different government agencies: the Bureau of the Budget, the Departments of Labor and Agriculture, the Council of Economic Advisors, and the White House staff. On the afternoon of 22 November 1963, Heller and his committee were working on their proposal, "Widening Participation in Prosperity," when they were interrupted with the tragic news of Kennedy's assassination.

The next day, Heller met with the new president. He presented Johnson with the grim facts their study had uncovered: 20 percent of American families lived below the poverty line, which the government defined as a family of four earning less than $3,100 a year. More alarming, the economy was no longer rising quickly enough to lift people out of poverty. The Council of Economic Advisors identified four groups of people most prone to living in poverty: blacks, people without a high school education, families headed by women, and Southern or rural families. The nature of poor, rural, undereducated, or single-parent families made it difficult for children in these families to pull themselves out of poverty, perpetuating what the advisers called the "cycle of poverty." Heller's committee was preparing several different strategies to combat poverty, but needed approval from the president. Johnson, after hearing Heller's report, told him "That's my kind of program . . . Move full speed ahead."

Heller and the task force moved ahead; in his State of the Union speech in January 1964, Johnson declared the War on Poverty. Later in the year, in a commencement speech at the University of Michigan, Ann Arbor, Johnson called on Americans to join him in creating a "Great Society," which would offer opportunities to all. Johnson believed in the power of government to correct social wrongs: he is the only president who spent his entire adult life working for the federal government, beginning in 1931 as an aide to a Texas congressman. Between 1931 and 1969 the only time Johnson spent outside of Washington was a two-year stint as Texas director of the New Deal's National Youth Administration. Johnson hoped that the War on Poverty and the Great Society would be his personal achievements, but he also intended them to be the culmination of work begun by Franklin D. Roosevelt's New Deal.

After the problems were identified and the war was declared, Heller's task force began preparing a legislative agenda. Johnson persuaded Sargent Shriver, former director of the Peace Corps and the brother-in-law of the late Presi-

A 1969 recruiting poster for a federally sponsored program

dent Kennedy and Attorney General Robert F. Kennedy, to take charge. Shriver quickly took on the responsibility and challenge of organizing the largest government effort to end poverty ever launched, as Johnson prepared to spend $1 billion to begin his program. Shriver called on government agencies and the private sector to contribute ideas, and the administration prepared the Economic Opportunity Act of 1964.

The act, which Johnson signed on 20 August 1964, created the Job Corps to help find jobs for the urban unemployed, the Neighborhood Youth Corps to provide work and training to urban youths, and the Volunteers in Service to America (VISTA) program, a domestic version of the Peace Corps. It provided aid to farmers and grants for education. It also established the Office of Economic Opportunity (OEO), which would oversee an ambitious Community Action

Program (CAP). In addition the Johnson administration created the Head Start program to prepare young children for kindergarten, expanded the Food Stamp program, began work-study programs, and created Pell Grants to help pay for college education.

The administration advanced a bold and ambitious agenda. Some features of the War on Poverty are today taken for granted and approved by even the most conservative thinkers. Head Start, Pell Grants, Food Stamps, and Vista are almost without controversy. Yet, the flagship of the antipoverty fleet, the OEO, almost immediately came under attack and did not last much beyond the 1960s. Its failure cast in doubt the entire Johnson enterprise of using the federal government to resolve a social problem. Its failure lies partly in the Vietnam War, which diverted not only the financial resources of the federal government but also the time and energy of the White House. However, a more plausible explanation must lie in the nature of the Washington bureaucracy and local bureaucracies, the changing temper of both Americans at large and the constituencies served by the OEO, and in the conflicting agendas of the men and women who organized the War on Poverty.

Though Shriver had been called into service as the director of the antipoverty program, he quickly found that his actual responsibilities would extend no further than the OEO. Head Start, Vista, and Food Stamps, the more popular features of the program, were taken over by other agencies. To the OEO was left the administration of Community Action Programs (CAPs), which proved to be the most contentious and unpopular aspect of the War on Poverty and ultimately undermined the whole thing. At a cabinet meeting Shriver proposed a five-cent tax on cigarettes, which would help the OEO establish a fund to create employment. The Labor Department had criticized earlier versions of the antipoverty program for not generating jobs–Shriver hoped through this tax to do the one thing certain to end poverty, putting people to work. Johnson, though, vetoed the idea.

Without a program to create jobs, how exactly would the OEO fight poverty? Actually, by the early 1960s some thoughtful Americans argued that lack of work was not really the problem. The change in thinking was reflected in the 1960 report of the Division of Juvenile Delinquency Service, a division within the Children's Bureau, an agency established during the Wilson administration to fight child labor. This study of delinquents, who had been perceived to present a social problem, and why youths gravitated to drugs and crime overturned current theories. Previously delinquency was thought to be caused by poverty, broken homes, poor education, race, or other factors. Not so, said the study. These things were concomitants of delinquency, not its causes. Developing on the ideas of society posed by French scholar Emile Durkheim, sociologists saw the real cause of delinquency as alienation or anomie–a feeling of powerlessness in society. Juvenile delinquents were the James Deans of American society, rebels without causes, listless and feeling unloved. Providing jobs, better schools, nurturing families, and ending racism would not be enough to end delinquency. Furthermore, the delinquents really were not the problem–society was, and the delinquents, through crime and drugs, were making a protest against a harsh and oppressive world.

That this argument turned prevailing social theory, as well as common sense, on its head seems clear. George C. Wallace, the governor of Alabama who was seeking support among urban whites in the North, criticized the "pointy-heads" and "intellectual morons" and the "bearded professor who thinks he knows how to settle the Vietnam war when he hasn't got enough sense to park a bicycle straight." The criminal who knocks you down, Wallace says, will be "out of jail before you're out of the hospital and the policeman who arrested him will be on trial. . . . But some psychologist says, 'Well, he's not to blame. Society's to blame. His father didn't take him to see the Pittsburgh Pirates when he was a little boy.'"

The sociological theory made an easy target for Wallace, and even for Republicans. It also created a problem for those sincerely interested in ending poverty. If delinquency is caused by anomie, if powerlessness, not poverty, is the problem, how can it be combated? The answer seemed to be in giving more power to these alienated youths. In the early 1960s, the Ford Foundation had joined with the City of New York and the Kennedy administration in forming the Mobilization for Youth, a community-based organization in New York's Lower East Side. The Mobilization for Youth represented a new idea in poor relief–instead of establishing jobs, it provided empowering opportunities and helped to organize the poor into agitation groups. The basic philosophy behind the Mobilization for Youth would also inform the Community Action Programs, formed under the OEO.

The case of Syracuse, New York, is instructive. A local reform organization, which had been established to combat juvenile delinquency, transformed itself into a Community Action Program when the OEO came into being. The Syracuse Crusade for Opportunity continued the work it had begun, but now sought to empower all the poor of Syracuse. Under the OEO the poor were to enjoy "maximum feasible participation" in these CAPs; they were designed to help them help themselves. Organizers attempted to address serious problems with most public welfare agencies–that the poor often did not feel in control of their own destiny and that welfare agencies and the police, the two government agencies with which many people dealt most often, were unresponsive bureaucracies. So the OEO determined that the poor would learn the benefits of participatory democracy through the creation of CAPs. An irony here was that many of the initial agencies, such as Mobilization for Youth or the Syracuse Crusade for Opportunity, were not created by the poor but rather by well-intentioned middle-class people, often under the auspices of a university, armed with the latest sociological theory.

In Syracuse the Crusade for Opportunity quickly found itself challenged by another CAP, this one emanating from Syracuse University. With the support of an OEO grant, Syracuse University launched a Community Action Training Project (CATP) to train the poor and mobilize them to take action. The Crusade for Opportunity was a white, middle-class philanthropic endeavor; the CATP was mainly a black and radical organization. Militant and radical activists of the 1960s saw organizations such as the former one as useful tools to take on the power structure, and the first step in a general mobilization of the poor would be to take over the Crusade for Opportunity. After all, the OEO had guaranteed "maximum feasible participation," and the poor would have control of their own destinies. By 1966 the CATP had taken over the Crusade for Opportunity, which ceased being an umbrella group drawing on disparate parts of the Syracuse community. It instead became a radical group that pretended to speak for the "dispossessed" of Syracuse. The goal of "empowerment" may have been achieved for some, though ending poverty was not, at least not for those who did not have the good fortune to be employed by CATP. Of some $8 million dollars spent by this CAP, $7 million went to salaries of its staff.

Though critics of the CAPs, such as Moynihan, have argued that the phrase "maximum feasible participation" ultimately destroyed the entire War on Poverty, James Sundquist, deputy undersecretary of agriculture and, like Moynihan, an original architect of the antipoverty policy, argues that the real key word to explain the radical nature of the CAPs was not "maximum," "feasible," or "participation," but rather "unconditional." Johnson had declared an "unconditional war on poverty," and members of the CAPs regarded themselves as warriors in an unconditional war, not as bureaucrats in a government agency. Members of these groups had been working under the auspices of private grants to study or combat poverty before the president joined the battle; their mandate was to get at the causes of poverty, not simply to ameliorate the living conditions of the poor. So it is not surprising that when the federal government seemed to promise its resources to combat poverty, these activists would seize the opportunity. It seems strange that the U.S. government would support organizations committed to revolutionary change, but the War on Poverty was in this sense a real war. In this case the federal government was moving away from state and local bureaucracies, creating or trying to create new power structures in communities.

The undermining of existing structures of power had another dimension. It provoked a backlash from established bureaucracies, who fought back. These bureaucrats, unlike the young revolutionaries and poor people they organized, understood more effective means of fighting bureaucratic war. Instead of a frontal assault on the OEO, the enemies of the CAPs sought to create a competing program that had the same goals, the Model Cities Program. This project, launched in 1966, gave grants directly to cities and towns to create antipoverty programs in their jurisdictions, under the auspices of the local government. The Model Cities Program, though considered part of the Great Society, had the effect of draining resources from the OEO and the CAPs and thus offered a bureaucratic victory to the welfare establishment.

Another instructive example of flaws in the CAP approach comes from a related movement, the Economic Research and Action Projects (ERAPs), funded by a United Auto Workers grant in 1965. The ERAP, as activist Sara Evans has recounted in *Personal Politics: The Roots of Women's Liberation in the Civil Rights Movement and the New Left* (1979), sought to empower the poor and dispossessed, organizing them into an active political force that could take on the establishment. In fact, ERAP workers were also members of the Students for a Democratic Society (SDS) and saw their work with the poor as part of a general revolutionary movement. In approaching their work in the urban ghettos, though, the members of ERAP unconsciously divided along gender lines. All had gone into the communities they sought to organize with the idea that the juvenile delinquents were a potential revolutionary force. The men attempted to "organize" the gangs of youths who hung out on street corners; the women, on the other hand, concentrated on females in the housing projects and turned their skills to organizing welfare mothers and working women. From the experience of ERAP the women saw that juvenile delinquents were not necessarily a revolutionary force, and also that women, as women, needed to be organized. Their experience helped direct the feminist movement of the late 1960s, which rejected the power structure imposed by men.

Though CAPs lent themselves to ridicule and provoked a political backlash against the Great Society in general, it would be a mistake to label them a complete failure. In the 1960s these organizations had a somewhat bizarre relationship both with the communities they hoped to serve and with the local power structures; the basic program evolved into something much more interesting. At first the leadership was in the hands of white middle-class intellectuals and activists, armed with good intentions and clear ideas about what was best for the communities they sought to empower. Implementation of the programs was a disaster, but the basic intention was the fundamental idea of American government—power should be in the hands of the people, or their elected representatives. By organizing people in communities, the CAPs created political bodies that could use the political system to achieve goals. Ultimately the inner-city communities "organized" by the young white activists could use their newfound political voice to achieve their own goals. These communities did not become, as some white organizers had hoped, the vanguard of revolution. Yet, community organization did ultimately lead to political power and improved social services for previously underserved communities. The poor in America now had organizations of their own to agitate to improve their lives. This goal was a modest one, far short of Johnson's aim to end poverty and create a "Great Society." The achievement was the creation of this more vocal political constituency.

—ROBERT J. ALLISON, SUFFOLK UNIVERSITY

DECLARING WAR

Because it is right, because it is wise, and because, for the first time in our history, it is possible to conquer poverty, I submit, for the consideration of the Congress and the country, the Economic Opportunity Act of 1964.

The Act does not merely expand old programs or improve what is already being done.

It charts a new course.

It strikes at the causes, not just the consequences of poverty.

It can be a milestone in our one-hundred eighty year search for a better life for our people.

This Act provides five basic opportunities.

It will give almost half a million underprivileged young Americans the opportunity to develop skills, continue education, and find useful work.

It will give every American community the opportunity to develop a comprehensive plan to fight its own poverty—and help them to carry out their plans.

It will give dedicated Americans the opportunity to enlist as volunteers in the war against poverty.

It will give many workers and farmers the opportunity to break through particular barriers which bar their escape from poverty.

It will give the entire nation the opportunity for a concerted attack on poverty through the establishment, under my direction, of the Office of Economic Opportunity, a national headquarters for the war against poverty.

Source: *"Proposal for a Nationwide War on the Sources of Poverty, Lyndon B. Johnson's Special Message to Congress, 16 March 1964," in* Public Papers of U.S. Presidents, Lyndon B. Johnson, 1963–1964 *(Washington, D.C.: Government Printing Office, 1965) I:375–380.*

Viewpoint:
The War on Poverty failed because it did not focus on the one sure way to eliminate poverty: creating jobs.

Lyndon B. Johnson is a tragic figure in U.S. history because he is the only president to launch two wars that America could not win: the War on Poverty and the Vietnam War. Until the language of "welfare reform" gained currency in the United States, however, Johnson's public memory lay almost exclusively with Vietnam. Terms such as "Tonkin Gulf Resolution," "Tet" and "POW-MIA" have meant more to high-school and college American-history students in the past twenty years than "VISTA," "CAP" and "OEO," largely because textbook authors emphasized the foreign-military policy dimensions of Johnson's presidency over his domestic agenda. Thus, the names of people such as Ho Chi Minh and General William Westmoreland became fixed in American minds, while those of Ted Sorensen and Sargent Shriver faded quickly for all but a handful of economists and sociologists whose careers were cut from the cloth of social reform.

Those who grew up during the 1960s can usually answer three where-were-you-when questions: the assassination of John F. Kennedy, Johnson's retreat from the 1968 presidential race, and Woodstock. Johnson withdrew his candidacy for reelection after the Tet Offensive, the "surprise" attack by North Vietnam on scores of South Vietnamese cities and towns during the Lunar New Year. Although Tet took place on Vietnamese soil, the political fallout occurred in the United States. Led to believe that the government was winning the Vietnam War, Americans found out—seemingly overnight—that victory was by no means assured. Televised nightly news turned living rooms into sidelines, enabling people to witness what no other generation of American civilians had seen: their own soldiers at war. These repeated images toppled any chance Johnson had to secure four more years in the White House. On 31 March 1968 he told voters that he was finished with presidential politics.

Johnson had sent American troops into combat just two weeks before the 1965 Watts riots. By then "War on Poverty" was an eighteen-month-old slogan from Johnson's 1964 inaugural address. Moved by the plight of the Appalachian poor, Congress had passed the Economic Opportunity Act of 1964 and the new implementing agency–the Office of Economic Opportunity (OEO)–was advancing Johnson's $350 million antipoverty strategy from paper to practice. The act authorized several initiatives, some administered directly by the OEO and others by local Community Action Programs (CAPs).

It was no accident that the War on Poverty's original concern was low-income youth. What compelled Kennedy and later Johnson to make poverty a major national policy issue was juvenile delinquency, largely because of Richard A. Cloward and Lloyd E. Ohlin's *Delinquency and Opportunity: A Theory of Delinquent Gangs* (1960). Michael Harrington's *The Other America; Poverty in the United States* (1962) supplied the remaining proof liberal Democrats needed to put an antipoverty campaign at the top of their agenda. By removing educational barriers and building hope for the nation's youth, Johnson believed government could reduce delinquency and school dropout rates and ultimately stem the tide of poverty.

The president and his advisers also believed in the ideology of American exceptionalism. From their perspective, poverty did not suggest extant or emerging deficiencies in either the economic system or postwar economic development trends. It was a problem, but not a systemic one. Johnson envisioned a "Great Society" anchored in the capitalist free-market system that worked well for the American mainstream. Thus, the War on Poverty excluded from its long list of initiatives any formal or federally coordinated approach to economic and industrial development. The American economy was stable and relatively strong in the early 1960's. Even John Kenneth Galbraith's *The Affluent Society,* published two years before the 1960 presidential campaign season, gave only a modicum of attention to national poverty.

Suffice it to say that because Johnson thought poverty could be cured by removing the social and educational hurdles that kept a minority of Americans poor–35 million people–administration policy planners paid almost no attention to job creation and new business development in the design of War on Poverty programs. To Johnson, the ghettos and Appalachia were anomalous in an otherwise exceptional nation.

Under the organizational plan contained in the Economic Opportunity Act of 1964, the OEO directed the Job Corps, which supplied job training to low-income youth; Volunteers in Service to America (VISTA), an inner-city public service and teaching program modeled after the Peace Corps; and the Work Study Program for lower-income students to work their way through college. While OEO was administratively responsible for CAP agencies, these nonprofit organizations were steered by residents of designated high-poverty target areas. They administered their own Head Start and Upward Bound programs (education for preschoolers and youth from low-income households); "Foster Grandparents" and the Work Experience Program, which made day care and social services available to the poor; and several smaller efforts.

If anything stood in the way of a broad endorsement for the War on Poverty, it was the CAP concept and, in particular, the statutory call for a program "developed, conducted and administered with maximum feasible participation by the residents." By giving the poor the institutional capacity, funding, and power to design and run their own antipoverty programs, portions of the Economic Opportunity Act drew almost instant wrath from state and local officials who thought Washington was making an end-run around federalism on one hand and local control on the other. It comes as no surprise, then, that the theory of community action became a major practical obstacle to the War on Poverty's success: resident boards had their share of "respectable" civic leaders, but the boards also gave power, prestige, experience, and jobs to minorities. In December 1965 Democratic mayors from across the country held a special meeting in Miami, all because of shared resistance to community action. Eventually, federal policymakers took heed.

The interdependence of urban politics, the White House, and Capitol Hill is exemplified well by a "second generation" War on Poverty initiative that Johnson put before Congress in 1966: the Model Cities Program. Although Appalachian poverty was on the public's mind in the early 1960s, it took little time to shift the emphasis toward decaying American cities. Federal highway construction, urban renewal, and suburbanization had already siphoned whites and middle-class African Americans out of inner-city areas, leaving behind the poorest urban residents. In late 1964 Moynihan, assistant secretary for policy planning in the Labor Department, discovered that although unemployment among black men was declining, welfare cases and births to unmarried urban black women were rising.

Moynihan saw a connection between these two phenomena and produced a well-known, but hotly contested, report on black families and black family structure. Although Moynihan's report was discredited by angry African Americans and leftist whites, it reinforced age-old beliefs about the "Negro problem" and gave support to the "culture of poverty" framework that shaped future planning by the Johnson administration. More significantly, it put the spotlight on African Americans and urban ghettos as key elements of the poverty profile in America.

The Model Cities Program, which Congress agreed to create in 1966, brought a "bricks and mortar" element to the War on Poverty—something Johnson had wanted from the beginning. Model Cities was not "community action," but "community development." It introduced massive amounts of federal aid to the most economically distressed urban centers, where city officials could use Washington's money to rebuild ghettos and provide comprehensive social services. Although city leaders had to consult with residents during the planning and implementation of Model Cities projects, local government had the final say: the grants belonged to city hall. In less than two years anti-CAP forces in Washington had succeeded at convincing the Johnson administration to pull back on resident control and let the mayors take charge.

The Model Cities legislation was a scaled-back version of an earlier proposal, the Demonstration Cities and Metropolitan Development Program, which differed in two respects from the bill that finally cleared Congress. "Demonstration Cities" would have reached more than one hundred American cities, large and small, while the Model Cities authorization gave the Department of Housing and Urban Development (HUD) enough money for grants to about fifty communities nationwide. The more important distinction, however, was race policy. Owing to enormous congressional resistance to a proposed requirement that Demonstration Cities public-housing units be racially integrated, the amended Model Cities plan included no such mandate. Unsurprisingly, some Model Cities housing projects were blocked later when community organizations, backed by the NAACP and the Urban League, sued city governments and HUD under the Civil Rights Act of 1964. Their charge was that the Model Cities Program was racially discriminatory. It is altogether ironic, yet telling, that the only means of redress against discriminatory housing practices in the early days of federally financed community development lay with the federal courts and the doctrine of strict scrutiny. Equally ironic, perhaps, is that an important source of legal support for housing discrimination complaints was OEO's Legal Services Program.

Although War on Poverty administration eventually called upon a complex arrangement of about eighty public agencies as the number of antipoverty programs and services grew, the original design involved a new department with direct access to the president—the OEO—and the local CAPs. When Food Stamps, Model Cities, and Income Maintenance were added to the mix, the bureaucratic dimensions of the War on Poverty changed. Indeed, as the reach of the antipoverty campaign increased, the risk of winning a few battles at the expense of the war also increased. The risk was real not because of cost but rather because the War on Poverty transformed and diversified in ways that brought politically conservative, racist, and patriarchal forces together in a counterassault under the banner of "Welfare Reform." Their strategy was to shore up faith in capitalism and invoke the trademark of American self-consciousness, "exceptionalism." Their ammunition was morality, money, and middle-class values. What had been a moderately palatable "hand up" for the nation's "underprivileged" in 1964 became a "hand-out" for "the undeserving poor" in the mid 1980s. Americans were accustomed to the concepts of an upper class, a middle class, and a lower class. By 1982, America had an underclass.

Throughout the 1960s and until the mid 1970s, there were indicators that the quality of life for lower-income Americans had begun to inch upward. In several antipoverty arenas—housing, health services, social services, educational, and economic opportunities—the statistics looked cautiously promising. Medicaid and Medicare caused enormous declines in the percentage of poor Americans who had never seen a physician for a routine medical examination; the infant mortality rate dropped by more than one third between 1965 and 1972; and life expectancy among the poor rose dramatically in the same period. Despite fraud, discrimination; and other problems in federal housing programs, the reality is that by 1976 America had reached a record low for the proportion of families living in overcrowded or substandard housing units. Food Stamps and other federal nutrition programs all but eliminated hunger, which in 1960 had been a serious national problem especially, but not exclusively, in rural areas.

A combination of declining federal resources (attributable in part to Vietnam); Richard M. Nixon's dismantling of OEO; the conversion of many antipoverty programs to federally funded, state-run public service systems; and the virtual gutting of CAPs contributed to the collapse of the War on Poverty. There were other problems, however. The 1970s decline in manufacturing increased overall joblessness, particularly among workers with limited employment skills, and caused a number of small-business closures as well. In fact, a fundamental restructuring of the U.S. economy was underway. As the transformation continued during the 1980s, it became clear that the American workplace and its workforce were at fundamental odds.

Working-class people who had spent most of their adult lives in a particular industry found themselves unemployable. High-tech industrial growth created jobs, but they required new, specialized skills. Service jobs swelled during the same period, but they paid poorly. As the 1970s progressed, not only did America retain its traditional poverty base of minorities and women, but it also gained dislocated workers. The scope of poverty had grown to overwhelming proportions by 1980. Incredibly, the federal government's response was to reduce overall assistance spending, blame the "welfare state" for America's economic woes, and call for a return to traditional (some would say, "antiquated") solutions to social needs: private charitable relief, the business community, churches, and other nonpublic institutions. Welfare had made life too easy, the arguments went, as evidenced by the steady rise in single-parent households on AFDC since the War on Poverty initiatives materialized in the 1960s.

In short, President Ronald Reagan and the far-right coalitions he represented laid the blame on Johnson's doorstep. Known causes of poverty among women (especially, but not only, black women)–occupational segregation, limited skills, the shortage and cost of quality day care, domestic violence, divorce, displaced homemakers, and unequal pay for equal work–were submerged beneath the rhetoric of welfare reform. Further, the competition for a shrinking pool of jobs forced many Americans to work longer hours at distant locations, often for considerably less than they had made before. As Michael B. Katz expresses in his book *In the Shadow of the Poorhouse: A Social History of Welfare in America* (1986):

> In the late 1960's, the federal government expanded social welfare primarily to insure social order and mobilize the votes of black Americans; in the 1980's, another of welfare's historic goals–the regulation of the labor market–and an attempt to mobilize political support among affluent and middle-income voters combined to fuel a war on poverty.

Hindsight permits us to see common cultural roots in a set of 1960s events that seemed almost unrelated at the time. The War on Poverty, the Civil Rights Act of 1964, uneasiness-turned-resistance against the Vietnam War, urban race riots, protests and liberation movements, and the height of the Cold War all occurred contemporaneously. The leftist-liberal-conservative ideological confrontations that germinated in the early 1900s and escalated during the 1930s were rekindled at the close of the 1950s. These confrontations, reenacted under 1960 circumstances, played out in a wide political pendulum swing that put a liberal Irish Catholic Democrat with an engaging smile in the White House, only to replace him with a scowling, impersonal, conservative Republican by the end of the decade (and a far-to-the-right candidate one decade thereafter). The country Nixon inherited in January 1969 differed significantly from the one that narrowly elected Kennedy nine years earlier. By the time Watergate forced Nixon to resign in 1974, the War on Poverty was an all but abandoned federal agenda, put aside for more pressing international problems that fell to presidents Gerald Ford and Jimmy Carter to resolve.

When welfare reform became a major campaign issue in 1996, the conservative Heritage Foundation was probably correct when it estimated total War on Poverty spending at $5.4 trillion. Yet, by ascribing War on Poverty failures to government-sponsored "behavioral poverty," mainly unwed welfare mothers who taught their children bad morals by example and became grandmothers to the next generation's poor, the Heritage Foundation took an indefensible leap of faith. It committed what William Ryan recognized as "blaming the victim" nearly thirty years ago.

Indeed, "blaming the victim" served as the rallying call for partisans committed to an anti-welfare issue network. Right-wing political leaders joined forces with religious organizations that opposed aid to single parents on moral grounds, leading the Heritage Foundation to claim that "illegitimacy is a social catastrophe." Similarly, Libertarian congressional candidate Ken Bisson blamed the victims in 1996 by concluding: "We give handouts to single mothers, we get more single mothers. We give a blank check for Medicaid recipients. Medicaid spending explodes." When Republican allies of former House Speaker Newt Gingrich endorsed the "Contract with America" manifesto in 1994, they agreed to enact laws in order to change "destructive social behavior" among welfare recipients and reverse the "illegitimacy, crime, illiteracy and more poverty" that Johnson's Great Society initiatives had spawned. As one caught up in the groundswell of "blaming the victim," Gingrich chose a revealing name for the welfare reform legislation he promised to put through once Republicans regained control of Congress: The Personal Responsibility Act.

Notwithstanding the rhetoric of welfare reform, the U.S. government did not "cause" poverty, illegitimacy, idleness, or an underclass. Rather, "in poverty discourse, moral assessments have nearly always overlain pragmatic distinctions. The issue becomes not only who can fend for themselves without aid, but . . . whose behavior and character entitle them to the resources of others." Johnson's concept, molded after the theories of Cloward, Harrington and others, was to empower American's poor, not to blame them. The proliferation of low-income advocacy organizations during the past thirty years attests in part to the success of Johnson's efforts, yet he stopped short of creating sustainable economic opportunites because he thought the poverty problem could be solved by equalizing access to political, educational, and social institutions rather than by fundamentally restructuring the nation's economic system. The War on Poverty should be criticized not for what it did accomplish, but for failing to address the one measure that lifts people from poverty by giving them the means to earn a living: jobs.

–JUDITH A. BARRETT, DUXBURY, MASSACHUSETTS

References

Ken Auletta, *The Underclass* (New York: Random House, 1982);

Liva Baker, *Miranda: Crime, Law, and Politics* (New York: Atheneum, 1983);

Richard A. Cloward and Lloyd E. Ohlin, *Delinquency and Opportunity: A Theory of Delinquent Gangs* (Glencoe, Ill.: Free Press, 1960);

Sara Evans, *Personal Politics: The Roots of Women's Liberation in the Civil Rights Movement and the New Left* (New York: Knopf, 1979);

David Farber, *The Age of Great Dreams: America in the 1960s* (New York: Hill & Wang, 1994);

John Kenneth Galbraith, *The Affluent Society* (Boston: Houghton Mifflin, 1958);

Herbert J. Gans, *The War Against the Poor: The Underclass and Antipoverty Policy* (New York: BasicBooks, 1995);

Michael L. Gillette, *Launching the War on Poverty: An Oral History* (New York: Twayne, 1996);

Newt Gingrich, *Contract with America* (New York: Random House, 1994);

Michael Harrington, *The Other America; Poverty in the United States* (New York: Macmillan, 1962);

Lyndon Baines Johnson, *The Vantage Point: Perspectives of the Presidency, 1963–1969* (New York: Holt, Rinehart & Winston, 1971);

Michael B. Katz, *In the Shadow of the Poorhouse: A Social History of Welfare in America* (New York: BasicBooks, 1986);

Katz, *The Undeserving Poor: From the War on Poverty to the War on Welfare* (New York: Pantheon, 1989);

Nick Kotz, "Discussion," in *A Decade of Federal Antipoverty Programs: Achievements, Failures, Lessons*, edited by Robert H. Haveman (New York: Academic Press, 1977), pp. 48–51;

Nicholas Lemann, "The Unfinished War," *Atlantic Monthly*, 262 (December 1988): 37–56; 263 (January 1989): 53–68;

Sar A. Levitan, *The Great Society's Poor Law: A New Approach to Poverty* (Baltimore: Johns Hopkins University Press, 1969);

Peter Marris and Martin Rein, *Dilemmas of Social Reform: Poverty and Community Action in the United States* (New York: Atherton, 1967);

Allen J. Matusow, *The Unraveling of America: A History of Liberalism in the 1960s* (New York: Harper & Row, 1984);

Daniel P. Moynihan, *Maximum Feasible Misunderstanding: Community Action in the War on Poverty* (New York: Free Press, 1969);

Nancy A. Naples, "From Maximum Feasible Participation to Disenfranchisement," *Social Justice*, 25 (Spring 1998): 47–67;

James T. Patterson, *America's Struggle Against Poverty, 1900–1980* (Cambridge, Mass.: Harvard University Press, 1981);

Charles F. Peake, "A Perspective on Economics, Poverty and Policy," *National Forum*, 76 (Summer 1996): 5–7;

Marc Pilisuk and Phyllis Pilisuk, eds., *How We Lost the War on Poverty* (New Brunswick, N.J.: Transaction Books, 1973);

Frances Fox Piven and Frances Fox Cloward, *The Breaking of the American Social Compact* (New York: New Press, 1997);

Piven and Cloward, *Regulating the Poor: The Functions of Public Welfare* (New York: Vintage, 1971);

Jill Quadagno, *The Color of Welfare: How Racism Undermined the War on Poverty* (New York: Oxford University Press, 1994);

Robert Rector, *Issues '96: The Candidate's Briefing Book* (Washington, D.C.: Heritage Foundation, 1996);

Rector and William F. Lauber, *America's Failed $5.4 Trillion Dollar War on Poverty* (Washington, D.C.: Heritage Foundation, 1995);

William Ryan, *Blaming the Victim* (New York: Vintage, 1971);

James L. Sundquist and Corinne Saposs Schelling, eds., *On Fighting Poverty: Perspectives from Experience* (New York: BasicBooks, 1969).

WARREN COURT

Coming to terms with the Warren Court: Judicial activism or constitutional evolution?

Viewpoint: The U.S. Supreme Court, dominated by liberal justices under Chief Justice Earl Warren, rejected prevailing constitutional theory and ushered in an era of judicial activism.

Viewpoint: The Warren Court adhered to the highest standard of constitutional government.

Was the chief justiceship of Earl Warren (1953–1969) an aberration in the U.S. Supreme Court's history, or did the Court under Warren merely extend the work of previous Courts in determining the law? While some previous and subsequent Court decisions have been controversial (*Dred Scott* v. *Sandford* in 1857, *Plessy* v. *Ferguson* in 1896, *Lochner* v. *New York* in 1905, and *Roe* v. *Wade* in 1972), the Warren Court's distinction is that it cohered around a particular philosophy that redefined the American political and social fabric. Some Americans welcomed these decisions; others did not.

Earl Warren seemed an unlikely candidate to lead a judicial revolution. A moderate Republican from California, he had been a tough prosecutor in Alameda County. As state attorney general he had led the campaign to remove Japanese Americans from the Pacific Coast during World War II. During and after the war he served as governor, one of the most popular in the state's history, and in 1948 he was the Republican candidate for vice president. If, as had been expected, Thomas E. Dewey had defeated Harry S Truman, Warren would have been vice president. At the Republican Convention in 1952 he was California's favorite-son candidate for president, though Sen. Richard M. Nixon maneuvered to have the California delegation switch to Dwight D. Eisenhower.

Before 1953 Warren had never served as a judge. Eisenhower did not name him to the Court, the first Republican appointee in more than twenty years, for his judicial philosophy, which was unknown. More likely, Eisenhower wanted to reward a political ally and bring some moderation and conciliation to the Court. Though all of the justices had been appointed by Franklin D. Roosevelt or Truman, the Court in the early 1950s was divided under the competing standards of Hugo Black and Felix Frankfurter. Both were stalwart liberals and intellectual giants, and both disagreed fundamentally about the role of the Court. Frankfurter, a disciple of Oliver Wendell Holmes and Louis D. Brandeis, believed the Court should restrain itself and not strike down state or federal laws unless the Constitution clearly and unambiguously warranted it. Black, on the other hand, believed that the Court's role was to prevent any state intrusion into the liberties of citizens. Black and Frankfurter had differing legal views, and each also regarded himself as the proper leader of the Court.

Warren thus needed all of his considerable political skill to unify the Court and to conciliate Black and Frankfurter. Warren did this with considerable grace, and the first major decision of his chief justiceship, *Brown* v. *Board of Education of Topeka, Kansas* (1954), was both unanimous and a judicial milestone. Subsequently, though the Court under Warren did not make as many unanimous decisions, it did make many significant ones, extending the protections of the First Amendment (*Yates* v. *United States* in 1957, *Engel* v. *Vitale* in 1962, and *Brandenberg* v. *Ohio* in 1969), Fourth Amendment (*Mapp* v. *Ohio* in 1961), Fifth Amendment (*Escobedo* v. *Illinois* in 1964, *Miranda* v. *Arizona* in 1966), Sixth Amendment (*Gideon* v. *Wainwright* in 1963), and the never before cited Ninth Amendment (*Griswold* v. *Connecticut* in 1965) as well as opening up areas into which the Court had never before ventured, such as voting rights and reapportionment (*Baker* v. *Carr* in 1962). While Black and Frankfurter approached these cases as judges or legal scholars, Warren's question always was, "Is it fair?" As chief justice, he made fairness the basic principle of American justice.

In these two essays, scholars Judith A. Barrett and Robert J. Allison disagree, not about the significance of the Warren Court, but about its legacy. Both scholars welcome the effect of many of the Warren Court's decisions, and while Barrett forcefully argues that the Court was simply doing what a Court was supposed to do in upholding the Constitution, Allison suggests that the Court was invading the political sphere, and while its decisions had the appearance of upholding democratic principles, in the long run these decisions undermined the idea of democracy. No chief justice since John Marshall has left such an impressive, and such a controversial, legacy.

Viewpoint: The U.S. Supreme Court, dominated by liberal justices under Chief Justice Earl Warren, rejected prevailing constitutional theory and ushered in an era of judicial activism.

The Supreme Court under Chief Justice Earl Warren tilted too far to the left. In several landmark cases involving voting rights, the rights of the accused, obscenity, and school prayer, the Court deviated from its traditional role as a judicial body and instead became a permanent Constitutional Convention, enshrining into Constitutional principle the judges' own predilections. This tilt had severe repercussions. First, by appearing to be partisan, the Court invited criticism from those who disagreed with its judgments. The 1968 election, in fact, was more a repudiation of the Court than of the Johnson administration, as both American Party candidate George C. Wallace and Republican Richard M. Nixon attacked the Warren Court for its breach of Constitutional faith. The Court invited this political backlash and had no political weapons with which to meet it. By completing the nationalization of the Bill of Rights through the due process clause of the Fourteenth Amendment, the Court left the states with little to do in the way of making public policy, increasing the centralization of American government. And by encouraging those who wanted to change public policy to bring their issues to court, rather than debating them in political forums, the Warren Court had the unintended consequence of making the left complacent, trusting in judges to solve their problems rather than in building political alliances.

William Rehnquist, clerking for Justice Robert Jackson in 1952–1953, as what was then the "Roosevelt Court" (all the justices had been appointed by either Franklin D. Roosevelt or Harry S Truman) was becoming the Warren Court, warned that "liberals should be the first to realize . . . that it does not do to push blindly through towards one constitutional goal without paying attention to other equally desirable values that are being trampled on in the process." Liberals should have remembered that the Court in 1935 and 1936 had gutted the New Deal, as the justices, according to Roosevelt, read their own economic and political ideas into Constitutional law. The greatest virtue taught by that experience, as with the experience of the early part of the century, was that judges should exercise restraint when reviewing legislation, that the unelected judiciary should defer to the elected branches of government. This was the message of Justice Oliver Wendell Holmes's dissent in *Lochner* v. *New York* (1905), when the Supreme Court struck down a New York law limiting the working hours of bakers. The justices believed that the Fourteenth Amendment was meant to ensure unlimited liberty of contract. Other Americans, including members of the New York legislature, believed that the state could protect the health and safety of its citizens by limiting the number of hours they were made to work. When the Court struck down the New York law as unconstitutional, Holmes wrote a blistering dissent: "This case is decided upon an economic theory which a large part of the country does not entertain. . . . Some . . . laws embody convictions or prejudices which judges are likely to share. Some may not. But a constitution is not intended to embody a particular economic theory. . . . It is made for people of fundamentally differing views, and the accident of our finding certain opinions natural and familiar or novel and even shocking ought not to conclude our judgment upon the question whether statutes embodying them conflict with the Constitution of the United States." In 1925, when the Court made an uncharacteristically liberal decision in striking down a Nebraska law, Harvard law professor and future justice Felix Frankfurter warned that "In rejoicing, we must not forget that a heavy price has to be paid for these occasional services to liberalism." If the Supreme Court could give, it could also take away.

One of the most important opinions, *Baker* v. *Carr* (1962), illustrates this dilemma. Tennessee's legislative districts had been drawn, and representatives apportioned, in 1901. By 1960 the ninety-nine members of the state House of Representatives were elected from districts widely different in size. More than five times as many people lived in Hamilton County as in tiny Moore County, meaning that each voter in Moore County had as much political voice as nineteen voters in Hamilton. Because the rural counties of Tennessee had more representatives, they dominated the state's politics, and the rural minority governed the urban majority. Voters and elected officials from the cities filed suit in federal court, maintaining that the Tennessee system of apportionment violated both their voting rights (under the Fifteenth Amendment) and their equal protection of the law (under the Fourteenth Amendment). The problem, though, was that the courts had long ago decided they would not decide political questions. They would allow legislatures and Congress to work out these political problems, since the courts had no way to force the political branches of government to act and since trying to move against political bodies would give the courts the appearance of having political motivation.

In this case, however, the Supreme Court decided to act. In *Baker* Justice William Brennan wrote that merely because the people of Tennessee were filing suit to protect a political right, it was not a political case. The Supreme Court ruled that the district court in Tennessee could hear the case and that Tennessee must reapportion its legislature in order to ensure more equality between legislative districts. On the surface this was a wise decision—now the majority would rule.

Yet, as Frankfurter had warned in 1925, before one rejoiced one should consider all the implications of the decision. Frankfurter, an associate justice in 1962, cautioned that the Court's involvement in this issue "may well impair the Court's position as the ultimate organ of 'the supreme Law of the Land' in that vast range of legal problems, often strongly entangled in popular feeling, on which this Court must pronounce. The Court's authority—possessed of neither the purse nor the sword—ultimately rests on sustained public confidence in its moral sanction. Such feeling must be nourished by the Court's complete detachment, in fact and in appearance, from political entanglements and by abstention from injecting itself into the clash of political forces in political settlements." John Marshall Harlan, also dissenting, said:

> one need not agree, as a citizen, with what Tennessee has done or failed to do, in order to deprecate, as a judge, what the majority is doing today. Those observers of the Court who see it primarily as the last refuge for the correction of all inequality or injustice, no matter what its nature or source, will no doubt applaud this decision and its break with the past. Those who consider that continuing national respect for the Court's authority depends in large measure upon its wise exercise of self-restraint and discipline in constitutional adjudication, will view the decision with deep concern.

The Court had, these two justices contended, overstepped its authority. But were the long-range implications of the decision as dire as Harlan and Frankfurter predicted? The answer is yes. First, the Court followed *Baker* with a string of decisions arising from other redistricting cases and ultimately settled on a precise mathematical formula, one person/one vote, as the only acceptable criteria for apportioning representatives in legislatures and in city councils. Some states, whose legislative chambers would have been overwhelmed by representatives if they maintained the old election formula, reduced the sizes of their legislatures and so increased the size of legislative districts. More important, by the early 1970s, when the one person/one vote mandate had been carried out, population had shifted yet again, to the suburbs. So city people, who had hoped thanks to *Baker* finally to have their voices count in legislatures, found themselves outvoted by suburbanites. If the goal was majority rule, of course, that was an acceptable and appropriate end. But if the proponents of *Baker* were trying to get more power for their cities, they failed miserably.

Next, the Court's meddling into the apportionment fray bore out one of Frankfurter's warnings, that this would keep the Supreme Court and lower courts constantly occupied in mathematical quagmires trying to draw boundary lines of exact population equality. This problem has come to exist, and no state legislature can draw new district lines without running into legal problems. Furthermore, attempts by states to protect particular interests, to guarantee that people who may not be able to command a majority in a geographic district can still have their voices heard

The 1967 Supreme Court, with Chief Justice Earl Warren seated third from the left

(U.S. Supreme Court Photo)

in the legislature, have failed to pass judicial muster. One can imagine many possible scenarios where this could happen, but recently the most glaring have been when states try to ensure that African Americans or Hispanics have the opportunity to elect representatives.

After the 1990 census North Carolina, Florida, and Georgia all drew up new congressional districts. Each state has significant African American populations, and Florida also has a sizable Hispanic population. The legislatures recognized that simply drawing up districts with equal numbers of people would not ensure that people of color or Hispanics had a majority in any single district; instead, these ethnic minorities would be scattered throughout many districts in which they would be a minority. Legislatures then drew districts that would have majority populations of blacks or Hispanics. The Supreme Court said this was unconstitutional, that creating districts to represent particular minority interests violated the equal protection rights of everyone else.

Two questions now arise. Is there any way to protect minority interests? And if the Court had not become involved in *Baker,* would states have reapportioned their legislatures? The answer to both is yes, and both answers rest on the same fundamental premise. Harlan was right—the Supreme Court is not intended to resolve every possible problem. There are other ways to resolve problems of discrimination and hardship. While one can look at the Warren Court as a great restorer of rights, in fact the real rights revolution in American society was not taking place in the Supreme Court chambers but in the streets of Selma and Birmingham and in churches in Mississippi and Harlem. As Frankfurter noted in his dissent, "Appeal must be to an informed, civically militant electorate. In a democratic society like ours, relief must come through an aroused popular conscience that sears the conscience of the people's representatives." The Voting Rights Act of 1965 did more to transform the American political system than did *Baker,* and the Voting Rights Act did not spring from an amicus curiae brief from the American Civil Liberties Union, but from mass mobilization that seared the conscience of the nation.

In *Griswold* v. *Connecticut* (1965) the Court also entered new terrain. Here it was not an area previously considered off-limits but was in fact inventing a new constitutional right. At issue was whether Connecticut could prohibit the sale of birth-control devices or the dissemination of birth-control information. Estelle Griswold, director of Connecticut's chapter of Planned Parenthood, was arrested for distributing birth-control devices and information. She charged that the Connecticut law was unconstitutional, as it abridged her freedom of speech. Further, lawyers argued that the law intruded into marital relations, where the state had no business. In his opinion for the Court, William O. Douglas said that "We do not sit as a super-legislature to determine the wisdom, need, and propriety of laws that touch economic problems, business affairs, or social conditions. This law, however, operates directly on an intimate relation of husband and wife and their physician's role in one aspect of that relation." The Court ruled that the law was an unconstitutional violation, not of any single right protected by the Bill of Rights or the Fourteenth Amendment, but of a whole range of rights that created "emanations" and "penumbras," among which was a right to privacy. Justice Hugo Black, since 1938 the Court's staunchest protector of Constitutional liberties, could not agree. "I like my privacy as well as the next one," Black wrote, "but I am nevertheless compelled to admit that government has a right to invade it unless prohibited by some specific constitutional provision." Privacy as a right is protected by common law, Black noted, and the Supreme Court does not have common-law jurisdiction. As for Planned Parenthood's contention that the law was silly, archaic, and at odds with prevailing opinion in Connecticut, Black and Potter Stewart said that the Court did not have power to strike down laws the judges found silly. If a law was at odds with community opinion, then certainly the community could persuade the legislature to repeal it.

In this decision, as in *Baker,* the Court interposed itself as an arbiter of policy, making a constitutional issue out of a political difference. Should contraceptive devices be publicly accessible? In Connecticut this was the subject of a fierce debate between the Catholic Church and Planned Parenthood. Each year the legislature considered repealing the contraceptive law, and it refused to do so. Planned Parenthood, instead of mobilizing politically, took the matter to Court, which made this political issue a constitutional one. Instead of mobilizing public opinion and competing in what Justice Holmes called the marketplace of ideas, Planned Parenthood and other liberal groups found it more expedient to litigate, and this had the long-range tendency of making both the Court seem political and liberal groups seem less adept at working in the political system.

Griswold also established a national standard, making it impossible to restrict the sale of contraceptives anywhere. While Planned Parenthood had maintained that ready access to contraceptives, which prevent pregnancy, would have the socially beneficial result of making abortion unnecessary, just a few years later Planned Parenthood was pushing to make abortion more accessible. While *Roe* v. *Wade* (1972) was decided after Warren, Black, Abe Fortas, and other liberal stalwarts had left the bench, it rested on the premise of *Griswold.* States could not restrict access to abortions, except during the final trimester. Though many in the states found this morally reprehensible, the Court had to protect the Constitutional right it had discovered in *Griswold*.

Cases such as *Griswold, Baker,* and others involving rights of the accused, most notably *Miranda* v. *Arizona* (1966), opened the Court up to criticism that it was intent on changing the Constitutional system. In the 1966 midterm elections Republicans gained seats in the House of Representatives and Senate, running on fear of crime. The *Miranda* decision, which mandated that suspects being questioned had to have legal counsel present and which severely restricted the power of police officers to question suspects, made an easy target for Republicans. In May 1967 Judge Warren Burger of the U.S. Court of Appeals for the District of Columbia spoke at Ripon College in Wisconsin, charging that America's underlying "fear of the power of government and . . . great concern for underlying liberty" had distorted the criminal justice system, making it "very difficult to convict even those who are plainly guilty." Burger, a thoughtful and meticulous judge, did not like the way the Supreme Court was revising state legal codes based on a few cases such as Ernesto Miranda's or Danny Escobedo's trials. His arguing that the Court had gone too far brought Burger to the attention of Nixon, then planning a campaign for the presidency.

Nixon and Wallace, both running for presidency in 1968, used the fear of crime as a potent campaign issue, and Nixon pledged to appoint "strict constructionists" to the Court. When Warren announced his plan to retire, Republicans in Congress, confident that Nixon or another Republican would be elected in November, blocked the promotion of Fortas to chief justice and the elevation of Homer Thornberry to the Supreme Court. On his election, Nixon appointed Warren Burger to be chief justice.

The Court under Warren had overstepped its authority, and though in some cases the results were laudable—ending segregation, forcing the reapportionment of state legislatures, protecting the rights of the accused, protecting the free exercise of religion and freedom of the press—in the way the Court reached these decisions it badly erred. It would have been wiser to seek those ends that had political solutions through the political process rather than through the courts. By overstepping the proper boundaries of the judiciary, the Court invited a public and political backlash, and thus it unwittingly helped to elect men determined to curtail the Court's powers and influence and undermine the freedoms the Court hoped to protect.

—ROBERT J. ALLISON,
SUFFOLK UNIVERSITY

Viewpoint: The Warren Court adhered to the highest standard of constitutional government.

Owing to its defense of equality and the civil liberties protected by the U.S. constitution, the Warren Court sparked enormous controversy about the powers and role of the federal judiciary. Throughout Chief Justice Earl Warren's sixteen-year tenure, the Supreme Court issued a number of pathbreaking decisions on racial equality, free expression, the rights of the accused, and separation of church and state, thereby establishing a doctrinal foothold for post-Warren rulings on abortion, school busing, and gender discrimination. Against the backdrop of the socially and politically explosive 1960s when Warren held the highest judicial post in America, the Supreme Court was a highly contested institution.

Today's historians, government scholars, lawyers, and judges remain divided over the legitimacy of the Warren Court's constitutional adjudication. Some critics of the former Chief Justice assail him for pursuing a left-of-center ideological game plan, and they argue that the Warren Court placed politics ahead of impartiality. Others claim that Warren, who was no legal scholar, substituted "creative constitutional development" for jurisprudence of original intent, meaning that under his direction, the Supreme Court effectively made new law by applying modern ideas to the intent of old words. Recently, the Warren Court has been chided for doing too little and for its failure to effectuate fundamental changes in constitutional interpretation because Warren and his colleagues were blinded by their own American liberalism.

The issue most frequently debated about the Warren Court concerns "judicial activism," however. Asking whether the Court "overstepped its bounds or adhered to the highest traditions of Constitutional government" draws scholars inextricably into the same dispute, one polarized by the language of "judicial activism" and "judicial restraint." Heated exchanges about judicial activism persist among professionals, scholars, politicians, and the press, suggesting that the Warren Court's significance transcends the political moment of the 1960s and raises several questions of historical and contemporary importance.

First, what was the "Warren Court"? Does it encompass all of Warren's time as chief justice, beginning in 1953, or is it restricted to the period between 1962, when judicial restraint defender Felix Frankfurter retired, and 1969, when Warren left the Court? If Warren had a "liberal agenda," or a desire to effectuate social welfare state policies through the judicial process, did his success depend on Justice Arthur Goldberg (Frankfurter's replacement) for a crucial fifth vote? Further, was there ever a "Warren Court" at all, or should the activism associated with Warren's name be attributed instead to Justice William Brennan, who joined the Supreme Court three years after Warren's appointment and remained until failing health forced him to retire in 1990? Brennan's admirers (and some critics) claim that he deserves the credit (or blame) for the legal revolution referred to as the "Warren Court" because he kept the egalitarian thrust alive while a succession of retirements and new appointments gradually changed the composition and philosophy of the Court. However, Warren's admirers, notably his loyal judicial biographer Bernard Schwartz, claim that it was "Super Chief" who brought unity, leadership, and an "institutional ethos to a court that was sorely in need of it."

Another question scholars ought to ask is whether an activist court inherently oversteps its bounds, for it soon becomes clear that "bounds" are neither as fixed nor as certain as the judicial restraint community would have us believe. Does activism distort or develop the Constitution? Is a court of restraint the only one that adheres to "the highest traditions of constitutional government?" Surely what Alexander Hamilton called "the least dangerous branch"—the Supreme Court—was never intended to be the least effective branch, for when the Framers designed a system of shared powers they were cognizant of the unique power (indeed, the historic legal tradition) of judicial review. And although such esteemed constitutional scholars as Learned Hand and Herbert Wechsler would disagree, a court that exercise judicial review is a court engaged to some extent in judicial activism.

Evidence of Warren Court "activism" lies foremost in a collection of major constitutional questions that the Supreme Court considered between 1953 and 1969, although the vast majority were taken up by the late period Warren court of 1962–1969. Arguably, the Warren Court decided many questions in ways that changed the way America thinks about the amended Constitution—specifically, the Bill of Rights and Reconstruction-era amendments. At the same time, some of the Court's most memorable holdings—*Brown* v. *Board of Education of Topeka, Kansas* (1954), *Cooper* v. *Aaron* (1958), *Mapp* v. *Ohio* (1961), *Baker* v. *Carr* (1962), *New York Times* v. *Sullivan* (1964) *Griswold* v. *Connecticut* (1965), and *Miranda* v. *Arizona* (1966)—confronted long-standing practices of federal, state, and local authorities; overturned laws on constitutional grounds; and spawned new debates about the separation of powers, federalism, and American civil liberties. By striking down state laws and overturning state court decisions, especially but not only in the South, the Warren Court changed the distribution of national-state powers and built a formidable bridge between the Fourteenth Amendment, the Bill of Rights and the Constitution's "Supremacy Clause." Warren, then, was (and is) controversial not only for specific decisions that came out of his years at the Court's helm but also for his "activist" strategy.

The terms *judicial activism* and *judicial restraint* have invited several, although not altogether conflicting, definitions in theoretical and practical literature on the courts, and some of them are found in mainstays of American jurisprudence. At the risk of substituting common sense for the venerable body of scholarship in which these terms are explicated, extended, and modified, judicial activism refers to a philosophy of constitutional adjudication that argues the Court's right to engage equally with other branches of government in the shaping of public policy; interpret the Constitution in light of current realities and not be constrained by either the doctrines of "original intent" or stare decisis (precedent); and intervene assertively in order to safeguard constitutional protections encroached upon or violated by other federal branches or the states.

Judicial restraint, on the other hand, argues that courts should: defer wherever possible to traditionally democratic means of resolving policy conflicts, for example, recognizing policy as the purview of legislatures; avoid the impulse to choose cases on appeal that present contemporary issues rather than enduring or fundamental constitutional questions; adhere to precedent; and generally, limit constitutional interpretation to the intent of the framers (or to those who authored and shaped constitutional amendments).

Such are the polemical contours of judicial activism-judicial restraint, and they shape the major themes in Warren Court discourse. How we define and apply these terms affects our understanding of constitutional law and the relationship between the Constitution, culture, and the judiciary. One cannot help but consider modern arguments about activism and the Warren Court against Hamilton's call for permanent judicial tenure (especially since calls for Warren's impeachment echoed throughout his sixteen years with the Court):

> The complete independence of the courts of justice is peculiarly essential in a limited Constitution [meaning] one which contains certain specified exceptions to the legislative authority. . . . There is no position which depends on clearer principles than that every act of a delegated authority, contrary to the tenor of the commission under which it is exercised, is void. No legislative act, therefore, contrary to the Constitution can be valid. . . . the courts were designed to be an intermediate body between the people and the legislature in order, among other things, to keep the latter within the limits assigned to their authority. The interpretation of the laws is the proper and peculiar province of the courts.

The Warren Court is not the first example of an activist judiciary in American history, and its brand of activism is not the only one that has attracted scholarly disagreement. Scholars such as Wallace Mendelsohn have debated the "activism" of chief justice John Marshall and in particular the case of *Marbury* v. *Madison* (1803), questioning whether Marshall's Court acted assertively or followed suit with the expectations of his day. Similar issues have been raised about the wave of judicial activism that extended from the late 1880s through the mid 1930s, a wave that peaked with the William Howard Taft Court and ultimately subsided during Chief Justice Charles Evans Hughes's term. Warren Court activism is usually considered the third wave, and its judicial trademarks include equality and the nationalization of the Bill of Rights.

The Warren Court commentaries published during and after the chief justice's tenure supply a record of received wisdom about the judiciary at this critical juncture in American history. They also bespeak enduring American concerns about political power—who has it, and for what ends—and centrally, who has the last word?

MIRANDA V. ARIZONA (1966)

In the late 1960s the U.S. Supreme Court heard a case that would have a profound impact on how law enforcement officials apprehended, interrogated, and prosecuted criminal suspects. The case involved Ernesto Miranda, who, in the presence of two Arizona police officers, made an oral confession to the charges of kidnapping and rape. The Supreme Court of Arizona held that Miranda's constitutional rights had not been violated. The U.S. Supreme Court determined otherwise. Earl Warren wrote:

. . . The cases before us raise questions which go to the roots of our concepts of American criminal jurisprudence: the restraints society must observe consistent with the Federal Constitution in prosecuting individuals for crime. More specifically, we deal with the admissibility of statements obtained from an individual who is subjected to custodial police interrogation and the necessity for procedures which assure that the individual is accorded his privilege under the Fifth Amendment to the Constitution not to be compelled to incriminate himself. . . .

At the outset, if a person in custody is to be subjected to interrogation, he must first be informed in clear and unequivocal terms that he has the right to remain silent. For those unaware of the privilege, the warning is needed simply to make them aware of it—the threshold requirement for an intelligent decision as to its exercise. More important, such a warning is an absolute prerequisite in overcoming the inherent pressures of the interrogation atmosphere. . . .

The warning of the right to remain silent must be accompanied by the explanation that anything said can and will be used against the individual in court. This warning is needed in order to make him aware not only of the privilege, but also of the consequence of forgoing it. . . .

The circumstances surrounding in-custody interrogation can operate very quickly to overbear the will of one merely made aware of his privilege by his interrogators. Therefore, the right to have counsel present at the interrogation is indispensable to the protection of the Fifth Amendment privilege under the system we delineate today. . . .

If an individual indicates that he wishes the assistance of counsel before any interrogation occurs, the authorities cannot rationally ignore or deny his request on the basis that the individual does not have or cannot afford a retained attorney. The financial ability of the individual has no relationship to the scope of the rights involved here. . . .

Source: *Henry Steele Commager, ed.,* Documents of American History, *2 volumes (New York: Appleton-Century-Crofts, 1973),* II: *713–717.*

In an important essay published three years before Warren retired from the Court, Bradley C. Canon suggested that judicial activism be defined by six characteristics--ranging from the extent to which the judiciary negates legislative actions and articulates new public policy to substantive differences between constitutional interpretation by the courts and other branches of government. Under Canon's criteria the Warren Court overstepped its bounds when the justices nullified age-old voting-district practices that left racial minorities unequally represented in Congress, yet by reconstructing old questions about the meaning of "representation," the Court found room (power) to intervene where legislatures had systematically frustrated the plain language of the Constitution.

Baker v. *Carr* (1962) and *Reynolds* v. *Sims* (1964) confronted what no prior Supreme Court had been willing to face: legislative malapportionment. The consequences were felt immediately, not only in the lower courts that had to oversee the dismantling of suspect voting district lines, but also at the polls where African American and white citizens, urban rural and suburban, finally cast votes of equal weight—"one man, one vote." As Warren stated bluntly in *Reynolds* v. *Sims,* "Legislators represent people, not trees or acres."

Canon's scholarly essay was not written in a vacuum. Throughout the 1960s the Warren Court accumulated professional and partisan enemies and yet its work won sympathy, and at times praise, in high places as well. In an attempt to place the complex demands on the

Supreme Court in perspective, former U.S. Solicitor General Archibald Cox suggested in 1967 that the "storm" over the Warren Court centered on continued disagreement about the judiciary's proper role in a democratic society. His introductory remarks in a lecture series that year shed light on how difficult it is to square one's perosnal sense of justice with the neutral objectives of the law:

> Should the Court play an active, creative role in shaping our destiny, equally with the executive and legislative branches? Or should it be characterized by self-restraint, deferring to the legislative branch whenever there is room for policy judgment and leaving new departures to the initiative of others? . . . The extraordinary character of questions put before the Court means that the Court cannot ignore the political aspects of its task, yet the answer to the question "what substantive result is best for the country?" is often inconsistent with the responses obtained by asking "what is the decision according to law?"

Constitutional historian Kermit Hall points out that for yielding to a personal sense of justice in the collective, the Warren Court was victimized further for giving more than "lip service" to the "professed ideals of equality, fairness and justice" because a majority of the justices sought "to end the process by which such ideals had been compromised, qualified, and even destroyed."

Accordingly, Hall attributes the backlash against Warren's activism to the Court's "reconciliation of professed values with behavior," a situation that brought into high relief the "hypocrisy" of Warren's own contemporaries. *The New York Times* columnist and Supreme Court reporter Anthony Lewis made a similar observation years ago. In a 1968 essay, Lewis told Americans that once Warren had been attacked for his honesty, the Chief Justice apparently became "liberated from the habit of political compromise . . . In an age of character assassination, he saw good in other people. In an age of government indecision, he was decisive."

Bernard Schwartz agrees. "For Chief Justice Warren, the issue on judicial review was not *reasonableness* but *rightness*. . . . He consciously conceived of the Supreme Court as a virtual modern Court of Chancery–a residual 'fountain of justice'–to rectify individual instances of injustice, particularly when the victims suffered from racial, economic or similar disabilities."

Another group of Warren Court observers is represented by Mark Tushnet, who argues that activist politics both inspired and ultimately decimated the "liberal" Supreme Court of Chief Justice Warren. Reminding us that the judiciary's "independence" hardly removes the Court from the rest of the federal government or from the political climate of the day, Tushnet suggests that society's "falling out" with the liberal New Deal/Great Society agenda spawned simultaneous contempt for Warren Court activism, yet he also concludes that what subsequent courts have never rejected is the notion that "the Supreme Court could help shape public policy."

Indeed, Chief Justice Warren Burger and his successor, William Rehnquist, continued the judicial policy tradition, at times barely concealing their "restraint." In contrast to the 1954 school desegregation cases (*Brown* and *Bolling*), the use of school busing to achieve integrated schools was not mandated by the Warren Court, although clearly it hailed from Warren doctrine. Rather, the more conservative Burger Court ruled on all of the crucial school busing cases: *Swann* v. *Charlotte Mecklenberg* (1971), *Keyes* v. *Denver* (1973) and *Millikan* v. *Bradley* (1974). While at the time many Americans objected vehemently to theses dicisions, Frederick Lewis reminds scholars that "the cruder forms of official racism are now almost nowhere sanctioned. A great part of this accomplishment [stems from] the broad thrust of the Warren Court equal protection jurisprudence."

Separate was not equal, and even Warren's harshest critics stop short of questioning the legitimacy of *Brown*. Harvard Law Professor Mary Ann Glendon, who crafts cogent arguments against judicial activism, nonetheless calls *Brown* "a great act of statesmanship. Those academics who downplay [its] importance in the struggle for racial justice have underrated its effects on attitudes about race relations," which in turn fostered a successful climate for the Civil Rights Act of 1964. Warren's legacy, then, is that his Court adhered to those "highest traditions of constitutional government," for if judicial activism is unprincipled, surely Congress would declare war on the courts, and surely the work of an activist court could not survive under later jurists committed to restoring Wechsler's "neutral principles."

Without *Griswold* v. *Connecticut* (1965), the Warren Court decision that invalidated an anticontraception law and decreed a constitutionally unstated right to privacy, the Burger Court would have had a great difficulty crafting its opinion in *Roe* v. *Wade* (1971). Ironically, most of today's antipathy toward judicial activism–dubbed by one federal judge as "a lack of fidelity to the Constitution"–emanates more from the abortion right in *Roe* than from any single decision handed down by the Warren Court. In fact, the Burger Court followed *Roe* with several decisions that radically changed gender power in the United States. *Frontiero* v. *Richardson* (1973) overturned a U.S. Air Force policy that denied female military personnel certain dependent benefits granted routinely to male servicemen. The Burger Court's unanimous decision in *Reed* v. *Reed* (1971), invalidating an Idaho law that gave preference to men in intestate proceedings, supplied the constitutional footing for *Craig* v. *Boren* (1976), which struck down an Oklahoma statute that set a higher age for the sale of beer to males over females. Finally, the same Court ruled unanimously in *Califano* v. *Westcott* (1979) that the Social Security Act violated the Constitution by granting benefits to families with dependent children because of a father's unemployment–but not a mother's.

Notably, Chief Justice Burger created the Supreme Court's standards for reviewing gender-based classifications. It is important to recognize, however, that what became known as Burger's exacting scrutiny test for "quasi-suspect" categories of discrimination–laws and regulations that create gender inequality or discriminate against illegitimate children–was a direct response to the two-part system of judicial review developed by the Warren Court. Burger contributed an intermediate (third) standard, thereby preserving Warren's strict scrutiny for race classifications and minimal scrutiny for age and indigence laws on one hand, and economic regulations on the other. All of these developments occurred, of course, because of Warren Court activism in the constitutional arena of equality.

Contemporary views about freedom of expression also attest to the Warren Court's enduring legitimacy. Two important Rehnquist Court decisions, *Hustler Magazine* v. *Falwell* (1988) and the famous flag-burning controversy *Texas* v. *Johnson* (1989), owe a debt of doctrine to such Warren antecedents as *New York Times* v. *Sullivan* (1964) and *Brandenburg* v. *Ohio* (1969). Still, Chief Justice Rehnquist has taken a dim view of Warren Court safeguards for the rights of the accused, such as those set in *Mapp* v. *Ohio* (1961), *Miranda* v. *Arizona* (1966) and *Gideon* v. *Wainwright* (1963). None of these cases has been overturned, but the famous "exclusionary rule" under *Mapp* lost some of its power in two Burger Court decisions, *U.S.* v. *Leon* and *Massachusetts* v. *Sheppard,* (1984).

Lewis fondly describes the Warren Court as a "second constitutional converntion" with "courage" and "judicial heroism," and laments that the Rehnquist Court is stacked with "more cautious contemporary Justices" who take "a more traditional–which is to say more limited–view of the role of judges." Ignoring standard polemics of activism versus restraint, of interpretivism versus noninterpretivism, Lewis argues that the Warren Court's significance lies in its defense of democracy–an outcome that can hardly be characterized as antithetical to the highest traditions of constitutional government, even though the Court strayed frequently from original intent in order to make room for democratic ideals in a modern era.

Lewis's claims echo a point Cox made to his lecture hall audiences in 1967: "Law must be binding even upon the highest court, but it must also meet the needs of men and match their ethical sensibilities." Similarly, Frederick P. Lewis argues that Warren Court activism was ". . . coherent because it expressed an integrated and principled perspective on what civil liberty should mean in a modern era." It became the job of an activist judiciary to shape a "fair, neutral and proper way to order liberty in America. [Warren Court] activism attempted to dismantle a different and older perspective, also fair and neutral by its lights. Both perspectives flow from the dynamics of the American political system and are legitimate within it."

More than a decade ago, former Justice Thurgood Marshall chastised judicial restraint and its conservative twin original intent, in an essay about the then-upcoming Constitutional Convention's bicentennial. "The government they [the Framers] devised was defective from the start, requiring several amendments, a civil war, and momentous social transformation to attain the system of constitutional government . . . we hold as fundamental today." What he did not say directly, yet clearly he knew, was that the "constitutional government" he revered was the product of activist petitioners like himself–as a major architect of the National Association for the Advancement of Colored People's (NAACP) litigation strategy–and an activist court like the Warren Court, which he ultimately joined at President Lyndon B. Johnson's behest.

Stated differently, Marshall's democracy was not the democracy of the Framers. Rather, it was a "redefined democracy" that Morton J. Horwitz describes as the product of debates about the relationship between political, social, and economic equality. These debates were born during the Progressive Era and persisted throughout the twentieth century, paving the way for a reconstructed, egalitarian definition of democracy. Participatory and inclusive, the political blueprint for the 1960s, the "new democracy" created fitting circumstances for Warren Court jurisprudence:

> . . . the Warren Court did not regard constitutional rights as in conflict with democracy but rather as constitutive of democracy. Much of the standard interpretation of the Warren Court depends on seeing it through a . . . Federalist understanding, [which] assumes that the central dilemma of American constitutional law is how to reconcile a conflict between majority rule and minority rights and prevent a passionate minority from dominating majorities. . . . Such a simplistic definition of democracy is inadequate to understand the theory of the Warren Court . . . [, which] attempted to give substantive content to democracy through its decisions privileging dignity and equality for all people.

No wonder, then, that an aging Marshall would take a dim view of celebrating the Constitution's two-hundredth anniversary. By 1987 the Supreme Court had downshifted from activism on behalf of a new democracy to restraint on behalf of an old mainstream, having all but abandoned the proposition that activism is the agent by which the judiciary acts coequally with the legislative and executive branches of government.

Does the Burger-Rehnquist transition represent the "highest principles of constitutional government" more than the Warren Court? The Rehnquist Court won praise in many circles for demonstrating "judicial restraint" or deference to legal precedent and to the legislative branch (or as some would argue, to state legislatures). That Rehnquist's retreat correlates with America's gradual loss of liberal momentum from the 1960s explains why countless interest and advocacy groups worried about losing "Warren Era" victories: on balance, the Rehnquist Court is politically conservative.

Still, while Chief Justice Rehnquist will hardly be remembered for championing civil rights, he and his "judicial restraint" colleagues have done relatively little to reduce the constitutional promises of Earl Warren's day and at times, they, too, have "made" law. In 1997 alone, the Rehnquist Court struck down all or key parts of three federal laws—the Brady Act (federal gun control) in *Printz* v. *U.S.;* the Religious Freedom Restoration Act (RFRA), in *City of Boerne (Texas)* v. *Flores;* and the Communications Decency Act, in *Reno* v. *ACLU.* These and other Rehnquist Court rulings signal less philosophical consistency between the Supreme Court and Congress, but they raise an interesting question. Is the Rehnquist Court restrained, activist, or bowing to the "states' rights" fervor that produced the very inequities the Warren Court tried to extinguish?

It takes little imagination to see that without judicial activism to nudge the process of "creative constitutional development," African Americans might still live under the rule of *Plessey* v. *Ferguson* in 1896, penniless defendants in criminal cases would be tried without counsel owing to *Betts* v. *Brady* in 1942 (overturned by *Gideon* v. *Wainwright* in 1963). Accordingly, the Warren Court needs to be understood for the ways in which it reinvigorated constitutional debate in the United States, adapted the concepts of liberty and equality to a society that had changed drastically after World War II, and articulated principles of enduring validity to Americans—including, it appears, to the more conservative, restrained federal judiciary. Hall suggests that while academics and practitioners continue searching for new threads of argument about the Warren Court, Americans "should at least honor the past on its own terms. If we do so, then we will appreciate that the Warren Court . . . is and will continue to be the ghost present at the constitutional banquet served each year on the first Monday in October."

—JUDITH A. BARRETT, DUXBURY, MASSACHUSETTS

References

Alexander M. Bickel, *The Least Dangerous Branch: The Supreme Court at the Bar of Politics* (Indianapolis: Bobbs Merrill, 1962);

Bickel, *Politics and the Warren Court* (New York: Harper & Row, 1965):

Bradley C. Canon, "Defining the Dimensions of Judicial Activism," *Judicature,* 66 (December–January 1983): 236–246;

Archibald Cox, *The Warren Court: Constitutional Decision as an Instrument of Reform* (Cambridge, Mass.: Harvard University Press, 1968);

Ed Cray, *Chief Justice: A Biography of Earl Warren* (New York: Simon & Schuster, 1997);

Mary Ann Glendon, "Partial Justice," *Commentary,* 98 (August 1994): 22–27;

Kermit Hall, "The Warren Court in Historical Perspective," in *The Warren Court: A Retrospective,* edited by Bernard Schwartz (New York: Oxford University Press, 1996), pp. 293–312;

Alexander Hamilton, James Madison, and John Jay, *The Federalist Papers,* introduction by Clinton Rossiter (New York: Penguin, 1961);

Morton J. Horwitz, *The Warren Court and the Pursuit of Justice: A Critical Issue* (New York: Hill & Wang, 1998);

Michael Kammen, *A Machine That Would Go of Itself: The Constitution and American Culture* (New York: Knopf, 1986);

Philip B. Kurland, *Politics, the Constitution and the Warren Court* (Chicago: University of Chicago Press, 1970);

Anthony Lewis, "The Legacy of the Warren Court," in *The Warren Court: A Retrospective,* edited Bernard Schwartz (New York: Oxford University Press, 1996), pp. 398-406;

Lewis, *Make No Law: The Sullivan Case and the First Amendment* (New York: Vintage, 1992);

Lewis, "A Man Born to Act, Not to Muse," in *The Supreme Court Under Earl Warren,* ed. Leonard W. Levy (New York: Quadrangle Books, 1972), pp. 151-163;

Frederick P. Lewis, *The Context of Judicial Activism: The Endurance of the Warren Court Legacy in a Conservative Age* (Lanham, Md.: Rowman & Littlefield, 1999);

Clifford M. Lytle, *The Warren Court and Its Critics* (Tucson: University of Arizona Press, 1968);

Thurgood Marshall, "The Constitutional Bicentennial: Commemorating the Wrong Document?" *Vanderbilt Law Review,* 40 (1987): 1337-1342;

Wallace Mendelsohn, "Was Chief Justice Marshall an Activist?" in *Supreme Court Activism and Restraint,* edited by Stephen C. Halpern and Charles M. Lamb (Lexington, Mass.: Lexington Books, 1982), pp. 101-119;

Paul L. Murphy, *The Constitution in Crisis Times, 1918-1969* (New York: Harper & Row, 1971);

Bernard Schwartz, *Super Chief, Earl Warren and His Supreme Court: A Judicial Biography* (New York: New York University Press, 1983);

Schwartz, ed., *The Warren Court: A Retrospective* (New York: Oxford University Press, 1996);

Martin Shapiro, *Law and Politics in the Supreme Court: New Approaches to Political Jurisprudence* (New York: Free Press of Glencoe, 1964);

Shapiro, "The Supreme Court from Warren to Burger," in *The New American Political System,* edited by Anthony King (Washington, D.C.: American Enterprise Institute for Public Policy Research, 1978);

William F. Swindler, *Court and Constitution in the Twentieth Century,* volume 2: *The New Legality, 1932-1968* (Indianapolis: Bobbs Merrill, 1970);

Mark Tushnet, ed., *The Warren Court in Historical and Political Perspective* (Charlottesville: University of Virginia Press, 1993);

Herbert Wechsler, "Toward Neutral Principles of Constitutional Law," in *Principles, Politics and Fundamental Law,* edited by Wechsler (Cambridge, Mass.: Harvard University Press, 1961), pp. 3-48;

J. Skelly Wright, "The Role of the Supreme Court in a Democratic Society–Judicial Activism or Judicial Restraint?" *Cornell Law Quarterly,* 53 (April-June 1998): 5-22.

WHITE FLIGHT

Did busing hasten white flight and weaken the Civil Rights movement?

Viewpoint: Yes, busing hastened white flight from urban areas and weakened some Civil Rights gains by essentially resegregating city schools.

Viewpoint: No, busing of schoolchildren was an effective way to correct racial discrimination in public education.

It could be called a tale of two cities. In 1970 a federal district judge in Charlotte, North Carolina, found that the school board had maintained a racially segregated system of education. He ordered the board to correct the situation, and though there was tremendous opposition to busing of children, the schools were integrated. Twenty years later, when it was proposed that the judge's assignment plan was no longer necessary, the citizens of Charlotte, white and black, resisted attempts to end it. These citizens, many of whom had grown up and been educated in Charlotte-Mecklenburg's integrated schools, think the system works.

In 1974 a federal district judge in Boston, Massachusetts, found that the school board there had also maintained a racially segregated system of education. He ordered the schools integrated, and the violent opposition to his order left the city even more divided than it had been. Twenty years later the local paper, which had supported Judge W. Arthur Garrity Jr.'s order, proposed a public forum to debate the busing issue. But no one was willing to defend it publicly. Boston's public schools are overwhelmingly black, more segregated than they were in 1974, and both blacks and whites have fled the system. Garrity, who wrote the original decision, in 1999 overturned the school department's integration plan for Boston Latin School, because it was too rigid. Parents throughout the district, and throughout Massachusetts, are currently challenging school-assignment plans that look only at race.

What happened? Why the difference? In these two essays, David I. Finnegan and Robert J. Allison look at busing and try to come to terms with this complicated topic. Finnegan is uniquely qualified to comment on the Boston controversy. As a parent of children in the Boston public schools in the early 1970s, Finnegan became active in a group determined to save the system from itself. He was elected to the Boston School Committee in 1975, at the height of the controversy, and served as its president for the next four years. He has since been active promoting racial understanding in the city. Allison, now a constitutional scholar, was a student in the Pinellas County, Florida, schools that were peacefully integrated by court order in 1971. He now lives in South Boston, the center of antibusing sentiment in the 1970s.

Finnegan and Allison are both classic liberals. They believe in a just society and that the state has a role in achieving justice. This debate was one of the most violent and ugly political controversies of the twentieth century. It has not been entirely resolved, and the verdict of history perhaps will never be unanimous.

Viewpoint: Yes, busing hastened white flight from urban areas and weakened some civil rights gains by essentially resegregating city schools.

No aspect of the Civil Rights movement caused more protracted opposition than busing to achieve integration in the public schools. One observer called it "a domestic Vietnam." As bitter and violent as the events of the 1960s may have been, a substantial majority of Americans supported the goals of equal opportunity and an end to legal segregation. Part of this situation could be explained by the regional context of the battleground. Legal segregation was confined to the Southern states of the old Confederacy. By 1970 the ten-state region was considered out of step with the rest of the country, which was not measurably impacted by federal enforcement policies. Until busing was ordered for the nation, the South was seen as virtually alone in its opposition to civil rights.

In 1954 the U.S. Supreme Court declared segregation in public schools unconstitutional. The doctrine of "separate but equal" was dead, and all laws requiring segregation by any method were a denial of the equal-protection clause. The *Brown* v. *Board of Education of Topeka, Kansas* case impacted the states of Kansas, South Carolina, Virginia, and Delaware. The case contained an original finding: it accepted psychological evidence of the harmful nature of segregation to the self-esteem of black children and, accordingly, found racially segregated schools unconstitutional without regard to the intent of the local school board. With *Brown,* the high court provided a blueprint for future application of desegregation to northern cities with large minority populations, which invariably lived in residentially segregated neighborhoods. After the passage of the 1964 Civil Rights Act these neighborhoods and their local schools were on a collision course with *Brown,* a collision almost totally unanticipated by the residents.

In 1968 the Supreme Court outlined the new direction in *Green* v. *School Board of New Kent County.* The Court struck down a school-choice plan on grounds that it was not the most effective remedy to bring about integration. Not only was the school system required to desegregate, it was obligated to employ a method most likely to produce integration. In the same year, the Court addressed the effect of residential segregation in *Swann* v. *Charlotte-Mecklenburg Board of Education.* The Charlotte-Mecklenburg School District represented the typical residential pattern in America. Whites predominated in suburbia; blacks were largely residents of the central cities. The district in *Swann* required massive busing to achieve racial balance. The neighborhood school was effectively swept aside, and cases following *Swann* henceforth were characterized by arguments over who would bear the brunt of busing. That is, the burden of busing could not adversely affect blacks. Public schools were now subject to redistricting by the federal Court, a move that severely underestimated parental attachment to the neighborhood school.

The residential pattern of *Swann* revealed an Achilles heel of the Court's remedies. How would the Court implement integration if their prescription were to accelerate the movement of white families to suburbia, a demographic pattern that had been clearly identified since the 1950s? Charlotte shared a school district with its suburb of Mecklenburg, but this situation was exceptional. Boston, New York, Denver, and Detroit were the norm—separate school districts for suburban and inner-city areas.

Strategists with the National Association for the Advancement of Colored People (NAACP) were well aware of the developing difficulty and sought to reduce the potential impact of "white flight" by enlarging the scope of the integration orders. Under this approach whites in suburbia would be annexed to central cities for purposes of racial balance. In 1974 the Supreme Court, in *Milliken* v. *Bradley,* rejected the "metropolitan" approach on grounds that only the offending school district was subject to a racial-balance remedy. The Court's earlier embrace of the harmful effects of segregation on blacks was effectively set aside, and henceforth only urban public-school systems would be subject to desegregation mandates, while white suburbs would remain exempt. The *Milliken* strategy had backfired. Instead of creating a pool of students to ensure racial balance, the effect was to guarantee that those who moved from the city were in no danger of losing their neighborhood schools. White flight of middle-class families to suburbia did more than defeat efforts toward integration; it left poorer whites, who were unable to afford a suburban home, bitter and disillusioned. Cities such as Boston and Denver lost the moderating influence of their once-powerful middle class, and poor people, black and white, were left to face the new reality through a devastating admixture of fear and resentment. To a climate already infected with racism came the insidious sentiments of class and conflict characterized by envy and hatred. By 1974 Boston and Denver were suffering the effects of this terrible alchemy.

"White flight" is a phrase used to describe the large-scale movement of whites from urban

Antibusing protestors at the Capitol, circa 1972

(United Press International)

school systems to suburban or private-school systems in order to avoid the effects of school busing to achieve integration. There are two schools of thought on the subject: one supports the above stated definition; the other, while acknowledging the trend of whites to suburbia, denies its causal link to school integration, arguing instead that a pattern of white migration preexisted the busing controversy by decades and accelerated, owing to economic growth. To one it was a largely unnatural event directly linked to busing and civil unrest; to the other, it reflected a natural tendency of affluent people to seek a better life in a newer, different setting.

While a pattern of affluent people "moving up" to suburbia had developed as far back as the 1930s, it simply cannot explain the dramatic exodus of white families from American cities that were subject to school-integration orders. Attempts to explain this demographic phenomenon as an extension of the suburban movement of the 1960s ignores the history of the 1970s, particularly that of Boston and Denver, which became poster children of the busing controversy. Efforts to reconcile the catastrophic effects of busing in these two communities with the earlier, modest migration spurred by Federal Housing Authority (FHA) mortgages and highway programs, fail to answer the statistical evidence of white flight. Not only did whites leave urban schools precipitously in cities undergoing desegregation, but families with children under age eighteen departed urban centers in numbers that were nothing short of alarming.

As many as one hundred school districts implemented desegregation plans between 1970 and 1985. Nowhere can one find substantial evidence that busing enhanced racial integration. On the contrary, the major cities are a testament to the opposite: there was increasing racial isolation. Chicago, New York, St. Louis, Houston, Dallas, San Antonio, and Baltimore all have substantially fewer white students today than before desegregation and considerably more racial isolation.

No city encountered more violent disruption concerning the desegregation of schools than Boston. Once considered the "Athens of America," Boston shocked the nation with its violent reaction to the 1974 federal court order to bus students. Parent groups throughout the city waged a five-year battle to keep their children in neighborhood schools. Every known method of opposition, from boycotting schools to stoning buses carrying black children, was employed to combat the busing order. By 1979 Boston's public schools had lost 35 percent of its student body: 70 percent of its white students and 45 percent of its families with school-age children. Almost all of the out-migration was the white middle class, leaving the school system to poor blacks and whites who remained subject to racial-balance orders until the year 2000. In the five years preceding busing, Boston experienced a drop in white enrollment of 10 percent: 72,000 to 64,000. In the ensuing five years, fully 70 percent of whites left the schools. These statistics present compelling evidence of the acceleration of white flight, clearly establishing busing as the principal cause.

Further analysis of population figures reveals an interesting profile of the population moving to suburbia. The 1985 Boston Redevelopment Authority Report on Demographics shows a net loss of 131,040 whites between 1970 and 1979. More significantly, those who left were married couples with children under eighteen. Whites without school-age children were not leaving the city, and unmarried whites actually increased in number. By 1990 there were a mere 12,000 white students in Boston's public schools, while the city reported a 58 percent non-Hispanic, white population.

It may be tempting to assume that Boston, because of its prolonged opposition to busing, is an exceptional case. The evidence, however, shows that Boston's pattern of white flight was repeated in many urban centers, not the least of which was Denver, Colorado. In 1974 Denver had 119 schools with a population of 88,000 students, 66 percent of whom were white. In 1980 the overall population was 68,000, with 36 percent being white students. By 1995, the final year of busing, the number of white students in Denver's schools had dropped to 32 percent, only 66,000. The number of whites had decreased by 69 percent; black students by 7 percent, while Hispanics increased by 37 percent. By 1995, 70 percent of the students were minorities: 47 percent Hispanic, 23 percent black, and only 27 percent white. Once again statistics indicate a substantial population shift in the number of white students in the immediate aftermath of a desegregation order. The cause of Denver's accelerated white flight, as with Boston, was busing. Finally, a review of enrollment data from the U.S. Department of Education, Digest of Educational Statistics for 1995, reveals the following percentages of whites in public-school systems in the North: Detroit, 6.6; Chicago, 11.4; New York, 17.5; and Philadelphia, 21.7.

Resentment over busing did not end with the departure of whites from urban public schools. Civil unrest, falling home prices, and neighborhood displacement created an urban constituency heretofore unknown in American politics. White working-class Democrats, disenchanted with the effects of busing and racial policies of affirmative action and so-called quotas, turned to the Republican Party and its standard-bearer, Ronald W. Reagan. "Reagan Democrats," as they were known, had a significant impact on the 1980 presidential campaign, helping Republicans to unexpected gains in states such as Massachusetts, Illinois, Michigan, and New York. The Democratic Party suffered particularly from the defection of its labor-union base, who shared Reagan's view on busing and affirmative action.

The classic working-class neighborhood of South Boston, a Democratic stronghold throughout the twentieth century, went Republican in 1976 and overwhelmingly supported Reagan in 1980 and 1984, as did the Commonwealth of Massachusetts. White males, Catholics, and working mothers in major Northern cities believed that the federal government had gone too far in racial matters. Largely supportive of integration, they disapproved of racial balancing and quotas, and these issues together with the nation's crime policies created new pockets of support for the more conservative Republican Party, which responded to their new constituency by promising an end to busing and a rollback of affirmative action quotas. Appointments to the Supreme Court of the United States took a decidedly conservative turn and contributed to a particular reluctance to support race-conscious remedies. Accordingly, race-based school assignments and related issues in the workplace have all but ended.

Surely, many changes in American life have contributed to this trend. But it is also true that discontent with busing created the atmosphere for a wholesale shift in party politics and with that a growing constituency in opposition to civil-rights gains of the 1960s.

—DAVID I. FINNEGAN, BOSTON, MASSACHUSETTS

Viewpoint: No, busing of schoolchildren was an effective way to correct racial discrimination in public education.

In the 1950s the school bus had been a symbol of educational progress. Three-fifths of schoolchildren in North Carolina, which proudly called itself the "school busingest state in the Union," rode buses to and from school every day. Expending so much effort and money in transporting these children was a symbol of the state's commitment to education. State officials were dedicated to getting children from rural areas into modern classrooms in the cities every day so they could become the good citizens and leaders of tomorrow.

Yet, school buses were also used to maintain racial segregation. Both black and white children were bused past schools closest to their own homes, so that they could attend schools only with children of their own race. *Brown* v. *Board of Education of Topeka, Kansas* decreed that separate school systems for black and white children violated the children's constitutional rights. In 1955 the Court, in *Brown II,* considered how best to implement its decision. As a concession to states, which argued that overturning long-standing systems of education and school policies would be difficult, the Court said that segregation had to be dismantled "with all deliberate speed." States took this wording as an invitation to move slowly, or they pretended to act while actually blocking the decree. States such as North Carolina dismantled their separate school systems, but in their place created systems that maintained segregation in other ways. Instead of sending children to the school nearest their home, the school districts created "attendance zones" to direct children to single-race schools, so that by the late 1960s, fifteen years after *Brown*, virtually all schools in the Southern states continued to be segregated.

Some school districts created "freedom of choice" plans, so that students could choose which school in the district to attend. Though these plans did not employ race nor on the surface promise to maintain segregation, they effectively did so, as black students were discouraged from choosing white schools, and white students were dissuaded from attending schools that had once been set aside for blacks.

Brown had been decided unanimously, and the Court maintained unanimity in all its decisions on school segregation thereafter. Chief Justice Earl Warren knew that this issue was too politically important to allow the Court to seem partisan. All the justices agreed, and the Court stood united in holding that segregation was wrong and that the various state methods to circumvent integration orders were also wrong. The Court had to decide if it was to permit states to get away with constitutional violations, even if they were done under the guise of "freedom of choice" or "attendance zones." Was an organized evasion of the law less severe because it had the words "freedom of choice" attached or because the state did not overtly declare it wanted to maintain separate races in the schools? By the end of the 1960s the Court was losing its patience. Having school systems openly flout the law and ignore the Court was damaging to both it and the Constitution.

The Charlotte-Mecklenburg school district, a combined precinct encompassing the city of Charlotte and the surrounding rural areas of Mecklenburg County, became the test case for implementing *Brown*. After *Brown*, North Carolina had taken some small steps to ending segregation, but these seem token in retrospect. There were 84,000 students in 107 schools: 71 percent of the students were white; 29 percent were African American. Of the 21,000 African American students in Charlotte, only 490 attended schools with white pupils, and of these, 392 were in one school with 7 white pupils. The other 98 black students in "integrated" schools were in 7 of the district's schools, and the rest remained in all-black schools.

When black parents challenged the continued segregation of the Charlotte-Mecklenburg schools and the inferiority of the all-black schools, the school board responded by closing the all-black schools, instituting in its place a "freedom of choice" plan, under which students in an attendance zone could choose any school in the zone that had room, but they had to provide their own transportation. Transportation, black parents knew, would put the burden of integration on them rather than on the school board, so they challenged the board. The case of *Swann* v. *Charlotte-Mecklenburg Board of Education* (James Swann was a seven-year-old boy whose father taught theology at Johnson C. Smith University) was heard in a district court in 1965 and made its way through the federal courts in the late 1960s, as the U.S. Supreme Court was considering plans similar to Charlotte-Mecklenburg's.

In April 1969, Federal District Judge James B. MacMillan, a native of Charlotte and a conservative pillar of the local community, concluded that the school district had maintained a segregated school system and in so doing had violated the Constitution. Heeding the more-recent directives from the Supreme Court, that merely dismantling the old system of segregation was not enough and that school districts were now required to take active steps to achieve integration, MacMillan ordered the school board to come up with a desegregation plan. The school board dragged its feet, missing a June deadline, and then submitted a weak plan at the end of July that MacMillan reluctantly accepted as an interim measure. He ordered a more comprehensive plan to be presented in November, which would be implemented at the beginning of the 1970–1971 school year. In November the school board asked for an extension, which the judge denied. He then rejected the plan the board submitted, saying it would permanently relegate two-thirds of black children in Charlotte-Mecklenburg "to this kind of separate but unequal education." The school board prepared another plan that would have left half the black students in segregated schools and provided no transportation for those attending integrated schools. MacMillan also rejected this plan and appointed Dr. John Finger of Rhode Island College, who had been an expert witness for the plaintiffs in *Swann*, to devise an acceptable plan. Finger's plan desegregated the system by grouping three or four outlying suburban elementary schools with one inner-city elementary school, busing black students in grades 1 through 4 to the suburban schools and white students from grades 5 and 6 to the inner-city schools. In the junior and senior high schools, black students from

SWANN V. *CHARLOTTE-MECKLENBURG BOARD OF EDUCATION* 402 U.S. 1 (1971)

This case and those argued with it arose in states having a long history of maintaining two sets of schools in a single school system deliberately operated to carry out a governmental policy to separate pupils in schools solely on the basis of race. That was what *Brown* v. *Board of Education* was all about. These cases present us with the problem of defining in more precise terms than heretofore the scope of the duty of school authorities and district courts in implementing *Brown I* and the mandate to eliminate dual systems and establish unitary systems at once. Meanwhile district courts and courts of appeals have struggled in hundreds of cases with a multitude and variety of problems under this Court's general directive. Understandably, in an area of evolving remedies, those courts had to improvise and experiment without detailed or specific guidelines. This Court, in *Brown I*, appropriately dealt with the large constitutional principles; other federal courts had to grapple with the flinty, intractable realities of day-to-day implementation of those constitutional commands. Their efforts, of necessity, embraced a process of "trial and error," and our effort to formulate guidelines must take into account their experience. . . .

The central issue in this case is that of student assignment, and there are essentially four problem areas:

(1) to what extent racial balance or racial quotas may be used as an implement in a remedial order to correct a previously segregated system;

(2) whether every all-Negro and all-white school must be eliminated as an indispensable part of a remedial process of desegregation;

(3) what are the limits, if any, on the rearrangement of school districts and attendance zones, as a remedial measure; and

(4) what are the limits, if any, on the use of transportation facilities to correct state-enforced racial school segregation.

Source: Documents of American History, *2 volumes, edited by Henry Steele Commager (New York: Appleton-Century-Crofts, 1973),* II: *756–760.*

the inner city would be bused to suburban schools. The plan was to bus an additional ten thousand students (thirty thousand were already being bused) and was to take effect by May 1970.

MacMillan predicted that "This will raise a lot of hell," and he was right. He was burned in effigy; picketers staked out his house; eighty thousand Charlotte citizens signed petitions against the court order; and Julius Chambers, the black attorney who had argued the case, had his house, office, and car bombed by anonymous attackers. This public pressure was dramatic and expected. Less dramatic was the decision of the Court of Appeals, staying MacMillan's order: it affirmed his plan to integrate the junior and senior high schools but blocked the elementary-school integration. It was not clear how the Supreme Court would decide the case. When *Swann* reached the Supreme Court, Warren had been replaced as chief justice by Warren E. Burger, a more conservative judge appointed by Republican president Richard M. Nixon, who had condemned what he called "forced busing."

On 20 April 1971 the Supreme Court, once again unanimously, upheld MacMillan's order. MacMillan had rightly found that the Charlotte-Mecklenburg school board had maintained racially segregated schools, and his plan was a reasonable and appropriate one for ending racial segregation. The plan did not mandate a strict racial balance in each school—had it done so, the Court said, it would not have survived judicial scrutiny. The burden of proving that its attendance plans were not discriminatory fell on local school boards, as did the remedy for discrimination. Simply dismantling the old segregated systems was not enough. "All things being equal," the Court said, "with no history of discrimination, it might well be desirable to assign pupils to schools nearest their homes. But all things are not equal in a system that has been deliberately constructed and maintained to enforce racial segregation. The remedy for such segregation may be administratively awkward, inconvenient, and even bizarre in some situations and may impose burdens on some; but all awkwardness and inconvenience cannot be avoided in the interim period when remedial adjustments are being made to eliminate the dual school systems."

With the *Swann* decision the Charlotte-Mecklenburg school district was desegregated. The Court insisted it was not requiring racial balancing–all schools did not have to have the same black-white ratio as existed in the community at large, but no school could be all black or all white. The real goal, the Court insisted, was racial diversity, not adherence to a mathematical formula. This idea was later buttressed in *Regents of the University of California* v. *Bakke* (1978), when the Court allowed policies that took race into account along with other factors in admissions to graduate schools and colleges but would not allow race to be used as the single factor.

The Court's new mandate in *Swann* required the dismantling of segregated systems immediately. Segregation and racism, however, were not simply Southern problems. Virtually every American city had a large black population, and by 1968, when the Kerner Commission issued its report on urban disorders, it had become clear that the North was no more integrated than the South. In the North, whites had migrated to the suburbs while blacks entered the cities, and by 1970 most urban centers were overwhelmingly black, while the suburbs were predominantly white. Along with this racial difference, the suburbs and cities had a profound class difference. Those remaining in the cities tended to be poorer, and consequently urban schools were not as well maintained as suburban ones.

In *Milliken* v. *Bradley,* the Court struck down a Michigan plan that required the busing of students between different school districts. In Charlotte-Mecklenburg integration was possible because one school district encompassed people of different races; schools in Detroit's single district were overwhelmingly black, while the white suburbs had their own district. Thus, integration would not be possible within district lines.

In Boston the School Committee had maintained grossly inferior schools in African American neighborhoods. Boston, a city of strong neighborhoods, still had a large white population in 1974 but was already undergoing a racial transition that was not the result of busing. African American migrants to Boston, which had been economically depressed after World War II, mainly settled in the South End (not to be confused with South Boston) and then began moving into the contiguous neighborhood of Roxbury, then home mainly to Jews and Irish Catholics.

Gerald Gamm, in the most recent study of the transition of Roxbury and Dorchester from being predominately white to predominately black, *Urban Exodus: Why the Jews Left Boston and the Catholics Stayed* (1999), argues that the notion of "white flight" is too simplistic. What happened in Boston in the 1960s was not white flight so much as the continuation of a process under way since the 1920s. Boston's Jewish community had been migrating to the suburbs at the same time as blacks were moving into Roxbury and Dorchester. Boston's Catholics, on the other hand, were predominately urban. The Catholic Church focuses on local parishes that are defined by geography, while Jews and followers of other religious traditions are not geographically defined. Until after the early 1960s, the Roman Catholic Church strictly adhered to parish boundaries, and communicants in one church would not attend mass in another. Life for Catholics was rooted in the parish, where one was baptized, confirmed, married, and buried. Catholic parishes also maintained schools, so many Catholics worshiped and attended school in one place, at the center of their community. In Dorchester, the largest of Boston's neighborhoods, the answer to the question, "Where do you live?" was often St. Ann's, St. Peter's, or St. William's, rather than Neponset, Mount Bowdoin, or Savin Hill.

The Jewish community began leaving Roxbury and Dorchester in the 1920s. By the 1950s Roxbury was predominately black, though it still had a large Irish Catholic population. Boston's legendary mayor James Michael Curley grew up in Roxbury; so did Malcolm X and Louis Farrakhan. The out-migration accelerated in the 1950s, and boomed at the end of the decade and in the 1960s. The various programs that created the real Jewish out-migration are chronicled in Hillel Levine and Lawrence Harmon's *The Death of an American Jewish Community: A Tragedy of Good Intentions* (1992). Gamm argues that the transition was not a sudden one, that Irish Catholics stayed longer, rooted as they were in their parish institutions. Even after they left certain areas, the parishes remained and today still serve the neighborhoods. African Americans wary of using Boston's public schools, and who have the means to do so, send their children to the parochial schools, just as white Bostonians do.

Busing to eliminate racial discrimination worked in Charlotte-Mecklenburg; it was a disaster in Boston. Arguing from the Boston case that busing was a failure in all cases would be as misleading as extrapolating from Charlotte's example that it was a success in every case. Contending that busing created white flight is also too simplistic, just as it would be to argue that busing was the only means to overcome racial discrimination. Social policies may influence change, but they cannot force changes.

If separate education was inherently unequal, was it any less so if the separation was caused by economics rather than by law? In *Brown,* the Court struck down de jure segregation, or segregation by law. By 1970 Americans were coming to recognize de facto segregation–that is, segregation not mandated by law but that had come into being for other reasons. In *Swann,* the Court acknowledged that it could not by its decree eradicate every form of prejudice, but by acting to prohibit discriminatory admissions policies, it could begin to educate students to the virtues of a racially diverse society.

–ROBERT J. ALLISON,
SUFFOLK UNIVERSITY

References

Emmet H. Buell Jr. and Richard A. Brisbin Jr., *School Desegregation and Defended Neighborhoods: The Boston Controversy* (Lexington, Mass.: Lexington Books, 1982);

Robert A. Dentler and Marvin B. Scott, *Schools on Trial: An Inside Account of the Boston Desegregation Case* (Cambridge, Mass.: Abt Books, 1981);

Paul R. Dimond, *Beyond Busing: Inside the Challenge to Urban Segregation* (Ann Arbor: University of Michigan Press, 1985);

Ronald P. Formisano, *Boston Against Busing: Race, Class and Ethnicity in the 1960s and 1970s* (Chapel Hill: University of North Carolina Press, 1991);

Gerald Gamm, *Urban Exodus: Why the Jews Left Boston and the Catholics Stayed* (Cambridge, Mass.: Harvard University Press, 1999);

Hillel Levine and Lawrence Harmon, *The Death of an American Jewish Community: A Tragedy of Good Intentions* (New York: Free Press, 1992);

J. Anthony Lukas, *Common Ground: A Turbulent Decade in the Lives of Three American Families* (New York: Knopf, 1985);

Bernard Schwartz, *Swann's Way: The School Busing Case and the Supreme Court* (New York: Oxford University Press, 1986);

Stephan Thernstrom and Abigail Thernstrom, *America in Black and White: One Nation, Indivisible* (New York: Simon & Schuster, 1997).

REFERENCES

1. Civil Rights

Baldwin, James. *The Fire Next Time.* New York: Dell, 1963.

Baldwin, *The Price of the Ticket: Collected Nonfiction, 1948–1985.* New York: St. Martin's Press/Marek, 1985.

Bates, Daisy. *The Long Shadow of Little Rock: A Memoir.* New York: McKay, 1962.

Branch, Taylor. *Parting the Waters: America in the King Years, 1954–1963.* New York: Simon & Schuster, 1988.

Buell, Emmet H. Jr. and Richard A. Brisbin Jr. *School Desegregation and Defended Neighborhoods: The Boston Controversy.* Lexington, Mass.: Lexington Books, 1982.

Carson, Clayborne. *In Struggle: SNCC and the Black Awakening of the 1960s.* Cambridge, Mass.: Harvard University Press, 1981.

Chafe, William H. *Civilities and Civil Rights: Greensboro, North Carolina, and the Black Struggle for Freedom.* New York: Oxford University Press, 1980.

Chappell, David L. *Inside Agitators: White Southerners in the Civil Rights Movement.* Baltimore: Johns Hopkins University Press, 1994.

Clegg, Claude Andrew III. *An Original Man: The Life and Times of Elijah Muhammad.* New York: St. Martin's Press, 1997.

Cook, Robert. *Sweet Land of Liberty? The African-American Struggle for Civil Rights in the Twentieth Century.* London: Longman, 1998.

Dentler, Robert A., and Marvin B. Scott. *Schools on Trial: An Inside Account of the Boston Desegregation Case.* Cambridge, Mass.: Abt Books, 1981.

Dimond, Paul R. *Beyond Busing: Inside the Challenge to Urban Segregation.* Ann Arbor: University of Michigan Press, 1985.

Dittmer, John. *Local People: The Struggle for Civil Rights in Mississippi.* Urbana: University of Illinois Press, 1994.

Du Bois, W. E. B. *The Autobiography of W. E. B. Du Bois: A Soliloquy On Viewing My Life From the Last Decade of Its First Century.* New York: International Publishers, 1968.

Du Bois. *Dusk of Dawn: An Essay Toward An Autobiography of a Race Concept.* New York: Harcourt, Brace, 1940.

Du Bois. *The Oxford W. E. B. Du Bois Reader,* edited by Eric J. Sundquist. New York: Oxford University Press, 1996.

Du Bois. *The Souls of Black Folk: Essays and Sketches.* Chicago: McClurg, 1903.

Fairclough, Adam. *Race & Democracy: The Civil Rights Struggle in Louisiana, 1915–1972.* Athens: University of Georgia Press, 1995.

Fairclough. *To Redeem the Soul of America: The Southern Christian Leadership Conference and Martin Luther King, Jr.* Athens: University of Georgia Press, 1987.

Formisano, Ronald P. *Boston Against Busing: Race, Class and Ethnicity in the 1960s and 1970s.* Chapel Hill: University of North Carolina Press, 1991.

Garrow, David J. *Bearing the Cross: Martin Luther King Jr., and the Southern Christian Leadership Conference.* New York: Morrow, 1986.

Greenberg, Jack. *Crusaders in the Courts: How a Delicate Band of Lawyers Fought For the Civil Rights Revolution.* New York: BasicBooks, 1994.

Hall, Raymond L. *Black Separatism in the United States.* Hanover, N.H.: University Press of New England, 1978.

Horwitz, Morton J. *The Transformation of American Law, 1870–1960.* New York: Oxford University Press, 1977.

Horwitz. *The Warren Court and the Pursuit of Justice: A Critical Issue.* New York: Hill & Wang, 1998.

Jones, Charles E., ed. *The Black Panther Party Reconsidered.* Baltimore: Black Classic Press, 1997.

King, Martin Luther Jr. *Why We Can't Wait.* New York: Harper & Row, 1964.

King, Richard H. *Civil Rights and the Idea of Freedom.* New York: Oxford University Press, 1992.

Kluger, Richard. *Simple Justice: The History of Brown v. Board of Education and Black America's Struggle for Equality.* New York: Knopf, 1976.

Lewis, John, and Michael D'Orso. *Walking With the Wind: A Memoir of the Movement.* New York: Simon & Schuster, 1998.

Nieman, Donald G. *Promises to Keep: African-Americans and the Constitutional Order, 1776 to the Present.* New York: Oxford University Press, 1991.

Payne, Charles M. *I've Got the Light of Freedom: The Organizing Tradition and the Mississippi Freedom Struggle.* Berkeley: University of California Press, 1995.

Quarles, Benjamin. *The Negro in the Making of America.* New York: Collier, 1964.

Raines, Howell. *My Soul is Rested: The Story of the Civil Rights Movement in the Deep South.* New York: Putnam, 1977.

Robnett, Belinda. *How Long? How Long? African-American Women in the Struggle for Civil Rights.* New York: Oxford University Press, 1997.

Rosenberg, Gerald N. *The Hollow Hope: Can Courts Bring about Social Change?* Chicago: University of Chicago, 1991.

Sarat, Austin, ed. *Race, Law, and Culture: Reflections on Brown v. Board of Education.* New York: Oxford University Press, 1997.

Scott, Daryl Michael. *Contempt and Pity: Social Policy and the Image of the Damaged Black Psyche, 1880–1996.* Chapel Hill: University of North Carolina Press, 1997.

Sitkoff, Harvard. *The Struggle for Black Equality, 1954–1992.* New York: Hill & Wang, 1981.

Tushnet, Mark V. *Making Civil Rights Law: Thurgood Marshall and the Supreme Court, 1936–1961.* New York: Oxford University Press, 1994.

Tushnet. *The NAACP's Legal Strategy Against Segregated Education, 1925–1950.* Chapel Hill: University of North Carolina Press, 1987.

Tuttle, William M., ed. *W. E. B. Du Bois.* Englewood Cliffs, N.J.: Prentice-Hall, 1973.

Van Deburg, William L. *New Day in Babylon: The Black Power Movement and American Culture, 1965–1975.* Chicago: University of Chicago Press, 1992.

Van Deburg, ed., *Modern Black Nationalism: From Marcus Garvey to Louis Farrakhan.* New York: New York University Press, 1997.

Von Eschen, Penny M. *Race Against Empire: Black Americans and Anticolonialism, 1937– 1957.* Ithaca, N.Y.: Cornell University Press, 1997.

Weisbrot, Robert. *Freedom Bound: A History of America's Civil Rights Movement.* New York: Norton, 1990.

Wicker, Tom. *Tragic Failure: Racial Integration in America.* New York: Morrow, 1996.

Woodard, Komozi. *A Nation Within a Nation: Amiri Baraka LeRoi Jones & Black Power Politics.* Chapel Hill: University of North Carolina Press, 1999.

2. Cold War Foreign Issues

Beschloss, Michael R. *The Crisis Years: Kennedy and Khrushchev, 1960–1963.* New York: Burlingame, 1991.

Beschloss, and Strobe Talbott. *At the Highest Levels: The Inside Story of the End of the Cold War.* Boston: Little, Brown, 1993.

Bowie, Robert R., and Richard H. Immerman. *Waging Peace: How Eisenhower Shaped an Enduring Cold War Strategy.* New York: Oxford University Press, 1998.

Caldwell, Dan. *American-Soviet Relations: From 1947 to the Nixon-Kissinger Grand Design.* Westport, Conn.: Greenwood Press, 1981.

Digby, James. *Strategic Thought at RAND, 1948–1963: The Ideas, Their Origins, Their Fates.* Santa Monica, Cal.: RAND, 1990.

Divine, Robert A. *Eisenhower and the Cold War.* New York: Oxford University Press, 1981.

Dobrynin, Anatoly. *In Confidence: Moscow's Ambassador to America's Six Cold War Presidents 1962–1986.* New York: Times Books & Random House, 1996.

Doenecke, Justus D. *Not to the Swift: The Old Isolationists in the Cold War Era.* Lewisburg, Pa.: Bucknell University Press, 1979.

Feffer, John. *Beyond Détente: Soviet Foreign Policy and U.S. Options.* New York: Noonday Press, 1990.

Gaddis, John Lewis. *The Long Peace.* New York: Oxford University Press, 1987.

Gaddis. *Strategies of Containment: A Critical Appraisal of Postwar American National Security Policy.* New York: Oxford University Press, 1982.

Gaddis. *The United States and the Origins of the Cold War, 1941–1947.* New York: Columbia University Press, 1972.

Gaddis. *We Now Know: Rethinking Cold War History.* New York: Oxford University Press, 1997.

Garthoff, Raymond L. *Détente and Confrontation: American-Soviet Relations from Nixon to Reagan.* Washington, D.C.: Brookings Institute, 1985.

Garthoff. *The Great Transition: American-Soviet Relations and the End of the Cold War.* Washington, D.C.: Brookings Institute, 1994.

Glaser, Charles L. *Analyzing Strategic Nuclear Policy.* Princeton: Princeton University Press, 1990.

Goncharov, Sergei N., John W. Lewis, and Xue Litai. *Uncertain Partners: Stalin, Mao and the Korean War.* Stanford, Cal.: Stanford University Press, 1993.

Hogan, Michael J., ed. *The End of the Cold War: Its Meaning and Implications.* New York: Cambridge University Press, 1992.

Holloway, David. *Stalin and the Bomb: The Soviet Union and Atomic Energy, 1939–1956.* New Haven: Yale University Press, 1994.

Hosking, Geoffrey. *The Awakening of the Soviet Union.* Cambridge, Mass.: Harvard University Press, 1990.

Kull, Steven. *Minds At War: Nuclear Reality and the Inner Conflicts of Defense Policymakers.* New York: BasicBooks, 1988.

Lafeber, Walter. *America, Russia and the Cold War, 1945–1990.* New York: McGraw-Hill, 1991.

Lebow, Richard Ned, and Janice Gross Stein. *We All Lost the Cold War.* Princeton: Princeton University Press, 1994.

Leffler, Melvyn P. *A Preponderance of Power: National Security, the Truman Administration, and the Cold War.* Stanford, Cal.: Stanford University Press, 1992.

Leffler, and David S. Painter, eds. *The Origins of the Cold War: An International History.* New York: Routledge, 1994.

Levering, Ralph B. *The Cold War: A Post-Cold War History.* Arlington Heights, Ill.: Harlan Davidson, 1994.

Mastny, Vojtech. *The Cold War and Soviet Insecurity: The Stalin Years.* New York: Oxford University Press, 1996.

Mastny. *Russia's Road to the Cold War: Diplomacy, Warfare and the Politics of Communism, 1941–45.* New York: Columbia University Press, 1979.

May, Ernest R., and Philip D. Zelikow, eds. *The Kennedy Tapes: Inside the White House During the Cuban Missile Crisis.* Cambridge, Mass.: Belknap Press of Harvard University Press, 1997.

McMahan, Jeff. *Reagan and the World: Imperial Policy in the New Cold War.* New York: Monthly Review Press, 1985.

Mills, C. Wright. *Listen, Yankee: The Revolution in Cuba.* New York: Ballantine, 1960.

Mueller, John E. *Quiet Cataclysm: Reflections on the Recent Transformations of World Politics.* New York: HarperCollins College Publishers, 1995.

Naimark, Norman M. *The Russians in Germany: A History of the Soviet Zone of Occupation, 1945–1949.* Cambridge, Mass.: Belknap Press of Harvard University Press, 1995.

Nathan, James A., ed. *The Cuban Missile Crisis Revisited.* New York: St. Martin's Press, 1992.

Naylor, Thomas H. *The Cold War Legacy*. Lexington, Mass.: Lexington Books, 1991.

Paterson, Thomas G., ed. *Meeting the Communist Threat: Truman to Reagan*. New York: Oxford University Press, 1988.

Paterson. *Cold War Critics: Alternatives to American Foreign Policy in the Truman Years*. Chicago: Quadrangle, 1971.

Peeters, Paul. *Massive Retaliation: The Policy and its Critics*. Chicago: Regnery, 1959.

Prados, John. *The Soviet Estimate: U.S. Intelligence Analysis & Russian Military Strength*. New York: Dial, 1982.

Pringle, Peter, and William Arkin. *SIOP: The Secret U.S. Plan for Nuclear War*. New York: Norton, 1983.

Schweizer, Peter. *Victory: The Reagan Administration's Secret Strategy that Hastened the Collapse of the Soviet Union*. New York: Atlantic Monthly Press, 1994.

Talbott, Strobe. *The Russians and Reagan*. New York: Vintage, 1984.

Ulam, Adam B. *The Rivals: America and Russia Since World War II*. New York: Viking, 1971.

Walton, Richard J. *Cold War and Counter-Revolution: The Foreign Policy of John F. Kennedy*. New York: Viking, 1972.

White, Mark J., ed. *Kennedy: The New Frontier Revisited*. New York: New York University Press, 1998.

Young, John W. *The Longman Companion to America, Russia and the Cold War, 1941- 1998*. London & New York: Longman, 1999.

Zubok, Vladislav, and Constantine Pleshakov. *Inside the Kremlin's Cold War: From Stalin to Khrushchev*. Cambridge, Mass.: Harvard University Press, 1996.

3. Cold War Domestic Issues

Caute, David. *The Great Fear: The Anti-Communist Purge under Truman and Eisenhower*. New York: Simon & Schuster, 1978.

Fineberg, S. Andhil. *The Rosenberg Case: Fact and Fiction*. New York: Oceana, 1953.

Freeland, Richard M. *The Truman Doctrine and the Origins of McCarthyism: Foreign Policy, Domestic Politics, and Internal Security, 1946- 1948*. New York: Knopf, 1972.

Fried, Albert, ed. *McCarthyism: The Great American Red Scare: A Documentary History*. New York: Oxford University Press, 1997.

Fried, Richard M. *Nightmare in Red: The McCarthy Era in Perspective*. New York: Oxford University Press, 1990.

Garber, Marjorie, and Rebecca L. Walkowitz, eds. *Secret Agents: The Rosenberg Case, McCarthyism, and Fifties America*. New York: Routledge, 1995.

Gardner, Virginia. *The Rosenberg Story*. New York: Masses & Mainstream, 1954.

Goldstein, Alvin H. *The Unquiet Death of Julius and Ethel Rosenberg*. New York: Hill, 1975.

Griffith, Robert. *The Politics of Fear: Joseph R. McCarthy and the Senate,* second edition. Amherst: University of Massachusetts Press, 1987.

Griffith, and Athan Theoharis. *The Specter: Original Essays on the Cold War and the Origins of McCarthyism*. New York: New Viewpoints, 1974.

Haynes, John Earl. *Red Scare or Red Menace?: American Communism and Anticommunism in the Cold War Era*. Chicago: Ivan R. Dee, 1996.

Hixson, Walter L. *Parting the Curtain: Propaganda, Culture and the Cold War, 1945- 1961*. New York: St. Martin's Press, 1997.

Horne, Gerald. *Black and Red: W. E. B. Du Bois and the Afro-American Response to the Cold War, 1944-1963*. Albany: State University of New York Press, 1986.

Hyde, H. Montgomery. *The Atom Bomb Spies*. New York: Atheneum, 1980.

Kahn, David. *The Codebreakers: The Story of Secret Writing*. New York: Scribners, 1996.

Lamphere, Robert J., and Tom Shachtman. *The FBI-KGB War: A Special Agent's Story*. New York: Random House, 1986.

Meeropol, Robert and Michael. *We Are Your Sons: The Legacy of Ethel and Julius Rosenberg*. Boston: Houghton, Mifflin, 1975.

Meeropol, Michael, ed. *The Rosenberg Letters: A Complete Edition of the Prison Correspondence of Julius and Ethel Rosenberg*. New York: Garland, 1994.

Navasky, Victor S. *Naming Names*. New York: Viking, 1980.

Neville, John F. *The Press, the Rosenbergs, and the Cold War*. Westport, Conn.: Praeger, 1995.

Nizer, Louis. *The Implosion Conspiracy*. New York: Doubleday, 1973.

O'Reilly, Kenneth. *Hoover and the Un-Americans: The FBI, HUAC, and the Red Menace*. Philadelphia: Temple University Press, 1983.

Oshinsky, David M. *A Conspiracy So Immense: The World of Joe McCarthy*. New York: Free Press, 1983.

Pilat, Oliver. *The Atom Spies*. New York: Putnam, 1952.

Powers, Richard Gid. *Not Without Honor: The History of American Anticommunism*. New York: Free Press, 1995.

Radosh, Ronald, and Joyce Milton. *The Rosenberg File*. New Haven: Yale University Press, 1997.

Reuben, William A. *The Atom Spy Hoax*. New York: Action Books, 1955.

Rhodes, Richard. *Dark Sun: The Making of the Hydrogen Bomb*. New York: Simon & Schuster, 1995.

Root, Jonathan. *The Betrayers: The Rosenberg Case–A Reappraisal of an American Crisis*. New York: Coward-McCann, 1963.

Schneir, Walter and Miriam. *Invitation to an Inquest*. Garden City, N.Y.: Doubleday, 1965.

Schrecker, Ellen. *The Age of McCarthyism*. New York: Bedford Books of St. Martin's Press, 1994.

Schrecker, *Many Are The Crimes: McCarthyism in America*. Boston: Little, Brown, 1998.

Sharp, Malcolm P. *Was Justice Done?: The Rosenberg-Sobell Case*. New York: Monthly Review Press, 1956.

Sobell, Morton. *On Doing Time*. New York: Scribners, 1974.

White, John Kenneth. *Still Seeing Red: How the Cold War Shapes the New American Politics*. Boulder, Colo.: Westview Press, 1997.

Toledano, Ralph De. *The Greatest Plot in History*. New York: Duell, Sloan & Pearce, 1963.

Weinstein, Allen. *Perjury: The Hiss-Chambers Case*. New York: Knopf, 1978.

Wexley, John. *The Judgment of Julius and Ethel Rosenberg*. New York: Cameron & Kahn, 1955.

4. Domestic Politics

Anderson, Terry H. *The Movement and the Sixties*. New York: Oxford University Press, 1996.

Bacciocco, Edward J. Jr. *The New Left in America: Reform to Revolution, 1956 to 1970*. Stanford, Cal.: Hoover Institution Press, 1974.

Bernstein, Carl, and Bob Woodward. *All the President's Men*. New York: Simon & Schuster, 1974.

Caro, Robert A. *The Power Broker: Robert Moses and the Fall of New York*. New York: Knopf, 1974.

Choate, Pat. *Agents of Influence*. New York: Knopf, 1990.

Collier, Peter, and David Horowitz. *The Destructive Generation: Second Thoughts About the Sixties*. New York: Summit, 1989.

Diggins, John Patrick. The Rise and Fall of the American Left. New York: Norton, 1992.

Emery, Fred. *Watergate: The Corruption of American Politics and the Fall of Richard Nixon*. New York: Times Books, 1994.

Farber, David. *Chicago '68*. Chicago: University of Chicago Press, 1988.

Farrell, James J. *The Spirit of the Sixties: Making Postwar Radicalism*. New York: Routledge, 1997.

Gitlin, Todd. *The Whole World Is Watching: Mass Media In the Making & Unmaking of the New Left*. Berkeley: University of California Press, 1980.

Himmelstein, Jerome L. *To the Right: The Transformation of American Conservatism*. Berkeley: University of California Press, 1990.

Kutler, Stanley. *The Wars of Watergate: The Last Crisis of Richard Nixon*. New York: Knopf, 1990.

Lukas, J. Anthony. *Nightmare: The Underside of the Nixon Years*. New York: Viking, 1976.

Magnet, Myron. *The Dream and the Nightmare: The Sixties' Legacy to the Underclass*. New York: Morrow, 1993.

Matthews, Christopher. *Kennedy & Nixon: The Rivalry That Shaped Postwar America*. New York: Simon & Schuster, 1996.

Nye, Joseph S. Jr., Philip Zelikow, and David King. *Why People Don't Trust Government*. Cambridge, Mass.: Harvard University Press, 1997.

Phillips, Kevin. *Arrogant Capital: Washington, Wall Street, and the Frustration of American Politics*. Boston: Little, Brown, 1994.

Rangell, Leo. *The Mind of Watergate: An Exploration of the Compromise of Integrity*. New York: Norton, 1980.

Rector, Robert. *Issues '96: The Candidate's Briefing Book*. Washington, D.C.: Heritage Foundation, 1996.

Reich, Robert B. *Tales of a New America*. New York: Times Books, 1987.

Rich, Michael J. *Federal Policymaking and the Poor: National Goals, Local Choices and Distributional Outcomes*. Princeton: Princeton University Press, 1993.

Safire, William. *Before the Fall: An Inside View of the Pre-Watergate White House*. Garden City, N.Y.: Doubleday, 1975.

Sandel, Michael J. *Democracy's Discontent: America in Search of a Public Philosophy*. Cambridge, Mass.: Belknap Press of Harvard University Press, 1996.

Vickers, George R. *The Formation of the New Left: The Early Years*. Lexington, Mass.: Lexington Books, 1975.

Woodward, Bob. *Shadow: Five Presidents and the Legacy of Watergate*. New York: Simon & Schuster, 1999.

Woodward, and Carl Bernstein. *The Final Days*. New York: Simon & Schuster, 1976.

5. Foreign Policy

Almond, Gabriel A. *The American People and Foreign Policy*. New York: Harcourt, Brace, 1950.

Bliss, Howard, and M. Glen Johnson. *Beyond the Water's Edge: America's Foreign Policies*. Philadelphia: Lippincott, 1975.

Crabb, Cecil V. Jr., and Kevin V. Mulcahy. *Presidents and Foreign Policy Making, From FDR to Reagan*. Baton Rouge: Louisiana State University Press, 1986.

DeNovo, John A. *American Interests and Policies in the Middle East, 1900–1939*. Minneapolis: University of Minnesota Press, 1963.

Destler, I. M., Leslie H. Gelb, and Anthony Lake. *Our Own Worst Enemy: The Unmaking of American Foreign Policy*. New York: Simon & Schuster, 1984.

Dimbleby, David, and David Reynolds. *An Ocean Apart: The Relationship Between Britain and America in the Twentieth Century*. New York: Random House, 1988.

Dulles, Foster Rhea. *American Policy Toward Communist China: 1949–1969*. New York: Crowell, 1972.

Dumbrell, John. *American Foreign Policy: Carter to Clinton*. New York: St. Martin's Press, 1997.

Dumbrell. *The Carter Presidency: A Re-Evaluation*. Manchester, U.K. & New York: Manchester University Press, 1993.

Forsythe, David P. *Human Rights and U.S. Foreign Policy*. Gainesville: University Presses of Florida, 1988.

Gendzier, Irene. *Notes from the Minefield: United States Interventions in Lebanon and the Middle East, 1945–1958*. New York: Columbia University Press, 1997.

Gerges, Fawaz A. *The Superpowers and the Middle East: Regional and International Politics, 1955–1967*. Boulder, Colo.: Westview Press, 1994.

Heikal, Mohamed Hassanein. *The Cairo Documents: The Inside Story of Nasser and His Relationship With World Leaders, Rebels, and Statesmen*. Garden City, N.Y.: Doubleday, 1973.

Henkin, Louis. *The Age of Rights*. New York: Columbia University Press, 1990.

Hersh, Seymour M. *The Price of Power: Kissinger in the Nixon White House*. New York: Summit, 1983.

Hill, Dilys M., ed. *Human Rights and Foreign Policy: Principles and Practices*. New York: St. Martin's Press, 1989.

Hoffman, Stanley. *Duties Beyond Borders: On the Limits and Possibilities of Ethical International Politics*. Syracuse, N.Y.: Syracuse University Press, 1981.

Hoffman. *Primacy or World Order: American Foreign Policy Since the Cold War*. New York: McGraw-Hill, 1978.

Hogan, Michael J. *The Marshall Plan: America, Britain, and the Reconstruction of Western Europe, 1947–1952*. New York: Cambridge University Press, 1987.

Holland, Matthew F. *American and Egypt: From Roosevelt to Eisenhower*. Westport, Conn.: Praeger, 1996.

Hunt, Michael H. *Ideology and U.S. Foreign Policy*. New Haven: Yale University Press, 1987.

Isaacson, Walter. *Kissinger: A Biography*. New York: Simon & Schuster, 1992.

Johansen, Robert C. *The National Interest and the Human Interest: An Analysis of U.S. Foreign Policy*. Princeton: Princeton University Press, 1980.

Kaufman, Burton I. *The Arab Middle East and the United States: Inter-Arab Rivalry and Superpower Diplomacy*. New York: Twayne, 1996.

Kennan, George F. *Memoirs*, 2 volumes. Boston: Little, Brown, 1967–1972.

Keohane, Robert O., and Joseph S. Nye. *Power and Interdependence: World Politics in Transition*. Boston: Little, Brown, 1977.

Kepley, David R. *Collapse of the Middle Way: Senate Republicans and the Bipartisan Foreign Policy, 1948–1952*. New York: Greenwood Press, 1988.

Kern, Montague, Patricia W. Levering, and Ralph B. Levering. *The Kennedy Crises: The Press, the Presidency, and Foreign Policy.* Chapel Hill: University of North Carolina Press, 1983.

Kerr, Malcolm H. *The Arab Cold War: Gamal 'Abd al-Nasir and His Rivals, 1958–1970.* New York: Oxford University Press, 1971.

Kissinger, Henry. *Diplomacy.* New York: Simon & Schuster, 1994.

Kissinger. *White House Years.* Boston: Little, Brown, 1979.

Kolko, Gabriel. *The Politics of War: The World and United States Foreign Policy, 1943–1945.* New York: Random House, 1968.

Kunz, Diane B., ed. *The Diplomacy of the Crucial Decade: American Foreign Relations During the 1960s.* New York: Columbia University Press, 1994.

Lenczowski, George. *American Presidents and the Middle East.* Durham, N.C.: Duke University Press, 1990.

Lesch, David W., ed. *The Middle East and the United States: A Historical and Political Reassessment.* Boulder, Colo.: Westview Press, 1996.

Lipset, Seymour Martin. *American Exceptionalism: A Double-Edged Sword.* New York: Norton, 1996.

McCormick, Thomas J. *America's Half-Century: United States Foreign Policy in the Cold War and After,* second edition. Baltimore: Johns Hopkins University Press, 1995.

Miscamble, Wilson D. *George F. Kennan and the Making of American Foreign Policy, 1947– 1950.* Princeton: Princeton University Press, 1992.

Morgenthau, Hans J. *In Defense of the National Interest: A Critical Examination of American Foreign Policy With a New Introduction by Kenneth W. Thompson.* Washington, D.C.: University Press of America, 1982.

Muravchik, Joshua. *The Uncertain Crusade: Jimmy Carter and the Dilemmas of Human Rights Policy.* Lanham, Md.: Hamilton, 1986.

Murray, Anne. *The United States, Great Britain, and the Middle East: Discourse and Dissidents.* Boulder, Colo.: Social Sciences Monographs & New York: Columbia University Press, 1999.

Newsome, David D., ed. *The Diplomacy of Human Rights,* Lanham, Md.: University Press of America, 1986.

Nichols, J. Bruce, and Gil Loescher, eds. *The Moral Nation: Humanitarianism and U.S. Foreign Policy Today.* Notre Dame, Ind.: University of Notre Dame Press, 1989.

Nutting, Anthony. *Nasser.* London: Constable, 1972.

Oye, Kenneth A., Robert J. Lieber, and Donald Rothchild, eds. *Eagle in a New World: American Grand Strategy in the Post–Cold War Era.* New York: HarperCollins, 1992.

Paterson, Thomas G., ed. *Kennedy's Quest for Victory: American Foreign Policy, 1961–1963.* New York: Oxford University Press, 1989.

Patterson, James T. *Grand Expectations: The United States, 1945–1974.* New York: Oxford University Press, 1996.

Plummer, Brenda Gayle. *Rising Wind: Black Americans and U.S. Foreign Affairs, 1935– 1960.* Chapel Hill: University of North Carolina Press, 1996.

Roberts, Brad, ed. *The New Democracies: Global Change and U.S. Policy.* Cambridge, Mass.: MIT Press, 1990.

Rosenau, James N., and Hylke Tromp, eds. *Interdependence and Conflict in World Politics.* Aldershot, U.K. & Brookfield, Vt.: Avebury, 1989.

Rosenbaum, Herbert D., and Alexej Ugrinsky, eds. *Jimmy Carter: Foreign Policy and Post-Presidential Years.* Westport, Conn.: Greenwood Press, 1994.

Schoultz, Lars. *Human Rights and United States Policy Toward Latin America.* Princeton: Princeton University Press, 1981.

Schulzinger, Robert D. *Henry Kissinger: Doctor of Diplomacy.* New York: Columbia University Press, 1989.

Schurmann, Franz. *The Foreign Politics of Richard Nixon: The Grand Design.* Berkeley: Institute of International Studies, University of California, 1987.

Smith, Gaddis. *Morality, Reason, and Power: American Diplomacy of the Carter Years.* New York: Hill & Wang, 1986.

Smith, Michael J. *Realist Thought From Weber to Kissinger.* Baton Rouge: Louisiana State University Press, 1986.

Smith, Tony. *America's Mission: The United States and the Worldwide Struggle for Democracy.* Princeton: Princeton University Press, 1994.

Stephens, Robert. *Nasser: A Political Biography.* London: Allen Lane, 1971.

Szulc, Tad. *The Illusion of Peace: Foreign Policy in the Nixon Years.* New York: Viking, 1978.

Taft, Robert A. *A Foreign Policy for Americans.* Garden City, N.Y.: Doubleday, 1951.

Turner, Stansfield. *Caging the Nuclear Genie: An American Challenge for Global Security.* Boulder, Colo.: Westview Press, 1997.

Vitas, Robert A., and John Allen Williams, eds. *U.S. National Security Policy and Strategy, 1987–1994: Documents and Policy Proposals.* Westport, Conn.: Greenwood Press, 1996.

Williams, William Appleman. *The Tragedy of American Diplomacy.* Cleveland: World, 1959.

Woodward, Peter. *Nasser.* London & New York: Longman, 1992.

6. Gender Issues

Babcox, Deborah, and Madeline Belkin, comps. *Liberation Now! Writings from the Women's Liberation Movement.* New York: Dell, 1971.

Cozic, Charles P. and Stacey L. Tripp, eds. *Abortion: Opposing Viewpoints.* San Diego: Greenhaven Press, 1991.

Davidson, Nicholas. *The Failure of Feminism.* Buffalo, N.Y.: Prometheus, 1988.

Denfeld, Rene. *The New Victorians: A Young Woman's Challenge to the Old Feminist Order.* New York: Warner, 1995.

Djerassi, Carl. *The Politics of Contraception.* New York: Norton, 1980.

Duberman, Lucile. *Gender and Sex in Society.* New York: Praeger, 1975.

Dworkin, Andrea. *Right-Wing Women.* New York: Coward-McCann, 1983.

Echols, Alice. *Daring to be Bad: Radical Feminism in America, 1967–1975.* Minneapolis: University of Minnesota Press, 1989.

Elshtain, Jean Bethke. *Women and War.* New York: BasicBooks, 1987.

Evans, Sara. *Personal Politics: The Roots of Women's Liberation in the Civil Rights Movement and the New Left.* New York: Knopf, 1979.

Faludi, Susan. *Backlash: The Undeclared War Against American Women.* New York: Crown, 1991.

Farganis, Sondra. *Situating Feminism: From Thought to Action.* Thousand Oaks, Cal.: Sage, 1994.

Farrell, Warren. *The Myth of Male Power: Why Men Are the Disposable Sex.* New York: Simon & Schuster, 1993.

Firestone, Shulamith. *The Dialectic of Sex: The Case for Feminist Revolution.* New York: Morrow, 1970.

Fox-Genovese, Elizabeth. *Feminism is Not the Story of My Life: How Today's Feminist Elite Has Lost Touch with the Real Concerns of Women.* New York: Nan A. Talese, 1996.

Friedan, Betty. *The Feminine Mystique,* new introduction and epilogue by Friedan. New York: Dell, 1983.

Friedan. *The Second Stage.* New York: Summit, 1981.

Harding, Sandra. *The Science Question in Feminism.* Ithaca, N.Y.: Cornell University Press, 1986.

Harding, ed. *Feminism and Methodology: Social Science Issues.* Bloomington: Indiana University Press, 1987.

Hooks, Bell. *Ain't I a Woman: Black Women and Feminism.* Boston: South End Press, 1981.

Howard, Angela, and Sasha Ranaé Adams Tarrant, eds. *Reaction to the Modern Women's Movement, 1963 to the Present.* New York: Garland, 1997.

Hull, Gloria T., Patricia Bell Scott, and Barbara Smith, eds. *All the Women are White, All the Blacks are Men, But Some of Us are Brave: Black Women's Studies.* Old Westbury, N.Y.: Feminist Press, 1982.

Langer, Cassandra L. *A Feminist Critique: How Feminism has Changed American Society, Culture, and How We Live from the 1940s to the Present.* New York: Icon, 1996.

Lednicer, Daniel, ed. *Contraception: The Chemical Control of Fertility.* New York: Marcel Dekker, 1969.

Linden-Ward, Blanche, and Carol Hurd Green. *American Women in the 1960s: Changing the Future.* New York: Twayne, 1993.

MacKinnon, Catharine, and Andrea Dworkin, eds. *In Harm's Way: The Pornography Civil Rights Hearings.* Cambridge, Mass.: Harvard University Press, 1997.

Mansbridge, Jane J. *Why We Lost the ERA.* Chicago: University of Chicago Press, 1986.

McClary, Susan. *Feminine Endings: Music, Gender, and Sexuality.* Minneapolis: University of Minnesota, 1991.

Millett, Kate. *Sexual Politics.* Garden City, N.Y.: Doubleday, 1970.

Mohr, James C. *Abortion in America: The Origins of and Evolution of National Policy, 1800–1900.* New York: Oxford University Press, 1978.

Morgan, Robin. *Sisterhood is Powerful: An Anthology of Writings From the Women's Liberation Movement.* New York: Random House, 1970.

O'Barr, Jean, and Mary Wyer, eds. *Engaging Feminism: Students Speak Up & Speak Out.* Charlottesville: University Press of Virginia, 1992.

Paglia, Camille. *Vamps & Tramps: New Essays.* New York: Vintage, 1994.

Patai, Daphne, and Noretta Koertge. *Professing Feminism: Cautionary Tales from the Strange World of Women's Studies.* New York, BasicBooks, 1994.

Roiphe, Katie. *The Morning After: Sex, Fear, and Feminism on Campus.* Boston: Little, Brown, 1993.

Rossi, Alice S., ed. *The Feminist Papers: From Adams to de Beauvoir.* New York: Columbia University Press, 1973.

Schlafly, Phyllis. *The Power of the Positive Woman.* New Rochelle, N.Y.: Arlington House, 1977.

Schneir, Miriam, ed *Feminism in Our Time: The Essential Writings, World War II to the Present.* New York: Vintage, 1994.

Shalit, Wendy. *A Return to Modesty: Discovering the Lost Virtue.* New York: Free Press, 1999.

Sommers, Christina Hoff. *Who Stole Feminism: How Women Have Betrayed Women.* New York: Simon & Schuster, 1994.

Wolf, Naomi. *The Beauty Myth: How Images of Beauty Are Used Against Women.* New York: Morrow, 1991.

Zinsser, Judith P. *History and Feminism: A Glass Half Full.* New York: Twayne, 1993.

7. Judicial Activism

Barrett, Edward L. Jr., William Cohen and Jonathan D. Varat. *Constitutional Law: Cases and Materials,* eighth edition. Westbury, New York: Foundation Press, 1991.

Bickel, Alexander M. *Politics and the Warren Court.* New York: Harper & Row, 1965.

Bickel. *The Least Dangerous Branch: The Supreme Court at the Bar of Politics.* Indianapolis: Bobbs-Merrill, 1962.

Cox, Archibald. *The Warren Court: Constitutional Decision as an Instrument of Reform.* Cambridge, Mass.: Harvard University Press, 1968.

Garrow, David J. *Liberty and Sexuality: The Right to Privacy and the Making of Roe v. Wade,* revised edition. Berkeley: University of California Press, 1994.

Horwitz, Morton J. *The Warren Court and the Pursuit of Justice: A Critical Issue.* New York: Hill & Wang, 1998.

Kammen, Michael. *A Machine That Would Go of Itself: The Constitution and American Culture.* New York: Knopf, 1986.

Lewis, Frederick P. *The Context of Judicial Activism: The Endurance of the Warren Court Legacy in a Conservative Age.* Lanham, Md.: Rowman & Littlefield, 1999.

Murphy, Paul L. *The Constitution in Crisis Times, 1918–1969.* New York: Harper & Row, 1971.

Noonan, John T. Jr., ed. *The Morality of Abortion: Legal and Historical Perspectives.* Cambridge, Mass.: Harvard University Press, 1970.

Schwartz, Bernard. *Super Chief, Earl Warren and His Supreme Court: A Judicial Biography.* New York: New York University Press, 1983.

Schwartz. *Swann's Way: The School Busing Case and the Supreme Court.* New York: Oxford University Press, 1986.

Schwartz, ed. *The Warren Court: A Retrospective.* New York: Oxford University Press, 1996.

Shapiro, Martin. *Law and Politics in the Supreme Court: New Approaches to Political Jurisprudence.* New York: Free Press of Glencoe, 1964.

Swindler, Willaim F. *Court and Constitution in the Twentieth Century,* 2 volumes. Indianapolis: Bobbs-Merrill, 1970.

Tushnet, Mark, ed. *The Warren Court in Historical and Political Perspective.* Charlottesville: University of Virginia Press, 1993.

Woodward, Bob, and Scott Armstrong. *The Brethren: Inside the Supreme Court.* New York: Simon & Schuster, 1979.

8. Labor

Boyle, Kevin. *The UAW and the Heyday of American Liberalism, 1945–1968.* Ithaca, N.Y.: Cornell University Press, 1995.

Clark, Gordon L. *Union and Communities Under Siege: American Community in the Crisis of Organized Labor.* New York: Cambridge University Press, 1989.

Dark, Taylor E. *The Unions and the Democrats: an Enduring Alliance.* Ithaca, N.Y.: Cornell University Press, 1999.

Davis, Michael. *Prisoners of the American Dream: Politics and Economy in the History of the U.S. Working Class.* London: Verso, 1986.

DuBofsky, Melvyn. *The State and Labor in Modern America.* Chapel Hill: University of North Carolina Press, 1994.

Goldfield, Michael. *The Decline of Organized Labor in the United States.* Chicago: University of Chicago Press, 1987.

Lipset, Seymour Martin, ed. *Unions in Transition: Entering the Second Century.* San Francisco: Institute for Contemporary Studies, 1986.

Moody, Kim. *Workers in a Lean World: Unionism in International Economy.* London: Verso, 1997.

Tomlins, Christopher L. *The State and the Unions: Labor Relations, Law, and the Organized Labor Movement in America, 1880- 1960.* New York: Cambridge University Press, 1986.

Zieger, Robert. *American Workers, American Unions, 1920-1985.* Baltimore: Johns Hopkins University Press, 1986.

9. Popular Culture

Asbell, Bernard. *The Pill: A Biography of the Drug that Changed the World.* New York: Random House, 1995.

Boddy, William. *Fifties Television: The Industry and Its Critics.* Urbana: University of Illinois Press, 1990.

Bower, Robert T. *The Changing Television Audience in America.* New York: Columbia University Press, 1985.

Campbell, Robert. *Media and Culture: An Introduction to Mass Communication.* New York: St. Martin's Press, 1998.

Corrigan, Timothy. *A Cinema Without Walls: Movies and Culture After Vietnam.* New Brunswick, N.J.: Rutgers University Press, 1991.

Czitrom, Daniel J. *Media and the American Mind: From Morse to McLuhan.* Chapel Hill: University of North Carolina Press, 1982.

Eliot, Marc. *Death of a Rebel.* Garden City, N.Y.: Anchor, 1979.

Ellis, John M. *Literature Lost: Social Agendas and the Corruption of the Humanities.* New Haven: Yale University Press, 1997.

Gamm, Gerald. *Urban Exodus: Why the Jews Left Boston and the Catholics Stayed.* Cambridge, Mass.: Harvard University Press, 1999.

Garreau, Joel. *Edge City: Life on the New Frontier.* New York: Doubleday, 1991.

Habermas, Jürgen. *Communication and the Evolution of Society,* translated by Thomas McCarthy. Boston: Beacon, 1979.

Hood, Clifton. *722 Miles: The Building of the Subways and How They Transformed New York.* New York: Simon & Schuster, 1993.

Kay, Jane Holtz. *Asphalt Nation: How the Automobile Took Over America, and How We Can Take it Back.* New York: Crown, 1997.

Fishman, Robert. *Bourgeois Utopias: The Rise and Fall of Suburbia.* New York: BasicBooks, 1987.

Gans, Herbert J. *The Levittowners: Ways of Life and Politics in a New Suburban Community.* New York: Pantheon, 1967.

Glenn, John. *Letters to John Glenn.* Houston: World Book Encyclopedia Science Service, 1964.

Jackson, Kenneth T. *Crabgrass Frontier: The Suburbanization of the United States.* New York: Oxford University Press, 1985.

Keats, John. *The Crack in the Picture Window.* Boston: Houghton Mifflin, 1956.

Kunstler, James Howard. *The Geography of Nowhere: The Rise and Decline of America's Man-Made Landscape.* New York: Simon & Schuster, 1993.

Lazere, Donald. ed. *American Media and Mass Culture: Left Perspectives.* Berkeley: University of California Press, 1987.

Levine, Hillel, and Lawrence Harmon. *The Death of an American Jewish Community: A Tragedy of Good Intentions.* New York: Free Press, 1992.

Marc, David. *Demographic Vistas: Television in American Culture.* Philadelphia: University of Pennsylvania Press, 1984.

Martin, Joel W., and Conrad E. Ostwalt Jr. *Screening the Sacred: Religion, Myth and Ideology in Popular American Film.* Boulder, Colo.: Westview Press, 1995.

McCurdy, Howard E. *Space and the American Imagination.* Washington, D.C.: Smithsonian Institute Press, 1997.

Meyrowitz, Joshua. *No Sense of Place: The Impact of Electronic Media on Social Behavior.* New York: Oxford University Press, 1985.

Michael, Robert T., and others. *Sex in America: A Definitive Survey.* New York: Little, Brown, 1994.

Miller, James. *Flowers in the Dustbin: The Rise of Rock and Roll, 1947-1977.* New York: Simon & Schuster, 1999.

Mumford, Lewis. *The Highway and the City.* New York: Harcourt, Brace & World, 1963.

O'Connor, John E., ed. *American Television: Interpreting the Video Past.* New York: Ungar, 1983.

Paglia, Camille. *Sex, Art, and American Culture: Essays.* New York: Vintage, 1992.

Paglia. *Sexual Personae: Art and Decadence From Nefertiti and Emily Dickinson.* New Haven: Yale University Press, 1990.

Polan, Dana. *Power and Paranoia: History, Narrative and the American Cinema, 1940-1950.* New York: Columbia University Press, 1986.

Rose, Mark H. *Interstate: Express Highway Politics, 1939-1989,* revised edition. Knoxville: University of Tennessee Press, 1990.

Rosenblatt, Roger. *Life Itself: Abortion in the American Mind.* New York: Random House, 1992.

Rudy, Kathy. *Beyond Pro-Life and Pro-Choice: Moral Diversity in the Abortion Debate.* Boston: Beacon, 1996.

Schumacher, Michael. *There But for Fortune: The Life of Phil Ochs.* New York: Hyperion Press, 1996.

Scott, Allen J., and Edward W. Soja, eds. *The City: Los Angeles and Urban Theory at the End of the Twentieth Century.* Berkeley: University of California Press, 1996.

Sears, Hal D. *The Sex Radicals: Free Love in High Victorian America.* Lawrence: Regents Press of Kansas, 1977.

Shelton, Robert. *No Direction Home: The Life and Music of Bob Dylan.* New York: Beech Tree Books, 1986.

Slotkin, Richard. *Gunfighter Nation: The Myth of the Frontier in Twentieth-Century America.* New York: Atheneum, 1992.

Snow, Robert P. *Creating Media Culture.* Beverly Hills, Cal.: Sage, 1983.

Sobel, Robert. *The Manipulators: America in the Media Age.* Garden City, N.Y.: Anchor Press, 1976.

Solinger, Rickie. *Wake Up Little Susie: Single Pregnancy and Race before Roe* v. *Wade*. New York: Routledge, 1992.

Stanton, Frank Nicholas. *Mass Media and Mass Culture*. Dartmouth, N.H.: Dartmouth College, 1962.

Stein, Maurice Robert. *The Eclipse of Community: An Interpretation of American Studies*. Princeton: Princeton University Press, 1960.

Sugrue, Tom J. *The Origins of the Urban Crisis: Race and Inequality in Postwar Detroit*. Princeton: Princeton University Press, 1996.

Teaford, Jon C. *The Rough Road to Renaissance: Urban Revitalization in America, 1940–1985*. Baltimore: Johns Hopkins University Press, 1990.

Thomas, G. Scott. *The United States of Suburbia: How the Suburbs Took Control of America and What They Plan to Do With It*. Amherst, N.Y.: Prometheus, 1998.

Thompson, John B. *The Media and Modernity: A Social Theory of the Media*. Stanford, Cal.: Stanford University Press, 1995.

Watkins, Elizabeth Siegal. *On the Pill: A Social History of Oral Contraceptives, 1950–1970*. Baltimore: Johns Hopkins University Press, 1998.

Watson, Mary Ann. *The Expanding Vista: American Television in the Kennedy Years*. New York: Oxford University Press, 1990.

Whitburn, Joel. *The Billboard Book of Top 40 Hits*. New York: Billboard Books, 1992.

White, Richard, and Patricia Nelson Limerick. *The Frontier in American Culture: An Exhibition at the Newberry Library, August 26, 1994– January 7, 1995*. Edited by James R. Grossman. Berkeley: University of California Press, 1994.

Williams, Raymond. *Television: Technology and Cultural Form*, second edition. Hanover, N.H.: Wesleyan University Press and University Press of New England, 1992.

Wright, Frank Lloyd. *The Living City*. New York: Horizon, 1958.

10. Presidential Memoirs,

Biographies, and Documents

Abrahamsen, David. *Nixon Vs. Nixon: An Emotional Tragedy*. New York: Farrar, Straus, & Giroux, 1977.

Aitken, Jonathan. *Nixon, A Life*. London: Weidenfeld & Nicholson, 1993.

Ambrose, Stephen E. *Nixon*. 3 volumes. New York: Simon & Schuster, 1987–1991. Comprises volume 1, *The Education of a Politician 1913–1962* (1987); volume 2, *The Triumph of a Politician 1962–1972* (1989); volume 3, *Ruin and Recovery 1973–1990* (1991).

Anson, Robert Sam. *Exile: The Unquiet Oblivion of Richard M. Nixon*. New York: Simon & Schuster, 1984.

Bernstein, Barton J., and Allen J. Matusow, eds. *The Truman Administration: A Documentary History*. New York: Harper & Row, 1966.

Brinkley, Douglas. *Unfinished Presidency: Jimmy Carter's Journey Beyond the White House*. New York: Viking, 1998.

Brodie, Fawn M. *Richard M. Nixon: The Shaping of His Character*. New York: Norton, 1981.

Bush, George. *Public Papers of the Presidents of the United States, George Bush: 1989–1993*. Washington, D.C.: GPO, 1990–1993.

Chesen, Eli S. *President Nixon's Psychiatric Profile: A Psychodynamic-Genetic Interpretation*. New York: Wyden, 1973.

Clifford, Clark. *Counsel to the President: A Memoir*. New York: Random House, 1991.

Eisenhower, Dwight D. *Mandate for Change, 1953–1956: The White House Years*. Garden City, N.Y.: Doubleday, 1963.

Eisenhower. *Waging Peace, 1956–1961: The White House Years*. Garden City, N.Y.: Doubleday, 1965.

Greenstein, Fred I. *Hidden Hand Presidency: Eisenhower as Leader*. New York: BasicBooks, 1982.

Hoff, Joan. *Nixon Reconsidered*. New York: BasicBooks, 1994.

Hutschnecker, Arnold A. *Drive for Power*. New York: M. Evans, 1974.

Johnson, Lyndon Baines. *The Vantage Point: Perspectives of the Presidency, 1963–1969*. New York: Holt, Rinehart, & Winston, 1971.

Kaufman, Burton I. *The Presidency of James Earl Carter, Jr.* Lawrence: University Press of Kansas, 1993.

Kutler, Stanley, ed. *Abuse of Power: The New Nixon Tapes*. New York: Free Press, 1997.

Mause, Lloyd de, and Henry Ebel, eds. *Jimmy Carter and American Fantasy: Psychohistorical Explorations*. New York: Two Continents, 1977.

Mazlish, Bruce. *In Search of Nixon: A Psychohistorical Inquiry*. New York: BasicBooks, 1972.

Morris, Kenneth E. *Jimmy Carter, American Moralist*. Athens: University of Georgia Press, 1996.

Morris, Roger. *Richard Milhous Nixon: The Rise of an American Politician*. New York: Holt, 1990.

Neustadt, Richard E. *Presidential Power and the Modern Presidents: The Politics of Leadership from Roosevelt to Reagan*. New York: Free Press, 1991.

Nixon, Richard M. *RN: The Memoirs of Richard Nixon*. New York: Grossett & Dunlap, 1978.

Nixon. *Six Crises*. Garden City, N.Y.: Doubleday, 1962.

Pach, Chester J. Jr., and Elmo Richardson. *The Presidency of Dwight D. Eisenhower*. Lawrence: University of Kansas Press, 1991.

Parmet, Herbert S. *Richard Nixon and His America*. Boston: Little, Brown, 1990.

Reeves, Richard. *President Kennedy: Profile of Power*. New York: Touchstone, 1993.

Rippert, Wesley G., ed. *The Spiritual Journey of Jimmy Carter: In His Own Words*. New York: Macmillan, 1978.

Sorensen, Theodore C. *Kennedy*. New York: Harper & Row, 1965.

Strober, Gerald S. and Deborah H. *Nixon: An Oral History of His Presidency*. New York: HarperCollins, 1994.

Volkan, Vamik D., Norman Itzkowitz, and Andrew W. Dod. *Richard Nixon: A Psychobiography*. New York: Columbia University Press, 1997.

Voorhis, Jerry. *The Strange Case of Richard Milhous Nixon*. New York: Eriksson, 1972.

White, Mark J., ed. *Kennedy: The New Frontier Revisited*. New York: New York University Press, 1998.

White, Theodore H. *Breach of Faith: The Fall of Richard Nixon*. New York: Atheneum, 1975.

Wicker, Tom. *One of Us: Richard Nixon and the American Dream*. New York: Random House, 1991.

Wills, Garry. *Nixon Agonistes: The Crisis of the Self-Made Man*. Boston: Houghton Mifflin, 1970.

Woodstone, Arthur. *Nixon's Head*. New York: St. Martin's Press, 1972.

11. Science and Technology

Berardi, Gigi M., and Charles C. Geisler, eds. *The Social Consequences and Challenges of New Agricultural Technologies*. Boulder, Colo.: Westview Press, 1984.

Blank, Robert H. *The Political Implications of Human Genetic Technology.* Boulder, Colo.: Westview Press, 1981.

Chaikin, Andrew. *A Man on the Moon: The Voyages of the Apollo Astronauts.* New York: Viking, 1994.

Chrispeels, Maarten J., and David E. Sadava. *Plants, Genes, and Agriculture.* Boston: Jones & Bartlett, 1994.

Clarke, Arthur C. *The Exploration of Space.* New York: Harper, 1951.

Crabb, Alexander Richard. *The Hybrid-Corn Makers: Prophets of Plenty.* New Brunswick, N.J.: Rutgers University Press, 1947.

Davies, Owen, ed. *The Omni Book of Space.* New York: Kensington, 1983.

Doyle, Jake. *Altered Harvest: Agriculture, Genetics, and the Fate of the World's Food Supply.* New York: Viking, 1985.

Dudley, William, ed. *Genetic Engineering: Opposing Viewpoints.* San Diego: Greenhaven Press, 1990.

Dunn, Frederick S., and others. *The Absolute Weapon: Atomic Power and World Order,* edited by Bernard Brodie. New York: Harcourt, Brace, 1946.

Evans, J. Warren, and Alexander Hollaender, eds. *Genetic Engineering of Animals: An Agricultural Perspective.* New York & London: Plenum Press, 1986.

Fitzgerald, Deborah. *The Business of Breeding: Hybrid Corn in Illinois, 1890–1940.* Ithaca, N.Y.: Cornell University Press, 1990.

James, Clive. *Global Review of Commercialized Transgenic Crops.* ISAAA Brief No. 8. Ithaca, N.Y.: International Service for the Acquisition of Agri-biotech Applications, 1998.

Kaplan, Fred. *The Wizards of Armageddon.* New York: Simon & Schuster, 1983.

Kauffman, James L. *Selling Outer Space: Kennedy, the Media, and Funding for Project Apollo, 1961–1963.* Tuscaloosa: University of Alabama Press, 1994.

Kloppenburg, Jack Ralph Jr. *First the Seed: The Political Economy of Plant Biotechnology, 1492–2000.* New York: Cambridge University Press, 1988.

Krattiger, Anatole F. *The Importance of Ag-biotech to Global Prosperity.* Ithaca, N.Y.: International Service for the Acquisition of Agri-biotech Applications, 1998.

Krug, Linda T. *Presidential Perspectives on Space Exploration: Guiding Metaphors from Eisenhower to Bush.* Westport, Conn.: Praeger, 1991.

Launius, Roger D. *NASA: A History of the U.S. Civil Space Program.* Malabar, Fla.: Krieger, 1994.

Launius, and Bertram Ulrich. *NASA & The Exploration of Space.* New York: Stewart, Tabori & Chang, 1998.

Lewis, Richard S. *Appointment on the Moon: The Inside Story of America's Space Venture.* New York: Viking, 1968.

Logsdon, John. *The Decision to Go to the Moon: Project Apollo and the National Interest.* Cambridge: MIT Press, 1970.

Logsdon, and others, eds. *Exploring the Unknown: Selected Documents in the History of the U.S. Civil Space Program,* 2 volumes. Washington, D.C.: National Aeronautics and Space Administration, 1995.

McDougall, Walter A. *The Heavens and the Earth: A Political History of the Space Age.* New York: Basic-Books, 1985.

Miller, Henry I. *Policy Controversy in Biotechnology: An Insider's View.* Austin, Tex.: Landes, 1997.

Molnar, Joseph J., and Henry W. Kinnucan, eds. *Biotechnology and the New Agricultural Revolution.* Boulder, Colo.: Westview Press for the American Association for the Advancement of Science, Washington, D.C., 1989.

Murray, Charles, and Catherine Bly Cox. *Apollo: The Race to the Moon.* New York: Simon & Schuster, 1989.

Newell, Homer E. *Beyond the Atmosphere: Early Years of Space Science.* Washington, D.C.: National Aeronautics and Space Administration, 1980.

Owen, Meran R. L., and Jan Pen, eds. *Transgenic Plants: A Production System for Industrial and Pharmaceutical Proteins.* New York: Wiley, 1996.

Rachie, Kenneth O., and Judith M. Lyman, eds. *Genetic Engineering for Crop Improvement: A Rockefeller Conference, May 12–15, 1980.* New York: Rockefeller Foundation, 1981.

Raeburn, Paul. *The Last Harvest: The Genetic Gamble That Threatens to Destroy American Agriculture.* New York: Simon & Schuster, 1995.

Rifkin, Jeremy, and Nicanor Perlas. *Algeny.* New York: Viking, 1983.

Rifkin. *Declaration of a Heretic.* Boston: Routledge & Kegan Paul, 1985.

Zimmerman, Robert. *Genesis: The Story of Apollo 8: The First Manned Flight to Another World.* New York: Four Walls Eight Windows, 1998.

12. Social Welfare

Auletta, Ken. *The Underclass.* New York: Random House, 1982.

Baker, Liva. *Miranda: Crime, Law, and Politics.* New York: Atheneum, 1983.

Cloward, Richard A., and Lloyd E. Ohlin. *Delinquency and Opportunity: A Theory of Delinquent Gangs.* Glencoe, Ill.: Free Press, 1960.

Gans, Herbert J. *The War Against the Poor: The Underclass and Antipoverty Policy.* New York: BasicBooks, 1995.

Gillette, Michael L. *Launching the War on Poverty: An Oral History.* New York: Twayne, 1996.

Haveman, Robert H., ed. *A Decade of Federal Antipoverty Programs: Achievements, Failures, Lessons.* New York: Academic Press, 1977.

Katz, Michael B. *In the Shadow of the Poorhouse: A Social History of Welfare in America.* New York: Basic-Books, 1986.

Katz. *The Undeserving Poor: From the War on Poverty to the War on Welfare.* New York: Pantheon, 1989.

Levitan, Sar A. *The Great Society's Poor Law: A New Approach to Poverty.* Baltimore: Johns Hopkins Press, 1969.

Marris, Peter, and Martin Rein. *Dilemmas of Social Reform: Poverty and Community Action in the United States.* New York: Atherton, 1967.

Moynihan, Daniel P. *Maximum Feasible Misunderstanding: Community Action in the War on Poverty.* New York: Free Press, 1969.

Patterson, James T. *America's Struggle Against Poverty, 1900–1980.* Cambridge, Mass.: Harvard University Press, 1981.

Pilisuk, Marc and Phyllis, eds. *How We Lost the War on Poverty.* New Brunswick, N.J.: Transaction Books, 1973.

Piven, Frances Fox, and Richard A. Cloward. *The Breaking of the American Social Compact.* New York: New Press, 1997.

Piven and Cloward, *Regulating the Poor: The Functions of Public Welfare.* New York: Vintage, 1971.

Quadagno, Jill. *The Color of Welfare: How Racism Undermined the War on Poverty.* New York: Oxford University Press, 1994.

Rector, Robert, and William F. Lauber. *America's Failed $5.4 Trillion Dollar War on Poverty.* Washington, D.C.: Heritage Foundation, 1995.

Ryan, William. *Blaming the Victim.* New York: Vintage, 1971.

Sundquist, James L., and Corinne Saposs Schelling, eds. *On Fighting Poverty: Perspectives from Experience.* New York: BasicBooks, 1969.

13. Vietnam War and Antiwar Protest

Berman, William. *William Fulbright and the Vietnam War: The Dissent of a Political Realist.* Kent, Ohio: Kent State University Press, 1988.

Buzzanco, Robert. *Vietnam and the Transformation of American Life.* Oxford: Blackwell, 1999.

DeBenedetti, Charles, and Charles Chatfield. *An American Ordeal: The Antiwar Movement of the Vietnam Era.* Syracuse, N.Y.: Syracuse University Press, 1990.

Ferber, Michael, and Staughton Lynd. *The Resistance.* Boston: Beacon, 1971.

Friedland, Michael B. *Lift Up Your Voice Like a Trumpet.* Chapel Hill: University of North Carolina Press, 1998.

Garfinkle, Adam. *Telltale Hearts: The Origins and Impact of the Vietnam Antiwar Movement.* New York: St. Martin's Press, 1995.

Goulding, Phil G. *Confirm or Deny: Informing the People on National Security.* New York: Harper & Row, 1970.

Halstead, Fred. *Out Now! A Participant's Account of the American Movement Against the Vietnam War.* New York: Pathfinder, 1978.

Hayden, Tom. *Reunion: A Memoir.* New York: Random House, 1988.

Hennessy, Michael A. *Strategy in Vietnam: The Marines and Revolutionary Warfare in I Corps, 1965–1972.* Westport, Conn.: Praeger, 1997.

Herring, George C. *America's Longest War: The United States and Vietnam, 1945–1975.* New York: McGraw-Hill, 1986.

Hoopes, Townsend. *The Limits of Intervention.* New York: McKay, 1969.

Horowitz, Irving. *The Struggle is the Message: The Organization and Ideology of the Anti-War Movement.* Berkeley, Cal.: Glendessary, 1972.

Isaacson, Walter, and Evan Thomas. *The Wise Men: Six Friends and the World They Made.* New York: Simon & Schuster, 1986.

Kahin, George McTurnan. *Intervention: How America Became Involved in Vietnam.* New York: Anchor Press, 1987.

Kolko, Gabriel. *Anatomy of a War: Vietnam, The United States, and The Modern Historical Experience.* New York: New Press, 1984.

Powers, Thomas. *Vietnam: The War at Home.* New York: Grossman, 1973.

Rotter, Andrew. *The Path to Vietnam: Origins of the American Commitment to Southeast Asia.* Ithaca, N.Y.: Cornell University Press, 1987.

Schlesinger, Arthur M. Jr. *The Bitter Heritage: Vietnam and American Democracy 1941– 1966.* London: Andre Deutsch, 1967.

Scigliano, Robert. *South Vietnam: Nation Under Stress.* Boston: Houghton Mifflin, 1963.

Simpson, Howard R. *Dien Bien Phu: The Epic Battle America Forgot.* Washington, D.C.: Brassey's, 1994.

Small, Melvin. *Johnson, Nixon and the Doves.* New Brunswick, N.J.: Rutgers University Press, 1988.

Small, and William D. Hoover, eds. *Give Peace a Chance: Exploring the Vietnam Antiwar Movement.* Syracuse, N.Y.: Syracuse University Press, 1992.

Unger, Irwin. *The Movement: A History of the American New Left, 1959–1972.* New York: Dodd, Mead, 1974.

Vogelgesang, Sandy. *The Long Dark Night of the Soul: The American Intellectual Left and the Vietnam War.* New York: Harper & Row, 1974.

Wells, Tom. *The War Within: America's Battle Over Vietnam.* Berkeley: University of California Press, 1994.

Wittner, Lawrence S. *Rebels Against War: The American Peace Movement, 1933–1983.* Philadelphia: Temple University Press, 1984.

Young, Marilyn B. *The Vietnam Wars, 1945– 1990.* New York: HarperCollins, 1991.

Zaroulis, Nancy, and Gerald Sullivan. *Who Spoke Up? American Protest Against the War in Vietnam, 1963–1975.* Garden City, N.Y.: Doubleday, 1984.

14. General Histories

Brinkley, Alan. *The Unfinished Nation: A Concise History of the American People.* New York: Knopf, 1993.

Farber, David. *The Age of Great Dreams: America in the 1960s.* New York: Hill & Wang, 1994.

Galbraith, John Kenneth. *The Affluent Society.* Boston: Houghton Mifflin, 1958.

Gitlin, Todd. *The Sixties: Years of Hope, Days of Rage.* New York: Bantam, 1987.

Goldman, Eric F. *The Crucial Decade–and After: America, 1945–1960.* New York: Vintage, 1960.

Kane, Joseph Nathan. *Presidential Fact Book.* New York: Random House, 1998.

Lukas, J. Anthony. *Common Ground: A Turbulent Decade in the Lives of Three American Families.* New York: Knopf, 1985.

Matusow, Allen J. *The Unraveling of America: A History of Liberalism in the 1960s.* New York: Harper & Row, 1984.

Rosenberg, Norman L. and Emily S. *In Our Times: America Since World War II.* Engelwood Cliffs, N.J.: Prentice Hall, 1999.

Sayres, Sohnya, and others, eds. *The 60s Without Apology.* Minneapolis: University of Minnesota Press, 1984.

Steigerwald, David. *The Sixties and the End of Modern America.* New York: St. Martin's Press, 1995.

Thernstrom, Stephan and Abigail. *America in Black and White: One Nation, Indivisible.* New York: Simon & Schuster, 1997.

CONTRIBUTOR NOTES

ALI, Omar: Doctoral candidate in U.S. history at Columbia University; adjunct professor in history at Long Island University, Brooklyn campus.

ALLISON, Robert J.: History professor at Suffolk University and at the Harvard University Extension school; author of *The Crescent Obscured: The United States and the Muslim World, 1776–1815* (1995); editor of *The Interesting Narrative of the Life of Olaudah Equiano* (1995), *American Eras: Development of a Nation, 1783–1815* (1997), and *American Eras: The Revolutionary Era, 1754–1783* (1998).

ANTHES, Louis: Doctoral candidate in history and law at New York University.

APEL, Patrick: Executive director of the Plymouth County Development Council, Boston, Massachusetts; M.A. in Russian/East European Studies at Harvard University.

AUSTIN, Thomas H.: Independent scholar, Toronto, Canada.

BARRETT, Judith A.: Public policy planner; graduate student in American studies at the University of Massachusetts, Boston; instructor of English and government at Massasoit Community College, Brockton, Massachusetts.

BARRETT, Margaret Mary: Independent scholar, Ann Arbor, Michigan; textbook publishing, W. W. Norton; M.A. in history at Arizona State University.

BELL, Jonathan W.: Doctoral candidate in history at the University of Cambridge, Great Britain.

BENSON, Erik: Doctoral candidate in history at the University of Georgia.

BERGMAN, Margaret Carroll: Freelance writer, Provincetown, Massachusetts; editor, *Provincetown Arts.*

BLAIR-ESTEVES, Heidi Jo: Doctoral candidate in the Women in Politics and Government program, University of Massachusetts, Boston.

BOURICIUS, Pleun (Clara): Lecturer in history and literature at Harvard University.

CARTER, James M.: Doctoral candidate in diplomatic history at the University of Houston.

CONNORS, Anthony: Doctoral candidate in history at Clark University; author of "Science and Medicine," in *American Eras: Development of a Nation, 1783–1815,* edited by Robert J. Allison (1997).

COOKE, Douglas: Independent scholar, freelance writer, and translator, New York; librarian, Brooklyn Public Library; M.A. in Classics and M.L.S. at State University of New York, Buffalo.

DOUGLASS, Lonna: Independent scholar, Boston, Massachusetts.

ESTEVES, Alexander M.: Attorney; Juris Doctor, New England School of Law; author of "The Serving of Arrest Warrants After 'Guaba,'" *Massachusetts Lawyer's Weekly* (12 June 1995) and "Changing of the Guard: The Future of Confinement Alternatives in Massachusetts," *New England Journal on Criminal and Civil Confinement,* 17 (Winter 1991).

FINNEGAN, David I.: Managing partner of Finnegan, Underwood, Ryan, and Tierney of Boston, Massachusetts; president of the Boston School Committee, 1976–1979.

FLYNN, Robert J.: Doctoral candidate in history at the University of Kentucky.

FOLEY, Michael S.: Lecturer in history at the University of New Hampshire.

HANGEN, Tona J.: Adjunct professor in history at Brandeis University and Bentley College; author of "A Place to Call Home: Studying the Indian Placement Program," *Dialogue: A Journal of Mormon Thought,* 30 (Spring 1997).

JOHNS, Andrew L.: Doctoral candidate in history at the University of California, Santa Barbara; associate director, U. C. Santa Barbara Cold War History Group (COWHIG).

KIRK, Hanno: Adjunct professor at Bluefield State College; chief researcher for Stansfield Turner's *Caging the Genies: A Workable Solution for Nuclear, Chemical and Biological Weapons of Mass Destruction* (1999).

LEDNICER, Dan: Independent scholar, North Bethesda, Maryland; retired chemist, National Institute of Health; author of the series *The Organic Chemistry of Drug Synthesis,* six volumes.

MACK, Adam: Doctoral candidate in history at the University of South Carolina.

MANGUS, Susan Landrum: Lecturer in American history at Ohio State University.

MASON, Matthew: Doctoral candidate in history at the University of Maryland, College Park.

MEZZANO, Michael Jr.: Graduate student in history at Northeastern University.

OGBAR, Jeffrey: Assistant professor of history at the University of Connecticut.

OSGOOD, Kenneth A.: Doctoral candidate in history at the University of California, Santa Barbara; fellow at the Institute on Global Conflict and Cooperation.

PUGLIESE, Elizabeth: Independent scholar, Rosetta Research, Austin, Texas; M.A. in international relations at St. Mary's University.

ROSENBERG, Jonathan: Assistant professor in U.S. history at the University of Virginia; research scholar at the Miller Center of Public Affairs, University of Virginia; co-editor, with John Lewis Gaddis and others, and contributor to *Cold War Statesmen Confront the Bomb: Nuclear History Since 1945* (1999).

SCHAFER, Elizabeth D.: Independent scholar, Loachapoka, Alabama; author of "Godspeed and War Eagle: Auburn University's Astronautical History," *Quest: The History of Spaceflight Quarterly* (Summer 1998); co-author, with others, of *Women Who Made a Difference in Alabama,* edited by M. Abigail Toffel (1995).

SCHEUNEMANN, Jürgen: Doctoral candidate in history at Yale University and DFG scholar at the John F. Kennedy Institute for North American Studies at the Free University of Berlin; Fox International Fellow at the Yale Center for International Studies.

SCHMIDT, Christopher W.: Doctoral candidate in History of American civilization at Harvard University.

SNEH, Itai: Doctoral candidate in history at Columbia University.

SNYDER, Amy Paige: Graduate student in science, technology, and public policy at the Space Policy Institute at George Washington University; research assistant at RAND Science and Technology Policy Institute; author of "NASA Astronomy at Age 40," *Space Times,* 38 (March/April 1999).

STEIGERWALD, David: Associate professor in American history at Ohio State University, Marion; author of *The Sixties and the End of Modern America* (1995).

UPTON, Bryn: Doctoral candidate in American history at Brandeis University.

VAN RIPER, A. Bowdoin: Assistant professor of history of science and technology at Southern Polytechnic State University; author of "From Gagarin to *Armageddon:* U.S.-Soviet Relations and the Cold War Space Epic," *Film and History* (forthcoming, 2000); author of *Men Among the Mammoths: Victorian Science and the Discovery of Human Prehistory* (1993).

WEHRLE, Edmund F.: Assistant professor of history at the U.S. Coast Guard Academy; author of "A Good, Bad Deal: John F. Kennedy, W. Averell Harriman, and the Neutralization of Laos, 1961–1962," *Pacific Historical Review* (August 1998).

WILENSKY, Robert J.: Doctoral candidate in history at American University; physician; Vietnam veteran.

WOLD, Robert N.: Independent scholar, Laguna Niguel, California.

YAQUB, Salim: Visiting assistant professor in history at the University of Chicago; contributor of two biographies to *American National Biography,* edited by John A. Garraty and Mark C. Carnes (1999).

INDEX

C

G

H

I

N

O

P

T

U

V

W

ISBN 1-55862-396-5
90000
9 781558 623965